Run to the Mountain

THE JOURNALS OF THOMAS MERTON / Volume I: 1939–1941 / Patrick Hart, O.C.S.O., General Editor

Thomas Merton

Run to the Mountain

The Story of a Vocation

EDITED BY PATRICK HART, O.C.S.O.

HarperSanFrancisco
A Division of HarperCollins*Publishers*

Grateful acknowledgment is made to:

Farrar, Straus & Giroux for *The Secular Journal of Thomas Merton*
(New York, © 1959), which makes up a small part of this complete
journal of the pre-monastic years.

Excerpt from "The Waste Land" in *Collected Poems 1909–1962*, by
T. S. Eliot, copyright 1936 by Harcourt Brace & Company, copyright
© 1964, 1963 by T. S. Eliot. Reprinted by permission Harcourt Brace &
Company and Faber and Faber Ltd.

Dylan Thomas: *Poems of Dylan Thomas*, copyright 1939 by New
Directions Pub. Corp., 1945 by the Trustees for the Copyrights of
Dylan Thomas, 1952 by New Directions Pub. Corp. and Daniel
Higham, Ltd. (formerly Dent, U.K.).

Book design by David Bullen

FIRST EDITION

Library of Congress Cataloging-in-Publication Data
Merton, Thomas, 1915–1968.
    Run to the mountain : the story of a vocation / Thomas Merton ;
edited by Patrick Hart.— 1st ed.
        p.   cm. (The journals of Thomas Merton ; v. 1)
    "1939–1941."
    ISBN 0–06–065474–0 (cloth : alk. paper)
    ISBN 0–06–065475–9 (pbk. : alk. paper)
    1. Merton, Thomas, 1915–1968—Diaries.   2. Trappists—United
States—Biography.   I. Hart, Patrick.   II. Title.   III. Series:
Merton, Thomas, 1915–1968.   Journals of Thomas Merton ; v. 1.
BX4705.M542A4   1995
271'.12502—dc20   94-43414
[B]   CIP

95 96 97 98 99 RRD(H) 10 9 8 7 6 5 4 3 2 1

Run to the mountain;
Shed those scales on your eyes
That hinder you from seeing God.

DANTE, *Purgatorio*, II, 7

Contents

Preface

Thomas Merton occasionally wrote of keeping a journal in his youth, and how wonderful it was to reread entries at a later date, tearing them out and discarding them. Unfortunately, Merton must have destroyed not a few journals of the premonastic years, because the earliest we have are from 1939 to 1941, just before he entered the Abbey of Gethsemani. Sporadically, as a young monk, Merton kept a journal, but only a few fragments of the novitiate journal remains. The most sustained journal writing was done during the rest of his monastic life, from the *Sign of Jonas* period until *The Asian Journal*. But even then we find some gaps, long periods when time prevented him from keeping a regular journal and even (unfortunately) some missing pages.

When in 1990 the Trustees of the Merton Legacy Trust asked me to be general editor of the Merton journals, the first thing I did was visit St. Bonaventure's and have copies made of these early journals. It has taken several years of research to determine the amount of journal material that was available. Once I had gone through the various collections – especially the monastic journals (written for the most part at Gethsemani and now housed at the Thomas Merton Center of Bellarmine College, Louisville), as well as the fragment from Merton's novitiate days, and three other journals from 1947 to 1951 (which are now a part of Columbia University Library's Special Collections), and St. Bonaventure University's Merton archives – it was decided to have seven volumes of Merton journals.

The Merton Legacy Trust, which was drawn up the year before Merton's death, includes the indenture that the journals may be published "in whole or in part" at the discretion of the Merton Legacy Trust, but not until after the official biography had been published and twenty-five years had elapsed since his death. The authorized biography, *The Seven Mountains of Thomas Merton*, by Michael Mott, had been published in 1985; and December 10, 1993, marked the twenty-fifth anniversary of his passage through death to life. The journals could begin to appear anytime after that date.

The next step was to appoint editors for the respective journals. The task was difficult because there were so many qualified people from which to choose. Only recently was it possible to determine the number of volumes in question, and then to appoint men and women who would be willing to undertake a segment of the entire project. I am happy to announce that the editors for subsequent volumes of the Merton journals will be Christine M. Bochen, Lawrence S. Cunningham, Robert E. Daggy, Victor A. Kramer, and Jonathan Montaldo. In addition to this first volume, I have reserved for myself the last volume, 1967–1968.

During his lifetime Merton drew upon these journals, choosing excerpts for a number of his books, including *The Secular Journal, The Sign of Jonas,* and *Conjectures of a Guilty Bystander.* He edited heavily, omitted a great deal of material, and substituted fictitious names in the monastic journals. After his death a number of books based on the journals appeared, such as *A Vow of Conversation, Woods, Shore and Desert, The Alaskan Journal,* and finally *The Asian Journal.*

The editorial decision was made early on to publish the journals just as Merton wrote them, following the chronological sequence, beginning with the premonastic journals, with a bare minimum of editing.

There is no denying that Thomas Merton was an inveterate diarist. He clarified his ideas in writing especially by keeping a journal. Perhaps his best writing can be found in the journals, where he was expressing what was deepest in his heart with no thought of censorship. We must be grateful that in drawing up provisions for the Merton Legacy Trust he made it clear that these journals could be published *in toto* or in part, at the discretion of the Trustees, and that they have decided to make all the extant journals available. With their publication we will have as complete a picture of Thomas Merton as we can hope to have.

Acknowledgments

First of all, I am grateful to the Trustees of the Merton Legacy Trust, Robert Giroux, James Laughlin, and Tommie O'Callaghan, for their faith in asking me to be general editor of Thomas Merton's journals. Also, my thanks to Anne McCormick, secretary for the Trust, who greatly expedited matters throughout the entire project. Then, too, I must acknowledge my indebtedness to Abbot Timothy Kelly and the Community of the Abbey of Gethsemani, who have provided me with the time and space, not to mention a computer and printer, to complete the work.

Among those who have provided the greatest assistance was Robert Lax, who agreed to read the manuscript alongside copies of the holographic journal, in helping with names and places that were nearly impossible to decipher from Merton's own hastily written entries. In addition to this work, which spanned several years, he welcomed me to Patmos, where I spent some days in an effort to establish a certainty regarding the journal transcriptions, especially of the middle missing journal dealing with Merton's Cuban sojourn in the spring of 1940. Bob Lax, the perfect host, made my time at Patmos very fruitful in every way.

One soon discovers the use Merton made of foreign languages, in particular Latin and French, in this early journal. I was fortunate to discover Dr. Robert Urekew of nearby Springfield, Kentucky, who was able and willing to translate all the passages in Latin and Greek as well as modern languages. Others who assisted me during the research were Brother Elias Dietz and Father Chrysogonus Waddell of Gethsemani, Dr. Lawrence S. Cunningham of Notre Dame, Dr. Michael Downey of Bellarmine College, Msgr. William Shannon of Nazareth College in Rochester, and Professor Ron Seitz of St. Catherine College, Kentucky.

Among the various Merton archives, of course, I am deeply indebted to Dr. Robert Daggy, Director of the Merton Center of Bellarmine College, for his assistance throughout the project, as well as to his student assistants. Dr. Paul Spaeth and Lorraine Welch of St. Bonaventure University's library staff were most helpful in providing me with copies of the journals and photographs of Merton drawings housed at St. Bonaventure's. The friars welcomed me warmly and shared their home with me while I was researching the Merton papers at Olean. Dr. Patrick Lawler and Kenneth Lohf made my time at the Columbia Library Special Collections very rewarding. Dr. Lawler was especially helpful in looking up books in the stacks that Merton referred to in his early journals, so we could check out quotations for their accuracy.

A word of thanks is in order to John Loudon and Karen Levine of Harper San Francisco, who have been tireless in pursuing optimum publication of this long-range project.

Finally, I want to express my gratitude to the editors of the later volumes of Merton journals, who have agreed to undertake this gigantic task in spite of already busy schedules: Christine Bochen, Lawrence S. Cunningham, Robert E. Daggy, Victor A. Kramer, and Jonathan Montaldo. May the Lord reward them all for their generosity by the satisfaction of having been a part of a group dedicated to making Thomas Merton's journals available in the best possible way.

Introduction

This first volume of the Merton journals covers the years from 1939 through 1941, the only extant journals discovered from his premonastic years. The first part, which has been called "The Perry Street Journal," begins with an entry dated May 2, 1939: "This is May. Who seen any birds?" Interesting that he should begin with an ungrammatical question.

The journal reflects the life of a young intellectual living at 35 Perry Street in Greenwich Village, and teaching at Columbia University Extension. He had received his Masters from Columbia in 1938 on "Nature and Art in William Blake"[1] and was contemplating a doctorate on the poetry of Gerard Manley Hopkins, but it never became a reality. We see here a twenty-four-year-old writer, clearly ambitious and eager to get published, offering his first novels to any number of publishing houses, only to be greeted with a rejection slip. Some of the more compassionate publishers actually read the manuscripts and commented on them, encouraging Merton to continue writing.

After his reception into the Catholic Church in 1938, he must have discarded his previous journals, as he mentions in the introduction to *The Secular Journal:*

> These are a few selections taken from a diary that I kept when I was a layman, a graduate student at Columbia, teaching in University Extension there, and later when I was an Instructor at St. Bonaventure University. This was written, like most diaries, informally, colloquially, and in haste. The whole diary filled two or three large manuscript volumes. Only one of these still exists, the others were thrown away or destroyed after I had typed out a few excerpts which are given here, along with parts of the surviving volume[s].[2]

---

[1] See Appendix I in *The Literary Essays of Thomas Merton*, edited by Patrick Hart (New York: New Directions, 1981), 385–453.
[2] *The Secular Journal of Thomas Merton* (New York: Farrar, Straus, 1959), vi.

Merton was mistaken in the above statement, since there were two holographic journals given to St. Bonaventure's University Archives by Mark Van Doren to add to their collection of Thomas Merton's notebooks and art work. These two journals appear to be the first and third of what must have been three premonastic journals. The first begins on May 2, 1939, and ends with February 13, 1940. The third journal, which has come to be known as the "St. Bonaventure Journal," begins on October 19, 1940, and ends with an entry for December 5, 1941.

But what about the missing journal, from February 13, 1940, to October 19, 1940? When packing his bags at St. Bonaventure's in early December 1941, preparing to enter Gethsemani, Merton was passing out manuscripts, poems, and drawings to friends; one of these, Richard Fitzgerald, a seminarian who had been on friendly terms with Merton, was given a treasure trove. Many years later Fitzgerald, retired from the ministry after having become a Monsignor Fitzgerald, was living in Florida. He wrote to St. Bonaventure's asking if they might be interested in these unpublished Merton materials. Father Irenaeus Herscher, a Franciscan friar and librarian at St. Bonaventure's, was delighted to receive the gift. And so are numberless Merton scholars today.

In the contents of the so-called "Fitzgerald File" at St. Bonaventure's was a transcription of the missing journal (from February 13, 1940, to October 19, 1940). It included Merton's month in Cuba, and so came to be known as "The Cuban Journal." There were other articles, for example, one on the lay apostolate, which was obviously influenced by the Baroness Catherine de Hueck.[3] We also discovered fragments of unpublished novels, such as *The Labyrinth* and the opening part of *The Man in the Sycamore Tree*, which never found a publisher. We can only conjecture here that Merton himself made the transcription of a part of, or the whole of, the holographic journal, which was then apparently discarded.

One question still remained: Were these actually transcriptions of the missing journal, or did Merton work them over as he typed them up, hoping that at some future time he might incorporate them or transform them into a novel? This dilemma was finally solved with the assistance of Robert Lax. This journal was written at a time when Merton and Lax were very

---

[3] Catherine de Hueck was born into a wealthy Russian family in 1890, and at fifteen married Baron Boris de Hueck. When she was twenty, they fled, penniless, to Canada. After some years, they founded Friendship House in Toronto, and later Harlem, New York. Merton felt called to do volunteer work at the latter during 1941, as described in part 3 of this journal.

close friends, and he had actually spent several summers at the cottage that belonged to Lax's family. I felt strongly that if anyone would be able to help discern the chronological sequence of these journals, it would be Lax.

For nearly twenty years, Lax had been living in self-imposed exile on the Greek island of Patmos. I wrote him asking if I might visit him in an effort to establish some order in these transcriptions of journals found at St. Bonaventure's, and he readily agreed. In the spring of 1992, I set off for Athens, and then embarked on the ten-hour-long ferry ride out to Patmos in the Aegean Sea.

After going through these transcriptions page by page, Lax and I agreed that the transcriptions were made directly from the journals and not re-worked at a later date. The immediacy of the writing convinced us that the transcriptions were authentic and could be included in this premonastic journal.

The third part, known as the "St. Bonaventure Journal," was written for the most part at St. Bonaventure's while Merton was teaching English and creative writing. Before leaving St. Bonaventure's for Gethsemani, Merton had given to Mark Van Doren two bound volumes of journals, along with other materials for an anthology of poetry, and a few typewritten pages from a journal. In January 1944 Van Doren wrote to St. Bonaventure's ask-ing if these journals might find a home there. They were indeed interested; and so on January 15, 1944, the two journals that comprise this volume were transferred to St. Bonaventure's for safekeeping. It was only years later, when Michael Mott, the official Merton biographer, wrote of having discovered these journals and other Merton manuscripts in the library at Olean, New York, that I realized what a gold mine was to found at St. Bonaventure's.

Toward the end of the journal there are references to the Baroness, who had given a talk to the friars and students of St. Bonaventure's on her lay apostolate with the poor at Friendship House in Harlem. As the journal brings out very well, Merton was torn between a possible vocation as a vol-unteer staff worker at Friendship House and a vocation to become a friar or monk. The matter is finally resolved as the journal closes and he departs from St. Bonaventure's for the Abbey of Gethsemani in the knob country of Kentucky, where he would spend the last twenty-seven years of his life.

PART I

Perry Street, New York

May 1939–February 1940

Bad guy in a window. Decoration day.

Tuesday, May 2, 1939. New York

This is May. Who seen any robins?

Cicero, *De Oratore*, recommends stamping your foot during your speech. At least at the beginning of the speech and at the end. Caius Gracchus[1] had a servant stand behind him with an ivory flute to play the proper note, and regulate the pitch of the orator's voice if he were getting too low or too high or too furious.

A girl on a street corner stamping her feet to make the men turn around.

Saint Augustine's problems are everybody's, except he did not have a war to worry him. The 12th Chapter of Book VII is magnificent. Evil the deficiency of good. Everything that is, is good, by virtue of its mere existence. Corruptibility implies goodness.[2]

Would have gone to the World's Fair today but did not. Yesterday was New Haven day at the Fair. Some thousands came from New Hampshire with books of tickets. On each book was pasted a dime for the Long Island R.R. turnstile. The glue on the dimes mucked up the slots in the turnstiles and the whole damn business was put out of order.

[John] Berryman is right about Wordsworth being a good poet. I read his sonnets in the *Oxford Book* today. "The Trosachs" is good, so is "Nuns fret not," which I should have remembered. Then I had forgotten "Or hear old Triton blow his wreathed horn" which is a swell sonnet – a good last line to a good sonnet. "The Trosachs." Three sentences.[3]

May 3

The Columbia Writers Club: run by the Extension English Department, proud of courses in playwriting, poetry writing, short story writing, etc. I was one of some twelve speakers, and had to talk about poetry, so named some poets I liked and said poetry was serious, and people who wanted to

---

[1] In the first book of Cicero's *De Oratore* (c. 55 B.C.E.), chapter XXXIV, reference is made to Caius Gracchus, whose speeches were studied as models in the rhetorical schools of the Empire.

[2] Saint Augustine, *Confessions*, Book VII of chapter 12. Merton found this chapter especially moving, and it may have influenced his own confessional autobiography.

[3] Wordsworth, "The Trosachs" in *Oxford Book* (possibly the *Oxford Book of Verse*), a text Merton was using with his students at Columbia University Extension.

write poetry should read poetry and sat down feeling horrible. Peter Munro Jack who made the first, biggest, and after mine the most nervous speech came up and said I had done a good thing. He had said poetry was the best thing being written now.

I still wish I were teaching English even if it meant going to every Writers Club Banquet ever given. Beef all night, and one glass of wine to every writer.

May 4

Beer after the nightmare society's banquet did me ill but I walked in the sun and went to the World's Fair. I like fairs. The colossal statues are awful, the trees and gardens good, the Turkish Pavilion, with music by real violins and pianos, and Pilav for 80 cents was a good place to eat. The Amusement Place is all jagged and has gaps between its teeth that let us see Flushing and its cemeteries. The hours on the busses that play part of "East Side West Side" will kill the Fair dead in the middle of August. So will all the canned Tchaikovsky that blows around among the fat statues. In the Amusement Section, an exhibit of "Natures Mistakes" – lambs with five legs, cats with two, etc. Oh no, I did not go.

May 11

I suppose I am not reading Croce on Vico[4] very carefully. I am not getting the steps in the law of reflux so well down. Yet as to *Finnegan's Work*:[5] The very first sentence says it's Vico. So *Finnegan* is the history of the world, seen Vician. And that is clear enough, what with Jarl van Hoother and the Norses and Outlanders. I like the interviews in pp. 60's. But Jarl Van H. and the Prankquean made me happy to the point of singing all weekend, notwithstanding Pernod, rum, scotch, beer, *arroz con pollo*, coca cola, roast beef sandridges and about everything except barley candy out at the Fair.

I like the fellow Amasis, who before being King would drink and sing and steal for fun, and then they would take him to the oracles and some would say guilty and some not guilty. So when he was King he rewarded

4 Giambattista Vico's *La Scienza Nuovo* (1725) is a philosophy of history on which James Joyce based his *Finnegans Wake* (along with Giordano Bruno of Nola and Nicholas of Cusa). See William York Tindall, *A Reader's Guide to Finnegans Wake* (New York: Farrar, Straus & Giroux, 1969) for an excellent introduction to Joyce's masterpiece. Merton was reading Croce's *La Filosofia di G. B. Vico* at this time, also.
5 A wordplay on Joyce's *Finnegans Wake* (Merton refers to it in one place as *Finnegan's Work* and another place as *Finnegan's Walk*).

the oracles that had said "guilty" and spat on the others for a troop of phonies, and so had his intelligent jest. This one is from Herodotus, but *Finnegan* too I suppose. For *Finnegan's Walk* is all around the world, and that has Egypt.

May 12

Today has the sort of clean sky and coldness of air and brightness all over, to make all things sharp and every line keen shapes firm colors bright that fall has. The effect was funny on me; I have been playing spring and so has the weather so that I had ceased to remember everything about last fall or almost any fall, and certainly stopped believing in last fall. Then I was tutoring the fat girl at Central Park West, and would go with my Cicero, and afterwards walk in the sun and go to Saint Gregory the Great for a few minutes, that being a dark flat basilica with no windows and so outside and more cold sun.

Or I would sit at a desk mornings in the Tutoring School reading or typing, and so I typed the Thesis and did an article on Crashaw. Last fall I worked hard and today I am up and working too – getting notes on Bridges' *Milton's Prosody* and everything is pretty gay.

Always forgetting the beginnings of fall, you always hit a day like them early in summer and you are pleased and that means it is the first time you really have put winter away out of your mind. Never think of fall in winter, yet in summer you think of it: it is going to be cool. And it is too. September and October are fine months.

So is May a fine month. But today is funny. Even scratch yourself and it is more like scratching yourself in autumn. And oh yes, last fall I was riding the busses up to the Hispanic Society Museum and looking at the El Grecos. And I keep coming out of High Mass at Corpus Christi into this very fine bright sun on Sundays and eating a (Lord knows!) bad breakfast in Childs on 111th Street and still liking it. Very early fall, I went on Sunday afternoons to the Metropolitan. Labor Day I was in Philadelphia with [Joe] Roberts. Early fall in between being in love with Pat Hickman and meeting this Doris Raleigh was a fine space.

May 14. Sunday

For Mother's day outside Saint Joseph's and I suppose all other churches they sold large artificial looking carnations. At least the pink ones were dyed. And a little girl who had just bought one was complaining to the vendor, "But this one doesn't smell nice. Flowers smell nice."

So then I read some more Vico – this the original. As to *Finnegans Wake* – there is this fight that reproduces itself more and less obscurely, between Earwicker and one Festy King and maybe also Finnegan; besides it's Cain and Abel, and it is the same argument rarefied in the Mookse and the Gripes. What it is here, the fight is in the light. Mostly it is in the dark. Then there is a wall and a gate, sometimes Eden gate, and also a gate in Dublin. The wall brings with it a lot of masonry talk and that leads to Pyramids and Tombs and that leads back to Finnegan. Festy King is at one point covered with stucco, so I think Finnegan and Earwicker are enemies. There is generally a girl in the background from Superca Latouche to Newoletta. Except M. and G. pay no attention to her, otherwise it is a fight of rivals – for a whore. So maybe Troy, but no indication of that yet. I expect the fight business will recur through Part one. (Part one is Norse and Finns and Huge Outlanders and Dutch swearing – Tacitus' Germania. Looking ahead I notice Part three, begins with Gascons.) Then too there is stone throwing. Who threw stones besides David? Deucalion – that's different.

Friday [Robert] Gibney[6] and I were at the Cuban Village again. Then we found who the two best dancers are: Antonio y Marquita, they do a fine rumba bright as fires! Marquita is small and very lovely and neat and I love her very much. We made them come and have drinks with us, and Marquita asked for "Some Tom Collins please." She walks very straight and smiles fine and talks in pretty Spanish and not much English at all, only more than Antonio.

May 18. Thursday

Sunday it was more Cuban Village and this time I met Wilma Reardon and I guess from now on she will be one of my favorite girls to meet for she is very pretty and nice. I stayed at Forest Hills on a couch in her house, and Monday walked in good hot sun to Flushing.

Tuesday was the day I found the fine passage in Joyce telling everybody how to read the book or any other book. Anybody comparing Joyce to a crossword puzzle must not think that he is describing Joyce or anything at all worth reading. Crossword puzzles by invariably foggy definitions and bad synonyms make language diffuse and kill it. Joyce gets a dozen rich and sharp associations from each word and the words are always alive and then go and give new life to new words.

---

6 Robert Gibney, one of Merton's classmates at Columbia, worked on *The Jester* with Merton and Robert Lax. He dated Peggy Wells, who was doing theater work at the time, but later married Nancy Flagg.

But on the other hand the dog population has gone and invented a machine to form sounds, syllables, and reproduce human speech – exactly. All that does to words is strain them through a machine and bring them out dead at the other end. It is horrible. I saw it in a newsreel. Besides it is idolatrous.

And today is Ascension Day, and in a week the Paraclete comes down like fires to be among us, bringing the gift of tongues. Now all Christ's lessons have been taught in His sermons and His miracles, His crucifixion and Resurrection. Now he ascends to heaven, and there is nothing left but for us to praise His glory, and meditate upon His teaching, and go about and proclaim God. I think poets owe a special adoration to the third person of the Holy Trinity, for by these tongues of fire all men are made poets and philosophers, and that is the way Christ would have it on earth. Yet the tongues of fire came down at the end of it all, and before that came the scourging and the thorns and Golgotha, so we must ever be after scourging pride. But here it is the Holy Spirit again, that has come down to tell us not only how to proclaim God, but even before that, to help us always to remember and understand the lessons He taught when He was on earth. This is really a momentous feast for the fires that came down are always among us, and we should pray now always to turn where those fires are, for although they are everywhere there is a kind of turning away from them so complete that it seems being inside out in a shell to close out the fires and get only what pride feeds on. So we must pray to be led where the Holy Spirit is, although He is right with us and in and out of us and all through us we have to go on journeys to find him. And it is bitter journeys without God's grace to walk peacefully about in the world loving created things because God created them but not loving them beyond their station in the order of being because they are imperfect yet make captives. When you love them for themselves then you get only bitterness. So it is good to beg for grace to go in the world the way the air does and the light loving the whole world and not stopping at any part of it and being in and out of all of it and not holding jealously to anything of it, but being brothers among all the other created things like you loving others as yourself, which you cannot possibly do if you love yourself the way you should love God.

May 30. Decoration Day

I would like to be at the beach today but it costs too much money. Anyway, Long Island is crazy. When I was at Long Beach and saw Seymour

[Freedgood][7] killing himself running his newspaper, it was bad. Then, Douglaston is full of crazies: and it was certainly a weird congregation in Saint Anastasia's: beating it out of church as fast as they indecently could right after the communion of the priest.

Long Beach was partly built by elephants but now it is a ghetto: and the bar that all the fellows there like best is the dirtiest and worst and chilliest, and is half underground in the mud. Out there they love the pin ball gambling games and they have some very pathetically stupid communists and the only decent place in Long Beach is Saint Ignatius Martyr Church and Father Brown inside of it is one of the four decent fellows in the town.

The Cuban Village is getting crowded and a bit bad too: but very crowded. Wilma tells me good stories about the various kinds of sicknesses, since she is a nurse. Everyone in the Aquacade has had colds: but the Amazons wound each other with their blunt spears and wooden swords, and the other night one of them fell downstairs and twisted her ankle. One of the Amazons let go of a disars and it went clean through the wall of the building. A Seminole Indian in the Seminole Indian exhibit comes in frequently with alligator bites.

It sometimes occurs to a fellow to talk about music. That is, talk about the kinds of people that like kinds of music. In the first place I do not know how to talk to the people who know a lot about music, go to many concerts and have a lot of fat albums. These people generally like Sibelius and are far from bored with Beethoven. Then, I hate Wagner. I do not know if [Robert] Lax[8] and Gibney hate Wagner: he belongs to a whole class of things they never mention at all.

Digression: List of some neutral things I have not thought of or mentioned or even heard mentioned well, this year.

Mendelssohn.

Sir P. Sidney.

Ann Dvorak (but I did, she is in a movie and scared me away).

Crap Games (but yes, too, in the Pastoral).

---

7 Seymour Freedgood and Robert Lax shared a room at Columbia's Furnald Hall, and became close friends with Thomas Merton. They succeeded in smuggling the Hindu monk Bramachari into their room, and he became an influential friend to all three through his spiritual wisdom.

8 Robert Lax was to become one of Merton's closest friends at Columbia, and throughout their lives through letters and visits. Their work together on *The Jester* and the Columbia yearbook allowed them the time to enjoy and appreciate each other's gifts. Thomas Merton and Robert Lax, *A Catch of Anti-Letters* (Kansas City: Sheed and Ward, 1994) captures something of their zany correspondence between 1962 and 1967. A volume of their complete correspondence is being planned.

Change this to list of things it would not be easy to imagine talking about for a minute: (One way or the other. You might easily laugh at, say, Kipling, or use him in a joke).

Anthony Trollope.

Camden, N.J.

West Virginia.

Radiators.

All right: to make the list easier; things I never really could believe existed:

Towns between Paris and Orleans.

Victor Herbert, Schumann, Schubert, Tolstoy, Bridge, Poland, Lapland, Jules Michelet (except he became real when I found out he translated Vico), Taine. 23rd Street. Yorkville. Zito, the world's worst dirty cartoonist: even though I spoke to him, I don't believe it is possible for anyone to do those drawings.

The Belgian Fascist Party. Rexists?

Evanston, Ill.

The King and Queen of England, but especially, Danish and Norwegian royalty.

Claimants to the throne of France.

Any movie studio in England (Hitchcock makes movies in some special, private country).

Milton's father and mother. Fichte, Hegel, Schlegel, Schleiermacher; Heinrich Heine, Heinrich Mann. Herder.

Camelias.

Babas-au-rhum, Danish Pastry, Napoleons, all the luxuries I can't tell apart but simply hate.

More things that simply do not exist:

Australia.

St. Pancras Station – or, well, Euston. The inside of St. P sure exists and it's all right. I'm sorry. Maryleybone Welwyn-Garden-City. Weston-super-Mare.

Wm. Morris' paintings in the Oxford Union.

The Tea Room at the Victoria and Albert Museum.

The Barber of Seville (Figaro?)

Arnold Bennett.

E. A. Robinson – Robert Browning – Ezra Pound.

Norman Dunfee, who lived in Great Neck and is now a London policeman.

Augustus John. Puvis de Chavannes.

The Paris Conscience.

Gambetta, and his balloon. Clemenceau.

Ausable Chasm. Saratoga Springs. French Lick, La.

Modernage books.

John Philip Sousa. The Howdy Club.

All the fellows in Russia except Stalin.

Animals that do not exist.

Man. Man is not an animal: individual men are individual animals – dogs, bears, monkeys, sheep, chickens. Man is not an animal.

Animals that do not exist:

I guess, for me, all the animals exist except gila monsters.

Places that do not exist:

West Philadelphia. Rangoon. Far Rockaway. Most of Long Island – Queen's Village, etc. Lille, Troyes, Dieppe, Dunquerque, Ostende, The Saar. Dusseldorf. Essen. Lichtenstein. Montevideo, and the country it is in (whichever of those two).

[Pages 13–16 are missing from the original journal. Pages 17–19 have five drawings.][9]

Those meanings again:

What Herodotus writes about:

There would be a lot of ways of talking about the Bakery on Hudson Street. You could say it was on the West Side of the Street. Frontage about 50 feet: two dining rooms. 350 tables. 350 menus. 2000 chairs etc. etc. Kitchen etc. etc. That's all right: you say that's what it has when you are trying to sell it.

But that isn't what you say when you want to say it has good cheap food. It might be Life Cafeteria from this.

Or you could say me and Gibney and Jinny Burton went there and the German waitresses told Gibney the German rhyme about baking a cake.

You could say roast chicken is 45 cents.

Herodotus[10] used figures when he was the only fellow who knew those numbers: e.g. how far it is from Susa to the Mediterranean. He was one of the few people who had been able to find out. And here was a case where

---

[9] Merton, the cartoonist, inserts three pages of drawings here, beginning on page 17 of the holographic journal. The first is entitled, "Bad guy in a window. Decoration Day." Below this, on the same page, is "War Lord's costume, for War Lords leading a Decoration Day Parade." On page 18 there is a large drawing of the War Lord from the previous cartoon. Page 19 has two small drawings, the top titled "Cuban Village" and below it "Renaissance War Lord." Three of these cartoons are used as graphic dividers for each of the three parts of this book.

[10] Merton was reading Herodotus's *Histories*, the first great prose work in European literature. Herodotus (died 425 B.C.E.) was known as "the Father of History" by Cicero, among others.

(a) it was important to have the world measured, (b) the numbers were so big they meant something over against the error he was correcting (e.g. the Lacedemonian King may have thought he could go to Susa in three days instead of three months).

Ordinarily, the way to tell somebody *nothing* is to tell him a number: just one number.

To get any meaning you have to have at least two numbers. The Empire State is 1200 feet high. So what? Well, my house is 30 feet high. Still, so what? But this time with a different kind of a shrug – a shrug for the not important, yet meaningful relationship – not just for the stupid meaningless kind of a fact.

But as soon as you get away from numbers, and words that mean just about as little, you get into significance.

Herodotus tells what they do in Egypt. Or he tells how they (Persians) shaved slaves' heads and wrote messages on them, telling the slave it was some medicine they were putting on, and let the hair grow, and the slave never knew he had a message: just went to the bird at the other end and asked for another treatment and the receiver shaved the hair off and read the message.

This is pretty different from saying how many slaves there were in Persia, point blank, and expecting a reaction.

This statement means a lot not only because you can compare it with all the other ways of sending messages, but all the other reasons for getting a haircut as well: then also all the relations of masters and servants you can think of, and all the faith in medicine you ever thought of. Here is your slave running half across Asia with a note written on his scalp, and all the time congratulating himself because he has such a healthy head.

And of course, you think in terms of other rebellions for why else would they use such a trick except in time of rebellion?

Herodotus is full of what: wars, migrations, rebellions, conquests, embassies, journeys, spies, subterfuges, local customs, weddings, sacrifices, oracles, building buildings, making laws, etc. The journey of a slave across Asia Minor with a message on his head relates directly to all these topics except weddings and building buildings. And both of these are generally only *mentioned.* So and so married so and so, daughter of a neighboring King, thus . . . relationship to wars, conquest, rebellions, etc. (It is an alliance.)

Herodotus says so many things that scholars have taken to reading him the way you read the World Almanac. Looking up things in him. (The *World Almanac* is all right too, but only if you have nothing to do and like to play Guggenheim against yourself.) So there has arisen a confused idea that Herodotus' facts are of the same kind, though of course much less *reliable* you understand! as the *World Almanac*'s.

He tells us Phoenicians circumnavigated Africa, but not because he wanted to edge Vasco de Gama out of first place in the race to get around Africa – He didn't put down his pen and say, "Well we beat that Portuguese by nearly two thousand years."

He tells it because he is describing the world, and it is one of the things about the world that there is water all around Africa except at Suez. And it is also a thing about the world that fine guys go off in their ships: and it is of the nature of man to be filled with the courage and patience and the strength and the wonder it takes to sail around a great hot fierce place, for three years going on and on and never knowing where.

So, too, it is one kind of a fact that there are tall natives in Ruanda having Egyptian cows, and another that they brought through the wastes, out of Egypt, great sweetness and nobility four thousand years ago. Herodotus is interested in the second kind. But in telling a fact of the first kind he would communicate the idea of the second all right. Otherwise why so many "legends" your science-hat does not go off to?

Now no kind of historian is much interested in this kind of truth today. Your romantic biographer is a low beast precisely because he too would shun like the devil Herodotus' kind of truth: he is simply trying to build bad little idols, and idolatry, naturally, involves error, necessarily.

June 1

I like Wordsworth's later poetry more and more. Some of it is very difficult. "Soft as a cloud on yon Blue Ridge," is not easy. "Sonnets to a Painter" have fine writing, also "Most Sweet It Is with Unuplifted Eyes." A splendid piece of writing is a sonnet "On the Departure of Sir Walter Scott from Abbotsford, for Naples." One reason why I think all Wordsworth's sonnets are his best work is because I think he is at his best in a five beat line. His earlier use of four beat iambic lines give too much of a namby-pamby dancing effect. However, he is damn good and powerful and condensed in that same four-beat iambic in "Extempore Effusion on Death of James Hogg." One reason for that is perhaps that he is writing *by the beat*, not syllabically. e.g. Syllables max. With elisions.

	9	9	Nor has the rolling year twice measured
(normal)	8	8	From sign to sign its steadfast course
	11	9	Since every mortal power of Coleridge
	9	8	Was frozen at its marvelous source.

It is funny that the last line gives an impression of being syllabically the longest of them all – probably because the crowded syllables of the line before pile up against its first word "Was."

One of the things that gives *Laodamia* dignity is its five foot line and the possibility for fine writing it gives Wordsworth.[11] From the subject matter alone it might easily have been a very silly poem: Protesilaus comes back from Hades for three hours, and spends them giving a lecture on Platonic Love!

The Perry Street kids are fine kids but all the same I wish that little bastard would put away the bugle that he doesn't know how to play.

I have never read more than a few short passages of the *Iliad*. I am always finding myself in stupid situations like that: read monkeys like Dos Passos (well, that's normal) or James Farrell; or have read *La Mothe le Vayer*, Crebillon *fils*, Richard Watson Dixon, Tristan l'Hermite, but not the *Iliad*.

Books I want to get:

The Iliad.

Boswell's *Life of Johnson*.

Herodotus.

Merely to read soon:

Coleridge's *Biographia Literaria*.

Richards on Coleridge.

Sophocles, Aeschylus.

Bradley on Shakespeare again. G. W. Knight, too.

Which reminds me: The English Department won't let me write on G. M. Hopkins for my Ph. D. I don't know what other subject I'm going to pick. They'd never let me write on Joyce.

Tonight I walked through the streets, and the Baer-Nova fight was on all the radios, and came out of all the windows: the same voice at the same time coming from in front of you and behind you and from both sides, and what did that do? The city having this one voice made the buildings become liquid and unsubstantial, and the most solid thing was this voice that flowed constantly through all the stone buildings at once.

The only thing that did not change its position relative to yours as you moved was this voice of Clem MacCarthy; you walked away from it and you found you were walking into it, and never knew when you were walking past it, or to one place where it actually was. And it was actually possible to wonder at the logical fact that all the radios were naturally

---

[11] Wordsworth, *Laodamia* and other poems on classical subjects were published in 1814–17.

synchronised. It was actually possible to expect, for a second, that the same voice coming out of two radios would blare against itself, or echo itself as if it were on two phonographs.

So, all through the city was this voice very confident of itself and very confident of science, making all the old stone buildings unquiet and unsubstantial with a pleasant kind of liquid quality. The town turned to water, and it was a bad fight: Nova won on a technical knockout.

August 24

> *Dio ti salvi Maria, piena di grazia;*
> *il Signore e con te; tu sei benedetta fra*
> *le donne e benedetto e il frutto del*
> *ventre tuo, Gesu.*
> *Santa Maria Madre di Dio, prega per noi*
> *peccatori adesso e nell' ora della nostra morte.*
> [Hail Mary, full of grace,
> the Lord is with you; blessed are you among women,
> and blessed is the fruit of
> your womb, Jesus.
> Holy Mary, Mother of God, pray for us
> sinners, now and at the hour of our death.]

So I owe Larbaud a debt – for putting in his novel the Hail Mary as it is in Italian, which is magnificent (on the same page he kids "Excelsior" even better than Thurber did in one of this year's *New Yorker*s.) All this tied up, too, with what a fine sweet girl full of grace is Celeste de Bellis – same eyes all full of a special good kind of light that good people have. Today, watching the morning of light through the leaves on the brick walls of the house across the garden, light in the little fish pond, same time record of Beiderbecke's "In a Mist" ending, very complicated perfect ending, intricate, suspense, perfectly satisfying; last bar of that, movement of light, it flashes into my head what kind of light and grace is in people like Celeste de Bellis, and for a tenth of a second it was like being lifted right through the sky: and things almost all stopped and lost their diversity and knit themselves together as they ought to be, and then I caught my breath and fell out of it laughing and crying; boy it was fine what I just missed; it was a thing to be happy and thankful for and laugh and be glad about.

There is not so much else to laugh about today. Walking along Forty-Second Street seeing the headline that the citizens have been told to leave Paris for fear of war – walking in the hot damp street with the signs on the movie theaters disguising the titles of old movies and trying to entice people in that way – it was terrible to feel so sad and desperate.

I saw _Modern Times_, everybody in the theater laughing. I don't remember when lately I have been in a theater where everybody laughed together so spontaneously as over this three or four years old Chaplin picture. Seeming more than that: it really talks more about the twenties than the depression, in spite of the strike material, etc. It feels that anything that ever had any happiness about this civilization – all the happy things this civilization has produced like Chaplin movies, are all gone and done with. Nothing left but the wars. The West Wall. The Maginot line. The bombers: bombers are our only shining things.

> Christ, have mercy on us.
> _Dio ti salvi, Maria, piena di grazia. . ._
> [God save you, Mary, full of grace.]

Precious Thoughts for August 29

I could write down a number of precious thoughts: but it seems silly to do it because it has just occurred to me that the thoughts that strike you (when you are walking along the street) as something you might conceivably write down (when you get home) are thoughts that you don't really forget, or aren't such good thoughts anyway, or ideas you have had all along.

Take for example a precious thought: that Ezra Pound's new book _Culture_ is perfectly lousy, his writing is disgusting, his opinions stink, his conceit is unbearable, his pettiness is an affront, his middle class vanity is only equalled by his lack of perception, and he parades the acquisitions he has found in museums and libraries with all the cheap pride of a Cincinnati grocer back from Paris with a lead paperweight representing the Trocadero.

But what would be the point of putting that down? Everybody knows it. People have read Pound since he has contributed to _Esquire_ and small sticky smart magazines (Pound and _Esquire_ are on exactly the same level, both bad in the same offensive and frightening way).

Precious thought: Pound's stuff, lately all written, scribbled down like this stuff here. If this stuff were to get into print would it look as bad as Pound?

What is this stuff written for? If I started examining that I would stop writing it. But it helps to put things down if you want to remember them. I will never forget that Pound is lousy. So why put it down?

Remember what?

Like the *"Dio ti salvi Maria"* I found in Larbaud.

Like names, dates, pages, verses, ideas, addresses, references, maps, snapshots.

The Museum of Modern Art – film library. Harold Lloyd – *The Freshman.* Dated. Robt. Benchley – *The Sex Life of the Polyp* (1928) dated surprisingly.

1. Exactly like 1928 *New Yorker* – only it is still funny. 1928 *New Yorker* liable to fall very flat in spots. Thin too in the same way: the cough before mention of the word "sex" has become insipid.

2. Benchley himself – thinner – darker slicker hair, exactly like someone in an Arno cartoon. The straight knee length dresses – every dress Arno draws looks like a 1928 dress.

3. Harry Rosenstein – a kid always worrying about what 1928 was like, looking up facts in books etc. Harold Lloyd, after being beaten up by the whole football team, staggers to his feet, dumbly, bravely, like Harry Rosenstein looking for 1928.

Great spirit that kid.

[Page of calligraphy.]

Germany has (calligraphy?) recalled her ships from off the ocean, issued food cards, stopped running trams beyond frontiers, mobilized everybody, stopped mail service, sent all foreigners away except a couple of commentators, now cries on France's lap, Britain strikes a stern pose, America shouts, Roosevelt girds himself up as Zeus, and still there isn't going to be a war.

Viva la Calligrafia!

Maybe if I translate Pierre Reverdy's *"La Pean de l'Homme"* I will

1. remember it better (it is so fine)

2. write better poetry.

Bad translation by Stuart Gilbert of something by Reverdy on Poetry in a *Vogue* out at Gibney's. Joyce let such a fool as Gilbert act as satellite?

Boswell wasn't by any means a fool.

I could write down what I think of Kathy Bailey, but reasons for not doing it are:

1. I have told seven or eight people, and now it gets to be like a set speech. So will certainly not forget it.

2. It is a dull commonplace anyway.

3. It does not concern anyone but those I have told: no: it concerns everyone in the world.

4. I will eventually say the same thing about five or seven people.

Note: the precious thought about K.B. (funny, Kay Boyle's initials) is what is so good about her, for the benefit of any mean bastard reads this thinks I want to rip anybody up the back.

If Doris Raleigh never said she liked Middleton's "Roaring Girl" I sure bet she does. I say this for no purpose at all except I have said it to myself all day, and am now putting it down in writing. Maybe one point of this book is to get things down in writing because they look different on paper than inside your head – Lax's idea all summer.

What was the least significant thing I did yesterday, August 28 (Monday)?

Of course, anything insignificant will not even be remembered.

1. In Dillon's Bar and Grill – mint in a glass – *Lone Ranger* on the radio, beer tastes bad – outside, red steel framework new building going up N.E. corner Sixth Ave and 48th – nobody good comes in bar yet – Coca Cola ad: big picture dame in white bathing suit nearly bursting out, on one breast a guy wrote "Phil" (or some name). I get cigarettes, look out at street; think maybe it would be good idea leave beer a moment. Walk out to street stand in door say one and one-half minutes in the air look around come back, but do not.

[A missing page here.]

Back in Dillon's Jinny Burton[12] says she is leaving for Virginia where she lives – for a while. I say it sounds like fun, or something of the sort and she says why don't I come along then? And so I accept.

Bright sun Friday morning (Sept. 1) for the first time in days and newspapers full of the bombing of Warsaw. Jinny and I and Joyce Ryan meet in Penn Station. The train is crowded. Right away on the train Jinny and Joyce eat salad. I eat a sardine sandwich. We read our magazines, talk.

At Washington, a stupid old man goes to pass from one car to another although we know the next car is just about to be taken off; he gets back in time, as the floor parts under his feet, after ignoring everybody's shouts (six or seven of us standing on the platform, doors closed, waiting to be let out on to the station).

From Washington to Richmond, in the Club Car – drinking Tom Collins.

[12] After her graduation from Barnard, Jinny Burton began acting in Center Theater productions, and she and Merton became good friends at this time. Both Lax and Merton considered her one of the most promising actresses of the group of friends. She and Merton traveled to her home in Virginia over Labor Day weekend.

We go through Quantico: straw dummies lined up along the track full of holes and gookes made by bayonets, in bayonet practice.

I don't know the secret of why we got Tom Collinses in this Club Car. I thought they didn't serve drinks going through Virginia. He made them in the kitchen, brought no bottles (little one shot bottles) out on the table.

Richmond: I lose my sense of direction. I get the impression of a very extensive, dull town.

Dome of the station exactly like that of the Columbia Library.

We go to see Hedy Lamarr in *Lady of the Tropics.*

Next morning there is supposed to be an extra saying Britain declares war but I see no signs of it. We drive to Urbanna. At Urbanna we hear no radios and see no papers. There is a rumor about the *Bremen.* Monday we hear about the *Athenia.* The weekend is devoted to sailing: for me, I have an impacted wisdom tooth – am half alive, mostly drinking all the time to keep standing it and to keep up with the Virginians. Hot sun.

Urbanna

Rappahannock River. Saluda. West Point. Protests about the regatta, fouling buoys etc. Joyce Ryan clamorously saying how her favorite boat is a schooner, the *Nighthawk.* Motorboat races. Labor Day, outboard races in the creek; Brunswick stew; the coastguard cutter *Commander Maury,* the *Old Tub* with a stupid old captain. Labor Day we watch the races from the *Maury* and see nothing. Barclay's house near Irvington; the Drugstore; Southside.

Sunday morning, yes, a radio in Southside saying Britain has declared war. Describing London quiet as on any Sunday. I hate it.

That is before the 12-mile race to Barclays which we follow in the committee boat.

Missie. Some girl, like Jinny said. The awful drunk guy who came to see her. The party Sunday night – "scotch type whiskey." Swimming in the creek 3 a.m. Everyone furiously drunk.

Back in the city – war has settled into a routine. Coming back on the train: on our way from Richmond to New York Tuesday, we know Roosevelt is proclaiming neutrality in such a way we are sure to have to be sore over every slight violation and so will go to war soon.

I did not get around to writing the book review until today.

September 8, 1939

The other night we saw *A Nous la Liberté* and *Modern Times* all over again, this time up at Thalia – 95th Street full of ugly intellectuals including a

Jewish dame with a laugh like a demented sheep which she probably got from being thrown out of Germany with whips.

Remember above all from seeing *A Nous la Liberté* this time the scene where they are hiring men for the factory and the little guy is marched in with the rest – they stand in front of a loudspeaker, which recites, over and over again, in a voice on a record just a little too slow a wonderful rhyme. They turn away from the loudspeakers, a lot of milling around, what with weighing machines and the little guy saying he doesn't want to work, and the overseer being tough and saying "it isn't what you *want* around here . . ." and in intervals, you can hear this rhyme going on and on and on in counterpoint to the whole thing.

The pattern of that scene is magnificent: it is one of [René] Clair's very best,

[other side of the page]

as much as I can remember of the rhyme.

> *Vous qui desirez de l'emploi*
> *Donnez nous votre nom, votre age*
> – – – (I forget)
> *Retournez vous et marchez droit*
> [You who want work
> Give us your name, your age.
> – – – (I forget)
> Turn around and walk straight.]

The pitch of lines 1 and 2 goes like this

> *Vous qui desirez de l'emploi*
> *Dites vous votre nom votre age*

Which all by some kind of association or other brings me to the point where I am bound to say that I think the best poet of this century in any country is

Guillaume Apollinaire.

I ought to write it in prettier letters:

Guillaume Apollinaire [larger script]

The only poet of any account writing in English has been W. B. Yeats. Auden, [Stephen] Spender, Eliot – not too much account, I must say. Talent, you know, talent! As for America . . .

[Two sheets are missing here; they seem to be have been torn out.]

The air outside my window is quiet, and light hangs among the leaves and the sky is soft and blue and warm. In one of the next houses, I can hear pots in a kitchen, and water running from a tap, and I can hear the voices of kids.

That is not an airplane, but the motor of a Goodyear balloon going down the North River, with sightseers. This sunlight, this warm air, the sounds of kitchens, speak of God's goodness and His mercy. I can sit here all day, now, and think of that, and ask God to show me everywhere more and more signs of His mercy, and His goodness, and help me to regain my liberty. Peace.

I know they are hearing confessions now at Saint Francis' Church. Everywhere, tomorrow morning, Masses.

Here on my shelves, Pascal, Saint Augustine, Thomas à Kempis, Loyola, The Bible, Saint John of the Cross (no – Lax has that).

Here is liberty, all I have to do is to be quiet, sit still.

Liberty: menaced most of all by the war. But by other disproportionate things I am more familiar with than war – which I don't know anything about really. All the restlessness I can create for myself looking for liberty where I know I have never been able to find it. Why?

The answer is, not only in war but always liberty is menaced: only not so brutally. And the solution only this, to abandon all things, only love God and thy neighbor. First: abandon all things. That, at least, if the only one thing, is the clear answer.

Several Vanities – September 13

1. When I kept a diary before – this is dignified by the name of a journal (oh no. I won't make that joke against myself. It isn't dignified by the name of anything) – one of the things I was always doing was picking a date – say September 13, and looking back over three or four years to compare what happened on the various pages of various books. I remember too, for no good reason, riding in a car along a shaded road towards Bournemouth in 1932 (August), saying to myself I wonder where I will be this time next year. That time the following year I was in America getting ready to go to Cambridge. But I did not think of it. I do not remember anything else about the ride in the car except that, along the road, was a wall.

2. One of the most shocking kinds of diary is a self-improvement confession diary. Mine was rather an "experience" diary, which is only schoolgirlish and ridiculous. The Benjamin Franklin trick: schedules for

self-improvement. Checking up on a schedule. Cf. André Gide – *Caves du Vatican.*

Extremes: crazy *actes gratuits,* for self-discipline.

Egoism – Stendhal, Alfieri. Perhaps that was what Lax was thinking about when we had all those arguments about "mortification" in Olean.

The guy who stuck a knife in his arm (Gide) just to show he could do it: naturally he turned into a criminal.

3. All this ties up with Egoism – ambition. Stendhal could get away with writing about ambition. I guess Gide did too, but it makes you uncomfortable to read it, because ambition today is becoming absurd. Because ambition has become absurd in literature, Hitler gets away with it in life. After that?

The stock arguments against ambition – (Shelley's "Ozymandias") have even come to be absurd too. Because an ambitious man is simply a bloody fool.

Because ambitious men are absurd, the same suspiciousness towards ambition literature has fallen upon confession literature. (By ambition literature – not Horatio Alger: Stendhal.) That is upon all confession literature indiscriminately. Rousseau as well as Saint Augustine. The *Confessions* of Rousseau belong with ambition literature: these of Saint Augustine do not. The difference is that Saint Augustine confesses God, Rousseau proclaims himself.

Confessions are only valid (in literature) if they confess God.[13]

7 P.M. A model sentence from Pascal. Maybe everyone who wants to write should, before he even starts, consider this sentence as much for its balance and its construction as for what it says: it is the beginning of all writing.

"Il ne faut pas avoir l'âme fort élevée pour comprendre qu'il n'y a point ici de satisfaction véritable et solide, que tous nos plaisirs ne sont que vanité, que nos maux sont infinis, et qu'enfin la mort, qui nous menace à chaque instant, doit infailliblement nous mettre, dans peu d'années, dans l'horrible nécessité d'être éternellement ou anéantis ou malheureux." Pensées III. 194. ["We do not require great education of the mind to understand that here is no real and lasting satisfaction; that our pleasures are only vanity; that our evils are infinite; and lastly, that death, which threatens us every moment, must infallibly

---

[13] The *Confessions* of Saint Augustine of Hippo was one of the books the Hindu monk, Bramachari, had recommended for Merton to read to deepen his knowledge of the Western tradition. He not only meditated on the *Confessions,* but also read Augustine's *City of God,* which made an enormous impression on the young convert to Catholicism.

place us within a few years under the dreadful necessity of being for ever either annihilated or unhappy."[14]]

Thursday, September 14, 1939

Two Quotations:

    1. Valéry Larbaud – *A. O. Barnabooth, Son Journal Intime*, p. 121 (cf. yesterday remarks on ambition, confessions, Gide etc.)

    "Curieux: l'aversion que j'éprouve à l'égard de ce que l'on appelle vertu. Il faut que j'examine cela aussi. Je suis bien obligé de constater qu'il y a en moi une emulation au vice. La vertu me semble négative et facile. Le mal me semble positif et difficile; et comment n'irais-je pas vers le mal? Constamment je l'entends qui me parle et me crie à grande voix: Paresseux! sors de ta chambre et viens me trouver; tu sens bien qu'il faut te surmonter et refouler en toi mille peurs, cent préjugés et un million de timidités pour t'élever jusqu'à moi. Je suis difficile et haut, viens!" ["Odd: the aversion I feel toward what is called virtue. I must examine that too. I am quite obliged to note that there is in me a rivalry with vice. Virtue seems negative and easy to me. Evil seems positive and difficult to me; and how could I not go toward evil? I constantly hear it speaking to me and shouting at me with a loud voice: Lazy! leave your room and come find me; you're well aware that you have to overcome yourself and suppress within you a thousand fears, a hundred prejudices and a million timidities in order to raise yourself to my level. I am difficult and high, come!"]

    2. Pascal – *Pensées* – VI. 408.

    "Le mal est aisé, il y en a une infinité; le bien, presque unique. Mais un certain genre de mal est aussi difficile à trouver que ce qu'on appelle bien, et souvent on fait passer pour bien à cette marque ce mal particulier. Il faut même une grandeur extraordinaire d'âme pour y arriver, aussi bien qu'au bien." ["Evil is easy, and has infinite forms; good is almost unique. But a certain kind of evil is as difficult to find as what we call good; and often on this account such particular evil gets passed off as good. An extraordinary greatness of soul is needed to attain to it as well as to good."[15]]

    1. These two quotations are obviously not contradictory, but say exactly the same thing.

    2. Neither compares absolute good and absolute evil – which cannot be compared because absolute evil does not exist and perfect good is only truly apparent to God, and we only know it imperfectly, from revelation.

---

[14] Blaise Pascal, *The Provincial Letters, Pensées, Scientific Treatises*, translated by W. F. Trotter, in *Great Books of the Western World* (Chicago: Encyclopedia Britannica, 1952), 207.

[15] English from Trotter, *Great Books of the Western World*, 207.

Both compare "evil" – "*le mal*" (a thing we can judge of by the light of conscience) with (a) "*ce que l'on appelle vertu*" (V.L.) and (b) "*ce qu'on appelle bien.*" (P.)

3. The difference: Pascal considering man in the light of the fall, original sin, redemption, etc. recognizes as "*le mal*" something easy in the fallen state. It is diverse; it is everywhere. *Le bien est unique.* cf. Saint Thomas. II – 1.2. – Q70 – A.4.[16]

But the good belongs to the true nature of man, is part of the heritage cast away in Eden, is single, is always sought after, is found by love, courage, patience, humility. In the sense that it is not for the slothful, it is "hard." In the sense that we must rise above our "fallen" nature to achieve it, it is "hard." V.L. uses the term "*te surmonter.*"

4. Saint Mary Magdalene: in her, the capacity for great "sinfulness" was the capacity for great saintliness. Also in everybody else. Pascal not speaking directly of that kind of instance. Larbaud is. Many so-called virtuous people are "virtuous" from sloth, out of inertia. Sloth is "*négative et facile,*" it is "*aisé.*" Virtue, without charity, is not virtue. Charity and sloth incompatible. N.B. The opposite of sloth is not "activity" or industriousness in a business sense. It is fortitude – including patience and long-suffering.

September 14. Thursday

Today: neither happy nor comfortable until I got in bed. Wisdom tooth (out Monday) and beginning of a cold. But with Gibney saw Sacha Guitry in *Story of a Cheat.* That was very fine. Monagasque Army – forwards and backwards!

New words – from places both in Guitry and Larbaud: *Monagasque.*

In Larbaud: Sammarinois (Saint-Marin-San Marino)
Salernitain (Salerno)
Also Gnossienne (Knossos – Satie)
Tarentaise – (dance – that's easy)
Bergamasque (Bergamo)

Now I'm tired of making that list. It would be a good one if I knew more of the good words – Oh –

Madrid – Madrilene.
Chypre – Cypriote.
Smyrne – Smyrinote (Val. Larb.)

---

[16] The *Summa Theologica*, one of the major works of Saint Thomas Aquinas, was read and meditated upon by Merton during this period of his life in New York. He undoubtedly worked easily from the Latin text, as this journal makes clear.

Sparte – Spartiate –

Corse – Corse (followed by all the unimaginable bad puns in English, for any funny fellow who wants them)

All good adjectives. Compare how poor and dull English adjectives taken from place names are. In fact – how few – you say a *London fog*, there is no adj. Then take it for nouns. Londoner, New Yorker, Oxonian and Cantab (hell!) Oakhamian, Nottinghamian – Chicagoan – (refuse to use that!). Can't even call to mind one ending in -ite – there must be some horrors. Well – Brooklyn*ite*.

Auverguat	Montalbanais
Breton	Toulousain
Picard	Albigeois
Perigourdian	Pallois (Pan)

September 26. Tuesday

Saint Francis in his sermon to the birds told them first of all how grateful the birds must be to God who gave them their coats of fine feathers for which they did not have to toil and spin, and for giving them the air as their element. So they should never, then, be ungrateful to him: but they should go everywhere praising him.

Thus first he told them what they already knew, of the great love and goodness of God. After that he told them never to be ungrateful to God, but always to praise him and glorify His Name.

It is easier to begin praying by glorifying God and remembering his goodness and his mercies, for they are obvious. Obvious, for example, in the consolation of the cool air, or the sun or the rain which falls on the just and the unjust alike – or in the stories of the Saints, or in the miracles of the Gospel, or in Christ's preaching, or the miracles of the Saints, or the great solace of Mass and prayer. But in continually asking for things without glorifying God and first being unmindful of his mercies, then prayer becomes sometimes dry and barren and harsh and without solace, and is reduced to a mumbling.

Fear: the greatest fear of all, of being ungrateful to God and betraying him. For it is comparatively little to sin without having confessed God – or known him, that is, in blindness and ignorance and confusion. But to confess Christ and then sin and so betray Christ by ingratitude (knowing His love and great mercy) and then to justify yourself and your sin, what a terrible damnation! That is worse than Pilate's sin, or the horror of the executioner who drove the nails in, or of the soldiers who pierced Him with the spear – it is the betrayal of Judas.

The greatest fear of all is the fear of this betrayal; it is horrible and black and without hope.

The fear, then, attends anyone thinking he has a vocation for the priesthood, very manifestly. The priest has declared himself, has been accepted by Christ as an apostle, has given up himself and the whole world and all it holds, for the service of Christ. Then to turn again into the world is to give over the incarnation of almighty and most merciful God to the executioner for thirty pieces of silver. That is putting your hand to the plough and looking back. The fear of the pit of Hell.

But Saint Francis saw in a vision that Brother Elias would betray him and die out of the order and be damned. Yet because Brother Elias begged Saint Francis to pray to God for mercy, God told Saint Francis he would not be damned. And although he betrayed the order and the Church and was excommunicated, repenting, and begging again for the intercession of the prayers of Saint Francis, it was granted him to die in the Church and in the habit of the order. Thus his Faith and Hope saved him, and gained him the prayers of the Saint and the loving mercy of Christ.

But no man is without sin, and although every sin is the denial and betrayal of Christ, yet in his mercy our true contrition and confession of our sins with meekness and humility and the long-suffering desire of amendment brings us forgiveness.

Nowadays the utterance of confessions on paper bears the stigma of hypocrisy, for it is too easy to cry out for our sins without true contrition, and to proclaim them without ourselves believing them to be sins. And those who read about them also do not believe those things to be sins.

[Pages 65–68 are missing from the original text.]

. . . and glorifying His name. If we do not, but begin immediately with asking him for a list of things we want, we are liable to forget that he is the creator of all things, and that he created us too, and that he sees into our hearts and knows what we need long before we can ask for it. We are liable to forget that he created everything and has all power over everything, but rather seem to ask him as if he were a kind of an intermediary reaching things to us off of a shelf. Rather than saying "Now pass me the dollar bill on the top shelf" – Thy will be done.

We cannot possess things – we die and they are lost, or they are stolen, or they perish. But more than that, we ourselves cannot even enjoy the things themselves. To think we can is idolatry.

When I smell a flower, is it my nose enjoying the tiny physical particles that carry the smell to it – if that's how smells go? Is it my nose that knows the difference between good and bad smells, or is the distinction an intellectual one? (Psychologists say there is no intellect. I suppose they have simply given it some other name, for that is all they have done so far, to obscure things by changing their names for the worse.) My intellect, which is good, in me, recognizes the smell of the flower for something it remembers as good (not something good in itself. Suppose you have rose-fever, then the mixture of good and bad in the smell of a rose is quite marked) – something that has good associations. The smell of the flower is good by virtue of the fact that God created it. Our intellect is part of what is most Godlike in us: the smell of the flower is no better and no worse, in itself, than the smell of a skunk. What our intellect likes, in the smell of the flower, is the associations it carries. But the smell of flowers reminds the intellect only of its own previous happiness, and the only real happiness it can have is in the love of God. What the soul enjoys in the world is still only itself and God, not *things*. The soul enjoys God, not the smell of the flower. Your nostrils enjoy a smell, or perceive it: but they don't know whether they enjoy it or hate it. They can only catch it, they cannot make any decisions about it, although I suppose there are some smells too much even for the nose, that is not a decision made by the nose, not to like that smell, it is the nose's weakness and deficiency, that it can't stand the smell: it might be either excruciatingly bad or excruciatingly good; all the nostrils know is, it is too much.

The nostrils catch whatever physical particles carry a smell. Eyes take in the waves of light bearing the image of things seen. Those physical particles, that actual light, do not get to the soul, the soul does not possess the things, only their images, and, even, only the reflection of their actual images. And the images themselves are only valuable not for their own selves, which the soul cannot capture, but for their association with something unseen and unheard.

We cannot possess, or even enjoy anything in itself, but only in God.

On the other hand, when we see things as they are in God (or as we think they are in God) in relation to the goodness and love of their creator, then the things are filled with more beauty and more significance than would be possible if we just looked at the thing for its own sake. If we look at an object, a creature: say, a tree, for itself, its own sake, it means either nothing at all, or else something not very important – an obstacle not too difficult to get around as we walk through the woods on the way to sell our Grandmother to the pimps.

Or else the tree may mean planks for tables and chairs and floors and walls that we need, and then we begin to be grateful to God, a little, for filling the world with things which we, who can no longer sleep under the hedges, may feed and clothe and house ourselves.

We have – not stopped loving the tree for itself for we have scarcely begun to love the tree at all: but stopped considering it as it is in itself, that is, cells of wood.

Or else the tree offers us shade, which is pleasant, and so reminds us of God's mercy and love which is pleasant and full of solace, and the tree appears to be the instrument of God's mercy and love for the just and the unjust alike.

Or else, the tree is a living thing, nourished as we are by the Lord God, and holding up its leaves and branches loving the air and the light that move around and among it, and nourished by the sun and the rain and the rich ground: and so, loving the tree, not for itself, we are able to achieve the imaginative self-identification with it poets and Saints both seek after and we love it in something of the same kind of way as Saint Francis loved and understood the birds and all living creatures.

But we cannot possess or enjoy or love trees for what they are in themselves alone, for in themselves alone they are really nothing, or very uninteresting. The soul cannot enjoy things, it can only enjoy itself or the love of God. It cannot enjoy trees: but God and his mercy and love are everywhere in the air, in the trees, in our hearts. So we can be struck with love and sympathy and understanding for the Godliness that is in all the things around us, that proclaim the immense and unfailing love of their creator.

Today, a fine rain, very gray, a little raw outside, like days in England. I remember – keep remembering the road from Ealing to Ripley – I used to go back and forth between terms, to school at Ripley Court, from Aunt Maude's.

First: Brentford; dirty little brick houses: a gap in them, you see down a lane to the river where there is a gray stone monument the shape of a pillarbox commemorating a battle between Caesar and the Britons. A ferry, a rowboat, to Kew Gardens (Once in Kew Gardens, you will look across the river to Sion House). Then you cross Brentford Bridge to Kew. On the left, on the Brentford side, a theater. On the right, on the Kew side, a place to rent boats. A common.

(Surrey: wide flat village greens criss-crossed with dirt paths – the grass drying and yellowing, clumps of gorse, a game of cricket. Along the common a line of low houses, one or two stories, brick, whitewashed, white and green. Behind: tall elms.)

After the village, along the edge of Kew Gardens, right. Then, the Pagoda, the field where some rugby team or other played, Richmond coming: Richmond, crowded street, Southern Railway Station, signs – Borial, Players Please, Every Morn I fill my Pipe – with St. Julien rich and ripe.

In Richmond there is a store belonging to a Merton. I forget what – a grocer? a baker? a tailor? a butcher?

Then, to Kingston. The King's Stone. Under the railway right by the station, bus ducks quickly under a bridge. Before Kingston, on one side a soccer field, on the other a factory, seeming closed, made some car Harvey Crystal once had one of – *what* car (Torture!)

Outside Kingston. The river on one side, on the other waterworks or sewage disposal or something. Then, fork left under some trees, along a green, and under the railway – sign on the flat metal bridge advertises Stutz or Reo cars.

Then out into Esher Common and

The Marquis of Granby [in flowery penmanship]

right, at a crossing. Very soon, Esher: on the right. Again, the racetrack – called what? The grandstand backed up against the wooded hill. We climb into Esher and stop at the crossing where on the right are bucks and on the left, I think,

The Bear [in flowery pen as above]

Out of Esher, then, at the top of the hill the road bears right, a garage I see very clearly but cannot describe and on the right the immaculate white-washed walls of either a nursing home or a girls school or a convent.

The road straight down a hill and straight up the other side. Woods both sides. At the top of the next hill is, I think, a place with sandbanks and rocks which I refer to in my practiced prep-school Latin ringing always in my head from having been learned by heart, the

Locus insidiis idoneus
[place suitable for ambushes]

Thus on to Cobham, what with one thing and another, we come up a hill, on the left a big white house with I forget what to distinguish it, on the right, a common: gorse. Then, houses begin, and the Cobham cottage hospital, and down hill to the pub I clearly see before me with green lattice work over grayish stucco, and the barrels and the red and black sign for

Friary Ale [flowery penmanship]

and it is, maybe the

Red Lion. [flowery pen]

Turn right then sharp, and we pass a place where Tom Bennett[17] and Iris [Bennett] and Hugo Anson and I had tea after being down to see his aunts at a town whose name I clearly remember but not just now, and it is over towards Aldershot, and maybe it is over in Hampshire and begins with a W.

Then we cross the river, and up the hill between high banks, and high over the road a metal suspension footbridge joins the halves of the estate the road, in its deep cut, divides. At the top of the hill

Feltonfleet School. [in flowery pen]

To the right a road that leads, as the sign says, straight to the motor races at Brooklands.

Down the hill through the trees and rhododendrons on the left, at the bottom, the cricket field where I made, batting for the second XI.

32 not out. [flowery pen again]

(Soccer there, too. The prickly, woolen black-and-green striped jerseys for Ripley Court.) Then on through the woods, pines, sandy ground, the road then sweeps down a curve to

Hut Pond [flowery pen]

smooth and glassy, black pines all around it. So on into Ripley. Ousie's house. The Anchor. Garages. The common. Left: the cottage. Ripley Court. Just before the cottage: British Legion Post. At night, sleeping in the cottage, in summer, waking up, hearing the British Legion singing

Old soldiers never die
They sim-ply fade a-way.

Little box hedges along the flowerbeds. Red brick walls, fruit trees trained against them to branch like candlesticks so all the fruit will hang against the wall in the sun. The tall elms. The ha-ha. Kedgerle for breakfast. The three

[17] Dr. Tom Bennett was a surgeon and friend of Tom's father, Owen Merton. He was appointed Tom Merton's legal guardian at the time of Owen's death, when the sixteen year old was a student at Oakham School in England. After winning a scholarship to Cambridge University, the young Merton proceeded to dissipate his time and energies during his first year. Dr. Bennett urged Merton to move to the United States and take up residence with his maternal grandparents – Samuel Jenkins (Pop) and Martha Baldwin (Bonnemaman) – in Douglaston, New York, and he subsequently enrolled at Columbia.

pieces of dry bread on everybody's plate you had to eat up before you could take buttered bread off the plates in the middle of the table.

And now, troops and tanks and guns along the Portsmouth road, and all those kids at the school are probably soldiers. Clifton-Mogs who got the scholarship to Eton. And the Steeles who went to Aldenham and Irving who went to Glenalmond and was at Cambridge when I was, and Romanoff, and Lansdowne, and Yates and R. G. G. M. Marsden, and Percy Major who had the lead plate in his head. . . .

But the papers do not say where the British soldiers are or who they are: the latest report described British officers having tea somewhere in France, and the English are angry at their "Ministry of Information" for giving no information.

If only there could be peace before they start to get killed. Now 12.15.

September 30. Saturday

Last night, began teaching an English class in Extension [Columbia University].

Tonight it is wet without raining. Walking into the room like walking into a pool. Anyway this is a damp room and gets no sun. But what does that matter?

I don't really feel like writing anything much at all. Can't feel that anything I would write down would have any importance.

Yet there is one very good thing to be thankful for to God: reading in the Henri Ghéon book about the Saint who was priest of Ars – found out also about Saint Philomena, blessed little Saint, flower of martyrs: a child who was martyred in Rome, and whose bones were not discovered until the nineteenth century. And by her grave a phial (the martyr's blood), and around the grave were painted an anchor and an olive branch and three arrows: the olive branch for the peace and joy of heaven, the anchor for her safety there and the arrows for the arrows of her executioners. Also three clay cakes, each bearing one word of this salutation:

Pax Tecum Filumena
[Peace be with you, Philomena]

No sooner were the bones of this blessed martyr discovered than they began to work the most wonderful miracles, and through her intercession many miracles were done at Ars where the Saint had a chapel to her in his church.

And it was impossible for me, reading this, not to suddenly feel the great power of this blessed martyr, kept, by Almighty God, so many centuries in oblivion. The words of the salutation are full of beauty and consolation and power.

What excuse is there for misery and unhappiness then, when there is the intercession before the throne of God of such a saint as this, who seems to be filled with such great love for all sinners and especially for those that love her that they at once feel it themselves, moving deeply within them, a sudden and obscure answer, bringing tears.

Not only her, then, but all the Saints; not only the saints, but the angels, and above the angels, their Queen, Mary, the Mother of God and Queen of heaven sitting before the throne of God above the nine choirs and the seraphim, all filled with love and mercy and interceding for us before God himself who loves us most of all, because in Him is all love, and he gave his body and blood in sacrifice for us upon the Cross.

But that body and blood, that sacrifice is daily perpetuated in the churches, and the church herself is there, a great everlasting source of wisdom and consolation.

Then, if our sins blind us to all this, we deserve our misery, but we must not let them do so: we must go to the church and pray to the Saints and to Mary and to Christ our Lord that the blindness of sin be healed in us and we must first of all love and glorify them, and though we are full of sin, we must not therefore be full of despair, but pray continually with humility and meekness for forgiveness of our sins and for increase in Love and Faith and Hope.

The whole world is filled with the blood and anger and violence and lust our sins and self-will have brought upon us, my own sins as much as anybody else's: Hitler, Stalin are not alone responsible. I am too, and everybody is, insofar as he has been violent and lustful and proud and greedy and ambitious. The world is very unhappy and terrible now, but beyond it and in it and around it is still the Love and Mercy of God, that only waits for our prayers. And now I am glad to have written something.

October 1. Sunday

Church had the atmosphere of a Feast. There is a novena to Saint Francis, and there are flowers: but that is every day, too. Today, completely jammed instead of half filled at 10, as usual, and also music. Very happy place, this morning. And that is so: every Sunday is a great Feast and a time of joy; which incidentally I did not use to believe so much. London and Cambridge, dreary Sundays. Enervating walks in the country.

I remember the feeling around tea time, at Oakham. Hunger and no prospect of anything but that doughey, heavy bread cut in chunks: the feeling that all the joints in my legs were loose and unstable – the feeling you get from walking a long way not normally or fast but listlessly, kicking stones. Sunday in France was never that way but always a feast, too.

In a corner of the upper church – but tucked away – a statue, much better than the others, although the same plaster type: yet it seemed at once different from them too; right away, I wondered what saint: an anchor – arrows – it was Saint Philomena. But of course there is a shrine to her in the lower church too, which I knew some time before finding out anything about her.

Today has the smells of a feast. A girl sitting opposite me in the restaurant at breakfast: some perfume on that reminded me of several things. First, the perfume and the softness and complexion of her skin reminded me of a whole class of girls I had been in love with from fourteen on. The kind that are rather thin than plump, rather blonde than dark, seem at the same time soft and sad: their sadness, a kind of mystery; melancholy which makes them appear, also, intelligent and good.

Then the perfume too reminded me of all sorts of Sundays and feasts and the rich smells going with them at Douglaston. The smell of powder and perfume in my Grandmother's room. The smell of the same room, with all the heat on, in the morning, with my Grandfather having breakfast in bed: so the room smelling of perfume, powder, coldcream, radiator heat, fried eggs, toast, strong coffee. All at once.

Other feast smells: brilliantine I bought in Bermuda this year. Good, fat smell, lavender. Means sun and the white coral houses and the dark cedars. That nostalgia now complicated by the fact that there's no going to Bermuda now, because of the war.

Feast smells at Douglaston: cigar smoke, meaning Uncle Charles and the funny sheets: (he brought the *Tribune:* Pop took the *Times*). Candy. Smell of dinners, of course. Smell of Christmas tree: noise of steam chirping in the radiator, at the same time.

Noises:

Outside, now, it is raining.

Noise of a cocktail shaker at Douglaston, first with a martini being stirred in it, then with something being shaken in it. Generally, sun outside, or late slanting sun through the French windows.

Noise of a toy electric train going around its tracks. Noise of winding up a clockwork locomotive – slower turn of the key, and thickening catch of the spring.

Noise of the cook chopping or pounding things in the kitchen at Douglaston.

Noise of tires singing past the house on the road outside, in winter or in autumn when the road is light and bare and hard.

Noise of a fire, cracking and snapping in the grate, just lit. The sheaves of sparks, that rush up the chimney from time to time.

Noise of the dog jumping up inside the door and scratching on it as you come up the steps.

Noise of Pop walking upstairs, beating with his hand on the banister halfway between the beats of his feet on the hollow sounding wooden steps.

Noise of someone (never me!) shovelling coal into the furnace downstairs, the shovel chunkily bites in under the coal, which smothers its sound: then the coal rushing off the shovel into the fire, leaving the shovel ringing slightly, full of a load.

Noise of someone opening up the legs of a card-table – a drag and a sudden catch.

Noise of starting the radio: click of the knob, and the light comes on, then, half a second later, a sudden swell of hum that dies again a little, while the radio settles down to think up a real sound. After that: nothing very interesting comes out of the radio, as a rule.

Noise of the cellar door banging shut: never one bang, but a bang and a quarter because of the bounce. Noise of footsteps on the cement steps leading down to the cellar. Noise of dragging ashcans up the cellar steps, step by step, the heavy, muffled bumping, muffled by the weight of the fine pinkish gray ash. All this took place under the window of the room I slept in: that room was Pop's den. It had an office desk and a swivel-chair. Noise made by the swivel-chair when you turned on it completely. First no noise at all, then a kind of slight, singing protest. (Noise of the drawers opening and shutting.) The protest of the chair comes not from making it turn, but it is uttered by a tough spring as you lean back in the chair and tilt it quite a bit.

Noise of raking leaves, of mowing the grass, of digging with a spade, of raking ground or hoeing. Sweeping the sidewalk and the brick front steps.

Noise of the sprinkler, as it turns scattering whirling threads of water around the air over the front lawn. Twenty or thirty feet away the leaves of the privet hedge move where you would not have suspected water was falling.

Thank God, then, for all good smells and good sights and good sounds; but what is the good of being attached to them, and sitting and turning over their memory and dwelling on the recollections they bring to you, and cherishing a sadness for these things which are gone away. Pop and Bonnemaman are dead, and it will never again be the same as being sixteen and eighteen and living at Douglaston, in vacations. And as to that, what a vanity it would be anyway to moan over the happiness of those times, because, at eighteen and twenty and twenty-one, while I was active and rushing about after all sorts of things, who can say those were very good or happy years for me when I was full of anger and impatience and ingratitude towards my family to an extent it is horrible to think about now. Then I was proud and selfish, and denied God and was full of gluttony and lust. And was so filled with all these things that even now the unhappiness of them does not leave me at all, but keeps forcing itself back upon me in thoughts and dreams and movements of anger and desire, and I am still full of that same pride and wretchedness, which is very strong and very hard to get rid of because of the strength of self-will which weakens love and prayer and resists God.

But all these things were much stronger then because I did not resist them at all; because of them, then, I was very confused and unhappy. So it would be a lie to look back on those as happy days. But it is vanity to desire anything that is past because you cannot bring it back again. Besides, if pleasure now is vanity, pleasure in the past is twice as much a vanity: the pleasure of making love, now, is poor enough by itself (that is, without enough love to want to marry the girl, which is not much!) but the pleasure of a first love when you were sixteen. . . . You will never be sixteen again and you will never be in love again for the first time, and anyway, it was fairly silly and certainly not at all satisfactory. As to its injustice – seeing she was married – I think that doesn't matter, because of my own innocence anyway. I did not conceive it was possible to do more than declare that I loved her, and give her one kiss. The misery afterwards, was, of course, a luxury. It was all very well and very nice, but to want such a stupid kind of thing to happen again would be crazy. Stupid: not the being in love part, but all the dramatics and excesses and luxuries of sentiment that surrounded it when the object of my love was on her way to the other side of the earth.

Yet there are many good things to look back on because, before I had my first year at Cambridge, anyway, although I was always full of crazy pride, yet I did love God and pray to him and was not completely full of sins. So there were good days at Oakham – and at Strasbourg and at Rome, and earlier, in France, and in London on holidays from school. But I think that

even as a child I was too full of anger and selfishness for me to want to recapture my own childhood at all now! In fact, then, to want to recapture
anything you have had or owned or experienced is a bigger vanity and unhappiness than to want to possess some present good that is before you.
And of course, Saint John of the Cross says the memory must be completely darkened, as well as the intellect and will.

Of course it is not really true that I am sentimental about things I remember. That is not it: but I find them easy and interesting to write about.
They come readily and run fast off the pen, for me they have a kind of life
and interest. I have been bothered, however, for a long time, wondering
just what place they have – what place anything has I write down here. 1)
To begin with – if this stuff is written to be remembered, to remind *me*
then it is nonsense: it is not worth remembering, or not worth going to any
trouble to remember: especially when nothing at all is worth remembering, really: not even Divine Truths, because the Faith and Hope in the
Love of God are inspired directly by his grace in the darkness of the intellect, the memory and the will: and the memory is to be utterly darkened
and turned to Hope which is the darkness of the memory, that is, true
light. 2) But, writing these things down, they clarify themselves, they move
in words and sentences, and so take shape while in my own mind they are
formless and not articulate. 3) The urge to speak and write, compared with
Faith, Hope and Charity themselves, is vanity. But we are given tongues
and words to praise God with and to proclaim him with, and we should
love to study how to use our tongues and our words. So while this stuff is
not written for anybody to read, yet it is practice and it is helpful and good,
so long as I do not think of it in terms of its being published and read, and
so a source of pride to use.

Yet this is obviously not practice in *writing* – that is, in expression, or
clarity or style or beauty or conciseness or what you will.

It is hardly practice in *thinking*, because there, too, it is loose and ram-
bling and incoherent: but it is at least practice in being, somehow, articulate. And it is a release for the things that I am full of and must try to say.
As to pride, it is obvious that anything good in this is nothing done by me,
but thanks to God only, and so how should I take pride in it? And yet, I always find myself taking pride in things that are not my own but God's (for
nothing is my own).

Yet it is good to write about and try to articulate all such things, not for
the sake of remembering them, because if God wills that you should hear
them again he will tell you them: but yet the next time I will come to talk

about these things they should be clearer and better for my having at least tried to articulate them now.

As to all the physical things and sensations I remember: it is not good to remember them for themselves; it is not even possible, really, to remember them for themselves – or to yearn after them as if you could re-possess them when you can't really possess anything anyway.

But nevertheless, words themselves have sound and color and life: and the things you make with words, sentences and verses, should also be physically attractive and beautiful, please readers and attract them to the spiritual beauty inside the words – that is their Truth. So, writing attractive words is not altogether vanity, even though it is no more important to salvation than knowing how to make a shoe (shoemakers probably have fewer temptations to pride) – and reflecting on physical things and words about them is a helpful exercise for a writer as craftsman. That is all.

But even the craftsman does not possess his craft: the art is a virtue, nourished, and infused and entertained by God.

The craftsman cannot get, or learn his craft himself: he himself can only lose it, just as we cannot learn or get any virtue ourselves, but must rely on God's grace for it: but it is our *selves*, our self will, that can turn us away from God, and make us lose our virtues that we have.

The craftsman who thinks he possesses his craft, and loses his patience and humility and love that are necessary to it, loses his art: the theory today is that artists by their own will and own supreme human understanding can be artists: so there is very little art and a lot of pride and bad pictures and quarrelling.

(Evening–Sunday)

[October 1, 1939] [18]

When Blake said some of his work was dictated by angels he did not mean that, because all other poetry was merely written by men, his was superior to theirs. On the contrary he meant that all good poetry was "dictated by angels" and that he himself could not claim any praise for "his" verses. They were not really his.

But nowadays, since men are supposed to be the highest of *all* creatures, because they are at the top of the ladder of evolution, we are very careful to

[18] Pages 5–6 are the opening lines of *The Secular Journal of Thomas Merton* (New York: Farrar, Straus and Cudahy, 1959).

guard that position against anything higher – angels – God. To presume that poetry could be dictated by a creature higher than man, then, seems an affront: and since angels are only "symbols," Blake seemed to be speaking by symbols to say he was the greatest of poets. But his statement was not one of pride but one of humility, because, as it happened, he believed in angels.

The only thing he meant was, he was at least a poet, while other writers, to whom the angels did not dictate (Klopstock, for example) were not poets. But to be a poet and not to recognize it would be a false humility: the only humility a poet is not allowed. The poet's humility is to write "in fear and trembling" (as he said to S[amuel] Palmer, if I have the reference right) and that he must.

This afternoon, read a few pages of Guillaume Apollinaire's *Anecdotiques* up in the Library.

It is an enterprise something like this – that is a notebook. Of course he is not particularly concerned with his cares. On the contrary, he looks around him and what he says is, I suppose, material for history. I was once set an essay at Oakham on "What is a Historian?" but I don't believe I ever wrote it. At any rate I am not sure now what a historian is. I will ask Seymour; he ought to know after years with Randall and writing papers on Thucydides. Everybody in the world is interested in what history is because they like to think that all around them "history is being made." To blind yourself with the cliche about this war being "history in the making" is a poor and sinful attempt at consolation! *The March of Time, Life* magazine, peddle their various noisy excitements as history. And perhaps it is true, they have something to do with history except that I should think history is written after the events have happened – we are too busy in trying to write it before. (We are writing ourselves into the war quite busily.) If that is so, why, then, it is a bitter shame we are so much concerned with history and so little with the salvation of our own souls.

That goes, too, I suppose, for the history of manners as much as of politics. But at any rate Apollinaire [is] not engaged in politics. *Anecodotiques* – writing his memories while they happened. My novel and memories, I am ashamed to suppose! I did never want to think of them as that, and would hate anybody else to think so and anyway it is a novel and not memories and not autobiography altogether. *Portrait of the Artist* – material all autobiographical, but it is not autobiography, it is a novel.

Setting that aside, biography is tremendously interesting and fascinating.

Therefore, too, *Anecdotiques* – with its information about Douanier, Rousseau, etc. is also very fascinating. My favorite kind of history: Herodotus; the lives of Saints.

Merton's political memories.

(G. Apollinaire lists some kings and princes he saw and they are funny.)

1. At a football game at Twickenham I was privileged to see the ex-King Edward VIII, at that time Prince of Wales. I was seated very high up in the North Stand behind the goalposts and naturally it was difficult to see a man who came out in the middle of the field to shake hands with the two teams. (I believe they were the English and the Welsh.) He had on a dark overcoat and held his hat in his hand, and even from the immense distance from which I strained to view him, I recognized the true prince's posture, slightly stoop-shouldered. I believe I would have recognized him by myself even if one of my neighbors had not called my attention to the fact that this was the Prince of Wales.

2. The late King George V and Queen Mary – they went by me quite fast in a closed car on Oxford Street as I stood on the kerb among a group of silent people waiting to cross and wondering at the inexplicable delay. Rev. F. H. Jerwood, chaplain of Oakham school, was once walking in Hyde Park when the Queen passed. He took off his hat and stood still as she walked by and she gave him a nod. I had my hat off and was standing still, too, but they went by too fast to give me a nod. The King has passed away but the Queen still lives.

3. I was in Germany at the time of Hitler, and Thaelmann and Hindenburg were running for president, but it was very dull. I got a sore foot which later developed into blood poisoning from which I was very sick.

4. I was riding a bicycle in Surrey when Philip Snowdon rode by in a closed car. He was then Chancellor of the Exchecquer and he looked sick.

5. I was walking in Saint James' Park when a gentleman came by in gaiters and my Uncle Ben whispered "That is a Bishop." I never found out what Bishop, although I took a snapshot of twenty or thirty bishops walking two by two out of Westminster Abbey in their vestments at the time of the Lambeth Conference, which T. S. Eliot thought about after.

6. I was walking on Rockefeller Plaza when a car stopped and the mother of President Roosevelt got out. For no reason except perhaps uncontrollable excitement, I remarked to two strange men who were picketing the building "That is the President's Mother." They had their

backs to me, and perhaps did not catch what I said, for they turned around with puzzled expressions and gave no answer and paid no heed to the President's mother. Meanwhile I was busy wondering if I was at last going crazy.

7. People I got autographs from (mostly by mail) when I was 14. Jack Hobbs, Rudyard Kipling, Alan Cobham (2), Billie Dove, Anita Page, Evelyn Laye, Madeleine Carroll; I think Edgar Wallace did not answer. G. K. Chesterton's secretary said he was abroad and so couldn't write his autograph until he came back.

8. In Rome I saw an Italian movie star, whose name I have forgotten, in a cafe, the name of which I have forgotten. Near that cafe was a store where I bought a lot of socks and neckties. They cost a lot and I said so and the man was offended and told me they were very good socks and neckties. As it turned out they were perhaps the best socks and neckties I ever had.

I guess that brings to a close my memories of famous people, except, of course, the evening I exchanged politenesses with Heywood Broun and Robert Benchley in the Stork Club, making a total of four "good evenings."

Two cruel and bitter movies: *The Women* and *The Old Maid* all about hatred.

In *The Women* the women are furies, but Rosalind Russell is so good that her part is at any rate humanized. Well, Norma Shearer – the first time I have ever been able to look at her, too, because her part was human enough all right. She did love somebody. But the men, not admitted to the picture, only seemed to stand outside it not as men but as wax dummies in a store window. Wax dummies because it was impossible to believe in them; store window because attention is drawn to them by their absence.

As for *The Old Maid* – completely horrible for the bitterness and hatred in it. Oh, it was well enough done. Great little actress!

In any picture in which there is a war – and in most of them there is – Civil War, Spanish American War, Crimea, etc. – they always take the opportunity to slip in a quick shot of a man being bayoneted. Then the whole audience literally gasps with horror, not liking it at all. In the *Four Feathers* it was a Sudanese. In *Old Maid* a Confederate.

As for the part, and Joan Crawford in it, of the shop girl in *The Women* – completely horrible and frightening.

———

A young Cuban, learning to be a waiter in Rossoffs. He talks English very badly, seeming to be insulting.

Recommends hamburger, brings it back in a minute; it has been keeping warm for an hour. Disappears around dessert time. I call another waiter who also can't talk any English. I say: "Please send my waiter."

"Send my waiter? Sure, sure, sure" and he ambles off to the other side of the room and pays absolutely no attention. Then my waiter appears. After dessert, spots me reaching for a cigarette, rushes up: says "Want a match?" confusing me badly. I say I have some. He puts his back in his pocket and rushes away embarrassed. So I find out he is not being a bad waiter, but trying to be a very good one and not succeeding, for tripping over himself, and being confused and defiant about language difficulties. I hope he will be a very good waiter, I sure do; because that is liable to happen to anyone wanting to be a good anything, a good poet, a good priest.

October 4. Wednesday – Feast of Saint Francis

The church at 31st Street was full of flowers and music and people.

There is nowhere I would rather have been than among the monks singing on the balcony above where I was. There is no kind of satisfaction or happiness even in what I am doing now. I have a job, I work hard reading when I am not correcting papers – Augustine, Anselm, Grosseteste (neglecting Elizabethan plays for the time being), yet it all seems a waste of time, because it has no kind of fulfillment.

Last night after my class – thirsty. I had a beer but only felt physical disgust for it and didn't want it. Don't even want food either, which sounds exaggerated: the reason, it doesn't matter one way or the other. Anyway I always spent too much time wondering what I was going to eat at meal times.

I did read Peele's "Old Wives Tale" last night and found it good. Also more of Apollinaire's *Anecdotiques* – full of wonderful stories – the man in prison at Ocana – the Albanian, who lived in Brussels, Rio de l'Albanie and ran a magazine called *Albania* – and so on.

But anyway, soon I will have all the necessary documents together and will write to the Father Provincial.

October 6. Friday

Yesterday, for many reasons, was filled with incidents that, though they were not essentially so, presented themselves to me as ludicrous.

Eating supper at a Gateway Restaurant – Grand Central Station. I order pineapple juice. Meanwhile I notice my reflection in the mirror, opposite. I am sitting on a low stool: between me and the mirror, the bar, or whatever, the low thing I sit behind: but it does not extend to the floor: below it, my feet gathered up together by the one central support of this stool: there, head, shoulders, elbows on the counter: the counter itself. Beneath, no apparent support, but these feet gathered together and crossed, by the leg of the stool. I thought this was very amusing and was laughing to myself about it: then the girl brought pineapple juice on a doily on a plate.

I lift the glass, take a very small sip, put it down: pick it up the second time for an equally refined sip: the doily comes up with the glass, sticking to the bottom of it, and simultaneously, a string orchestra begins a polka on the radio. It was like beginning a scene in a Chaplin movie.

Next to me, two old ladies, with a lot of bundles, one of them deaf. She wears a hearing apparatus. Between them they order one sandwich and a helping of pie. They divide the sandwich and the pie, each take half. The deaf one ordered the pie. The other takes her half of pie from the deaf one's plate – perilously: then the custard teeters and falls off the crust.

They say nothing to each other, but eat their food rapidly, with every appearance of complete understanding between themselves.

Filled with ideas to talk to the class about – grammar and usage. That grammar is not the art of speaking *correctly* but of speaking *logically*. What is speaking correctly? Where is your authority for correct speech? There is no man who is your authority: no man can make the law. Correct writing means writing that pays attention both to grammar and to usage: that is, it is logical and in good taste. But it is not, for that, correct, an eternal pattern, something to base a law on. It is simply proper to its surroundings – its context. Really there is no such thing as "correct" writing in the strict sense. That is, right instead of wrong.

That we think grammar tells us how to distinguish *correct* from *incorrect* speech means that we have ceased to understand grammar: for this is completely turning upside down what grammar is: the art of saying things logically, rationally. Grammar is that art which describes the logic of language to us – the innate logic of language: it is not an art that *prescribes logical laws*, imposes them *on* language.

That we have ceased to understand grammar is another sign of our decadence: by that I mean we are in decadence (not because our speech is loose and ungrammatical: that is the only healthy thing about our speech today, ordinarily – its looseness, slang, life, activity), but because we have ceased to understand

  1. the kind of thing grammar is
  2. that such a kind of thing exists or has a place.

It is the same old group of processes that began with the Renaissance: heresy – to schism – to atheism – to religion of the state – humanism – to materialism – to capitalism – to communism.

This one began when the Renaissance decided *the correct* Latin orator was Cicero. How was Cicero any more correct than – Tacitus, Saint Augustine – why classical Latin more *correct* than medieval Latin. It is simply more *classical*. Cicero's Latin is no more correct than Augustine's, it is simply more Ciceronian. The error, the pride, then of saying *"Ciceronian"* and *"correct"* are synonymous epithets when applied to Latin.

You may like one or the other better. I have, I admit, read more of Cicero's Latin than Augustine's: but, to judge by Augustine in translation, I like his prose better, although I am a great sucker for Ciceronian periods and love them most fondly. Yet rather for parody. But Augustine is simply too good to like that way: not a suspicion of liking him for possibilities of parody.

To impose on language rules from the outside (call that grammar), to deny language its own life and logic as a living, growing thing. What does that reflect? The imposing, on man, of rules from the outside: standardize him, stamp him with rubber stamp characteristics. In a (democracy, Nazi state) he must be such and so: his soul, character, must be formed according to rules formulated outside him, not dictated within him by a conscience inspired by God and directed by the milder and widely flexible rules of a Church guarded and instructed by the Holy Spirit, which believes that every moral case should be judged on its own merits, and has immense respect for the *individuality* of every man's soul. (For there is only true liberty within the Church. I say it; and funnily enough – *Blake said the same of temporal rule by Rome*.)

The modern incomprehension of the *kind* of thing grammar really is – reflects the modern incomprehension of *respect for liberty and life*.

The substitutes for charity in a democracy are not so much evil as they are pathetic and well meant.

Take the case of the beavers in Connecticut. Some have built a dam, and it is flooding the neighborhood of the stream. The matter was brought to court: the Highway Department sought the right to remove these beavers and their dam.

The Attorney General's decision, at Hartford, says: the rights of rational animals are inferior to those of the state: so much more then are the *rights of irrational animals inferior to those of the state*. However, in the case of humans, there is just compensation (in a case like this) so too "these little animals should be compensated." So they are to be removed to another home where they will be "able to perform and exercise their natural skill and ability."

Naturally, you can either take the beavers away or let them go on building their dam. The best thing is probably what is done: let them build their dam somewhere else: but why all this pathetic hooey about the relation of the beavers to the state, their rights before the law etc. It makes you want to cry: it means that nobody really has any rights, any freedom, any liberty anyway. Nothing is guaranteed, the state is lunatic. If it can soberly discuss an obvious thing in terms of the *"rights of rational and irrational animals"* then it means that "liberty" is a farce.

In a state where "liberty" is based on the "rights" of each individual there can never be true justice. But in a state where you get to discussing the *rights of beavers*, then there is the danger not only of injustice but of violence and general ruin, through a kind of contagious madness that could sweep the country as the fear of the Martians swept New Jersey.

(Rights: if a state guarantees the Rights of all men: men either will or will not demand the *extreme limit* of what they are entitled to. Furthermore, it is even their *right to keep more than they have a right to* if they can get it legally (or even illegally, as long as the injured party doesn't complain and demand his rights). Now everybody does not demand the full extent of his rights. Most people, to tell the truth, don't care. But some get as much as they can get; more than they have a *"right"* to; they take over the "rights" of many many others who don't really care. Thus they become so big that they are monuments, and everyone looks up to them, and makes it his ideal to get that much more of his *rights* too (if he only could!). The ideal is greed and avarice. How can there be justice or liberty in such a state? Yet imagine the pandemonium if *every* man set out to demand at once the full extent of his (nebulous) *rights*, and the whole nation were swept by completely active and murderous avarice!)

But the state, no man, can ever take away the liberty of him who loves and serves God in meekness and humility and charity. That is, no man can take away the liberty of saints. Even though we are not saints now, but terrible sinners, weak and without courage or cleanness: yet even for us although the state can give or take away our "right" to worship God in public – yet no state can give or take away the right to love Him, and no state, for that matter, can really stop the saying of Masses and the administration of sacraments, if the faithful remain faithful.

The substitutes for charity in a democracy are not so much evil as they are pathetic. And of course Nazism makes no pretence at substituting anything for charity, although it might conceivably come to pass that Nazism, for a space, might enjoy one or two of the cardinal virtues for ambition's sake, just as Augustine said early Rome did when, for ambition's sake and for the love of glory men were at least temperate and courageous, even if they were also barbarous and full of pride. (But wait until the enforced temperance breaks down, and wait until the vicious barbarism of the fall, not of the rise of Nazism! Or of all the allied movements – that is, all the atheist-totalitarianisms.)

The substitutes for charity in a democracy: to begin with, what the word charity has come to mean: giving a nickel to a beggar, a hundred dollars to a hospital. Charity – you can claim exemptions on your income tax for "charities." But, substitute for charity the theological virtue, not the modern (protestant) word. Well, for one, the love of animals. A curious, well-meant, hopeless sort of thing that I used to get sore at, foolishly. Women who love their little dogs and lavish money on them, who would not give anything to a man who needed it.

And yet, perhaps they realize they could not give to that man without pride, and so would be ashamed to do so, for fear of pride (that shame too, is pride), but still, in their animals there is something they can really love and be lavish upon quite spontaneously, loving cats. So perhaps it is better for an old hag to give her money to cats, which she really loves, than for a rich man to give his money to a hospital to make himself feel good (rather than for love of other men) and to avoid some more taxes: that is, from the point of view of the virtue. But that is a sickening subject.

Talk about rights – is meaningless, really: but it is a substitute for "charity" – and it shows people want to love God and one another, but have forgotten how.

The love and care of animals – people are afraid of loving one another, for fear of being hurt themselves in their pride. But animals can hardly strike at their pride, and the love a dog gives you is simple, understandable, not complex. So people are full of pride, but they must still love some creature.

In the war – yesterday the Germans buried, with military honors, three unknown English airmen brought down in a fight over the Teuterborg Forest. A substitute for charity: it got some outlet in the pomp and bugles and speeches of a stupid military funeral. And by the way – Bill Hemmings who sat in the back row at Oakham, next to me, when we read Tacitus, and who was my studymate one term, – we read of the battles in the Teuterborg Forest: he wrote two years ago he was in the R.A.F. Was he one of these men?

It is terrible and incomprehensible, this sort of thing! But God give us peace!

Sunday, October 9

Began reading Dante's *Paradiso* today, out at Douglaston, after Mass. More splendid than anything else before it. He starts by praying to achieve a much higher kind of writing than in the *Hell* and *Purgatory*, to fit his much higher subject: and he does.

Everything is now made plain: movements are swift and easy (arrows) and the "keel" of the poetry cuts the water in a swift, straight furrow now.

Perhaps it is easier to write well of difficulty – the hard climb of the mountain of *Purgatory* – than of the swift and breathtaking and yet unnoticed movement through nine spheres of heaven.

The difficulty of *Purgatory*, the horror of *Hell*, make it seem Dante's difficulty is in his progress through *Hell* and *Purgatory*, and not in the writing of it. But now the ease of the writing must be more nearly equal to the ease of his progress. The vision he gives us must be as clear as the vision he himself enjoyed.

It is easier to communicate a clear idea of the obscurity of hell than a clear idea of the clarity and brilliance of heaven.

But because heaven is, of itself, a better subject than hell and a higher one, so, with the writing being good enough and high enough to reach the height of this subject, the *Paradiso* is the greatest of the three books.

The wonderful image at the beginning – Beatrice looking on the Sun, Dante upon Beatrice, then feeling himself to be filled with the power to look upon the brightness of heaven.

> *Nel suo aspetto tal dentro mi fei,*
> *Qual si fé Glauco nel gustar dell'erba,*
> *Che il fé consorto in mar degli altri dèi*
> ["At the sight of her I became, inside me,
> What Glaucus was, on tasting grass that made him
> Companion in the sea of other gods."]

To begin with, the audacity of the sudden image from a pagan story: and it is perfectly appropriate, by its very audacity.

Not only Glaucus, by eating the strange sea grass became one of the sea gods (pagan gods) but also, besides the memory of paganism is the memory of earth, even though the memory of sin and the very existence of water (as compared to almost supersubstantial dew) is left behind in the earthly Paradise.

After the tremendous marching line, in major-key

> *E di subito parve giorno a giorno.*
> *Esser aggiunto . . .*
> ["And suddenly it seemed that day to day
> Was joined . . ."]

and what follows, this has the effect of a sudden, haunting, minor discord, with its "dying fall." That is, there is a "dying fall" of sense as well as sound: Glaucus – unknown half-forgotten fisherman – humble grass (here where the food is the bread of angels), and the poor forgotten very minor pagan sea gods, all the more obscure because they lived hidden in the sea, an element livable only to creatures lower in the scale of being even than man.

Also, a man who disappears into the sea, has gone to live forgotten by the earth in an element where everything is dumb and muted, in a slow dream. This adds to the *"erba"* all the connotations of the lotus plant.

Now all these connotations are implied, too, in Wordsworth's line –

> "Or hear old Triton blow his wreathed horn."

The "old," and the quaintness of "wreathed horn" carry the same sort of feeling.

> Have sight of Proteus rising from the sea
> Or hear old Triton blow his wreathed horn.

"Have sight of . . ." that is, Proteus is rarely seen: you have to catch a glimpse of him. He himself is the most elusive of living things. Besides – "horn" rhymes with "forlorn" – and there, of course, "The very word is like a bell . . ."

These are remote things Wordsworth *longs after.*

However, Dante is in the presence of what he has longed after. He has entered Paradise, and is about to look upon the shining spheres, the joys of the Saints, the great glory of Almighty God. Yet, by this minor key, this memory of pagan things, introducing an utterly different kind of remoteness (the remoteness of the bottom of the sea and its forgotten gods) he *reminds us of the force of his longing* which is now about to be satisfied.

It is interesting to compare the Wordsworth and Dante lines again, in a different connection.

What it is natural for man to long after is the joy of Heaven.

Wordsworth, in his sonnet, turns from the world in despair and disgust – but does not know where to go, what he longs after, and would be satisfied, he says, with the remoteness of paganism: when what he is looking for all along is the remoteness of Heaven: the things he seeks are beauty and peace: but we know by revelation that these are to be sought after in God, and are only perfect in heaven.

Perhaps atheists and agnostics have substituted the fear of disease and sickness to the fear of Hell and Sin. It is certain that the doctrine of the withering away of the state into "pure communism" is a pale communist reflection of the Christian belief in Heaven and eternal salvation.

It is certain what we long after is our own salvation and what we dread is our destruction, in whatever terms you care to look at it. But the only way we can be destroyed is to have our souls damned in Hell: we cannot save our flesh, but our souls may be saved in Heaven.

Since this fear of destruction is inevitable, if the fear can be transferred from the soul to the body, then we become utterly preoccupied with ourselves, and filled with self-will and selfish fears, and one true destruction is an easier matter.

But sickness and death cannot, of themselves, destroy; sickness and the fear of death are sources of temptation. (Yet to the Saints, the *resisting* of the temptations, in sicknesses, by patience and humility and meekness and faith is an aid to perfection.) We must care for our bodies reasonably, that is, not neglect our bodies, because sickness is a source of temptation: but if we are sick we must pray for patience and courage and faith and meekness, that we may always fully trust in God, and never cease to love him and glorify him.

For we are scarcely ever really afraid of the sicknesses drunkenness and gluttony and lust may bring upon us – oh, we are afraid, because in proportion to our *desires* for the flesh, our fears for the flesh grow too: but we have confidence that doctors can heal our ulcers and cure us of horrible rotting diseases, or allow us to die more slowly of them, all gobbling as we go, cramming our bellies to the last second before the grave itself swallows us up.

Yet, our fears of the consequences of gluttony and lust are no fears at all in comparison with the truly *pious* horror we feel in the face of what we believe are the terrible consequences of fasting and asceticism and chastity.

To ease our "nerves" we are told to smoke more cigarettes, not give them up. To re-establish our peace of mind, we should go out and possess a woman at once. The idea of seeking to sleep with a woman because that will have a therapeutic effect is a ghastly ugly heresy. Heresy, because it is after all true that men and women were made for the love of one another, body and soul too, and they should all either marry or renounce physical love in the service and love of Christ, in whom all love is exalted above the flesh.

The terrible thing is that people who are so empty of *love* that they make love for its wholesome physical effect on themselves, get deeper and deeper into the confusion and misery they are trying to get out of. That is, the misery of pride and selfishness and selfish lust.

I have been praying for chastity purely out of shame and confusion over my own unchastity. But today perhaps for the first time it occurred to me that chastity, refined with the fire of its sisters charity and humility and meekness, is a very exalted and beautiful thing, and I first began to ardently desire it for the love of God, and not simply for fear of my own loss of grace by lack of it.

That is, although I have always been struck by the loveliness of a truly chaste person, one in whom chastity and charity are become the same thing, so that these people are almost transfigured by a kind of unearthly and peaceful and spontaneous innocence. So – Bramachari, Father Moore, Maritain, etc. (Maritain – wedded chastity)

But people are not only foolish, they are unjust when they talk about the vow of chastity priests take. While on the one hand they say that chastity is a dreadful, harmful, dangerous and "unnatural" thing, and asceticism and mortification of the flesh are perversions and horrible abnormalities, yet they turn around and condemn priests as a class for being secret lechers and full of lustfulness. Some priests have been and are; and this does not take away from their sin and the general scandal. But the injustice lies in condemning in the same breath "mortification" of the flesh and the priests who do not practice it, do not mortify their lust.

The implication is the obvious one that there should be no vow of chastity at all: but to argue against the vow of chastity is to argue against religion, because religions that allowed their priests to marry have degenerated and wasted away and all but denied God. Protestantism has, in effect, ceased to be a religion: the protestants lock up their churches but for one hour on Sundays; Anglicans keep their churches open but get nobody in them; some sects deny Christ altogether – to all but Aramaeans he is only a "wonderful man." But in the Catholic Church, and in Hinduism and Buddhism, etc., the chastity of the priests goes with the ardor of Faith, and the continual preaching of the love of God and his incarnation, or incarnations, to redeem the world. (The idea of redemption is in Oriental Mysticism, because all mysticism depends on the idea of redemption – or is that false? Maybe not literally true: have to find out.)

Today: 8 o'clock Mass at Saint Anastasia's in Douglaston. Everyone in Douglaston condemns the pastor for asking for money "all the time." But it is a rich parish and the people do not give what they could. However, I had been much meaner and more unjust, judging the congregation for being full of people who did not seem to want to be there and who rushed out of Mass as soon as they could, even before the blessing. (I had not realized the depth of my pride until seeing it written down! It is a kind of pharisaic snobbery!) This morning, at the 8 o'clock Mass, the men of the parish were finishing a mission, and besides them there were a hundred others, 40 went to the altar rail to receive the most Blessed Sacrament, and the crowd of people was really enormous. And that is a very good and joyful thing, and not to have been joyful all day on account of it is a kind of deep ingratitude to God.

Note: a terrible sentence to write: "I was unjust," I mean in a matter where you judge people, not a piece of writing or a building. It is just as bad as saying openly "I am just." It implies not merely that you are capable of judging and being right some of the time, it even implies you are capable of judging and being right practically all the time! But who shall judge at all – *et tu, guare judicas fratrem tu'um?* [and you, why do you judge your brother?] Who can even *see* to judge, for it is not a question of charitably withholding a judgment you are capable of pronouncing, or refusing to make a judgment you could make: you are utterly incapable of making a judgment at all. You cannot see to do it.

In judging *things* that are made by art – you can compare them with standards made by art, too, and say something right or wrong. But how can you judge people? By comparing their actions with the tables of the old law? Compare your own actions in judging first with the two Commandments of Christ, that you should love God with your whole heart and whole soul and love your neighbor as yourself. And then there is no room left for judging. You cannot see to judge. Who am I telling this? Who is *you?* You – that is "a man," "one" – but that is "me." It is a terrible thing to see that you have written down "I was unjust" – but "more unjust" (than other people) is a double judgment against myself: but yet there is *no* judgment in the light of justice. I have not *pronounced myself* unjust. I have pronounced myself full of sin and pride without meaning to by 1) implying that I *could* judge justly and by 2) already judging others as *unjust* by saying I myself was "more unjust" than they. And this *on top of* "judging" specific people for leaving Mass early!

But we are so incapable of judging that I cannot possibly "judge" *myself* to have been "unjust" anymore than I can decide that I have been just.

So the words are not only sinful but intellectually absurd, and what a pile of sins they involve. First, the pride of thinking I could judge at all.

Second: the pride and uncharity and self-will of thinking others unjust.

Third: the pride and uncharity I thought I was being sorry for – "judging" the people who left the church.

Fourth: making a meaningless and absurd statement, without logic and reason.

Fifth: even, perhaps, priding myself on writing it.

Sixth: adding now unnecessarily, sin number 5 purely for the sake of rhetoric – and seven this one and so on! I am glad it is more absurd than intentionally wicked and I pray my pride could make such a farce of itself immediately every time I fell into it! So we should be equally thankful to God for laughter and for tears, for both laughter and tears are holy. I don't mean the laughter of hatred or the tears of envy. Blake said "A tear is an intellectual thing"; he meant tears are holy and he did not mean the tears of rage.

October 14. Saturday

Newspapers announce the sinking of the *Royal Oak*, an old tub – fought at Jutland. All *Royal Oak*s are supposed to have had bad luck; this one has been in scandals and accidents. The scandal I remember but not clearly: and I was surprised to learn it involved a jazz-band. I knew before that it involved grave accusations of dishonor. The *Royal Oak* was a skittish, dissipated, disreputable old battleship. Also, a bomb got dropped on her in the Spanish Civil War. Now she has been torpedoed and sunk. She, and all her predecessors, were named after the Oak Charles (the second, say the papers, but I believe Charles I) hid in Shropshire somewhere. Probably a disreputable old tree, too.

In returning the novel, Farrar and Rinehart announced they were not enthusiastic enough about it to publish it. Trying to find out more, I repeatedly got on the telephone, and talked to a woman whose job it is to say "we never discuss refused manuscripts." Then, quite by chance, she suddenly relented, half hoping I would not turn out to be a maniac after all, and let me talk to a man who had not read the novel, but whom, at any rate, I saw. From the notes of one who *had* read it, he told me the story was impossible to follow, and shoddily written. That it often got dull and boring. That this man had not bothered to finish it. That the names of the characters were ugly and disconcerting, and the characters themselves were unreal.

Looking at the thing again, I find all that is true.

He said it was obvious enough I wanted to write a novel, and that it showed promise. I believed that in the first place.

He asked: what was I trying to do, create some utterly new kind of novel structure? The name of Joyce slipped into one of his sentences, intimating that sort of thing was all right, perhaps, in Joyce. I hastened to deny that I was striving after originality. That is, originality for its own sake, and apart from the novel.

Coming home I rearranged all the chapters in a different order, and now I haven't any idea what to do with the thing. That was Thursday.

About prayer.

It is written, "take no thought for the morrow; sufficient unto the day is the evil thereof."

The past and the future, not real. Only the present is real. In eternity "all is present." (Saint Augustine. *Confessions.* XI, 11)

". . . my childhood, which is now no more, existeth in the time past, which now is not; but when I remember and recount it, I behold the image thereof in the present time, because that still remaineth in my memory." (XI, 18)

". . . it might be properly said that there are three times, a present time of things past, a present time of things present, and a present time of things future." (XI. 20)

Prayer is a way of bringing man close to God. God is eternal: to him, all things are present. So, in prayer, there is no past, properly speaking, *no future*. But in prayer, always present, is a present tense of things past –

[Four pages are missing from the journal.]

October 15. Sunday

It was perfectly natural and right for it to be the fifteenth of October in the city. Cold, absolutely brilliant light: on the newspapers it tells the scores of football games – (Columbia 6 – Army 6) and so on. But out at the World's Fair, to see "Oct 15" on the white, small tower of the Chase and Sanborn Coffee place was a kind of shock. Because I remember seeing, without noticing them, dates in May and June on that tower: it was as if, going back to the Fair, it would still be May on the Chase and Sanborn small white tower.

It definitely is not. It is quite a different Fair. The silly statues are getting to look shabby instead of all bright and slick. The people are all different. Then there is the war, which seems to have taken the foundations right out from under the French building, although it is still shiny and crowded: and, oh, it is solid: it doesn't really shake or really tilt or sway!

The Fair does not seem as bright and as rich and as happy as it did in May, although in this light everything had to be brighter than ever, and was. Perhaps it was because there was no longer the softness of the May air, and May foliage and spring flowers, and a brand new fair.

For the first time today I went to the Art Exhibit and was surprised to see how fine it really was: a wonderful exhibition, marvelous things. But the El Grecos were hung in a small room where you could not see them properly because, if you got more than three feet away from them, people crowded in front of you, peering at the name of the painter, or the little plaque on the bottom of the frame, and then rushing on.

It would be utterly commonplace to say that almost all the people going through the exhibit rushed from room to room reading the names of painters off the frames, and not looking at the pictures at all. That is getting to be a very corny old joke: the *Punch* jokes about American tourists in the '90s, and so on.

"Remember the Leaning Tower in Florence?"

"Naw, that wasn't Florence, it must of been Venice, because the day we was in Venice it rained, and we couldn't see the Leaning Tower."

Jokes like that keep Irwin Edman's course in Esthetics hobbling along from day to day. The trouble is that Edman's Esthetics, and Columbia's new darling, "Humanities," do exactly the same thing as the Sunday fellows in the Museum: rush from picture to picture reading off the names, not looking at the pictures.

The Sunday fellows hope they will remember the names but don't. Columbia makes a stern effort to remember the names and connect them with the appropriate works. Columbia succeeds in remembering a list of names: that is all.

Among the best things there:

First of all, the Fra Angelico *Temptation of Saint Anthony*. Completely perfect composition. The Figure of the Saint a little left of center of the picture, caught in a kind of slow dancing movement away from a leaf on the dry ground, the only thing that seems to be tempting him. Perfect movement of the drapery, a black cassock, and kind of luminous deep gray cloak: his face: not much less melancholy serenity than that of an ancient Greek statue. Behind, a bright red church on a hill: some towers against a perfectly luminous sky – a line of trees with enamelled, dark foliage. Sharp outlines of the brilliant, pure-colored fantastic landscape around him.

Looking at this picture is exactly the same sort of thing as praying.

The *action* of the picture has no past and no future: it is full of movement and life and joy as well as utter peace and serenity: but it does not *move*. It has been still for seven centuries, obviously. In *time* we follow an action from its beginning to its end – from the time it is insensibly born out of some other action, until it is insensibly lost in another action with a different meaning still. This continual change from action to action through movements all more or less imperfect in meaning, and never ending anywhere, is the way time shows itself to us.

But in eternity, movement is perfect: there are no transitions between perfect significance and perfect significance. The *movement* in the picture is pure and chaste and as near to perfect significance as human technique can achieve because it is *still* at its most perfect point. In life, too, that perfection in movement may be achieved for one second but then it is immediately lost again: but in the painting it is always *present*, not remembered, not hoped for, continually *there*.

This is only comparatively speaking, naturally, because that picture itself has changed and will eventually perish too, for it is made in paint on wood (I suppose) and these tarnish and warp and decay. Yet the form it reflects will never die. Created things can perish, "forms cannot" because it *is* in eternity, *sicut erat in principio et nunc et semper* [as it was in the beginning, is now and ever shall be].

The painted Saint has been still in this quiet landscape for seven centuries, but his movement is more perfect than the movement of any dance because it is *still*: more perfect than any dance, that is, that is not also stilled at last at its most perfect "movement" which, by being still, includes the whole dance and all its movements (cf. the article in *Verve*). So it is in eternity where prayers are not uttered as we utter them (for words imply time), but perfectly. For example, imagine uttering an exclamation point: "!" In

Heaven, the short Gloria or the longest psalm are uttered perfectly so: "!"
(by analogy. But of course even this ! cannot by us be conceived out of time
or space).

Yet in this "!" the words are more perfectly and beautifully *sung* than we
can conceive. But we can begin to conceive how by looking at such a painting as Fra Angelico's *Temptation of Saint Anthony.*

If I were to say which painting I looked at in the whole exhibit appealed
to me most and seemed to be the most perfect, I would say this one: that is,
better than the El Grecos, than the whole pile of Rembrandt, Rubens, etc.
(I did not get to look at these so much) than the Andrea del Sarto near it
(very obviously!). By comparison, how sloppy and shoddy the Veroneses
and Titians and Tintorettos looked! The first time I have completely
agreed with Blake on that!

Better than Breughel, than the Goya of the child in the red suit, etc.

The Breughel *Wedding Dance* also a very perfect picture. The gaiety of it
is the gaiety of its form, not of the people in it (for there too their drunken
"gaiety" twists their faces more with pain than with joy. They are not
happy, they are drunk. But the picture is happy).

The formal arrangement of the picture is very exciting and moving.

You start by seeing the dancers in a round in the foreground, their whole
group is like a living organism: in a pyramidal arrangement △. At the
Apex, two couples, *flat* and like Thurber: both in the same kind of motion.
Then, right: a *line* of people, along the edge of the dance, curving down to
the pipers, lower right hand corner. This line closes off a crowd that seems
at first to be just a crowd: red coats, white kerchiefs on the women's heads,
etc. Some roofs. That, at a glance, seems flat. The first pyramid is carried
on, in a wedge, back into the picture, by trees, and another line of people
standing etc. Then, at the apex of this pyramid, suddenly, far away, in a dull
gray coat, back to everybody, standing perfectly straight and looking off
out at the back (and top) of the canvas, the figure of one man: paying no attention, doing nothing, standing, rigid, his back to everything. This is so
challenging that it offers itself as a key to the whole picture, and, indeed,
travelling back from him the eye suddenly sees all the depth and movement
of the whole crowd on the right; and we see into two barns that we had not
noticed before – and they are full of people.

Then you begin to find out all the amazing things he has done with
white aprons and white caps and kerchiefs. And the simplicity of the figures in the foreground is much more meaningful: not just "modern looking," that is, familiar.

Everybody in the crowd seemed at least to pause at this big canvas, and those who said anything, seemed to be liking it at once. So there goes a lot of snobbery, right away, down the drain! Maybe they liked it for its subject matter, or thought they did, but who cares? It isn't good because it's "earthy" and "real" at all: that is only secondary. (Note, it is by no means realistic.) What everybody liked was its humor and its joy and its life, no matter what they said. I am sure of that. And these are some of the things they said:

1. Two girls – Jewish (I guess) students: "It looks like one of the early French Impressionists."

2. One Jewish guy, with a crowd: "Excellent reporting. Look at those knees."

3. One of two girls, giggling: "Look at them kissing, there."

4. A man: "That one's drunk, I guess."

5. A man: "That's a Dutch painting: not a skinny guy in the bunch of 'm."

6. A man, foreign accent: "Country Dance."

7. A woman: "Look at those white aprons."

8. A man: "Some paunch."

9. A man: "Look at the pipers."

A lot of people, of course, just read off the name: "Broogul." Well, why not? I bet there were a lot of pictures did not catch their attention enough to make them curious about the name.

In the first rooms, where the Angelicos were, there was a boy of 18 or so and an older man: at each picture the boy said: "The hands are good." At the Angelico *Annunciation* he said, of the angel "one hand is better than the other," but the older man contradicted him mildly, saying "No, both the hands are good."

While I was looking at the *Temptation of Saint Anthony*, a fairly old lady with a harsh voice said, behind me, "Look, nobody laughs in these pictures: they must of been awful unhappy people in those days." But here were three Angelicos, the Angel, the Virgin, the Saint, all luminous and joyous and peaceful. It does not make you mad; it makes you want to preach the Gospel, for sorrow and fear at the end of the world.

In the El Greco room, people were shocked and violent and bitter, especially women, and one made a loud social blunder she was sorry for when she found out. It was referring to the *Descent from the Cross:* I can't write it down, for it was a great inhuman scandal and she was sorry, anyway. Another one, an old lady, said of the figures in *all* the El Grecos, generally: "They're all dying of TB." And more comments about the unhappiness of the age the painter lived in. The instinct to ask her at once "What is the world dying of now? Are we so healthy? Are *our* pictures dying of anything? Can they die if they aren't even alive?"

The El Grecos really floored everyone, and seemed to bring out *blunders* (The TB gag was no blunder: it was quite deliberate, and a different thing) but there was the man who came in and saw the *Agony in the Garden* – Christ confronted with the Angel and the chalice, and he said at once "Here is the Temptation in the Desert" and then corrected himself, in a hurry, from the catalogue.

The El Greco room seemed to force people to name the devils that possess the world, and hunt souls into Hell.

Then some people came in, and looked around and one said, tired: "Religious pictures again!" But two young girls, suddenly ran, with quite a surprising gaiety, to the *Vision of Our Lady* and remarked on the pretty colors in the vision: and they weren't anybody's obvious pretty colors – but oh, yes: the TB lady remarked on "Those ugly pastel shades."

After that, I only stopped for the Goya boy in the red suit with his cats and his birds, a swell amusing picture, but amusing in a literary sort of way, and at the other end of the pole from Angelico completely: seeming so weak and thin and empty and unfinished and hasty by comparison. Literally, a canvas three quarters empty and meaningless.

A man stooped, and read the name "Goy-ay." But a child ran to the still life of a lot of fruit and said "Look, a dinner" but I guess she was just being cute, because kids know very well what a dinner is.

Yet, so many people were articulate about the pictures, and shouted at them, anyway. And what's the difference between the dame with the TB gag and the ones who like El Greco because he is in fashion, provisionally, before finding out? Because nowadays El Greco is not for a lot of people and perhaps he never was. That is, he is plenty complex, and most people cannot get at him all at once because they are not all that complex themselves. Anyway, El Greco has a lot of weaknesses, too, compared to Angelico for example. (Yet, do not deny anything of the power and perfect form of the *Adoration of the Shepherds* in the Metropolitan.) But when he fails the failures are striking. People honestly liked the Breughel. I guess they all had an acquired respect for Rembrandt. No boast, no false humility either.

Outside, a lot of people buying postcard reproductions: but what a crummy choice they had!

———

I went to the Linguaphone booth in the Communications Building: and listened to a Portuguese lesson and found out the things I didn't believe about the pronunciation were true – and more than that!

Portuguese – they pride themselves on pronouncing everything the way it is spelt, and so do the Hungarians: in neither language can I find out that the pronunciation has any connection with the spelling. In both, "s" is often (in Hungarian maybe always) "sh." "A" in Hung. is nearer "oh" and in Portuguese nearer "e" or "uh." Amusing dipped effects in Portuguese where "e" is dropped out – it sounds like a good language, on the whole.

When Gibney and I and Lax and Freedgood were in the Brazilian Building a couple of weeks ago, looking at the tropical birds (they were too certain the birds were ridiculous and stupid and were being rude to them), a child with his father came down the steps above the cage. The kid, pointing down into the cage, shouted "Look daddy, there are the pigeons" and the Father, pretty heartily, shouted back, "Sure, Sure, Sure, Sure!"

Proust and memory: to Proust experience seems to be valuable only after it has been transformed by memory. That is, he is not interested in the present: and I suppose while he was writing his other possible present experiences did not appeal to him: sick in bed. The "present time of things present" was unbearable. What kept attracting him was the "present time of things past." Actually what was important to him was writing – that is, writing was the one "present" he could put up with.

How close are "imagination" and "memory" – are they more or less the same thing? That is – in principle? A child can be imaginative yet how much does he have to remember? More than you might suspect.

Imagination deeper than memory: the transformation more complete. Memory – an easy and partial transformation. I suppose memory, as opposed to recollection, includes selection, interpretation, and so on. Aristotle says memory is the higher faculty: animals recollect, men have memories.

On the Long Island Train today: going through Sunnyside Yards. On top of a factory, the sign "Karpen" (I guess furniture). Of course I have seen it a hundred times, but it never meant anything. I recognized it as something I had seen before, but I happened to be thinking about it, in relation to some telegraph poles moving in front of it. Then, I recollected it. Now, for the first time, I remember it. It is part of a pattern of my own, not part of a series of things that just happen to be there in Long Island City.

What would you call "remembering" dates in history? I suppose it depends on how much meaning they have in a pattern. Learning a list of dates, parrotlike, is not using memory, I suppose.

However – I cannot get anywhere now trying to make these distinctions in a thing I only understand confusedly.

What is this terrific importance that memory seems to have for me?

Perhaps I am interested in it because it was so easy to write such a lot of autobiography this summer: but that may be putting the cart before the horse.

Is it a new interest? Or have I always been preoccupied over memory ever since I was a little boy?

October 16. Monday

Saint Thomas, in the *Opusculum* XVII, "Refutation of the Pernicious Teaching of those who would deter men from entering Religious Life," quotes Saint Gregory, *Morals*, saying: "When my conscience was urging me to leave the world, many secular cares began to press upon me, as if I were to be detained in the world, not by love of its beauty, but by that which was more serious, viz, anxiety of mind. But at length, escaping eagerly from such cares, I sought the monastery gate."

When I first knew I must be a priest, I went to Father Ford, who put the idea in my head that I had never had: of being a secular priest. But it was not long after that, that I went to ask Dan Walsh[19] about it, and he told me to go into an order, suggesting that, from what he knew of me personally, I should go to the Franciscans.

He knows me better than Ford. I had his course in Saint Thomas last year: after classes we would talk and I would tell him about ideas that I was enthusiastic about, and in our conversations I am sure he found out enough about my intellectual and spiritual temper to give advice to me on such a subject. He introduced me to [Jacques] Maritain, and after Maritain's lecture last spring at the Catholic Book Club, Walsh and I were both very stimulated and went off talking about miracles and Saints. When I first

[19] Merton attended Dr. Dan Walsh's classes at Columbia, where they became close friends, a friendship that continued throughout their lives. Dr. Walsh was the first person to mention the monastery of Gethsemani to Merton. Years later, upon his retirement from Columbia, Dan Walsh followed Merton to Gethsemani, and lived in the Guest House.

mentioned my vocation he said immediately he had always expected I would want to go into the religious life.

On his advice, after he had arranged an interview for me, I went to see Father Murphy, at the monastery. On the way down, happening to be wondering and anxious about what would happen, I opened the *Little Flowers of Saint Francis* I was carrying and read "Brother, this offer *(profferta)* of yours I accept in the Name of God" or words like that, and I was very happy. Then before seeing Father Murphy I stopped at the Chapel of Saint Philomena to pray (I did not know who she was) and prayed. I said the prayer of Saint Thomas, *Concede*[20] and the word *perfecte adimplere*, seemed to ring out, and to hang in the air near me, and I prayed I might serve God perfectly. Father Murphy advised me to apply to the Provincial.

But the document, the application, has to be accompanied by documents I could only get from Father Ford. Going back to him, he urged me again against an order. He said I would not be happy in an order. He said the orders were the source of "all the evils" that have come into the Church. He said the orders had degenerated and were not doing any good work, especially in this country. He mentioned what fine men were going into the diocesan seminaries now.

I returned to Father Murphy, who told me strongly enough he was sure mine was a Franciscan vocation. Then I went to Saint Joseph's rectory, because I live in Saint Joseph's parish, to get a letter. Father Cassery was fine and enthusiastic and kind, and, of a remark I let fall, said I seemed to have the Franciscan spirit which was a kindness I was floored by.

But then I had to go back to Corpus Christi for my certificate of baptism, and I went straight to the rectory, avoiding Father Ford. Then I happened to find Father Kenealy on duty, and he began telling me much the same things as Ford did – that I would not be happy in a monastery. His arguments were diocesan life was full – you were "your own boss"; you were working in the city (in this diocese) not in the country . . . very personal reasons.

---

[20] Saint Thomas Aquinas's *Concede mihi* prayer is quoted by Merton here, with a reference to the recurring theme of fulfilling perfectly those things that would be pleasing to God. The opening of the prayer is: *"Concede mihi, misericors Deus, quae tibi sunt placita, ardenter concupiscere, prudenter investigare, veraciter agnoscere, et perfecte adimplere ad laudem in gloriam Nominis tui."* [Grant me, O merciful God, to desire eagerly, to investigate prudently, to acknowledge sincerely, and to *fulfill perfectly* those things that are pleasing to You, to the praise and glory of Your holy Name."] The entire prayer can be found in *The Raccolta* (New York: Benziger Brothers, Inc., 1957), 567–72.

Father Ford arranged an interview with Father Furlong at Cathedral College today. And I saw him. Ford had not told him of my desire to go into a monastery: he too was in favor of diocesan life, but by no means so emphatic. He said we must try to follow the will of God in this, as in anything else. Then tonight, I called up Dan Walsh, and asked his advice and he repeated what he had said before, and told me to get the Saint Thomas book. Rather he told me of it, and I rushed at once to get it out of the Library.

Nothing Ford or Kenealy had said had changed my mind, but I was beginning to worry if I were not being stubborn and self-willed as I so often have been, always! Then, I began to wonder if the life in the monastery would not be too hard, and I had to take that to confession (but did not mention a vocation) but the priest was good and I came out with a high heart. Anyway, now I remember what Cardinal Newman said to Hopkins: "Do not say the Jesuit discipline is hard. It will save your soul."

Thus everything I have found in the Gospels, reading them again, is so clear. "Give everything to the poor and follow me!" All the counsels. And, what Walsh said: it is easier to follow them in a monastery than when you are on your own in a diocese.

As to the orders being the source of all evils – that is a false generalization, obviously. Besides, it was comforting to find out again, from Walsh, how long that argument had been argued! What Saints we would not have had if everyone had believed it!

The degeneration of the orders – same old argument too. Besides, if that were an argument against going into the religious life, why did God say to Saint Francis: "You see my house is in ruins! Go and repair it"? I talk about the argument, not my own ability to do anything, for by myself I cannot even pray, but God must first make me want to, and without God I am nothing but dust. As to the orders doing no good work – Saint Francis' is the busiest church in New York, all day long confessions, and prayers, and the Way of the Cross, and Novenas, and Benediction, and Sermons and help to the poor and the sick and the unhappy, and praise of God.

And I am sure what Ford means by the finest type of fellows going into seminaries would be equalled by the young Franciscans I have seen at Saint Bonaventure's and so on . . .

But now, on top of this, the arguments in Saint Thomas: that the man who has repented of great sins should forsake even lawful things and give up even more than those who have always obeyed God, and sacrifice *everything*. Nothing was ever so near certain. *Deo Gratias!*

October 19. Thursday

It is very hard to know what kind of a day it is from this room. That is unless you get the blinds right up to the tops of the windows. Then sun glows on the walls of the other houses, and on the barnlike back of the Baptist Church that blocks off the small garden, small as a hole, with a towering blind wall of bricks.

Diagonally, though, to the west of my windows, are interesting dirty terraces, of other houses – iron steps going up and down. A picket fence painted blue on a flat roof of a terrace at my level – second floor. Further, a trellis, completely bare now. The trees, no leaves. I forget what kind of trees they would be, and that should forbid me forever to think this notebook is in the tradition of G. M. Hopkins! But these trees are the kind which, like sumach, when they lose their leaves seem to dry up and be made of brown sour twigs like papier-mâché. These trees have hanging in their tops brown dirty clumps of some rubbish or other: from here it looks like dried seaweed, as if the trees had just come out of a pond or a flood. But that is their fruit.

I don't know why I should have been a little surprised when Ed Rice[21] said he had sometimes thought of being a priest. But that serves me right for wondering why people seemed surprised when I told them about my vocation.

Rice's difficulties are the same as mine. Astonishing how much they follow the same pattern.

First: he thinks of the Jesuits. That's what I started out with, too. I suppose in my case it was because of working on Hopkins.

Second: he is afraid he will no longer be able to "write the way he wants to." That is, freely, using any kind of language that presents itself.

Third: he is not particularly anxious to get married, any more than I am. And so it goes. I wish Rice would come and be a priest too, and I know it is God's will he should because every vocation is of God, Saint Thomas says:

1. If Satan "transforms himself into an angel of light" and inspires good desires in order to deceive us, yet if we are faithful, he cannot deceive us,

---

[21] When Merton decided to become a Catholic, he turned to Ed Rice, a fellow student at Columbia, to be his Godfather. Of the "in group" at Columbia, most of whom were Jewish, Rice was one of the few Catholics. He later founded the Catholic cultural magazine *Jubilee*, with the encouragement of Lax and Merton. Rice published his reminiscence of Merton, *The Man in the Sycamore Tree: An Entertainment* shortly after Merton's death, illustrated with many of his own striking photographs, taken over the years at Gethsemani.

but he does the work of a *good* angel: that is, if he leads a man to good work and the man does that good work, the error is not harmful.

2. No suggestion to enter a religious life from man or Satan has any efficacity unless it be accompanied by interior attraction from God. So Augustine says: "All the saints are taught by God not because all come to Christ, *but because no one comes to him by any other means.* Thus the desire to enter religion, from whomsoever such suggestion may proceed, comes from God."

October 22. Sunday

If I had more humility and did not rush to write things down so fast, and did not assume that everything is interesting if you put it in writing I would make fewer crazy statements and say some things so that they are as true as I see them. But what presumption, when I know nothing about philosophy – know so little about it that I can't even read it carefully. But anyway, I do not aspire to be a philosopher – but go after allegorical theology which is not argumentative: but there: I am not sure what allegorical theology *is*, but only know one thing it is *not*. And that thing – argumentativeness: well I am always obviously trying to be argumentative. Perhaps I had better not argue with myself anymore about the validity of writing things down in this book. All right: it is not for reading: and the embarrassment of reading some of the stuff over again comes under the heading of mortification of pride.

What is the "mild yoke" of Christ's service? The love of God is blessedness, and that is joy, and to love God is to be full of joy. Loving God and serving Him is done by imitating Him in His Incarnation as man, that is, by being Christlike, and following Christ's example.

To follow Christ, and to serve him, is to be full of joy. Unhappiness, to one who would serve Christ, comes when you fail in His service. Therefore the "yoke" of the service is mild, and to be patiently and joyfully under the yoke is sweet and peaceful, but to be out of it is *hard* and bitter.

But what is it, more precisely, to be under the "mild yoke" of Christ's service? Christ's service is begun and ends and is all included in "Thou shalt love the Lord thy God with thy whole heart and thy neighbor as thyself."

But the principal occasions by which we fall out of that love, are the seven deadly sins: Pride, Covetousness, Lust, Gluttony, Envy, Anger and Sloth. The reason these are sins (or more properly incitements *to sin*) is that they lead us away from the love of God.

The love of God is light within us: the sins take that light and darken it.

The love of God is a talent we possess within us: the sins keep us from multiplying that talent, and would take even that away, but that God's presence remains in the heart of even the worst sinner.

The love of God is the cleanness of our heart, and its joy: but that is made foul and sad by sin, taking away the love of God.

The love of God is that which sweeps our house clean, and makes it neat: but if we then turn back, the devils come and find the house free and clean, and all the better for them, and that is all the worse and more bitter for us.

But the mild yoke of God's love only says that we should love Him above all things, always. That is sometimes hard because no man can serve two masters, and love idols and God, too; and who leans to the Devils will find how hard they make it to beg God's love.

And to try to be happy by being admired by men, or loved by women, or warm with liquor, or full of lust, or getting possessions and treasures: that turns you away, soon, from the love of God; then men, women, and drink and lust and greed take precedence over God; and they darken His light, and hide the talent, so it shall be taken away at the end, and make us foul and sad, and open the door to the legion of devils. And then we are unhappy and afraid and angry and fierce, and impatient, and cannot pray, and cannot sit still. That is the bitter yoke of sin: and for this we leave the mild and easy yoke of Christ, and make it so that it is hard, and necessary to go through pain and sorrow and tribulation to get back to the easy service of Our Lord.

But we serve Christ by praying to Him and glorifying Him and His Blessed Mother and His Angels and His Saints, and by clinging to the service of Holy Mother Church, and by doing good works of charity and mercy (but I cannot think of one good work of charity I have ever done) and loving and helping our neighbors and brothers, and perpetually forgiving those that would hurt us, and by being poor in spirit, desiring nothing of the world, and no man's harm (not our own either!).

And this means, especially, that all day whatever we do the Holy Name of Christ should be on our lips, and His Holy Cross before us, and these are sources of humility and joy; then we may go about our work, or any of the things we do, full of joy and unconcern, not attached to anything we are doing, yet seeming to do that better still than before, not desiring or dreading or anticipating the next task or amusement or duty that we have ahead of us, but forgetting the past and the future, and not attached to the present, being still full of simplicity and sweet joy, by reflecting on Christ or His Saints.

So it has been at church and coming out of church, and sometimes in all sorts of other places.

[Two pages are missing from the journal here]

. . . learning well, being full of pride, and falling back all the time, can yet feel this kind of joy, and serve God this little that I can keep going to Mass and trying to pray and keeping close to the Holy Sacraments; if I can feel this peace and this joy sometimes in spite of my unclean and selfish heart, what must it be to serve God truly, with unremitting sacrifice and prayer and good works!

It must be the kind of joy that I can once in awhile catch at here, where everything is unified in proper harmony, and there is no barrier between yourself and what is around you, for you simply seem to exist in some same not quite important or interesting medium that is nevertheless pleasant and gentle because of something that shines all through it and through you. And then there are sharp movements of happiness in pronouncing the names of Our Lord and His Saints, or saying, for example, the poor quiet ancient salutation to the little Roman martyr

"Pax Tecum Filumena"

in which there is a particular strength and blessedness: for she is a particularly blessed intermediary for us before the throne of Christ in this day, the sweet Saint who had no glory or no reputation at all of her martyrdom but was buried into utter hiding, with her bright light hid and her voice unheard, that even the lovely example of her saintliness be kept from men for centuries until our own time. Then this *"Pax Tecum"* is as a "peace be with you" on a long and patient journey; and for all this time this child, martyred before her service on earth had time to really begin, was left to wait meekly and patiently for centuries more before she could even help those on earth by answering their prayers, nor serve God by adding the prayers in her honor to her own offering of prayers and psalms glorifying Our Savior, Christ.

But think of her joy in being a special chosen instrument of God's providence, selected by a kind of wise husbandry from an age that was fruitful in Saints, to be saved as it were, to be one of *our* Saints, as if adopted in our age that is so wicked and needs so badly such reinforcements of Saints. Thus the Saint of Ars, by no coincidence, seemed to attribute his own miracles to Saint Philomena, and paid her special reverence for he knew she was a Saint of our time and not of her own: and he was a kind of guide that led her among us, showing us her miracles and his own, that is: God's miracles.

And she is a Saint who is brought to us as an example of innocence (for she was a child, like our other child Saint Theresa of the Child Jesus) and humility (for she was so long obscure and hidden) – and she is indeed a treasure that was hidden in the ground many years: that is, of course, the *knowledge of* her in the relics and phial of blood and the symbols and the salutation were hidden like a treasure, in the ground. So her name, even, was buried.

But besides all this she is a very joyous Saint, for she brings us such blessedness and joy by prayers and her swift answer to her salutation, when God wills it.

Then it is particularly right that the Friars Minor, in whose ideals innocence and humility and joy are so prominent (witness the rule and the Little Flowers and the character of Saint Francis and his companions) it is particularly just and right that the Franciscans should give Saint Philomena special love and honor and reverence; and so I pray, too, that she will protect me, and ask God to make me chaste and meek and perfect in my vocation, and bring me then to the Monastery and serve Him perfectly there. And then I know I will see great joy: but if I am proud and vain and arrogant and not humble and not chaste and not patient, then I will not have rewards but tribulations: and I pray God to give me patience and undying perseverance under temptation and to deliver me from these and all my sins.

(Evening)

Pictures of French towns and villages, out in the French exhibit at the Fair, kept drawing me to look at them all summer. I have always thought that plain French houses – the commonest of "domestic architecture" were about as good as anything in the world and are the sign of the most civilized country in the world. Houses in the small towns in the South of France – almost flat tile roofs, blank walls, plain, yellowish stucco, windows oblong with solid wooden shutters, just about as functional as anything could be: make modern buildings – pronounced modern architecture – look fantastic and exaggerated rather than functional.

Even the worst of the second Empire, in Paris, France did better than England, Germany.

Farm houses are good everywhere, in every country.

I think the best modern poetry is being written in France, has been for the last fifty years. Between 1880 and 1920 perhaps the only good poetry was being written there.

This week, for the first time I read the *Complaintes* of Jules Laforgue: or some of them. They are very fine and very moving: more moving than anything in English since then, except by Yeats. I make a big exception for Yeats, because he is very good, too.

The use of the ballad form, and nursery rhyme meters and the language of speech seems to imply a much greater freedom than there is in other forms. As a matter of fact this really exercises a great emotional restraint upon the material of the poem, and condenses and strengthens and canalizes it in the utter simplicity of the language and the meter – what do I mean, utter simplicity? Not simple to understand; maybe *innocence*. It makes everything seem very impersonal in tone, although the language is familiar and personal. Laforgue, using sung meters, nursery rhyme meters, ballad meters, gets the same effect as the Provencals and Dante did using vernacular instead of Latin, Innocent, sincere, and especially impersonal, because a form that belongs to the whole people at once (as the ballad and nursery rhyme do) can hardly do anything but restrain the personality of tone. But any form tends to impersonalize the things said in it.

The *"Complainte du Pauvre Jeune Homme,"* where he commits suicide:

> *Lame,*
> *Fine lame,*
> *Soyez plus droite que la femme!*
> *Et vous, mon Dieu, pardon! pardon!*
> *Digue dondaine, digue donaine,*
> *Et vous, mon Dieu, pardon! pardon!*
> *Digue dondaine, digue dondon.*
> ["Blade,
> Sharp blade,
> Be straighter than woman!
> And you, my God, forgive what I do!
> Fiddle-dee-dee, fiddle-dee-doo,
> And you, my God, forgive what I do!
> Fiddle-dee-dee, fiddle-dee-doo!"]

is utterly formal, impersonal, terrific in its restraint. So, anyone thinking it flippant and irrelevant would be quite misguided – the apparent flippancy and lightness of the burden only add to the poignancy of what the lines say, and they express a complete hopelessness, a profound tragedy.

The contrast of this most informal language and the depths of the tragedy it is used to relate produces a very *formal* effect and displays a gesture that is perfectly significant not by its freedom but by its restraint – like a very formal movement in a dance.

The photograph of Laforgue, in his top hat and his neat, elegant clothes, nevertheless surprised me. He seemed to be walking very precisely and carefully, although as I remember it the photograph did not show his feet or legs, but was only three-quarter length.

In the French building was also a photograph of Apollinaire in his soldier's uniform, bearded, a bandage around his head: taken, I suppose, in a military hospital. A very solid and stocky and powerful looking fellow.

Portraits of all the writers and poets are in the French building, in a not too good photomontage mural of facsimiles of picture and manuscripts and pages (manuscripts?) There are – Pascal, Rabelais, Rimbaud . . . I didn't look at it all very carefully.

In the next room, beautiful modern missals on display, with swell leather bindings and work on the bindings, on one a very good crucifix: one leatherbound missal, edited by Dom Cabrol, was priced at only $2.20 and I would have bought it there, only they only took orders, did not give you the book to take away. It was all in French, except for important parts of the Mass, like the Preface etc., where there was also the Latin.

The French building is the one where they have the biggest and best exhibit of books that I have ever seen at the Fair. But I have not looked closely in the British building that I was only in and out of. The South American countries also exhibit their books and magazines; but the literature – the national literature of a place like Chile – seems to be made up entirely of bound volumes of political editorials reprinted from their newspapers. Gibney says that only accounts for half their national literature: the other half deals with *psychopathia sexualis*.[22]

I went to the Fair again Friday with [Bob] Gerdy and Rice. Then it was a little like it had been in spring: few crowds, the air soft and mild and slightly misty; the music in the singing towers sounded the same, only they cut out the Tchaikovsky and play jazz, thank heaven. The horns of the

---

[22] An allusion to the book *Psychopathia Sexualis*, by Baron Richard von Krafft-Ebing, a German neurologist known for his work in forensic psychiatry. The seventeenth edition of the book appeared in 1924.

busses sound the same, and behind all the noises of the Fair you could hear the sort of siren (more a claxon, or some like a foghorn) of the big locomotive at the R.R. building no matter where you were. In the summer it seems to have been drowned out. Only in the Amusement Area, which was bad even then, has everything changed completely for the worse.

We tried to see the Art exhibit but it was still too crowded to see anything properly: but this time we found the Hieronymus Bosch *Temptation of Saint Anthony* which is surely one of the best things there and surely also the best Bosch I ever saw. Best – well, most interesting, anyway, of the things in the exhibit.

I had missed it the first time by rushing through that particular Flemish room without paying any attention to anything.

Today I went to the Museum of Modern Art with Jinny Burton and Celeste and Lilly Reilly. There was a special show of [Charles] Sheeler which Jinny wanted to see for some reason, but she was disappointed and well might have been. I did not recognize him until I saw some pictures of factories that looked as if they came out of *Fortune*. I never saw anyone so neat and so precise and so completely uninteresting. His photographs were better than his paintings because the things photographed had an interest of their own (i.e. Chartres Cathedral) but if the things in his photographic paintings ever had any interest, the paintings lost it all; and neither the pictures nor their subjects were anything but dull. However he designed a nice drinking glass and a good spoon and a fair textile thing.

Another thing about France: I can't conceive of them attaching any importance to such trash as those Sheeler paintings.

Before going to the Museum, Celeste would go in to the Rehearsal Club (an actors' boarding house) on the same street. There was Kathy Bailey who had just come back from Boston where she has a small part in the new Saroyan show, *Time of Your Life*, and is full of fantastic stories of people being fired, and new parts being written in here and there, and Arabs, and drunks and what not in the play. I have an idea Bailey will be a great famous actress though I have never seen her on the stage. I just had a terrific argument about religion with her the first time I ever met her. In that argument she was completely hairbrained, yet in the middle of all that were flashes of intuition that were so right that you were amazed: then a whole pile of cant again!

October 23, Monday

Today it was colder: everywhere I went the sun seemed to be shining on buildings near me, showing them up bright and cold against dark slate clouds that sailed fast, torn into long patches of deep blue sky, behind them.

Going up 114th Street East of Amsterdam – there is a slight slope up, towards where there are a couple of trees and the wall of the heights and the drop; beyond that nothing but this sky and parades of slate and purple and pigeon colored cold clouds: bright pale can on the limestone of the Nurses Home, and my shadow going alongside of me on it, I can see by my shadow my hair is blowing, and thinking of the sky up ahead dark and turbulent as a sea, and a tree with a rim of leaves left scattered along the top of its fan of branches, nods and bends all northward, against that sky, "publishing," I think (making up a line but no poem to go with it) the trees ". . . publish the stern intentions of the fall."

Tonight, not so much heat in the radiator. I do not turn around to see the good fire I have lit because I am writing very fast, and presently want to read Richard Rolle.

The fire is built with wood I got from an Italian peasant on 10th and Greenwich. He is a peasant [who] keeps logs and kindling in a cellar, and is very swarthy and broad and quiet and seems all over coal dust, though he is a woodman not a coal man. I guess he has an ice business of a sort, too. But he seemed always gruff and sour to me.

Tonight his collar smelled of crushed fermenting grape. There was a line of barrels and they were mostly lying tilted a little, and the crushed mess of grape was "cooking," and wine was dripping slowly into white enamel pans and pots set under the barrels. There was a winepress, too, still choked up with a squashed mass of grape, tilted and patient, dripping out wine, too.

So I said I hadn't smelled that smell since I was a kid. He said where? His English was very hard to understand, in fact maybe he wasn't talking English at all, or Italian. Maybe he invented an incomprehensible Neapolitan English and mixed it with an incomprehensible Neapolitan Italian, and I only understood by a minor miracle. Yet it was easy to understand. I told him: France: how they made the wine in the streets. Well, if they pressed it in the streets did they cook it in the streets?

I said I thought they let it cook in the houses, or the courtyards of the houses. (The Bonnette, the little stream, would be stained like ink with the rubbish of the old squashed grape that was all dried out, in barrels and thrown away in the stream.)

Then I noticed he was a true peasant, with a good face and the eyes of a child. He was very happy to talk about his wine. The kindling he sold me was smashed up from boxes and crates that had brought the grapes from

California he had made the wine with. So then he got a glass, and poured me some wine out over the edge of a pan: it was raw and new but good enough; while I drank it, I guess he was saying you'd pay 15 cents for a glass of wine like that if you was to go to the saloon.

When I left, I said I guessed he would have a good time drinking his wine Christmas and New Year and Easter, and he said I should come back whenever I wanted some wine.

He is a very remarkable guy, to be a peasant in the middle of the city and still completely a peasant. He has been here 28 years. Knows hardly any English: in fact I am sure our conversation took place in no language at all, although there *were* sounds. And a very good guy, with a very good peasant face, but so swarthy and dusty as if it were covered over and hidden and embarrassed at being seen in the city, especially *this* city.

The kind of a guy that is the same as though he were still on his land with his wife and kids and his vines and his olives and his beasts. The kind of man [who] actually exists on bread and wine and olives and garlic and sausage and greens, and never says anything and never understands the crazy political fellows, and is humble and poor in Spirit too and loves God and prays to Him like a child (for we all should). And from such came many Saints, from the poor that are also poor in Spirit, and love God and His gifts and tend the earth and care for God's good beasts, the slow, heavy steaming oxen.

If I were to be a good Franciscan, that is, Christlike, I would first of all have to be in almost all points as this peasant appears to be. That is – to set no store on pride in knowledge, or possessions, or ambitions, but completely obscure looking and acting: and with all that not envious, not ambitious, but quiet and good, and giving people things, and being patient, and working and living on little food. But being, first, *nobody:* this peasant, obscure and dark, and silent, and not knowing much how to talk: of such were Christ's Apostles.

October 29. Sunday

Instinct to write about apparently unimportant things today. Like Gibney calling at Douglaston, saying he was reading the "best book in the world" – "His Monkey Wife" by John Collier. The long correspondence with Gibney (not under the same heading – unimportant) this week. Monday I write him a note: Wednesday I get a long letter about religious questions, as they say. I write him another, Thursday I get another, Friday I write another. There the matter rests. Controversy: what, he asks, do I really believe? What about asceticism? Do I just take that on principle because the church says so? etc. How about the popular blasphemies – the Buck Mulligan blasphemies of the fellows? Thursday I had talked with Jinny Burton who couldn't understand Gibney complaining about being unhappy all the time, nor his suddenly saying in the middle of a party or a conversation or just walking, "I'm happy."

These things are almost impossible to write about. Why? In the first place (well, almost saying the same thing over again) I don't at all know what to say. That is about Gibney's scrupulous perplexities and inhibitions about believing anything definite.

That he likes Pascal fine, loves him, and despises him for holding out salvation in a way that seems to him (Gibney) to be saying: "since you can't know, what can you lose?" That is one of the things I don't understand.

About the things in Gibney's position I don't understand, I have inadequate words: words I don't properly understand either: but his position is one of extreme protestantism, in a technical sense. Protesting against the church. Sounds like Calvin, but is all Gibney, obviously not Calvin.

That the fellows are repelled by "asceticism" is easy to catalogue; perhaps too easy though. It is easy to be repelled by false "mortification of the flesh" where people shout against sin and have in their hearts nothing but hardness and uncharity, and really are so busy *hating* sin that they have no time to love God. This they see into very clearly. Because of that, however, they conclude since there is some good in drinking, that [there] is some happiness however unsteady and futile, and some pleasure in loving a woman's body (although that almost always ends in dissatisfaction and restlessness and disgust if you are not in love with her so that you want to be with her always, married) then you can get some inkling about the love of God through these pleasures and stimulations. And yet Gibney is utterly unsatisfied and unhappy and restless and disgusted. But try to say that "mortification of the flesh" means turning away from temptations to God so that you will not be attached to pleasures – and therefore will not be unhappy and desperate when they elude you. That mortification of the flesh does not mean concentrating your intellect, will and memory to whipping your body, but a means to give your intellect, will and memory over utterly to God and the love of Him; that mortification of the flesh does not mean that you deliberately weaken and destroy your body with the same intensity of purpose as an athlete builds his life, so as to end up being proud of your emaciation, just as a bad athlete might be proud of being musclebound, just because his muscles were large; that shutting out desire is like going into a quiet room where you can pray in peace and be calm and ask God for His love, to do good works, patiently and happily full of that Love.

They see very well that this kind of false and disastrous recitation of asceticism leads only to pride: but do not believe there can be a true self-denial; Lax, who loves God, was horrified at the first chapters of Saint John of the Cross – as horrified with them as transported with the rest of them that came later.

When I said that it was hard, if you were attached to drink and women and pleasures and ambitions, to love God and even to pray to him. Lax said nothing should be hard. That is of course true: what he meant is, just as I did, that you should be so full of the love of God as to be no longer attached to these pleasures, so that it would no longer be *hard* to abandon them. Nevertheless you have to abandon them, and because of our weakness and selfishness, when God calls us to Him (as he always does, always, every minute), we go to these pleasures which turn us aside, hold us back from Him. But Christ came not to call the just but sinners to repentance – and saying, whoever thought he was just should throw the first stone at the woman taken in adultery – so who of us is just? We are all weak and selfish and proud, and all bear the burden of Adam's sin; but Lax does not hold with any doctrine of original sin. And he would have the love of God be easy, and so would Christ and so would the worst sinner, the unhappiest of all: and so it is easy, that is plain. Ask and it shall be given you, seek and you shall find. What is the way? Go sell all that thou hast, [give] to the poor and follow me, take up thy cross and follow me. It is easy – that is plain. And it is easy: that is it is the mild yoke of Christ. The cross is heavy and the way of the cross is hard for the flesh to follow, but prayer makes that light and easy too.

But it is hard to try to carry the weight of this burden and the weight of sins and desires and lusts too, in fact you go two steps under the combined burden and fall down in despair, because you cannot carry them both without trying to be a camel getting through the eye of a needle.

But when you have put down your sins and desires, then it is easy.

A man going to the house of his lover, which is at the top of the hill, does not carry a sack of scrap iron and old junk to sell to junk peddlers he may meet on the way, especially when he really knows nobody wants the junk and scrap iron anyway, least of all himself or the junk peddlers, who are all somewhere else hurrying to the houses of their various loves. As he throws his sack of scrap iron into the ditch and hurries up the hill to the house where his love is, and doesn't know whether the sun is hot but only that it is bright, and hardly knows that because all he yearns for is to be at the house where his love is.

That I didn't want to write about any but unimportant things meant there were a lot of things to be writing about and that I did not know where to begin.

The unimportant things might have been:

1. The new maid, at Douglaston: called Victory, who follows Father Devine, and is there replacing Satisfied, who does too, but is sick, poor thing – great and fat and mild and quiet. I don't believe Father Devine to be God, but Victory and Satisfied are gentle and mild and quiet, and do love God, the true God, because there is only one happiness, that is, in serving the one truth. But how would writing about them have been writing about anything unimportant? Yet I do not know anything about them, while Gibney and Lax are my good friends and I know them and what I could write about them would mean more than what I could write about Victory and Satisfied.

2. Another "unimportant" thing I could have described – riding down to Flushing with my cousins Pat and Frank [Priest].

3. Or the kind of day it was.

But the reason it is hard to write about Gibney's complicated state of mind is that: first I may "understand" the reason for the blasphemies, but I can't like them. Second, his crossing himself under stress I can sympathize with but don't too much bother to understand because that is not so much of my business anyway, and if anyone is to write it down and describe it and talk about it he is: and he is willing enough to. Third, why write anything about your friends except to them, not that this wouldn't be for them as much or more than for anybody, but that it is better to write it directly to them and only for them (and the angels) to read.

This summer, I thought I had been saying the same things to Lax in conversation and to everybody in the Pastoral. He disagreed with the things in conversation and agreed with them in the Pastoral, saying I had never said those things in talking. In the same way I had argued verbally with Gibney and not made him see that I meant anything, and said, as I thought, the same things in two letters and he apologized saying maybe I was offended at him not understanding that was what I meant. Of course I don't know what the reasons are, but perhaps the most obvious one is that the convention of tough talk and slang and colloquial accents, used to cover up embarrassment at talking about things about which bad cliches have been used, is not my medium: not my vernacular even. Neither my Latin nor my common speech, or my *volgare*. Whereas this, which doesn't seem to be different, evidently is. In the vernacular I can put things down faster, so that they are communicated. But it is probably quite crazy to think that this is the same as my speech when I am talking to Lax, Gibney. To begin with, I am fluent enough at the vernacular that is really theirs when it comes to jokes. Maybe in other things it becomes nobody's vernacular – least of all mine. Maybe my speech is completely different from this writing which I think is like my speech. I now realize that the way I talk to my class is not the way I talk to Lax or Rice. [John] Slate has different gags, and his vernacular has a different tempo too from the average Lax-Gibney vernacular. But there is a Lax-Slate vernacular they developed on a train in France, that includes modified barking and a lot of happy dog gestures. Gibney has none of that at all and won't bark in the least, but I use it with him, not thinking until now. There is no barking in anybody's writing, obviously. It is fantastic to think I never much observed any of this before, but also unimportant that I should now. So that is enough: now the thing *is* getting unimportant.

October 30. Monday

Some words that occur to me in a list of out of the way and uninteresting things, expressing our interesting civilization.

Pari-Mutual,

Totalisator.

Crematoria-ory.

glider (for a kind of hammock).

helicopter.

depth bomb.

time clock.

spigot, winch, gaskett.

cylinder, coil, carburetor, feeder, fan belt.

Break lining. Soy beans. Crude oil. Pyrene fire extinguishers. Antiphlogistine (this smacks of alchemy though, when they used it on me). Acetphenetidin. Chrome. Chromium. Anti-aircraft, pom-poms – casemate, blockhouse, conductor, car barn, operator, operative, meridian;

Alimony, beaverboard, white lead, red lead, yerba mate, Sanka coffee, caffein, adrenalin, scalpel, ex-ray, ultra-violet, infra-red, shutter, tele-photo lens, esperanto (Eh! Portisto!) goalkeeper, polevault, Messer-schmidt, A.R.P., tanktrap, camouflage.

Televisor, voder, diaphragm, Klieg light, macadam, guava, carbonifer-ons, vadose water level, panda, electrocution, electrolysis, insulin, vi-tamin, trauma, erg, volt, election, carbonated, dynamite, peroxide, mercurochrome, novocaine, forceps, pneumatic, emery board, sand-paper, ping-pong, gyroscope, bathysphere, white slaves, gladstone bags, zippers, denicotinized cigarettes, condensed milk, rodeo, rib-bon microphone, barge canal terminal, alfalfa, excelsior, jack, raffia, burlap, burley, cottonseed oil, diathermy, therapy, hydrogen, im-pulses; investigator;

Checker, engineer, air conditioning, acetylene, coke and blast furnace, rolling will, rayon, TNT, shredded wheat, nitroglycerine, Rye Crisp, ballot box, box office, ticket taker, voting machine, curtain rod, fire engine, vita-glass, linoleum, Ovaltine, celanese, stadium, grand-stand, starting gate, puck, cleet, hammer (in athletics) racquet, foot-fault, linesman, touchjudge, bailbondsman, pawnbroker, catcher's cage, movie projector, sound track, gamma ray, watertight door, caucus, cell, convention, piston-ring, piston rod, observation car, roundhouse, transformer, switch, real-estate, pyrex-glass, coffee percolator, mixmaster, toaster, Dutch cleanser, formaldehyde, toothpaste, Lysol, Iodine, Lint, silicosis, coalbreaker, occupational therapy, infantile paralysis, typewriter ribbon, carbon paper, sodium lamp, black light, silex, waffle iron, incandescent lamp, outboard motor, surfboard, aquaplane, Vickers (plane of some sort), lathe, whipsaw, jigsaw, fretwork, Baby Ruth, Mars, Phenol, Ambulance, skywriting, halftone, projection room, projector, negative, devel-oper, fixer, screen, pica, unit, carbon dioxide, incinerator, sulphuric acid, plate (photography), linotype, blow torch, airbrush, paint gun, French curve, T square, U tube, diving bell, Florence flask, Wasser-mann test, vaccine, anti-toxin, glucose, chlorophyll, chloroform, chloride, chlorine, zinc ointment, borax, margarine, altimeter, speedometer, propeller, aileron, carbonated water, pepsi-cola, card-board, gasoline, donkey engine, power station, powerline, etc. etc. etc.

That is about all the modern words and objects I can bear to think up just at the moment.

October 31. Tuesday

It came me to write a list of snatches of songs and jingles and stupid catches I can remember.

1. The wren the wren the king of all birds
    The ran the ran the kick of all bards
    The rain the rain the kin of all bores
    The rum the rum the coin of all beers
    The rune the rune the cane of all bears,
    The rim the rim the kind of all bars
    The rat the rat the claim of all beards,
    The root the root the cling of all burrs,
    The rant and rant the clang of all bawds.   1938.

2. *"Dein Vater war ein Graf."*
    ["Your father was a Count."]
    > My father spoke of this line of a song to Mrs. Stratton, in a restaurant in Marseilles. He referred to its poignancy. I thought I understood the poignancy, but felt that when he was saying "count" he meant "cow" (I did not hear) so I corrected him saying it should be "kuh," only I pronounced it "kuh," and Mrs. Stratton thought I was saying "cul" and so told me I mustn't say that. I will never forget this line of a song as long as I live.   1927.

3. *"Du Bist meine Greta Garbo*
    Bist die schonste frau der Welt
    Du bist blond' wie Greta Garbo
    Sondern du hast nicht zu viel geld."
    ["You're my Greta Garbo,
    The prettiest girl in the world;
    You're as blond as Greta Garbo,
    Only you're just not as rich."]
    > The time I thought Marek Weber had a good orchestra, 1931.

4. *"Elle avait des tout petits petons . . ."*
    ["She had tiny little feet . . ."]
    > Marius, age 12, drags a wagon along in front of the Hotel Dieu: I am waiting along the balustrade of the Jardin des Themes, Marius comes by, stops in front of me. In the wagon is a little kid. Marius says: sing: the kid begins to sing "Elle avait . . . etc." We laugh. (M. = my enemy) 1927.

5. *"J'ai deux amours*
    mon pays et pain"

["I have two loves
my home and my bread."]
    La Baker Strasbourg. 1930.

6.   "The world is so full of a number of things
I am sure we should all be as happy as kings."
    R. L. S. Annoyed me from a child. 1920(?)

7.   On the road to Mandalay.
Where the flying fishes play
And the dawn comes up like thunder
Out of China, cross the bay."   1930–31–32.
    Mr. Duesbury who taught history and had a solemn dead pan,
    recited this in a deep and hollow voice at the Old Boys' concert
    every end of term. Then we would shake the ginger beer bottles
    and let go the cork and try to hit the ceiling with it.

8.   "Owls go by and they give me the eye
Walkin' my baby back home."
    Ted Weems Orch. 1931.
    Still have the record.

9.   "There'll be pie in the sky when you die."
    A communist gathering in somebody's rich Jewish apartment, in
    very bad taste furnishings on Park Avenue. They give out little
    books with the words of all these songs, but nobody sang then . . .
    I had a long argument about whether Swift was an atheist (I said he
    was), then they got me drunk, and although I offended everybody
    by saying "but what's so wrong about Trotsky?" They tried to sign
    me up for the Y.C.L. If they did, it didn't take. 1935.

10.   "You're the tops
You're the . . . ?"   1935.

11.   I love Louisa, Louisa loves me,
when we ride on the merrygoround
    I *Kiss:*
      Louisa
    Fred and Adele Astaire, *Bandwagon.* 1931.
    That was the first time I was in the New Amsterdam theater. The
    second was two weeks or so ago when we walked in and saw a
    Charles Boyer Irene Dunne picture about a flood, for about two
    minutes and then walked out again.

12.   "Can't go on, all I have in life is gone
Stormy weather."
    Going to Jones' Beach. 1933.

13.   "Lazy Bones, lying in the sun."
        Identical.
        1934.

14.   *"A, ab, absque, cor am, de*
    sine, tenus, pro and prae
    Palam, clam, cum, ex and e . . ."[23]
        Rhyme for remembering what Latin prepositions take the ablative.
        Ripley. 1929.

15.   "Con-stantinople
    C-O-N-S, T-A-N, T-I-N-O, P-L-E."
        Ripley. 1928.
    . . . and Saint Malo, and Rye.   1928.

16.   Chicago – that city – of brotherly love
    of brotherly love. . . .

17.   Valencia. . . .

18.   Toodle-oo. . . .

19.   I want to be happy
    But I can't be happy etc. . . .

20.   Tea for two and me for you etc. . . .

21.   *Mon Paris.*
        1925–1926–1927.

22.   "Don't despair, use your head, save your hair
    Get *Fitch-Sham-Poo.*"
        Radio. 1938.

23.   "Every morn I fill my pipe
    with Saint Julian, rich and ripe."
        Along Southern Rye – England. 1928–29.

24.   "If you don't know Minnie
         don't know Minnie
    She's tall and skinny
         tall and skinny . . ."
        Walking along the Rhine, towards Anderbach. Feet beginning to
        hurt. A pipe, in which I put dutch tobacco. (Piet Hein Grun) 1932.

25.   "God – Bless – Ameri – cuh"
        Leaning in a car through Saluda, Virginia, singing this at tops of
        voices, the day we didn't know if Britain was fighting Germany yet
        or not. Sarcastical. 1939.

---

[23] Latin prepositions that take the ablative – "from, away from, far from, before, of, without, as far as, for, in front of, in the presence of, unknown to, with, out of, out . . ."

26.   "But I'll love my baby
Till the day I die"
My favorite lines of "Saint Louis Blues." 1933–39.

27.   "Mr. Gottlieb, Mrs. Claypoole
Mrs. Claypoole, Mrs. Gottlieb
Mr. Gottlieb, Mrs. Claypoole
Mrs. Claypoole, Mr. Gottlieb."
G. Marx, *A Night at the Opera* – 1937.

28.   "Too-la-too-la-too-la
troi-i-re."
C. Chaplin's song, *Modern Times.* 1937.

29.   *"Vous qui desirez . . . etc."*
"Le travail est obligatoire
car le travail, c'est la liberté."
["You who desire . . . etc."
"We have to work
because work is freedom."]
R. Clair's *A Nous la Liberté* – 1934.

30.   "Come landlord fill the flowing bowl
Until it doth run over."
The people on the "American Banker." 1934.

31.   "I'm singin' in the rain
Just singin' in the rain."
Sunday afternoons my first year at Oakham. 1930.

32.   "I want a pretty girl
To hug and hold."
Same. 1930.

33.   "Oh no John no John no John
no."
West country folk song we learned to sing (against our protests)
at Ripley Court. 1928.

34.   "I'm in a heat wave
A tropical heat wave."
The Boat Race ball (Cambridge), at the Savoy, Elaine Jennings. 1934.

35.   "Oranges and lemons
Say the bells of Saint Clements."
I don't know.

36.   "Christian dost thou see them, on the holy ground
How the hosts of evil, prowl and prowl around."
A Protestant hymn that has a good tune. Oakham. 1931.

37.   *"Nous n'irons plus aux bois*
    Les lauriers sont coupés."
    ["We won't go into the woods anymore;
    the laurels have been cut down."]
        Out of some intellectual book. 1937.

38.   "Lilies of all kinds, the Flower de luce being one."
        (*Winter's Tale*) I thought I would get a title of a novel from this.
        1933.

39.   *"Siena mi fé, disfecemi Maremma."*
    ["Siena gave me life, Maremma took it away."[24]]
        Dante.
        Remember it because Huxley plays on it in *Those Barren Leaves*.
        Read that. 1937.

40.   "This is the way the world ends
    This is the way the world ends
    This is the way the world ends
    Not with a bang but a whimper."
        T. S. Eliot.
        Used it as a smart quotation in an essay on the "End of the World"
        in my scholarship exam for Cambridge. 1932.

41.   "To languish in his slow chapped power."
        Marvell.
        It just occurred to me to put it down. I remember more lines from
        that than from most other poems. But I am not supposed to be
        putting down things that are amazingly good here.

42.   *"Viridesque manu siccata capillas."*
    ["And lustrous hair with a dried-up hand."]
        Some point of syntax the name of which I have forgotten. Oakham.
        1934.

43.   "Did you ever see a dream walking?
    Well I did."

44.   "Is this the record office?
    Yes.
    Well give me 'I'm a dreamer aren't we all.'"
        Excruciatingly dull joke in *Punch* – 1932 or 3.

45.   "He puts boot polish on his heel
    And thus the aperture conceals."
        End of an excruciatingly dull poem of my own about a man with
        a hole in his sock. Oakham. 1932.

---

[24] *Purgatorio* V, 134. Maremma was a malaria-ridden swamp on the shores of Tuscany.

46.   *"Gall, amant de la reine, alla, tout magnanime*
    Gallamant de l'arène a la tour Magne, a Nimes."
    ["Gall, loving the queen, goes to the magnanimous tower
    Gallamant of the sand at the Magnus tower, at Nimes."]
        V. Hugo.
        Because of Cocteau's *Grand Écart.* 1939.

47.   *"*Touching is spoiling."
        Various buildings, N.Y. Worlds Fair. 1939.

48.   *"Blanc sur rouge, rien ne bouge*
    Rouge sur blanc, tout fout le camp."
    ["White on red, nothing said
    Red on white, you're in for a fight."]
        Advice to wine drinkers. Saint Antonin. 1926.

49.   *"Mene mene tekel euphasin"*[25]
        On a desk in the Examination rooms, Cambridge. 1933.

50.   *"Ehen [Eheu?] Fugaces"*
    ["Alas, O fleeting (hours)."]
        On an old clock, Fletchers' House, Rye. 1928.

51.   *"Leu sui Amant que plor e van cautan."*
    ["I am Arnaut, who weeps and sings while walking."[26]]
        Dante, *Purgatorio*
        Because it is good because it was used in the novel because I like
        it etc. because it is Provencal. 1939.

52.   *A Sainte Blaise*
    à la Zuecca
    Nous etions
    Nous etions bien là.
    A Sainte Blaise, à la Zuecca
    Nous etions bien là.
    ["On the feast of St. Blaise,
    at the Zuecca
    We were there,
    We were truly there.
    On the feast of St. Blaise,
    at the Zuecca

---

[25] Cf. The "Writing on the Wall" in Daniel, 5. 24ff. "MENE, TEKEL, and PERES": [God] numbered (your days); [God] weighed (and found you wanting); [God] divided (your kingdom).

[26] Dante, *Inferno, Purgatorio*, XXVI, 142. Arnault Daniel was a twelfth-century Provençal poet and troubadour.

We were truly there."]
> De Musset.
> Because it's pretty and easy to remember, ever since Oakham –
> 1931–2.

53. *"Splendide Mendax."*
["Magnificently mendacious."]
> Example of an Oxymoron. Oakham. 1932.

54. "And bowled the round nave down the Hill of Heaven."
> *Hamlet.*
> A swell grandiloquent nonsense line by the Player King. 1938.

55. "Want matches, yes, yes, yes.
Want matches, no.
Want matches, yes, yes, yes.
Want matches?
No."
> Blake. 1938.

These things are easy to remember. So I put them down. All the good lines I know I can't remember to put down, so much.

November 2. Thursday. All Souls

The other day, in Grand Central Station, a tired little rich 20 year old dame with nothing better to do, collecting for the Cancer Fund. There is, in fact, a crew of them taking over parts of the station: near the information booth is a table and an old lady at it, directing them all. They wear their simple hats and, all over them, the look of the furniture in their parents' comfortable living rooms.

They betray a kind of well fed anxiety in their eyes; a look that rich 20 year olds get that make them look, under their not too fancy clothes and not thin flesh, lean.

One of the girls, in a mouse colored coat, shakes the little white tin box and cries:

"Help the Cancer! Help the Cancer!"

Ed Rice has a couple of girl cousins of this type – nice well brought up girls in well to do Brooklyn families. One day we are crossing Madison Ave, and Rice blanches as if to turn around and run, and his two cousins are standing on the sidewalk, side by side, their feet together, smiling with a kind of awed surprise, even giggling. Here comes their funny cousin Ed whom they admire but don't know what to make of.

The two cousins are not beautiful and not ugly, they are funny looking.

Ever since then, in all sorts of places, Rice will start to walk fast looking straight ahead, and say "Come on, my cousin's back there. She didn't see me." And he will give a kind of helpless laugh.

There is a logic of language and a logic of mathematics. The former is something like experience: it follows it closely, is not rigid but supple, imitates life. The logic of mathematics is abstract, more certain, if you like, but achieves certitude at the expense of truth. That is, it is less real.

The "logic of language" – that is – follows language, grammar, rhetoric, living things that grow in the same way as a tree, spreading out into the light, not spreading out into a geometrical shape: the tree grows into what it loves to be, not into what mathematics would like it to be.

Saint Augustine is a rhetorician – he persuades: he is a preacher; his logic is the logic of language, of literary expression, of poetry etc. His books move and grow and are full of their own life and they grow towards the truth and embrace it the way a tree grows up reaching into the light and air and embracing it in an "airy cage" where light and air move sweetly and freely in and out.

Walsh quotes Gilson or someone saying what Augustine is interested in is his own religious experience: he narrates it over and over. The center of his philosophy is the Confessions. He addresses himself to Christians; he is a rhetorician; he does not need to bother with philosophy, the truth is already established in revelation, it is there. You do not have to go far looking for it and worrying about it as the ancients did. The truth is there, he expatiates on it, talks about it beautifully, pays it the tribute of beautiful words and rich love and great understanding. No emphasis on *Logic* in the Platonic sense (Plato's metaphysics was Logic) or in any systematic sense. The truth is established. Words grow out of it.

Saint Thomas, addressing Saracens and Averroists, has a different task, has to go back to metaphysics and logic, and define and establish the truth in philosophical terms since he is dealing with pagan philosophers: then comes the theology.

Thomas is a teacher and not a preacher, too. He is arguing against the Gentiles. Everything that is in Augustine needs to be put on a different basis if you are talking to a Gentile philosopher in order to *convince* him, intellectually. Saint Augustine was writing to *persuade*, to move the will toward Faith and Love.

Where Saint Augustine takes Christian truth and expounds it, Saint Thomas takes Christian (Augustinian – it is the same) truth, and systematizes it for the purpose of theology and philosophy.

This clear metaphysical structure was something necessary to Christian thought in the times that were to come. Luther's utter lack of metaphysics has reduced Protestantism to the position where it can have not only no metaphysics but no theology: and, actually, no religion either any more.

Now, the Historians of Philosophy keep talking about the Augustinian and the Thomist traditions as two fundamentally opposed movements. Ramon Lull, for example, is an Augustinian: yet Saint Thomas and Saint Augustine are much closer together than Augustine and Ramon Lull. Lull, to begin with, in his exaggerated Platonism, fills the air with mathematical problems, strives after diagrams and mechanical systems that will prove everything without fault, lay down the rules for everything, state that such is definitely *so* and must be so; order everything that is by mathematical formulas. But to impose this on top of the thought of Saint Augustine, which is an altogether different type of thought, means destruction. Lull ends up with no metaphysics and only logic: hence he is abstract, unreal, talks about things that don't exist.

The value of the distinction in *De Ente et Essentia*, cap. II, where Plato's separate forms are attacked and disposed of, I think, conclusively. At any rate it appears that way to me, although I do not follow the whole thing as clearly as I might. Distinction between a *metaphysical* and a *logical* definition. First and second intention. The first, metaphysical, deals with things as they are, in fact: the second, logical, treats them as they are, abstractly, in the mind. In other words, a metaphysical definition is stated in terms of *act* and *potency* and a logical definition in terms of *genus* and *species*, which are second intentions. They are the means of understanding things but not the things we understand.

Platonists say a thing *is* its (logical) definition. To them, man is made up of rationality and animality. Body and soul. Independent.

Thomas, on the other hand, thinks the addition of *form* (soul) to *matter* (body) makes a third thing, a rational animal, not rational and animal. The *soul* is not purely rational: it is also sentient and vegetative. The body is the subject of all the operations of the soul, is ruled over by intellect and will, and so this *animality* is quite different from the animality of a dog.

The genus (animal) has a unity only of indeterminateness. You can only make it a unity by ignoring the specific difference of separate animals.

Matter is common, too, to all "animals," rational and irrational. But matter is a first intention. Prime matter is called *one* (is a unity) by the re-motion of all forms. Genus is called one through the indeterminate unity of signified forms: remove this indeterminateness, we find there are as many essences as there are species – As there are specific differentia. *No genus is an essence* except by virtue of this indeterminateness, which is merely a liberty of language.

The nature of species is indeterminate in respect to the individual genus: specific differentia = essence: individual.

The essence of Socrates is signified by the name of man, and that name is predicated of Socrates. The essence of Socrates is not Socrates.

Logically, we predicate humanity of Socrates, but humanity does not signify that in virtue of which Socrates is a man. It does not include designated matter. It is a logical abstraction, the name man contains matter implicitly, the name humanity excludes the designation of matter, and so it cannot (ontologically) be predicated of individual men.

The consequences of this are easy to see – and the dangers it leads into: the people who are always preaching about humanity and preaching about something which doesn't exist: but that is the beginning of this whole business of state worship. Everything is subordinated to the good of humanity: that is the ideology. And for the sake of this ideology individual men lose their liberty, their worth, their lives, everything, are treated not like men but like beasts, are beaten, sent out to kill, used as chattels, made slaves, submitted to filth and indignity and dishonor and torture, lose their freedom, their children, their own liberty to read what they like, their freedom to praise God – all in the name of "humanity." If humanity existed that would not be possible.

The essential Christianity of Saint Thomas' point of view is that it ties right back with the New Commandments of Christ, who did not tell us to love abstractions but to love our neighbor. To love our brother; to love our enemies: "do good to them that hate you."

But it is perfectly easy to hate and kill any individual in the name of "humanity", which does not exist.

Who will not say "but Augustine is a Platonist and believed in separate forms?" Augustine and Thomas are prevented from deviating from the same end which is the Divine Truth they both serve. Augustine can no more fall into the "humanity" error than Thomas himself; the truth he serves keeps him from doing that. The difference between them will be entirely in the very minor point of psychology: or not entirely so, perhaps, Saint Bonaventure uses some argument about separate forms to uphold Divine Providence and the Creation of the World against Averroists. Thomas' answer I should know but don't. Augustine is kept from error because after all he is not a philosopher: he is not trying to distinguish truth and error and argue about them: he knows the truth and is only interested in the *experience* of it. Let Saint Thomas do his arguing for him.

I guess what Gilson called him was an "empirical psychologist."

Thursday. November 8

In the last three days I have written another 60 or 70 pages of new stuff for the novel which I reread and found dull. Jinny Burton came around a couple of times and this morning I stopped by at the monastery. Tonight taking a bath I was led to reflect that this fall, since I am going into a monastery, is quite different from other autumns. Reading my diary for 1931, which I ought to destroy, I am surprised at my childish paganism. Announcing what I wanted: to be drunk.

To the end of useful notes for novel: in my 16 year old unquietness, what things stirred me, and seemed to be connected with desires.

"Autumn Crocus."

Omelet and rhine wine at the Trocadero.

Edna Best, Madeleine Carroll, etc.

Picture of Clara Bow on a beach in *Sporting and Dramatic.*

Cocktail Bar at the Mayfair. Side cars.

Grogs in Strasbourg.

Maison Olivier, Strasbourg.

Anita Page in *War Nurse.*

"Echoes of the Jungle," by Duke Ellington.

"Georgia on my Mind," by McKinney's Cotton Pickers.

T. S. Eliot's "Waste Land."

Oxford.

Cambridge.

Ezra Pound's "Lustra."

Chagall's paintings.

Marie Laurencin.

Cézanne.

Thursday. November 16

That list never did get finished.

There may be a war in Europe and the mayor of Long Beach may have been murdered but nobody can convincingly say this is such a bad age.

This is not a completely sterile age at all. Perhaps today for the first time I realized that, for painting, this has been *so far a very great age.*

There has been better painting in the last 80 years of Europe (*not* of America) than in the last 300 years – since El Greco.

Today I saw the Picasso exhibition. I have never seen such a one man show in my life. Room after room of his paintings, and each room better and more exciting than the last. It was a terrific and tiring and bewildering experience. The man is an immense and unheard of genius.

Afterwards, reading the two interviews prefacing the catalogue, was as good as seeing the pictures: he talks as straight as he paints, and there is absolutely no fooling about him.

In the same room – "Rose Period" – the women with loaves and the *Woman with the Fan* – both completely wonderful. They are so wonderful that there is absolutely no formula for them, no fooling with the wedges and spirals like Miller and his Rubens. They are pictures that are perfect because they are the way they are.

He was as old as I am now when he did them. If that isn't reason for humility . . . ! The second floor is tremendous: full of things, room after room gets better and better, and I didn't know what to do when I came to the drawings – so I let them go until the next time. Room after room – more color. The three musicians – various guitars, the wonderful seaside stuff.

The little beach scenes – at Dinard, were 1928, when father and I were at Saint Malo! Even that coincidence is exciting. The Three Graces: but especially in the room before that *Le Tapis Rouge* (with the bust and the watermelon and the mandolin) what a gorgeous thing, in the same room: *The Fish Net* and *Woman* (pink) *with Mandolin.* The room with the three graces has also three dancers and the Ram's head. Some Picasso year, 1925!

The Minotaurs – I hadn't seen any – are wonderful. And also, as I say, the bathers. Then, all of a sudden one of the gayest and happiest pictures in the world is two girls and the toy boat. Completely lovely and charming and humorous and swell.

Very impressive – Plaster head and a Bowl of Fruit, some swell picture. You could go and list all the things there, saying some swell picture, except the big fat dames period leaves me a little cold. The very latest frontal eyes stuff is lovely! Such fine innocence, those girls, writing letters with frontal eyes and crowns of leaves!

There is a terrific fuss about the *Guernica* mural and it is a terrific mural. But I think the fuss is a phony: now they can let themselves go: something that doesn't have to do with art can be talked about. Hoopla!

The catalogue is fine, all full of good reproductions and Picasso's own words and complete bibliographies and lists of exhibitions and places he has lived in, etc. I read where he says: "To me there is no past or future in art. If a work of art cannot live always in the present it must not be considered at all."

Picasso – Catholic. In a definite sense: he does in painting more what Joyce, Dante, do in writing than what Thomas Wolfe, D. H. Lawrence do in writing. He is a religious artist in the sense that all great artists are religious. What is more Christian than this: "We all know that art is not truth. Art is a lie that makes us realize truth, at least the truth that is given us to understand. The artist must know the manner whereby to convince others of the truthfulness of his lies . . . Nature and art being two different things, cannot be the same thing. Through art we express our conception of what nature is not."

But no use going around proving Picasso is "Catholic" and so antagonize good and wise men who are afraid to be Catholics. What is good is of God, and what is true is His. The truthfulness of Picasso's lies is a god-like thing.

Today the fellow upstairs had a piano moved in. He does not play well but it sounds wonderful. I think it sounds wonderful just because it is clean and clear, and not the muffled stuff that comes out of a radio.

Picasso says: "I want to get to the stage where nobody can tell how a picture of mine is done. What's the point of that? Simply that I want nothing but emotion to be given off by it."

He got to that stage in his 24th year with the woman with the fan – before, with the old man and the guitar: before: as soon as he stopped painting like Degas, Lautrec, etc. – Paris vile life. *Moulin de la Gallette.*

Sunday. November 19, 1939

Now look you: there have been three important things that have happened this year.

1. The publication of *Finnegans Wake.*
2. The War in Europe and the Russian German pact.
3. The Picasso exhibition.

Compared with these three things everything else has been trivial.

Each one of these things proves something different – in its own way.

Nothing is more definitely proving that nobody wants to fight than the present war. On the other hand its inactivity may be a ruse to teach people to like war a little better. Anyway, it is probably the transition from an argumentative peace to a continuous argument with a show of arms to support it, a state of affairs that may last another twenty years – the truce that must come will not make much difference to the state of affairs either.

1. *The Picasso exhibition* proves beyond a doubt that the greatest living artist is Picasso. Proves that he has to be accepted as such. It proves more than that to me. With the exception of Cézanne and possibly Gauguin he is the greatest artist since El Greco.

2. The Picasso exhibition proves that the living work of this greatest living artist is something tremendous, fantastically good and great and rich and alive and pure. It proves that, not only is Picasso good, but the art of our age is very great.

3. In the same way *Finnegans Wake* proves Joyce is the greatest writer of our time, and that the writing of our time is not poor, but very good and rich and exciting and fine.

4. Of everybody at the exhibition, to which I went again yesterday, there was not one who did not seem to be forced to admit Picasso's greatness. Most of them, however, were admitting it very unwillingly.

Most of them expressed out loud, and in no indefinite language, their deep hatred of Picasso. These expressions of hatred were excited, almost hysterical; they were shameful and transformed the people who uttered the opinions into beasts.

I saw one old man, highly excited, running among the pictures like a dog with his tail between his legs.

With him was a youth, about 21, Harvard type, very pimply, who read out the names of the pictures very loudly and then laughed after each name. As he laughed he would cast nervous glances around him from the corners of his eyes.

Even more despicable than these people, who could not be expected to know anything anyway, were two fat, blackhaired guys with glasses, artists, obviously. They too ran from picture to picture, obviously whipped white inside; their lips trembled with fear; they tittered like high school girls. One of them would stick his nose an inch from the picture and cry "Look, Look, he put one coat on top of the other too fast, and now the paint's cracked" and he would giggle nervously and rush on to the next one, where, if the paint happened to be cracked, he would say exactly the same thing.

(Sure, the paint cracked:

But these men: 1) did not look at the pictures at all

2) wanted them destroyed, so that they would never have to see anything so good. So they were glad about the paint cracking.)

5. In the same way, I reflected that the old man and the Harvard boy – yes, they were fools, but you could do nothing to blame them for not liking Picasso: it is their misfortune. But you are stung yourself by the loudness of their folly, which is an offense, produces an indignation that is a necessary by-product of love of the good things Picasso did. And eventually this becomes a battle of prides and you end up not seeing the pictures but just being blindly angry at the other people around you: that is of course terrible.

But nevertheless, that old man, that fatuous pimply guy, the two terrible artists: they wanted (not even secretly) to see every picture destroyed. The terrible thing is, they are perfectly capable of destroying them, or having someone else do so. And in the end they probably will.

6. Of course, all the wiseguy fat people with their witty remarks were there.

One fat woman, before one called *Woman in an Armchair* says:

"I bet it's an ear. Let's all make a guess what it is now. I say it's an ear. What do you say! I say it's an ear."

And she says it's an ear loud enough to make sure every person in the gallery hears it.

Her voice is nervous, excited.

The fear of these people in front of Picasso is terrible, utterly painful.

7. There were the good people, who would go about saying "Well, I like that anyway." And I love *them*, anyway.

8. There were some horrible intellectual-type scraggly dames with their fellows, who shrieked and snorted with laughter (laughter that sounded like strangulation) when they saw some phalluses in a picture of some dancers.

9. All these people were about the same as the reviewers – Royal Cortissoz etc. and as the reviewers who reviewed *Finnegans Wake*. They all

1) secretly hate the artist and openly denounce his admirers as members of a cult.

2) wonder if they are being tricked. They are in mortal fear of being tricked into seeming ridiculous: duped by a piece of clowning.

3) they grudgingly admit "the man is a good technician" but only do so in order to state that he is "nothing but a technician." They admit Joyce and Picasso are technicians. They deny they are artists at all. This

is their way of getting around the difficulty of the tremendous effect these artists have on everybody.

4) or else they go so far as to say they are trying to be "shocking," but "Is that art?" etc.

10. This gang, the intellectuals, the "cultured" people, the fops, the Yale fribbies and the hundreds and hundreds of bleak ugly wives of Park Avenue dentists, and the whole club of reviewers, and the Village boys, are far far more horrible than the base populace that didn't understand the pictures at the fair. What a difference! To begin with, the worst ones at the fair were of this semi-intellectual gang anyway. Oh no! No more cracks against the populace: the populace doesn't *pretend* to know! That's something! The crazies aren't there, at all.

11. There must have been dozens of quiet people saying nothing but loving the pictures. I am sure there were. You would not notice them, because you did not go there to see people anyway: these other loud babies you simply couldn't get away from: they were always crowding in between you and the pictures in order to make their loud remarks. But I did see two girls go quietly across one of the rooms with very shining eyes and expressions of wonder and delight: they were as beautiful as anything, just because of that.

Monday. November 20, 1939

I think everybody in the world wants the people to read his autobiography, or his letters or his diaries or his state papers or even his account books.

Everywhere I look people are full of their autobiography or their own collected notes or something of the sort.

To start perfectly simply – something quite straight. Lax spent the summer writing an autobiography after he had spent the spring writing a journal. The best novel of the age – *Ulysses* – is autobiography. D. H. Lawrence – autobiography and he is, anyway, important.

Today and autobiography.

I took part one of my novel (the non-autobiographical part of an autobiographical novel) back to Farrar and Rinehart. Honestly I don't know why. Saturday I thought why not just get the thing printed and Sunday I thought, what I should do is burn it: the thing's a scandal. Besides, it hangs around my neck like a millstone, and it offends me. But still I think it has some good and I know it is as good as so many things that are published.

Today, there was a picture of Roosevelt dedicating a Library or something he has had built at Hyde Park to house his state papers. In 1941 the

Library will be thrown open to scholars. The world thinks this means Roosevelt won't run for a third term, but all I care about is: here is another guy who realizes that the medium the whole age seeks expression through most readily is autobiography, and he is jumping right in with the others.

I have spent weeks telling my class to write out of their own experience: and they write best when they do, too. They write almost good autobiographical short stories sometimes.

I showed them some from Thurber's *Life and Hard Times* and some from Clarence Day: autobiography; now Day's autobiographical sketches have been put together and made into a play on Broadway, *Life with Father*.

Last night I was reading Ernest Dimnet – autobiography; this time, of a priest. And it is interesting and good. The stuff about Cambrai is wonderful.

Today I bought Saroyan's *Inhale and Exhale* and opened it – very exciting and poignant and funny and terrible autobiography.

Auden and so on: *Letters from Ireland, Journey to a War*. Gertrude Stein – by the way I want to read that. What she is most interested in is autobiography, biography (the good one of Picasso).

Take *The Seven Pillars of Wisdom*, great fat monumental thing, very impressive. I must read it: autobiography. Also the Picasso exhibition: the way it stands is, especially in its early rooms, clearly autobiography.

The big monuments of these years are all autobiographies.

Joyce, D. H. and T. E. Lawrence, Thomas Wolfe, Saroyan, G. Stein, etc.

Then all the minor stuff. Henry Miller. Henry Seidel, Canby's *Mona Mater*, Irwin Edman *Philosopher's Holiday*. N. M. Butler.

More autobiographies: J. C. Powys, – a ghostwritten autobiography of Corcoran or Cadigan or Madigan – I guess, Corrigan; who flew to Ireland in a tin airplane. Ghostwritten autobiographies of everybody: everyone who even opened a grocery store has written or thought of an autobiography.

Bob Sherwood – (fake) old clown, ran or runs a bookstore, and knew Pop. His autobiography even made pages of the *News of the World* (London) for a couple of months.

Pop himself, at Lake Placid, in the summer of '36, dictated a lot of autobiography and reminiscences to a public stenographer.

Mark Van Doren has avoided autobiography, but not Carl. T. S. Eliot has not written much autobiography except the last editorial in the last *Criterion:* but then, who is T. S. Eliot?

Good guys who have written no autobiography: Richard Hughes. E. M. Forster. But Hughes has at least done an autobiographical sketch in *Omnibus*.

Sidney Horler – wrote a pile of detective stories and they served as an excuse for the autobiography of a writer of detective stories.

How autobiographical is Larbaud?

The big and significant "monument" of the '20s in France and out of it too: Proust.

Every fellow has built his own dumb pyramid. But it's not so dumb either. There has been wonderful autobiography in this age (and terrible stuff, too – like this Joseph Freeman).

That comes from the fact that people know you can write about everything, everything is important, or can be. Everything was important to Saint Francis.

I guess where we really know how to talk is in autobiography. We can't write *Iliad*s or Greek plays but we can write autobiography – and poetry.

Tuesday. November 21

It is very interesting and exciting to read Saroyan and it is certain enough that he has some good even if nobody knows what. For example I guess his romanticism and Eliot's classicism are about equally important and unimportant. They both certainly wear tags neatly and easily or I wouldn't of mentioned it.

His tough shouting grandiloquent sentimental tough talk sometimes gets him into some sentences that are completely fine. Nobody knows what they mean and that doesn't matter. What matters is their tenderness and pathos: and I guess the fake tough defensive attitude is what doesn't matter at all. What is good in the tough talk is only the tough Damon Runyon carefulness about big words, a kind of tough politeness: the contrast there (conventional) is OK.

The tough talk on the other hand and the combination of tough and sentimental is a lot of the time just turgid and a bore.

"International Harvester" is no success for my money – crap about J. P. Morgan, etc. Facile social conscious blurbs. On the other hand, "Two Days Wasted in Kansas City" couldn't be better. Some fine story. The manner is very strained but that is all right: it is strained to the limit but that doesn't make any difference, it holds up fine.

A lot of the kid stuff is pretty terrible, yet the thing about the theater is again fine, couldn't be better, ("The World and the Theater") is a beautiful fine story.

Some fine stuff, a lot of this Saroyan stuff is, and then a lot of it is just nauseating. Only once in a while are there stories, whole stories that stand up. He is convincing in sentences, terrible a lot of the time.

Nobody could call Saroyan "brilliant." He is stupid, maybe. He is a great fool, but that doesn't matter at all. He doesn't want to be brilliant, he wants to be brave and good. He is not an artist, he is a moralist and he is yelling after some moral beauty all right and it is the only moral beauty, too: Love. He is looking for it, and a lot of times he finds it and then he's good, but he flounders around and gets up and falls down and rolls around drunk and he doesn't care. Probably doesn't drink a drop. Sounds like a moralist: but that's praise. Sometimes, the times he's good, he's full of Love. That's where everyone likes him, too. Everything else about him is foolish and ridiculous (and he doesn't care and neither do I. It happens to be one of the ways of salvation to be a fool for the sake of Love) but yet, too, he is such a fool a lot of the time! I don't know. He's too often corny.

The thing about most of it is: it's already outdated. The whole 1930s are already dated although the decade isn't even over.

The war, something about it, just the fact that it has been declared, has made this William Saroyan stuff I am reading right this minute sound old fashioned. Are Saroyan, [Thomas] Wolfe, relics of the '30s as Scott Fitzgerald and Mencken are relics of the '20s? (Where do I get all this history talk?)

When I came to America in 1931: went away impressed by 14th Street, etc. etc. having run into Reg Marsh and so on. Coming back in 1933, 1934 met the Miller crowd, and so on. The 14th Street crowd.

The 1930s – Important for – characterised by –

14th Street (The Depression – focus of attention here)

New Masses.

American Communism – especially Communism at Columbia, student Communism. The *Daily Worker* first gets a Sport Page. The C.I.O. sitdown strikes, Peace strikes, etc.

Albert Halper's "Foundry," "Union Square," Thomas Wolfe, William Saroyan. John Steinbeck. J. M. Cain, the final Hemingway stuff. "It Can't Happen Here."

WPA plays.

WPA art. Woikers.

Repeal: Calverts, Schenleys, Seagrams, form the taste of the nation.

G men (instead of gangsters)

Studs Lonigan.

Midwestern Aristotles: Hutchins, etc.

Thurman W. Arnold.

Pareto.

Archibald MacLeish.

Auden and Spender and C. Day-Lewis, etc.

"Murder at the Vanities."

Photographic annuals with a lot of montage showing the state of affairs: Bums

Sleeping on newspapers, etc.

Breadlines.

Benny Goodman, Gene Krupa.

Time magazine.

The new *Life*.

When I went to Columbia in 1935:

Ad Reinhardt; Jimmy Wechsler; the *Communist Spectator*. Bob Smith's and [Robert] Giroux's review (35–36). Strong Saroyan Hemingway influence in Smith.

My own Studs Lonigan period.

My Constitutional Law and Thurman Arnold period. Even up to 1937 – when I took Economics!

The war is really a new thing alright. And it has put a date on a lot of things: most emphatically it has dated

Studs Lonigan stuff.

American Communism of the United Front stamp and before.

Archibald MacLeish? (not the war, Washington).

14th Street.

Pictures of bums sleeping on newspapers.

I had always thought of the war as being fought in the same uniforms as 1914–18. But the uniforms are more modern. So are the planes. There is the Maginot line. It is a new kind of war. They haven't rushed millions of men at once into an attack: but Poland was wiped out in the old manner. This is a shiny new war. I knew it was going to be utterly different: I even guessed it would be a matter of engagements between small units: mostly aerial. But who knows what is going to happen? Anyway, a letter from Bennett tells how England is haywire with regimentation. All these things imply a strictness and reticence which makes Saroyan sound out of date. And now the war may make us all, who knows, tight-lipped!

Before this war was started I could not think I would be interested in Guillaume Apollinaire's war stuff (Calligrammes) etc. Now I suddenly understand how it was possible for him to write calmly about a war.

Voyage au Bout de la Nuit [Journey to the Bottom of the Night] was a product of the '30s, not of wartime or of the '20s.

December 8. Feast of the Immaculate Conception

I wish nobody had ever told me it was a good thing to attempt to know myself. I used to write it down in my diaries in Greek – γνωθι σεαυτον ["Know yourself"]. (Never knew anything about the accents.) I carted my diaries from Oakham to Rome to New York to Cambridge and knew – not myself or anything else – nothing. No-*thing.*

"No Foundation – all down the line." (like the Turk in Saroyan's play says). I read Jung and tried to figure out what psychological type I was, and figured I was an "extraverted sensation type," whatever that is. I was certainly afraid of being an introvert. That is because introversion is a sin for materialists, and what is more it is used conversationally almost as if it were synonymous with "perversion."

I read some Virginia Woolf novel and thought I was one of the characters. I thought I was like George Gissing as he is described in Wells' autobiography. (What a ridiculous thing it is to take oneself so seriously!)

But it is completely embarrassing to come upon such examples of vanity and pride. It is more pitiful to think how miserable and ignorant I continued to be while I was so unhappily engaged in the futile business of trying, in a reasonable and humanistic manner, to know myself. What floundering around! It was a wonder I remembered my own name! It was a greater wonder I remembered the names and faces of people around me.

Knowing myself – it was really a sort of a desperate substitute for confession and penance. That was why it was so silly and so lamentably useless. For the only valid kind of self-knowledge is the amount needed for a good examination of conscience to make a good confession. But both these are something God will give us if we pray humbly to Him for grace and love, and the important thing is God's love, not ourselves and what is in us. We don't want to know what is in ourselves in order to dwell upon it, treasure it, meditate upon it unless it is not of ourselves but of God. So everything that is of our own worldly desire and fear must be cast out so that we can see God within us and everywhere outside of us too. What we want to know is not ourselves but God.

"Know thyself" – it was proposed that if a man knew himself, he could manage himself so as to do just as much as he was capable of doing, etc. and be at peace just occupied enough to avoid boredom, not so busy as to get tired or flustered or excited – amused enough to be pleasantly stimulated, not enough to be choked and saturated. What a stupid ideal, but above all what a crazy idea to think it can be reached! It is a reflection of the peace and blessedness we all long for, however. That peace is not in knowing ourselves but in knowing God. But we must know ourselves, too: we must know this much: that we are not God. We already know we are unhappy: the amount of self-knowledge we need is simply what will help us find out the reasons for our unhappiness: that is in what ways we have loved silly and inferior and imperfect things and preferred them before God.

Saint Theresa [of Avila] – _The Interior Castle_ – says we must not dwell on self-knowledge alone, but pass on from it at once and go seeking God's love above everything, because every other desire is a traitor and every other knowledge is vain without God.

Without the love of God, or the explicit desire for Him, self-knowledge is futile and makes one very miserable, because one seeks this way to get out of a blind alley – and never does. We only think we want to know ourselves, but we really want to know God.

I was so preoccupied with self-knowledge that I didn't know anything about anybody else's feelings.

Tonight I saw some old letters from various people. I wondered how I ever deluded myself that I knew how to read when I had simply not read one third of the things that were said in those letters although I read the words over and over again.

One batch from a girl who, I thought, didn't love me, and was all the time very plainly saying she did without actually saying so literally. Another batch from a girl I hoped loved me, and just as plainly didn't but was even patronizing about the situation, as if she wanted to see how much I would stand. The letters are really very good and very amusing: but it is fantastic that I, so touchy and full of pride with those other letters, was completely taken in by these! Completely meek!

If I could only be meek when meekness is a virtue! It is really very funny: but the other letters are very saddening and make you completely ashamed: it feels horrible to know how stupid and beastly and clumsy and proud and selfish you could be! And with people whose every word and the look of their handwriting shows were good and unselfish and gay and full of grace and beauty!

But it is long past the time for writing out an analysis of that: yet perhaps it is good I didn't burn all that stuff before.

But it is liable to turn into a silly bad thing to dwell on these embarrassments too: for then you get into a state of false humility, beating your head and saying "O how I have hurt other people" and that is more frightful than whatever selfishness or pride it was before. What is painful is the blow to your present pride, as if the offense still persisted.

I remembered the other day how I was walking down Senate House Passage at Cambridge with some people, going to hall in Clare. I had been drinking beer and was a little tight: did not notice some people who made as if to smile and say hello. One of the others said "Those people seemed to know you." I turned around and recognized a man and his wife and daughter: they had asked me to tea that very afternoon and I had forgotten all about it. Oh! . . .

It is the same kind of shame in all these cases. It is completely horrible. It is not "Oh how I have hurt . . ." but just a complete deflation. I hope nothing like that ever happens again, ever, ever. Yet like this, all the bad confessions we make and all the half-hearted prayers and all the complicated stupid worries we get into with vile things coming into our minds, as if it wasn't our own fault and something to be taken with humility and not with anger and elaborate plans – getting obsessed with filthy ideas (elaborately filthy ideas, too) that get mixed up in prayers and torment and confuse us . . . all that is itself a way to take us away from praying and loving God and to make us think about hating filth instead. So these ideas will come, and why shouldn't they, good heavens, after the things I have done for so long my head is full of crap! Half the images and most of the language that occurs to me is scatological, because I have been in all that up to the neck, wallowing about rather weakly, claiming to know myself.

So if all that, as it must, presents itself to me and scares and torments me sometimes, then I must above all things avoid playing the "know myself" game, because if I do it will surely mean losing what little I can find of a path to God.

This is the state, perhaps, where Saint Theresa says one hears God calling in the words of devout people and good books. And oh in her book so much, too! What a divine good writer! Saint John of the Cross is more precise and more integrated and more ordered and perhaps more subtle and profound but no more luminous and not quite as completely, continually, exciting. But what a book! And what exhilaration reading it! Exhilarating because the words *fly* off the page, just as they flew on to it. She wrote at a terrific speed.

People who "know themselves" are always the ones who can't see the beam in their own eye. In getting to "know themselves" they have studied their own faults so closely and with such loving care that they see them in every-body around them even if they are not there.

Got back today from being in Washington the weekend with Rice. Maybe I always was bad at picking hotels. Got a very bad one in Washington: the Harrington: not quite so modern or so comfortable as the Olean House. In fact, the Olean House had it all over this great firetrap. Bad rickety joint, people rattling on our doorknob all morning, dark black room on a court from which you couldn't see the sky. Crummy.

I wonder when I ever of my own choice picked a good hotel? I let the Cook's man sell me the Hamilton Hotel in Bermuda (what a ridiculous ramshackle depressing joint!). I stayed at the Alexandra Hotel near Hyde Park corner overnight once. I guess it wasn't so awful for the price, but then that was a hotel Pop had discovered and not I.

Where else? Stayed overnight at Oddenino's and The Regent Palace. Both horrible.

In Rome – a pretty vile place: although on the Via Veneto it was small and black and stuffy and cramped up and full of old ladies.

I suppose, come to think of it, I have never spent the night in a hotel in New York. I would probably pick something far worse than the Taft or the Lincoln.

Did all right in Germany but not in Brussels. Oh no! not in Brussels.

Every hotel I have ever picked has been full of a kind of spiritual squalor, sometimes accompanied by actual physical squalor, too. All these hotels frighten me. But I am happy about the hotels other people have picked, or are lucky enough to get sent to.

Cf. the spiritual squalor of _Look_ magazine.

Certain legations have more character than any other buildings in Washington. Apostolic Legation, British, Japanese. The White House has its dignity, even the Capitol, too. Even the Lincoln Memorial has a certain quality: except for the lousy monstrous statue in it.

The ridiculous Art Galleries of Washington. Certain pictures in the Corcoran Art Gallery, completely awful. Very funny collection in the Corcoran. _Lost Dogs_. Boats. Stupid American women of 1908–'09. Shocking to see so much completely awful junk in one place. A Portrait of Bismarck, in the middle of all of it, had startling merit, by comparison! A pile of junk, and then a Degas, or a Winslow Homer. Homer the only relief you could really depend on. Quite a lot of him.

A stinking piece of interior Decoration by Whistler at the Freer.

All that Public Building part of Washington seemed amazingly dead. The legations and the big hotels looked like fun. The part around the Catholic University was impressive.

The best thing of the weekend was hearing the Dominicans sing Vespers at their seminary. Very good, very fine songs, very good chapel, very swell happy looking friars, happier than anyone I have seen in five years, maybe except for fellows like Father Edmund and Father Joseph Vann, etc., Franciscans. But seeing these men in their chapel, kneeling facing the aisle (the benches run parallel to the aisle) but turning their heads so that their eyes are fixed on the Blessed Sacrament on the altar, and singing. Black and white Dominican habit. A wonderful litany.

The whole area around Catholic University, crowded with seminaries, full of priests and religious, seemed to be very busy and very gay, too. The whole place is impressive, but everywhere you get the appearance of something unfinished. Although many of the buildings are already 20 or 30 or 40 years old, the whole university seems to be in scaffolding. Unfinished – perhaps not even started. Sloppy mixture of architectural styles, several bad kinds of eclecticism. Yet a very busy seeming place: as though there were a lot of activity and happiness and wonderment about having a big Catholic center in America. When you have seen the solidity of things in Europe – when you have seen Rome, it is odd to see something so raw, so unbegun. But maybe it is already a big thing and the best thing in the country, and please God it may someday be very great and wise and solid and rich and a source of wisdom and riches and light for all this part of the world. Because this hemisphere needs it, and will need it more, because after the war, or as the war goes on, this country is going to be more and more lost as the civilization of Europe (on which America, being still a province, depends) destroys itself.

Disappointed in the Franciscan showplace. Seemed overdone; a little distressing in some ways. Did not know the seminary was in a different building. The Holy Land Church was so much of a museum it was a little hard to feel it was consecrated: especially the chapels and things downstairs.

Met Doctor Robert Connery and Father Charles Hogan. Connery used to teach at Columbia. Both now at Catholic University. Hogan a student. Very liberal, always talking about it, as if it embarrassed him somehow. Proselytizing for the left. But of course a very good Catholic, naturally.

Must be a pile of priests around who look on themselves as radicals. Left wing stuff and economics bore me at the moment. It all seems so dumb and futile: waste of energy. But tied up with theology it must have *some* life, *some* value, some force. Maybe a lot. That is something I will need to learn, I suppose. But just at present I am not interested: also it seems false and improper somehow. You get too much interested in unions and you forget about charity and get all tied up in beating the Ginsburg Sash and Door Company, or the next union. Pretty silly things can happen, if that once starts.

Only nothing indicates this Hogan is not a perfectly charitable guy. So what can you say? Being interested in unions is as proper an interest for a priest as the interest in writing and painting. Maybe more proper, because it is actually closer to charity if you do it right. The first duty of the Christian to his neighbor is towards the poor and the sick: writing books maybe comes a little after that, and then only for the saving of souls or for the full glory of God.

Trouble is, there are going to be too many half-baked liberals around now, talking their dumb heads off without knowing what they are saying. Completely irresponsible diluted radicalism divorced from Russia will probably sweep the country. It has already begun, producing bad WPA art in all the post offices – that was four years ago that started. (Due homage to Reg Marsh, who paints good. I mean the dopes.) Now Steinbeck's *Grapes of Wrath* is a movie. And more movies with John Garfield and Priscilla Lane. Dust bowls.

Liberal crap in the same squalid magazine *Look*, not for any purpose, just to help sales. Complete eyewash this issue about advertising to help neutrality: the ads all perfect *for* a war, too, as well as against it.

Coming back, I saw Father Edmund. He tells me I probably won't be admitted to the Novitiate until the regular new class goes in in August. It seems like a very long time. But on the other hand it is already three months since I decided and that has gone pretty fast.

More than a week ago I saw the Saroyan play *(Time of Your Life)*. Kathy Bailey had quoted me and Gibney an awful corny sounding prologue. That was not in the play.

Kathy's part itself was very corny. She wasn't as good as a fine girl who came on for quite a long bit, with plenty of dialogue with Dowling. Good idea having this other girl enter just as the curtain falls on Act I, and her scene begin when the curtain rises on Act II. Sure, Saroyan is a moralist.

I was at a cocktail party where I told everybody that. Enough! He is a moralist.

Some good toys in the play. Didn't like Dowling's part much. Liked Willie the Marble Maniac. The Arab. Not quite sure it was a good idea except the old country music. The Arab not quite convincing. Saroyan has to get one of the other characters to say with all the emphasis possible that this Arab is a *"very good guy."* Otherwise we'd just think he was a pretty good guy who didn't know English and played the harmonica OK. Which is, as a matter of which, all that is true about him.

Good scene between the bartender and his mother. She tells a long excited unintelligible story in Italian, they laugh, cry, embrace, laugh and laugh and she runs off again. When someone asks what it's all about he says: "Oh, that's my mother, she came to say hello!"

December 14, 1939

There could certainly be something disagreeable written about all the teeth I have had pulled out. But I am not going to do it. Another one yesterday – another wisdom tooth. Not so much hammering as the last wisdom tooth: not any stitches. Same smell of disinfectant mouth wash all around my room now, same sick feeling from swallowing blood all night.

But why should I detest it so much, and fear having teeth pulled so much? There is really not a very good reason. Sure, it is disagreeable and, afterwards, it hurts, and you bleed. But the hurt isn't much worse than a hangover, nor is the sickness from drinking your own blood half as bad as a hangover. You'd think after all this time I'd have learned to have my teeth pulled patiently, without fear. But remember the last wisdom tooth. Chopping and hammering for a half hour; could feel pain in spite of the novocaine. Then stitches – five or six, and blood and iodoform in my mouth for a week. And the ache. This one is nothing. It is nearly over already. A little aching left where they hammered. You'd think I'd be more patient and grateful. Disgust at the tooth being so rotten. Disgust with so many of my teeth being rotten.

Fear before going to the dentist. All very silly. Maybe I'll learn to be patient with such things some day.

Whatever I said about *Inhale and Exhale* doesn't apply to the *Daring Young Man.* Very good. Much better than "I. and E." Fewer corny parts. Good prefaces. Good stuff about writing. Still haven't hit an individual story as good as the one about "Two days wasted in K.C." except Daring Y.M. itself. Very good business about the teletype machine (story – 12345678) and the music in it. Saroyan very close to everybody. Closer than any other writer.

I remember hearing a girl usher, in the theater where *Time of Your Life* was playing, saying to someone: "Listen, William Saroyan writes very good." and I never in my life heard an usher say anything like that.

I wanted to write to Joyce last spring and I got sore at Lax for writing to Dorothy Baker this summer, but now I want to write to Saroyan. But Joyce doesn't invite letters: Saroyan does. His writing is that kind of writing: it demands letters. Saroyan is very earnest, and is always looking around saying "Do you get exactly what I mean?" and he wants people to say "Yes, sure" and agree with him. And I do, and maybe everybody who does should write him a letter saying so.

This business of writing letters to people involves a very delicate question of pride and humility if you look at it objectively. In the first place it would be possible to write such letters as if you yourself were important. You would be doing the writer a favor, as a clever intelligent acute fellow, telling him his book is OK and you approve. When you realize that it is possible to write a pompous letter, you can go one step further, and humble yourself by writing the letter anyway, if you still have something to say. If you really want to say it, then humility demands you do so, knowing it is going to look like the letter of a pompous, contumacious guy, or like the letter of a maniac or anything. Only you do it of course because you love the guy and need to say so: not because you want the autograph letter of a successful author. So I think I will write to Saroyan.

I left the window open all afternoon to let in the air and let out the stink of antiseptic mouthwash and now I sit in bed and the room is cold, but I am very comfortable. Sore jaw. I drink grapefruit juice. I have a lot of books on my bed.

When I wrote this first sentence I seemed to remember the way it was sitting in bed in a rather cold room writing my diary, the Christmas holidays at my Aunt Gwyn's at West Horsley. 1929. Already ten years ago!

I rode on a bicycle to Farmham, to Godaliming. The Wye was flooded, at Guildford. Where are the boys who were at school then at Ripley Court? Where is Steele Major? Ingram who went to Felsted (a tough red headed guy), Romanoff, Clifton-Mogs who had a round freckled face and a surly disposition and got a scholarship to Eton? R. G. G. M. Marsden? Hooley? Lansdowne? Irving whom I later met again at Cambridge?

I remember how it was walking across the field to Church. Everybody believed the Vicar was crazy. Ten years.

Today was the day of the big battle in the South Atlantic between the *Exeter, Ajax* and *Achilles* and the *Graf Spee*. They drove the *Spee* into Montevideo. It was a very clever battle, very exciting to read about. Very tricky business. The *Spee* attacked a French steamer – or began to chase it. The *Ajax* came up to help. Laid down a smokescreen, maneuvered shoreward, got the *Spee* on the horizon and then the *Achilles* came up and finally the *Exeter.* The *Exeter* was put out of action in four hours but after a running fight that lasted all day the *Spee* ran into Montevideo. People had been driving along the shore following the sound of cannon. A large silent crowd was there when the *Spee* came in, silent, battered, after midnight.

So there we go reading about the war – everyone has been taking a very active interest since Finland was invaded. This is a different kind of war. Maybe people will get used to it and tolerate it. Maybe the newspapers will try to keep us out of it and we will talk ourselves into it *against* the propaganda everybody fears.

The *Spee* fight – no propaganda necessary: everyone knows where his sympathy is. Absurd to think there is any necessity for propaganda over Finland. People are demanding pro-Finnish news stories, Finnish victories, etc. Everybody likes Finland, and that is right. Finland is brave and fine. But that doesn't make war any finer or better. Unfortunately, people will soon be quite ready to fight: asking for it themselves. No propaganda, just give them what they want.

The propaganda *for* this war was all laid down firmly before by the *antiwar* people; they pointed out exactly how hateful Nazis and fascists were. Those on the other side did a good job of making Russia hateful. Russia joins Germany: no need of propaganda. Everybody thoroughly hates them both already.

The books on my bed are Grierson's *Metaphysical Poets*, Bossuet (whom I haven't read a line of yet), Saroyan, the *New Yorker* and F. García Lorca. Lorca is fine. A swell poet. For that reason I stop writing this and go back to reading him. Flamenco poetry. Very fine stuff.

Some splendid words in Spanish: *marfil* (ivory), *cojín* (cushion) *carmesí, puñal, girasoles, madrugada, yerbaluisa, reyerta* (quarrel) *naipe* (playing card) *liris* (lily), etc. etc. Every individual word in Spanish is very interesting all by itself. Interesting – provoking, fascinating by itself. Maybe I have been seeing a lot of good words, since I have been reading Lorca. But compare not *naipe* and "playing card" but, say, lily and *lirio. Lirio* is a fascinating word.

December 17, 1939

Spanish words: *Manzana, piel, nervio, charol* (varnish), *imperador, luciernaga, ribera, lucero* (morning star), *maravilla, domador, brunir* (burnish), *alfenique* (almond paste), *una bruidis* (a health, a toast), *tibio* (tepid), *cabriolear* (caper, somersault), *almendra* (almond), *escotero* (free), also *escueto* (disengaged), *escudunador* (a man who pries into things), *carbebecor* (to astonish), *sabana* (sheet), *amortajar* (to shroud).

The news of the crew scuttling the *Graf Spee* spelled itself out on the Times Building this evening, early, while I was in Times Square. Nobody paid any particular attention.

Nevertheless, the war is nothing but the biggest spectacle of some years, and is being treated as such. Only maybe not so many people are interested. Maybe, too, more than you'd think. The scuttling of the *Spee* certainly ended *that* part of the spectacle abruptly. It was a very good thing. At least that many men are saved, and that many British sailors are saved. It would save a lot of trouble if Hitler would scuttle his whole darn government. And it is good for those poor German guys who will now have a nice peaceful time in Uruguay – and maybe they'll live a civilized life and get some civilized ideas.

The Germans learn bad things so fast and so well, maybe they learn good things fast and well, too, when they get the chance. They are devoted, loyal to a phony ideal; they should certainly be capable of tremendous devotion and loyalty to a true one. And it is so: all the German priests I ever saw are apparently very very fine priests, wonderfully good. Or who could be better and finer than Nanny?

A nation that is capable of being trained to cruelty and arrogance is by that very fact also capable of being trained to kindness and patience and love and humility. Maybe it happens to be a little harder, but it is certainly very possible. They all want a messiah: they take the first one that comes, and the first ones that come are not always so good: Luther, Bismarck, The Communists, Hitler . . . Quite a little club of messiahs! Add Frederick the Great and his flute.

It is the poor crazy Russians that are the helpless ones! No shoes, cotton uniforms, their shells don't go off, they aren't trained, they don't know what they're fighting for, they get slaughtered by the thousand, they were drafted out of their factories and given no reasons, they are, some, nearly 40 years old. Maybe it is just a way of getting rid of all the poor guys that remember when there was a religion. It is obvious the Russian government isn't terribly concerned over what happens to them. No good, first class, well trained troops are being sent in to help these poor dumb helpless half-starved and completely frozen conscripts. None of them, it is said, are communists. Thousands, thousands and thousands are frozen, starved, shot, drowned in lakes, ponds, rivers, puddles and any body of water deep enough to cover them if they lie down flat where they fall.

Lorca is easily the best religious poet of this century. I wish I could stop trying to make judgments – "best in the century" etc. Never got over the sin of editing a college yearbook. (What an embarrassing thing that was. Would like to buy back all the copies and burn them.) He is a "flamenco" poet. Flamenco music is terribly religious: Lorca's poetry is very very deeply religious.

The poems of arrests are fascinating in the *Romancero Gitano*. There are certain attitudes in *Prendimiento De Antonito el Camborio en el Camino de Sevilla* which are the primitive and formal attitudes of figures in a Douanier Rousseau painting. The Arrest itself seems to be a kind of Douanier Rousseau treatment.

> *Antonio Torres Heredia,*
> *hijo y nieto de Camborios,*
> *con una vara de nuinbre*
> *va a Sevilla a ver los toros.*
>
> *A la mitad del camino*
> *corto limones redondos,*
> *y los fue tirando al agua*
> *hasta que la puso de oro.*
> *Y a la mitad del camino,*
> *bajo las ramas de un olmo,*
> *guardia civil caminera*
> *lo llevo codo con codo.*
>
> *A las nueve de la noche*
> *lo llevan al calabozo,*
> *mientras los guardias civiles*
> *beben limonada todos.*

Y a las nueve de la noche
le cierran el calabozo,
mientras el cielo reluce
como la grupa de un potro.
[Antonio Torres Heredia
son and grandson of the Camborios
with a willow staff
goes to Seville to see the bulls.

In the middle of the trip
he picked some ripe lemons
and was throwing them at the water
until the water seemed golden.
And in the middle of the trip,
under the branches of an oak tree
the police came along
and took him away.

Early in the evening,
they took him to jail,
while the police
were all drinking lemonade.
And early in the evening
they locked up the jail
while the heavens glistened
like the rump of a wild horse.]

The more you read the read the better he is: *San Gabriel* is tremendous and fine. *Preciosa y el Aire* may be one of the most fascinating things I ever read in my life. Best Spanish poetry for my money since the early *Villancios* and old Romances.

Maybe someday soon there will be flamenco records, of singers – La Nina de los Peines – doing Lorca's poetry.

In the nineteenth century the career of the artist ended in suicide. In the twentieth the artist ends in murder. Lorca, murdered. Bix Beiderbecke, murdered. It is terrible and frightening, but not so completely trivial as an artist's suicide. I have never been able to think of the Chatterton story as tragic. Or the stupid death of Lionel Johnson – drunk, he falls under a cab or some vehicle – convert and all, with his top hat, run over in a gutter. Ugh! That is a really shameful one.

The deaths of artists are never satisfactory. Marlowe – murdered, or killed in a fight or what. The death of Shakespeare – satisfactory: he died and made a will. The death of a writer, to be at all proper, should result in some kind of document, something written. If not, at least something spoken. But better, a will leaving your wife your second best bed.

What I don't know about the deaths of artists would probably fill several very uninteresting books.

The death of Blake, on the other hand – perfect: seeing angels, singing at the top of his voice, very happy and excited and full of joy seeing the doors of heaven open in front of him.

To tell the class: important what a writer's attitude towards life is. Cf. the Preface to *Daring Young Man*, which I will probably read to them.

If a man writes remembering we must all, at some time or other, die, it is very important. It will greatly affect the way he writes.

This is a much better formulation of the problem than T. S. Eliot's way of putting it in terms of original sin.

In this the confusion between an attitude and a belief is done away with. Not everyone believes in original sin, but everyone knows we must die. What is important and characteristic about a poet or a novelist is determined not by what he believes as much as by what his attitude is, where he stands to look at things from. That is where you must begin.

But after that, it is important, all right, whether he believes in God, and in the redemption of the world by Christ. But a poet who does not start out by remembering we must all, some day or another, die, is not going to be so clearly faced with the need of believing things about God one way and another.

A writer who merely takes the attitude that every citizen has ten cents to spend on Wheatena and five to spare for a chocolate bar is not going to be affected much by the question of original sin, if he sticks to this one simple attitude. His style will not be directly influenced by such remote doctrines, or by any of the mysteries.

Remind myself to remind them this is not the difference between an optimist and a pessimist, which is what they will all take for granted.

Ask them if it is morbid. Is that morbid? is a swell question for classes. I asked them once if Thomas Stanley's *Exequies* was morbid, having read it to them. One of them said yes, another said, no, it was satire. Another said it was hardly morbid because he said "exactly what flowers" he wanted on his grave, and you could only do that in fun. The reference is to

"Yet strew
Upon my dismall grave,
Such offerings as you have,
Forsaken cypresses and sad Eve;
For kinder flowers can take no birth
Or growth from such unhappy earthe."

I got them to admit this was not only not "morbid" but also not especially "sad" either, but really rather light hearted after all. I am sure that
was very important if only they remember it.

Attitudes a writer may take – a selection by no means, of course, exhaus-
tive:

1. That happiness *is* found on the Staten Island Ferry.

2. That we must all die, and that after death we are useful to the plants
as nourishment and manure.

3. That children are suckers for cops and robbers stories.

4. That you can always sell a lyric having the rhyme of "love" and "stars
above."

5. That you can sometimes sell a lyric that kids the trick of rhyming
"moon" and "June" but ending up with "Anyway that's how I feel about
you."

6. That the guy picketing the pin-ball machine in a drugstore knows
what he is doing.

7. That the sooner a machine is invented to compose everything we
write for us, as well as write it down, the better.

8. That it is possible to take all these attitudes at once.

9. That the only important thing in the world is not being caught
drinking a glass of buttermilk.

10. That although we must die, it is better to forget it and get drunk.
These attitudes are all very popular, I am sure.

Someday I am going to find a good place to eat in the Times Square dis-
trict that is not as expensive as Sardis and is nevertheless good. Make a list
of the places I have tried. Rosoffs – never again. LaHiffs, never again. Several places in those side streets, never again. Guido's Italian Best, Monte
Rosa, etc. etc., not if I can help it ever again. Taft Tea Room, sometime
when I want a sandridge. Jack Dempsey's Broadway Bar – never again. The
place next to the Capitol, not if dragged in dead. The Hotel Lincoln, not
to save my own life from starvation, maybe. Huntsman Room at the Astor,

OK, maybe. Italian Restaurant next to Dinty Moore's – maybe. Dinty Moore's, how do I know, I never was there? Penn Drugstore at the Astor, all right for cokes, ain't it?

That leaves Sardis. Because not the Brass Rail and not that other joint near it or any of those stinking bars, baby, with their log cabin marquees. Also the automat and the Times Square Childs and the Mirror Candy store and Maxwell House, etc. but NEVER that cafeteria on the corner of seventh and something, north side, just past the Mayfair – not the Bristol.

In fact such a list of lousy horrible places to eat outstrips that around Piccadilly Circus by a mile! As a matter of fact, facing the top of the Haymarket was one quite good place which I forget the name of and I don't mean Lyon's corner house.

Zuttis'? Zucco's? Zelli's? – what's the matter with this pen? [ink blot on journal].

Modern words – of our great century.

Sterile, sterilize, oxidise, carbonate, calcimine, lubricate, lubricant, colonic irrigation, sterile gauze, bauxite, cordite, phenol, synchro-mesh, cutting room, projection room, glassbrick, radiophoto, antenna, Lockheed, dive bomber, magnetic mine, heavy and light machine guns, tommy guns, minesweeper (dated – last war), minelaying seaplanes, aircraft carriers, balloon barrage. I guess I don't know many technical words. I don't know the language of my time very well. Sulphanilamide is talked of a lot. Wonder what it is. Someone in my class wrote an essay describing it. I still wonder what it is. Adhesive tape, torpedo tube, rotolactor – I don't know. Football helmets. Brace, truss, shoulderpads, whatnot, Liniment: what's so new about all this? Seems I can't think them up out of my head: have to look some up sometime.

Thought of a couple more: photo offset (Joe Roberts just called up, that's why), mimeograph, manila folders, cardboard binders, linotype, hypo, inlay, four color photo engraving, denture, hacksaw, wind gauge, altimeter, ameter, sound box, tone arm, compass shutter, photoelectric eye, exposure meter.

December 18. Monday

Short stories and journals have something in common – short stories and entries in a record, that is. If I impose a rudiment of form on what has happened so far this morning, there is some sort, I guess, of a short story. But it can't be the kind of journal entry saying "Got up 8:30," etc.

III

On the other hand, to say what I want to say in a short story would be very hard. To say anything in a short story would be easy, to say anything properly in a short story would be hard. I have never written any short stories.

Maybe if I turned this journal into one short story a day about what I saw happen or what I did I would soon learn to write short stories, but the catch is this, I don't want to be a writer of short stories, I want to be a priest. For instance now I don't conceive of myself as writing a short story at all because I am writing in a clothbound ledger called "Record" instead of on the typewriter. Writing in this ledger is all right. Journal form, not short story form. Part of a long collection. Journal is something between an epic and an encyclopedia, both unfinished and badly done and careless, but happy. Completely, however, formless. Writing on a typewriter a thing you think of as a short story has its difficulties. It has its difficulties if you *think* of it as a short story. "I am writing" you say "a short story." Okay, where's the plot? What happens? That's not the least of it:

If it is a short story, it is for everyone to read: it is directed at an audience. You care to get it read. But that means you must think about getting it published, because if you have something you want people to read, it has to be published for them. There are two ways of getting a thing published.

1. Selling it to someone who will publish it.
2. Publishing it yourself.

Now if you are to sell it to a publisher, that is if you keep reminding yourself you are to sell it to a publisher, you start having business worries, maybe. You ask yourself, "Will this sell?" And since you then try to modify your stuff to fit a market and since you have no earthly idea what the market wants you write a bad story. Then you go and brush it up for the market and rewrite and rewrite for the market and you have several bad stories and are well on the way to writing things you'll hate for the rest of your life.

If you plan to publish it yourself there is all the embarrassment: it has got to be so important that it is worth your looking like a nut to get it said and understood. Because nuts print their own stuff – only rich nuts, naturally (I'm not rich, but I can pretend to be, for the sake of argument). Therefore it has to be more than a short story, it has to be some kind of a message, or a superlatively beautiful piece of work or something. But anything I would write in a short story this morning would be neither.

I do not want to write a short story, really. A short story is for publication and I would worry all the time because I wasn't keeping a carbon.

You keep a million carbons of poems, because that's easy. But it's tiring to keep changing sheets of carbon paper for a story or a novel, page after page. You let it go. The things I did this morning do, and do not, belong in a short story. Anything belongs in a short story, depending what you want to say about it. Only the unimportant things about this morning go nicely in a short story. The important things belong somewhere else. Either that or I am about to revolutionize the short story.

What did I do so far this morning? Only went to Mass. But that is very important. How is it important to a short story? If it is important to me it is important to a short story. But I have to find out a way to bring it in, and that is what is hard.

Very easy to think of all the stupid things that have no importance: but wait a minute: maybe I'll write the short story.

Maybe anything does belong in a short story, especially a short short one. However, maybe short stories are what I know least about of almost any literary form except perhaps some small types of poems.

I have really read very few short stories. The short stories I really like are all, mostly, funny. Ring Lardner, Thurber, the "Man Who Corrupted Hadleyburg."

Incidentally I used to read all those at the time I lived in Douglaston. Maybe there is something about the conditions imposed on a person living on Long Island in a suburb that makes it necessary for a person to read a lot of light and humorous short stories in order to preserve his peace of mind. Gibney, who is now every day at Port Washington, spends a lot of his time reading John Collier stories. I guess you have to.

Serious short stories have never interested me much. Even the liveliest. Until reading Saroyan, I mean. For example, Hemingway's short stories never meant much to me. They are probably less interesting than Sherlock Holmes short stories which used to interest me considerably at the age of 14. I have never felt the slightest desire to read O. Henry. And I have never read him, although everybody says he is very good. I don't even get very far with Richard Hughes' short stories. I have always had a prejudice against buying a book of short stories. I steered clear of Huxley's *Those Barren Leaves* for years because I thought it was a book of short stories.

On the other hand I find peoples' notebooks and diaries intensely interesting, and I am perfectly happy writing in a notebook of my own. And I like reading novels and I was perfectly happy writing one this summer and this fall.

I have always liked volumes of letters but I have at the same time generally always been impatient of epistolary novels.

I have always been fond of guide books. As a child I read guide books to the point where it became a vice. I guess I was always looking for some perfect city. Some city where there was absolutely everything. This ideal city was something of this sort. It was situated at the bend of a large river. It was near a range of mountains; it was full of fine buildings. It had two or three railway stations. A cathedral, many gothic churches, abbeys, monasteries. A medieval university. Many schools and palaces. Big hotels and department stores, several museums. Famous men were born there. It was the seat of an archdiocese, it was the headquarters of an army corps, it manufactured something or other. It had an important rugby team.

I tried to make out Grenoble was a city of this type but many things were lacking. I never went there. Clermont Ferrand I loved, and finally got taken there. It had volcanic mountains around it. It had a cathedral. Great black lycées and colleges. A famous man, Pascal, had been born there. It had snow on the streets in winter. It had romanesque churches built out of fantastic red lava, or something. It had small trolleys, and cafes, and a bookstore that was narrow and full of books and seemed like an 18th century bookstore. I liked Clermont Ferrand fine. It had no rugby team, but Mont Ferrand, a suburb, a manufacturing town where they made tires, sure did.

I never loved Toulouse, but I remember it with awe. Vast red city, hot and big and in some way, fierce and grand, too. A very impressive city, great and sprawling, and southern in a different, a much more arid way, than Marseilles. Toulouse has a sort of asceticism Marseilles lacks: the asceticism of a town that is huge but not cosmopolitan. Toulouse is completely southern French, homogeneous. There are, of course, Spaniards and Arabs: but they do not really mar the homogeneity of the city.

I looked for my cities in the South, but I read about Stockholm and about Dresden. About the only two northern towns that attracted me. I had a period of raging over English cities, of which Exeter was my favorite for a long time. I never went there. The city I like best in the world is Rome.

December 19. Tuesday

The rule for learning how to write short stories: write one a day for two months. Then burn almost all of them and rewrite three or four ten or twelve times each. Of course this is pure fancy on my part, I have never written a short story, really. Part of the rule would be: all that time you wouldn't be thinking of this as "writing short stories" – or I wouldn't, because there is something a little appalling to me about the *difficulty* of writing short stories. You would be thinking of this, a spending each day writing something that had a beginning and an end and maybe even a middle.

I just thought of writing a short story about a hermit: it has neither beginning or middle nor end. But it goes like this. I am walking along. I see this hill, with some trees and rocks on the top of it. Facing east is a cave. The rocks are very slick and neat, a flat, sharp rock face, shiny, yellowish. Like in a Bellini painting, is what I mean. No geology.

Beyond the hill, across a valley is an Italian town. Beyond that the Appenines, the hills of New Jersey, who knows: The Poconos. (cheap!)

(As soon as I go to write a short story I get cheap.)

Across the mouth of this cave is a trellis upon which a grape vine grows. The broad grape leaves make a pleasing dappled shade in the summer. The hermit has an old drawing board set up on a stand. It was given to him by a man who used to work in a drafting office. (What on earth is a drafting office?) He puts, on this drawing board, a book. He sits upon a gasoline drum. He leans his elbows on the drawing board and reads his book. Behind him, on the wall of the cave, is written in charcoal: *Du bist ein Esel* ["You're an ass"].

In front of him, all over the walls, are wonderful primitive religious pictures, in charcoal also: a crucifixion, Our Sorrowful Mother, Saint Francis preaching to the birds, the Assumption of Our Lady, the Resurrection of Our Lord, the Last Supper, the Baptism of Jesus.

The hermit is preparing to do a picture of the martyrdom of Saint Sebastian also. And other Spanish subjects. The end of the cave has space for a triumph of the Blessed Sacrament. The drawings are very good, like those of a child.

As I approach, the hermit leaves his book, and picks up a violin and comes out of the mouth of the cave, playing and singing a hymn he has just composed, which sounds partly like a Gregorian Chant, partly like an Arab Chant, is sung like a Flamenco song. Its words are:

Silet mons,
Silent arva
silent aves,
Magna, parva
Nunc eamus
Nunc eamus

Benedicamus
Benedicamus.

Silet Wald
Silet Hugel
Silet grossmud
Kleine Flugel
Alle treten
Alle treten
Gott zu beten
Gott zu beten.

Silet wood
Silet river
Silet gift
Silet giver
Nunc eamus
Nunc eamus
Benedicamus
Benedicamus.

Allons dans ce
Beau silence
Ave Maria disons
Ave Maria disons
Dans ce fin silence,
va:
Prends tou essor élance
toi
Nunc eamus
Nunc eamus
Benedicamus
Benedicamus.

Mi alma huye
En las colinas
Y alla canta
Sus complinas
Nunc eamus
Nunc eamus
Benedicamus
Benedicamus.

Nunc fideles vadimus
Nunc fideles vadimus
Alla montana para orar
Alla montana para orar.
Benedicamus
Benedicamus
Alla montana para orar
Donde los santos solitarios
Renden gracias al senor,
Con sacrificios diarios
En las llamas de Amor.

Nunc fideles glorificamus
Sanctum Patrem, Filium,
Atque Sanctum Spiritum
Trino dominoque damus
Totam salis saporem
Totam cordis amorem
Totam almae ardorem
Per omnia saecula saeculorum.

[The hill is still
the plain is still,
the birds are still,
great and small
now let us go
now let us go
let us bless
let us bless.

Still is the forest
Still is the hill
Still are the tired
little birds,
all going
all going
to pray to God
to pray to God.

The wood is still
the river is still
the gift is still

the giver is still
now let us go
now let us go
let us bless
let us bless.

Let us walk in
this beautiful stillness
let us say "Ave Maria"
let us say "Ave Maria"
Walk in the precious stillness:
Take up your own delicate flight.

My soul flees
into the hills
and there sings
its evening prayer.
now let us go
now let us go
let us bless
let us bless.

Now we faithful go
now we faithful go
to the mountain to pray
to the mountain to pray
let us bless
let us bless
to the mountain to pray
where the solitary saints
give thanks to the Lord,
with daily sacrifices
in the fire of Love.

Now we faithful glorify
the Holy Father, the Son,
and the Holy Spirit
and we give this triune Lord
all the taste of the salt
all the love of the heart
all the fervor of the soul
for ever and ever.]

And that, I guess, is the end of my short story.

One reason why I can't write short stories to other peoples' formulas: I can't invent a character fast enough. I have to write twenty or thirty pages before I have any idea what kind of a character I am writing about. Then I go on and on and on pages and pages and pages and maybe never get to the point when the character means anything to anybody else.

Another thing is that I have tremendous preoccupations of my own, personal preoccupations with whatever it is going on inside my own heart, and I simply can't write about anything else. Anything I create is only a symbol for some completely interior preoccupation of my own. But symbols I have difficulty in handling, these are! I start to write a short story, creating something new, I get distressed in the first paragraph and disgusted in the next. I try to create some new, objective, separate person outside myself and it doesn't work. I make some stupid wooden guy.

Give me a chance to write about the things I remember, things that are in one way or another piled up inside me and it is absolutely different. There are a whole lot of rich and fabulous and bright things in that store: whether things I remember or things that just make themselves there: deep and secret and well ordered and clear and rich and sweet thoughts and ideas are there, but they are all about things that are so close to me that I love them as myself. Some actual people – not enough of my neighbors, however; this makes one thing very apparent, doesn't it? Such things as I love as I love myself I can write about easier than about things that don't exist and therefore can't be loved. I guess I could write a much better short story about angels I love than about some purely fanciful person who cannot be conceived as having any of the characteristics of anyone I ever loved. I can start to write if they are symbols of something I love, but as symbols they are hard to handle.

Since there is a curiously close relationship between love and fear, I also write very readily but without pleasure about the things I fear, but then I am rarely happy about what I have written. I only know I am writing well about the things I love: ideas, places, certain people: all very definite, individual, identifiable objects of love, all of them, because it is impossible to love what doesn't exist.

Today in History

Today is the day the general public rushed to see *Gone With the Wind*, at two theaters – the Astor and the Capitol: all for fabulous prices. 75 cents,

$1.10 etc. Not so fabulous. I had no particular trouble getting a seat at the Capitol.

Why is this so important? It is a great big long film of a great big long book and everybody believes it to be important. That is enough for me. I believe it too. I still believe it.

Although the second half of the film is terribly dull and even vicious, I think it is very fine for someone to have made a movie four hours long. Because the second half drags it seems even longer. Because they showed a lot of completely stupid newsreels that were already a week old. Anyway the show dragged terrifically at one point.

Newsreels of dresses made out of spun glass. Dresses made out of "milk and water and air," jewelry made out of coal or something. Then monkeys playing Santa Claus, in a small house with a Christmas tree, and finally, publicity stuff from Florida – people aquaplaning behind a seaplane. Horrible phony voice. I guess I remember the commentary by heart. I've seen it everywhere for the past ten days (three movies).

"It's *grand* fun but look out for the *bumps*. . . ." One of the people falls off, then another.

"And now here's a motorboat to the rescue" (motorboat to the rescue).

"But oh no, no one's hurt. The aquasports just want a lift, that's all. . . ." (The plane and the aquaplaners again).

"Ah, but down here it's *June* in January . . . etc. etc."

I don't know whether I felt more like vomiting for the "aquasports" or for "June in January."

Gone With the Wind – OK. It's an immense long picture. The second half is about very mean people who kick each other continually in the face; the picture is very tremendous and impressive as a whole. It bears you down by sheer weight. The first half is very interesting and a lot exciting, too, in fact quite some bit harrowing in places.

It is a very heavy solemn picture but in the business of the siege of Atlanta, or all the Civil War stuff, its solemnity is matched by a lot of terrible adventures and big spectacle and its solemnity is OK. Later on when the solemnity surrounds a lot of cheap junk and a heap of wife-beating the violence is just vicious and repellent. So is the straight face humorlessness. Some awful hammy scenes.

The character of Melanie, although hammy all the way through, gets good as everything gets good in the part immediately following the siege of Atlanta: the picture divides in the middle of its very best part: the part about the Southern Estate that has been destroyed in the war. That is not only good, it is very good.

(Funnily enough in the H.G. Wells' *Things to Come* which is in no way to be compared with this, the movie was only halfway good in the parts where it showed a civilization that had been destroyed.)

This picture is really two or three pictures or an infinite number of pictures, yet it was a very good thing to do it up in one picture.

To judge the book by it, it must be a better book than *Anthony Adverse* appeared to be from the movie they made of it. I have not read either one, but this movie makes *Gone With the Wind* seem at least a little interesting and I am really curious to take a look at it and see what it is like.

The scenes of southern society at the very beginning looked pretty stupid. It is a pity only a few minor characters had any southern accent at all.

I believe *Gone With the Wind* to be just as good and just as important as any big fat book written by Thomas Wolfe. OK, Thomas Wolfe has a lot of yearnings and shouts a bit and is lyrical and is by no means vicious in the way the Rhett Butler-Scarlett O'Hara household turned out to be. But *Gone With the Wind* is a more exciting story, and characters mean something in it. Not much, but something.

I have no interest whatever in Leslie Howard, or old man O'Hara or any of Scarlett's minor husbands or half the minor characters. Vivien Leigh was, I guess, very impressive. She was much prettier in newsreels than in this. Her face was too often given green highlights and the last shot of all, of her, in the film, was completely horrible. I am glad I did not see it from beginning to end. Maybe I will in a few months. It will probably be excruciating, and I dare say, I won't support it for ten minutes. But I would be curious to try. That is enough.

All the part about the Civil War was very harrowing and it is scaring to think how near the whole world is to having just that happen to it: it is already happening in Poland and Finland.

December 21. Thursday

Peter Munro Jack's story about the Spaniard here in the Village somewhere: the Spaniard owns a siamese tomcat and he rents it out to Jack for his two siamese females: this Spaniard has a whole lot of Lorca papers dating from the time Lorca was in New York. Something he was writing for a ballet, it appears. Not such a story. But the guy has papers.

Three 16 year old guys standing on the corner: laughing a lot, fatuously; one of them is imitating orchestra leaders. He imitates Clyde McCoy, they guess. He imitates Ted Lewis, the others guess "Cab Calloway." Loud fatuous laughter. They are all three terribly bored.

Very wonderful clear sky tonight as deep and bright as paradise, full of chaste and clear stars shedding their light like water all down the brilliant air. On Eleventh Street (the good part of Eleventh, back of where I live and where I now sit writing in bed) along the block of the Baptist Church. This was like a different and more refined and pleasant city. The houses looked neat and the lighted windows made them look like the houses of eighteenth-century merchants, not of twentieth-century socialist kindergarten teachers.

Down at the corner of Eleventh and Bleecker – piles of cake and trays of cookies and pastry in Sutter's window. On the opposite corner, on the block where Van Doren lives, a girl with an armful of parcels posts a letter. A well-to-do married couple, drunk and unsteady, stand by the florist store. The man looks at the store: the wife says "Don't buy anything more, don't buy anything more" and he answers "Why not? Why not?"

I opened up Grierson's *Metaphysical Poets* and saw on the page Donne's "Nocturnal upon Saint Lucie's Day": today being the winter solstice and the shortest day I thought it must be Saint Lucy's: but looking into my Daily Missal I found Saint Lucy's Day on the 13th and that today is the Feast of Saint Thomas the Apostle.

Then this is really my Saint's day. I went to Mass and received [Communion] this morning but didn't know anything about it, and I am sorry. The Epistle, which I now read, is glorious for today.

"*Fratres, jam non estis hospites, et advenae: sed estis cives sanctorum, et domestici Dei: superaedificati super fundamentum Apostolorum et Prophetarum, ipso summo angulari lapide Christo Jesu. . . .*" ["(Brothers) You are strangers and aliens no longer. No, you are fellow citizens of the saints, and members of the household of God. You form a building which rises on the foundation of the apostles and prophets, with Christ Jesus himself as the capstone" (Ephesians 2.19–20, New American Bible).]

The Gospel is of course the story of Thomas' doubt. The Communion prayer:

"*Mitte manum tuam et cognosce loca clavorum: et noli esse incredulus, sed fidelis.*" ["Take your finger and examine my hands. Put your hand into my side. Do not persist in your unbelief, but believe!" (John 20:27, New American Bible).] And all this is beyond words. For I went very long without belief in Christ, but insulting him and reviling his name; and ever since my baptism I have been of small faith, weak and insecure and impatient and without strength or courage, and only by grace of God's kindness and grace and his care in sending me often to confession to good priests have I gradually got enough strength in my legs to walk a little. But how weak that is still. But why is it?

Saint Thomas didn't doubt that Christ was the son of God or that Christ was crucified for love of him. Saint Thomas doubted that Christ rose again from the dead, and that He who appeared to the apostles in the upper room was really Christ. So, too, I haven't been strong enough or humble enough in faith in the resurrection of Christ, symbol of the resurrection he can bring about in our own souls in this life, as well as of the resurrection of our souls to heaven in the next and of our bodies at the last day. For if I had more love and more faith and more humility and patience, my soul would be cleaner and not so full of fears and impurities and lack of courage and full of temptations and full of impatience under temptation, but would be stronger and calmer, and fuller of Christ's love instead of my own selfishness and my own confusion.

None of us can actually see Christ the man in the appearance under which Thomas saw him, but we receive Christ man and God and partake of his body and blood, manhood and Godhead in the Sacrament of the Eucharist. *"Mitte manum tum et cognosce loca clavorum."* Christ speaks these words to us, actually, at every elevation of the host, and it is with the words of Thomas that we reply in our hearts: "My Lord and my God."

Blessed Saint Thomas, who are blessed because, seeing the risen Christ and handling His wounds you believed in Him: pray to Him that I, seeing His body and the blood of His wounds each day may also believe Him, and be filled with His love. And may the image of the five wounds go with me wherever I go; and may the blood from them purify me utterly so that every earthly fear, desire or temptation may be driven out of my heart, and so that I may be wholly filled with God's love and become His servant and the fellow citizen of the Saints. Amen.

January 4. 1940

REFLECTIONS ON THE MEANING OF 1940

A New Year – it feels like a New Year: a new decade. In his book about *The Medieval Mind*[27] which I have been reading, Henry Osborn Taylor can tolerate practically everything in a Christian philosopher except the interest in numbers. Augustine, fascinated by the symbolic meaning of numbers, drives Taylor wild. Alcuin, or someone else, following after him, drives

---

[27] Henry Osborn Taylor (1856–1941), *The Medieval Mind: A History of the Development of Thought and Emotion in the Middle Ages* (Cambridge, MA: Harvard University Press, 1911).

Taylor crazy again. You could collect book-review blurbs about it: preoccupation over numbers gives us passages which represent, says Taylor, "Augustine at his worst." etc.

And yet numbers have curious effects, outside their proper province as mere numbers. They symbolize many more things than quantity. Or different quantitative abstractions themselves seem to symbolize different states of mind.

Numbers have a lot of literary value. Take the difference in dignity in a place name:

1. The Oaks.
2. Seven Oaks, Twelve Oaks.

Dignity conferred on (2) by the number. That is not because of any intrinsic merit in the number itself: this, by the way, suggests a good list.

Four Roses
Aux Trois Quartiers
The Seven Sisters (Pleiades)
Seven Dials
Ten pins
Nine pins
Nine mile Airport (Allegheny)
Quattro Fontane (Rome)

As a piece of bad fantasy I thought of the following as a fiction name:

Peter Sixpence,
The Four Feathers,
Three Feathers (Pub Name),
Seven Against Thebes (Fantasy Pub Name),
Seven come Eleven,
The twenty-four elders of the Apocalypse,
The Seven Hills of Rome,
The Nine Choirs of Heaven,
The Fortyniners,
The Roaring Forties,
Seven league boots,
The Seven Dwarfs,
The Hundred Days,
A seventy five
A three ring circus,
A two ton truck,
Goody twoshoes,
The Seven Brothers (A Moving Van Company in Brooklyn).

The good things in this list, the mysterious sounding and important sounding ones are:

The seven sisters, Seven Dials, Nine mile, Quattro Fontane, Seven Brothers, also the Seven Hills and the Nine Choirs.

Quattro Fontane is more quaint than anything and then it is Italian and I have a personal good feeling about the actual place.

Seven – is an important number: I don't know anything about it, but it is the number legends are supposed to love best. It is a natural in any legend, or any fiction – even now – Seven Keys to Bald Pate (?) and Seven Dwarfs, etc.

What are there fours and forties of?

1. A child on all fours.

2. Four Roses, Four Feathers, Fourfooted denizens of the Jungle, Four Evangelists, Four masted schooners, Four sides of a square, rectangle, etc.

3. The 1840s. Gold Rush, 1848 revolution.

The 1840s – early Victorian age in England.

The 1640s – English Civil War.

The 40s of a century is when you suddenly realize you are in the middle of it, and that the century is not young anymore.

I am sure a lot of the yelling and shouting and gaiety of the 1920s came from a kind of superstition that the number 20 belonged to everybody and everybody was 20 years old, or ought to try to be.

I guess the 1940s look pretty serious.

4. Forty-second Street.

The Forty-second Parallel.

The Roaring Forties.

All have the same sort of literary value to me – all carry with them the same kind of mental image: a sort of shoddiness, a rubbishy quality. That is because the street has a shoddy character and the book was disorganized and rubbishy, like a rubbish heap, and the Roaring Forties mean a lot of wetness whipping over a disabled vessel all tangled in ropes and spars. Untidy roaring forties.

5. But 1940 is brand new, and is clean as a new penny, in spite of all the untidiness in Europe.

6. There is the completely unwarranted feeling of relief you get ending something you have arbitrarily started to count off as a "decade."

7. Carlyle's *Past and Present*. 1843.

Macaulay's *Lays of Ancient Rome*. 1841

Ruskin *Modern Painters.* 1843–1846. etc.
Dickens – *Old Curiosity Shop*
>> *David Copperfield,* etc. '40s.
Thackeray – *Vanity Fair* – 1847–48.
Thomas Hardy – born 1840.
C. Brontë. *Jane Eyre* – 1847.
E. Brontë. *Wuthering Hts.* 1847.
Tennyson – *Locksley Hall*
>> *Lady of Shalott* 1842.
Three romances(?) *Pippa Passes* – 1841.
>> *My Last Duchess.* 1842.
>> *Spanish Clyster.* 1842.
>> Etc. 1842–3–4.
(Browning – b. 1812. born in the same part of his century as I am in mine.)

8. By this we may tell nobody knows what 1940 holds: we think about Picasso, Joyce, etc. being the ones responsible for everything now: but the future will hold us responsible. I don't mean that corny phrase to be so important sounding. But what the physiognomy of 1940 will look like in a museum of cultural relics depends on fellows as old and a little older than I am. Soon matters will be out of the hands of the generation that is 50 or 60 now – Stalin, Hitler, Mussolini: our fathers.

It is hard to realize that these men will not be our contemporaries in our maturity, and that, in our maturity, we will not be able to hold them responsible any longer for the way the world is. Which shows we must not be too ready to hold them entirely responsible now.

9. How ridiculous we would think it was to find a document of some man comparing the years 440 and 540 a.d. To us those years seem exactly the same: but that is because most of us only know how the Roman Empire had fallen, and the "Dark Ages" had come. It would not seem 440 was so absolutely different looking as 540 to a man living in 540. Maybe that is because it really didn't look different to such a man. Perhaps he didn't care. Perhaps no one kept any record of such differences. Perhaps the only distinctive trait of our culture, beneath the obvious things, machines and the war, is that we are very preoccupied with recording the differences between this year and last.

But that was very much part of the temper of the 1840s too. Ideas of Progress, Labor trouble, mechanical advances, scientific ideas, evolution, Marxism, Oxford Movement, Liberal Christianity, [John Henry]

Newman's Conversion – all this was coming to a head in the 1840s. But all those things dominate us now. Really we have changed very little from that age we thought (in the 1920s) we were *least* like.

Now we imitate their clothes, corsets, bustles. Or is that some other period?

What have we got that's so new now? A lot of shining Lockheed bombers and Curtis Hawks and Vickers Spitfires and a lot of Messerschmitts.

Tremendous interest in *arms*. The fight is represented as a fight of arms against arms. What is tentatively bombed now: places where arms are *stored* (not where arms are *made*). The religion of this age is devoted to the manufacture of arms. The 1840s probably had no such concept. They were all full of ideas about peace and justice. The inadequacy of their ideas about peace, justice, free trade, empire, etc. have led to all factories being devoted to work for war.

Germany is fighting the 1840s: the 1840s were terrible, the future is unthinkable! Progress down a steep hill, very fast, toward the pit.

But maybe that is the reason Russia tied up with Germany: and the reason why she imitates Germany in everything, right down to the way she words her communiques. Germany is fighting 1840: Russia thinks 1840 was to be destroyed: Russia now in fact abandons her loyalty to 1840, the womb the Soviets were gestated in, and makes her world among the chief wolves, learning from them, or trying to.

10. What happened between 440 and 540? The Romans in 410 left Britain utterly. 449 – the Saxons began coming – to Kent. By 549 the Angles were invading the north of England. Not a very wide difference, it would seem to us.

No wider a difference than there probably really is between the things that manifested themselves in the 1840s and those that happen now: just two different incursions of barbarity.

In the 430s – Rome was sacked by the Goths. In 493 – Theodoric is King of a sort of fusion of Ostrogothic and Roman elements – Clovis [marries Clotilde and in 496] was converted – so between 440 and 540, in that century, the course of the next thousand years, maybe even the fate of the whole world had been decided. The fate of the whole world is decided, perhaps, every second of every day: but in that century it was finally decided that the Church would stand and that Europe would be Christian – at least until now.

Maybe now it is being decided in the other direction: maybe this time the barbarians will win. If they do, it is partly at least the fault of the Christians: the individuals themselves, because if the Christians are good enough, the barbarians can't help becoming Christians.

11. I am not at all sure that history repeats itself, except in the sense that every time I take a breath, history repeats itself. But my breathing is not a matter for a historian. A lot of things repeat themselves, but they are not historical, all of them. The Battle of the Marne is not a repetition of the Battle of Marathon, and yet it is, too. It is a kind of repetition of any other decisive battle you care to mention. But it is only a repetition of a battle because that battle was *decisive*, not because it was the battle of a free people against the army of an Oriental Monarch. The Kaiser was not an Oriental Monarch; however, he was a monarch.

The thing that makes the Marne and the Marathon opposites and not the same is that England and France were the big imperial powers on one hand and Persia was the big imperial power in the first battle.

Friday. January 5, 1940
Yesterday I took the novel, with all the new stuff in it from October and November to another publisher. This time Macmillan.

The reason I took it there is that Macmillan's is within walking distance of my room where I live: and I have been inside the building before. More palatial sort of a place than Farrar and Rinehart. Nice to take your novel into a place that looks as rich as a bank – not a bank, either, a treasury. Because that is what Macmillan's place looks like: a treasury.

I gave it to a fellow called Purdy, who seemed to be a very good guy. He in turn goes and gives it to somebody to read. I was startled to realize this morning that this reader would probably be some guy in very much the same position as myself.

1. He is probably not any fierce expert fellow with the brain of a wizard and the salary of a chamberlain living in a magnificent house where, with bright instruments, he will examine and analyze my book and judge it infallibly.

2. He is probably not on the other hand some dim-witted illiterate, with a rolling head full of teeth that snaggle and snarl at my book, and my book is not something he will instinctively detest as the mean detest the lofty and beautiful.

3. He is a guy who wants to be happy and wants to go to heaven and be blessed, and he wants to love people and he makes mistakes that confuse him and he gets embarrassed and he gets sick and has pains and wonders where his money is coming from next. And he sure wants to read a good book: maybe through my fault my book cannot talk to him; maybe it is not

written so that it means anything or communicates anything. Maybe he will think: "This could have been a good book" or something like that. Maybe he will have a curious feeling that it might be good but that he might be mistaken because it isn't exactly like his favorite book – *Ulysses*, *Gone With the Wind*, or some book. Maybe he is tired of reading long manuscripts, maybe he is ill and my book won't do anything to make him pleased. I guess I can't imagine myself, even myself, with all the advantages I have for making the most of my own novel, recommending it to a publisher at any rate as a commercial venture; I can see myself right now, on the bed, with my collar open and my tie undone and glasses on and that worried frown reading the novel just as if it were something handed in by my composition class. I guess I wouldn't be any happier about it.

On the other hand, maybe now because it is my own novel, I am hard on it. I guess if those some 500 pages with the same words on them came to me from someone else and I hadn't seen them before, I'd like them – oh yeah? What about the football novel I reread (in part) and burned last month? Was it awful! I have never seen anything so bad, published or unpublished, by anyone. Completely embarrassing.

The other evening I was to Ad Reinhardt's. I think Ad Reinhardt is possibly the best artist in America. Anyway the best whose work I've seen. I am glad he does so many good pictures. I am glad he gets at least some jobs here and there. I am particularly glad he is doing a mural for *Cafe Society* and it will probably be the very best mural there. I wonder which one they are wiping off to put his on top of.

Reinhardt still sticks with the communists. Certainly understandable: a religious activity. He believes, as an article of faith, that "society ought to be better," that the world ought to be somehow changed and redeemed. That in the world there is so much good, so much energy that could be liberated and allowed to run toward a good end, so that people could live happily and at peace. In such a state artists would be free to paint what they were really impelled to paint by a kind of inner necessity, or by the light of grace or whatever it is that makes painters love a certain kind of form.

Reinhardt's abstract art is pure and religious. It flies away from all naturalism, from all representation to pure formal and intellectual values. Reinhardt said the other night that what form a bird like Ingres got, was by mistake: painting representation.

Reinhardt admires Ingres a lot. So did father. So have I, I guess, always, except for the brief period of snobbery between 16 and 21 when I admired mostly what was fashionable. As a kid I liked Ingres fine: Ingres is the right kind of artist for kids who like things to be neat and realistic. Reinhardt's abstract art is completely chaste, and full of love of form and very good indeed. He is already abandoning the pretense of trying to reconcile that with the usual communist feeling about art, because he admits that he doesn't want, really, to do any more cartoons and that he doesn't like cartoons, and doesn't want his art to tell people anything or teach them anything or instruct them in anything.

He is perplexed because life is tough. Didn't seem beaten down or anything, but nevertheless perplexed and said he was confused, but didn't give the appearance of being so. But he doesn't much like the painting he has to do for money and wants more time for the painting he would do for love: then he doesn't make any money anyway. He spoke as if he would go and get drunk, or something. Of course he doesn't pay any attention to the idea that, at any rate in Russia, the kind of painting he does for love would not be loved by the Russians, who, just like the Nazis, are tossing all that stuff out. Reinhardt doesn't belong on that side, and maybe sometime he will realize it. He already realizes there is a wide gap between his painting and the CP. He refuses to compromise with cartoons, says that if he wanted to teach and work directly for the CP he would drop cartoons and art altogether and be an organizer. That makes it a pretty clear dilemma. He'd make a pretty good priest: a better priest than Gibney or Freedgood or Lax, not because of the dilemma but because he wants to really do something like a priest. Seymour has some of the same instinct with his smalltown newspaper.

I think I understand the religious element in what Reinhardt is doing as a communist and as an artist. He and Pat were not too impolite about me and my monastery either. Pat seemed to think it was reasonable on the grounds that I was assuring myself a bed and three meals a day for life: as if it were the WPA art project, which is the comparison she herself made.

I suggested there was "something else," besides that, that impelled me to apply for admission to the Order of Friars Minor. She said that was probably "something emotional." I agreed and then remembered "emotional" is a term of reproach in a communist. Indeed, she was looking at me reproachfully.

The interesting and confusing thing is this: Communism and Christianity are supposed to be bitter enemies. And indeed, in their theology, they have to be opposed. Communism says there is nothing but the visible material world: that there are no transcendentals – or maybe they *do* exist – for one always appeals to justice, liberty, etc., transcendentals. Nature is blind. Man has superior, infallible reason. Since man's reason and will are perfect, it is absurd that the world hasn't so far been perfect for man to live in. The reason for this has been economic determinism – a sort of Calvinist predestination operating through forces let loose by the wickedness of a few selfish and crafty men.

For the world to avoid damnation, the masses must come to life, realize that they are all powerful, that their reason is mighty and perfect, and take over from the self-destroyed capitalists. Perfect liberty will be in the distant Paradise where the state has withered away and there is no more government in Eden. For this to happen, the Church, the tool of the oppressor, must be destroyed. The belief of Christians blinds men to the fact that they can have everything they want on earth: the belief of Christians denies, in fact, that perfect happiness is possible to be achieved through material goods, bread alone. This, argue the communists, is a ruse to keep bread from the people, on the theory that there is pie in the sky after you're dead.

In point of fact every Christian wants to be blessed and every communist wants to be blessed. Both look for the state of perfect happiness and peace and blissfulness – for *all men*. The communist says show it to me? And then denies he can *see* angels and saints and heaven, and God so where is all that happiness? The Christian says show me, too: the communist points to Russia.

This is rather an unfortunate time to point to Russia. A few thousand Russians went into battle yesterday with guns in one hand and handbooks on how to shoot in the other: and this morning their bodies lie freezing on the ground. But that is the sin of the capitalists: well, show me your happiness:

- In the future: world revolution: the state withers away: perfect communism.
- You hand me a laugh with your pure communism. It's pretty far away. Further than heaven.
- You hand me a laugh with your heaven. Show me where you get that "happiness"?
- Saints, charitable people. Look about you.
- Screwballs. Nuts. Maniacs. Exploiters, too, living on the blood of the poor.
- They themselves are not rich; and what they have, they give away. They have nothing.

– Private charity is a lie, a deception. . . .

– They are poor: all they have is Christ. . . .

– Yeah! All Christ and no bread. Look at their starving kids. Why don't you teach them birth control?

And so it goes. I didn't argue with Reinhardt. There is a very good agreement floating about, that nobody argues with Reinhardt. He himself is bashful about it anyway and doesn't want to argue much or at all.

So, the interesting and confusing thing is this: Communism and Christianity are supposed to be bitter enemies. Communists like to burn down churches and shoot priests; Catholics all too often like to see the Communists shot up, too.

But Ad Reinhardt, if he would get over a lot of stumbling blocks that are practically all matters of language, would in ten minutes be a very good Christian because he is naturally a very good guy. This same guy would cease to be a Communist and become a Catholic and still be the same guy, the same artist, etc. In what way does it change you and in what way does it not change you? Why do you have to travel so far in order to change, outwardly, so little?

When I was fourteen I discovered something about learning to ride a horse. The first few days you don't know anything about it at all. You keep falling off. You can't sit in the saddle properly, you get jogged to pieces while trotting, etc.

After about one week, suddenly, you find you can stay on, you post when the beast trots, don't fall off, canter about, gallop through woods and underbrush, etc. But you are still not a decent rider. Not a good one. You can simply stay on a horse. That is after one week. You learn very fast to stay on the horse. After that it takes a very long time to learn how to ride: how to make the horse obey any little pressure of the rein, of the leg, of the heel. How to guide the horse through hard places, how to take him to a jump, how to make him walk on hard roads and down steep roads, etc. That takes months and months and months and even years.

It takes a week to learn how to stay on, but years to become a rider. The difference between a man who continually falls off a horse and one who stays on is much greater than the difference between a man who stays on and one who can really ride and control the horse. Outwardly, anyway, the difference is greater. Probably the horse, who is the important one, finds the relationships more nearly as they be. He probably knows what the real differences are.

In one week you travel apparently a vast distance: from a man who can't stay in the saddle you become one who can.

After that, for months and months, there seems to be no change, no progress at all. Note a. What is the application of this to a Communist who becomes a Christian? It is not a direct parallel at all. It has nothing to do with anything before conversion, only with something after conversion. It is easy to learn the elements of catechism and get baptized. After that, what is harder begins. It is hard to keep, patiently and humbly, away from temptations and sins: and you seem to make no more progress at all, you wonder if you have changed at all. It is easy enough to love God, especially if you have always loved some aspect of Him, and everybody does, and must love God under one aspect or another. But that love must sooner or later stand the test of adversity and trouble if we are ordinary people. It must stand the test of temptations.

A communist is already in love with one aspect of God, if he is a communist for the right reason: that is not out of hatred of capitalists but out of love for men, workers. So it will be easy enough for such a man to love God if it can be pointed out to him without too much trouble over language that what he loves is God: that "God" expresses it better than "humanity" or "the proletariat" which are feeble and inaccurate general terms that don't mean much, and are never precise. (The attributes of God are precisely defined, and the love of God is an easily recognizable thing, because it is really at the center of everybody's experience whether he knows it or not.)

But after he knows God the convert is likely to have some trouble because of certain habits by which he was falsely led to seek some substitute for happiness before. Altogether, communist habits differ widely enough in some respects from Christian virtues. Communism is sporadically violent, although here the emphasis has been on "peaceful" picketing and sit-down strikes and the violence has tended to start on the other side. However, this violence business has nothing much to do with the question. I suppose it would be nonsense to try and compare communist techniques of activity and Christian. In neither case are we specifically concerned with virtue. Communism is on the world's side; so any communist has everybody else's troubles as to keeping the virtues. Greater than some; both Communists and Nazis although especially the latter are systematically trained in pride, even in arrogance: their discipline begins with the fact that they *know all the right arguments*, and can use them. Catholics also have truth behind them and know it, but you find a Catholic refuses to argue, very often, because he doesn't believe he knows the arguments of his faith himself, or that he can do anything by argument.

On the other hand, most good Communists are fairly temperate people: don't drink much, are not always as great lechers as they would appear to be by their talk, and are as often as not as connubial and faithful and settled as any bourgeois, but they would be ashamed to admit it. It might not be hard for the Communist to resist these temptations but others – pride, fear, anger, etc.

[At this point 20 pages are missing from the holographic journal.]

. . . The progress toward that end is not only possible, it is imperative, it is our only reason for being alive. It is to seek Him that God created us, for a God that is perfect cannot create anything for any other end than Himself.

ON THE OTHER HAND:

a. all that is still an abstraction. It only fits the future; properly speaking the future does not exist. Only the present exists.

b. It is never possible to really see or understand progress that has happened to us from some point (a) in the past to now. The past does not exist either. The present exists: it changes all the time. Lot's wife, not realizing the past had no reality at all, turned into a pillar of salt.

As long as we are in the world we are in some way imperfect. As long as imperfection withholds the complete love of God from us, that imperfection must appear so important that no trivial, light modification in it brought about on our habits and affairs can seem of much consequence in comparison to it.

c. Thus it is confusing and futile to try to realize how we have progressed since some past moment. But the future is just as illusory as the past. God's love does not belong to the future but to the present. Our limitations force us to abstract, and to form a general view of our life in terms of a progress into the future, for in the present we always realize our imperfection. But we must continually pray for God's love *now* (not tomorrow) – hence the parable of the wise virgins.

d. The great sin is *counting up your progress* minute by minute, and forgetting everything else.

Saturday. January 13, 1940

If there is no important change in our lives as we go on there is no point in keeping journals. Journals take for granted that every day in our life there is something new and important. I am not going to try to justify what I am writing here.

A person's expressions change, but I guess his face doesn't. Even if he grows a beard, it is still the same face, and then, what is the importance of a face? Who cares how he looks? Too many people, including me – including everybody, maybe.

Every time anyone has ever asked me "what's new?" I have answered "nothing." I am forced to. I realize there is nothing new. Not because things aren't always changing, that isn't it. Only if there *is* anything new I start telling people before they get a chance to say "Well, what do you hear from the gang, eh?"

"What's new in Consolidated?"

"Yeah, live outfit."

"Yeah."

"Yeah. Going concern!"

"Yeah."

"Well, what's new?"

"Nothing."

"Yeah."

"Ain't it so?"

"Yeah."

"Yeah."

"Yeah." etc.

If I was to force myself to answer that question I would remark on the following things.

1. At least three members of my class have started trying to write like Saroyan – and not succeeded. They have written like him, not as to quantity, only as to *structure* of the stories. To write a story with as little structure as a Saroyan story and still say something you have to have written a lot of practically the same thing just before you got around to this particular story. No good to read one book of Saroyan and then write a one-page story and get disgusted because it only resembles his stories in shortness and in lack of event in the O. Henry tradition (lack not so much of plot as of *problem* which is formulated, then complicated, then solved in the last paragraph).

2. I have got Curzon's *Monasteries of the Levant* from the Library and right away I am going to read it. The seven sentences I have read look fine, the pictures look fine. Maybe then I'll read *Arabia Deserta*, only I don't think so. I think I'll read Duchesne's *History of the Early Church*, or Gasquet on *English Monasticism* or more of Gabriella Cunningham Grahame on Saint Theresa (there where I wrote Grahame it looked like my Grand-

mother in New Zealand's handwriting – mostly that kind of "Gr." G. and R. Grandmother. Your loving *Grand*mother. Yep. G & R. Georgius Rex. Grandmother. Interesting).

3. Ed Rice has lost 12 pounds and some money. He has made an oil painting and given it to three girls and they will take it and cut it into three parts, each taking what she likes from the picture.

[No 4. Not in the journal manuscript.]

5. Got to write letters. Glad I thought of it. Some good has come of this list!

6. Coming out of the Subway I dreamed Macmillan had accepted my novel. Crossing Greenwich Avenue, by the movie theater, I dreamed I went to Havana and rewrote the ending, making the scene Havana.

7. Once again I have Vico from the Library – Michelet's translation. This time I am going to read the book. Last time, I confess, I didn't read a word of Vico himself, and only a few pages of Croce about him. Looking at the card in the book, the other person who has had Vico out in the last 10 years is Lionel Trilling. And I guess he is the guy I would pick to be reading him, too. Trilling or Tindall.

Other names on cards. A fellow called C. Farrar – he has had out almost all the books on mystics that I have taken out. I wonder who he is, what he is doing. Never saw him. Be a joke if I met him beginning Novitiate in August!

I have been going through the *Spiritual Exercises* of Saint Ignatius. Not giving them four hours a day but at any rate two and a half.

The first day, didn't know where I was getting; didn't seem to see what I was supposed to *get out* of the meditations quite clearly. Just read what the book said and put the book down and repeated the words back.

Second and third days: temptation to think the thing was doing us harm. That is to be expected.

It is true that the exercises are quite tiring. The completeness of the meditations on mortal sin is impressive and also efficacious. The meditations on death are nothing new to me!

But aside from brief moments in the consideration of mortal sin, I was most of all moved in the short meditation on venial sin today, thanks to God. It seems to me to be a singular proof of God's mercy and forbearance that, although venial sin is, in His sight, still fuller of ugliness than we can imagine, and although one venial sin takes away more from His glory than *all* the good actions of all men ever added to it (and no good action of men was ever theirs, but only His), yet it is only *venial* sin, and He allows us to recover from it by His grace, which it does not rob us of altogether. In spite of the fact that venial sin is a greater offence against His love than we are capable of imagining, yet He does not take His love away. How much greater must be his forbearance in forgiving us mortal sins which are infinitely ugly and displeasing to Him since they are what is most opposed to His love! How much must we increase our humility, and abnegation in order to be full of love for God when all the half-willing movements of lust and fear that come to us continually, all our selfish thoughts and desires that are only half repressed are exceedingly displeasing to Him, and offend Him in His infinite love. How much does Mary overlook, in her deep love, to intercede for us, when to her, in her beauty and purity and perfection of love, our selfishness and ingratitude is actually horrible: but how much more horrible to Christ, Who is all perfect.

Whoever really loves Christ, knowing that love to be actually all our liberty, all our life, all our joy, all the goodness we know of and guess at and long for, and knowing that venial sin is a step towards the prison, is a step towards the *death* of the soul which is mortal sin, knowing all this, he will pray most fervently to fear and avoid venial sin as much as he was careful to defend himself against mortal sin *before:* as much! how much more, for how careful are we, how strong are we in our defense against mortal sin, always falling into it, and sacrificing the life and joy and liberty and whole being of our souls!

Not until I did the meditation on venial sin did the full impact of the greatness and horror of mortal sin really strike me, in spite of all that had gone before this meditation. And now I most fervently pray that I may altogether amend my life, utterly and completely, forsaking all things.

Never, before this consideration, was the real necessity of renouncing *everything* so clear to me: before, I only really knew the words. Never, before this consideration on venial sin, was it so clear to me there was such terrific urgency for an unrelenting and complete sacrifice and struggle against temptation, for before this I had always half expected that when the time came for me to amend my life, God would take away temptation altogether and all at once. Not that the *"mild yoke of Christ"* isn't a mild yoke, but the liberty to bear that mild yoke and not to give up for the heavy one of sin and the unbearable one of damnation, the liberty to serve Christ is one to be defended at the price of torture and death of the body.

Then it seemed most fruitful, too, to meditate on the notion that the fires of Hell and Purgatory are the same fire which the damned bear with hatred and impatience and the saved with love and patience and humility. But the pain is the same for both, in intensity, if not in duration. And that is liable to be true of the tribulations of the flesh on earth, also. Some bear them with hatred and anger and fear, and try to escape by drinking and chasing women, etc. Others bear them with patience because of the great love they cherish in them for Christ. And I pray most fervently with all my heart to be able to begin to love Christ so.

There is an absolute urgency for unrelenting combat with the passions and weaknesses of our flesh. As far as I have been concerned, all the psychoanalytical arguments have only served me as the excuses my laziness and cowardice required to avoid the struggle, and so continue in misery. The only happiness I have known in the last six years has had some connection with my conversion, and has been tied up with the increase in my belief and desire to serve God.

There is utter necessity for giving up all things, taking up the cross and following Christ. Everything else is imprisonment and death. Before, I knew this intellectually: now I *know* it, I assent to it with my whole soul and heart, not only my understanding.

There is an utter necessity to sacrifice yourself completely. Any argument against that is an argument that you should give up your soul and consent to be miserable, to be damned. Whether it is *hard* or *easy* all depends. Whether it is good homiletics to stress the fact that the struggle is heroic, I don't know. The truth stands so, absolutely: any arguments around it, as far as I am concerned, are either with it or against it. If they are with it, there is no longer much conflict of language, either. There is no compromise with the truth.

However, there is no need to meditate on death every day of one's life. To make that a rule would be unnatural. The greatest *rule* is to love Christ and your neighbor with your whole heart and your whole soul. How do you do this? By taking up your cross and following Him. But taking up the Cross means the relentless battle against the flesh – there are various techniques to be used: one of the ways *not* to overcome drunkenness is to continue drinking as if it didn't matter.

Precisely the greatest temptation that confronts someone trying to overcome his flesh in this age is to listen to the arguments against mortification. Of course it is "bad" to carry mortification to extremes, irresponsibly. But we use the arguments to persuade ourselves that it is morbid to deny our slightest desire, it is morbid to deny our desire to seduce a woman, or to have a drink, or to overeat, or to gamble. The ones who listen to the arguments and feel the greatest terror of extreme mortification, are the ones who deny themselves nothing – the ones that aren't even temperate, let alone ascetics! A drunkard goes two days without a drink – he *knows* he is going to pieces physically because of the morbid ascetic strain he has imposed on himself. The proof? He feels terrible. And, as a matter of fact, he probably does. I felt terrible the first two days I went without cigarettes, too. Nervous and even sick.

When we get near the point where mortification is dangerous, someone else will soon stop us. Who am I to talk? I never mortified my flesh for two seconds, really.

Actually, "mortification of the flesh" is comparable to training for athletics: and no more harmful if it is done the way we are meant to do it: we eat only what we need, the barest essentials. We cut out smoking, drinking, we inure ourselves to hardship by sleeping on hard things, wearing rough clothes, etc. We get up early, etc., we do things that are a little painful and tiring. What is there about this that is different from the life of a poor laborer? Or of an athlete in training? And, as a matter of fact, the frequency with which that comparison appears, even from the earliest times, is startling.

But as I say, who am I to be talking? Except I rarely smoke or drink and I have stopped eating meat because I don't particularly like it! Some hardships!

Sunday. January 14, 1940

The most ordinary meaning of a journal is a book in which separate entries investigate what differences there are between one day and the day before it. What makes each day different, what makes each day what it is, each experience unlike any other experience, etc. Every day is different, but also every day is the same. Every man is different, all men are also the same.

I guess if I want to I can work this down to the old familiar (to me) dilemma of Plato and Aristotle – which one looks at things from the right end. This dilemma can never mean anything to me until I read both Plato and Aristotle. I have never read either – except the *Poetics* and *De Memoria* of Aristotle and parts of *The Republic* and the *Ion!*

One kind of autobiography establishes how *different* the writer is from everybody else, another how much the same everybody is. It is too bad you can't realize you are a person, sometimes, without assuming that means you are a more important person than everyone else: the most important person in the world. Saint Theresa thinks everybody is the same as she is, because we are all sinners. Hitler thinks everybody is different from him, because they are, some of them less pure, some of them less noble, some of them less intelligent, some of them less beautiful, all of them less godlike, all of them less perfect. It is the Hitlers who think they are perfect – because nobody else thinks so. It is the saints who know they are not perfect, although sometimes other people say of them that they are saints: the saints themselves know themselves only as sinners, liable to lose their love and the sight of Christ through a movement of impatience or selfishness or pride.

Hitler writes a biography of himself in which he is better and more powerful than anybody else: people don't believe it entirely: very well, they have to be shown. Start a war! Whatever he does, Hitler does it to prove that whatever his autobiography (written or unwritten) says about him is true.

I am not talking about *Mein Kampf*. I haven't read it.

I just looked out of the window into the dark well of a courtyard behind the house. Music from the Baptist church has ceased. The thin rain has not. It falls lightly, cold, crisscrossing in the air. The branches of the tree are stripped absolutely bare: they look like rubber, in the wet.

Water drips on the stones.

I cannot tell if there is still thin unmelted ice in the goldfish pool – or not. Ice pockmarked by the thin cold rain. The snow is all gone.

Over beyond the church, the houses on Eleventh Street – their roofs shine with rain. The sky is black.

I like it when it rains, when the sky is black, when the rain is light and thin. It does not make me feel sad, particularly.

I remember walking along a road towards Caylus with my father. The sky was dark. It was not yet raining, though. The road ran along the top of a ridge, and for a long distance you could see hills, the tops of hills, the gray causses, dry and dotted with white outcrops of rock. When we came upon the valley where Caylus is, the village and its castle, in the gray air, built of gray stone, against the hills, was camouflaged. You could hardly see it for protective coloring.

That was on a Sunday, too. We had eaten an omelet at the inn at some little village. When I got home, I probably wrote down in a book about the places we had seen. The villages, the chateau – its name I forget. Not much more than a fortified farmhouse.

All the castles in that country – Penne, Bruniguel, Caylus, Montricoux, Najac – what a difference from Montricoux to Najac! Montricoux is in the plains, the houses are red brick, the belfries are red brick, too, in the style of the Romance or whatever you call it – architecture of Toulouse (*"Roman"*).

But Najac is in the deep gorges the Aveyron cut in the causses. Built on a rock, a tough, gray castle. And not changed since the Hundred Years' War or the Albigensian Crusade – except gutted and a bit ruined. But the same aspect, from the outside, anyway!

The habit of going and looking at places: some habit. Probably dates from the Renaissance, when men went and admired Roman Ruins. (Yet the Anglo-Saxons, too, were tremendously impressed by Roman ruins.)

People from Marseilles going out to Cassis to drink wine and look at the sun on the water of the little harbor.

Old Sargant driving us over to – what was the name of the house? A ruined Jacobean manor house near Stamford (I don't mean Burleigh) began with a K. maybe.

I walk to see Ightham Moat in Kent. It is twenty-one miles there and back. (I am fourteen.) It is also Sunday and a gray day.

People from Paris going out to Versailles – *"un jour de grandes eaux"* ["a day of great tides"].

Going for a ride on the Staten Island ferry is different. It implies a whole lot of phony gaiety and insouciance: here we are gay people getting fun out of a conveyance. We are immeasurably clever because we get all this fun for ten cents. There is no such self-consciousness about a whole family of London people going out to Windsor to see Windsor Castle.

Riding with Uncle Ben to see some churchyard in Middlesex because there was an old yew tree there.

The instinct to go twenty miles to look at a tree has been balled up in this country, to some extent. Sunday drivers are despised: they are dopes. But I was glad when Father Joseph and I drove up past Yonkers to see the gardens at the Untermeyer place this fall. The instinct exists and flourishes after all.

Lax and I had fun going to look at Nyack. We had fun going to look at New Haven; had fun with Rice going to look at Washington.

But as a matter of fact if I were to go to the Metropolitan Museum now, I guess I would find a whole lot of people who had come there just to see – not pictures, but something: a museum.

Going somewhere to see a house, gardens, a tree, a bridge, a picture: a very good and healthy and civilized kind of recreation, a better one than I ever realized. I don't include running somewhere to see an accident: I refer to the class of things you can plan ahead of time. If a picnic goes with it, all right. A picnic as an end in itself has never seemed to be much fun though.

One Sunday afternoon when I went with Tom and Iris Bennett (who had come up to Oakham) and Tabacovici, the Rumanian who had a study across the hall, to Burleigh House, and sat under a tree and looked at the place from about ¼ mile off in the park. Then we went to tea at the George, in Stamford.

Some day, make a list of all such places, such afternoons.

Thursday. January 18, 1940

Start out by saying: "I think my besetting sin is . . ." so start out absurdly, ruin everything by a bad beginning. That is the trouble with all kinds of confession literature.

It is written by people who read books to find out how much they themselves resemble the characters in the books. They write their own story with the assumption that other people will want to be like them, know themselves by the same label. Assumption that people are all the same, that one sin covers a multitude of cases, being the same in every one.

Well, it is so and it isn't.

To say my besetting sin was a vicious love of *independence* (i.e. a kind of pride), would be ridiculous. The ridiculousness is not in the fact that it would be actually false, but the sentence would be phony in a literary sense. Bad style, bad taste, false sounding, etc.

1. "besetting sin." Cliche. I guess almost any way of saying the same thing with two words – sin and an epithet – would sound like a cliche.

2. "My principal sin" how can you know? How can you talk about it as if you knew it objectively, mention it in a detached manner?

3. "My principal sin is a love of independence" so, indeed. How novel! Love of independence! Make it sound as if it were a new sin and therefore a rather slight one, a kind of personal eccentricity, a foible. Love of independence? Why it sounds so little like a sin it might almost be a virtue. Indeed it is a virtue: raise yourself above the mob. Be *independent* of conventions, prejudices, be free, have personality, individuality, be the master of your soul, control your fate, do as you please, *fay ce que vouldras*. Independence! That and the Fourth of July, too. That is no sin, that is a virtue: it is by independence that one asserts himself, gets ahead, etc.

Yet this independence, pride, is not only a great sin, it is the *principal sin*, the root, the heart of mortal sin.

Satan and the fallen angels fell because for a moment it entered their hearts to question the goodness of God, to think "I will not serve," to have a feeling of *independence*, of existing by their own right.

Adam and Eve the same way: the sin was the same. They knew the goodness of God and the perfection of peace and the conditions on which that peace depended: the everlasting contemplation and glorification of peace and love itself for its own sake.

Having everything in perfection, they were tempted to believe for a minute that there was something more than this perfection, that it was thus not perfect, that God was not all wise, all seeing, all powerful, all merciful and all good – there was something more that He had not provided and that they could get *independently* for themselves.

So now there is an angel guards the Gate of Paradise with a flaming sword, and man's eyes cannot bear the tremendous piercing brightness of it; it fills the air a hundred times whiter than lightning.

This independence, this pride, is the very expression of the root of sin, the longing for independence is the movement of sin itself in the soul: then it shows a curious complacency in me to discover that this "love of independence" is my "besetting sin" when that is original sin itself! Attempting to rebel and say "I will not serve."

Yet there is a paradox.

In proportion as this desire for *independence* from God and His law and His love, and the voice of our own conscience increases, so our real *dependence* on creatures, on the affections and aversions of our flesh increase, and this independence is no independence at all, but actually slavery.

So in a sense there is an independence we should seek, that is, independence from the fears and desires of the flesh: non-attachment to creatures. But that is found by seeking *dependence* on, obedience to the Word of God, His law and His example in the Word incarnate Christ, and His teaching through the Church and His help through the sacraments and the voice of His grace as it speaks in our own heart, in our conscience. He who loses himself finds himself. If you would possess everything, desire nothing. If you would be full, bind yourself in utter obedience and servitude to God.

To think then that this desire for physical "independence" will make it hard for me to submit myself to discipline in the monastery, when I have always hated and avoided all kinds of discipline outside it, is only to say that I am a man conceived in sin and born into the tribulations of the earth where we are restless and rebellious, always seeking independence, our own way, that is, our own way to become our own prisoners, prisoners of our own will, and of our own desires for material things.

And, once again, I remember what Cardinal Newman wrote to Hopkins: "Don't say the Jesuit discipline is hard – it will save your soul."

Tuesday. January 23, 1940

That long and distressingly confused consideration "of moral progress": I still haven't reread it. What do I mean people do not change? Where is the trouble? There is some phenomenal confusion right at the beginning of the whole thing.

What kind of a confusion?

One between moral and intellectual problems. Since everybody is potentially good, everyone can be saved, everyone can love God and serve Him instead of hating Him and filling the world with injustice and violence. It is easy enough to see this goodness in everybody. In their opinions it is easy enough to see more or less truth; nobody, I guess, is completely wrong in everything!

However, perhaps it is too easy to assume that because everyone is potentially good, and his opinions are not completely wrong, he is not far from being right. It will not take much of a change to make him right, just as it will not take much of a change to make him good.

For him to start to be good, all that is necessary is the right movement of his will in the direction indicated by God's grace. Yet even then, he has a tremendous long way to go before he is at all good.

But it takes no such movement of the will to make a man's opinions immediately sound or true, or make what he says reasonable and in accordance with what is.

Perhaps I have taken too readily for granted that everybody must apprehend the same things because the same things are all around everybody.

Then perhaps I have too easily assumed that since everybody apprehended the same truths the only reason they could not agree as to what the truths were is because they used more or less correct words to express what they saw.

Everybody would agree, one thinks, if each person used words in the same sense: or if everybody used words accurately or vividly or something.

But it isn't as simple as that.

Not only do people apprehend things more and less clearly, and not only do they express themselves some well and many not well at all, but in between apprehension and verbal propositions exist the purely mental act of judgment, and its mental, immaterial product – the proposition as it is not in words in time (spoken) or in space (written).

Beyond judgment lies purely mental, again, reasoning which also has its products – argumentation, first mental, then verbal.

Then not only are verbal propositions and verbal arguments the mere products of things I had never considered at all, but also they are *distinct from them*, and the two must not be confused.

Now not only are there vast differences between the way different people apprehend things, but also even vaster differences between their judgments and far vaster than ever are the distances between their different kinds of reasoning.

I had imagined the matter of everyone's reasoning was essentially the same, and most people needed only to perfect the form of their reasoning – especially the form of the final verbal product, argumentation.

But everyone's judgments are so confused and falsified by insecure perspectives we have today, how can they be true? And not only the form of their arguments but their matter is completely haywire.

That is why there is so much absurdity passed out every time anyone opens his mouth to attack or defend anything in politics or religion. Everybody has been educated to read and write, but nobody has been educated in the things a man reads and writes *about*. People have forgotten about that. Consequently the only writing that makes much sense is writing *about writing*. Saroyan is a fool. He doesn't know anything. He never learnt anything: but what he can write about convincingly is – writing, and the relationship of writing to not starving in San Francisco. (I don't refer to Joyce, who was decently educated.)

– Why do I write so much about things about which I know so little?

January 24. Wednesday

W. H. Auden's trick: ratio-announcers: parody of banal radio announcements – parodying trivialities of commercials and musical comedy songs, etc. Done well enough for once in *The Dance of Death* and yet not too well either. Since then, done to death. The complete and uninteresting and flat and stupid banality of *On the Frontier*. Dull as could be. I only dipped into it, however. But it sure looked awful. Ostuia – Westland. "I see where it says in the paper that our leader . . ."

"Hello T. J. now about this contract, this shipment of munitions from your country to mine although we are at war, ha! ha! . . ."

Maybe it is a bad trick or maybe Auden just does it badly. Lax does it better than Auden: I guess a whole lot better. Maybe Auden is just a dull stupid dope after all. I guess *The Orators* is as good as anything he did, and then, what's so good about that?

One night Melville Cane (or Cain) came to Columbia to read some of his poems to Philolexian in a little social room in Hartley. He sat in a chair and read his appalling stuff for a while, and appealed to us for comments on this pleasant light trash, and I guess I remarked on the way he kept talking about spiders in his poems. I didn't even say it was effective although it was giving me the creeps. I don't know whether spiders was the image or not. Something like it. Maybe rats.

Anyway he finally folded up the last triumphant morsel from the *New Yorker* and looked around the room with a sort of feeble expression of challenge you might expect from, say Irwin Edman[28], and then asked if anybody in the room liked Auden, Spender and Day-Lewis. And I who had just been reading some Lewis said Yes, I liked them. Not much of an argument developed. I think he didn't want one, anyway.

I suppose if Melville Cane was to repeat the question to me this minute I'd give back the same answer. On the other hand I believe if W. H. Auden was to walk in the room and dare me to like the works of Melville Cane I would stand up and like them fine.

No I wouldn't, I was just fooling.

January 25. Thursday

Most days begin the same way: I come home from Mass and breakfast and then begin a long and agonizing hunt for some small object without which, apparently, I cannot do any work – if it isn't reading glasses, it's a pencil or a pen or some paper.

Just now I filled my pen: I had been using little scraps of paper to clean it after filling it – now couldn't find any. Yesterday, lost a red pencil.

Remember the times at Douglaston you would look up and down all over the house for a shoe, a hat, a sock, a book, a brush. In the matter of books, especially, it meant war. My Uncle and my Grandmother always suspected my Grandfather of picking up books and throwing them out or giving them to taxicab drivers – and a lot of times they were right.

However, today doesn't begin this way. I just had lunch; and there is no necessity to write in a journal. I could read, or draw, or think up a new way to make the novel end, or study some time. Anything.

When my handwriting gets smaller – not neater, just smaller – it seems that I have been reading something that requires a lot of concentration, or that I have been trying to follow something that requires discipline.

The times at Cambridge when I got zealous for the reformation of my ways and started to work hard – (for instance, Easter vacation, 1934) handwriting got smaller. Just before Christmas, 1933, when I was in a pretty bad way I made a deliberate effort to make my handwriting neat and precise. It didn't help very much. On the other hand I may write smaller and neater when I have been writing a lot with a pen. Maybe the handwriting

[28] Irwin Edman (1896–1954) was one of Merton's professors at Columbia.

is more regular after I have been writing a lot. Nowadays there isn't much difference.

My handwriting was smaller, too, my first term at Columbia. Then I was working quite hard and trying to read a lot – and as a matter of fact read tremendously but not very carefully. Covered more ground than I had before, ever; but not since. After 1938 I have read even more. Between 1935 and '38 I didn't read so much.

Gasquet's *English Monastic Life*[29] which I am skimming through, though plain and pedestrian in its tone, is a very interesting book – an extremely attractive book because of its material.

What is fascinating about the life he describes in English Monasteries has really little to do with monasteries as such. What is fascinating is the material side, the physical aspect of the life in medieval English abbeys: the *techniques* of living and techniques to do with housekeeping, etc. are what is so appealing about the book.

For example, it was among the duties of the refectorian to change the straw on the refectory floor – in spring to scatter bay leaves on that floor to freshen the air, in summer to scatter flowers, mint on the floor to sweeten the air – to provide fans for cooling it. He had to see that no wood-ash blackened the under side of the monks' loaves of bread: he had to wrap these loaves in a napkin. He had to see that the salt was dry.

The cellarer, besides supervising the feeding of the monks – had to take care the locks on the granaries were sound, had to supervise the threshers and winnowing women who came to thresh out the abbey's grain. He had to look after the women who came to make oatmeal. He had to get wax for candles, and supervise the making of them by itinerant candlemakers, he had to get nails, etc. The under cellarer put straw around the beer-barrels in frosty weather . . .

All these make monasteries attractive because, I suppose, in them we can find the perfection of ordinary medieval living, the perfection of techniques governing a domestic economy that was simple and clean and pleasant: (at any rate the monasteries appear to have been cleaner than the castles, from the rules about scouring pans, etc. perfectly). The pleasant side of all this is in the simplicity and apparent wholesomeness of that kind of life, but also in the techniques that are hinted at and that have been lost

[29] Abbot (Cardinal Francis Aidan) Gasquet's (1848–1929) *English Monastic Life*, 1904. He was the Abbot of Downside Abbey, Bath, England, and Prefect of Vatican Archives from 1918.

to home life: threshing, candlemaking, baking, brewing and so on. I guess it is true all this is done less well by large-scale manufacturers – it is an extraordinary pleasure to get home-made bread, and so on.

Of course that has nothing to do with the essential part of a monk's life. All these things are accidents, and anyone longing for a religious life because of them would be longing for some kind of an illusion, would be deceiving himself in the worst way. Nevertheless, there is something about the techniques of medieval social and domestic life that is in its way perfect – something that still was not lost in parts of France and England, and something that belonged to all pre-industrial times – you find it in the outbuildings at Mount Vernon, where there is a smokehouse and so on, perhaps even a smithy.

Also, more than likely you will find almost everyone has a good feeling for that kind of thing, look back on it with regret – whoever has any idea or conception of what it was like, whether from reading [William] Morris or from living in the south of France or from any cause.

Incidentally, English public schools are much more reminiscent of the monastery as it was in the Middle Ages than are the schools of other countries. Many of them were built around the actual remains of an old monastery. There is daily chapel: of course, refectory. Little rows of studies like cells, and generally pseudo-gothic architecture. French Lycées are possibly close to monasteries as they actually are now! Not so much chapel of course: but strict discipline, early hours; you are more or less cloistered inside the Lycée walls. The courtyards at Montauban were surrounded by actual arched galleries. You went everywhere marching two by two in line.

So much of this feeling for old traditional techniques is preserved in the English and French countrysides. The oast houses and hop gardens of Kent. Winepresses in every house in the south of France. Strings of sausages and onions and garlic hanging from the rafters in a French kitchen.

The techniques we have developed are capable of being just as sound and just as good as soon as our systems of production get less haywire, and as soon as we stop producing entirely for war and entirely for money, instead of producing the things we need, and distributing what we had made to the people who *need* them. I guess what is attractive about medieval techniques, is that they worked admirably, succeeded admirably. Of course they had their limitations: but they were, within these, remarkably successful. And that is what we naturally yearn after! Imagine a society actually producing good things for itself quietly and successfully! But then there were plagues and famines; yet these were not the fault of the way things were made and distributed. And now, when we are immeasurably more capable of making all sorts of things, everything we make seems to turn itself into a weapon. So what's the good of it? At least the plagues and famines were not directly the result of our ill will!

January 26. Friday

I miss my novel. Macmillan has had it for over two weeks – no, three weeks. I telephoned Mr. Purdy this week and he said the first reader had given a favorable report on it and so it had gone on to someone else. So now instead of being suspicious of my novel, and growling at it and kicking it around, I am happy about it. I would like to be kind to my novel, and make up for the way I have scolded it. Maybe it is not so bad after all: I wish it was here so I could pat its shaggy head.

However, probably tomorrow – no, Monday is a better guess, I get a polite note from Macmillan's Mr. Purdy and I go over there and drag back my big heavy novel, not speaking to it; then I'll get it home and whip it and throw it in a corner and be mad at it; then after about a week I'll make five corrections with this pen and re-type the title page and haul the whole thing off to – who? Harcourt Brace? I wish Macmillan would take it: I'd like the book to be published by a place that's as big and solid and shiny as a sub-treasury or at least as a Federal Reserve Bank.

Today when I came into my room I didn't have a long agonizing hunt for anything except the heat. The window had been open wide about eight hours last night and no heat on at all and it's around 15 to 20 outside: for this reason the room got rather cold.

February 13. Tuesday

The Village, which has been pretty ugly and unpleasant all fall and most of the winter too, is turning into an attractive sort of a place again. It was this way when I moved down here last spring. I don't dare go near 8th Street any more – the place is too shocking by reason of its phoniness: but last year, at noontime, on the false spring days of February, it was pleasant around here. Streets all quiet and sunny. And now it is the same way all over again.

But at the end of August the place was a nightmare!

I don't remember anything about October and November. I was rewriting the novel all the time – at any rate in November. October – busy with my own class, and trying to do some reading at the same time and I don't remember whether I did any. It seems a long time ago. Time has gone very quickly and nothing much has happened. That I can't seem to remember anything – suggests that I ought to be ashamed of having led a sort of vegetative existence. But I haven't. I have done a lot of things: what? I don't know. But I must have – I was busy all the time.

In the last week – since Ash Wednesday – a list of things that have happened.

1. Have shaved off my mustartch.

2. My brother comes home from Cornell, with a Buick. He doesn't want Uncle Harold to know about it, for fear of getting criticised for extravagance: so he keeps the car parked at the station.

3. We drive to see Gibney who sits in his house at Port Washington carving an African mask.

4. Thoughts in connection with T. S. Eliot: I am walking in Penn Station and reflect that it's Ash Wednesday and that Eliot wrote a poem by that name and the two don't really have an awful lot to do with each other.

I am finishing this pastoral in Joyce doubletalk. I think: as a dedication.

> To J. Joyce – *il miglior fabbro* ["the finest craftsman"].
> (or to W. Shakespeare
> D. Alighieri – *il miglior fabbro*)

That dedication to Pound always made me helplessly mad. Irwin Edman writes in his present of a Random House "Donne" to Lax. "To Robert Lax – *saluti affettuosi*" [heartfelt greetings]. Almost anything written in a book is liable to be awful – but especially if it is in Italian. Gerdy,[30] three years ago, thinking of being a convert, gives Lax a Bartholomus Angelicus, and on the flyleaf, "Yours in Xt," wherever he got that! Lax gives Gerdy some book back, but is a bit embarrassed although he was also thinking of conversion, replies "Yrs in Him," spelling embarrassment all across the page. All of this could be called "Thoughts in Connection with T. S. Eliot." It also applies to everybody who is so sure the Mass is "beautiful and artistic" and who admires "Thomas" because the *Summa* is a magnificent work of art "like a Gothic Cathedral." All that stuff is sure no good.

5. Reading Huxley's new book – *After Many a Summer* and being very uncomfortable about it – it is so bad.

---

[30] Robert Gerdy was another of Merton's friends at Columbia, who along with Lax, Gibney, Rice, Slate, Freedgood, and Ad Reinhardt, were members of the "in group."

6. Reading Maritain's *Introduction to Philosophy* and finding it very exciting, stimulating, entertaining, clear, forceful. It must make anyone but Aristotelians or Catholics terribly angry, but why not? It is necessary for the truth to be defended without compromise and without a lot of polite philosophical doubletalk. The thing for the other side to do is write something a little more forceful than Edman's *Candle in the Dark* or a little more coherent and less impotently raging than Communist pamphlets. Maritain can be high-handed because he is completely competent and sure of himself and *right*. And it is right that people should start philosophy from something as good and clear as this.

PART II

Cuban Interlude

February 1940–May 1940

Cuban village.

February 18, 1940. New York

There is a new biography of Joyce out which has confirmed what everybody probably suspected: that his personal life has been dreary and rather uninteresting. I suppose he has been too much whipped. His pictures show him to be a slight, skinny, small-boned Irishman; blind, gray, sharpnosed, sharpchinned, a bit arrogant. One picture which showed him in a very stuffy looking smoking jacket, surrounded by his friends, who are all nonentities.

He is fastidious looking too, though. He has long fingers, small feet. In a lot of ways he reminds me of a Redemptorist missionary I know who has spent the last six years riding around in the Matto Grosso in the wilderness and heat bringing the sacraments to Indians.

Joyce certainly looks like an Irishman who resisted a vocation to the priesthood, but he also looks more like a book keeper than a writer. That he happens to be the best writer in this century is quite apart from this, and nobody ever said that his looks had anything much to do with what he wrote. It is too bad he made the same mistake that the people who hate him have always made: that of making no distinction whatever between the culture of the Irish middle class and the sacramental life of the Church.

He is always attacking the former, and very rarely the latter: but he makes so little distinction between them that when he makes fun of the Irish middle class, he leaves it to be clearly understood that he is including everything they might possibly want to believe in.

But to the people who hate him, the middle class is as sacred as the Mystical Body of Christ, so *everything* he says seems to be blasphemous.

March, 1940. New York

I just picked up *Pale Horse, Pale Rider* by Katherine Ann Porter, and read the first story, while the afternoon sun, spring sun, came through the bare branches and the window into the warm room. I went into the kitchen and half filled a glass with ginger ale and put some ice in it and sipped it very slowly.

The fact is, K. A. Porter writes well.

The neatness of her sentences is amazing, and so are her immaculate images and all her refined technical tricks – and so is the complete unimportance of whatever she seems to be talking about. So the book is a good book merely to have around so that you may pick it up from time to time and read four or five very clean and pretty sentences.

Her work is like sewing or embroidery or crocheting or whatever it is women do well. Or if that sounds mean: then it is interesting in the same mild way a good issue of *Harper's Bazaar* may be interesting to a man: pages of good montage, pretty pictures that don't mean much except that some subtle girl is standing in a landscape with something subtle on her head and it looks interesting.

March 19, 1940. New York

Graham Greene's *Brighton Rock* is good all the way from the quotation on the flyleaf, from *The Witch of Edmonton:*

> "This were a fine reign:
> To do ill and not hear of it again."

The book is full of terrific images, witty and complex and metaphysical. He is putting to its very best use a kind of modified surrealism, and the framework of the "thriller" is perfect for what he is trying to do.

I like the song that Ida (a character who thirsts after justice 'like the British fleet,' but is otherwise the least successful in the book) keeps singing over and over in her beery voice:

> "One night – in an alley – Lord Rothschild said to me . . ."

The Boy, the fierce central character, is not just a psychological study, because if he were the book wouldn't have all the meaning it has: it is a parable, and you can't make parables out of realistic, psychological studies. Therefore his fear of sex is more than just a glib trick of the author in characterizing him: it carries with it the notion of chastity turned inside out into a kind of Satanic sterility, which is a kind of imprisonment imprisoning him in evil yet liberating in him one terrible power: to kill people swiftly and almost surgically, with complete coldness. All this is comprehensible in terms of the doctrine of *"corruptio optimi pessima"* ["The corruption of the best is the worst"] and the whole thing has implications that are important for our society which worships a kind of surgical sterility itself, but cannot connect up that worship with all the dirt and cruelty and misery that are forced, harder and harder, upon the poor.

The best characters in the book are Colleoni and his gangsters. There is a scene where Colleoni comes walking grandly through the lobby of a hotel, where he lives in splendor, followed by a secretary running behind him and putting down on a pad names of flowers and fruits which Colleoni calls out as fast as they come into his head. They are to be sent to Colleoni's wife, from whom, of course, he has been separated for years.

There is another scene, where one of the gangsters, who is worried sick because he is in danger of being killed by his own gang, is mooning around on a pier and gets his character read by a slot machine. The card, maybe, comes in the form of a love letter, not a fortune: anyway it begins "Your wondrous winsome beauty and culture . . ."

Good Friday, 1940

"For in that she hath poured this ointment on my body, she did it for my burial."

SAINT MATTHEW 26

"He has poured out His soul in death."

ISAIAH

The apostles and, specifically in one Gospel, Judas, complained that this ointment was _wasted_ in being poured upon Christ instead of being sold and the money given to the poor.

Let the people, the so-called Catholics who argue against the "imprudence" of certain actions – like, for example, admitting a Negro child to parochial school for fear all the white parents take away their children – remember the "prudence" of Judas and freeze with horror!

The Pharisees and Judas gave openly to the poor. They knew how much to give to the poor, and at what season. They know how to give to the poor so that it wasn't embarrassing, or imprudent, or rash. They knew enough not to give the poor so much that they preferred to live on alms and gave up working altogether, the lazy sots. The Pharisees knew all this, perfectly. They had a system all worked out, and a lot of special prayers for every penny given away. It was a very efficient system, almost like some modern "charity" with a huge filing system and a big sucker list of names and a lot of little dames with glasses hopping around in an office like birds, and a lot more dames like mice, scratching at the doors of the poor with notebooks, and asking them their grandfather's birthplace, and do the children have the rickets or tuberculosis, and how much money do the kids all make between them shining shoes and selling papers?

The Pharisees knew how to take care of the poor in such a way that the poor would be always with them.

Therefore Christ said to those who objected the ointment should have been sold for the benefit of the poor that, for such gifts, the poor would be always with them.

There is a distinction between charity, the theological virtue, and charity a modern word meaning a mechanical and impersonal kind of almsgiving, as, for example, when a millionaire leaves all his money to "charity." The poor will be always there for this kind of almsgiving, where the rich man, infinitely distant from the poverty of the poor, scratches with a pen on a paper and starts a long series of book-keeping entries and abstract transactions which ends up a long time later with a nervous little social worker scolding a group of little kids who are trying to play baseball in a fenced-in gravel plot in a slum, somewhere.

Without love, almsgiving is no more important an action than brushing your hair, or washing your hands, and the Pharisees had just as elaborate a ritual for those things as they had for alms, too, because all these things were prescribed by law, and had to be done so. But love does not give money, it gives itself. If it gives itself first and a lot of money too, that is all the better. But first it must sacrifice itself.

If everyone had such charity as the woman who wasted, sacrificed this ointment that could have been sold for the poor, the poor would be much better off, and in fact would not be poor at all, or no poorer than anybody else. And what if the ointment had been sold? What about it? What would become of the ointment? What would the next buyer do with it? Pour it on his own dirty head, probably. But because this woman poured out this ointment and "wasted" it all for Christ, her story shall be told until the end of time.

The perfect charity of this woman's action is all the clearer when we see how it reflects the perfect charity of Christ's sacrifice for us, which was about to be consummated, and which she (and nobody else that was there), clearly foresaw, or she would not have done this, as Christ Himself bears witness: "She did it for my burial."

Thus He signalized the perfect charity of her gift by comparing it to His own passion, which it foretells and illustrates. The preciousness of the ointment testifies to the infinite preciousness of Christ's body and blood, offered up for us on the Holy Cross, a sacrifice that *infinitely* exceeds the object (our souls) for which it was offered up.

Yet if the woman had poured out this ointment, not upon God but only upon a prophet, the sacrifice would not have been perfect, and the significance of Judas' objection (that it should have been sold for the benefit of the poor), is that he did not believe Christ to be God, and, indeed, disbelieved in advance the very possibility of the redemption of man by Christ's Passion. He was already hardening his heart in stubbornness and suspicion and pride against the words of the One he was about to betray. And what he thought he was doing was being virtuous, prudent. He was caring for the poor. He was impatient of this crazy, wasteful, imprudent action; it repelled him, and scared him.

Let the people who are repelled and scared by the charity of saints, and the Catholics who fear those who try to help the poor by giving up everything they have, including their lives, to them, let all these remember the "prudence" of Judas when the woman poured out the ointment, and let them shudder. Because the woman knew she was in the presence of God, and gave him everything she had while Judas stood by giving a lecture on prudence, and one that was instantly answered and confounded by God Himself.

March 27, 1940. New York

I saw a Negro workman riding happily on the Long Island train, wearing a woolen cap on his head and reading a Negro newspaper, the *Society Page:* and down one side of the page he was reading a great big advertisement reading "Panic Stampede for *Native Son.*"

"Panic Stampede" is some phrase! However, I guess it is right, all right. However, at the bottom of the ad was a coupon you could cut out and send in, so that you would have the book: the idea being that you were a Negro and *Native Son* was by a Negro and naturally you were going to think this was the best book in the world for these reasons.

And then I got very sad, thinking how these people who can do so many good things instinctively, like playing pianos and dancing, should have to start imitating the dullest, stupidest tricks of all the crafty, snobbish, petty, absurd little classes and groups that make up the rest of society. I thought of all the Socialists walled up in their rooms praising Socialist novels, and all the Communists growling in their hutches the praises of Communist novels and then I thought of all the Catholics praising the works of some feeble pompous little idiot who had just been converted to the Church, and I thought of the Jews praising novels by Jews, and my mind returned to the polite and soft voiced and smiling and slightly awkward and intensely earnest Negroes gathered in fairly livable apartments on Edgecombe Avenue, talking about *Native Son*, but not really succeeding in being as stupid as the Communists and the Socialists and the Catholics and the Jews and everybody else. But give them time: they will succeed: they will get to be as dumb as we are.

The terms Communist and Socialist are nothing but social classifications. The term Catholic can refer to a social classification or to a religious one, and I am talking about the social one, the way the term is used in conversation. You say so and so is a Catholic. Maybe you just mean he has an Irish name, and was once baptized, and when he blasphemes he blasphemes the name of Christ without giving the impression at all that he doesn't know what he is talking about. Or when you say Catholic, maybe you mean someone who reads a lot of rather messily got up little magazines written in bad English and full of extremely sentimental illustrations and obscure snapshots of missionaries standing with their arms around little Chinese children. You are still talking about Catholics in the cultural and not the religious sense, because it is one of the singular disgraces attached to Catholics as a social group that they, who once nourished with their Faith and their Love of God the finest culture the world ever saw, are now content with absolutely the worst art, the worst writing, the worst music, the worst everything that has ever made anybody throw up. All this, far from being caused by their Faith, only weakens and ruins their Faith. It is something of Middle Class culture which is poisoning the Faith instead of slaking our thirst to honor God. And those who cannot distinguish what is bourgeois, in what they believe, from what is Christian are crucifying God all over again with their trivial, complacent ignorance and bad taste and materialism and injustice.

I heard of a fairly devout Italian woman (I say she is fairly devout at least because she has a lot of those crazy holy chromos insulting the Sacred Heart and the Blessed Virgin on the walls of her apartment) and this woman read a book called *Black Narcissus* which was about some kind of a nun falling in love with some kind of an Indian native. Well, the good woman got excited and wept and bawled a lot and read the book over a couple of times and for a long time it was her favorite book, and I wouldn't be surprised if she thought it was a devotional work.

Then there are all the Communists who think Shakespeare was a kind of a Communist, and all the Jews that think he was definitely a Jew, and the Irish who think Shakespeare was really a man named O'Neil. And, of course, earnest Catholics (there is nothing wrong with what they do except that it is stupid) work hard to try and prove Shakespeare was Catholic when all that is important is whether or not Shakespeare wrote great plays, because if they are great they are true, and if they are true they are Catholic.

So personally I don't care whether Shakespeare's father was ever signed up by the Jesuits in some underground Catholic club, nor whether Shakespeare was poaching in the preserves of a "new man" in order to get even with him for stealing the house and lands of a hunted Catholic nobleman, and I don't think it affects the value of Hamlet if Shakespeare never went to Mass. Dante didn't fiddle around wondering if Vergil was Catholic (except the Middle Ages were pretty excited about the Messianic Eclogue's being a Prophecy of Christ's coming!) and Saint Thomas wasn't trying to make Aristotle out to be a Christian, nor Saint Augustine Plato.

Truth is Truth and whoever beholds the Truth sees God. Catholics did not manufacture the Truth, but Truth was given to the Church by God through Christ, His Word incarnate, Truth Himself, that we might come to Him more easily no matter who we are, peasants or street-sweepers or washwomen or cooks or firemen or soldiers or kings or writers or priests or even politicians. But the Church did not create the Truth, and never held any monopoly on that mode of it which is accessible to man's natural reason.

You do not have to be a Christian, you only have to know life, to write a play which, like *Hamlet*, is ultimately incomprehensible except in terms of the doctrine of original sin, and illustrates the consequences of it. And if the play is true, it doesn't matter how immoral the hero is, the immorality will appear for what it is, and even more clearly than it would in life.

Catholics should stop demanding what the Communists demand of plays and books: that they conform to some abstract ethical system imposed upon them by force, not that they should merely tell the truth and be good books or plays.

March 29, 1940

There exists a figure in American literature who is a very interesting sort of figure, in his own strange way, and that is one T. Philip Terry, a writer of guidebooks to Mexico and Cuba. I have just come across him, and his imitation Baedekers.

His books are bound like Baedekers and organized like them and printed like them: but there is a difference. Terry has a curious personality which dominates the way his guidebooks are written, and makes them entirely different from Baedekers. Sometimes you wonder whether this personal touch is very desirable: but it is, it makes his guidebooks good and funny.

I can't say I admire his opinions about the Mexicans, whom he continually refers to as the "Mex." Nor am I happy with his notions of the religious backwardness of these superstitious natives, and I am not totally entranced with his elaborate analogy between the Mexican insult *"cabrón"* [cuckold] ("which is apt to provoke instant physical retaliation") and a "certain inelegant and disparaging accusation (referring to ancestry and moral purity) frequently bandied about by certain American tongues." But anyway it is quite easy to see that this Terry is a wag and a card.

He has a classic little article on Mexican beggars, based on the following concept: "The average Mex beggar is a chrysalis usually ready to develop into a full fledged thief." And, he adds, with a relentless and cynical severity, "Children are taught to beg from infancy, and though one pities the bedraggled and poorly clad mites, it should be constantly borne in mind that money given them goes directly into the hands of shiftless parents who as promptly spend it for drink."

This is followed by some lofty but practical moralizing which explains that the demand for labor in Mexico, at the same time as all this begging continues, far exceeds the supply, and we should neither pity these worthless idlers, nor those "foreign tramps who have no passion for clean linen and make Mexico their winter rendezvous during the season."

The whole article on beggars can be resumed in the following sentence: "There is no lack of charitable organizations in the Republic."

All this is written in the fine spirit of that practical Yankee morality which long ago put thrift and prudence at the top of the moral ladder and lowered "charity" from being the Name of the Third Person of the Trinity to a word meaning mechanically dispensing some money to the poor, in a purely abstract fashion, and incidentally giving the "charitable" organizers a nice cut on the way between the giver and the far less blessed receiver.

The article on thievery deserves a crown of laurel more than anything any humanist grammarian ever wrote in the Italian renaissance!

He begins with the "degenerate Spaniards" who not only cut their way into houses through the roof, but rob the poor boxes in the Churches (a temptation which has since been put out of their way in many of the provinces of Mexico where the Churches are either destroyed, or else, if open, not allowed to have anything to do with "charity," which has become a function of the government in the more scientific form of insurance. This is because of the well known fact that Christianity has two aspects: one in which it is a racket practiced by the priests, tools of the Capitalist class, on the unsuspecting poor; another where it is a true ideal, cherished by a few misguided enthusiasts: but an ideal that is totally absurd and "unscientific." And anyway, these idealists only play right into the hands of those scheming clerics!)

Terry doesn't get around to expressing such ideas as these, however, but the intellectual descendants of the liberal puritanism he comes from certainly do.

The important thing, though, is his warning against these rapacious Mexican thieves, these Homeric larcenists: They "steal wire cable by the mile, notwithstanding the risk of electrocution." They take it away and hide it along with "bolts from freight cars, engine fittings, . . . lead pipe, bathroom fixtures, potted plants, door plates, push buttons and whatever portable thing can be lifted or wrenched from the house." I like "lifted or wrenched."

As for tourists, they will be more concerned with this warning. Let them beware of ground floor rooms, even with barred windows, because thieves with "telescopic poles or long canes with hooks at the end" reach in through the grating and fish, indiscriminately, for any object in sight.

Speaking of thievery, it has its source in alcoholic stimulation, he feels. "The consumers (of *pulque*) are chiefly the idle and common laboring classes to whom it is meat, drink and a constant stimulus to crime."

This bourgeois prejudice would have to be erased from the sentence to describe the present drinkers of pulque in the New Republic of Mexico, and it would only be necessary to substitute for "idle and common laboring classes" the words "idle and counterrevolutionary kulak classes" and that would do the trick.

The similarity of bourgeois prejudices and Communist prejudices is always nearly as striking as the similarity between bourgeois bad taste in art and architecture and Communist bad taste in both (in Russia) which is, if anything, a bit worse.

And both the Communist and the middle class Puritan would be very happy about the following splendid period: "The zealous but oftentimes bigoted friars, who ruthlessly destroyed the early Indian manuscripts and idols, professing to believe them works of the devil, lost no time in replacing them with their own divinities in wood or plaster, and these, with singular inconsistency, they worshipped with even greater fanaticism."

Brave Terry! Noble Fellow! Think of those sinful old bigots committing the crime of destroying *art!* And being unfair about it too, being *inconsistent*, in fact singularly inconsistent. Noble satirist! Such crimes make your Puritan and your Communist weep with such hot mad tears of outraged justice that they will pick up their hammers and rush blindly to the nearest Spanish or Russian Church (the job was done in England and Germany long ago) and start breaking up the idols there – with singular, of course, consistency!

Immediately after this passage, we are startled by the change of tone, from bitter but noble satire to mild and perplexed severity: "Good music (military) is more often heard in the Mexican Plazas than in churches, where it is of a purely devotional character."

April, 1940. Miami Beach

The Leroy Hotel is an ok place. It has a particular smell about it which I find hard to identify, but it is a smell that seems to be appropriate to a seaside hotel, and indeed reminds me of some hotel I have stayed in sometime and somewhere, and I can't remember which one.

Venetian blinds, stone floors, coconut palms making a green shade in the room: the smell is a sort of musty smell of the inside of a wooden and stucco building cooler inside than out. It is a smell that has something of the beach about it too, a wet and salty bathing-suit smell, a smell of dry palm leaves, suntan oil, rum, cigarettes. It has something of the mustiness of that immense and shabby place in Bermuda, the Hotel Hamilton had: for the salt air had got into the wood and the walls of that place. It smells also like the Savoy Hotel in Bournemouth, which stood at the top of a cliff overlooking a white beach on the English channel. It had fancy iron balconies, and even when the dining room was full you could feel the blight of winter coming back upon it, and knew very well how it would look all empty, with all the chairs stacked.

I was in love there with a girl called Diane. The blight come upon our love that November, at which time they stacked up our chairs. I burned her letters in the fireplace of the Prefect's common room at Oakham: I tossed them in a packet into the flames with a grand gesture. Only once I wished I had them back to read.

The smell of this Miami room, my groundfloor room that looks out on a patio (my windows are kneedeep in bushes – if I were somebody's aunt I would lie: "Hibiscus"), is further complicated by the presence of leather. My good new leather gladstone bag, my saddle leather bag, bright, all leather, *limpio*, clean, unbanged, unstrapped, sweats aromatically in this heat, and gives off a good smell of leather. The fellow who sold it to me didn't have the wit to say this was the kind of a bag that would look better as time went on. However, the salesclerk in Rogers Peet (downtown New York) said just that of my new camelshair sportjacket.

Even the false leather suitcase I have had for a year, and bought for only five dollars as opposed to twenty, gives off its own kind of false leather happiness.

The shadows in the room, that is the shadows that green light through palm leaves makes upon cheap yellow stucco and woodwork all spanished up with cheap varnish, antiqued and renaissanced with a sort of a lacquer I presume, that kind of cool shadow in a room reminds me of a girl's house in Great Neck where I used to spend some time. She had a big cool living room with awnings on the screened windows, and some breeze circulated through it while we gently sweated in our tennis clothes and sat on the couch and sipped cocacola and giggled at each other.

The thing is, she is married and lives here in Miami Beach somewhere and has a child and I ought to call her up I suppose. Miami Beach is where she came from in the first place.

The smell and the light all belong to summer. And I suppose I am above all impressed with them because of the suddenness of my transition into them from New York, which just now has got a pretty raw April.

Here it is as hot as August. Coming here overnight, and stepping off the train into an August afternoon, and riding in a car along blue bays where there is a lot of greenery, lush greenery, is like the time I first got off the English boat in August and drove out on Long Island astonished at the heat and the haze and the profusion of weeds growing four and five feet high along the roads.

Driving out along these streets with shining new hotels and apartments everywhere (they put up forty-seven new hotels this year) was something like the time last spring I stepped out of the Long Island station into the garish brightness and gaiety and movement and the snoring tones of broadcasted music blowing about in the air of the Worlds Fair: and the musical horns of the busses, and the foghorn noise of the huge locomotive by the Railroad Building.

Miami must be typically American, because it is like nothing else on earth except, perhaps, a lot of places in America that I have not seen. To say that a place is typically American only means, after all, that it is completely unlike Paris or London or Rome or Madrid or Bucharest or Zurich or

Oslo. And it is certain that Miami Beach is nothing like Cannes, or Nice, or Spoleto, or Antibes, or Brighton or Dinard or Southend or Ilfracombe or Torquay or Weston-super-Mare.

It is not true that Miami is all Jews. It is true that it has a great street full of cheap drugstores that exactly reproduces the principal street of Long Beach, Long Island. Maybe that is all that anybody means: that and the racetrack and the dogtracks and the roulette joints. Nor is it truer of Miami than of anywhere else that it is full of gangsters, although yesterday there was a gunfight in front of a cigarstore, in which one man was killed and a cop had a bullet go through his cap. It is true that Al Capone's brother is running the waiters' union, and the papers are making a fuss the union is being, as they so colorfully say, "probed."

It is not true that Miami is ugly, or that the architecture is for the most part revolting. The new shiny storefronts along Lincoln Road are all white and functional and dressy and gay and sort of Worldsfairish in their lousy sculptured decoration but the effect of the whole is pleasant. A Hotel like the Pancoast looks very nice, and the fifteen- or sixteen-story hotels and apartments they have run up among the coconut palms are infinitely better than anything the whole length of Central Park West, which is one of the most forbidding streets in the world.

When you say functional, of the buildings: that means they are using designs that appear to be functional for the sake of effect, in other words, using non-functional tricks that appear functional but are only unnecessary decoration. That is the inevitable fault of the idea of the *"machine pour vivre"* ["device for living"]: because that is not the correct definition of a house, the result is that modern architecture is even more showy than baroque or rococo: but not nearly as good. I imagine that the rows and rows of little boxlike houses you see going through Baltimore are truly functional, in the unconscious way the factories everyone admires are functional. But those rows of houses are pretty ugly, all right. Nobody says they are particularly good machines for living in, but machines for living in is all that they are.

Miami is showy in a whole lot of ways, but in the last two years of building the fake Spanish has been swamped under the modern worldfair style, the showiness of mimic functionality. And that is a good thing: it is not an unbearable genre at all.

The reason the Leroy Hotel is Spanish, full of stucco and tiles and moorish arches, is that it is an old hotel: meaning it was built five or six years ago, or possibly, even as far back as the twenties, before the flood.

Of course it would be possible to do the cheap and easy trick of tearing Miami apart for its vulgarity, describing all the Mormon temples and the Bahaian shrines and the evangelists and the funeral parlors and unpleasant aspect of the city government. It would be very easy to copy down the signs you read along the road (I liked "Madame Taylor Trout's Theatrical Dance Studio," right by the railway in Hollywood by the sea – the friendliest town on earth) and be morally outraged at the vulgarity of hotdog stand architecture, and mortally offended by this or that villa, tortured even to death by a cigarette ad that you would see all over the place anyway, anywhere in America. All that stuff, since Huxley made such a fool of himself in *After Many a Summer Dies the Swan*, seems to be so superficial. I don't know why, but there seems to me to be something else you are obliged to do about an ugly hotdog stand besides making obvious remarks about it in a high state of moral indignation. If you don't like it, kick it down. Otherwise leave it alone and shut up and clean the hotdog stands out of your own heart, brother: this is the friendliest town on earth; I don't think the people with the most bleached hair in it are happy in it, for if they were, why would they try to sit in my lap on buses? But really, up at the North end of the beach everybody seems very tan and calm and peaceful, pleased with their cars and their many colored coats, quiet and without too much guile. Well if it is possible for some people to be tan and contented, it is possible for everyone. Maybe there is some cause of desperateness and violence that ought to be removed at the other end of the beach.

Once you get away from the hotels, and wander along the wide streets, say around fortyfirst street and Sheridan Avenue, the place is no different from a suburb of New York, say Great Neck or Bronxville, except that there are palms. The heat, the light, the sky, the atmosphere, the very feeling of the air is that of the North Shore of Long Island in August. Maybe the South end of the beach is like the South shore in August. In other words, almost anything you can say of Long Island is applicable to Miami Beach: they are the same people, wanting the same thing, living in the same kind of houses and driving the same kind of cars, equally recklessly. The reason people make a fuss about Miami is that it is not a place you come home to in the evening dead tired from your office, and it is warm all year. That is all.

But what is it that the smell in this hotel reminds me of? It is a typical summer resort smell, and maybe it epitomises all the summer vacations I ever had in my life. It is the way houses on Long Island smell in the middle of the afternoon in August. From the road outside the smell of cars (of cars themselves, not necessarily their exhaust), comes and contributes to the effect. The smell of Buicks is, I believe, quite individual. Or at any rate, big expensive sedans heat up when they are parked in the sun and smell stuffy and opulent in a way that a Ford coupe does not. On the other hand the upholstery of a convertible that has been standing out in the sun would smell the way the things do I am talking about. Rather it would not belong to this room, but to a whole vacation category, a series in which the smell, the atmosphere of this room figures.

Anyway this end of the beach smells of Buicks. The hotel also smells like the Grand Hotel de Parame, near Saint Malo. That was a Grand Hotel indeed, but the paint peeled and the parquet floors seemed unstable because of the way sea air gets into things. So I suppose the sea air gets into things here, too: the wind off the ocean all day has been quite moist, the sun itself being blinding and hot and dry.

Another thing about this room: it smells like some place where I have read a lot before, some place where I have had books. At the Savoy Hotel in Bournemouth I read *Saint Mawr*, by D. H. Lawrence, and got bored to death by *Jude the Obscure*. It may well be that the place merely reminds me of one of the front rooms in Douglaston, shaded and cool, where I have read God knows what.

It doesn't hurt to bring books to Miami either. When you have been swimming, and sitting in the hot sun, or lain in the sand listening to wind clatter through the dry palm leaves with the noise of rain, or sat up and watched the unending procession of cumulus clouds white in the sun, it makes you like what you read more than usual. I admit freely that I looked at a couple of García Lorca's poems, from the *Poema del Cante Jondo*, on the beach, and saw even more clearly than before how good he is and – how many of the Spanish words I don't know. That is not just a gag, either. That before I had only realized both these things confusedly is a sign that I had read him, then, with a less clear apprehension.

If Miami Beach is to be put in a category, or assigned some place in a tentative European series (the American seaside places I know are either like Coney Island and Long [Island] or Sakonnet, the Cape or Urbanna or the Rappahannock, in Va.). I should say it resembles Cannes more than Brighton, but it doesn't resemble Cannes much. Only at least it doesn't have the completely horrifying squalor of Brighton: only a certain part of the place is squalid, and it is the temporary jerrybuilt squalor that a good stiff breeze could make into matchsticks, whereas Brighton is built of brick and its uncleanness and misery is as solid as stone and mortar can make it.

There is no comparison between this place and Brighton, except that certain people talk as if there were. Perhaps there is some relation in terms of analogy, although I think Atlantic City is a better bet in that case.

So now that this is clear it is time to send off a couple of postcards announcing to people that Miami Beach is not as bad as the Florida publicity men have made it seem after all.

It is as easy and as dull to expose the falseness of clichés as it is to wisely show up how advertisements mislead the public and falsify the truth. Everybody knows that ads are misleading: indignation on that subject may be the prerogative of every decent thinking person, but it certainly is boring to listen to now that it is one that every decent thinking person exercises with complete abandon. However there is a cliché that Florida and Southern California and New York are not America. Presumably Saint Louis and Chicago and Dubuque *are*. But that is silly: Miami and Hollywood and New York are even more America than any of the workaday places, because they objectify all the desires of the people in those places: Miami is more America than Dubuque because Miami is what everybody in Dubuque dreams about.

I do not say that to be superior. Is it so bad to want to be handsome and sunburned, to go about in nice sport clothes, bright shirts, *alpargatas* and so on; to ride around in a green Cadillac convertible with girls who dance well and are very pretty and prettily dressed? Is it so bad to dream about having time to go swimming and to sit around on verandas and look at the palm trees? Is it so vulgar to want to have peace and leisure and friendship and certain mild pleasures like playing golf and drinking rye highballs on the terrace of the club afterwards? That is what Dubuque dreams about, or must dream about because it comes here at some expense to get all those things. I wonder what those forgotten intellectual colossi, H. L. Mencken and Sinclair Lewis dreamed about? Well, it's a little obvious to wonder that, too, because Sinclair Lewis loved all the things Babbitt loved, or he wouldn't have described them with such loving patience. And that he loved those things is a point in his favor, too. That, like Babbitt, he never loved anything else in particular was his weakness.

Miami Beach is still full of vacant lots, and anyone who wants to start a nightclub simply takes one of them and puts a night club on it. The consequence of this is you are allowed a certain architectural freedom in this venture: your nightclub can be polygonal or even round, or it can ramble about. This is completely different from New York, where nightclubs have to be fitted somehow into the cellars of brownstone houses. So the night-clubs in Miami Beach are rather gaudy and unsubstantial looking polygonal boxes standing about in vacant lots. There is a little nest of them scattered about near the towering pink bulk of the Roney Plaza.

These most of all, these little one-storied slicked-up white buildings with neon lights all over them, look like the amusement area of some world's fair; but when I went into El Chico too early for rumba music, and sat down to wait for the orchestra, it was really more like the dull and serious part of the fair. The illusion of that was created by the horrible blue educational looking murals of Mexican peons draped in their serapes and loaded down with baskets, going to the market: all these had been faithfully copied from photographs, the photograph lights and shadows being considerably exaggerated. The place is circular, and has a circular bar. It was empty. You expected that when people filled the place, not music, but some half-magic, half-scientific educational travelogue with the help of electrical tricks and subdued recorded organ music, would begin.

The next person to come in was the manager of some other nightclub which had just closed for the season: he invited the cigarette girl over to the bar, where he bought her several B and Bs and told her that this was the most successful season he had ever, ever had.

Finally a door in one of the murals opened, cutting a blue *peón* in half. A musician's face looked out at the empty room and the circular bar: then it vanished and the door closed with the sound of a drum. It took half an hour for some more people to come in, and then the music started. When it did it wasn't bad.

I went on to the Five O'clock Club, where they give you a drink on the house at five: unfortunately it was then nine. The Five O'clock Club was bigger and shinier and more crowded, whiter, brighter, and having many more tall mirrors and a taller ceiling. Two men in white dinnercoats and black ties were playing accordions and singing to the people at the bar, and when the orchestra came on there wasn't any improvement either, so I left and went home. So much for night life in Miami Beach.

Miami

I had not known what a city it was. Coming from the station we did not go through it at all, but only along the piers where the Clyde Mallory Liners docked, and the Merchants and Miners line tied up. Looking back at it across the bay, as we went out upon the windy causeway to the palm-covered spit where the hotels of Miami Beach are, it was a fair looking skyline against the blue sky, everything clean all about you what with wind and water and sun, you would have thought it was a pleasant city. But it is not. It is a fantastically shabby and squalid and rather fierce city, a cheap city, a vicious one, and still very crowded too, even though it is well on into April as I write.

The measure of the city is the Church of the Gesú, on First Avenue, down near Flagler Street, that is, right in the heart of the place. In the same way, the measure of Miami Beach, or of the good end of it, is the Church of Saint Patrick which is more than a measure of it, as a matter of fact because it is one of the nicest churches in America.

The Church of the Gesú is as huge as a hall, a great immense hall you would expect band concerts to be given in. You could get thousands of people into it. It is huge, as big as an armory. Facing you as you come in is a great battery of altars lined up against the immense back wall, and the whole wall above and around them is thick with blue and white plaster statuary, and the completely naked and desperate melodrama of the place is frightening, as if this huge cheap makeshift had to be run up like an ark to accommodate the whole city of Miami, which might be expected to run to it for refuge in a sudden flood or in a storm of fire and brimstone: a storm of brimstone, any day, any time.

It is at the same time the biggest and shabbiest and most impermanent looking church I ever saw in my life, as if it had been run up for one and only one vast holocaust.

The Church of Saint Patrick, on the other hand, is a beautiful church, also quite big, but a very good romanesque basilica, simple good high sweeping arches, a splendid sanctuary, splendid in its simplicity. The rector, Monsignor somebody or other, is a fine fellow and a good preacher, and his priests are nice guys, from their looks. Sunday it was full of communicants, and there were many communicants this morning, too. Sunday it was bright with pretty dresses, and happy looking, guileless people. In the loft is a great organ, and a choir of schoolgirls sang, a Gregorian Kyrie, and Sanctus, and so on, and not badly. It seems to be a very pleasant sort of parish, a good parish.

The reason it was so good to be in that church, too, was that you could see how if all the parishes in the country were like that things would be good enough for one to say we had a Utopia: because that would mean everyone in the country had enough to eat, and leisure to rest and be healthy, and get tanned up, and wear nice clothes. Even one or two colored fellows in the church were that way, nicely dressed, happy, serene.

On the other hand, the Gesú is the church that is fitted out to serve a parish of desperate and violent souls, and to save them. It is not necessarily a question of one parish being richer than the other, just because one is safer than the other.

At the same time I can hardly say I know what is in the Gesú parish: the center of Miami is: cheap postcard stores, bars, fruitjuice places, movies, beauty parlors, barbershops, banks, offices, bus stations, five and tens, cut rate drugstores, and cigarstores like the one where, the other day, there was a gunfight between the cops and robbers. Probably also gambling joints and brothels and bookmakers' offices and places where men concern themselves with the smuggling of dope and Chinamen into the country from the Caribbean islands.

Romantically speaking the Gesú is the more exciting parish, and the one where a priest would be more likely to become a saint . . . if it is possible to say such a thing. The mere physical aspect of the church at the Gesú is enough to frighten you out of complacency, it is at the same time so ugly and so adapted to its purpose – saving souls in holocausts – so comically melodramatic and so serious. Saint Patrick's is a finer, cleaner place, and in it it is much easier for the quiet and gentle devotion of an ordinary person to grow and bear fruit in patience and joy and a certain kind of contemplation of God that becomes possible when you are simply grateful for His gifts.

April, 1940. La Cabana, Cuba

To get to La Cabana and the Morro you have to get in a launch or a rowboat at Cavalleria wharf. That is just behind El Templete, which stands under a big Ceiba tree of some historical significance, facing the Plaza de Armas. This is right across the narrow entrance to the harbor from La Cabana fort. Four or five launches ride in the blue water, tied up to the stone quay. Offshore there are generally a couple of schooners at anchor waiting for some cargo to take along the coast to Matanzas or Cardenas or further. If you are American they will charge you forty cents to go to the Morro and twenty to the Cabana: but the real fare to the Cabana by rowboat or launch is only a dime, and you can walk from Cabana to the Morro, as it is only about half a mile. Besides, it is a nice walk, along a footpath at the top of the bluff, from which you get a view of the whole city across the harbor mouth, with its domes and churches and towers and white buildings and avenues full of palmtrees. The view of Havana from La Cabana or the Morro is as good as that of Rome from the Pincio, of Florence from San

Miniato, of Paris from the Sacre Coeur, and a whole lot better than that of New York from the top of any building, because New York, from the top of a building, is impressive but not beautiful. The best view of New York is from a boat in the harbor.

You can see the whole city, from the sweep of the flat shoreline where the Vedado runs out to the point just beyond the big Hotel Nacional, to the principal fort on the hill behind the university, to the big white spire of La Reina and on over to the chimneys of the powerstation and the docks and masts of the inner harbor. But it is in front of you that the most important part of the city lies, gathered around the big Capitol dome in its center: and directly in front, along the sea wall lined with coconut palms, runs a wide avenue for cars to go fast on, and behind it are toy houses and the towers of churches and beyond that taller buildings still. It is a very pretty city.

La Cabana itself really is a fort. At the dock, one of the soldiers who is leaning in the shade with his hat on the back of his head will take away your camera and stick it in his pocket while you go on up the path to the top of the hill. Then you will go through a heavy iron gate that has been let into the thick wall, and a sentry will stare at you wondering what to do about you being there: so he will send you across the green grass of the parade ground that is lined with trees, to an office where you will wait for some time while sergeants, lottery ticket salesmen, politicians, workmen and nondescript friends of the men garrisoned there, walk in and out. Then you will be turned over to some party member in good standing, depending on who is in power across the way, and he, dressed in a rumpled white linen suit like all the other guides hanging around the street, will take you around the fortress. You have to have a guide. That is on account of the military secrets. The whole of Havana walks in and out the gates of this fortress selling ice cream and small cookies and lottery tickets: photographs of its most vital defences may be bought on postcards: but the law says that American tourists must have a guide to take them through the forts. And a very sensible law, too, as a matter of fact. Otherwise they would probably go blundering into great primitive showerbaths that have been installed in some of the old dungeons.

Since La Cabana is a proper fort, or rather a big fortified barrack where a regiment of gunners is stationed, there is nothing much interesting about it, except the view you get from the walls, looking over Havana. It is a pretty place, inside, with its flat lawn of a parade ground. Soldiers sit about on benches under the trees. The place is neat and well kept and cool and airy. It would be a pleasant enough place to be stationed, I should think, if one had the misfortune to belong to a Cuban artillery regiment. Everybody seems fairly happy. As I was going through, a great negro bugler strolled under the trees blowing with a great flourish the call that brings race horses to the starting gate at all American tracks, and probably Cuban tracks too. A negro sergeant walked out of his way so as he could pass me by and grin and say "'Ullo Mister."

The Morro, on its rock, with its drawbridge and great deep moat and its thick walls and bastions and tunnels and passageways and lighthouse and dungeons is a pleasanter place, and the view is even better from it. It houses a military college that exists in its underground passages and extends far in under the rock in many mysterious places I have no doubt.

There are, for the public to see, several dressed up dungeons with wax figures in them of chained Cuban prisoners and stern Spanish guards. The central piece of the whole waxworks they have rigged up in this old fort is a torture chamber where a Spaniard is garrotting a Cuban while a priest stands by with a rather hypocritical expression of pity and disgust upon his face. The guide takes you to the highest carat on the wall, and shows, on one side, a drop of some fifty feet to the sea where he points out what he calls a "shark's nest." On the other side there is a drop nearly as deep to the bottom of the dried up moat: of this drop the guide says, "Boy, if anyone fall down there, he die."

Cuban conversations are excited, rapid, witty and they never end. They do not get carried on as much with the help of gestures as one might suppose: and the Cubans accuse the French of being the people that talk with their hands. What gestures there are are very stereotyped and belong to particular occasions: when these proper occasions come up, then the gestures are used, but the Cubans do not embellish their words by sketching out meanings in the air in front of them. However, they do emphasize their best jokes by slapping each other on the shoulder quite a lot.

Cubans don't argue much, at any rate in public: you can walk around the streets for weeks and never see a quarrel. Cuban children laugh and yell a lot, but they do not cry as much as you might expect them to. If the howling of babies is not one of the more noticeable noises in a Cuban city, it may be because it is drowned out by all the other noises going on in the place: but I do not think so. There is certainly no lack of children: and they are nice kids, too. Pretty, happy, friendly, a lot of the time dirty but who cares? And they make a lot of noise, too: when they are happy they run up and down with very shrill and happy yells. So if they were to cry a lot, I am sure you would have to hear it.

You get the feeling that the gregariousness of the Cubans is not only different from that of Americans, but also that it answers to a more genuine necessity. One of the reasons for this is that while Americans get restless and like to mix with their own kind and talk in lobbies and pullmans, that talking does not solve anything, does not satisfy anything or end any loneliness or distress, that distress is exemplified in a million other needs for stimulations that are also inadequate.

That is why American conversations rapidly take on a synthetic character, become an instrument for the injection of a lot of cheap ready made good humor by means of dirty stories, handies, Confucius sayings, knock knocks, and all that stuff that ends in such empty and sad sounding laughter you wonder they all don't go out and kill themselves. To hear a party of Americans sitting around over their drinks, coughing and laughing at their traveling salesman stories is about as gay as watching a bunch of fraternity boys swatting each other in the arse with big wooden paddles. It sure doesn't seem to answer any human necessity I can think of, but of course it proclaims the presence of a craving for friendship and mutual love and sympathy all the more poignantly because it is so ludicrously inadequate to do anything about it.

All this is even truer of England, but it is not so noticeable there because the English have trained themselves to appear outwardly as if they didn't need to love anybody but themselves. Anyway, the value of making your conversation out of dirty jokes is that it makes it all more impersonal: underneath this outside covering you can withhold your reserve of suspicion and mistrust and malevolent, critical satisfaction at the difference from yourself you notice in the people around you. And you don't have to give them anything of your own, or take anything of theirs: it looks like love because everybody's mouth is stretched out into the shape of a smile, but it is saved from really being love because nobody has given or received anything from anybody else.

The Englishman's house is his castle, and it seems as if all those related to him or descended from him or converted to his standards of materialism or defending any other standard of materialism equal to his find themselves always defending a castle, walling themselves and all their possessions in with a concrete ring of privacy that no one must come through or all will be lost. Or perhaps it is a human necessity that everyone knows, to have in himself a fortified sanctuary: but your feelings about it will be determined by what you are keeping inside of it. You will defend the castle according to the kind of enemy that is likely to want to destroy what is inside of it. And if it is a heavenly treasure you have laid up there you will not be afraid of thieves or, indeed, of any human enemy, for the Christian loves his enemies precisely because the treasure the enemy covets will never be diminished by being shared: rather it will be increased. If, on the other hand, you have a heap of corruptible goods locked up in a safe deposit box in your middle somewhere, you will fear every natural agency as a potential danger to it: and you are likely to see every man as a thief, and so hate everyone.

Whether Americans are more afraid of such thieves than Cubans are would be silly to try and say: but in any case privacy is something that doesn't have much value to Cubans: they are not interested in hiding their feelings any more than they are embarrassed to let people look through their windows and into their houses, and they do not get nervous at being looked at themselves, nor do they hesitate to look at anybody or anything that interests them, either.

Every Cuban city centers around a public square or an avenue of some kind that serves as a *paseo*. The *paseo* expresses the very essence of Cuban, and I suppose Spanish life: In a city where everything is wide open to the street, churches, houses, cafes, hotels, banks, offices, stores, the center is a big open square with trees and innumerable chairs and wide walks: on Saturday and especially Sunday evenings the whole town comes out here, and this becomes the town. Specifically, the whole town walks around and around and everybody looks at everybody else. In some places, like Matanzas and Camaguey, they keep to the proper custom of the *paseo*, which is that the men walk around the square clockwise and the girls counterclockwise, so that they can all see each other properly, and smile and wink and larf and flirt. If you see someone you know, you drop out of your clockwise circle and join them walking counterclockwise conversing very gallantly.

Cubans would rather walk around in the *paseo* than go to a movie any day. They would rather walk in the *paseo* than get drunk, or possibly even than get into a crap game. I think they would rather spend their evening in the *paseo* than any other way, except going to a big dance. And that the *paseo* itself is a happy and delightful thing shows that it is a thoroughly good and successful custom. It answers a real necessity that all the young people and many of the old in a town seem to feel for being in the same place at the same time, where everybody can see everybody else, and talk to everybody else and live completely as a community at least for two evenings a week. It would take an almost superhuman persuasion to get a Cuban to desert the *paseo* before it broke up at ten o'clock. And even if the square is lined with cafes where you could sit and drink coffee and watch everyone going past, yet most of the tables are generally empty. What is important is to be a part of the community that is moving around and around in concentric circles like the souls of the prudent in heaven.

The power that moves these circles is, as I have now said about seventeen times, love. That explains why Cubans are satisfied with the *paseo*, and do not need to get drunk or anything else of the sort. Because the only reason why a really gregarious person gets drunk is that he is in a situation where in order to be with a lot of other people, all laughing and talking or looking at each other, he has to be in a bar or at a party. But on the other hand if there is so much drinking in America it may mean that Americans love drink at least as much as each other, if not more. Or maybe they are so scared of each other that they don't believe they can be happy in a group in the same room unless they are all plastered. Cubans are not that shy, or that uncouth.

On the other hand, another reason why the *paseo* is a success (and this is very important) is, after all, that the people who take part in it are beautiful themselves. No one can imagine a crowd of several hundred people all walking around and taking pleasure in the sight of each other if only one or two of their number was beautiful. On the contrary they would all go and hide in their houses, or sit in the movies where they, the ugly ones, would be in the dark, and only the pretty ones would be visible, greatly magnified up in front of the others, on a screen.

It would be an exaggeration to say that Americans are ugly; in fact it would be a lie; American girls are very pretty and American boys are very handsome. Only it just came into my head for a minute of a Saturday night crowd in Times Square in terms of the *paseo*. To think of so many ugly people liking the sight of each other is ludicrous: no wonder they swat each other in the stomach with their arms and fists as they walk along. On the other hand it is hard to say which of these events is prior in a causal series: does the ugliness cause the bad temper or the bad temper the ugliness? Every time you compare Cubans and Americans you get into a strange and absurd mess and yet there must be some grounds for making the comparison: the reason I am always trying to make it is precisely that people seem so much prettier and so much happier in the Parque Agramonte, Camaguey, than they do in Times Square, New York. This may be partly an objectification of my own state of mind here on a vacation: but surely, only partly.

It may be just my own taste that says the people are more beautiful here: but it is an incontrovertible fact that they laugh more and talk gayly with each other, and make friends with a complete stranger immediately: and everybody really does like everybody else. And while there is a lot more calm in small towns in America than there is in Times Square, and while there is more show of friendliness, yet small towns cannot compare with Cuba either for the amount of laughing and gaiety and friendliness. I myself would go so far as to say that the friendliness that people in small towns in America believe they have is almost entirely an illusion. No people who are really friendly to strangers would ever imagine there was any point in putting up signs saying "Welcome" at the edge of their towns. Nor people who really loved strangers would leave signs on the road out of their town saying "Glad you passed through, Come again" because such signs only proclaim how aware they are that the stranger actually did pass through as fast as he could without breaking the law, and that he would rather be seen dead than come through such a mean little town again.

When a stranger comes into a small town in America, everybody gets a good look at him, and criticizes his clothes and his manner behind his back. If someone talks to him it is with a mixture of servility and insistence and fright that is appalling to see. When I had been half an hour in Matanzas, I was driving out to Monserrate hermitage with three young Matanceros I had just met in the public square, who were taking me to see the one important sight in the town, and at the same time persuading me to stay another day and come with them to Varadero beach.

The next day, one of these fellows spent the whole morning showing me everything there was in the town: the college of the Marist Fathers, the high school, the cathedral, several churches, the river, *Pueblo Nuevo* and the rope factory and the new baseball park. We walked all over the place. By the second evening there I had met at least twenty people, men and girls, not counting about twenty more white and black children who were my very best friends for life.

The town of Sancti Spiritus didn't have any signs on it saying Welcome or Come Again, brother. When we got there in the bus I got down to get a drink of some *gaseosa* [soda], and this small boy came up smiling and said hello. I asked him what town it was, and he said it was Sancti Spiritus. I said it looked very beautiful. He said yes indeed it was: where was I going? To Camaguey? Why didn't I get off the bus and stay and see Sancti Spiritus? But I said no, I couldn't. Maybe I would on the way back, in a couple of weeks. So when the bus pulled out of Sancti Spiritus there was I with a friend waving good bye, saying he hoped I would really come back to Sancti Spiritus in two weeks. If I hadn't been so bored with Cuban buses and with the heat inland I would have come back, and Sancti Spiritus was really very pretty, sitting in the plain with high blue mountains behind it like a stage set.

At Santiago, once again, within the first twenty minutes I had made friends with a seventeen or eighteen year old student who served as acolyte in the cathedral, who showed me all over Santiago, and took me to the best place to swim near the city (which I would probably not have found by myself), and everywhere I went they would come bringing small presents for me to take along when I left, as remembrances. In Matanzas I got a Mexican magazine because I had happened to remark that I was interested in magazines. In Santiago they gave me some little religious cards.

The *paseo* does not exist in its pure and proper state in Santiago or Havana. The Parque Cespedes at Santiago was hot and dusty and noisy at night, the air filled with the blaring of the world's only flamenco saxaphonist being broadcast over a public address system, interrupted by the noise of all the little bells of the kids selling ice cream. The crowd was mostly negroes, and they sat dejectedly around on the benches: but really there was not much of a *paseo* at all. In Havana there is plenty of room for a *paseo*, all up and down the Prado, around the big Parque Central, and along the *paseo* de Marti across the street from the Capitol. But Havana is too big and too fashionable a city for the *paseo* to be the center of its life for everybody. Once again, here the *paseo* does not really express the authentic life of the city. In Camaguey the poor, the middle class, everybody all belong to the same *paseo*, all move about in it together, all knowing one another. In Havana, the people who walk about are mostly poor. A lot of them are whores. A great number of them are trying to sell things to tourists: a lot more are themselves tourists. Anybody with any social pretensions at all is either off at some party in the Vedado, or out at the Havana Yacht Club, or else going up and down the Prado not on foot but in a car. The *paseo* in Havana is not a *paseo* at all: but still, there are a lot of people walking up and down in it.

The crowd is very animated and gay, too: and as you pass along the Paseo de Marti, along the front of the rather shabby arcaded buildings facing the big, white Capitol, there are a lot of cafe tables out on the sidewalk, and three or four of the cafes have orchestras, orchestras made up largely of girls, playing every night. I saw three rather poor but respectable looking girls pass one of these cafes and turn and give a very dirty look to three whores who sat together at one of the tables without escorts and dressed in splendor.

Here the crowd does circulate back and forth along the sidewalk in front of these cafes where people sit an hour or two over a cocacola listening to the music. But on the other side of the wide street, in front of the Capitol, where there is all the space in the world, nobody walks at all.

In Camaguey, though, they really had a *paseo*. The Parque Agramonte is rather small, and consequently it got terrifically crowded. The Band (every *paseo* needs a military band) was jammed up against the side door of the Cathedral, and around and around went the concentric circles of girls three and four together, arm in arm, and boys, four and five together going in the other direction. Most of the girls who had sweethearts did not walk in the *paseo*, but sat with them on little iron chairs that are lined up around the concrete walks, their arms around each other watching everybody else walk around and around. This is not just because of the crowding in Camaguey, though. It seemed about the same in Matanzas: if you knew a girl, you walked with her and her girl friends a couple of turns around the park: if you had a sweetheart, rather than walk with her, to be looked at, you sat with her on a bench, off to one side, and looked at everybody else. Standing around the edges of the circulating crowd were more young men, two and three deep: and as soon as the band had finished a number, the uniformed players would drop their instruments and jump up and stand in a line at the edge of the crowd, looking at everyone go by.

April, 1940. Havana, Cuba

There is a popular superstition about Havana which says that the first thing you see when you approach it on the boat is the Morro Castle. That is not true. I don't know what was the very first thing anyone saw, but the first individual thing on the low shore that got my attention was a big yellow square which turned out to be some building or other in a little village a few miles to the east of Havana.

The next thing was, beyond that, the city itself, the color of a pearl in the morning haze. In the other direction, a low long line of fertile hills stretched along the shore, tapering off eastward into haze and beyond that, suddenly, it led out into a mirage, a second horizon, a second sea hanging low in the sky, and on that sea a small ship steaming north, never seeming to move, just hanging there in the white haze, knocked cockeyed by the reflection of itself, high in the bows and low in the stern and looking something like a trawler.

Behind the line of low hills, and beyond them was a line of clouds look-ing like a fabulous range of jagged blue mountains, and I had already be-gun to feel the curious feeling one feels about such cloud mountains, such impossible lovely ranges of mountains, when all of a sudden as we got closer to shore, it became apparent that these were not cloud mountains at all: but they were, on the contrary, quite real although they might have been a mirage. They must be the mountains I have read of, that lie north of the town of Trinidad, in the province of Santa Clara.

Long before you could pick out the Morro at all (for at that hour in the morning with the sun falling on it from the shoreward side – to which side it has only low bastions and earthworks to show – the ramparts over the harbor mouth were in the shadow), long before that, I had seen the Capitol dome standing above the city, and could follow the line of white buildings stretching out along the Malecon toward the Vedado and beyond that.

They were beginning to pile out luggage out on the narrow and crowded and sunny deck, and I walked in and out among the people, getting, when I could, to the rail, and looking still over at those hills and those mountains, thinking of what Columbus said (the words are quoted in any guide, in any travel folder you pick up), "The loveliest land that eyes have ever seen." Al-though it was lovely land, it was all cultivated, and probably is less exciting than it was when Columbus came upon it all palm trees and flowering jun-gle. And anyway he landed at the other end of the island.

From out at sea, I don't imagine Havana looks much better than Miami, because Miami from the sea looks all right. Havana is a pearl colored city, you don't know what's going to be in it. From the sea you can't tell.

As you get closer, and begin to enter the harbor, it looks like one of the duller places along the Mediterranean. There are lines and lines of white and pink and pale orange colored houses with arcades and arcades and archways running along the street, and the houses are shuttered, and there is a sea wall, and it does not appear to be very animated. If you care to, you can look at it as if it were painted in a two dimensional sort of a way on a Dufy screen, and throw in some bright colors of your own into the picture, and it gets to be fun. But that side of Havana isn't animated. It is when you see the Prado and the parks and the low towers of a church standing here and there not much above the level of the surrounding buildings, that Ha-vana suddenly becomes a very charming city: but it still isn't particularly animated.

The truth is, you have to leave the dock and get into the streets before, all of a sudden, the city overwhelms you, and you are overcome by its brilliance and the lights and shadows and the noise and the cries of the colors and the smells and the tremendous life that flows in and out of the dark shops that stand open to the street. Then comes the paradox that Havana in many ways appears to be more of a city than even New York, because it is a city in the real sense that Mediterranean and Levantine and perhaps oriental cities are cities. There it is not the buildings that are important but the life in them, and they are full of life, crammed with it. Negroes with cigars in their mouths and great bloody aprons, carrying huge sides of beef out of trucks and into dark cavernous butcher shops that open right out on the narrow street. Clusters and clusters of bananas and papayas and coconuts and God knows what different kinds of fruits hanging up in the fruiterer's. Piles of cigarettes, shelves and shelves of books, cigars, medicines, sheets and sheets of numbered lottery tickets hanging up over a tobacconist's counter, and more magazines than I ever saw at once in my life: dozens of newspapers.

It is a city that, although it is physically dirty and full of poor people, is much more a city, and more truly a rich city than New York because it seems to be richer in multitudes of material things, fruits, meats, sugar cane, coffee, tobacco, newspapers, rum, bread, machinery, musical instruments. New York is only rich in gold and silver and account books full of figures and ledgers and fancy printed stocks and ticker tape and nervous energy and electricity. Havana is more of a city because it is flesh and blood, bread and wine, matter charged with life.

It is the nature of a city to be full of people doing things for some immediate end, commercial, esthetic, sinful, what you will. They are doing this in a city because each man, there, can supply someone else with at least one thing he might want. A city is, from a certain point of view, a place where proximate satisfaction for almost every order of need or desire is immediately to be had for the asking: you clap your hands, whistle, beckon to the proper person.

If the nature of a city is such that it makes it possible for men to satisfy one another's needs directly and speedily in its streets and marketplaces and its cafes, it follows that it is better for the city to satisfy needs that already exist and to provide for these well, than for it to *create* artificial needs in order to dispose of new objects, while neglecting to fulfill men's ordinary needs properly. Or, a city that ignores half of men's needs and desires, and concentrates on only one aspect of life, say the commercial, to the exclusion of the esthetic, the moral, etc. is a poor kind of a city. It is of the nature of a city to attempt to satisfy every class of need. Also, a city where large numbers of people are deprived of even a poor imitation of certain kinds of satisfactions, esthetic or religious or something of the sort, is a failure as cities go, because it is also of the nature of the city to try and provide some sort of satisfaction for everybody's needs. I can only conclude that a city in which simple needs for everybody are more easily satisfied, in which even the poor have the chance of getting and enjoying more and more of the things that are not essential to bare existence, like amusements etc., and in which more kinds of needs in general are satisfied in more different kinds of ways with less trouble for everybody, that city is better than one where the food is bad for everybody except the rich, where there are only one or two standardized kinds of amusement, where religion is neglected, where more than half the houses are ugly.

Havana is a thoroughly successful city, it is a good city, a real city. There is a profusion of everything in it, immediately accessible, and, to some extent, accessible to everybody.

The gaiety of the bars and cafes is not locked in behind doors and vestibules: they are all open wide to the street, and the music and laughter overflow out into the street, and the passersby participate in it, and the cafes also participate in the noise and laughter and gaiety of the street.

That is another characteristic of the Mediterranean type of city: the complete and vital interpenetration of every department of its public and common life. These are cities the real life of which is in the market place, the *agora*, the bazaar, the arcades.

A negro, laden down with round red and yellow maracas, and, in his hands rattling castanets with a gay sharp roll, circulates in and out the bar, the lobby of the Hotel Plaza: the dining room, which is not separated from the lobby by any dividing wall, shares not only the life and commotion of the lobby but the air [and] the coolness as well as the noise of the arcades outside. You can hear the roll of the castanets as this negro goes on out and under the arcades, in and out a barbershop, a cafe, in between the tall chairs of the bootblacks, in and out the pitches of the newsboys with their hundreds of magazines.

Sellers of lottery tickets, of postcards, or late extra papers (there is a new edition of some paper almost every minute) go in and out of the crowd, in and out of the bars. Musicians appear under the arcade, and sing and play and go away again.

If you are eating in the dining room of the plaza you share in the life of the whole city. Out through the arcade you can see, up against the sky, a winged muse standing tiptoe on top of one of the cupolas of the National

Theater. Below that, the trees of the central park: and everybody seems to be circulating all about you, although they do not literally go in and out the tables of where the diners sit, eating dishes savory of saffron or black beans.

Food is profuse and cheap: as for the rest, if you don't have the money, you don't have to pay for it: it is everybody's, it overflows all over the streets: your gaiety is not private, it belongs to everybody else, because everybody else has given it to you in the first place. The more you look at the city, and move in it, the more you love it, and the more love you take from it, the more you give back to it, and, if you want to, you become utterly part of it, of its whole interpenetration of joys and benefits, and this, after all, is the very pattern of eternal life, it is a symbol of salvation, and this sinful city of Havana is so constructed that you may read in it, if you know how to live in it, an analogy of the kingdom of heaven.

I don't know why I had imagined that, just because the Cubans speak Spanish it would be fairly easy to get a Spanish edition of the works of Saint John of the Cross in Havana. It turned out to be practically impossible: as a matter of fact I still do not know if it is possible at all.

The first day I was in Havana, I was coming up the Calle O'Reilly when I saw a bookstore, a second hand bookstore, and walked in, asking not for John of the Cross, but for philosophy books. The nearest thing to philosophy on the shelf they pointed out to me were a couple of shabby volumes of literary criticism by Menendez y Pelayo. Then, when I asked for Theology, they said they didn't have any.

Another store of the same kind a little further up the street did have a couple of shelves of philosophy: I had to climb a ladder to look at them. I shouldn't have been surprised to be confronted first of all by none other than Nietzsche. A little further along, Max Nordau, whom I take to be some sort of a third rate Spengler. Schopenhauer, Ortega y Gasset: but these are respectable names while, for the most part, the shelves were full of Spanish and French nineteenth century liberals and radicals of the same sort of calibre as Jaures. I cannot seem to remember any of the names in particular: but once again, Menendez y Pelayo, too, on literary criticism.

The next place I went into was the Casa Belga with its big stock of French and English books, and its specialty in pornography and little editions printed in Paris, Henry Miller, Rimbaud's *A Season in Hell* (the salesman took offense when I mentioned that a translation of this had just been published by New Directions in Connecticut: he said this was the original. Not the original original, of course, since it was in English, but the "original translation"), and then things like the *Philosophy of Nudism*. The idea of a philosophy of nudism gave me to laugh somewhat in a quiet scholarly way, to which the salesman refused to grant even a minimum of complicity or assent of any kind. I have always had a certain instinctive respect for the native common sense of the Latin races, who do not indulge in half so many elaborate and sentimental delusions of themselves as do Teutons, and Anglo Saxons and Celts and Jews and so on. For this reason I too readily assumed that this salesman realized right away that the philosophy of nudism must be an absurd sort of a book, with a dressed up pompous title, which some dope of a tourist would buy for the pictures of nudists: and so waste his money. But on the other hand I had forgotten that Cubans and other Latin Americans are suckers for all kinds of sex books: but unlike Americans, they really seem to think seriously that there exists a philosophy of sex, and that "sexology" is a science. That is the way the matter stands, and I can't make up my mind who are the bigger fools, the Cubans or the Americans.

The next place I went to was a bookstore that looked like a bank and it did not even have books out on display on the counters: every book in the place was expensively bound and was locked in behind wired in doors. They couldn't help me any, either, in my search for something by Saint John of the Cross. Further down the same street (by now I must have been either in the Calle Obispo or Obrapia), I did finally come to a place where they sold books on philosophy.

When I asked for philosophy, they began first to drag out their John Stuart Mill and Herbert Spencer and Schopenhauer and so on, but besides that they had a whole lot of Maritain and Berdayev in translation, which they brought out very gladly. There I finally decided to see what Jaime Balmes was like, and took something by him, and also something by Juan Zaragueta, a modern Spanish Catholic (a book printed in Spain in the time when the Civil War was going on, and a neat, well printed book, which surprised me considerably: I had assumed books were not published in a country which had a war going on in it). The nearest he could get to Saint John of the Cross is the autobiography of Saint Theresa, which is such a universal classic that I guess you can get it for thirty cents on the Spanish shelf in Macy's. Anyway, I already have it.

I had given up hunting for Saint John of the Cross and was going off up the street when I saw a huge place with a great big sign saying "La Moderna Poesia" which rather astonished me: what a huge shiny big bookstore it was! Only when I looked into the window I saw a lot of straw hats, and in the next a lot of kids suits. It turns out La Moderna Poesia is a department store.

There is also another department store in Havana called "La Filosofia." It would have been funnier if I had run into that one first.

April, 1940. Havana, Cuba

Much of the shouting that goes on in the streets of Havana has to do with daily papers, naturally. I haven't counted them up, but it seems to me that Havana probably publishes more daily papers than New York does now (since so many papers took one another over there) if you don't count the little German and Russian and Yiddish papers they make in New York. Maybe even if you count them, Havana is still ahead.

Most of the noise is made about the *Avance* and the *País* which are afternoon papers. That is, they send their news boys out into the streets just before noon to shout not the headline but the name of the paper. If they had to shout the headline they would be hard put to it to know what to shout: there is no "the headline" because the front pages of both papers are entirely covered with huge headlines and tiny little stories to go with them. This is true of most of the other papers around Havana, and if you were to judge the news by them you would get a pretty fanciful idea of what was going on at present in the European war.

As I write the English have been forced to abandon their absurd halfhearted attempt to defend Norway against the Germans, which of course was no attempt to do anything except to make a kind of gesture, a sort of a little brave gesture for the neutrals elsewhere. When they found the Germans, on the contrary, were not making any gestures, the English had to make a disgraceful retreat, one that added more ignominy to their name than anything, even Munich, did: for after all, peace is something, and Munich was an attempt to keep it: but this was an act of war. If you are going to keep out an invasion of barbarians, if you have made up your mind to resist them, instead of letting them come on and invade you and take it patiently, if you are going to fight barbarians it is absurd not to fight them because barbarians won't be much impressed by a sort of a gesture, a sort of a song and dance. Barbarians, the fonder they are of violence, the more they fear cowardice, and the more they fear cowardice the more they scorn it in others: I don't think the English are cowards; I do think that they just want to be left alone, and don't want to have to fight at all: nor were they given any encouragement to fight in Norway, or even, apparently, anything much to fight with. The English soldiers were in a position where, even if they had been desperate for a fight, their government had, by its indecision, so mis-managed everything that fighting was useless. When fighting is useless, a soldier who does not care to be fighting will let the thing go. The English don't care very desperately about saving their empire, but it doesn't seem sporting to let it go without a gesture. I don't know, maybe the Germans are glad about that: if it were more than a gesture, Germany would be forced to really fight and it would be too bad.

However ignominiously the English were kicked out of Norway you couldn't tell it by most of the Havana newspapers. The headlines of the *Avance*, of *El País*, of *El Crisol* and even of the more or less objective *Diario de la Marina* (which is the best paper in Havana) are all desperately in favor of England and France naturally enough. But they are so much in favor of the allies that they are completely nutty in their arrangement of the news: and, when the English were getting out of Norway as fast as they could the biggest headlines on the *Avance* and *País* said that the Germans were sur-rounded in Marvik: which they had been, as everybody knew, for the past two weeks.

The first news that the English were evacuating Norway came in *Discussion*, a little sheet as crazily pro-Nazi as the others are pro-English, in *Hoy*, which is Communist and therefore pro-Nazi, and finally, in the *Havana Post* which is the paper they publish in English.

The *Havana Post* is the only paper that is anywhere near arranging the news according to its true value and importance. Of course they all get the same news over the wires, but the others put the reliable accounts of Ger-man victories back where they won't be noticed. But even the *Havana Post*, when compared to the *New York Times* and *Tribune*, themselves also vio-lently pro-allied, seems a little extreme. After a week of Havana headlines, to see the front page of the *New York Times* getting here three days late and to see how the Germans were really getting along was enough to take my breath away! For all week long the British had been advancing and cutting off the Germans' lines of communication and sinking so many transports that no German reinforcements could get within miles of Norway: all this I had learned from the Havana papers, until suddenly the British were pil-ing into their boats as fast as they could, and beating it for home, leaving equipment and even men, not to mention the disgusted Norwegians, be-hind them.

If this sort of thing goes on I imagine Germany, if she doesn't win the war outright, will certainly turn into everybody's new hero. That is because everybody is now under the illusion that there are two alternative kinds of lives to lead in society, one democratic and the other totalitarian. And since England, a democracy, is making such a spectacle of itself, everybody is soon going to be thinking that therefore Totalitarianism is good because England looks so silly. The attitude taken by violently pro-allied papers and propaganda will only make this all the more pronounced, because people will themselves suddenly call attention to the injustice with which Germany has been treated in the headlines, and all that will add to Germany's prestige. From then on, *everything* said against Germany will be "propaganda".

Look how things come about: and what elementary ideas we have on the nature of propaganda. Everybody wants the allies to win. Therefore both the publishers like to publish news about allied victories and the public likes to read it. What is published in the paper is what everybody wants. It is a cinch that, if you want the allies to win, you will like a paper that tells you they are winning: but when, at great personal sacrifice, you finally throw away the idea that this news is true, instead of blaming yourself for deceiving yourself, you blame the paper for deceiving you with propaganda.

That is one reason why it is so silly for the allies to try to overcome Germany with propaganda, telling the Germans they are deluded by the propaganda of their own government. Nazi propaganda will not, for the Germans, become propaganda until the Nazis are defeated or fall over from their own clumsy weight. But right now I am afraid the Germans have got a Nazi government because that is what they wanted, even if they didn't think so themselves.

When it comes time for the Nazis to fall on their dumb heads, it is a cinch the Germans will not blame themselves but will blame the Nazis for what has become of Germany: but in fact the Germans themselves will be to blame because they got something they themselves wanted to the extent that they were proud and conceited and violent and pompous and cruel and cowardly and all that in their hearts. And because of all these things in our hearts, too, we get wars and revolutions all over the earth, and that is what it means to say the wars are punishments from heaven upon us for our own sins because, if we loved God more and violence less, we would not have wars and revolutions.

War is the punishment that is visited upon earth for the cowardice of mankind, because the only true courage lies in the love and the hope and the belief of heaven which cannot be shaken by any other desire. But when men renounce heaven they become aware that they have lost love and courage and wisdom and happiness, and they try to replace them with substitutes: pretending to be courageous by overrunning some little country like Poland: Poland herself having less than a year before that thrown out its chest and pretended to be one of the big warlike states by grabbing its little slice in the dividing up of Czechoslovakia. War is the punishment that is visited upon earth for the cowardice of men.

All these papers, *Avance, El País, El Crisol, Hoy, Alerta, Discusion, Luz, Acción*, and I forget what else, are hawked about the streets by the shrillest voiced newsboys I ever heard in my life: and more of them, too. They swarm out into the crowd, climb on and off the trolleys, sprint after the buses, dart in and out among the tables of the cafes, crying out like birds, like foxes, like coyotes, like leopards: in and out the newsboys bark and bay, they run singing out the names of papers, pouring out the names in a long and chattering cry or giving to the air the brass sound of a buglecall interrupted by death from an arrow in the throat as one might imagine the call of the trumpeter of Cracow if only that actual call didn't turn out to be the dull thing it really is.

Behind them come chanting the sellers of lottery tickets, going everywhere with big red numbers written out on a card stuck in a hat, or carried on a board: waving sheets of blue tickets up and down the narrow sidewalks. In and out the legs of the walkers dart begging children who will beg not only from Americans but will trot along a block beside anyone at all, holding up their little dirty hands. Infamous custom, wretched, dishonest little creatures, no doubt they rush away and squander the tourist's grudging penny on some filthy candy, gorge themselves with a penny ice as if life were meant to be all laughs and fun and pleasure!

Added to the noise of all this is the noise of almost any conversation, for conversations between more than two people are liable to involve a great amount of shouting and laughter and excitement. Then the noise of maracas shaken by some vendor: the clang of trolleycar bells, the tooting of horns the loudest of which are usually on bicycles, the noise of radios playing in the houses with their wide open doors and windows and everywhere the little clanging and clattering handbells carried by the kids who go about with a box slung over their shoulder selling some kind of frozen candy.

Incidentally all bells, these handbells as well as the bells of trolleys, get run in a clattering syncopated sort of a rhythm that might fit a conga: and even the church bells in the cathedral at Santiago would go four fast beats with the accent on the last which is fundamental to both rumba and the conga, and upon which the elegant structure of all the other proper syncopations is built up.

There is an illusion that while life in New York is agitated and noisy, life in Cuba is restful and quiet. This is not something that people believe who have never been to Cuba; it is something the Cubans themselves will tell you with the greatest seriousness, right in the middle of the noisiest moments of this very noisy city Havana. But the statement must be qualified by another, and that is that Cubans, when they speak of "quiet," do not mean the absence of noise but rather the absence of any bitterly fixed intensity of purpose, they do not mean by rest the absence of movement, only the absence of struggle. Consequently, what is considered a quiet and restful atmosphere in Cuba is one of completely reckless and giddy absence of any kind of care or responsibility. This atmosphere is certainly very gay and very crazy but is the remotest possible thing from being either silent or inert! However once this is understood it is possible to see what people mean when they say Havana is restful when New York is not. Havana is not less noisy than New York, it is much noisier. But it is less grim and less worried than New York. It is a happier place, and a prettier one and a crazier one, and strangely enough it lacks all the coarseness and brutality of New York, and lacks all the bitterness and brashness of New York and has none of the vulgarity of New York except so much as New York and Miami themselves have exported to Cuba. Havana lacks both the true tragedy of New York's relentless materialism and the phony melodrama of the people who are trying to forget that materialism in the wrong way and in the wrong places. Physically the dirt and misery of the very poor in Havana may appear to be greater, but that is because for one thing Cuba worries a lot less about dirt than New York does. It is not my job to evaluate the relation of poverty in Cuba to misery in New York: but it probably comes, physically, to the same thing since, if the Cubans have less, yet in Cuba you can live on less, and, if there is no place in New York where people go in complete rags and their children naked, it doesn't mean that the poor in Cuba are that much poorer, or have that much more trouble getting something to eat. The poverty is terrible in both places, but in New York you don't notice it so much as poverty, but rather you see the ugliness and squalor under which the poverty hides. In Cuba the poverty is out in the open, because it is that kind of a climate. And however bad the poverty is in Cuba, you lack the sense of overwhelming gloom and despair that fills whole sections of those ugly cities in the north. Even more, the cities of England than those of the United States.

I had known in a confused sort of a way that Cuba wouldn't be all rumbas. The rumba is not the national music, and the great majority of Cubans do not dance to it, or to the conga, except in polite versions which are, incidentally, very good dances. The rumba and the conga danced in the "*típico*" manner as New York night clubs know it is suspect in Cuba as being for the negroes only. The Cubans themselves play and dance to *sons* and *danzons* more than anything else. For myself I would rather dance them than anything else in the world: they are the best dances I ever tried to do, but congas are swell, too. Of course I have my own private delight in the *paso doble* which is also one of the best dances in the world.

It was not only the representatives of the Cuban government in New York who got angry at the "Cuban Village" in the 1939 World's Fair. Most of the Cubans themselves are still talking about it, and very sore, too. They are not sore about the *comparsa* or the *zapateo* or the rumba numbers: but they are about the *nanigo* stuff, but especially about the mixture of *nanigo* and Broadway, the "*sacrificio.*" That was the number that was always getting publicity because they brought out a girl with her breasts uncovered. (She was, herself, from Wisconsin.) This makes the Cubans especially furious. They are incensed to think that they should be thought to get excited over anything so infantile as a nude show. A naked woman, for a Cuban, does not constitute a show. Either she is a singer or a dancer: if she does not sing or dance, what is the use of bringing her out before the public. But if she does, then it is absurd that she should not appear in costume, because costume is very important to the dance.

The Cubans have nothing against congas and rumbas and Afro-Cuban music and dancing in general. They dance them a lot, too, but do not go crazy over them. The attitude towards them is the attitude people take towards swing music who were brought up on the early, and modified, hot jazz of Paul Whiteman. They tire of it fast, and they think the jitterbugs are crazy. In the same way in the presence of a terrifically good conga, completely overwhelming with good drums, the average Cuban either laughs as though it were good but slightly absurd, or makes a face with the same expression that asks: "Oh, do you call that music?" Their attitude towards the negroes is exactly the American attitude towards jitterbugs, which is completely unfair. Afro-Cuban dancing is maybe the best dancing of its kind in the world, and the jitterbugs are, on the other hand, completely lousy.

Marianao, eight miles out from the center of Havana, is where all the little night clubs are with the best rumba and conga orchestras.

They stand in a string, these shacks, under the trees that line the broad highway. On the other side of the road are the bath houses of the beach, a couple of yacht clubs. Further along, the Casino, which is an extremely swagger spot only I never yet got to see it. Some of the shacks are physically the same as any hot dog stand along an American road, but they sell, instead of hot dogs, *gaseosa* and ices and beer and, if you want it, Cuban rum, straight, with water on the side. But the Cubans themselves are not great drinkers even of beer. They prefer *gaseosas* and fruitjuices and coffee.

Some of these shacks are shooting galleries. A lot of them have jackpot machines: and I kept away from those, although they were quite an attraction to my friend José Luis. He would dart off with a handful of nickels, and you would hear him play three or four times: sometimes pick up a couple of nickels, but then come back making confused and embarrassed gestures.

I was lucky to have met José Luis. He was a Spaniard, and a very good guy. He worked out of a famous restaurant in the country, about fifteen miles out of the city, called Rio Cristal. The place is run by the Cristal Brewery. It is a very good restaurant, and a very pretty place, standing on the edge of a deep glen full of flowers and palm trees, and banana trees and bamboo, at the bottom of which runs a stream. There is a weir built across the stream, and it is nice to sit down there and watch the water pour over the fall. Back up the hill you can hear the music of the three musicians as they play a *danzon* for the people eating lunch on the terrace. Well, José Luis worked at this place, as a bartender. And since Rio Cristal is only open in the daytime (people do not even come out there for dinner at night), he gets off work at seven. So, since I had said something about La Playa, he said why didn't we go out there together that night.

I already knew that La Playa is no place for a stranger to try and find his way around by himself, not because it is tough or dangerous or anything like that, but because he will be cheated right and left, and probably robbed, too, what with all the dance hostesses and gyp artists and so on hanging around, and besides, I suppose prices tend to vary, and if you don't know what you are about you will go paying cover charges.

I had no way of knowing scientifically that José Luis suggested going out there out of pure friendliness: but you can tell when some one is a good guy and when he means what he says. José Luis meant exactly what he said. He liked the Playa because he had some friends out there, bartenders, and he liked to go out and talk to them, and hear music and have a beer or two. And he said we wouldn't mess around with any girls and we would get home early because he for his part had a wife and kids. We rode out on the trolley and got there around nine thirty, and went to a couple of places where José Luis had friends, and heard a lot of rumbas and congas and *sons* and *danzons*, and even saw a floor show, and got home around midnight.

We saw the floor show because José Luis had a pal called Manolo who was headwaiter at one of the bigger nightclubs there, and he gave us a table to sit at, inside it, while the show was going on. As for music, the rest of the time there was a fine orchestra playing out in the open for the people at the bar. I think one of the secondary reasons why José Luis wanted to go out to Mariano that night was that he had a big brand new photograph of his wife and little boy and himself, and he wanted to show it to all his friends. Anyway we had a fine time. It turned out José Luis had a couple of brothers who were Franciscans back in Spain.

He is a fine gay guy, and slapped his knee and laughed with great delight at the best steps in the conga they did in the floor show, but on the way back in the trolley he showed me an open air place, no longer in the Playa but among the little neat houses of Miramar, where he said they had dancing with nothing but Spanish music: this being not a night club or a cafe, but a place where there was music and an open space to dance in: and it was public. There were cafes around about. He said that when I came back from Santiago I should come and have dinner at his house, and he and his wife and I would all go out there. I am going to do my best to hold him to that promise.

The word Florida is not a particularly beautiful one in English, possibly because it assonances with horrid, and yet in Spanish it has more than a lovely sound: it has lost none of its etymological content, and still means the place of flowers. The place of flowers, not the place of Daytona Beach or Boca Raton or Tampa or Miami or Saint Petersburg or Fort Lauderdale. It is interesting the way the word Florida, and even the name Miami, is bandied about in Havana as if Florida were still a good place, the land where De Soto went off to find the fountain of youth and where he caught fever and died.

One of the best restaurants in Havana is La Florida. The bar connected with it is called La Floridita. It is a fine place, open to two streets, very busy, as popular with tourists as with the people of Havana. The tourists drink Daiquiris and planters punches (La Floridita is "the Cathedral of the cocktail and the cradle of the daiquiri") while the *Habaneros* drink beer or coffee or fruit juices. Three negroes play guitars and maracas by the door, and once in a while one of them shyly comes around with a saucer for you to put nickels in. When they play, they sit at a table. There is no special place for musicians: these occupy a table in the doorway and in between songs they lay down the maracas on the table among the waterglasses. (Note on the Florida: the Spanish word for "flowering" has come in English to have the degenerate associations the word "florid" carries with it: more than full blown, too many vulgar blooms. The cliché "a florid complexion" is used everywhere, to describe the bloated red faces of men who stuff themselves with food they don't want, like swine.)

Another of the best restaurants in Havana is the restaurant Miami, a great big place right on the corner where the Prado comes out into the Parque Central. The food there is fine, and so is the food at a smaller place just across the small square from La Floridita: and that is called Le Petit Miami.

In La Floridita they make you an orangeade with just as much care as they do a daiquiri. They ice the glass, and they shake up the orange juice with sugar and ice in a shaker (an orangeade is pure orange juice and ice and sugar), and strain it out into the cold glass. This costs a dime. I don't know how much the daiquiri would be. Probably thirty or thirty-five cents, maybe only a quarter.

The Cathedral is the only Church in Havana that has any real historical or architectural interest. It has an interesting baroque facade flanked by unequal towers, one of them rather svelte and pretty, the other heavy and squat and full of great bronze bells. The gray limestone of the front is heavily weathered, and makes the place look very ancient and gives it a distinction which makes up for the fact that it is only a very little cathedral, hiding in an old square down by the harbor mouth.

Inside, too, it gets distinction not from any special beauty of the interior, which is cruciform, regular, rather dark, not large, [but] from the wonderful rich woods of which the High Altar and side altars and choirstalls and all the furniture of the basilica are made. There is also a lot of good old silver on all the altars, which shows up well against black mahogany and caoba wood. There is nothing gorgeous about all this, but it gives the place the sort of solid seventeenth-century opulence that you find in the Jacobean wainscoted halls of English manors or certain Oxford colleges. Only I don't like to mention England this morning: the Nazis just invaded Holland and Belgium, and I suppose the English will land a completely unarmed force of about one regiment of recruits, just enough to be kicked into the sea with the greatest possible disgrace, leaving Holland full of busy Nazis establishing air bases from which England can be completely destroyed.

The little church of the Cristo, the Santo Cristo del Buen Viaje presents plain, bare, buttressed walls to the trees of the comparatively quiet square outside it, and inside it is almost as plain as a Presbyterian church, except for the rich wood ceiling which was renovated at the expense of some Irish lady in Philadelphia. The church has connected with it a college and monastery which is run by Augustinian Fathers, and hence the connection with Philadelphia, because they are from the American province (only just now have they split up into two American provinces), and therefore Americans, and I suppose most of them went to school at Villanova.

The fact that these priests are Americans, and preach with a strong American accent to their Spanish, and the fact that the church looks so much like a Protestant church, all this throws into relief the differences, the superficial differences, because they are only superficial, between the practice of Catholic ritual in America and in Latin America.

The walls of the church itself are almost bare. Above the altar is a large but plain crucifix. (The fact that the crucifix is plain does not mean that it is not realistic in the Spanish manner, and indeed it is an old one brought there by Franciscans of the seventeenth century.) The altar itself is plain, bare looking. The sanctuary is wide and empty, and on either side of it are two uninspired looking statues, one of Saint Augustine with a mitre and a great black beard, and the other of the Immaculate Conception. Then there are two side altars flanking the sanctuary on either side of a wide, round chancel arch: one is dedicated to Saint Nicholas of Tolentino, and the other – I forget.

The sermon is preached in Spanish (or the ones I have heard there have been: there are probably some Fathers who preach in English) but in a more or less conversational tone of voice, by that I mean the conversational tone an American might take, and it has none of the exalted rising and falling of the voice that makes a sermon by a Spanish Carmelite so moving. Then, again, communion is distributed as it properly should be, I suppose, during Mass itself, right after the communion of the priest. In most Cuban churches the custom is for communion to be distributed before or after the Mass at a side altar unless there is some special occasion on which a whole big group like the Holy Name Society is going to receive communion and then they have a special communion Mass for them.

In very few Cuban churches is there a stoup of holy water at the door. It is not universal to genuflect before taking a place in a pew, either. A few people do it. A lot of people, especially men, stand up when everybody in an American church would be kneeling down, as for the blessing, or from the Sanctus to the Consecration or even during the Consecration. Most people do not kneel at the Sanctus bell, but wait until the one just before Consecration. They get up again and sit down after Consecration and kneel again when the bell rings for the communion of the priest. These are some of the things they do differently in Cuba. I write them down because I myself wondered about them before I came here. Also, before beginning a confession, they say *"Ave Maria Purissima"* instead of asking for the priest's blessing. That was one of the things I wanted to know, too. Also in Cuba there is no abstinence on Fridays.

> The *canonazo* (cannon shot) fired from Morro Castle at nine p.m. is the signal for many social functions to start. A host of *Habaneros* take out their watches and set them in accordance when this shot is heard.
>
> *Terry's Guide to Cuba*

I have no watch to take out and set in accordance when this shot is heard, and for me it has not been the signal for many social functions to start, in the proper sense of the word. But by reason of this fascinating sentence I have had occasion to notice the firing of the gun off the Morro as many times as I have been within hearing of it. And every time I have been filled with a scarcely suppressed excitement, a belief that I would see, all around me, doors fly open, a host of *Habaneros* issuing on every side from the houses into the streets, people coming out and getting into cars, or marching off in couples setting their watches in accordance when this shot is heard, and hurrying to brilliant social functions which have, at that precise instant, begun.

I think the first time I noticed the firing of this gun I was walking on the Prado. I had had dinner in La Zaragozana, I had taken to smoking a cigarette, the first one in about two weeks, and was not enjoying it in the least. I had made plans to attend a show called *La Conga de Madianoche*, in the Teatro Marti, which, for some peculiar reason, was scheduled to begin at midnight and in actual fact was given much later, so that it should really have been called *La Conga de las doce treinta y cinco* or the Conga of twelve thirty-five, and as it turned out, there was not much conga to it at all. The show stank.

But to return to the question of this nine o'clock gun. By nine o'clock I had fought my way through the crowd of bootblacks and American negro pimps and small seven year old ice cream salesmen with bells and a crowd of unelegant *Habaneros* waiting to set no watch and to attend no function: I had wormed my way through this mass of people and come out at the foot of the Prado where I crossed to the sea wall and stood for some minutes reading off to myself the signs: Canada Dry, Bacardi and so on. Then I turned once again to the Prado, planning to make once again that arduous journey along that hall of lowbranched and thickset trees and perhaps to have a drink of ginger ale up opposite the Capitolio.

That was the situation when boom: off goes this nine o'clock gun with a big dull thump.

Havana made no jump; Havana behaved as if it had been clipped behind the head with no pillow; not a door was flung open, not a note of music was struck with the small iron shoe of no cane, not a watch, as far as I could see, was wound.

What social activity began for me at that precise moment?

A small boy came up to me and remarked: "Gimme one cent."

Eventually I reached one of the smart fashionable cafes opposite the Capitol, where I had a bottle of ginger ale and listened to an orchestra of cheerful female musicians, and eventually went to this *Conga de Medianoche*. At the smart cafe, at the table next to me was a man who was drunk, and looked like an American only he talked pretty good Spanish. If he wasn't American he was giving the very best imitation of an American I ever saw. He had a pair of maracas which he did not know how to play, and to everyone that went by in the crowd he gave a great, noisy, and very moist raspberry. He was accompanied by a negro dwarf about three and a half feet high, whose thick bow legs were so short that his head and hat seemed to be as big as all the rest of his body, trunk and legs. This dwarf was annoyed at the behavior of the man, but obviously couldn't do anything about it. He sat there like a person, looking strict indeed, but all the time plenty sore about this drunk, because the fact of his drunkenness only emphasized the presence of a dwarf, and the fact that the dwarf sure was a dwarf. I guess he had a reason to stay with the hog: he was probably accompanying him to a house of ill repute for a certain fee. In other words, I am endeavoring to suggest in a nice way that this dwarf had flung open his door that evening and set his watch at the boom of the nine o'clock gun for an evening at pimping among the fashionable crowds.

Another time I happened to hear the gun, its muffled report reached me a good measure further down the malecon: beyond the Hotel Nacional, in fact, beyond the Maine monument, out in the Vedado. Possibly a watch or two was wound in the cars that sped by me, but I could not see any pedestrians within a mile to see if they jumped as if stung and hurried off as if to darnce.

At this precise moment I was walking along the empty sidewalk of the *malecón* [dike], next to the sea wall, in the cool breeze that blows in at night off the Gulf of Mexico. What was I doing? If you had been within earshot you would have heard me singing the following song:

> *"Mientras cami-na-a-a-ba*
> *En las orillas del mar . . ."*
> ["While walking
> along the seashore."]

which comprises almost the whole song. It was a flamenco song all my own, and its lack of sense was amply compensated for by the extremely eloquent presence of feeling, not to mention that special force which art may always borrow from aptness: for was it not indeed true that I was at that very moment promenading upon the banks of the sea?

Right then off goes this bloody cannon: Boom down there in the dark where the feeble ray of the Morro light attempts with two stabs a minute to pierce the murky bosom of the night.

What social function was presently initiated by me under the impulse of this stirring and so significant shot? I walked for several blocks in the warm, sweetsmelling treeshaded villalighted softvoiced Vedado until I reached the intersection of L and twenty-fifth street, at which intersection, opposite the Medical School of Havana University (a little gray building that looks like a nunnery) is situated the cafe known as Las Delicias de la Medicina or the Delights of Medicine.

Here, ensconcing myself upon an iron chair on the terrace, I ordered a *coco glace* which was duly brought, spoon and all.

I am about half finished indulging my sweet-tooth with this extraordinary creole delicacy when two small girls, aged about eleven, I should judge, made a gap in the privet hedge that separates the cafe from the sidewalk, and one of them with a great deal of friendly mockery addressed me in English with the following words:

"What-is-your-name?"

"Ha ha ha" I cried with a loud larf, "Thomas. What's yours?"

"Ha ha ha" she replied, "Wednesday, no, Tuesday," and made as if to run off. But she stayed, and presently said: "My – English Teacher name is Miss Gombold."

"Ha ha ha" I larfed, believing every word, for that sentence had the true ring of sincerity. "Where do you go to school?"

"Colegio de Luz" (Loo-oo-th) she replied with what was probably a first rate parody of Miss Gombold's Spanish accent. And at this they both larfed fit to kill. Then they went away, but they soon came back, and when they did, the other little girl, who had not spoken so much before, now made me a compliment upon my personal beauty, alleging that I was very "pretty" as she was pleased to term it. I could only reply in kind, which, of course, brought on a gale of laughter and an immediate proposition of marriage, which I was unfortunately unable to accept through press of other business.

I had noticed, all along, that this second little girl wore her hair short: I mean so short that it was what we call a crew cut, and I could only conclude that her head must have been completely shaved within recent months. As it turned out, I was right, for before we parted she took occasion to recount how some time before she had been in the hospital for having fallen out of a third story window on her head which was in itself extremely remarkable. I gallantly replied that I had just had my appendix out and we parted the best of friends.

Purses and belts made out of alligator hide, and bottles of Cuban rum are not the only specialties you can buy in Havana nor are maracas (but the ten cent maracas they sell on the street are no bargain: on the other hand they aren't bought because they are maracas, but because they are round and painted red and green and have the word souvenir written all over them. They contain about ten cents worth of souvenir value, I suppose). No: but one of the good things you can get in Havana is a shoe shine. For a nickel they give your shoes the whole works, from saddle soap on up, and including a preliminary polish with a serge cloth, then a waxing over of polish, the brushes, and a high polish with a soft cloth that leaves you to go walking off with your feet flashing in the sun like swords.

In this respect also Havana is superior to New York. There is no place in New York where you can get such a shine, let alone get one for a nickel. If you have white shoes, they will work on them for half an hour for twenty cents, and give you the whitest white feet to walk away on that you ever saw. The best bootblacks are not, of course, the kids that run around on the Prado with a box slung over their shoulder, and their brown and skinny backs only half covered by a ragged shirt: the really good ones maintain great chairs under the arcades along the Parque Central between the

Teatro Nacional and Calle Neptuno. These are so good that people bring their shoes here from the ends of the city, on their way to work, and leave them to be cleaned some time during the day when there is no one in the chair. These bootblacks then are always cleaning shoes, with or without people in them.

Another good thing to get in Cuba, even better than their daiquiris, are the fruit juices and the ices. They make great orangeades of pure orange juice with sugar shaken up with ice that is wonderful to drink and makes plain orange juice taste like vinegar in comparison: and everybody knows that even plain orange juice is one of the nicest drinks in the world. They make *"refrescos"* [refreshments] out of every imaginable kind of fruit, water-melon, papaya, *mamey, ananá* [pineapple], mango everything. It doesn't matter how little liquid the fruit is: if the drink turns out to have the consistency of Cream of Wheat they still drink it and call it a drink. *Refresco de Papaya* turns out to be of that sort; orange in color it is thicker than any thick soup I ever had, as thick as wheatena, and sweetish besides. Other fruits, besides turning into just as thick a drink, also have the sort of perfumed soap taste that many tropical fruits have, and *refrescos* made of them must be an acquired taste: *refresco* of mango is the color of the yolk of a reddish egg, and a lot thicker, and tastes like a heavily perfumed paste. *Mamey* is the same: these flavors are better in ice cream, and *guanaba*, which is also fairly sticky and perfumed, makes a very good sweet ice. Iced coconut-milk made into a *refresco* is one of the best drinks in the world, and they also sell you coconut ice, served in a half coconut shell which is easily the best ice anybody ever invented, and is called *coco glace.*

Papaya, which looks like cantaloupe but does not taste a bit the same, is a very good fruit, and it is even better with the juice of lime squeezed over it. All tropical fruits are very pretty to look at. In any bar where they are making daiquiris they have piles of fragrant sharpsmelling green limes sliced up in quarters lying around on a wet board waiting to be used: and the orange-red of the inside of a *mamey* is one of the most interesting colors I have ever seen.

Coming into Havana from the sea, the most prominent things on the city skyline besides the Capitol dome (which you see for miles), and the telephone building are the towers of La Reina and Nuestra Senora del Carmen, both big churches. La Reina has a tall Gothic spire of pure white stone, the Carmen, a square colonial tower with a great statue of the Virgin on top of it. Neither church is in the old section of the city, and both are fairly new.

La Reina is quite new, having been finished some time in the twenties, but I guess the Carmen is a little older, but not much. Both are very important churches, because they are in very populous barrios. La Reina is in a crowded sort of a slum neighborhood in which a great deal of commerce is carried on in cheap, small articles under big and shabby and crowded arcades. The Carmen is in a neighborhood almost as crowded but not quite as poor, and besides, it is near the University and therefore on the edge of the prosperous suburb called the Vedado, which is a very pleasant place full of houses and gardens and shining four- or five-story modernistic apartments.

The good thing about these neighborhoods, which are both about a mile from the Parque Central, is that tourists do not frequent them, and consequently neither do the pimps, guides, sellers of French postcards and so on. I found out an easy way to escape from all that was to get on a bus and ride with it until I got in the clear. Then I could get down again and walk about the streets and arcades, among the people, with no one to bother me.

The Gothic interior of La Reina is tremendous and dark and rather cold. Every man to his own taste, but I myself have never been particularly fond of the Gothic revival. As Gothic revival goes, I suppose La Reina is a pretty good job. I like the tower all right.

The sanctuary is a tremendous jumble of precious tropical woods and stones and metals carved out into symbols of the faith which I could not disentangle and all centering around a tremendous Christ. The whole thing was designed by a Spanish Jesuit, I suppose about twenty years ago. If I look in the guidebook I know where I will be able to find the tremendous figure it cost. The whole thing was carved by Catalans and shipped over to Cuba to be put together.

This was the first church I went into in Havana. Aesthetically I am not particularly fond of it, but nevertheless the place is impressive, and its impressiveness testifies to something of great importance. It strikes the person coming into it with great force, overwhelms him and fills him with a kind of awe so that at least the artists managed to communicate a tremendous sense of the power and majesty of God. But what is more important, that sense of awe is not adventitious or facile: it is something deep and unforgettable because this church communicates a terrific sense of the reality of God's power as something that moves with deep might in the most secret places of every person's self. I can imagine people who don't believe in God being scared to death by La Reina, and not knowing by what, but if they went out angry because of that and concluded the Jesuits had designed the place out of malice with the intention of scaring comfortable and sensible materialists they would be all wrong. The impressiveness of La Reina, and the way it awes you with a sense of the reality of God's power is only one aspect of the sense of the reality of God that the Spanish possess to a greater degree than many other people taken as a whole. The example of it that Anglo-Saxons are fondest of exclaiming against is the intense reality with which the suffering of the Crucified Christ can be expressed in the religious art of Spain.

For Protestants the crucifixion soon became a very different thing than it has always been for Catholics. To begin with, the terrible sorrow of the *Stabat Mater Dolorosa* is taken away, although there is an increased stress, a return of emphasis upon the two thieves. Then the crucifixion itself becomes bloodless, and insensibly the emphasis is shifted from Calvary back to the Palace of Pontius Pilate, and to the Trial, and soon one begins to wonder about the reasons for the condemnation of Christ. One turns to the study of how He happened to get condemned, and away from the fact of His crucifixion. The reasons for the condemnation of Christ to be crucified were foolish and He Himself was, of course, innocent. But then we begin to tell ourselves, of course, it was true He was innocent: but it is quite natural that, with the set of interests there were, that needed to have Him out of the way, He got condemned: as if the interests of a couple of tribes in one of the second rate provinces of the Roman Empire had some importance of their own! From there on, the next step is easy; we proceed from examining the reasons why Christ got condemned to reflecting upon the fact that, after all, Pontius Pilate wasn't such a bad fellow: he was a gentleman, a cultivated Roman, and he *saw* that Christ was innocent, didn't he? Well, we, too, see that Christ was innocent, and by now we have come to delude ourselves that this was all that counted. He was innocent, but then, what can you do? He had all the powerful and rich Jews against him, and everybody knows you can't defend yourself if the moneyed interests are out to get you. As long as you recognize the truth, that He was innocent, that is all that is necessary, let Him die. But why should He die? Well, that is an uncomfortable sort of a thing to talk about. Perhaps no one knows. But anyway, it is obvious that is the only fitting end to a dramatic story. Imagine if He had lived to a good old age, surrounded by disciples, He would have made no more popular impression on the world than some old Greek philosopher. The question of the Love of Christ is of course in completely horrid taste, and nobody would dare mention it.

So, finally, your good comfortable Anglo-Saxon materialist comes to recognize that Pontius Pilate was really a pretty good sort. Pilate was in a ticklish position, and he got out of it after doing his best to compromise. In the end he did a rather sporting thing. He recognized that Christ was innocent and washed his hands of the whole affair. Pontius Pilate is the hero of the nineteenth century. He was a great liberal.

When the story of the crucifixion has reached such a state of distortion that its hero has become Pilate and not Christ, then naturally the blood, which Pilate tried to wash off of his hands, must not come into it at all. Calvary is off the stage, and is not talked about. It must, if possible, be kept in the background, lest by chance the prophecy be fulfilled, "they shall look upon Him whom they pierced." Remember, we have tried to wash our hands of His blood: we have recognized Him to be without guilt: now let us alone, will you?

When we try to pretend there was no blood at the crucifixion, it means not that we are humane, not that we detest sadism and the thought of cruelty, not that we are so gentle and loving in our hearts that we cannot bear the sight of bloodshed, not that we are peacemakers who would turn away from the very thought, the very picture of the spilling of blood: those excuses are all lies, and all they mean is that we, like Pilate, are ready to acquiesce in the betrayal of Christ to spare ourselves trouble or pain or discomfort. When we pretend that there was no blood at the crucifixion it means we are trying, like Pilate, to wash our hands of that blood: and that is why we admire Pilate; he did what we would have done. But before Pilate's hands were dry, the Jews had laid the heavy cross upon Christ's shoulder and were driving Him up the path to Calvary. That night He had been scourged, and He still wore a crown of thorns; He fell three times upon the road. They drove nails in His hands and feet and then, when he had died, they pierced His side with a spear. "And then came there forth blood and water."

The Spanish know very well that this was so, and the crucifixions in their churches show it. The hands and feet and side of Christ are bloody: and generally the knees, too, because they have not forgotten that He fell three times, carrying the cross. That they have such a real sense of the sufferings of Christ brings upon the Spanish peoples accusations of cruelty, and it is pointed out that they also like bull fights and cockfights, that they are cruel to animals and that they are hot blooded and violent, and their arguments end in stabbings and they fight civil wars, hold inquisitions. Sometimes it is said the keenness with which they feel the sufferings of Christ is a sort of cause of the rest of this "Spanish cruelty," sometimes that they both proceed from one cause, but in any case there is an inevitable connection between this barbarous cruelty and the bloodiness of Spanish crucifixes. The Spaniards would do well, it is invariably suggested, to forget about the sufferings of Christ and [then] they might turn out more "humane." Well, the English are humane and love animals all right, but there are more kinds of cruelty than one. There is a certain kind of beastly, ice cold English spite that goes on and on and on until it blasts and withers everything within its reach, and is as terrible a thing as any murder, and just as often ends in murder as do sudden Spanish bursts of anger. The worst of this spite, too, is that it is relentless, and never alternates with any kind of love, as sudden anger does. But then, does the brutality of German concentration camps arise out of some necessary connection with meditation upon the sufferings of Christ? Or the cruelty of Turks, or Chinese, or Japanese, or Mohammedans, or of lynch mobs in the southern states of America or other parts of the country? There is so much violence and cruelty everywhere in the world that no conclusions one may want to draw about the connection of Spanish crucifixions with Spanish "cruelty" mean anything at all.

The truth is that, at the same time as possessing a keen sense of the reality of the suffering of Christ on the cross, they have just as keen a sense of the power and justice of Christ the King, and just as keen a sense of the reality of His infinite love and mercy for us, and of the reality of the love the Blessed Virgin has for us, too, and the saints, and the angels. It is absurd to talk statistics in a case like this: but let me point out the obvious thing that nine-tenths of all the statues in any Spanish church are statues of Saints and of the Virgin or of the Sacred Heart or the Christ Child, all of which display a sense of the reality and immensity of His love, and not merely of the intense suffering He bore on account of that love.

Nuestra Señora del Carmen is a big triumphant church, with wide arches and baroque ornament and plenty of light: and the reredos behind the High Altar is particularly fine. In the middle of it is the Virgin of Mount Carmel, triumphant, beautiful, merciful, wearing a crown and carrying the Christ child, the King, Her Son. On one side is Saint John of the Cross, carrying a cross and looking up directly into the light of heaven, and on the other side is Saint Theresa of Avila, enraptured, with the dove, symbol of the Holy Spirit, flying above her. On Sundays it is crowded to the doors all morning, like all the other churches in Havana, with Catholics. Girls with black lace mantillas covering their heads, and men and children, and among them an astonishingly big proportion of beautiful people, beautiful eyes and faces, beautiful gestures, people full of joy and kindness and grace. That is the same everywhere, in every church: the Cristo, La Merced, San Francisco, or the Cathedral of San Cristobal de la Habana.

April, 1940. Camaguey

Camaguey lies in the middle of a plain, a great wide plain covered with sugar cane and pasture land and, in some places, dense tangles of uncleared thicket: not jungle, but just completely impenetrable brush about twelve feet high: the stuff seems from the road to be so thorny and so tightly interwoven that only some small animal the size of a hedgehog could get in and out of it. It would take all day with a machete to go a quarter of a mile through such stuff. It is literally as close as a fence all the way through.

Crossing the plain, you see smoke rising from behind the level line of the horizon, like smoke from a ship at sea. Presently it turns out to be the stack of a sugar central. But now and then off along the side of a field stands a row of royal palms, delicate and tall like a line of ladies at a dance. Coming to Camaguey, you see several massive and solid looking church towers, heavily buttressed, standing above the houses on the plain. It seems to be a completely colorless city and completely flat.

You are no sooner engaged in the labyrinth of narrow and twisting streets than you realize the city is not flat, either, but is built upon a slight rise, a sort of dome shaped elevation about a mile or a mile and a half long, on the highest point of which is built the great big church of La Merced with its high and massive tower. Unnoticed, along the bottom of this slight hill, a stream called the Rio Jatibonico runs through its weedy trench, half dried up and choked with rubbish. But you wouldn't know it was there.

Camaguey is an old city, and a big railway junction in the middle of a plain rich in sugar and cattle, and a city full of activity and a city full of churches. But it is the last thing in the world from a tourist resort: it is a working town. They do not know that tourists exist in such a town. If you are a foreigner they take it for granted you have come there on some job or other, for some deal with some *estancieros* [cattle ranchers] which will be consummated in the stink of cigar smoke, while their horses hang their tethered heads to the dusty street outside.

The town is full of cowboys and plantation riders and soldiers in colorless uniforms. Cowboys clank along bowlegged with boots and spurs and wide brimmed hats and faces like leather: guns in holsters hang at their belts, or machetes swing in great leather scabbards and beat against their calves as they walk. If they don't have a gun or a machete, they will have a knife in a scabbard on their hip. But far from being fierce people, they go quietly about their business in the city, and then towards nightfall ride away into the plain again.

Nevertheless this is a grimmer sort of a place than Havana. There is less noise, less laughter, less light and many more people with all their front teeth pulled out. It seems to be a Cuban failing, to have weak front teeth: you see dozens of people, young men, young women too, walking about with only two canines left sticking out of their upper gum, and all the rest have been pulled out. They do not worry about getting false teeth, and besides, that is expensive. Camaguey is an active and industrious sort of a place, but a pretty poor one, too. In fact, at first, compared with Havana it seems terribly dingy and dusty and half ruined. It seems to be a strange and shabby city: or that was the way it looked at first to me. But that was because I arrived in the evening, and the street lighting is completely rudimentary: they do have electricity: but to light the streets they hang a naked bulb, the sort that would not adequately light a large room, up on a wire every two hundred feet or so along the street, and [they] let it swing and cast its feeble light upon the street. Then the houses are dusty and the streets narrow and the dimly lit shop windows are full of no splendor but necessities, and as cheap as possible, too. With all that the place is very crowded, but not animated in the way Havana is. So naturally the first night I came there I thought Camaguey was rather dingy, and didn't know whether I was going to like it much.

Besides that, I had been depressed by a misapprehension about the Church of the Virgin of La Soledad. It is a great big important church right in the middle of the town, in the busiest part of it: but as I passed it, it was locked up (as churches in Cuba are from one until about five-thirty every afternoon), and besides, the walls were in an awful state, great patches of plaster yards square had fallen off and exposed the brick underneath. Along the walls, too, hung tatters of old posters about movies and May Day parades and workers' meetings and elections. But worst of all under the tower, inside the ground floor of the church tower itself, a man had established himself and set up a flower shop: not that the flower shop wasn't pleasant. But I concluded that the church had been closed up for good and all, this great big church to the Virgin closed up and abandoned, allowed to fall to ruins. Or maybe this was a strong Communist town, maybe they had actually gone in and shot the priests and desecrated the sanctuary and nailed up the doors. The whole thing made me feel very miserable and sick inside, and I thought that this was going to be a very unhappy and wretched place to be in: and the sooner I got out the better.

As it happens, the reason for the shabby and half ruined appearance of the outside of the church is this (I found it out in my Terry's *Guide to Cuba*, which tells you absolutely everything!): In Camaguey lived, or maybe still lives, one Sir William Van Horne, a great Canadian capitalist, a Canadian railroad man who came to Cuba and was the one who got the Cubans to build a railroad on the island. That, naturally, was a good thing, not so much for travellers as for transporting sugar and other products to the sea where they could be shipped off to foreign markets. Van Horne seems to be, from what the guidebook says about him, an interesting sort of a character, a sort of a crazy nineteenth-century capitalist with big and strange ideas and unlimited opportunities for putting them into effect, good or bad. He built himself a big house just outside Camaguey, and called it San Zenon de Buenos Aires. Saint Zeno, of course, was no saint but the stoic philosopher: and that, my God, is such a perfect symbol of everything I can think of about nineteenth-century eclecticism: it is the most completely eclectic name I can imagine. Think of how much it includes: it is full of the completely misplaced optimism of the nineteenth century, it includes admiration for Greece and for stoicism, and drags in a whole string of republican and Jacobin associations, as did the paintings of David: but then the really clever joke of tacking "San" in front of Zeno and thereby eliminating all but the quaint aspects of Spanish Catholicism, but bringing them in full force that is the mechanism of a kind of Joycean wit, and all the more forceful because after all, it reflects and openly parodies the whole Christian attitude towards pagan philosophy, since the very beginning: first Plato, then Aristotle. Saint Zeno! Then add de Buenos Aires after it: everything in that from Bernardin de Saint Pierre, the Lakeists etc. to the idea of the Englishman's house being his castle. Some name for an estate, and all the better if you imagine it as being on the gate of some little villa on Ealing Common.

Anyway, whatever Van Horne did, this name he chose for his place suggests he must have been a pretty amusing sort. The condition of the Church of La Soledad today is, it appears, due to some silly romantic notion of Sir William Van Horne's that it ought to be "saved from the restorer," or "spared by the hand of the restorer." (Note: Terry's words, concerning the quaint and antique – that is, tornado stricken – appearance of the outside of the church are: "The unusual quaintness and age-old aspect of the high-roofed structure so appealed to Sir William Van Horne that through his friend Father Marinez Saltage, the parish priest, it escaped the work of the restorer and stands as it was when completed.")

Terry says that Sir William used his influence with the parish priest, his good friend, to bring it about that the outside of the church was not touched, but left in the lousy condition in which it still is, plaster falling off the bricks into the street, dirt, half torn posters and so on. This is supposed to be quaint, picturesque, that a church should give the appearance of being about to fall down utterly into ruins. Actually the church is very solid and is not falling into ruins at all: and the next morning, when I went inside, I found the interior very beautiful and neat and clean and imposing, too, with its huge arches as massive in their construction as the arches of Roman Thermae or of some medieval citadel. But finest of all is the sanctuary, with the steps leading up to it and, behind the altar, the mahogany reredos with the image of La Virgen de la Soledad in the center, in black robes and behind glass, for it is a miraculous image.

Out of the seven big important churches in Camaguey, five are dedicated to the Virgin, and of these, four are the biggest churches there. The Cathedral, Nuestra Senora de la Candelaria, La Merced (Our Lady of Mercy), La Soledad (Our Lady of Solitude), La Caridad (Our Lady of Charity) and La Carmen (Our Lady of Mount Carmel). The other two are San Francisco and the Church of the Christo: but the three big churches that dominate the center of town, forming a sort of a triangle in which they share the whole heart of Camaguey, marking it out with their three tall towers, are the Cathedral, La Merced and La Soledad.

Of these perhaps the largest and most important is La Merced, the tower of which dominates the whole city. Next to it is a monastery which once belonged to the Order of Mercy, but which was later secularized and turned into a barracks and later left to go to ruin until the Discalced Carmelites took it over.

La Merced is another church with massive pillars and great heavy round arches made of tons of mortar and brick. Two flights of steps and two altar rails separate the sanctuary from the body of the church and lead up to the high altar itself, which is Gothic in style and full of gilt and silver and gold, too. It is quite new, since it was built to replace an older altar which a fire consumed, and it cost a tremendous sum which some lady bearing the noble names of Betancourt and Agramonte presented to the church.

The side altars are all Gothic, too, to harmonize with the high altar, and are done in coaba wood, but the figures of the various saints on each one are very poorly done: these include two unpleasant statues, one of Saint Theresa of Avila and one of Saint John of the Cross. The central figure of the Virgin on the high altar, however, is quite a good one. However, if you turn and look up into the choir loft, you can catch a glimpse of another very impressive black robed Virgin, Our Lady of Sorrows, the kind carried in Holy Week processions, standing in a glass covered niche and facing a splendid crucifix.

The monastery, which has a three-sided cloister which connects with the church, is occupied by Discalced Carmelites of the Province of Castilla la Vieja: and they are mostly Spanish, except I suppose they have some novices once in a while from Cuba: quiet and polite men in brown robes, all wearing glasses, happy to talk to anybody that comes along, and happy to show one around their monastery. They are lucky not to have been in Spain! One of them told me how many Carmelites there had been scattered or killed: it was some phenomenal number.

This monastery of La Merced in Camaguey by no means gives the appearance of a prosperous foundation. It is an old building, but in pretty good order. It has a two-storied and three-sided cloister the fourth side of which is taken up by the wall of the church. They found all the floors falling in when they came to occupy the place after its secularization, and they put in good new tile floors. The cloister is quiet and cool and pleasant, and surrounds a garden shaded by mangoes, palms, papayas and banana trees. There also grow a number of boxed plants that can be taken into the church and arranged up the flights of steps in the sanctuary to decorate the altar for a feast.

But the building is too big by far for the small congregation that lives there and takes care of it: they are only seven or eight priests and a few brothers and a novice.

That all Cuban life is public, and that privacy is completely lost in the overflowing of public life into the rooms and patios of private houses, takes all sorts of forms. Not only do people wander in and out of hotel dining rooms selling things: that is not unusual, hotels are public. Not only do small boys run in barefoot off the street into cafes and clamber up on the bar rail and ask for a glass of water (which no one ever thinks of refusing them), that is all right, bars are public, too. Not only do people throw open the shutters of their houses in the evenings and have not the slightest objection to your looking inside through one room into another and still another: the whole house has become public, and everything that goes on in it. This complete loss of privacy in the victory of public life over everything else extends to churches and confessionals: and no reason why it should not, either.

There are no confessionals with curtains and doors to them, no confessionals you close yourself up inside of or hide in. The reason for this is probably that they would be unbearably hot. The priest sits in an alcove that is open to the front, and on either side are grilles let into the side of the alcove. The penitent kneels down before this grille and says his confession through it to the priest. He is right out in the open, and in many churches the confessionals are right alongside of the pews, and I suppose if anybody wanted to listen to the confession they could probably hear most of it. Nobody is in the least concerned about it, however, and there is no reason why the average person should be. I guess if a penitent murderer wanted to confess without being overheard, he would be able to find some quiet confessional off in a dark corner of a church. And, I suppose, the nature of things in Cuba is such that, if you were really interested in your neighbor's sins, life is so public that you would know all about them long before it came time for him to go and confess them to the priest.

There are, also, altars all along the side aisles of most important Cuban churches, and these are not there for decoration alone, or for a chance passer-by to pause in front of for a moment's devotion. Mass is said, some time or another, in front of all of them, particularly in front of altars to the Virgin of La Caridad, protectress of Cuba. They have no altar rails in front of them, and are not shut off from the church in any way. If communion is to be distributed in front of one of them, a pew will serve as altar rail. They do not only say Mass up at the top of the steps in the sanctuary, but also down in the body of the church, among the people. But I suppose there is really nothing in the least uncommon or extraordinary about that in a Catholic country. And this is one of the principal reasons why they have signs on the doors of many churches in Havana to ask parties of tourists not to come blundering in before nine-thirty or ten in the morning: they are just as liable to come in a side door and find themselves right on an altar where Mass is being said, and go trampling all around it in a great state of ignorant confusion.

In La Soledad there is a negro sacristan who not only serves Mass for all the priests all morning, but takes care of the church, and so forth. He walks about very busily, wearing spectacles and a white linen suit and takes his office very seriously. One morning, after all the Masses had been said and I thought the church was completely empty, I heard a tremendous racket, shouting and imprecations and violent words going on off on the other side of the church. It was the sacristan, who was furiously bawling out a little boy who was kneeling in front of La Caridad: he had brought a crazy looking fluffy white dog in with him, and the sacristan was commanding him to get the dog out of the church, but the boy won, because a priest came along and shrugged and said it didn't make much difference. The sacristan went away very sore.

Another protest against peaceful penetration of private by public life was a discreet and humorous sign I saw in the back of a Camaguey print shop. The shop, like all other shops, stores and so on, was wide open to the street, and in the doorway a group of people stood around with their hats on the backs of their heads, talking and laughing and spitting into the gutter. Back in the shop a sign on the wall read: *"No haga tertulia en mi puerta"* meaning, more or less, "Don't obstruct my door by holding lectures and debates in it." But nobody paid any attention to that.

A proof that Camaguey is no center for tourists is the difficulty one has in buying picture postcards there. There is no sign of a card anywhere in the Hotel Camaguey, which is, in its way, famous, and is the hotel most likely to attract anyone who had come to see interesting and beautiful sights. You go from one place to another in the town, and no one has any cards. In one place they say they used to have postcards, but they forget what happened to them. In another, they bring out, not photographs, but little cards with tinted pictures of palm trees, of courtyards full of bougainvillea, or of big earthenware *tinajones* standing about by a door to catch the rain water. These cards are not postcards, but semi-precious remembrances to be carefully mailed in an envelope on somebody's anniversary, I suspect. I went to the shop of the best photographer in Camaguey finally, and there they consented to sell me some old out-of-date postcards they had lying around. They said they were planning to make some new ones soon.

The Cuban landscape is not really tropical, although Cuba is a tropical country. By way of illustration, I will now record an imaginary conversation between two persons concerning the Cuban jungle:

A: Oh boy look at that jungle over there.
B: What jungle over where?
A: Over there, them woods.
B: Oh, over there, them *trees*.

That is the sort of conversation in which one might exhaust all the possibilities of Cuban jungle as a topic for enlightened discussion.

The Cuban jungle looks like any woods you might expect to see on Long Island except that the trees are smaller, and have some moss or other parasites hanging from them in grayish streamers, and are tangled up with more underbrush: but not a different looking kind of underbrush. Also, most of it, at any rate along the railroad and the Carretera Central, has been cleared away. Or maybe I didn't see any jungle at all: maybe I am only describing what I imagine would be the nearest approach to it that I saw.

You ride along in the train, you come to a concentration of small trees and large bushes, and you say to yourself: ah, maybe this is the beginning of some jungle. Then right away the bushes thin out again, and among them you see half a dozen stray horses and cows, scattered about nibbling on the dry grass. When I say the Cuban landscape is not tropical, I mean it is not in the sense I mean it in no way resembles any pictures I ever saw of Yucatan, of Honduras, of the Amazon country, of the Congo country or anything of that sort. It does in parts resemble pictures of the grasslands of Nigeria, the Matto Grosso of Brazil, the Chaco. But where there are royal palms, it is just a nondescript landscape, fairly pleasant, of the kind one might associate with almost any part of South America. There is a whole lot of sugar cane, a whole lot of pasture land, and everywhere groups of royal palms with their graceful silvery white trunks stand around and shake their dark green heads. They are a pretty tree, and coconuts look like slatterns next to them. The land is mostly flat, except in Oriente and Santa Clara and Pinar del Rio where you get blue mountains standing in the distance like a promise of Eden.

The promise always looks better than its fulfillment. The mountains themselves are full of pretty valleys and royal palm trees and flowers, too, and streams: but from far away they really look fabulous. That is what they turn out not to be.

Another thing about the Cuban countryside is that you soon get depressed by the miserable *bohíos*, little huts thatched with palm or palmetto that stand in a stamped out dusty patch of ground where chickens scratch and naked brown kids play in the dust. These huts are where the poor live: and it is not picturesque. It is just lousy and miserable.

That is true also of the poor sections of towns like Camaguey and Matanzas and Santiago. The very poorest people live in *bohíos* in a sort of garbage dump on the edge of town. Those a little better off live in shattered stone houses among some torn up streets where pigs and chickens turn up and turn over and over the garbage in the gutter and turkey buzzards wheel in hundreds in the hot sky. Outside of Havana, the cities are made up of streets and streets of such houses, dirty little one-story houses with dust blowing in and out the door and the gray stucco falling off into the street. Nevertheless, from the attitude of the people that live there you get the impression that they find life easier and better and happier than the poor in the slums of New York. The poor in Cuba live in misery and dirt, but their poverty lacks the mental quality of despair which makes the poverty of northern cities so completely and horrifyingly squalid, crying out to heaven for vengeance. And, of course, in Cuba all kinds of fruits grow wild all year, and you never starve: nor do you ever freeze, either. It is supposed to be theoretically possible for every Cuban to get some kind of work, but that is just what people say. One thing is certain and that is that foreigners in Cuba are strictly forbidden to do any work there.

Just because the streets are dirty and channeled up where torrential rains have carved out gullies in the rainy summer time, and the houses are gray and shabby-looking in a Cuban city, doesn't mean you are in a poverty-stricken neighborhood, either: you look inside the house, and you will see the upright piano, the picture of the Sacred Heart on the wall, the clean tile floor and the cool garden where two or three young girls sit in rocking chairs, with their braided hair and their white blouses and blue skirts, their school uniforms. These are houses of middle class families not rentiers, little shopkeepers, clerks, etc., who probably have less to live on than it would take to keep from starving in a New York slum.

Matanzas was the first place where I ever slept in a room with no glass in the window. The window was high up in the bare yellow wall, so high up you couldn't see out of it. You pulled a rope and that swung open a big wooden shutter, painted dark red, that closed up the window if you wanted to shut out the light or the rain. But this was not the rainy season: that doesn't begin until the end of May.

All through the interior of Cuba the houses do not have glass windows. They are protected, on the outside, by more or less fancy iron bars. Inside, you bar the window with wooden shutters. The purpose of the shutters is not to bar people's vision that are outside: they are used to close out the hot sunlight. As soon as that side of the house is shaded again, the wooden shutters are opened. What does it matter that people passing in the street can look right through the house? It means air passes through the house, too: and also it means that your friends can see you sitting there, and stop and talk to you, while you can call out into the street without having to open windows, too. But the most important thing is for the house to be cool.

April, 1940. Camaguey

The Teatro Principal held three surprises for me in Camaguey. The first one was that the lights suddenly went up, after the movie was over, and I discovered that the audience was full of white suits and pretty dresses, and that, therefore, my dismal apprehension that the town was falling to pieces and dying of starvation had been an illusion produced by the lack of electric light in the narrow and silent streets. The third was that I discovered, from the top of the tower of La Merced, that this theater was a huge whale-backed place, one of the biggest buildings in town: the second was the most agreeable: the Mexican Vaudeville troupe of Beatriz Nolesca.

Beatriz Nolesca, the signs said, that I afterwards saw: *"bailes, arte, juventud."* Dances, art, youth. What came on first was not youth but a middle aged Mexican Panurge, and I began immediately to laugh myself silly because I could just barely understand all his jokes, so that the pleasure at being able to understand them combined with the mediocre pleasure implicit in the jokes themselves to make them sound really humorous. But he was a good guy, and looked like a Marseillais, and his humor was the rhetorical *miles glorious* [glorious soldier] stuff the Marseillais make much of. Maybe I should not apologize for laughing.

He made a speech: then came three Mexican girls that looked like kitchen maids in everything, attitude, clothes, gestures and all, and did a dance with some big earthenware plates and some Mexican music. My curiosity about Mexico began to diminish rapidly, and yet I was gaga, fascinated by this dance. This was my first night in this strange town in this strange country and I did not yet know what to make of the place or any experience that occurred in it. I was open mouthed, like a cowboy in off the plain to see this same show, and I didn't lose a gesture of the dance. I will never forget it as long as I live, it was so bad, it was so beautiful. Plates on one side, plates on the other side, they swing their heads to this side, to that side, sway, turn, plates here, plates there, smiling all the time. Tan tan tan, tan tan tan: the sort of music all tin strings and ought to have a marimba to it also! This way, that way. One girl was round faced, the other was really fat, the third was slim and had slim legs and a sort of a catlike face that was mean and pretty, and she knew she was more graceful than the others. Without there having been much clapping at all, they did a whole encore, the whole thing all over, just as a matter of routine, as if they *had* to do it twice. It was so pretty and so awful: this side, that side, turn, sway. Tan tan tan; tan tan tan. At the end they twirl around and up go their skirts like light bells around their

[blank space in the journal]

up on tiptoe legs. Ding Ding. The end. They run awkwardly off the stage. I never saw anything so lousy or so unforgettable or so fascinating. It wasn't that they danced badly. They danced very well a dance that was so bad it made you want to cry, so bad, so meaningless. Some Mexicans!

It was even worse when the plump one came running out in a tight black shortcoated furry man's Mexican cowboy outfit, so black and tight and furry it made her look like a huge mouse, and all her movements were indeed those of a giant mouse, and that was what her smile wrote all over her face:

"Now you may see that I am a giant mouse."

This was really more awful than the other, and with no good dancing to contradict the badness of the whole conception. I was transfixed by this dance: when it was over I could have wept.

Really the funny scenes were good. One of the sketches was about a machine for rejuvenating old men. This machine belongs to the owner of a beauty parlor and this panurge of a janitor who has been given half a share in it for back wages. An old woman and a young girl come in to have the girl's ninety-five year old fiance reduced to a decent age: she wants him twenty, the mother wants him thirty. The panurge, after a lot of explaining about how the machine works, goes off, and comes back driving and whipping and kicking the old man across the stage and off the other side to where the machine is. You know that the machine rings a bell every time the man in it has lost five years. The bells start, count off some sixty years, and then start going furiously ding ding ding ding ding, while panurge comes dashing back saying he can't find the switch, can't find the key to get the old man out, etc. etc. Another interpretation of Huxley's problem! Nothing is left of the old man but his black suit and hat. The reason for this is that the old man was the giant mouse dressed up in another costume. Or maybe the giant mouse was the daughter: I think not.

There was another sketch about a birthday party. The giant mouse had a birthday party. The sketch wasn't funny, but the business in it was. A girl comes in with a great white dog under her arm and hands it to the other girl as a present. The dog is really just a little too big to be handed around, and it is funny. Then they say the dog's name is *Como tú* ["Like you"] and they work that gag until it dies of exhaustion, then the dog barks and runs around and raises a lot of fuss and goes off. The real part of the sketch is to do with panurge, all gallant and important bowing and larfing and guzzling all the beer and dancing with all the ladies, each lady in turn fainting with great screams because she is overpowered by his body odor. All the darncing and fainting is very funny.

I went to see them again the second night, in a different bill, but they were not so good at all: there was something strangely disturbing in seeing those same gestures all over again even in different contexts. Both times, however, the giant mouse managed to be a giant mouse: and both times, after a dance by two girls (again with a plate, which one of them dropped, on the second night), Panurge came out and held up his hands to still the dying applause crying:

"*Muchisimas gracias, respetado público, son mis hermanas las dos.*"

"Thank you, thank you, respected public: those girls are my sisters."

I suppose Cuba is too poor for a false feast like Mother's Day to be much of a commercial success, and for that very reason, Mother's Day has actually taken in Cuba. It is really something of a genuine feast, and it is certainly a religious one. It got mentioned from the pulpit, and you could see that it meant something to everybody, too. Mother's Day is really a success in Cuba, a success which it can never hope to be in America, precisely because in Cuba it is useless to try and make it into a big advertising gag for candy and small presents, as nearly everybody cannot afford that sort of thing.

Instead of that, everybody goes to church and everybody wears a flower in his buttonhole, a red rose if his mother is living and a white one if she is dead, the red and white each having a meaning which was explained from the pulpit in the church of San Francisco. So you see everybody walking about loving their mothers: while in America the sale of candy and the amount of talk about loving one's mother is out of all proportion to the actual love that is shared between mothers and their children. On top of that comes this great commercial insult, and so many other things of the same kind, that anyone with a grain of sensibility or decent feeling begins to wonder whether the love of one's mother is not a false and shameful thing if it lends itself, without any protest, to the exploitation of charlatans. One immediately wonders why, if Americans really do love their mothers, they should tolerate for an instant that that love should be made a great buffoonery, and Mother's Day is so cynically exploited in America that it is a perfect scandal: it makes people who really do love their mothers almost ashamed of that love on Mother's Day if they happen to be sensitive to charlatanry at all. I do not insist that a half a million other perfectly happy people can love their mothers and go on loving them without being corrupted by Mother's Day, and even giving Mother's Day presents out of love and not out of compulsion or false emotion. But all that does not apply to Cuba. And probably if the truth is known they do really love their mothers in Cuba, and that is why Mother's Day is a commercial failure there, but at the same time a great moral success.

This is not to say that there is not as much sentimentality about mother-hood in Cuba as there is in America, but even then, the sentimentality in Cuba is rather more sound and fundamentally closer to a more important kind of truth about motherhood. Take the front pages of the *Havana Post* and *El País* on Mother's Day, 1940. Of course most of the page is taken up by the German invasion of Belgium and Holland, a thing which demonstrates clearly that Hitler is diabolically inspired, is making war sheerly for its own sake, not even for the sake of conquest, but as an end in itself, his purpose being not to beat England and France without getting America in it, but, on the contrary, to get the whole world in the war again, to make sure the thing is really universal. Germany's defeat does not matter, because he will then have ensured the destruction of the whole earth besides: it is a fundamentally diabolical instinct for mass suicide. However, to get back to Mother's Day: the Dutch news cannot keep from the front page a certain tribute to motherhood: and it took typical forms in one paper and the other. In the *Havana Post* it was of course the silver haired old lady, sitting hunched up in a chair in a foggy, blurred sort of atmosphere so that you cannot see any of her features. That is the usual American version. Mother is wrinkled and frail but brave enough to bake a pie at the drop of a hat, and what America is really talking about all the time is grandmother-hood. Cuba, on the other hand, is not, and that is what makes Cuban Mother's Day one stage less remote from the truth than the American Mother's Day: I therefore propound this rule:

Rule: When the Cubans talk about Mother's Day and the love of mothers, they really mean mothers and not grandmothers: and also they really mean love, and not presents.

This is a fairly good thing.

Therefore the picture on the front of the *País* was under a headline saying: "*Las Madres, fuente de la vida*" or mothers the fountain of life, and showed a picture of a young mother with a lot of children around her, a very clear picture of a mother and her children all happy and smiling and having their arms around each other. Not a wrinkled up sweet old lady with no children, but mothers in as much as they are mothers, the source of life, not fountains of cookies and brownies and inexhaustible supplies of apple pie such as Cushman cannot hope to imitate. The sentimental reverence for fountains of life can also unquestionably be overdone, but it is so much harder to overdo something that after all has such a real importance! Life is one thing and apple pie quite another.

April 18, 1940. Camaguey, Cuba

This modern rat-race civilization having lost, at the same time, its respect for virginity and for fruitfulness, has replaced the virtue of chastity with a kind of hypochondriac reverence for perfect, sterile cleanliness: everything has to be wrapped in cellophane. Your reefers come to you untouched by human hands. Fruitfulness has no more meaning but has degenerated into a kind of sentimental and idolatrous worship of sensation for its own sake that is so dull it makes you vomit: the fat blondes in the dirty picture magazines are getting bigger and fatter and more rubbery, and all the people who think they are so lusty are really worshipping frustration and barrenness. No wonder they go nuts and jump out of windows all the time: such contradictions are completely unbearable and cannot be replaced by a lot of mental and sexual gymnastics, the way the mental cripples who have been psychoanalyzed seem to humbly believe.

There is more talk about Peace, Life and Fertility now than at any other time in the history of the world, especially, of course, in Germany and Italy (The Italian Fascists all talk like shrivelled up old men, mumbling between their gums, "Life, Life, Youth!") and at the same time the people who yell loudest about all these things are clearly responsible for the worst war that was ever heard of, and are also busy putting out of existence in lethal chambers everybody that has gone crazy as a result of this kind of thinking (gone crazy, that is, without getting into the government).

April 29, 1940

The complete interpenetration of every department of public life in Cuba, the overflowing of the activities of the streets into the cafes and the sharing of the gaiety of restaurants by the people in the arcades outside, also applies to churches. There, the doors being open, while Mass is going on you unfortunately get all the noise and activity of the street outside going on, too: the clanging of the trolleycar bells, the horns of the buses and the loud cries of the newsboys and the sellers of lottery tickets. Outside the church of Saint Francis the Sunday I was there, a seller of lottery tickets was going up and down and shouting out his number with the loudest and strongest voice in the whole of Cuba, and Cuba is a country of loud voices. It was a fine sounding number, four thousand four hundred and four:

Cuatro mil cuatro cientos CUA-TRO,
Cuatro mil cuatro cientos CUA-TRO

and so he went on, adding some half intelligible yell now and then that had something to do with Saint Francis: probably that Saint Francis liked the number, too. *Cuatro mil cuatro cientos CUA-TRO!* You could hardly hear the communion bell.

All that is, perhaps, unfortunate. It is a shame that a lot of noise from the streets should fill churches during the consecration of the body and blood of Christ, but after all it doesn't really make a tremendous amount of difference. It is unimportant because, after all, a person who is following the Mass is not distracted by it, and forgets about it altogether. Or if he is unfortunate enough to be distracted by it, it means that through some deficiency of his own, some lamentable lack of patience, some selfishness or other, he is preventing himself from following the Mass and is only thinking about himself.

And is it worse for there to be noise outside in the street than it is for there to be inattention and impatience and hearts and minds locked up against the sacrifice of the Mass inside the church itself? Which of the two dishonors Christ more? Is it a bigger shame that people should go about making noise in the streets, or that people inside the church should forget that Mass is going on and get angry at the people who are making the noise outside? But the problem doesn't really arise, because you soon cease to pay any attention to the noises in the street. Havana is so full of street noises, and they penetrate everywhere, everybody is used to them.

As I came in the front door of San Francisco, a crowd of children, from the school I suppose, filed in one of the side doors two by two and began taking their places in the front of the church until gradually the first five or six rows were filled. Mass had already begun, and the priest was reading the epistle. Then a brother in a brown robe came out, and you could see he was going to lead the children in singing a hymn. High up behind the altar Saint Francis raised his arms up to God, showing the stigmata in his hands; the children began to sing. Their voices were very clear, they sang loud, their song soared straight up into the roof with a strong and direct flight and filled the whole church with its clarity. Then when the song was done, and the warning bell for consecration chimed in with the last notes of the hymn and the church filled with the vast rumor of people going down on their knees everywhere in it: and then the priest seemed to be standing in the exact center of the universe. The bell rang again, three times.

Before any head was raised again the clear cry of the brother in the brown robe cut through the silence with the word *"Yo Creo . . ."* "I believe" which immediately all the children took up after him with such loud and strong and clear voices, and such unanimity and such meaning and such fervor that something went off inside me like a thunderclap and without seeing anything or apprehending anything extraordinary through any of my senses (my eyes were open on only precisely what was there, the church), I knew with the most absolute and unquestionable certainty that before me, between me and the altar, somewhere in the center of the church, up in the air (or any other place because in no place), but directly before my eyes, or directly present to some apprehension or other of mine which was above that of the senses, was at the same time God in all His essence, all His power, God in the flesh and God in Himself and God surrounded by the radiant faces of the thousands million uncountable numbers of saints contemplating His Glory and Praising His Holy Name. And so the unshakeable certainty, the clear and immediate knowledge that heaven was right in front of me, struck me like a thunderbolt and went through me like a flash of lightning and seemed to lift me clean up off the earth.

To say that this was the experience of some kind of certainty is to place it as it were in the order of knowledge, but it was not just the apprehension of a reality, of a truth, but at the same time and equally a strong movement of delight, great delight, like a great shout of joy and in other words it was as much an experience of loving as of knowing something, and in it love and knowledge were completely inseparable. All this was caused directly by the great mercy and kindness of God when I heard the voices of the children cry out "I believe" in front of the altar of Saint Francis. It was not due to anything I had done for my own part, or due to any particular virtue in me at all but only to the kindness of God manifesting itself in the faith of all those children. Besides, it was in no way an extraordinary kind of an experience, but only one that had greater intensity than I had experienced before. The certitude of faith was the same kind of certitude that millions of Catholics and Jews and Hindus and everybody that believes in God have felt much more surely and more often than I, and the feeling of joy was the same kind of gladness that everybody who has ever loved anybody or anything has felt; there is nothing esoteric about such things, and they happen to everybody, absolutely everybody, in some degree or other. These movements of God's grace are peculiar to nobody, but they stir in everybody, for it is by them that God calls people to Him, and He calls everybody. Therefore they do not indicate any particular virtue or any special kind of quality: they are common to every creature that was ever born with a soul. But we tend to destroy their effects, and bury them under our own sins and selfishness and pride and lust so that we feel them less and less. And when we do get struck with a strong movement of God's Grace, if He means to be particularly merciful, it shows us all the horror of our sins more clearly than we ever saw them before, by comparison with the effects of this mercy. The unhappiness of our sins shows up with all the more ugliness compared with the beauty of the joy we feel for one instant of God's Grace.

May 8, 1940. Havana, Cuba

Last night I was scared right out of a movie by an English picture that was so vile I am convinced England is done for forever. Although the picture has nothing to do with war, it is such a failure that it makes it totally comprehensible that the English should have failed in everything else they have undertaken in the political sphere also. It was Merle Oberon in *Over the Moon*.

Underneath the chirping, surface gaiety and self-possession of the lines (I have nothing against Merle Oberon), and the idea is the inhuman frigid cheapness of Tit Bits, Pantomime Choruses and all kinds of poor, frozen Cockney bravery that all cries out for vengeance because it was produced by the grinding materialism of the worst industrial slum-civilization that has ever yet been seen on the face of the earth. It is the cheerfulness of a people that have had all the life ground out of them, and are dead beat except for this heart-rending and useless birdtalk bravery! Those pitiful stiff upper lips and toothless smiles of the English working class!

May 21, 1940. New York

The room I had in Havana, in the cheap hotel up by the University, had a hard bed which frequently collapsed. It was on a corner of the building and windows opened, one towards the fake Columbia of the University, the other towards the Calle San Lazaro. Through that other came the reflection of the tower of Neustra Señora del Carmen, and the great statue of the Blessed Virgin was caught in the mirror of my wardrobe, and I could look at it when I woke up in the bed, reflected there, with the sky behind it unusually white in the glass.

I have been cleaning my stuff out of a room I had on Perry Street. I lived in it all winter, sitting at the desk, spending more time in it than in any other room I ever lived in, for the same period of time.

What was I doing?

Going through the *Spiritual Exercises* of Saint Ignatius.

Correcting papers written by my English Class in Columbia Night School: "My Favorite Movie Star." "Is It Possible to Be Happy without Money?"

Lying on the bed with five or six stitches in my jaw where a wisdom tooth had been torn and hammered from the bone: the sweet smell of Gilberts antiseptic filled the whole place for weeks afterward. As a consolation, I feebly turned over and over the pages of travel folders about Mexico, Cuba, Brazil. (I knew all along I would only be able to afford Cuba.)

Most of the time wrote and wrote: a Journal, longhand, in a ledger. A novel that has perplexed three publishers without any result. And also I read. Pascal, *The Little Flowers* and *Rule* of Saint Francis; Lorca; Rilke; *Imitation of Christ*; Saint John of the Cross and also William Saroyan, when I was too tired to read the hard stuff.

The world has become altogether too desperate for the writing of Auden, MacNeice and Day-Lewis to seem of any account. They were all right so long as we weren't quite sure whether we had nothing more to worry about than an economic crisis.

Now that it turns out that it isn't just a sickness of our bank books and time clocks, but a real plague and a real deluge moral, spiritual, physical, every other way: they get to look terribly thin.

I make an exception for Spender. I read something he wrote for Manuel Altolaguirre and it seemed pretty good.

It is said that while the Germans were desecrating a church somewhere in Poland, some German sergeant, cockeyed with the excitement, stood up in front of the altar and yelled out that if there was a God He would want to prove His existence at once by striking down such a bold and important and terrifying fellow as this sergeant. God did not strike him down. The sergeant went away still excited, and probably the unhappiest man in the world: God had not acted like a Nazi. God was not, in fact, a Nazi, and God's justice (which everybody obscurely knows in his bones, no matter what he tries to say he thinks), is inexpressibly different from the petty bloodthirsty revenge of Nazis over one another.

God, according to His inscrutable will, does occasionally strike such fools down: but who was struck down at the crucifixion of Christ? Christ's passion and resurrection are greater than any imaginable miracle, and Christ's transubstantiation into the bread and wine of the Blessed Sacrament is far more miraculous than God's striking down somebody who desecrates that Sacrament: it is a far greater and more terrifying thing that Christ in the Sacrament should *submit* to desecration.

Nobody was struck down on Calvary. The heavens split and the veil of the temple was rent and the earth shook, but all for those of us who are weak in faith, and who of us isn't? But who was struck down? The Pharisees? Was Judas blasted by lightning or did he go and hang *himself?*

The most terrifying thing that happened on Calvary was not that the earth was shaken to its foundations, but that the Son of God cried out "My God, my God, why hast Thou forsaken Me!"

May 26, 1940

The cause of England in this war can be said to be just only in-so-far as it is somewhat less unjust than that of the Nazis, who quite clearly wanted the war, and started it, and England has a natural right to defend herself. She has been attacked, yes, and she is defending herself it is true. Whether what she is defending is, in any other than a very superficial sense, just, is quite another matter.

And if we go into the war, it will be first of all to defend our investments, our business, our money. In certain terms it may be useful to defend all these things, an expedient to protect our business so that everybody may have jobs, but if anybody holds up American business as a shining example of justice, or American politics as a shining example of honesty and purity, that is really quite a joke!

And if this is a joke, it is also a bit blasphemous to get up and say that just because Germany started the actual fighting, ultimately Germany is to blame for everything, and God is on the side of England and the democracies and all enemies of Germany. That would make God the defender of more kinds of dishonesty and trickery and avarice and bribery and hypocrisy than a person with a tender conscience can bear to think of.

To try to make God the defender of any one side in this war is simply to reduce Him to the level of a Nazi, and no greater blasphemy is possible, but, besides that, it is irrational to the point of lunacy.

We know the Nazis half expect, from moment to moment, to be struck down by fire from heaven, because they have an ineradicable suspicion that there is a God somewhere, and if there is one, He must be like a Nazi, and ready to destroy even His friends at the first sign of anything that displeases Him.

But the tragedy is that the English and Americans and all the others are also disappointed because God is not a Nazi. Because if God were a Nazi, at the first false step of the Germans, their entry into Czechoslovakia, He would have blasted them into atoms for violation of an agreement.

If God allows the Nazis to attack England, and even beat her, it is precisely because He is not a Nazi. If He were a Nazi, the Nazis couldn't win.

As soon as we forget that God's justice is not the justice of a tough, erratic and rather venal police sergeant, but that it is synonymous with His love, we become incapable of understanding anything about God, because we are thinking no longer of Christ, but of Thor, or Odin.

The justice of a barbarian deity is not in the least inscrutable, although it may be a little crazy at times: but you do something that offends Him, and He breaks your neck. But the justice and love of a God who dies for those who offend Him, on a cross, the death of a slave, is totally inscrutable, and is to be adored and imitated before it can be understood, because it can only be understood when it has been to some extent imitated and loved.

But if God *were* just only in the sense that a cop is just: that is, you offend against his book of rules, and he arrests you: then instantly he would strike us all down for the very blasphemy of comparing him to an ordinary human policeman!

If God were a storm trooper, there wouldn't be a single storm trooper left in Germany. Berlin would be ashes.

Instead, some, not all, of the churches in Poland are ashes.

However, to say that God is punishing the Church is far worse than imagining that He ought, right now, at our wish, to punish the Nazis. God does not punish the Church: He punishes sinners – and how He does we cannot very well conceive. Wars, plagues, famines have something to do with His punishment, not so much because they are the punishment itself, but because they are warnings of the eternal punishment to come. Christ said of all these things:

"It shall happen to you for a testimony" (Luke, xxi. 13) and Saint Gregory the Great makes the comment that all these tribulations merely point to the Last Judgment and the tribulations in eternity for those who never consent to love God, but willingly cut themselves off from Him.

"Ultima tribulatio multis tribulationibus prevenitur; et, per crebra mala quae preveniunt, indicantur mala perpetua quae subsequentur." ["The final tribulation is preceded by many tribulations; and by the frequent evils which go before are shown the perpetual evils which are to follow."]

It is conceivable for instance that God's punishment of the earth should operate in some strange manner in which those who hate Him are allowed to torture and kill those who love Him and whom He loves: that is, the poor and the holy. For in this the Crucifixion of Christ is reenacted because, when He was crucified, He even bore the punishment and the suffering of those who murdered Him! He even bore the punishment of Judas, if Judas himself had willed to ask for forgiveness: but even after the betrayal Judas was only damned by his own despair, and therefore took the punishment upon himself.

It is even conceivable that God should let the whole Church suffer crucifixion as the world's "punishment" before the last day, that is, the world would crucify the Church, and the Church suffer in this crucifixion once again for the salvation of the world.

For Christ suffers in the Church: and there is nothing suffered on earth that Christ Himself does not suffer. Everything that happens to the poor, the meek, the desolate, the mourners, the despised, happens to Christ.

The only thing that can save us is an army of saints – and not necessarily Joan of Arcs or military saints. Where will they come from? Nobody can really say, except those who think about it seem to believe (like Maritain) the saints will come from the poorest of the laity, from the depths of the slums, from the concentration camps and the prisons, from the places where people are starving, bombed, machinegunned and beaten to death. Because in all these places Christ suffers most. Maritain adds, I think, that they will also be found in a few religious orders – the contemplative ones.

And the rest of us, what should we do? Fall down and pray and pray over and over to God to send us saints!

May 27, 1940. New York

I was reading a Paris letter in a copy of the *Partisan Review*, maybe a year old. It dealt with a whole lot of personalities and issues nobody had ever heard of except the writer stopped to sneer at Cocteau's *Parents Terribles*, which I haven't read. He covered himself up with elaborate protestations that he wasn't criticizing Cocteau on moral grounds, indicating that he knew the argument that says a work of art should be judged in its own terms, and then went ahead and criticized the play on political grounds, which is an even worse mistake. He never got around to talking about the play in its own terms at all. Which all goes to show that the people on *Partisan Review* have read a little more than the ones on *New Masses*, and know what is good taste and what is intellectually fashionable, and write a little more subtly, and yet make just as big mistakes, if not bigger ones, all the time.

But the most interesting thing in the letter was some grief over the fact that some idiot French Fascist had mutilated a statue by [Jacob] Epstein. Epstein must think by now that he is a very important artist, the way people make demonstrations over his statues: and that is very unfortunate, because he isn't much of an artist at all.

But there you are. Epstein is a Jew. Nazis hate Jews. Communists hate Nazis. Nazis hate Epstein, therefore Communists love Epstein because the Nazis hate him. French Fascists hate Communists, Jews, Epstein, and particularly Epstein's latest statue, which French Communists are thereby furiously prompted to love. If either side ran across the statue in a warehouse, with no label on it, and if they had absolutely no means of knowing who had made the thing, they probably wouldn't know whether they liked it or not. They would remain speechless. They wouldn't have a judgment.

This is called the Proletarian Theory of Art.

When the Fascists mutilated that statue, the Communists scream as if it were their own flesh. They explained their scream as the evidence of their horror at seeing art so despised and desecrated. However, if it happened to be the best picture of the year, but was signed Giorgio di Chirico, and somebody threw a brick through it, then your Communists would remain miraculously calm in the presence of something unpleasant happening to a work of art. In fact, you would probably find one of them had thrown the brick.

And, as a matter of fact, this same letter that laments the mutilation of the Epstein statue gloats over the fact that Chirico is supposed to be in trouble in Rome, with his bosses. Sure! They are just crazy about art, those boys! They judge it in its own terms!

And yet the *Partisan Review* is at least an important magazine: it is one of the only ones left in the country that, with all its mistakes, at least has something to say!

May 28, 1940

I am in no mood to read [Thomas Mann's] *The Magic Mountain*, which is the kind of book I find tedious anyway. I am only willing to be excited by its metaphysical symbolism and analogies if the elementary level of the book, the surface of meaning, is also interesting. But when the surface is as tedious as this, I don't feel much like going below it.

The book is full of characters that use expressions like "Sapristi" and "Sapperlot." You find sentences like "Doesn't your monism rather bore you?" and "What about quietism, a religion that numbers Fenelon among its disciples?" Then, with their mouths full of "chocolate-filled layer cake," they ask one another "fondly":

"Is time a function of space, or space of time? Or are they identical? Echo answers."

When echo answers, I lose interest. Metaphysics isn't any fun if it is all *sapristi* and very heavy clichés and very slow, self-satisfied speeches, and elaborate German witticisms as light as bricks. I will admit that the book is more interesting than the Princeton Senior Poll of student opinion about the universe, but not much more.

However, I like the point about the air on the mountain, or as much as I stopped to get of the point. The mountain air is good for tuberculosis: that is, it stimulates the disease, and forces it to declare itself, and after a certain point, checks it and helps it. So Hans Castorp, who thinks he is well, is seduced by the Circes of philosophy in this Berghof to stay around until the disease also declares itself in him. Well, that is good. And I suppose there are a lot of other analogies in the book that are interesting in the same way. The application of this to the world outside is, of course, obvious.

I am also willing to admit that all these people exist, since Settembrini obviously designed the Italian Pavilion at the World's Fair. But just because they exist doesn't mean that Mann has written about them very interestingly, or not to me. Anything that exists can be written about: but the mere fact that it exists isn't enough to make the subject of a book interesting.

The mixture of materialism, disease, disinfectants: the atmosphere of inner corruption and outward spotlessness: all that fascination for nightmare romanticism, pommaded moustaches, the tomb and military honor and afternoon coffee: all those exercises, *Geheimrats* [secret meetings], stiff collars, heavy meals, Sanskrit verses, moustached Russian women, amateurs of optics, botany and gooseliver, all these things would make a very interesting combination to anybody who was less complacent about them than Mann, who really doesn't see anything more dangerous in all that than Sinclair Lewis saw in Babbitt.

All the material in the book is important. That damp tubercular mountain, with its microcosm on top of it, faces the flat plains of Germany and Latvia and Poland and Russia, the places where the barbarian invasions have always come from, and that is what the book is all about. A record of the barbarian invasion up to the time of the last war, or whenever it was.

And still it is tedious.

May 30, 1940. New York

Instead of having faith, which is a virtue, and therefore nourishes the soul and gives it a healthy life, people merely have a lot of opinions, which excite the soul but don't give it anything to feed it, just wear it out until it falls from exhaustion.

An opinion isn't one thing or the other: it is neither science nor faith, but has a little bit of either one. It is a rationalization bolstered up by some orthodoxy which you happen to respect which, naturally, starves the mind instead of feeding it (and that is what people who have no faith imagine faith does, but they don't know what they are talking about, because faith is a virtue and active habit which cannot even pretend to rationalize anything: it seeks what is beyond reason).

In this situation, where there are hundreds of people with no faith, who don't really believe anything much, long inquiries are constantly being carried out as to what various persons "believe." Scientists, advertising men, sociologists, soldiers, critics, are all asked what they believe inasmuch as they are scientists, advertising men, etc. Apparently there is a separate belief appropriate to every walk of life. Anyway, they all answer with brisk one thousand word articles stating some opinion or other that they have picked up somewhere. The result is enough to make you break down and sob.

H. G. Wells has tried to spend his whole life telling people "what he believes," that is, trying to get them to accept his own confused opinions about the purpose of human life, if any. Since, from what I hear, he isn't even a particularly good scientist, he hasn't even got the basis he thinks he has for all his other statements: but even if he were a good scientist, his science isn't a sufficient basis for the metaphysical and moral statements he tries to make. At the same time he complicates his position very curiously by denying that metaphysics or morals are really relevant at all. His life work would be a spectacular failure if there could be anything spectacular about someone so completely unimportant as H. G. Wells.

It should be the great pride and strength of every Catholic that we have no ready, ten-minute, brisk, chatty answer to the question what we believe, except in the words of the Apostle's Creed which are not really comprehensible to scientists anyway. It should be our greatest strength that we don't have, on the end of our tongues, a brief and pithy rationalization for the structure and purpose of the whole universe, only a statement that, to a scientist, is a scandal: an article of faith. God created the world and everything in it for Himself, and the heavens proclaim His glory. It should be our greatest strength that we don't have any rationalization to explain the war "scientifically" and have no "scientific" solution to all our economic problems.

The greatest weakness of Marxists, for example, is the readiness with which they can explain absolutely anything in brisk and chatty and pseudo-scientific terms. They have not yet begun to feel ridiculous since their explanations have taken to contradicting themselves completely from one day to the next: they still believe that they are being scientific. Surely, the faith that science can contradict itself and still be science is a faith that doesn't honor science at all, because the only value science pretends to have is that it is certain and cannot contradict itself.

Faith on the other hand is always contradicting itself, because everything we say about God is so inadequate that it always runs us head first into a paradox.

In certain things, it is even more the glory of the Catholic than that of the skeptic to say "I don't know."

As a matter of fact, the true skeptic doubts in order that he may know. If there is no other certainty, he doubts so as to reduce everything to the level of his own, human, and fallible notions of certainty. But a Christian believes in order to submit all the products of his own fallible judgment to the test of a revelation that is infallible and divine and eternal – as obscure as it is infallible, obscure and mysterious because it is as simple as it is divine.

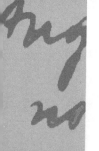

PART III

Saint Bonaventure's, New York

June 1940–December 1941

Renaissance
War Lord.

The French have been driven south to the Loire, and all my friends have gone to the lake, and I am sitting by myself in the middle of the driveway outside the cottage, looking at the woods.

Just because nobody I ever knew wanted a war, I imagined the Germans didn't either, and all the time they wanted nothing else. No, not all of them. But you hear of the tremendous enthusiasm of some of the German troops in this fight: they like it, and that is why they are winning. Nobody else likes war.

Here it is very quiet and sunny. In front of me there is a bush covered with pale white blossoms that do not smell of anything much. Somewhere under some thorns and weeds a cricket sings drily. Everything is quiet and sunny and good, but I am tempted to make no sentimental comparisons between this and the valley of the Loire.

It is possible to imagine a man coming silently out of these woods into the open grass space before me and aiming a gun and shooting me dead in this chair, and going away again.

Even though there is sunlight, the woods might well fill, all at once, with the clack and roar of tanks. The airplane that went by an hour ago might have been filled with bombs, but it just wasn't. There is nothing too fantastic to believe any more, because everything is fantastic. There is no fighting here now, but there could very well be plenty tomorrow.

The valley is full of oil storage tanks, and oil is for feeding bombers, and once they are fed they have to bomb something, and they generally pick on oil tanks.

Wherever you have oil tanks, or factories, or railroads or any of the comforts of home and manifestations of progress, in this century, you are sure to get bombers, sooner or later.

Therefore, if I don't pretend, like other people, to understand the war, I do know this much: that the knowledge of what is going on only makes it seem desperately important to be voluntarily poor, to get rid of all possessions this instant. I am scared, sometimes, to own anything, even a name, let alone a coin, or shares in the oil, the munitions, the airplane factories.

I am scared to take a proprietary interest in anything, for fear that my love of what I own may be killing somebody somewhere.

Even then, though, property is not the only thing wars are waged for. There are more than economic reasons for this one, obviously. The Germans are fighting because Hitler and some lunatics like him thought the French and English were persecuting them – and also because they had an idea they could beat the English and French and beat them badly, and thoroughly insult them afterwards, too.

The war is going on because the Germans were once scared and depressed and confused and full of hatred. Economic motives increased all these unpleasant emotions, but were not their only motives. Nevertheless, as long as the world is interested in nothing more than the exploitation of economic forces, all we are going to get is one terrific war after another until there aren't any but the most primitive economic resources left to exploit!

When the Germans say they are fighting for goods, and raw materials and for "*Lebensraum*" and colonies, none of these are the real reasons for their going to war with such enthusiasm, because, as a matter of fact, in the same breath they claim to be idealists, and say that only the dirty capitalist democracies would fight for such base things as money, goods, raw materials, etc.

I am not sure even the Germans themselves know why they are fighting. But children do not bully one another for economic reasons, and the Nazis and Fascists long ago announced they loved killing simply for its own sake!

June 25, 1940. St. Bonaventure, New York

All the papers tell how some cloistered nuns in New York are praying continually for peace in a novena beginning last Sunday, and, of course, all Catholics should be praying every minute for peace: but we are not. It is astounding how little we do, we who are supposed to believe that God hears and answers our petitions: we don't even ask Him anything, or when we do, it is something completely selfish. If a person prays an hour a day, it seems tremendous: he begins to think himself a monster of asceticism.

Mass once a week is the bare minimum of prayer, for avoiding utter damnation, but Mass so seldom as this becomes nothing but a helpless pause in the middle of a succession of brutal desires and actions, and it is a miracle, with so few people praying even that much that the world has any virtues at all! It is a miracle that the Battles of Flanders and France, instead of lasting a month or so, are not going on and on until every last man is wiped out. It is astonishing that, being the way we are, there should be any peace at all, on earth. But the answer is not in our wills, in our souls: it is in the weakness of our bodies.

Our bodies collapse, now, even in the anticipation of battles. Armies are full of young men going mad, even before they are blown to bits, or merely shell-shocked. This is the only reason why they don't go right on fighting until they wipe out everything: their nerves break down first, they collapse from exhaustion, and have to pause, from time to time, and recover.

Nobody wonders that those people never pray who don't believe in anything, but who lead their lives according to some obscure and arbitrary system of instincts and superstitions and rationalizations and prejudices and animal desires and social inhibitions. But the Catholics who are supposed to believe in the efficacy of prayer, and yet lead their lives by those same standards, and hardly ever pray at all, they are the ones that ought to be terrified, because they will be held responsible for what is happening, too! They are a stumbling block to the others, who only see in them rather cruder and poorer and less intelligent and more plebian versions of themselves!

We have no peace because we have done nothing to keep peace, not even prayed for it! We have not even *desired* peace except for the wrong reasons: because we didn't want to get hurt, we didn't want to suffer. But if the best reason we have for desiring peace is only that we are cowards, then we are lost from the start, because the enemy only sees in our cowardice his first and most effective weapon.

If we are ever going to have peace again, we will have to hate war for some better reason than that we fear to lose our houses, or our refrigerators, or our cars, or our legs, or our lives. If we are ever to get peace, we have got to desire something more than reefers and anaesthetics: but that is all we seem to want: anything to avoid pain.

It is terrifying that the world doesn't wake up to this irony: that at a time when all our desire is nothing but to have pleasant sensations and avoid painful sensations there should be almost more pain, and suffering and brutality and horror, and more *helplessness* to do anything about it than there ever was before!

June 28, 1940. St. Bonaventure, New York

What (besides making lists of the vices of our age) are some of the greatest vices of our age?

To begin with, people began to get self-conscious about the fact that their misconducted lives were going to pieces: so, instead of ceasing to do the things that made them ashamed and unhappy, they made it a new rule that they must never be ashamed of the things they did. There was to be only one capital sin: to be ashamed. That was how they thought they could solve the problem of sin, by abolishing the term.

Another vice of the last hundred and fifty years has grown out of all the facile rationalizations of cyclical movements in history, leading to the belief that with every new year we were witnessing the return of some pattern of events that had already taken shape once before in history. Now that we have got back to the rebirth of Druidism, the fall of Rome, the new Golden Age, and the plagues of Egypt, the whole thing is too complicated for anything but total destruction.

We are developing a new superstition: that people who think too much about a certain disease will give it to themselves by suggestion: we get ulcers from worrying about them. If we don't worry about them, says the converse of this argument, we won't get any diseases.

We have another superstition, like this one. If we all agree that war is unpleasant, and that we don't want it, then we won't have to fight. We think that, just because we don't want to fight, nobody will ever come and take away our ice cream sodas, incidentally killing us. This is bound to happen if, in the same breath, we accuse them of being black dogs for coveting our ice cream sodas.

Then of course we have the vice of thinking that because something is successful, it is therefore valuable: the worth of a thing is in its profit to us.

Also we love facts for their own sake, in contradiction to the superstition I just mentioned. The radio is full of question bees and information programs, and everybody reads the *Reader's Digest*, which pretends to give as many facts as possible in a little space. At the same time, the very hardest thing in the world to get is any real news about the war. We know the bare fact that France has been beaten. But what is going on there? It might as well be some country in the moon.

It is hard to conceive France as a nation which has now been crowded into its most despised provinces: the Auvergne, the Dauphine, the Limousin, etc. What will be the first public utterance of the government once the nation has collected itself together in its diminished and dishonored state? How will they express themselves, ever? What will be the first book printed in the new, captive France? What will be the first exhibition of paintings? All this is hard to imagine, particularly if the capital is going to be some place like Clermont-Ferrand.

July, 1940. Olean, New York

Every new headline – there is just one each day, an expansion of some sentence in some communique – tells me no more than that I know nothing about the war, and seem to be not only unable to conceive what it is all about, but even to find out anything that will help me to figure it out.

I ran across a *Harper's Bazaar* six years old, from 1934, in which there were a couple of pages of montage concerning London night life at the time. The whole thing not only didn't resemble anything I could imagine ever having seen (and yet I had seen it), but didn't even seem to represent any kind of reality whatever. Pictures of the same thing in 1925, when I was too young to see any of it except from a distance, would have been quite believable: not these, however. The pictures looked too dull even to be real: like something conceived by a person without any imagination at all.

Sometime I am going to realize the same thing, but seven times more emphatically, about the pre-war New York of 1937 and '38 and '39.

I wish I had something I could write down about the war, and make sense. I wish I knew something I could say about France.

For eight months the people of France complained only of boredom. Then suddenly there was an immense confusion, Germans appeared everywhere, and took away their outmoded pistols and hustled them into a dining car that had to be carted out of a museum for the purpose, and made them sign an armistice. All this, too, is like something thought up by a person with the dullest mind on earth: but behind this there is really a reality, and a terrible one.

Something actually did happen, behind all the meaningless stories we have read in the papers, but nobody is able to tell us what that thing was. The Germans may think they understand the Fall of France: they do not any more than we. But they don't have to understand it: it was something they had hoped for and are now pleased with, and all that is even better than understanding, subjectively speaking.

But the rest of us are left with a lot of very silly labels we have written out and have nothing to attach them to: these labels read: "all the facts; the truth about France; inside story; the real dope; the incredible truth; who was responsible? fatal indecision; deplorable waste; democratic inefficiency, German efficiency; the Jews and Freemasons done it; it was the dirty reds; it was the pro-fascist *Petit Dauphinois* (a Grenoble paper that is being quoted solemnly as *the* important source of news from France. The real news of France coming from Grenoble!); it was the Maginot Line, now a tourist attraction for German maids; and so on. All we have are these labels, the worst in the world, waiting to be tied tightly to all the wrong facts and silliest opinions, I have no doubt.

For the next two years, all we will get will be a set of facts such as we have been able to guess so far, and this set of labels, and they will be changed around in interminably different combinations until they become stupid enough to be put in a history textbook as the explanation of what happened.

August 21, 1940. Olean, New York

Maybe today was the day when I should have asked myself what has happened to the summer. But it was in many respects a good day, colder and very clear. Tonight when I was walking on the road in the woods, I saw the moon was well past full, and moonlight looked colder than I had ever seen it before. Streaks of mist, like bacon, hung over the valley.

Back in the cabin Ed Rice had been reading, in a pamphlet that had once belonged with an album of tangos, that many people had broken their legs doing the tango.

September 5, 1940. New York

This was the first time I ever went to Yorkville: to see the film of the war in Poland, a year ago. The Germans took a lot of trouble to get those pictures, and the propaganda, of course, was not in the pictures but in the cutting and the commentary. (The same pictures were used all over again against the Germans, later, by the *March of Time*.)

It showed no dead men, nobody getting killed, nobody even getting roughed up. A couple of Poles, in a great crowd of prisoners, appeared with bandages on. They showed one dead horse, with a great swollen belly. Otherwise, no death.

On the other hand there were hundreds of feet, it seemed, of destroyed material and houses. All this destruction was completely dehumanized. You saw a lot of razed buildings, blasted bridges, wrecked trains, piles of captured guns and other nondescript stuff. It was like watching hours of filming of a great garbage dump, and the whole thing soon got very nauseating and stupid. After that, when they did show men, even the men looked dehumanized, and appeared to be nothing but more equipment.

The Germans looked like good equipment, the Poles looked like cheap equipment, slightly spoiled. Otherwise they were the same. It almost seemed to be the point of the picture that these men had ceased to be people, and were nothing but very good equipment, sound, reliable and tireless German equipment, manufactured by the Fuehrer.

But there was one shot of some Germans riding by on caissons, dead tired, and some of them slumbering. Suddenly one man got in the eye of the camera, and gave back the straightest and fiercest and most resentful look I ever saw. Great rings surrounded his eyes which were full of exhaustion, pain and protest. And he kept staring, turning his head and fixing his eyes on the camera as he went by demanding to be seen as a person, and not as the rest of the cattle. The censors should have cut him out, because he succeeded. You began to realize how tired and disgusted all those soldiers must have been. It added great weight to the effect of all the garbage that had gone before. What a thing to be proud of! To have turned one whole country into a junk heap!

There was nothing insidious or subtle about the commentary, which was in English. It was dogmatic and blatant and clumsy, and wouldn't have fooled anybody except a German.

The general effect of the film was not terror, or anything at all dramatic: you just got oppressed by the drabness of a lot of tired soldiers and a lot of rubble and garbage.

The shots of Hitler himself were just as drab and dull as all the rest. He looks like nothing: an insignificant little guy with a pointed nose and a dejected mouth, down at the corners, like a tired wash-woman's.

Once in a while there would be a surprising picture: the sky above burning Warsaw (lying low on the horizon) was filled not with black smoke but huge white clouds, hanging still and piling up like thunderheads and filling that whole quarter of the compass. There was a telephoto shot of Gdynia under fire which was interesting because of the crazy telephoto perspective, but not much more. There is evidently nothing beautiful or exciting to be found in war at all, because these photographers must have tried their best. It was simply ugly, all the way through.

The really ugly parts were about the bombers. You didn't see anything repulsive happen, or terrible, or frightening: but the bombers themselves looked like big, malevolent, outlandish bugs.

The most actively obscene shot in the whole picture was one of a bomber releasing a stick of bombs which fell away from under its belly in a group: it was like some vile beetle laying eggs in the air, or dropping its filth.

There was nothing about the picture from beginning to end that wasn't squalid. I don't know what I expected: perhaps I thought the war had some new horror to it that I hadn't imagined. If it has, that never got shown, and isn't likely to be, either. This is a picture supposed to favor war, and show how much was accomplished by a war. The pictures were evidently truer than they meant to be. It is no joke that the world is going to turn into something infinitely repulsive and horrible when it is remade in the image of people who believe in this kind of thing: and the tragedy of that is, if we fight Hitler, we will become like him, too, we will turn into something just as dirty as he is. If we are going to beat him, we will have to.

Everybody in Yorkville looked very peaceable except the waiters standing in the doors of the restaurants and bars. Nazism is just the religion for waiters, stewards, taxi drivers, hospital orderlies, janitors, crutch salesmen, undertakers' helpers, garbage men, attendants in public toilets, barbers and dogcatchers.

October 19. 1940. Saint Bonaventure

It may well be that this big fat book begins with the snow. The sky was gray and heavy with it, it was a gray sky full of not clouds, but snow. You couldn't tell what kept it from falling. It was the color of pewter, a frozen mist, with a pale, lined patch, where you might expect the sun.

Now that the trees are bare, or almost all bare, with only a few still bearing leaves, for contrast, the landscape is more interesting. You see hidden roads: what used to appear thick forests, are curtains of straight trees with fields in between. You can see the solid structure of the hills, their rocky flanks, the hard talus. And, along the top of the ridge, through the bare trees comes light. The landscape is more like a drawing and less like a painting. Sometimes it is like an architect's plan for a landscape, and that is what is interesting about it. The leaves have fallen and the landscape has analyzed itself out and the essentials of its structure are bare and clear.

The air also was cold this morning, and the river was so still that I threw acorns in it, and broke the reflection of a hill in perfect concentric rings.

Along the bank of the river, as I walked, I scared up some wild ducks out of the bushes, under the overhanging bank, and they flew out with beating wings and a kind of whirring cry over the still water of the river, and wheeled so that they disappeared and flew away concealed from me by scrub and bushes along the bank.

Some of the errata listed in the English Edition of *Seven Types of Ambiguity* are funny.

To excuse one sentence in the Gline foreword, he has to say:

"For *From Mr. Robert Graves' analysis* read from *Miss Laura Riding's and Mr. Robert Graves' analysis*. It is regretted that *A Survey of Modernist Poetry* is erroneously referred to as by Mr. Robert Graves. It is by Miss Laura Riding and Mr. Robert Graves."

Then, after all this:

Page 8 line 24 For *Miss Gertrude Stern* read *Miss Gertrude Stein*.
Page 36 line 11 For *paths* read *pathos*.

I. A. Richards is too much a psychologist. For criticism he often substitutes little psychological intuitions about the writers he is writing about saying: "here he is being a snob," "here he chose these words to conceal his own ignorance," "here he chose these words to pretend he is better than everybody else." It may be all right, but with him it is too glib, and I am extremely suspicious of it. He rattles it off too easily.

Speaking of some neo-platonist he remarks that his psychology "*implies* discrediting of the senses" when all neo-platonists openly stated their discrediting of the senses. Why? The purpose of the statement is to indicate the importance of the senses to Richards' own system, which is perfectly all right. They are just as important to Aristotle, too, but Aristotle wasn't so huffy about it. So maybe Richards takes so much account of the snobbery and touchiness and huffiness of some one like [Walter] Pater because he is just as irritable himself.

Criticism should never have to rely on psychology even, but certainly it has no business making most of its points by little trick intuitions and guesses at character, no matter how accurate these flashy little intuitions may be.

Well, all right, Richards doesn't make most of his points that way. But clearly his points about *language* tend to be accompanied by little personal intuitions *ad hominem* and language is the thing Richards himself is touchiest about.

I intensely dislike some of his lingo – for instance his insistence on calling all general, abstract or universal terms "*metaphors*," and calling philosophical language "*figurative*." He only does it to be irritating. It is a deliberate sneer: but on top of that he always severely condemns people who use language to imply sneers and insults in some sphere like this where they are signs of extreme weakness.

He is a great case for the amateur psychologist himself!

October 21. 1940

"Eo fruimur, quo quietamur; sed quietatio respicit rationum finis, et finis rationem boni, et bonum est objectum voluntatis: ergo fruitio, quae ordinat ad illud, similiter." ["We enjoy it when we are still, but stillness calls for a reason, and its reason is the good. The good is the object of the will, and therefore enjoyment, which is ordered toward the good, does likewise."]

Saint Bonaventure. I. Sent. II. I.c.

Voluntas nec delectatur nec quietatur nisi in eo, quod cognoscit, vel per fidem vel per speciem (beatific vision) *et in eo, quod habet per spem vel* in re, *ideo actus aliarum virium ad hunc* disponunt, *non tamen sunt ipsum frui.* [The will neither delights nor is still unless it has knowledge, either through faith or through the reality *itself* (beatific vision) and unless it has that knowledge either in hope or *in reality.* Therefore, the actions of other powers *dispose* toward this, and are not the actual enjoyment of it.] *I. Sent. II. iii.*

Si quis videt aliquid et habet, nunquam delectatur, nisi amet; aliter tamen requiritur visio quam amor. Nam visio disponit, similiter et tentio (striving); *sed* amor *delicias suggerit. Unde* est quasi acumen penetrans, et ideo ei maxime convenit unire et per consequens delectare et quietare: *ideo essentialiter et non dispositive (amor) et fruitio.* [If anyone sees something and has it, he doesn't delight in it unless he loves it; for otherwise, we speak of vision, and not love. For vision disposes toward something else, as does *striving;* but *love* suggests delight. Hence, *it is like a sharp, penetrating sword, and therefore union with the object is especially appropriate, as is the consequent delight and stillness;* therefore enjoyment (love) is something essential, and not dispositive to something else.] *I. Sent. II. I. ad. 2.*

Ad illud "Visio est tota merces", dicendum quod illud non dicitur proprie, sed per concomitantiam, quia visio et complacentia in qua est perfecta ratio fruitionis, inseparabiliter se habent. [To the statement, "Vision is the full reward," it must be said that this is not stated properly, but through concomitance, since vision and the concomitant pleasure, which is the perfect motive of enjoyment, are inseparable.] *I. Sent. II. 1. ad 3.*

Visio beatifica[1]: the two notions are inseparable: Saint Thomas places the emphasis on *visio;* Saint Bonaventure on *beatifica.*

The creation, exemplarism, and the *Word* – according to Saint Bonaventure. For Saint Thomas, creation less active than as conceived by Scotus.

---

[1] *"Visio beatifica"* refers to the way the *blessed* or *happy* ones ("Come blessed of my Father") will enjoy the *vision* of God in eternity. Thus, "beatific vision."

Creative power inseparable from God's essence: an aspect of it. For Duns Scotus, a free act. For [William] Occam a completely free act, so free it can be misinterpreted as arbitrary.

For Saint Bonaventure – the Divine mind contains not so much static Platonic archetypes as active *significationes* of all things.

October 24. Feast of Saint Raphael

Saint Raphael I remember also by place names, Saint Raphael in France and Calle San Rafael in Havana – the buses travelled it a lot. This morning, walked along the pasture where sun slanted through the straight trunks of the bare oaks, casting their shadows upon the grass and hummocks. It was warm, and like spring. Many days in October and many days in October are like spring: I think it may even be silly to talk of "spring weather" at all. Maybe there is no such thing.

The story of Saint Raphael and Tobit is so fascinating I wouldn't know how to begin talking about it. The symbols in it, and the deep meaning, are marvelous. But it is especially wonderful, for its dramatic ambiguities: the angel is among them, they do not know him. He guides them through terrors safely, reveals himself at the end and leaves them. The theme is so good, its poignancy and wonder and significance strikes one on some deep spot where I can't find words to talk about it.

"*Tobias, plus timens Deum quam regem, rapiebat corpora occisorum, et occultabat in domo sua, et mediis noctibus sepeliebat ea.*" ["Tobias, who feared God more than the king, gathered by stealth the bodies of the slain, and hid them by day in his house, so that he buried them under cover of night." (Tobias 2.9 – Latin Vulgate)].

"*Contigit autem ut quadam die fatigatus a sepultura, veniens in domum suam, iactasset se iuxta parietem, et obdormisset, et ex nido hirundinum dormienti illi calida stercora inciderunt super oculos eius, fieretque caecus.*" ["It happened one day that, tired from burying the dead, he went into his house, lay down next to the wall of his courtyard, and fell asleep, and from a nest of swallows there fell warm droppings into his eyes, and he became blind." (Tobias 2.10–11 – Latin Vulgate)].

Thesis: 1. This strange blindness is brought into a kind of coincidental connection with the still stranger "reproach" of Sara the daughter of Raguel, in a distant city – who was accused of having killed seven husbands: who had died on their wedding night to her. Both she and Tobias pray at one time to the Lord, so he sends Raphael to heal them both.

The trials of these two are all the more terrible because of their *fantastic nature*. They are humiliations no one could possibly take the slightest pride in, because they also make one utterly ridiculous. But their charity is still perfect, in spite of that.

Act II

Tobias sends his son to Rages, the city where Sara is. Now, the entrance of Raphael is prefaced: it is as sudden as the appearance of a new figure in a Javanese dance.

"*Tunc egressus Tobias (Junior) invenit iuvenem splendidum,* stantem praecinctum et quasi paratum ad ambulandum. *Et ignorans quod angelus Dei esset, salutavit eum, et dixit:* Unde te habemus, *bone iuvenis?*" ["Then, setting out on his trip, (the younger) Tobias met a splendid young man, *standing dressed and ready for a journey.* Not knowing that he was an angel of God, Tobias greeted him, and said, '*Who are you,* young man?'" (Tobias 5.5 – Latin Vulgate)]

The greeting is as gay as something from Sir Gawain and the Green Knight. *Hilaritas* is the essential characteristic of all these stories of the Archangels: great joy! The sorrow of Tobias and Sara is as terrible as that of Job, but it seems almost humorous because it is caught up in the breathless excitement of this *hilaritas* appropriate to the story of an Archangel. The plot is geared to the speed and intellectual excitement of *hilaritas,* also. This is great joy and humor but with no laughter – it is too serious. If you laughed, it would be the laughter caused by the excitement of a tremendously successful serious passage in a poem!

"*Noli flere, salvus perveniet filius noster, et salvus revertetur ad nos, et oculi tui videbunt illum. Credo enim quod angelus Dei bonus comitur ei, et bene disponat omnia, quae circa eum geruntur, ita ut cum gaudio revertatur ad nos. Ad hanc vocem cessavit mater eius flere, et tacuit.*" ["Don't cry. Our son will arrive safely, and come back to us safe and sound. Your eyes will see him. For a good angel will go with him, and see that all goes well for him, so that he will come back to us in joy. At this, his mother stopped her weeping, and was silent." (Tobias 5.28 – Latin Vulgate)].

Tobias goes out with his dog and the angel; comes to the Tigris and goes to wash his feet in the river, and is menaced by a great fish.

"*Quem expavescens Tobias clamavit voce magna, dicens:* Domine, invadit me!" ["Fearful of the great fish, Tobias cried out with a loud voice, saying: '*Sir, he comes upon me!*'" (Tobias 6.3 – Latin Vulgate)]

The cry is tremendous, by its lack of any definite subject for the verb – and for the verb itself "*invadit.*"

"Sir, he comes upon me!"

October 26. 1940

Saint Thomas' *"Pulchrum est id quod visum placet"* ["Beauty is that which is pleasing to behold"] is not a definition of beauty, but a description of the *conditio sine qua non* [necessary condition, without which an event cannot take place] of aesthetic apprehension.

Similarly, to say aesthetic enjoyment is enjoyment of a thing for its own sake is also a description, not a definition.

The notion of the *coniunctio convenientis cum convenienti* [union of the harmonious with the harmonious] is misleading in the discussion of beauty.

There is a fear, not that the war will end civilization, but that the reaction after the war will. Now everyone is keyed up to a great effort: but the fear is that, after all is over, everybody will fall down and die of a mortal lassitude and the sickness of disgust. Maybe everyone will just die of weariness and shame and hopelessness. That was what was frightening about France. As if they just gave up in disgust, willing to do nothing but die of *accidie*.[2] Maybe the war will peter out and everything thereafter will rot with melancholy, beginning with Germany and England.

I read *Sir Gawain and the Green Knight* again today and it is one of the best books in the world, the gayest and the most healthy. Men in my class, realizing confusedly in an exam that it had so much more value than *Beowulf*, and was therefore *truer* in an ideal sense, groping for an explanation of this experience, could only catch on to the one criterion they knew, and described it as if it were truer in the literal sense, and *more naturalistic and realistic*.

But *Beowulf* only quantitatively exaggerates fundamentally possible things: the acts of strength are exaggerations of smaller acts. Swimming for three weeks is an exaggeration of swimming three hours. While in *Sir Gawain* a man walks about carrying his own head in his hand, talking to the people and making jokes, fundamentally impossible – but more credible than Beowulf fighting sea dragons.

But even better than *Sir Gawain* is the Book of Tobias: these two are, at present, my two favorite stories, but the Book of Tobias leaves me, every time, breathless, with all the depth of its symbols and analogies.

---

[2] In Cassian's list of the Eight Principal Vices, the sixth is *accidie*, in early English. Owen Chadwick translates this as "boredom with the life of prayer" (Owen Chadwick, *John Cassian*, 2d ed. [New York: Cambridge University Press, 1968], 89).

Apart from that, however, it is a series of the most striking and astonishing dramatic scenes.

It is spread all over many countries – the action moves in a sort of a geographic triangle; Nineveh, Rages, and Gabelum. Between all these points an emotional tension of yearning and expectation is set up.

At Nineveh, Tobias waiting and weeping and fearing his son is dead, and his wife watching the road from a hill outside the city. In Rages – Tobias Jr. and his wife, T., worrying because he knows his father is worrying about him, and also waiting for the angel to come back from Gabelum.

All this takes place with a sort of destroyed perspective, as if the three scenes were on one panel of a medieval painting all together, which gives the whole thing an economy and simplicity and power that is terribly effective.

Add the detail of the faithful dog's joy at the end, when he runs ahead of Tobias and the Angel and Sara to the mother of old Tobias, and it ties the whole thing together again.

What is the effect of this separation and reunion? It comes on top of the fact that they are all living in exile *anyway* – among Assyrians and Persians. On top of that, Tobias is separated from his only son. This double exile, this twofold separation accentuates our own pilgrim state on earth, and gains dramatic force itself from that notion, which is also emphasized by the presence of the Angel.

That is what it is all about, this Drama. It is a Drama of our Fallen State and, on the level of the *dramatic* statement alone, it is a drama of clarity among men wandering on earth in search of heaven, from which they are exiled.

But then there is the deeper mystical meaning: the fish which terrified Tobias, but had in him the salvation of Tobias and Sara and the cure of old Tobias' blindness.

There is the tremendous scene, where Tobias and Sara burn the fish's heart upon the coals and pray: He that this marriage be sanctified, she that they both grow old together in cleanness of health.

Characterization is done this way by sudden contrasts – as when Tobias speaks, and his wife, suddenly content and consoled, ceased weeping *immediately.*

October 27. Feast of Christ the King

Today I saw a movie of London under bombing, and heard recorded the sound of the air raid alarm and of the all clear signal. For the first time in my life, I think, I momentarily wanted to be in the war.

There is a sort of fascination about it, too: something behind patriotism or anything like that – and lower than that, too: a kind of animal curiosity to hang around the scene of danger and of killing, the scene of the most important and terrible killing that is being done in the world today.

The thing that shocked me as much as anything was the picture of Peter Robinson's store in Oxford Circus with a hole blasted out of the three top floors. In Peter Robinson's I bought a gray suit when I was sixteen, or fifteen, and wore it to Strasbourg and to Italy the first time I went there. I remember the suit very well. It was gray herringbone tweed. Just up the street, upper Regent Street, from Peter Robinson's, was the place where I used to take the Green Line bus to go to Ripley. Diagonally across Oxford Circus was Henry's Long Bar, where Roger Payne and I used to drink beer; where Julian Tennyson and I drank champagne my last day in England. It was from upstairs in Henry's Long Bar that I called up the Bennetts to say good bye. Further down from Peter Robinsons, eastward across Oxford Street, was the cinema where I first saw all the René Clair Pictures: *Le Million*, *A Nous la Liberté*, *Le Dernier Miliardaire*, as well as that strange Freudian movie I went with Tom Bennett to see there, and many other things. All this was struck when Peter Robinson's was struck. Bombs are beginning to fall into my life. That wasn't true with Warsaw. I had never seen, nor imagined, Warsaw. This was a terrible thing to see.

But more terrible was seeing the line of people going down into the air raid shelter at dusk. Then seeing the empty streets, and an air raid warden walking slowly with his hands behind him, in the sudden flash of a bomb: and hearing the sound of that air raid alarm. This, for the first time, made me want to fight.

Of course it was propaganda, and good propaganda. The talk was all understated. The air-raid alarm, the pictures of the people were enough: and there was nothing false about the sound of that alarm, nothing misleading about the falls of the people, who were not terrorized, not disgusted, but brave and patient and hurt, without any showiness, no fancy gestures, no exaggerated lip-biting and none of the coerced smiles I had imagined from the newspaper stories.

For the first time I imagined that maybe I belonged there, not here. I have responsibilities in England, I left my childhood behind there. Now that they are bombing it, perhaps I should go back to my childhood: except of course they don't, for the moment, need men.

Actually, all the propaganda needed to make me want to fight was uttered by the Germans. If they had never bombed any part of England I would never have given a damn for the whole war, no matter what. Perhaps a bombing of Paris for two or three weeks might have done it. I don't know. The bombing of Rotterdam rather repelled and scared me. But the bombing of London, where I once lived, where there are so many people that were my friends in school, and people that I loved, is certainly different.

I think this was one of the best photographed, best cut, best spoken documentary films I ever saw. No, some of the lines were pretty terrible: but the tone of the man's voice was good. The title was lousy: "London can take it."

It showed a big gash blown in Somerset House, something that might have been a new wing of the Middlesex Hospital, burst wide open. Some of those Bermondsey Houses for laboring men were shown blown up. There were many places I didn't recognize – probably in the city. But what was impressive was the amount of life going on in the city; buses, people going to work, hurrying around the piles of stone and brick in the daytime – then going underground at night.

The town hall in Allegheny, standing with its cupola among the bare branches, against a gray sky, and with its red bricks, might have been something in a Surrey village, a Victorian post office or something, the other day. In any case, I was reminded of Surrey, and felt strange. And I have been dreaming I was in London, often, at night.

November 2. 1940. All Souls

In three days there will be an election and that will be the last we'll ever hear of Wendell Wilkie, whose voice has already dwindled to a throaty whisper.

Some days ago, I can't remember how many, all our numbers were drawn out of the goldfish bowl in Washington. As a particular insult connected with this process, the bowl was not big enough to contain all the numbers, so instead of getting another one, they added on to this one with some kind of fake glass. The reverence for that lousy bowl in particular is a bad omen.

Then six numbers were left out, and called last in a separate lottery of their own: The guys drawing out the numbers were blindfolded with a piece of upholstery from a chair on which sat a signer of the Declaration of Independence when he signed the Declaration of Independence. The newspaper gave no further details, and left me believing that somebody got at that poor old chair with a razor blade and carried off the strip of cloth and left a hole in the chair and blindfolded the Secretary of Agriculture or whoever it was drew out the first number.

I still don't know my number, or if I was drafted.

Two months ago I would at least have imagined myself going daffy to find out.

I think they are trying to hypnotize us into a false sense of security by the ridiculous and undramatic triviality of all these ceremonies. It is as though they were trying to kid us by hiring a big billboard and then writing on it in pencil "Join the Army." But we are not fooled. We know you paid for the billboard!

E. B. White wrote a fine story on [Henry] Luce in the *New Yorker*. Luce had previously said he would never sit down to dinner knowingly with a man who had refused to vote in this election – to *affirm*. Everybody has to *affirm*, he insists. I was going to write him a crank letter. White has done far better. There is no use writing to Luce. I guess White will be shot when Luce is dictator.

What filthy lies come on the bottle with this ink! It is said to be pure and perfect, that it *cleans* the pen of the impurities left by lesser inks. It is said to dry before you can draw breath. It is said to do a whole lot of things. Actually it flows sluggishly at first, and then suddenly comes in a great rush and pours itself out, and you find yourself trailing seas of ink across the paper in a huge, insulting smear. And it has a funny smell. It is probably, also, extremely inflammable, and I wouldn't be surprised if it were explosive. Probably also, after a period of, say, six months, it fades, and with it my immortal works and undying witticisms are forever lost, and vanish in the air, to the great regret of posterity.

New words in Philosophy:

The distinction between *infinite* and *indefinite*.

Mathematical infinity is only indefinite.

Quantitative infinity is "infinite" (indefinite) only by lack of definiteness, is mere potentiality. Real infinity is infinity of being, infinite actuality, infinite from lack of any limitation, because it is beyond all conceivable limitation.

"*Infinitum dicitur dupliciter, scilicet per privationem perfectionis; et sic materia dicitur infinita, et* talis infiniti non est finire, sed potius finiri indiget, secundum quod est possibile. *Alio modo infinitum dicitur* per privationem limitationis; et quod sic infinitum est, *proprie habet finire quoniam ultra ipsum, cum non sit maius cogitare, non contingit aliquid appetere. Unde talis infinitas convenit ultimo fini, quae maxime habet finiendi rationem.*" ["Infinity is understood in two ways. First, through the privation of perfection. In this way, matter is called infinite, and *of such infinity there is no end, since it is lacking an end, being only possibility.* Secondly, infinity is understood as the privation of limitation; what is thus considered infinite, is already completed, since there is nothing beyond it. Since nothing greater can be thought of, it does not desire anything beyond it. It is this kind of infinity that is proper to the ultimate end, which has the greatest power to motivate."]

Saint Bonaventure I. Sent. I. III.I. a3.

There was fine movement of wind on the pasture today. The ground was drying after a lot of mist and rain. Wind moved the tufts of brown grass, over the still green clover. Leaves, caught in the stalks of taller, dead, priceless weeds, wagged in the wind like a multitude of small people. The sky, over the distant farms, was cold blue and full of mottled clouds, with gray and lavender shadows, like the sky in Manet's "River at Argenteuil."

Sunday. November 3

The other night I picked up and looked at some Paul Valéry, and was enjoying the Alexandrines when it came to me in a flash that probably, at last, I was capable of understanding Racine. I had never really seen anything in him, really, but had always been ready to admit there must be something there. I opened a book and came in the Fourth Act of *Berenice*, where Titus is speaking to himself.

> *He bien! Titus, que viens-tu faire?*
> *Berenice t'attend. Ou viens-tu, temeraire?*
> *Tes adieux sont-ils prêts? T'es-tu bien consulté?*
> *Ton coeur te promet-il assez de craute?*
> *Car enfui au combat qui pour toi se prepare*
> *C'est peu d'être constant, il faut être barbare . . . etc.*
> [Well, there, Titus, what are you doing?
> Berenice is waiting for you. Are you timid?
> Are your farewells ready? Have you talked
> this over with yourself?
> Has your heart promised you enough fear?
> For since it is for combat you are being prepared at least
> It is not enough to be faithful, you must be a beast.]

And I found I was right: I found all this tremendously moving in a very pure way. Not exciting, but nevertheless it was stirring, and almost entirely because of the writing. If you look for stimulus in the psychology, or the material that goes to make up the "characters," etc., you are disappointed. The play is made up of the interplay of *themes*, musical themes, extremely measured and refined and regular, that are carried, first of all, by the language, the meter, the rhythmical effects, the structure of the verse.

Therefore all the speeches are quite long, and two characters will hold the stage for some time, alone, exchanging 20-line, or 30-line speeches. Obviously, this is to exploit musical effects, symphonic effects. This is to show changes in modulation, developments of a theme (musical) etc. above all. With this going on, you find the same device is used to carry certain thematic *ideas* – very broad. The conflict of two kinds of love. Conflicts of "passions" also used for the same *symphonic* effect.

To say it is symphonic does not mean it is diffuse, or that the effect is achieved by the suggestions created by the sound of various words alone. It is symphonic not by virtue of the harmony inherent in individual words, it is a symphony of grammatical, syntactical, logical and metrical harmonies. The effect is consistently delightful, by continual limpidity and cleanness and purity of diction and writing that carries you surprisingly high, without your realizing it.

I wonder how much sense there is in quoting a single line of Racine: every single line, word, comma has an exact place in the whole structure, this symphonic structure.

If a line of Racine is to be quoted at all, the only way is to make it fit into another structure, take it and fit it neatly into a paragraph of critical prose, giving it a setting with all kinds of syntactical properties able to support it and show it off to advantage.

If anything is out of place in this age it is Racine. We are completely out of tune with anything so perfectly balanced and clean and harmonious as *Berenice*. We are so much out of tune with it that it simply doesn't make sense when we read it; it takes a kind of illumination to catch on to what a play by Racine is really trying to do.

In the book I had marked a couple of lines in *Andromaque*, about seven years ago, in pencil. They were the marks of a crazy man. I had absolutely no idea how to judge Racine, how to appreciate him.

Another writer who is poles apart from Racine is Pope. Racine is never epigrammatical – or I wouldn't expect him to be from this piece of *Berenice*. And he almost never writes a line that is quotable for some aphoristic statement about morals or philosophy. Everything in Racine is strictly part of a unity: the organization of ideas, verse, speeches, "passions" appropriate to a certain action. This is the most important sense of unity – and everybody points out Racine kept to the three unities without noticing this true unity to which he adhered perfectly. His plays are all perfectly integrated, down to the last detail. Therefore, every moral statement made refers only to this particular case, the particular action being described. No philosophical remarks having general reference are *ever* thrown off because absolutely no line is written that has reference to anything outside the action of the play.

Now to read Racine and expect to find the same kind of quotable lines as in Pope's "Essay on Criticism" is an absurdity. Racine, intellectually speaking, is a perfect artist. Nothing he says has any reference except to the unity and perfection of the work of art itself. Everything leads inward, and the work rests perfectly balanced upon itself.

Racine does not knock you over with fantastic signs of genius, yet he is a genius: only you realize it after you have finished talking about his play. Racine's personality and genius are completely hidden in his art. But they are there just the same.

Funnily enough Dante, who writes in the first person, vanishes in his work the same way. Not Shakespeare. Shakespeare is always doing marvelous things that are the products not of any recognizable personality, but of sheer imaginative overflow, a brilliant excess. Dante and Racine, Dante even in the highest imaginative brilliance, and his is the highest in the world, even above Shakespeare, still dominates it with his art and his order and the unity of the work. The porter in *Macbeth* is nothing but a brilliant interpolation. There are really no interpolations in the *Divine Comedy*. In Racine, interpolations are not even imaginable.

The other thing I have just understood for the first time is Donne's *Ecstasy*. I have been reading it for years and getting lost after the lines

> As twixt two equal armies, fate
> > Suspends uncertain victory
> Our souls, which, to advance their state
> > Were gone out, living twixt her and me.
> And whilst our souls negotiate there
> > We like sepulchral statues lay;

Beyond that I used to flounder around, not reading or misreading most of the lines. At least I recognize a meaning in the ending. But there is a middle part, still, where I lose most of the references.

Another thing: I am no longer sore at Herrick, or not as sore as I was. I think he is a Highschool boy, yes. But he has some fine lines and slick ideas.

The golden pomp is come;
For now each tree does wear,
Made of her pap and gum
Rich beads of amber here.

"The Argument of His Book" (Hesperides) is good. Some lines from a long epigram "Upon M. Ben Jonson" are very good. Some lines from the "Farewell to Sack" are fine. I take back what I have said about Herrick, except I am tired of poems about how drunk we all love to get.

One thing I didn't change my mind about is Carew's song "Ask Me No More Where Love Bestows." However, one stanza came to me tonight as rediscovery:

"Ask me no more where those stars light
That downwards fall in dead of night.
For in your eyes they sit, and there
Fixed become, as in their sphere."

The line "That downwards fall . . ." is some line. I think gabble about natural description in poetry is absurd; the function of such a line is not to describe nature, it is to incorporate the effect of a natural object, with all its analogical properties, into the unity of a poem. All right, to do that the thing has to be described. Let it. That description is not an end in itself, and must not be detached and treated so.

The force of "downwards fall at dead of night," suggesting the swift, silent, streak of a shooting star, is not meant to remind you of summer nights when you have caught your breath at seeing such stars, but is meant to lead you to the sense of the next lines, and to tie in, finally, perfectly, with the idea "fixed . . . as in their sphere." Reading this stanza wrongly might well come of going off on an emotional tangent from the suggestive effect produced by "downwards fall in dead of night" with its image of the night's stillness etc.

November 7. 1940

"*Vae prophetis insipientibus qui sequuntur spiritum suum et nihil vident!*" Ezech. 13–3 ["Woe to those foolish prophets who follow their own thought and see nothing!" (Ezekiel 13:3 – Latin Vulgate)]

"*Et dixit ad me: Fili hominis, quodcumque inveneris, comede; comede volumen istud, et vadens loquere ad filios Israel. Et aperui os meum, et cibavit me volumine illo; et dixit ad me: Fili hominis, venter tuus comedet, et viscera tua complebuntur volumine esto quod ego do tibi. Et comedi illus, et factum est in ore meo sicut mel dulce."* Ezech. 3:1–3 ["He said to me: Son of man, eat what is before you; eat this scroll, then go, speak to the house of Israel. So I opened my mouth and he gave me the scroll to eat. Son of man, he then said to me, feed your belly and fill your stomach with this scroll I am giving you. I ate it, and it was sweet as honey in my mouth." (Ezekiel 3.1–3, New American Bible)]

November 10. 1940

There are a lot of things I wish I had never said, because they were foolish, or because they hurt people, or because they were intended to. But mostly because they were absurd.

I said to Dan Walsh once that I thought G. M. Hopkins had been done in by the hard discipline of the Jesuits. I suppose I believed it. It was very stupid.

I also said to Dan Walsh that I had to have meat, for my health. He made me ashamed at once by saying I was lucky to know myself that well; right then I knew it wasn't true.

I wish I'd never told those dirty jokes in Virginia.

I wish I'd never argued with Lytton Strachey's brother, the psychoanalyst, about whether a certain manor house was Elizabethan or Jacobean: he knew and I didn't, and I insisted it was Elizabethan – it was Kirby Hall, Lincolnshire.

I wish I'd never argued with Fr. Joe Vann about art last summer – it resolved itself into an argument about words, very futile. Also I wish I'd never argued with him about James Joyce.

I wish I'd never said Joyce was "Catholic." I didn't know, and that is one thing he certainly isn't. But he is, in a certain respect, an Aristotelian. Aristotelian and Catholic are by no means the same thing!

I wish I'd never made the dirty crack about Peggy Wells' cooking last summer. I didn't mean to be nasty, but it certainly was nasty.

There is no real necessity to write down this kind of stuff. It is boring, even as I write it on the page.

The other day they showed the *March of Time* about the Vatican here: even the stones were beautiful. I was bowled over. It was the first beautiful architecture I had seen in months, even in a picture. All the triumphant statues around the great Piazza in front of Saint Peters, and those on top of the facade! They showed Saint John Lateran, and that day was the feast of its consecration!

I have an idea it would be valuable to write down stories in this – stories I hear, stories I invent. I am not terribly interested in telling stories. I always wanted to write down stories old Peter Hauck told, but they were obviously the stories one would want to write down and they weren't really stories – the Chinaman, dead, in a room across an alley from where he worked: he found out, his attention being attracted to this mysterious room by the swarms of flies all around and in and out its window that opened on the alley. Also, if I write anything down it had better not be backwards, like that.

Fr. James Murphy, a Redemptorist missionary in Brazil whom I went to see downtown one rainy day last winter, rides miles and miles through the Matto Grosso on a pony, unarmed, among fierce beasts, jaguars, poisonous snakes. His horse has fallen under him, stung to death by such snakes, miles away even from a village of straw huts. He never talks about these adventures, but loves more to talk about the people in the straw huts, whom he baptises, marries, shrives.

Fr. James grew up in the part of Brooklyn where Peter Hauck lived, and is an old friend of the family.

Br. Ferdinand, the gardener, entered the monastery after the wars, in which he had served in the German Army – if that is a story, then I don't know it.

November 12, 1940

Yesterday the English went through the mummery of placing a wreath on the cenotaph while German and Italian planes dropped bombs on London. (Planes is a stupid, weak and journalistic word – a word used not for its value or its meaning or even its usefulness, properly speaking, as a sign, but only used because it fits conveniently into a headline.)

Modern ceremonies are pitifully ridiculous. The participation of men in frock coats and trousers contribute to making them so, but nevertheless, uniforms do not help. No wonder no one believes in what these ceremonies are supposed to stand for – they carry no conviction. England has wisely almost abandoned ceremony altogether in the war. Nothing is left but the naked sterility of a world being ground up in the smoking rubble of bombed buildings – and a lot of terrifying dead, colorless jokes. The Nazis had a reason for saying the way England takes the bombing is not heroism:

and it is *not*. It is toughness, but nothing heroic about it. It is grim and barren and stupefied and not at all pretty the way heroism should be. But it is prettier than the garbage and stink of slavery in a concentration camp, and that is its virtue.

MODERN CEREMONIES –

A top hatted prime minister lights an undying flame to an unknown soldier, steps back, sticks out the round arc of his belly, removes his top hat and holds it over his lung.

At a dog cemetery, a group of the owner's friends gather for the funeral of a Scotch Terrier.

A wreath on the cenotaph.

Hitler makes a speech in a beer hall.

A Senator poses shaking hands with an Indian Chief. Both are wearing great crests of feathers.

Fiorello La Guardia winds up and throws the first ball of the season. Queen Mary releases an electric catch, and a bottle of a champagne, in a carefully aimed cradle, swings smack against the bow of a battleship and breaks.

A group of Communists carry signs: the Brooklyn College delegation of poets to the May Day parade.

Ribbentrop arrives at Moscow and shakes hands all 'round.

The handshake.

The lifting of the hat.

The Nazi salute.

The Communist salute.

Easter egg rolling on the White House lawn.

The drawing of the first number in the Draft.

Cutting a ribbon to open a bridge.

The Mayor's party taking the first ride on a new city subway.

Mayor Forness' speech to a St. Bonaventure pep-rally.

A reunion of old grads.

A pajama parade of freshmen being initiated into a fraternity.

The receiving line at a High School Junior Prom.

A girl hands over the colors to someone or other at Annapolis.

A beauty contest.

Dean Hawkes turns up the first spade full of earth for a new building.

The boy scouts plant a scraggly little tree in a park, dedicated to peace.

New Year's Eve, 12 o'clock, everybody yells and screams, whistles blow, etc.

The electrocution of criminals – a repulsive ceremony.

Cheerleaders at a football game.

An American Legion convention.

A Baptist minister pronouncing an "invocation" at a luncheon meeting of Rotary.

All these ceremonies are rotten because their only reason for existing is a vague feeling "that there ought to be some sort of a ceremony." The ceremonies of the Protestant church are futile because that is the reason for their performance, also.

Sunday and yesterday there were great earthquakes in Rumania and great windstorms in America. A radio tower was blown down in Detroit. That is a good combination for Nostradamus. Tomorrow, maybe Greece will cave in, or the Italian army run into the sea, or London be finally wiped out, or Hitler fall downstairs and break his hip.

I have an idea Hitler will die of nothing spectacular like a bomb, but probably old age or some children's disease like the mumps.

Further violence – there has been a big outburst against the freshmen on the campus here, involving all kinds of consequences. Further, I got a letter from Jinny inviting me to Richmond, that drunken city, for Christmas. I saw a shooting star. One of my students knocked out a freshman and then fell into a hedge and got a thorn so deep in his hand the doctor couldn't cut it out.

I gave my class some Chaucer to put into modern English and this will probably severely tax their brains, and do violence to their tempers. Father Cornelius is mad at the *New Yorker* for being anti-Catholic and I am mad at it for being anti-funny, and extremely dull. Gibney has got a cold. Lax is afraid to drive Gibney's car. The football coach has been bitten by Father Hugo's black spaniel. The football team has lost another game. Somebody told me that when a pig attacks a human being he (the pig) gores out the entrails and eats them, but that is all the meat a pig will ever touch. I saw what I thought was a photograph of the three Ritz brothers dressed as women, but on closer inspection, it turned out to be the three Andrews Sisters. Somebody said that they couldn't hold the College's Junior Prom in Bradford because nobody could drive back that distance afterwards without cracking up against a tree somewhere in those 20 miles. They tried it once and that was what happened. This is a violent world, in which I am not doing nearly enough work, although I appear to be busy all the time.

November 13

The first time I ever read the *Ancient Mariner* was in Saint Antonin, when I was about eleven. The Mayor's older son had had it in the Lycée and he lent the book – it was in a thin little book by itself, to me, or to my father and I read it. I pretended I liked it more than I did.

One thing I was impressed by:

That the wedding guest never got to the feast.

Another: that it was bad luck to kill an albatross.

Children are not good judges of poetry. Anyway, Wordsworth and Saint Augustine differ completely as to whether they "rest in Abraham's bosom all the year," and for Saint Augustine the screaming fury of babies is proof of original sin.

I think children are worst judges of poetry. They are extremely hide-bound and demand stark realism in formal literature, while seeming to cherish or desire to enjoy fantastically imaginative stories, but only if they seem to be able to be *proved* literally.

For children, whatever it is, it had to really happen. If it is only a story, then it is a lie. If it is a convention, then it is faked. But still they are suckers for the most transparent conventions: "Once upon a time there was a giant . . ." Oh! If it was in some "old days" or other, then that's all right. There used to be giants.

But Coleridge spoke as if the Ancient Mariner were his contemporary, as if the wedding guest were Coleridge himself. He didn't say "once upon a time." Therefore I was a little suspicious of the *Ancient Mariner*.

Sir W. Scott and H. Walpole are the same way! They, like children, demand, in effect, that you begin with "Once upon a time" as if you had to be ashamed of the "wonderful" the "sublime" the "wild" the "romantic" – and excuse it by giving it a setting in an age which "believed in such superstitions."

I have been very exercised about "literary truth" and "belief" since my classes thought that, because *Sir Gawain and the Green Knight* was *truer* than *Beowulf*, it was "more realistic." But a man riding around with his head cut off, holding it by the hair, and talking to people, is not realism.

Anyway, I reread the *Ancient Mariner* today – for, maybe, the tenth time since 1928, and for the first time realized what a really great poem it is! And for the first time I discovered the passage about the weird song of the dead men – who operate throughout as a chorus, always confronting the Mariner in a group – doing things as a group, but silently except this un-earthly and magnificent and exciting song:

For when it dawned – they dropped their arms
And clustered round the mast;
Sweet sounds rose slowly through their mouths
And from their bodies passed
A round, around flew each sweet sound
Then darted to the sun;
Slowly the sounds came back again
Now mixed, now one by one
Sometimes a-dropping from the sky
I heard the skylark sing;
Sometimes all little birds that are
How they seemed to fill the sea and air
With their sweet jargoning!
And now 'twas like all instruments:
Now like a lonely flute;
And now it is an angel's song
That makes the heavens be mute.

– rose *slowly through* their mouths – seems to suggest the *transparency* of the dead men, although they were not transparent as I remember.

– suggests that, in relation to this song, they were little more than *passive instruments*. They were not singing, the song was moving, through them and out of them and back into them, from some invisible source. They are nothing but more or less passive mediums for the passage of this unearthly music into time and *space* for this music moves as clearly in space as it does in time. (That is how its unearthliness is described: by the fact that it *moves in space almost visibly*.)

– The notes of the song were high pitched, but with the soft modulation of *the flute* or of the *lark*. These give that fullness of tone that keep this music from being just high and shrill: this was more than a whistle and yet higher than the ululation of classical ghosts or of H. G. Wells' Martians.

– Also the music is beautiful, and it is a kind of hymn in praise of the morning, a kind of *aubade* of Zombies, but it is beautiful and entrancing, not just frightening and weird – it was like an Angel's song.

Besides all this, the general tone of the *Ancient Mariner* is always humorous. That's as it should be. The wedding guest's impatience is humorous; so is the Mariner's insistence on his story. So is the Pilot's son going crazy. The supernatural events are not all humorous in themselves, but their wonder is set on a good shock absorber of humor. The wonder of the

Castle of Otranto – it is stupid in itself – but its stupidity is increased by the way it jars on its solid base of cement like solemnity. The water snakes and the slimy things in the AM are humorous and vivacious and gay, not solemn or horrible. The AM is saved from the fierce snake.

I often wonder if teaching literature hasn't been the first thing to make me really read the stuff. I feel as if I never had read any literature before! I wonder what I have been doing with books all this time. I certainly have to wear reading glasses, so I was using my eyes. But somewhere it all got lost, between the eye and the spirit. Or maybe that's fooling. But I certainly didn't read carefully all that I read: and I wonder how many things I've read can I remember? I certainly can't quote!

What snatches of verse can I remember?

> "Thou still unravished bride of quietness
> Thou fosterchild of silence and slow time . . ."
> *"Precepta regis sunt nobis vincula legis."* ["The commands of our king
>   have the force of law."]
> Age cannot wither her, nor custom stale
> Her infinite variety . . .
> The unimaginable touch of time.
> Nuns fret not at their convent's narrow room.
> Rob me, but bind me not and let me go.
> At the Round Earth's imagined corners blow your trumpets,
>   angels . . .
> The expense of spirit in a waste of shame
> Is lust in action. . .
> I'll tell you the story of Minnie the Moocher,
> She was a low down Hoochie Koocher . . .
> And custom is a spreading laurel tree.
> My little love in light attire
> O sing unto my roundelay . . .
> Save where the beetle winds
> His still but sullen horn
> Or where the weak ey'd bat
> On short shrill shriek flits by on leathern wing.
> O earth, O earth return
> Arise from out the dewy grass . . .
> When the stars threw down their spears
> And watered heaven with their tears. . . .
> The singing masons building roofs of gold.

The multitudinous seas incarnadine.
Por el mes, era de Mayo
Cuando hace la calor,
Cuando canta la calandria
Y Responde el ruisenor.
Cien jacas caracolean,
Suo juietes estan muertos.
[The month, it was May
When it gets hot,
When the lark sings
and the nightingale answers.
A hundred ponies prance around,
Their riders are dead.]
Let the death divining swan
That defunctive music can. . .
And tear our pleasures, with rough strife
Through the iron gates of life . . .
. . . she tames
The wilder flowers and gives them names.

November 26, 1940

A week ago today I got off the train and went marching off to the Literary Agent's with the new novel. As I suspected, I am now trying to think up a better ending. A week ago today I bought Kierkegaard's *Fear and Trembling* at the Oxford University Press, and have since talked about it so much I feel as if I had been reading Kierkegaard all my life.

A week ago tomorrow I saw Seymour, Helen, Slate, Mark Van Doren, Bob Mack, O. J. Campbell, Prof. Wright, Mrs. Mendelssohn of the English Office, Dr. Dobbie the same but not Prof. Tyndall and not Fr. Ford, neither of whom was in. Also I saw Miss [Naomi] Burton of Curtis Brown who had read the novel. Also I saw Marlene Dietrich in *Seven Sinners*.

Friday I went to Boston – or rather Thursday night I went to Boston.

Boston had a metal, pyramid-shaped bomb shelter parked in the South Station, for everyone to view and tap. The city is being surveyed for hiding places from bombs. Boston is much nearer to London than its distance from New York might indicate.

LIST OF THINGS IN BOSTON

The bus station near the Hotel Statler, buses pointing at the branching streets like big guns.

Boston Common: along which are piano stores; a Beachcomber bar; on the other side, nice houses, the State Capitol.

In Boston I discovered there is a small magazine being published in this country, in French, having the same layout and format as the *Reader's Digest*, attacking Petain, and called I scarcely know what. Also a paper-covered book by Maurois in French, put out by the French Library in Rockefeller Center.

The *Atlantic Monthly* office: a lot of old *New Yorkers*, and a pleasant view. I spoke to C. Kerr about the decline in the quality of the *New Yorker*, and about C. S. Pearce of Duell, Sloane and Pearce, and of the *New Yorker*. I knew all along that the scribbled poem in my pocket was going to be sent to Pearce presently: and, yesterday, it was!

C. Kerr took me to lunch at the Saint Botolph's Club. I had an oyster omelet, the first time I've ever been able to even swallow an oyster. Kerr seemed at first suspicious that I might fight over *The Labyrinth*[3] but soon calmed down and told me all the parts he liked in it. They were many. He did not like the fancy parody at the end.

He did like:
> The name Jato Gordon, and the character of the same.
> The character of T. Park.
> The stuff in Marseilles.
> The stuff about Religion in Rome.
> The character of Taylor.
> The incident in the Weylin Bar.
> Jato Gordon's letter.
> All about Columbia.

He was doubtful about:
> The Joyce part about Cambridge.
> Sneed, Fugaz.

He did not like:
> The character of Sally.
> The movie Taylor was in.
> The parody ending.
> The man from Hollywood (not Fugaz).

I forgot to ask him about:
> Sidney Dispatch.

---

[3] *The Labyrinth* was one of Merton's early novels that failed to find a publisher.

Summary: I wasn't going to rewrite the book. If I had, he might of wanted it. He said it had to be about me or Terence Park, one or the other. Not both: too confusing. I'm sure I don't know.

MORE ABOUT BOSTON

The incomparable dreariness of Harvard Square, and all Cambridge. The more incomparable dreariness of M.I.T. The squalor of Huntington Ave. The Uptown movie. The squalor of Washington Street.

The Catalonian Chapel in the Museum of Fine Arts. It was filled with a class of high school girls, sitting on all the benches and even on the floor while their young teacher dictated information that they busily took down in their notebooks.

"The central figure – is Christ in majesty – The scallop motif represents – (I forget what) – The stars symbolize the universe – His hand is raised for the Greek blessing – " and here she broke off and wondered aloud what was the difference between a Greek Orthodox and Roman Catholic blessing. She was very sober and serious, and all the little dames took down notes very meekly. It was very pleasant to see them with their bent heads, writing down what the teacher said – and not looking at all at the frescoes! But why be mad? Better they should meekly take notes than be full of proud and pugnacious opinions conforming absolutely with some arbitrary party-line of fashions, and equally unfounded on any true understanding. If they don't understand, better they should be meek and listen to something about the stuff. And the remarks were objective – not opinions, but facts about the frescoes.

THINGS I MANAGED TO COPY OUT OF KIERKEGAARD BOOKS IN THE BOSTON PUBLIC LIBRARY AND THE WIDENER LIBRARY AT HARVARD.

I. *Christian Discourses* VII.

"If the angels are God's messengers who obey His very behest, if He makes use of the winds as His angels – the bird and the lily are just as obedient, although God does not employ them as His messengers and it is as if He had no use for them. The lily and the bird have no occasion to become self-important in view of the use that is made of them, they feel humiliated, as though they were superfluous. In man's busy life it is no rare occurrence that precisely the unusually talented person more or less superfluous because he is not apt to fit into any of all the situations to which the bustle of business would assign him, with which it would occupy him and employ him – and yet precisely his superfluousness does more to magnify the Creator's honor than does all this self-importance and bustle."

II. *Philosophical Fragments.*

The subject of becoming remains unchanged in the process of becoming (undergoes a change in being but not in essence).

Can the necessary come into existence?

> "The necessary cannot undergo any change since it is always related to itself, and related to itself in the same manner."

> "Everything that comes into being proves precisely, by coming into being, that it is not necessary."

> "The actual is no more necessary than the possible, for the necessary is absolutely different from both."

> "The change involved in becoming is an actual change; the transition takes place with freedom. Becoming is never necessary. It was not necessary before it came into being, for then it could not come into being; nor after it came into being for then it has not come into being." (p. 61)

"All becoming takes place with freedom, not by necessity."

November 27

Today a lot of snow and very cold, very slippery. The buttons are coming off my very heavy overcoat. My cold is a little better. I have read more of Kierkegaard's *Fear and Trembling.* Fr. Philotheus laughed uproariously for happiness when I described Kierkegaard's image of the two dances illustrating his distinction between resignation and faith. He laughed with great happiness when I told him of Lowrie's sentence in his introduction saying Kierkegaard had not yet been read in China because China doesn't take account of anything that is still unknown to America.

I think Lowrie's introduction to his *Biography* is very good – even if he does talk about the man constantly as "S.K.," as if he were the head of a firm.

I like Kierkegaard's notions that the greatest saints probably look like the stupidest bourgeois.

I was driven in to the Boston Public Library, where I read some Kierkegaard, by a shower of rain.

The Fra Angelico of the Blessed Mother and Child with Saint George, among other saints, I saw in the Boston Museum and now have a postcard of tacked on my door. It is one of the most wonderful pictures I have ever seen. It is absolutely holy. It is a real picture of the Blessed Mother. It is a picture of God as He really appeared in the flesh. Fra Angelico knew how

He appeared. He knew: most artists never knew. Their babies are just hunks of flesh, containing no spirit at all, let alone the Word of God!

This is a baby no one would think of talking baby talk to, and kissing and mouthing. It is the Christ Child, to be adored with great gifts or such gifts as one possesses – as much as one has.

I am glad I am not in:

Thompson's Spa, Boston.

Or The Hotel Statler.

Pieroni's Restaurant,

The Hotel Essex, opposite South Station.

The Widener Library.

Harvard Square.

The German Museum at Harvard.

Joy Street.

Milk Street.

The Botolph Club.

The Copley Plaza.

Boyleston Street.

That half-finished New England Mutual Building, on Boyleston Street.

The Telepix Cinema.

The Bomb proof shelter in South Station.

The Fox and Hounds Club.

The Puritan Bookstore, or whatever it was called.

The State Capitol, illuminated by night, and unharmonious by day because the main building is brick and the new wings, flanking it, are stone.

The Ritz Carlton.

The Fenway.

Back Bay Station.

Crossing the perilous intersection of Stuart and Arlington Streets.

The Holland-American line office on Boyleston Street.

The kitchen of my brother's girl's house in Weston, watching that mad, pretty, awkward, police dog puppy.

I am glad I am in this room. Tacked on the door are pictures of Saint Dominic, Saint Francis receiving the stigmata, two of the Blessed Mother and Child, and one, a Dürer, of the Virgin of the Annunciation. Raphael, Fra Angelico, Dürer, Guido da Siena, The School of Giotto. On my desk,

Kierkegaard, The *Biographia Literaria, Metaphysical Poetry* – Donne to Butler, Saint Bonaventure, Saint Teresa of Avila, Hopkins, Lorca, Aristotle, *The Pearl, Little Flowers of Saint Francis,* Saint John of the Cross. Wait and see how fast I throw away Byron! Then also Saint Augustine, but waiting to be returned to the library. Two volumes of Skeat's big Chaucer, also. Somewhere – Blake: not my own. Modern Library, and its paltry edition!

November 28, 1940

England is being blasted right off the face of the earth and no one can comprehend it. What is happening is much more terrible than what happened to France, in a way. It is already as if England were buried under ruins. One ceases to hear much from her. It is as if her voice were being stilled – and then, all of a sudden, the English Ministers begin to cry out "We are getting beaten – help us!"

And that means we probably soon will. But she is obviously being beaten. It must be terrible, now. First, London was being bombed, and still persisting. Now, suddenly, piece by piece of England is being wiped out. England, who wasn't touched for centuries! Because the towns are so foul, that are being destroyed, because there was so much misery in them, because the whole thing is so strange, because it does not make a noise like history, it all seems incredible. We do not feel concerned. But then I am in the depth of the country, here. The trouble is that it is all too disgusting. The war is waged, now, impersonally, by bombers, by machines. There is not even much hatred. If there were more hatred the thing would be healthier. But it is just filthy, this destruction. In France, it was not terrible in this way: that was the amazing movement of an army, cutting up, scattering, capturing another army. But this is just a vile combat of bombs against bricks, attempts to wipe out machines and to bury men lying in tunnels under tons of stone and rubbish. It is not like a fight, it is like a disease: and the Germans will find that, if they overcome England not like men but like a pestilence, their own power will immediately rot, after the war: for they will all turn to killing themselves.

I wonder if all the German airmen, from the bombing they have done, have come to consider themselves as a kind of doctors?

I wonder if, when the war is over, they will all realize that they themselves are living, and sterilize themselves, wipe themselves out. Maybe medicine, without mercy, will come to consider its mission to be not to save men but to kill microbes, and so, doctors will want to sterilize everything.

That is the trouble, this bombing may appear to be medical. That is why it is so foul. But precisely in that is its danger to the airmen themselves.

Flying itself is a terrible thing, probably all fliers are atheists or tend to become atheists, thinking themselves angels.

November 29, 1940

Kierkegaard has an interesting notion of a vow of silence necessarily imposed upon a man capable of the kind of faith shown by Abraham in the trial over Isaac.

This faith is beyond heroism because it is incomprehensible. Heroism is only possible in the realm of the universal. This is beyond ethics, beyond the universal, beyond the intelligible, and once more *particular.* Abraham is an individual in the presence of an Absolute Personality. This relationship is incomprehensible.

To try to express it – for Abraham to try and express it, would be a terrible temptation to hypocrisy or sacrilege. Hence the vow of silence. He has to endure this martyrdom of being incomprehensible, *absurd.*

A similar vow of silence is imposed on the Blessed Mother by the incomprehensible mystery of the annunciation: "Be it done unto me according to Thy Word!" This dreadful and magnificent and terrifying annunciation of the Angel: "the Spirit of the Lord God will come upon thee:" "Be it done unto me according to Thy Word." This is beyond heroism: there is absolutely nothing theatrical about it, nothing spectacular. If it could be explained, this would be heroic. Because it is incomprehensible, – hence the vow of silence. She must remain completely alone with this immense and terrific responsibility which no one is able to understand. She cannot be a teacher, only a witness. That is the highest thing of all – silence: The final culmination of Christ's teaching, the test of our faith, beyond all teaching is his *disappearance* from the tomb. Nobody saw the resurrection.

Quia si confitearis in ore tuo Dominum *Jesus Christum,* et in corde tuo credideris quod Deus illum suscitavit a mortuis, salvus eris. [For if you *confess with your lips that* Jesus is Lord, *and believe in your heart that God raised him from the dead, you will be saved.* (Romans 10.9, New American Bible)]

Rom. 10.9

It is beyond words, beyond teaching: *"in corde tuo credideris."*

Kierkegaard distinguishes the "infinite renunciation" by which man becomes a tragic hero, a luminous example, a teacher by example because he loses his individuality in the universal, the most comprehensible, the most right, and "Faith", which is far beyond, incomprehensible, *absurd*, involving a teleological suspension of ethics, in the privacy of an individual once more alone with his dread in the presence of God. Hence the command to sacrifice Isaac supersedes all ethics, it is absurd: it must be done because it is absurd and dreadful, but *not because it is duty* and therefore pleasant, as Agamemnon's sacrifice of Iphigenia.

Now when Saint Francis came back from Mount Alvernia, we read in the story of a tremendous, overwhelming change that had come over him. He was no longer a teacher. He no longer said anything. *He is no longer a dramatic figure.* He is no longer a colorful, lovable figure, no longer charming, romantic, no longer the Saint Francis who preached to the birds, who played on the fiddle with two sticks and made songs for the Lord in French. On the contrary, he is a strange, colorless, hunched up little man, silent, seeming to be sick. He has his hands bound up in rags and won't show them to anybody, but hides them under his sleeves.

He carries upon him the stigmata; stigmata, as if really signs of shame. The shame of Christ, the most terrible insult ever perpetrated on earth, the wounds made upon the body of God by men: this insult, by virtue of the incomprehensible, Saint Francis also wore: and what a terrible thing it would have been if he had gone about showing these wounds to people: it would have been a more terrible act than the treachery of Judas.

Saint Francis' greatness is in this, that he bore the same insult as Christ – an insult beyond all comprehension, beyond all drama, beyond all speech, so extreme as to seem utterly neutral.

In the same way the Mystery of the Annunciation is so extreme that to men it seems strangely neutral, it cannot be grasped. Unbelievers can't even make much of scoffing at it; they try, and their insults never get anywhere near what they would like to say – they seem powerless. So also with the Resurrection: it is so incomprehensible that it is even beyond blasphemy.

Yet Our Blessed Mother, in the Annunciation, was left absolutely without protection from the insults of every unbeliever. She was the only one who ever saw the angel, and Kierkegaard says, the angel was sent to her: the angel was not sent to announce the mystery to the whole world that men might more easily believe. If we have any faith at all, we are able to share in that same insult: that those who blaspheme Our Blessed Mother may also think us mad for believing in the Annunciation. But it happens that those who have most faith are those who appear least heroic: Saint

Francis, before Alvernia was a passionate, wonderful saint: and after it, a silent, hunched up little man, hiding his hands.

December 2, 1940

This vow of silence idea of Kierkegaard's is something you keep coming across everywhere, because radios are forcing men into the desert. The world is full of the terrible howling of engines of destruction, and I think those who preserve their sanity and do not go mad or become beasts will become Trappists, but not by joining an order, Trappists in secret and in private – Trappists so secretly that no one will suspect they have taken a vow of silence.

We are surrounded by noise, so much noise that the statement that we will be silent will be drowned out, so there is no point in adding that statement to all the others, to the din of guns. . . What is the sense of opening your mouth in a bombardment to say you will be silent?

I am impressed and awed by the fact that I cannot join an order.

Yet at the same time, tomorrow is the feast of Saint Francis Xavier who preached the Word of God in China and Japan and Indo-China and is the Patron of the Propagation of the Faith. Before anyone makes a vow of silence, perhaps he must submit himself to God's Law, which is universal. As Kierkegaard says, if he loses his individuality in the universality of God's Law, a man's life will become an intelligible pattern for all. Of course if he tries to "be" something for others to look at, he asserts his individuality over against the universality of good works, and denies them. If he is good to be seen by men he denies his goodness. If he is good in secret, men will understand, openly, his goodness as universal and praise not him but our Father. Therefore there, too, secrecy is necessary.

The higher vow of silence is not for most people. I don't think it is to be sought after. The tribulation of the dreadful faith of Abraham alone in the presence of the Father, or St. Francis alone in the presence of the Son is not to be idly asked for by a terrible coward, afraid of a toothache. But a man must still lose himself secretly in doing good works of Faith and Love in the universal sense. This comes before any higher vow of silence, but this vow of silence is important too. It is by this silence that we preach: by that we cannot preach.

In either case, we must seek silence. I think that is indicated not only by the increase of unbearable sound in the world.

Why was Saint Philomena kept hidden for seventeen centuries? If not to teach us secrecy.

The prayer for the Beatification of Bishop Neumann, which was sent to me by a strange series of hidden causes, also stresses this secrecy.

December 3, 1940

Saint Thomas conceives God's essence as a blueprint of all created essences.

For the Franciscan school, even the exemplar causes of things are free acts of God and every exemplar cause is contingent. All the ideas in the Divine mind are contingent. For Occam, the Divine ideas are so free as to be almost arbitrary.

For the Franciscans, God creates the essence of, say, a tiger lily, and relates it to His own essence. He creates these forms and can annihilate them. They have no necessity.

For the Thomist, God contemplates His own essence and draws from that the form of a tiger lily which is present in it with a certain necessity already.

For the Thomist, the human soul can only understand what has first been presented to it in phantasms. Phantasms are transmitted to the intellect *only* through the five senses (of the *body*). When the soul is in heaven, before the Last Day, before its reunion with its glorified body, it has no body at all. Therefore no senses. Therefore receives no phantasms. Therefore it is blind in heaven – unless the active intellect is endowed there with special miraculous graces enabling it to overleap this natural barrier. But there is a natural barrier. Therefore the *philosophical* argument the Thomists have for the immortality of the soul can only say that if the soul is in heaven, it is completely inactive there, blind, *stored* so to speak, in unconsciousness, until the Last Day. There is no *natural* reason for it to enjoy the Beatific Vision: only a supernatural reason: that belongs to Theology.

Aeternum – Aeviternum[4]

For Aristotle, the intelligences are uncreated first movers moving the spheres. He only proves existence of a first unmoved mover, not a creator, consequently he goes on to admit the existence of many first movers.

This position is a little modified by Thomists, for God is a creator. The angels take the place of these movers of the spheres, they are created movers, but they are eternal – beyond time in the *aevium* [eternity], possessing their being at once, perfectly, totally – not successively in any respect.

---

[4] *Aeviternum* is the Old Latin form of *Aeternum*. Both words mean "eternal."

For the Franciscans, the angels do not possess their being at once, perfectly, totally, but in a *succession of moments* – if not of earthly time, anyway successively.

How does Saint Thomas explain something like the fall?

The angels enjoy their *substance* at once, totally, perfectly, yet also exist successively, too.

Time as we know it is a succession controlled and measured by the sun. The succession admitted by the Franciscans in Heaven and in Purgatory is not measured in this manner, but is a succession. Hence it is not really an *aeviternum* [eternity] at all, but still time.

In time, existence is successive, from moment to moment, a *forma fluens* [flowing shape, or changeable essence] controlled and recreated each instant by God as *causa conservans* [the cause that keeps something in being], not merely set in motion by God as *prima causa producens* [the first cause that brings something into being]. On this relies Occam's proof for the existence of God.

Man's identity, preserved from moment to moment, in spite of his change in being from moment to moment, is the product of the *causa conservans*, and man's being is more than the total of these successive moments, just as a poem is more than the sum of its parts. A man's identity is a total, a *gestalt* [the form, figure, or shape of an *ensemble* taken together], product of this *causa conservans*. Nevertheless his being is constantly changing, from moment to moment. I am not what I was a minute ago. Each *present* moment offers the possibility of completely free and contingent choices. Every past moment represents actions that have been done, and are now rooted in necessity. Meanwhile the *causa conservans* is more than a blind life force, it is God's eternal and free and loving will, that thought each moment of my existence before I was, and every second of my life, waking and sleeping, creates me, is crucified for me, rises again from the dead: this in eternity, and also in time, for every second, every moment, in the vast temporal life of the Church, God takes flesh before the tabernacle, and is offered up and nailed to the cross, crucified, dies, is buried, is resurrected somewhere on the earth. In the hurry and crowding of words, still this astounds the eye on the page. In the turmoil of thoughts, the brain is aghast at it. In the movement of desires the will is staggered by it, and exhilarated; and the mind cannot understand. But in the silence of thought and reflection, it will not be deliberately found, this truth: those who have found it, see this truth, then, as it really is, in the silence and darkness. In that silence you cannot walk about and come upon this truth in its reality. There is, after the words, an emptiness where curiosity is a blasphemy and where those who have retired into the deeper silence know there is dread: but beyond that, the only absolute certainty. I can read about the dread and the certainty, but only read because I only know words, not silences.

December 4, 1940

Cum enim secundum statum conditionis nostrae ipsa rerum universitas sit scala ad ascendendum in Deum, et in rebus quaedam sint vestigium, *quaedam* imago *quaedam* corporalia, *quaedam* spiritualia *quaedam* temporalia *quaedam* aeviterna, *ac per hoc quaedam* extra nos, *quaedam* intra nos; *ad hoc per quod perveniamus ad primum principium considerandum quod est* spiritualissimum *et* aeternum *et* supra nos *oportet nos transire per* vestigium *quod est* corporale *et* temporale *et* extra nos, *et hoc es*t deduci in via Dei; *oportet nos intrare ad mentem nostram quae est* imago *Dei* aeviterna, spiritualis *et* intra nos, *et hoc est* ingredi in veritate Dei; *oportet nos transcendere ad aeternum,* spiritualissimum *et* supra nos *aspiciendo ad primum principium et hoc est* laetari in Dei notitia et reverentia maiestatis. [For since according to the state of our condition, the very universe is a kind of ladder for ascending to God, and that in certain things there is *a trace*, or *image* of the *spiritual* in certain *corporal* things, and of the *eternal* in certain *temporal* things, and of certain things *inside us* in certain things *outside us;* thus, it is necessary to come to the first principle by considering what is *most spiritual* and *eternal* and *above us* in the *traces* that we see in things that are *corporal, temporal* and *outside of us.* This is what it means to be *led in the way of God.* It is necessary for us to enter into our mind, which is the *image* of God, *eternal, spiritual* and *inside us,* and this is what it means *to walk in the truth of God;* it is necessary to transcend to the eternal, the *most spiritual* and that which is *above us* by looking to the first principle, and this is what it means *to rejoice in the knowledge and reverence of the majesty of God.*]

The poem I got back from the *New Yorker* today at least looked as if it had been handled.

Somebody remarked today that it has snowed everyday since we got back from the Thanksgiving vacation. I haven't noticed. I have been busy learning how to read (aloud). Things I have thought up, cursorily.

Chaucer, in the introduction to his *Thopas* [an unfinished tale], implies that he is really Stephen Daedalus. Tendency of all Aristotelians to be Joyce.

I thought of sending to New Directions for Dylan Thomas' *Portrait of the Artist as a Young Dog.* Maybe the only good thing about the book is the title.

I thought of not leaving here immediately when the Christmas vacation begins, too early, on the 18th.

Learned how to read Blake's *To the Muses.* I read it to my sympathetic evening class. They shook their heads. I explained "The green corners of the earth." They fainted. I think they were shocked that, in another connection, the sun should come forth as a bridegroom from the bed chamber, rejoicing as a giant to run his course.

Any thought I put down here is liable to be complete as soon as it gets on paper, and never more touched. Therefore, no projects.

Last night I tore a handful of pages out of last year's journal. It is nice to have a journal, written at great length one year. The next you fall upon it as idle as a king and read a page and tear the page out and throw it away; you have read the day's news.

The reason is God's delegate to sit in judgment upon itself, says Saint Bernard.

When am I going to think about the things I have copied out of books?

The Octopus Tree crowds to my mind. Out! That is the worst of keeping a journal. It belongs in another list.

A postcard of the Cézanne *Avenue of Trees* in the Frick Collection turned up in some book. It had been used for cutting the pages.

Today was another day for believing Wordsworth a madman. Only his later poems, Duddon Sonnets etc., can persuade me that he wasn't a crazy phony. But today I read "Lines on a seat in the yew tree . . ." What confusion!

Outside, in the snow, I heard a rifle shot, under the pine trees, beyond the greenhouses. Out there, once, there was once a pen full of hounds nobody knew what to do with. They had just come here and multiplied, fed by the friars. It is very dark outside.

I have thought considerably about the morality of sleeping in the afternoon for an hour after dinner.

Why would I write anything, if not to be read? This journal is written for publication. It is about time I realized that, and wrote it with some art. All that screaming last year, to convince myself a journal was worth writing, but not to be read.

If a journal is written for publication, then you can tear pages out of it, emend it, correct it, write with art. If it is a personal document, every emendation amounts to a crisis of conscience and a confession, not an artistic correction. If writing is a matter of conscience and not of art, there results an unpardonable confusion – and equivocation worthy of a Wordsworth.

There was a time when I was a sophomore, and thought I was living in an ivory tower. So I took my copy of the *Selected Essays* of T. S. Eliot and sold it to the Columbia Bookstore, where later it was seen by H. Jacobson who seemed impressed that I could take Eliot or leave him alone so lightly. I rather wish I had the essays now, but scarcely know why, except to read about John Ford, perhaps.

Further things I think about while the snow whirls:

The *quem quaeritis trope* [whom do you seek]: will I teach a course in Pre-Shakespearian Drama next term? Probably not. I wish I hadn't mentioned.

What good would it do, anyway, if I *did* get hold of Harper's life of Wordsworth, which isn't in the Library?

Braque.

Chagall.

The Hieronymus Bosch *Adoration of Kings* that was in the World's Fair, not this year but last. The surrealism of Bosch is tolerated by people (who don't like art) on the grounds that Bosch lived in the old days and didn't know any better. In other words it must have been unconscious on his part. Nobody who could draw as *real* a Christ Child as Bosch – real in the sense that it is not realistic, but the incarnation of reality – of actuality, i.e. goodness, power – could do anything unconsciously in his painting!

I've got ink all over my fingers, after saying this and other things on paper.

Further reflections: England is being destroyed.

How did I not mention this in class? How do I not mention this in every class. I only barely refer to it and then seldom, unimportantly. Southampton was once one of my favorite towns. What book did I once buy on the platform of the Southern Railway station? I forget.

Ellington's "Koko."

Country Gal.

Sepia Panorama.

I opened a Grammar book, and a sentence for analysis read:

"Mr. Edison's motto is, '*If you hustle while you wait you will succeed.*'"

I have scarcely been so happy to read anything since the stuff about Victor Hugo in *Le Grand Écart*.

"If you hustle while you wait! . . ." consider the inhuman wisdom of the immortal Edison, whose wire trinkets are now being holed away for the

Krieg in a shelter able to resist the heaviest bombs. If the world seems to be coming to an end I think I will make my way to Rahway, N.J. and sabotage the Edison relics, lest they remain for the Martian archaeologists to admire in the future.

"Hustle while you wait!"

If you are forced to stand in one place, do not be idle! Turn somersaults, cartwheels, handsprings!

While waiting for that big business appointment, ceaselessly climb up and down all over the furniture of the outer office. Be in constant motion even while you should be still – Hustle while you wait.

When you sit down to dinner, do not waste the precious moments that elapse while the maid is serving up the food. Practice whisking the cloth off the table without disturbing the plates and knives and forks.

Waiting for the subway: do not stand in one place! Knock people down! Start a fight!

December 8, Feast of the Immaculate Conception

> *Vestimentum tuum candidum quasi nix, et facies tua sicut sol.* [Your garments are as white as snow, and your face shines like the sun. (Antiphon at Lauds for the Feast of the Immaculate Conception)].

This is one of the greatest feasts. Especially because it is a modern feast. It is a feast that has a special significance for us. But I wouldn't write about anything I didn't understand, or even think I understood. All I know is that we should all be especially devoted to the Immaculate Conception, whose feast was given us especially for our time. The feast of the purest of all created things and the most perfect and the most beautiful was given us, and Her doctrine, of whom it is said: *"Tota pulchra es, Maria, et macula originalis non est in te"* ["You are all beautiful, Mary, and original sin is not in you"] became dogma in a century which devoted itself to a singular worship of ugliness, and to a singular cult of that curiosity about the lower nature which was the material cause of the first sin. But *"macula originalis non est in te."* Now all that ugliness and all that curiosity and all that baseness has born its vile and terrible fruit in this war. Therefore we must turn with special reverence and devotion to the Immaculate Conception of Our Blessed Mother. This is Her Feast: not the feast of an innocent little girl. Not the feast of a sweet lady in a gown. This is the feast of the Immaculate Conception of the Mother of God, who crushed the serpent's head, whose purity and glory defy imagination, and demand, no idolatrous condescension, but absolute fidelity and love and reverence, so that we should all be agonized to be so incapable of the love and reverence this feast demands.

. . . *Facies tua sicut sol* [Your face shines like the sun].

December 9

No wonder nobody much teaches anything about literature in literature courses. Literature is hard to teach. You cannot explain what is good easily, any more than you can explain Faith easily or Love easily. Furthermore, to teach appreciation of literature is often as bad as teaching appreciation of Divine Charity! You must not talk about either in cliches: it is sacrilege, because it scandalizes anybody who has enough sense to detect the falseness of a cliche, and makes him turn away from literature – as from religion, for good!

Maybe it is less of a sin to just teach the biographies of poets. At least a biography is something: it is not pure subjective opinion. But who teaches *poetry* and not *opinions?*

Today there was a thaw, sunlight, and blueness and warmth in the air. The hills, still snowcovered, were lovely in the haze of the thaw. There were patches on the wet, soft ground, where the snow had melted, and it was good to see the ground. A stray red setter followed me out through the woods, acting as if I were his master, running off, coming back when I stopped and telling me to come on, very pleased when I whistled to him, and acting just like a dog being taken out to run in the woods. In the end, it turned out he had taken me for a walk; led, not followed me, out and back. I wish I could keep him and feed him in my room. How could I ever take care of a dog?

Today I was in Olean for the first time in a week. There are new buses. Lax went to New York with Gibney a week ago. The town is full of shoppers. The streets are wet.

Sitting in the chair, having a haircut, I reflected that I had finally got used to not talking to barbers. Before, I had always been fairly conscious of the fact I was not saying anything. Now, I am neither surprised when I speak to a barber, nor when I don't speak. I have finally become used to getting my haircut, and can sit in the barber's chair without embarrassment. Don't even give it a thought!

I can't wait to read Lervti [?] or the "Circassian Love Chant" (never did before, you know!).

Books that I have lost – they were in a box somewhere – Random House Blake, O.S.A.: Donne, Keats in a $1.00 edition, *Ulysses*, and other things I forget. Oh yes, Coleridge.

Down the hall, somebody drew a bow across a muted violin – it sounded like a distant horn. O.K. I'm wrong. It is a horn. It got louder.

December 10. 1940

The distinction between seeing God *per speculum* – by means of a glass and *in speculo* in a glass, in a mirror, present there not by reflection, but actually.

For Saint Thomas, the intelligence, memory and will are really distinct: they are separate accidents of a simple substance, the soul. By virtue of that fact there is communication between them. For Saint Bonaventure intellect, memory and will are neither distinct from one another nor from the soul itself. In this the soul is a more perfect image of the Trinity, of three persons, not distinct, one God.

For Saint Bonaventure there is no distinction between charity and sanctifying grace. Charity is sanctifying grace considered as oriented from man to God. Grace is charity considered as oriented from God to man. Grace is the beginning; without grace man cannot pray for grace. *Iustitia* [justice] is the directing and making use of charity, working in charity.

For Saint Thomas – sanctifying grace an entitative habit of soul and charity is a habit of that distinct faculty the will. Without grace the habit of charity is worthless: but charity does not occupy the whole soul. There is need of grace.

"*Secundum enim primam naturae institutionem creatus fuit homo habilis ad contemplationis quietem, et ideo* posuit eum Deus in paradiso deliciarum. *Sed avertens se a vero lumine ad commutabile bonum, incurvatus est ipse per culpam propriam, et totum genus suum per originale peccatum, quod dupliciter infecit humanam naturam, scilicet* ignorantia *mentem et* concupiscentia *carnem; ita quod excaecatus homo et incurvatus in tenebris sedet et caeli lumen non videt nisi succurrat gratia cum iustitia contra concupiscentiam, et scientia cum sapientia contra ignorantiam.*" *Itinerarium.* 1. 7. ["For according to the first institution of nature, man was created capable of the calm of contemplation, and therefore *God put him in a paradise of delights.* But turning away from the true light to goods that change and pass away, he was bowed down by his own fault, he and his entire race incurred original sin, which infects human nature in two ways, namely the mind through *ignorance* and the body through *concupiscence;* thus, because he is *blind* and bowed down, man sits in darkness and does not see the light of heaven, unless he is helped by grace with justice against concupiscence, and with knowledge against ignorance."]

———

I just wished the war was over so it would be possible to be in Rome. I just thought of being at the top of the steps, high up on the Capitol, at the entrance to Sancta Maria in Aracoeli.

If I go to the Columbia Library during this vacation – Christmas vacation, what books do I suppose I'll go looking for? Chambers' *Life of Coleridge*. Harper's *Life of Wordsworth*? Waste of time. F. L. Lucas – *Decline and Fall of the Romantic Ideal*? It seems silly that I can't think of anything better than these to look at when I am so short of books here. Perhaps I don't really need them; or probably the thing to do is read some Elizabethan Plays. Better to buy a little book.

I don't think they have Dekkers' *Plague Pamphlets* – not on the shelf among the English books, anyway.

Pretty editions:

The big – many volumed edition of [Walter Savage] Landor.

Painter's *Palace of Pleasure*.

Nonesuch Press Blake; Ed. Keynes. 3 vol.

Margolinth's *Marvell*.

Oxford Press. Crashaw.

What did I take from that Library last Christmas?

H. O. Taylor – *Medieval Mind*, vol. I.

Cunningham-Grahame *Life of Saint Theresa*, vol. I.

What else? Probably Christopher Dawson – something or other. I could get it here!

Maybe to the Columbia Music Library, listen to Scarlatti, Purcell, Byrd, Medieval Music in the Anthologie Sonore. But John Paul has Scarlatti.

In other words, I can think of no vital reason for going to the Columbia Library. But yes I can, too: Lowrie's Life of Kierkegaard. I know exactly where to find Kierkegaard on the shelves in tier three. I looked at him there before.

Wish I knew something about Scotus and Occam.

December 14. 1940

Concerning a theory of communication: begin with the mystery of the Visitation – this would also be a starting point for an aesthetic which would avoid the pure intellectualism of some more or less Thomist aesthetics and naive theories saying art must preach a moral lesson.

The Mystery of the Visitation implies a whole conception of communication based on charity, which lies behind the illuminationism of Saint Bonaventure. If we communicate, it is by virtue of sharing the same ideas, implanted in us by God; but by a loving God, so that we may love Him. The beginning of communication is the salutation: Peace be with you! God be with you. Peace, in this sense = the direct intuition of God, the mystical union (not vision, in Saint Bonaventure).

How the Mystery of the Visitation is a perfect starting point: in this, the salutation was also a sacrament; the salutation of Our Blessed Mother was the cause of sanctifying grace being poured down upon the babe, that leapt in the womb.

Saint Bonaventure's notion of Christian *conversatio* – not just talk, but charity as expressed by all acts of outward behavior, every word, every just act, every act, that is, that brings men to love and glorify God. (*Itinerarium* 1.8.)

Also, Saint Epiphane says in a sermon on the Blessed Virgin: *"Ave liber incomprehensus quae Verbum et Filium Patris mundo legendum exhibuisti."* ["Hail, incomprehensible book, which you gave to the world to read, the Word, the Son of the Father."]

Fr. Philotheus says one Gabriel Marcel has things to say about communication. I have already written to find out from a store in New York if they have anything by him.

Thus there can be such thing as a silent conversation: a conversation without words, more perfect than conversation with words. Donne's *Ecstasy* would be a quaint and rather awkward expression of it. Incidentally, how often was Donne deliberately quaint? Eye beams threaded on one string. Today I thought of some lines of Donne that I admitted were unsatisfactory. There comes a point where you can understand Donne's shortcomings (as Coleridge said there was a place where you ceased to be ignorant of a philosopher's understanding and understood his ignorance. Clumsy, because he sacrificed too much to the *chiasmus* [?]) but I forget what the lines were – oh yes:

> "I have done a greater thing
> Than all the worthies did
> And I shall do a greater still
> Which is: to keep that hid."

Now I look at the book: no wonder the lines were so bad; they were *my* bad lines, not Donne's:

> "I have done one braver thing
> Than all the worthies did
> And yet a braver thence doth spring,
> Which is to keep that hid."

And it comes out even better repeated in the last stanza, bringing the poem around in a perfect circle. I think I will learn to distrust such intuitions about poetry that come to me in the middle of the afternoon while I am hitch-hiking in to Olean! The best stanza in the poem . . . the above, by coming right after it, thus explaining it, complicating the general idea it expresses.

> It were but madness now t'impart
> The skill of specular stone,
> When he which can have learned the art
> To cut it, can find none.

"Done *one* braver thing" – makes all the difference. The indefinite article makes it very naive: "one" is much more serious and has some humility in it, too. As for greater – it has none of the gravity and compunction and depth imparted by "braver," which is a modest word by association with fear: therefore serious and not at all.

"Worthies" – the worthies are quaint, in a good way; just as the "sepulchral statues" are quaint, in a good way. They are old and humorously conceived. The "worthies" are reduced to a kind of anonymity by being named as a species – and the word "worthies" implies the added anonymity imparted by the idea of the (anonymous) popular tradition by which the worthies come down to us. The sepulchral statues have not only the incommunicativeness of stone and of the tomb, but they are the products of anonymous artists.

The notion of reticence is important to religious verse. Two aspects in Blake: the two poems – the poison tree, and "I told my love . . . love which never told can be." An opposition. Then there is the other opposition, in the Gospels:

> "Let your light so shine before men . . ."
> "A city which is set upon a hill cannot be hid"

and

> "Let not thy right hand see what thy left hand doeth."
> "When you fast, be ye not, like the hypocrite, sad."

There is only an apparent contradiction, but the appearance of contradiction scandalizes the weak. The first is *"conversatio"*[5] – confessing God before all men. But the second is keeping hid that which cannot be told. It is a very complicated and subtle distinction: that which can be told must be told. That which cannot, must be kept hid. St. Francis himself had to hide his hands, after Alvernia.

The Resurrection – was hid.

No one saw the Resurrection. Everyone saw the Crucifixion. Everyone does see the crucifixion. The cross is everywhere. But the resurrection is secret. The saints, who have understood it, in all its reality, cannot explain. The crucifixion can be explained to everybody.

December 18. 1940

It is extremely quiet – everyone has gone home for Christmas. I am grateful to this place. I stay in it a few more days to work alone. Perhaps read Peele's *Old Wives' Tale, The Shoemakers' Holiday, – Faustus, Tamburlaine,* etc. all over again. Certainly to finish notes on Wordsworth, Coleridge. Perhaps for the first time I am beginning to understand Wordsworth. That is, I have finally figured out how it was possible for the same man to have written "Three years she grew" and "Resolution and Independence," or "The Ode to Duty" and "The World is too much with us." That is some of the worst and some of the best poems in English.

Last year I was writing about the fact that I didn't know what a short story was or how to write one.

My students would probably be shocked at the lack of events in a *New Yorker* short story, so I hesitate to read them any. Besides, this is a course in literature. I lent one of them some Saroyan and he liked it fine.

The place is so empty that the ROTC man and a business professor are crowded in the next room, not talking, just sitting, to close out the emptiness of this great big building. But the priests are downstairs. Tonight, I like it empty.

What you don't hear when the building is empty:

The guy who goes by singing: "In my dreams I'm home again. Home where I be-long!" Now he's home where he belongs.

---

5 *Conversatio* is a technical term that means turning away from love of self or the world, or God *for* oneself, and so on. It means to love God *for Himself alone* (not merely turning from disbelief in God to belief in His existence, or anything like that).

———

Last night for the first time in my life I spoke on the radio. I was never less afraid of anything in my life than a microphone. I was more nervous at rehearsal than when I went on the air.

The things I had to say were not mine. I wrote the speech: gave it anonymously. I wrote the speech down. Therefore I had no call to be nervous over the speech because it was not mine and there was no question of trembling for fear I wouldn't be adequately praised.

It was a speech saying everybody should pray for peace, and therefore it was too true and too serious for me to worry about getting mike-fright. If I had written a comic sketch, then I would have had a right to be terrified with worry as to how it might go over.

The only thing that possibly could cause mike-fright is that suddenly one might become very conscious that the microphone was picking up all sounds – therefore that one was being heard. There are cases where I can see how I'd be afraid if I suddenly became conscious of the fact that I was being heard everywhere. Last night it was extremely important to be heard everywhere, not because of myself but because of the words. Therefore no mike-fright. I changed the speech while I was reading it. Sometimes I stumbled over a word, ad libbing. But it was good to be able to say exactly what seemed to be required, and know that it was going into effect *instantly* – not like something that can be written on paper and then crossed out, or reconsidered in some way.

I wrote the speech a week ago Saturday.

What happened in Olean today when I was in town.

I met Lax's father outside Oakleaf's.

I saw Fr. Peter Regulatus lifting a bundle out of a car down in front of the Five and Ten.

I ran into Ed Jantos the Freshman coach in front of Davis' [men's clothing store]. Later he picked me up in the car as I was walking back to college, out past the Nun's Hospital. I noticed that the Haven Theater was playing *The Ramparts We Watch* and in the paper Roosevelt was giving away things to England. Eating his cake and having it, getting England to fight for him without being in a war himself. It doesn't seem so much, to have asked over a small unheard of radio station for some people to pray for peace. What I wonder is, did anybody pray for peace? Maybe to wonder that is a sacrilege. All I had to do was give the message.

All the while the sky was very gray, of course.

The Salvation Army dames leaned in their booths looking mighty seedy, and rang their little bells.

A bus went by full of fellows from Saint Bonaventure going off to take the Erie train.

I saw Bob O'Brien in the lobby of the Olean House.

I noticed there was a portrait of Lincoln over the doors, in the splendid marble interior of the First National Bank where for once I was putting in money and not taking it out!

On the cover of *Look* was a girl in a white and skirted bathing suit upon a very tropical beach. It wouldn't be a bathing suit but a bathing dress.

The newspaper said Hitler made Petain let Laval out of gaol. I refuse to wonder what *that* is all about.

New words: Bardia, Solum, Fort Capuzzo.

Last year it was Mussolini. Very small victories compared with the Battle of France!

Thursday. January 2. 1941

I will not soon forget how happy I was to get back here from New York. Not that there was anything wrong with New York: but it was very delightful coming in to my room, and seeing the pictures tacked on the door, and the bed made up with clean sheets.

The room was full of the books as I had left them, hastily arranged along the back of the desk in a long, fairly orderly row. The room was full of the atmosphere of work. I was a little sad, all of a sudden, to think that the novel was supposed to be finished, but was consoled to think that I still really have to write a decent ending on to it and maybe revise a lot of it besides.

Looked at as a promising trial, it is a good novel. Looked at as a successful treatment of a tough, *Hamlet* subject, it isn't. I am not content, and never was to think anything I ever wrote was a trial. Nor am I content to leave this as a trial. It is too clear that something can be done with this one.

Equivocal use of the word trial.

Fr. Philotheus gave his speech on Occam in Detroit: he was surprised that there were more than 50 people! He returned through (to him) enemy country (Canada), but found no occasion to throw the bombs he didn't have with him anyway.

What new on the Erie R.R.?

Going down, I noticed there was a shack as you enter Corning near the bum's jungle, and on the outer walls of this shack are crude religious paintings.

There is a theater in Waverley with a crazy name which I have forgotten.

There is a very fancy farm on the climb between Susquehanna and Deposit.

The Delaware Valley is full of intuitions about the theory of knowledge. The big discovery I made there in 1938 when riding up with Lax was only, after all, that I was capable of reflecting upon an act of consciousness of my own. I had perceived the distinction between a nominal perception, and a reflection upon the consciousness of perception. But after all that is an important thing to find out. It is only since then that I have been able to write any poems.

It was not until lately that I found out the philosophical words to describe what I had discovered then.

This time I found something else and made a fable of it.

It suddenly struck me as a painfully offensive thing for me to ride whirling through those rocky valleys in a train exclaiming "I know all these hills!"

What do I know of them, or they of me?

It suddenly occurred to me that these real hills must be, to me, because of the peculiarity of my position, peculiarly, very painfully abstract.

What position?

I am sealed up in an air-conditioned train, whirled past the hills and the ice-jammed banks of the river and the woods streaked with white filaments of brick, and cliffs white with icicles.

In order to know these hills, I ought to set foot upon their earth in quietness, perhaps. At least that seemed something painfully necessary at the time. Instead I go through in the sealed train, looking out from behind glass. I am cut off entirely from the hills and they are fairly abstract. What do I know of them, or they of me?

There is no necessity for me to know them, or for them to know me. If I am to know those hills, if their rock faces are to be more than blanks, perhaps I have to climb them, be lost in their woods.

However, it is a terrible thing to ride encased in the glass, sterile, train asking the hills who they are, and being cut off from any real answer in a sealed tube of scientifically cleaned and heated air, not the same air as fills the bitter, hostile woods outside. When the hills go to answer, they are defeated; so is the questioner. The answer can't get through the glass.

Coming back the pine trees across from Narrowsburg pointed with their black hands to the dark sky. The trees at Narrowsburg station – locust trees along the river behind Calicoon station. If you say your prayers, the glass doesn't matter, doesn't stop anything from getting through: the defeat is only when you do not pray, and figure you can know the hills themselves, and not God through them. When you set yourself up to question the hill, what it is in itself, it gives you a stern wall for an answer – and you see the glass between you, and realize the air you breathe has been washed and warmed and you hate that air and its sweet, false, slightly suspicious trainey smell.

In New York – no movies, no plays, no circuses, no hockey games, no Heaven on Ice or whatever it was. No nothing but work, and the Columbia Library, and seeing Lax and Gibney before they went off to Virginia. And yesterday three egg-noggs, at Northport, among those giggling Jane Austen dames, pretty, flaxhaired, having visited Sweden, having studied music.

It was an old house on Church Street, Northport. The rooms were warm and much inhabited, comfortable. There was a trick radio-victrola, a ouija board, a Saroyan book, a Picasso book, a lot of other books, a portrait of the older girl herself very young.

They giggled. They flirted. How they flirted, o them little Jane Austen dames. They wanted to ask their ouija board if Ed Rice was in love. One of the dames knew Freddie Freedgood. Their mother liked the ruined churches at Visby and wanted to put more Seagrams in the egg-noggs. They offered to each and all, marzipan, on a plate.

One had a record from *Marriage of Figaro* for Christmas.

Foolishly I talked about Bloy's book *Celle qui Pleure [She Who Weeps]* and the old lady thought, concerning the apparition of La Salette, "Someone might have imposed on those children."

I spoke to her. On either side, just out of the range of direct vision, her two daughters sat, one in the outside corner of each of my eyes and listened.

It got dull when the talk got around to Roosevelt.

Gerdy was/was not peeved when everybody refused to leave at 9:30 just after we had got there. Gerdy fidgeted a lot. One of the girls was his girl.

As a matter of fact they weren't little, but tall. Their flax hair was uncut, and hung in hanks down their backs. They wore velvet dresses. They grinned a lot, continually. They figured me for a priest, at which I scarce knew whether to be delighted or annoyed, priest being in my eyes a good category, and in the eyes of little dames wanting to flirt around, a dull category. I think, happy, especially after getting back here tonight, to my room. I wish I only were!

This is the new year: I tried to tell myself: a year of terrors, but the sun was out. It may well be, just the same. I am the worst of all prophets: prophecy is the one thing, besides mathematics and being a soldier, I am certain I have no gift for. Being an ice-man I'm not certain of – never having tried.

January 3. 1941

I have already written a letter dated January 3. 1940 – or I think so. I can't verify that because the letter is sealed and ready to go.

There is all the difference in the world between the woods here and the woods on Long Island. I have nothing but the feeling that the very ground is artificial on Long Island – and it is really nothing more than a sandbar and a moraine. Here the earth is much more solid. But the woods also have a different, and a healthier smell. No marshes, no blue mud, no wet sand, no muggy warmish air, no sumacs all over the place. No sassafrass either, if I am sure what that is. I am probably less sure of that than of anything in the world.

Here the solid and rude and fine structure of hills, clad with bare woods, are all lightly powdered with snow today: that gives them a whole lot of beauty. The river was fine, with its silent eddies of cold, dark water.

And this pen, with its silent eddies of ink, science's perfect ink! Sickly smelling, ready to pour out in a great blob on the paper, any minute!

I reflected on the train, that I am glad I have no desire to spread around the article on Clare Boothe in this week's *New Yorker*. It is a vicious article.

[Merton had instructed Fr. Irenaeus to blank out several parts of this entry.]

But I'm glad I don't want to spread the article around just on that account! The article is her fault. If I spread it around and joined the attacks against her I would be working for her, and helping the processes. This imperishable thought came to me maybe around Addison, NJ.

What books seemed important enough to look at, at Columbia?
Schelling's *Elizabethan Drama* in 2 volumes.
Spens – *Elizabethan* something, *Tragedy* or *Drama*.
Colvin's – *Life of Keats*.
Kierkegaard – *Le Concept de l'Angoisse*.
Selliere – *Leon Bloy*. What a wicked book: and full of lies!
Dekker – *Christ's Tears over Jerusalem*.
Boas – *Marlowe and His Circle*.
Bloy – *Celle qui Pleure*.
Ellis. Fermon – *Jacobean Drama*.

Hazlitt's *Essays* (Dropped them quick!)

Catholic Encyclopedia.

Marvell's *Poems* – (just looked at the book, didn't read a line.)

An *"Age Book"* on the Period of Transition before Elizabeth.

Blair's *Grave* – for Blake's illustrations. Some pictures!

Byron's letters – (clapped the book shut as soon as opened!)

Peacock's *Reminiscences of Shelley.* A good book.

What books did my uncle have?

Count Ten by Hans Otto Storm.

The Renaissance by J. A. Symonds.

You can't go home again, or I can't come home again, or we can't get in again, or you mayn't come out again, or you won't get back again, or you don't go there again, or we shan't get here again, or they don't return again, or we never return again home by Thomas Wolfe. It looked terrible.

Not all that terrible. There seemed to be a fairly good scene about some firemen. But there was an awful room on 12th Street and an awful room in Brooklyn, and on one page he made love to four vile Park Avenue dames who never before or after appeared in the book and it was very stupid and dull.

But there was a scene interesting enough that I read three consecutive pages, about the Olympic Games in Berlin.

"I place no value in eating or not eating, because after all what is of importance? Only to come to the Lord. But those who do fast as well as those who do not fast come to the Lord." (Theresa Neumann)

"My father is a tailor; when he has made some article of clothing, and someone says to him 'a fine garment, well made' my father is pleased. So also is our Heavenly Father pleased when we graciously and gratefully admire the beauty of His creatures."

January 6. 1941

"Formerly mankind did not have such a need (for suffering). Things would be better if men would praise God more. Even a little flower can give us occasion to thank God and to praise Him. The Savior permits suffering, to punish certain sins, to test the fidelity of those who love Him, and to give man an opportunity to help others. The sufferings are never so great that a person cannot bear them or must be unhappy, if he has the Savior with him." (Theresa Neumann)

"Where obedience is lacking there is grace lacking too."

January 9. 1941

W. C. Fields under the name Mahatma Kane Jeeves, wrote a movie called *The Bank Dick.* The best things in it were the invented names.

The town – Lompoc.

The hotel – New Old Lompoc House

The Black Pussy Cat Cafe and Snack Bar.

Egbert Souse.

A. Pismo Clam.

Repulsive Rogar.

Filthy McNasty.

The Lompoc Picayune – Intelligencer.

Og.

There was a fine chase in several automobiles. There was a good ending. W. C. Fields has been given a million dollar job directing movies – and has sold a movie grown miraculously [rich] from a story he chanced to tell some press agent while they were making a movie in the earlier part of the picture . . . He doesn't have to work. He is walking around the grounds of his great estate in stupid pants and black coat and spats, nothing to do, swinging his cane. A white coated bartender comes walking in a businesslike manner down a path in the middle distance. Not even looking at Fields. The bartender turns down another path. Fields goes after him, walking briskly, and they go off into the distance and disappear in the trees, off to some fabulous bar. That is the end.

Otherwise, it wasn't the best picture in the world, except for Fields arresting a kid with a toy pistol in the bank and having a ketchup bottle bounced off his head by his little daughter and getting Franklin Pangbourn Mickey-finned.

January 11. Feast of the Holy Family

Just what is a *"Lebensgefuhl"* [full of life]? That seems a silly question to ask on the feast of the Holy Family.

The Feast of the Holy Family is the feast of a terribly important and mysterious truth: with all kinds of facets: and yet it has a surface very hard to penetrate.

The Hidden Life of the Lord at Nazareth is one of the things being celebrated here. Now if we try to imagine the Hidden Life of Jesus, living, obscure, obeying his earthly parents, working in a carpenter's shop, the imagination has no very interesting images to take hold of. A Galilean carpenter's shop – a workbench, of some sort, shavings on the floor – the Blessed Mother cooking in the kitchen – and what did poor Nazarenes eat?

The feast becomes ridiculous, becomes the feast of realism. But that is exactly the point: it is the feast of obscurity and obedience, of God subjected to man, obeying earthly parents, in *obscurity*. Realism has nothing to say about so great a mystery, and it is the fault of our imaginations that we skid about hopelessly on this external surface.

But this is the one, of all cases, where the externals mean absolutely nothing. The importance is that Jesus' life was *hidden:* it is the externals, such as realism may perceive, that do the hiding, but what is important is what is inside. The externals, the appearances, whatever the visual imagination has to take hold on are less to the truth of the mystery than the rind is to a fruit, the shell to a nut, the wrapping to a package containing a box containing a case containing a setting containing a diamond. The external surface is only there to be penetrated. Of course the Blessed Mother had to cook, and St. Joseph had to teach Jesus how to be a carpenter. These things are meaningless, because they only conceal, do not reveal, the unbelievable ecstasy in which that Holy Family lived. To think that the Word of Almighty God was their child, and lived with them thirty years or more in peace and obscurity, in a secret which defied all speech, all knowledge, even all wonder. I think Saint Joseph is the only human being who ever lived thirty years on earth in perfect ecstasy *all the time*, with Our Blessed Savior not only always in his presence, but loving him with an exceptional love, the love of a son, and receiving from him a special love, the love of a father. The Blessed Mother endured for us the whole sorrow of the crucifixion: St. Joseph was not at the Cross' foot, but in Heaven.

Kierkegaard speaks of those who carry with them the terrible secret of faith, a faith which has seen God directly and therefore can no longer be put into words: and he says that such people outwardly appear to us perfectly commonplace and even worldly. The paradox that the man of greatest faith, like Abraham, appears not a romantic hero but a common, worldly, dull old fellow, outwardly. Saint Francis hid the stigmata, because silent and completely obscure, like a little sick man, after Alvernia.

Yet stigmatisation involves a further complication, another convolution too, in this notion of obscurity.

Theresa Neumann's stigmata are not hidden. On the contrary, they are terribly public. They are there to be pried into, and observed, and checked and analyzed by every scientist or photographer or journalist that comes along. But this is the most terrible obscurity of all. Theresa Neumann is at once the most public and the most obscure figure in the world. She herself is nothing but a completely anonymous instrument. Not passive, by any means: any more than the Blessed Mother was a will-less instrument, for all this hangs upon her humble will, as our very salvation hung upon the active consent of Our Blessed Mother: "Be it done unto me according to Thy word!"

Yet Theresa Neumann is completely obscure, because we can see in her nothing special, nothing dramatically heroic, only the commonplace outer surface that is the exterior of a terrible mystery – and has nothing to do with the mystery.

Theresa Neumann has shown that this impenetrable obscurity that the person of greatest, most humble, most obedient faith must suffer, is impenetrable even when it is made most public.

So even the most exact description of the house in Nazareth, and a story telling every external action, all the dishes that were washed, all the clothes sewn, all the carpentry done there, would still mean absolutely nothing. That is also what is wrong with fictionized lives of Christ.

Lebensgefuhl – consciousness of some life-force, some natural power that has no further definition than that it is natural and a power? In an unhappy[?] sense, the kind of dejection that confused Wordsworth and imprisoned Coleridge in inaction. The kind of motiveless depression that sent Luther about his crazy scruples. The kind of thing I made such a botch of writing about in this last novel.

I don't approve the description of it in any such pseudo-physiological terms as that. St. John of the Cross does much better. It is not a sensation, so much as a temptation. The temptation to hopelessness and to scruples. Temptation to sin against Faith and Hope. A trial of some sort: and because everything has a good use, this temptation can be well used by being suffered in patience and obedience and humility. To start out on a chain of ideas that leads up as high as the dread of Abraham from some phoney concept like *"Lebensgefuhl"* shocks me. I probably don't understand it, or in what connection Fr. Philotheus used it last night. He wasn't talking about exactly that, although he did get into the discussion of people with scruples from this notion. Pleasure is, I suppose, also a *Lebensgefuhl*. I protest against such a word.

Horizon is a tiny magazine for British Intellectuals, and born of the war in England. May 1940 was Vol. I. No. 5, so it started in January 1940. I wonder if it still goes on. In the issue I got – there was a v. good poem by Dylan Thomas. Thomas is more of a poet than Auden, MacNiece, Day-Lewis and those birds. Not Spender, maybe. But there were pages of a journal of Spender's which were repulsive. "Tom Eliot took me to lunch at his club, we discussed our poems. How do you mean to pursue your lovely craft, Mr. Spender? O Mr. Eliot, these are hard times for we poets."

Then there was an unfriendly article on Graham Green saying he writes about "Greenlanders," which is true, but what of it? There's no need to sneer at Greenlanders: there are some in every house, in this enlightened age when the world is populated by Greenlanders: witness some of the other stuff in *Horizon*. R. H. S. Crossman, for instance. Anyway, interesting problems about democracy in Crossman's little article. The best of all was a review of some book by some guy named Sherard Vines by one Michael Nelson, beginning:

"From a Midland town of Rumpingham with its suburb of Mere, a selection from the middle class grow steadily more defined in their inability to grasp the political situation of pre-Munich, and in their inability to see themselves with the irony of Mr. Vines. Middle class with little or much money, dealing with the working class only so far as sex necessitates, they are representative enough of England's pre-war middle class."

I was going to say, on reflection, maybe a good writer on an off day, but I think not.

January 15. 1941

I renounce with the greatest alacrity in the world the following literary projects:

1. Writing a story about a man who owns a dog named *Caesar* – the whole purpose of this story would be to have someone come in with a pail of old bones and garbage and pieces of gristle, and chicken guts, and melon-rinds etc. etc. and say "What am I supposed to do with all these old bones, etc.?"

To which the man would wittily reply:

"Give unto Caesar the things that are Caesar's."
– or rather "Render – etc."

2. Writing a story about a bantam-weight prizefighter named "Kid Promiscuous."

3. Drawing a cartoon having the following caption:
"Where was you, playing volley ball?"

4. Writing a literary article beginning –

"I fear me there is a little of the Helen Hokinson in every one of us, and each literary genius, if he only allowed himself, could reveal himself to the world with as dull an imagination as that of Gluyas Williams." [*New Yorker* cartoonist]

5. Writing a radio speech that makes some sense. But I do not utterly renounce it, either.

6. Writing a story about four people, two old and two young, models who had never seen each other before, and who had to pose for a big color-photo for an advertising agency, as if they were a family, father, mother, daughter, grandson – or some child.

7. Another literary article beginning:

"Every man a Coleridge! Fill your journals with worthless projects! See what jolly sport!"

8. I never renounced, because I never thought of, the idea of writing a story about some people in an air raid shelter during an air raid. Now I have thought of the idea, and now I renounce it.

9. The story about a revolution on some Caribbean Island, which was to have been a *Collier's* story, was renounced in June 1939 and stays renounced. The Island was called San Jamie. I renounce the *Collier's* story as a literary form for me, forever.

I lately saw in my mind's eye, or in a dream:

Paris, France.

Paris, France, 1928. In front of the Chambre des Deputes.

Eton – a newish building a music school, maybe.

(Supposing I were not a professor of English at Saint Bonaventure but an English Master at Eton – in peace time. The thought fills me with awe. It is completely unbelievable. In the first place I would have to change back to an English accent, and worry about my manners all over again. All the same I would rather be a master at Eton than at any other school, except for the sneers at my tie.)

Epinal.

Avenue de la Grande Année, Saint Antonin, in front of the Hôtel des Thermes, Annexe – 1928. Father and I ran a race up the middle of the street and I was astonished that he beat me so badly.

Oakham, as seen from Brooke Hill. And the street in front of Greylands.

Us sitting in the Garden of Greylands, supposed to be going through Euripides, all getting fits of laughter at some cat.

The Gare Montparnasse.

Hôtel des Trois Rois, Basle.

The station platform, Köln. Big sign *"Echt Kölnisches Wasser."*

The movie in Köln where I was terrified by the syphilis movie.

Via Veneto, in front of the Ministro dei Corporazioni.

Pont de Kehl.

The Main Street of Kehl.

The Lake of Geneva, 1926.

Rocamadour.

The station at Caussade. Reg Marsh and Bett, who had left the train, getting on their bicycles and riding away on to the wintry causses. We go on to Montauban.

Cinema de la Madeleine, Paris.

Riding a bicycle on a road in Paget, Bermuda – the road that takes you to the Inveruril. [?]

The street outside the Hotel Camaguey, Camaguey. The plainest, dirtiest street in the world. I saw a rat a foot and a half long run across that street so lazily the bus got him.

Halifax, N.S.

Gettysburg battlefield

What you saw out the right hand window of a train going to Manton . . .

That old building standing on the hill over the river, in the Stevens Institute grounds, 1931 – as I was docking on the *Minnetonka.*

Standing on the station platform at Manton, where we changed to the express with the fancy dining car! Some bliss! . . .

January 16. 1941

Eia nunc homuncio, fuge paululum occupationes tuas, absconde te modicum a tumultuosis cogitationibus tuis. Abjice, nunc onerosas curas et postpone laboriosas distensiones tuas. Vaca aliquantulum Deo, et requiesce aliquantulum in eo. Intra in cubiculum mentis tuae, exclude omnia praeter Deum, et quae te juvent ad quaerendum eum, et, clauso ostio, quaere eum. Dic nunc, totum cor meum, dic nunc Deo: quaero voltum tuum; vultum tuum, Domine, requiro (Psal. XXVI, 8). Eia nunc ergo, tu, Domine Deus meus, doce cor meum ubi et quomodo te quaerat, ubi et quomodo te inveniat. Domine, si non es hic, ubi te quaeram absentem? Si autem ubique es, cur non video te praesentem? Sed certe habitas lucem inaccessibilem. (S. Anselmi *Proslogion*, Migne Cap. 1, c. 226.) [Now, little man, turn away a little from your cares, hide a bit from your anxious thoughts. Lay down your burdensome concerns, and put aside your worries. Give a little time to God, and rest a short time in him. Enter into the cell of your mind, exclude everything but God, and that which helps you to seek him, and, with your door closed, seek him. Say now, sincerely, to God: I seek your face, *your face I seek, O Lord.* (Psalms 26.8) Now, I ask you, Lord, my God, teach my heart where and how it might seek you, where and how it might find you. Lord, if it is not here, then where can I find you? If you really are everywhere, then why don't I see you here? But surely you live in inaccessible light. (S. Anselmi *Proslogion,* Migne Cap. I, c. 226)]

Quid faciet, altissime Domine, quid faciet iste tuus longinquus exsul? Quid faciet servus tuus anxius amore tui, et longe projectus a facie tua? . . . (*Proslogion,* Cap. I, c. 226.) [Most high God, what is this, your faraway exile to do? What is your servant, anxious for your love, and cast so far away from your face, to do? (*Proslogion,* Cap. I, c. 226)]

Deus meus es, et Dominus meus es; et numquam te vidi. Te me fecisti et refecisti, et omnia mea bona tu mihi contulisti, et nondum novi te. Denique ad te videndum factus sum; et nondum feci propter quod factus sum. O misera sors hominis, cum hoc perdidit, ad quod factus est! (Ib. c. 226.) [You are my God and my Lord; and I've never seen you. You made me and remade me, and you have given me everything that I have, and I still don't know you. Finally, I am brought to the point of seeing you; and I've not yet done what I'm made to do. O sorry lot of man, who lost that which he was made to be!" (*Proslogion,* Cap. I, c. 226)]

Quaesivi bona, et ecce turbatio. Tendebam in Deum, et offendi in meipsum. Requiem quaerebam in secreto meo, et tribulationem et dolorem inveni in intimis meis. (Ib. c. 226.) [I have sought the good, and behold anxiety. I reached toward God, and only came to grief. I sought inner peace, and only found trouble and sorrow within me. (*Proslogion,* Cap. I, c. 226)]

Doce me quaerere te, et ostende te quaerenti; quia nec quaerere te possum, nisi te doceas, nec invenire, nisi te ostendas. Quaeram te desiderando, inveniam amando, amem inveniendo. Fateor, Domine, et gratias ago, quia creasti in me hanc imaginem tuam, ut tui memor sim, te cogitem, te amem; sed sic est abolita attritione vitiorum, sic est offuscata fumo peccatorum, ut non possit facere ad quod facta est, nisi tu renoves et reformes eam. Non tento, Domine, penetrare altitudinem tuam; quia nullatenus comparo illi intellectum meum, sed desidero aliquatenus intelligere veritatem tuam, quam credit et amat cor meum. Neque enim quaero intelligere, ut credam; sed credo ut intelligam. Nam et hoc credo quia nisi credidero, non intelligam. (Ib. c. 227.) [Teach me to seek you, and show yourself to me, the seeker; for I cannot seek you unless you show me. I seek you by desiring, I find you by loving. I love by finding. I praise you, Lord, and give you thanks, because you created me in your image, so that I am mindful of you, think of you, and love you; but such is the harmful effect of vices, such is the obscuring smoke of sins, that I cannot do what I have been made to do, unless you renew and reform me. I do not try, Lord, to penetrate your heights, for in no way could my intellect be worthy; but I desire to know something of your truth, which my heart believes and loves. For I do not seek to understand, in order to believe; rather, I believe, so that I will understand. I do believe that unless I believed first, I would not understand. (*Proslogion*, Cap. I, c. 227)]

Deus est id quo nihil majus cogitari possit.... id quo majus cogitari nequit, non potest esse in intellectu solo. Si enim vel in solo intellectu est, potest cogitare esse in re: quod majus est. Si ergo id, quo majus cogitari non potest, est in solo intellectu, idipsum, quo majus cogitari non potest, est quo majus cogitari potest: sed certe hoc esse non potest. (Ib. c. 228.) [God is that than which nothing greater can be thought ... that than which a greater cannot be thought cannot exist in the understanding alone. For if it is in the understanding only, then it can be thought of as existing in reality as well, and this would be greater. Therefore, if that than which a greater cannot be thought is only in the understanding, this same thing than which a greater cannot be thought is that than which a greater can be thought. But clearly this is not possible. (*Proslogion*, Cap. I, c. 228)]

Vere est aliquid quo majus cogitari non potest, ut nec cogitari possit non esse: et hoc es tu, Domine Deus noster. (Ib. c. 228.) [There is truly something than which a greater cannot be thought, so much so that it could not even be thought of as not existing: and this is you, Lord our God. (*Proslogion*, Cap. I, c. 228)]

January 18, 1941

Aliter enim cogitatur res, cum vox eam significans cogitatur; aliter cum idipsum, quod res est, intelligitur. Illo itaque modo potest cogitari Deus non esse; isto, vero, minime ... Ita igitur, nemo intelligens id quod Deus est, potest cogitare quia Deus non est ... Deus enim est id quo majus cogitari non potest. Quod qui bene intelligit, [utique intelligit] idipsum sic esse, ut nec cogitatione queat non esse. Qui ergo intelligit sic esse Deum, nequit eam non esse cogitare. Gratias tibi, bone Domine, gratias tibi; quia quod prius credidi, te donante, jam sic intelligo, te illuminante; ut si te esse nolium credere, non possim non intelligere. (Ib. c. 229.) [For, in one sense, we think of a thing when we think of the word that signifies the thing; and in another sense, when we understand the thing itself. So, in the one sense, God can be thought of as not existing; but not in the second sense. ... For God is that than which a greater cannot be thought. Whoever understands this well knows that God exists in such a way that he cannot be even thought of to be non-existent. Whoever understands that God exists, cannot think of him as non-existent. Thanks to you, good Lord, thanks to you; for what I first believed, through your grace, I now understand, through your light; so that *even if I were to not want to believe that you exist, I could not fail to understand your existence. (Proslogion*, Cap. I, c. 229)]

Quae justitia est, mereati mortem aeternam dare vitam sempiternam? . . . Minus namque bonus esses, si nulli malo esses benignus. Melior enim est qui et bonis et malis bonus est, quam qui bonis tantum est bonus; et melior est, qui malis et puniendo et parcendo est bonus, quam qui puniendo tantum. Ideo ergo misericors es, quia totus et summe bonus es. (Ib. c. 231–232.) [What justice is it, to give eternal life to one who deserves eternal death? . . . For you are less good if you are favorable to no evil person. For he is better who is good to both the good and the evil, than one who is good only to the good; and he is better who is good by punishing and pardoning the evil, than one who punishes only. Therefore you are merciful, who are supremely and totally good. (*Proslogion*, Cap. I, c. 231–32)]

Parcendo malis ita justus es secundum te, it non secundum nos; sicut misericors es secundum nos, et non secundum te; quoniam salvando nos, quos juste perderes, sicut misericors es, non quia tu sentias affectum, sed quia nos sentimus effectum; ita justus es, non quia nobis reddas debitum, sed quia facis quod decet te summe bonum. Sic itaque sine repugnantia juste punis, et juste parcis. (Ib. c. 233.) [Pardoning the evil thus is considered just to you, but not to us; for you are merciful for us, and not for you; for you save us, whom you could cause to perish justly, because you are merciful, not because you feel any emotion, but because we feel the effect of salvation; you are so just, not because you repay us a debt, but because you do what is fitting for you as the supreme good. And so, without repugnance, you justly punish, and justly pardon. (*Proslogion*, Cap. I, c. 233)]

Adhuc lates, Domine, animam meam in luce et beatitudine tua; et idcirco versatur illa adhuc in tenebris, et miseria sua. Circumspicit enim et non videt punchritudinem tuam. Auscultat, et non audit harmoniam tuam. Olfacit, et non percipit odorem tuum. Gustat, et non cogniscit saporem tuum. Palpat, et non sentit levitatem tuam. Habes enim haec, Domine Deus, in te, tuo ineffabili modo, qui ea dedisti rebus a te creatis, suo sensibili modo; sed obriguerunt, sed obstupuerunt, sed obstructi sunt sensus animae meae vetusto languore peccati. (Ib. c. 236.) [Lord, you still hide my soul in your light and blessedness; and for that reason it still lives in darkness and distress. For it looks around, and does not see your beauty. It listens, and does not hear your harmony. It smells, and does not perceive your perfume. It tastes, and does not savor you. It touches, and does not feel your lightness. For you have this, Lord God, in you, in your own ineffable way, which you gave to things that you have created, in their own sensible way; but they stiffened and became paralyzed, and blocked the senses of my soul with the old weakness of sin. (*Proslogion*, Cap. I, c. 236)]

The *Sunday Times* is so full of horrors each Sunday that going through it is like being caught in a huge iron mechanical mangle.

I don't necessarily mean the series of speeches on the front page by Knudsen and Wilkie and Pillkie and Blimpson and Shimpson and other wealthy poltroons and *milites gloriosi* concerning the necessity of all us young fellow tightening our belts and winning this war.

It is the most vicious thing in the world the way we are told it is only a matter of selling aeroplanes, and not of fighting at all. The worst is, they all believe that. That is why Roosevelt is one of the most dangerous guys that ever set foot in a Packard to ride at the head of a parade. He actually believes we are going to enter and fight and win a war by means of factories! Or does he? Why all these speeches? If not to get us drunken, dissolute young men all steamed up to fight Germany, like the poor excited guys that ripped the flag down off the German Consulate in San Francisco yesterday.

This is a significant enough time to be writing this. It may just happen that Hitler and Mussolini might take a crack at America, start some kind of trouble, before spring. They are having a meeting, and it is thought that when they have a meeting, owing to the importance of melodrama in totalitarian policies, some action always follows, as a sort of symbolic reminder that this is no longer a question of conferences like those of Stresa and Locarno etc. where there was all talk and no action. Childish, you will say, Arthur, but indeed it is good theatah – so much for the world of treaties, armaments and policies, and I must say that today things move so *fast* that one scarcely knows what to *make* of it all, *does* one, does *one?*

That isn't what's so bad about the paper. It's the other stuff. The only thing that was funny was the picture of the three fat, sick, clumsy, big boned, rich ladies, simpering on skates very nicely (all three too big for their own legs) on the ice at Tuxedo Park. That was, in a sense, charming, because they looked such crazy old fools.

What is very bad is the attitude of small town cartoonists in the sticks towards international affairs. They have some misplaced idea that Hitler is shivering in his boots because "Uncle Sam" is training a tiny army with broomsticks and pieces of wood and baseball bats. All their cartoons are concerned with this fanciful situation.

Another rather disquieting thing: the news from Fort Dix, where they are training the guys that have been drafted from New York, is consistently horrifying. The other day they chanced to look over a lot of blank cartridges they had for some infantile kind of practice and found a good proportion of live rounds mixed in with them.

It is all right to die for your country, but it makes you feel a little queasy to think of dying from being tripped over by a couple of sergeants so fat and so drunk they can't see straight – or dying from having a radio fall on your head, or dying from poison candy in a clap-board canteen.

As for the art page there was a statue called "Shulamite" by one Louis Slobodkin that was one very precious work of art.

I got sore at some guy "revitalizing" Shakespeare in the *Sunday Times* a couple of months ago, too.

Then there's the story in the magazine section by an expatriate back from Paris after 21 years, saying New York is nice and genteel and also that it has a Whitmanesque quality, and that it is mature. Van Wyck Brooks was choking to get this remarkable dictum out of his throat in 1922 the year after this unknown tea drinker left our shores.

I was frightened by the book section where I am sure they are using the same photograph for Antoine de Saint Exupéry and Richard Aldington (two unknown authors). There was also a review of a book about a guy who, I am sure, is Beerbohm's *Enoch Soames*, showing that the Devil has a hand in newspaper publication.

Big article called "Busy Brain of the Army." Another: "His third and hardest term begins."

I have as much sympathy for the theater section as for any. All the horrors are not there. The Rotogravure had a lot of pictures of ugly deformed women with a caption saying in effect "Our Opera Stars used to be fat, now see how sweet and beautiful!"

I will go back to reading the *The Woman Who Was Poor.*

And the *Woman Who Was Poor* is *some novel!*

The second part is a better love story than Anthony and Cleopatra – the second part is magnificent, and ends with some mystical vision! All through the second part, or the last of the second part, there is a series of souls as simple and clean as pictures by Blake.

The very beginning of the book is muddled, and it is a little disconcerting until you look at it in relation to the end. Then you realize that the beginning of the book is the beginning of a journey of infinite distance. I was doubtful about the whole first part. Not a line of the second part was doubtful for a second.

The absolutely terrifying scene of the death of her child.

The scene at Parc-la-Valliere, with Mme. Poulot and Mme. Grand gesticulating and flinging filth and insults out of their windows, as on a sort of one dimensional stage set, in which the house is diminutive compared with the human figures. This is a marvelous episode.

The first part – I liked Leopold's galvanizing effect on cab drivers. I was a little suspicious of Gacongnol, whose death, however, was splendid.

Embarrassed by Marchenoir stroking the Tiger in the zoo.

But the whole book is fulfilled in the ending, which resolves all possible doubts about its structure etc. It is a very fine novel. Leon Bloy is a very fine writer, and that is only insulting him, for he is not a writer, but a Pilgrim of the Holy Sepulchre.

Selliere says Bloy never went to the Holy Sepulchre. I wonder how Selliere manages to drag himself around with the millstone he must have hanging on his neck? I wonder how he avoids falling into rivers and being dragged down by the weight of that burden. I dare say he can understand the newspaper. He should limit his reading to that, in future. Let him sit on his millstone and read the German ed. of *Paris Soir.*

The *Woman Who Was Poor* is some novel, even in English. I wonder what happened to my French copy I lost before I could get to reading it! I want to read it over and over.

January 21. 1941

S. Bonaventurae, *Itinerarium Mentis*, cap. II. #5–6.

Apprehensio [apprehension]

Oblectatio – [pleasure]

Diiudicatio [judgment]

Oblectatio – implies notion of "convenience"

"Delectatio est conjunctis convenientis unum convenienti."

Oblectatio follows the *apprehensio rei convenientis.*

It is a *sense* delight (?)

Delectatur sensus *per similitudinem* abstractam percepto.

(*abstractam* obviously does not mean the product of intellectual abstraction)

Delectatio	1. *speciositatis* – through the *forma* – [form]
	2. *suavitatis* – [through the] *virtus* [power]
Three kinds of	
proportionalitas	3. *salubritatis* – [through the] *operatio* [operation].

(. . . *species tenet rationem formae virtutes et operationis, secundum quod habet respectum ad* principium, a quo manat *ad* medium per quod transit, *et* ad terminum in quem agit.) ["(. . . the appearance holds the reason for the form, power and operation, insofar as it refers to the *principle from which it operates*, to the *medium through which it acts*, and to the *purpose for which it acts*.)"]

Omnis enim delectatio est ratione proportionalitatis. [For all delight in the measure of proportionality.]

The beautiful (1)	There is *proportionalitas speciositatis* when the thing itself *(id quod visum placet)* possesses beauty of form or *species*.
	"Pulchritudo nihil aliud est quam aequalitas numerosa, seu quidam partium situs cum coloris suavitate." [Proportion of Appearance (what pleases the eye). "Beauty is nothing other than harmonious equality, or a certain placement of the parts with the sweetness of color."]
The pleasant (2)	*prop. suavitatis*
	"Cum virtus agens non improportionaliter excedit recipientem, quia sensus tristatur in extremis et in mediis 237 delectatur." [Proportion of Pleasantness – "When the power acting does not improportionately exceed the recipient power, for the senses are saddened by extremes and delight in the mean."]
The wholesome (3)	*pro. efficaciae*
	"quando agens imprimendo implet indigentiam patientis." [Proportion of Effectiveness – "When the power acting fulfills a need in the thing being acted upon."]
	Diiudicatio – *"inquiritur de ratione delectationis, quae in sensu percipitur ab objecto. Hoc est autem, cum* quaeritus rationem pulcri, suavis et salubris *et invenitur quod haec est* proportio aequalitatis. [Judgment – "It may be asked what is the reason for the delight, which is perceived in the sense from the object. This happens when one *considers the measure of beauty, pleasure and wholesomeness*, and this is none other than a *proportion of equality*."]

Diiudicatio transfers the *sensible species to the intellect*.

January 25. 1941

Quick quick! Set down on precious paper the phenomenal results of my two minutes meditation. See the author analyze his inmost experiences! Pay a penny and see him beat himself in a debate!

Q: Don't you think you are old enough to write a short story?

A: As a matter of fact, now that you mention it, I just have written a short story – in fact two short stories.

Q: Ah ha! Allow me to photograph you for the motion pictures! (Podden! I was only joshing!) What did you say, Meesther? Two shog-sorries?

A: Yoats! I hear Jack's rote two shog-sorries. Very tidy, each one!

Q: Come now, not like those scurrile notes you penned last year concerning your meditations in the barber chair?

A: No. Each one hath a beguineing, a model, and a friend.

Q: You mean a beguileing, a muddle, and a find?

A: Yes, a Bourgignon, a Moselle, and a Flamand.

Q: Continue to narrate to me. How do you feel?

A: Rotten.

Q: Why?

A: O, because! . . .

Q: O be definite. Are you or are you not a grown up, professional man? Now that you're in professional life you've got to pull yourself up straight, and conceal that gap between your vest and the top of your pants, and brush your teeth and speak out.

A: I feel rotten. I never wanted to write the shog-sorries in the first place.

Q: Then why did you?

A: Sense of duty.

Q: Duty to whom?

A: Caesar.

Q: Come, come!

A: I mean what I say. Render under Caesar the things that are easier. And if I were to render these pitiful documents unto God I'd be a sad sinner, the Day of Judgment!

Q: What are they? Lewd?

A: No, stupid; imperfect!

Q: What is imperfect?

A: I feel like a card-cheat in the Atheneum: about to be kicked out by the Prime Minister.

Q: Cheating is allowed: the bombs are dropping.

A: Be quiet.

Q: How did you cheat?

A: I wrote a story with a plot.

Q: What's wrong with that?

A: When I was fourteen I wrote stories with a plot.

Q: All right, now you're twenty-six.

A: Second childhood? I should go back to that stuff?

Q: Maybe they'll sell.

A: That's the trouble.

Q: Oh, they're not highbrow enough?

A: You cheap weasel!

Q: Would you be sore if you wrote a story sounding like Richard Hughes?

A: Yes, you bet!

Q: Would you be sore if you wrote a story that sounded like one of Saroyan's?

A: Yes, you bet!!

Q: Why? Because he didn't answer your letter?

A: Thanks for the tip-off. Here's a statement: "Saroyan gets his effects by the simple trick of being sincere with himself. It's so simple that it looks extraordinary. He doesn't even write very well: he just speaks his own mind. People have never heard of such a thing, so they are bowled over. This is a very good thing to do, and a good way to write." If you, Q, say "may I quote you?" I'll bean you with a hammer.

Q: I won't say that at all. But I will ask you one thing, Meister: was your two stories speaking your own mind?

A: (blushing) No. They was not.

Q: Well, what did they do? Speak something else?

A: They are artifice.

Q: What's wrong with artifice?

A: It's a lie, that's all.

Q: Oh, a Platonist!

A: You confuse me.

Q: Come on: didn't you have to say anything

[several pages missing from ms.]

"Intolerance may be said to be a terrible virtue of primitive ages." (Valéry, p. 190)

"We find ourselves confronted with a confusion of the social system of the verbal material and of the myths of all sorts which we have inherited from our fathers, and of the recent, vital conditions – conditions of intellectual origin, conditions entirely artificial, furthermore essentially instable, for they are directly dependent upon ulterior creations of the intellect, increasingly numerous (some translator!) p. 191.

(The Crisis – ref. to World War) – (an age about to perish is worse than . . .)

"An extraordinary shudder has stirred the marrow of Europe. It has felt, in all its thinking cells, that it no longer recognized itself, that it had ceased to resemble itself, that it was about to lose consciousness – a consciousness acquired by centuries of bearable misfortunes by thousands of first rate men, by innumerable geographical, ethnical and historical hazards.

Then, as if for a definite defence of its physical self a richness, all its memory returned confusedly. Its great art and great books came back to it pell-mell. Never did we read so much or so passionately as during the war, ask the book sellers. Never did men pray so much, or so profoundly, ask the priests.

All the saviours were invoked; all the founders, protectors, martyrs and heroes; the fathers of every fatherland, the sainted heroines, the national poets.

And in the same mental disorder, at the appeal of the same anguish, cultivated Europe underwent the rapid revival of its innumerable creeds, dogmas, philosophies, heterogeneous ideals; the three hundred ways of explaining the world; the thousand and one shades of Christianity, the two dozen positivisms, the whole spectrum of intellectual light displayed *its incomparable colours – a strange contradictory light on the death throes of the European soul.*

February 4, 1941

This morning, sitting alone at a big empty table in the vasty hall of the caf' I reflected upon the elegant works of T. S. Eliot, particularly the part in the "Waste Land" where he says

> O, O, O, That Shakes-pearian rag
> It's so elegant
> It's so intelligent

and then I thought to myself, wasn't he *bold* when he wrote that. How *sly!* What an independent little old *elf!* How *cute!* The lines embarrassed me the moment I was sixteen, and I didn't realize, until this morning, how much.

Also, I think the important musicians who have introduced tissues of ragtime into their immortal works sound like nothing. Take the foxtrot in "Facade" – it's the saddest thing I ever heard. Stravinsky's foxtrot movement in one of those short, skinny works of his – then. I heard a Ballet Negre by whatever the French guy's name is who was on the back of Satie's "Gnossienne" and it was nearly as bad as the others – I mean Darius Milhaud.

All these poor jerks ought to kiss Duke Ellington's feet, and then throw away their metronomes and sit and listen to him for a while and maybe they'd learn something.

I found a good Bermuda down by the Allegheny river this morning in bright sunlight and snow. But the sun was warm, and sparkled on the water like a big flock of small silver firebirds and the sky was a good blue; and I guess all I ever wanted out of Bermuda was sun and blue sky and color. Here there were no aquamarine waters, no white sand, no purple patches in the green sea where the reefs would be. This morning the trees were all white with hoarfrost. By the time I got down to the river, after the nine o'clock class, the hoarfrost was gone off all the trees, down in the valley. But back on the hill by the Rock City fire tower the trees were still white.

While enjoying the delights of this Bermuda surrogate I questioned myself concerning the triviality of the two short stories I wrote last month and didn't have any answer except "Well, they were only exercises."

So then I said: "When are you going to stop writing exercises and write something real?"

"I'm sure I dunno!"

Secretly in my heart this morning I believe my novel to be not bad. Sure as anything that means it is now being rejected by somebody I never even heard of, and the splash of its rejection makes silent obscure waves that reach out blindly to my unseeing mind in an unheard cry for sympathy. "Help!" cries the novel, "I have been rejected again."

I do not mention which novel. It goes for both.

This time last year *The Labyrinth* had been rejected by Macmillans – just had been. Since then it has been to Viking, Knopf, Harcourt Brace; then to Curtis Brown who sent it to Modern Age – Atlantic Monthly Books – McBride – and now Carrick and Evans. Carrick and Evans' "no" has not yet reached me. I asked her [Naomi Burton] to send the new one to Harcourt Brace first, but haven't heard.

I don't think the publication of either novel has the slightest importance, except that it would be nice. I don't think any writing is finished until it is printed and read. I'd like to have a printed copy of each one in my hand. So many bad books get printed. Why can't mine?

Q: Well, make up your mind: is *Euphues* tedious, or isn't it?
A: Boy, some parts of *Euphues* are the worst stuff I ever read.
Q: Ha Ha, you've certainly changed your tune in the last few months.
A: Parts of it are still all right!
Q: So you finally found out the difference between *Euphues* and *Castiglione's Courtier*?
A: So what?
Q: *Castiglione's Courtier* is a real book and *Euphues* isn't.
A: You're Q. You should be asking questions, not making statements. But now I'll ask one: where's my copy of the *Courtier*? What thief has it?
Q: How do you know you didn't give it away according to your last year's well known plans? Hey?
A: You said it, how do I know?
Q: Incidentally, now that we have mentioned the plan you once entertained, this time last year, of you know what: How does it look now?
A: The same. But I think I'd be a Trappist.
Q: Now you're joking!
A: You think so?

Just before the Feast of Saint Andrew Corsini, patron, or anyway, protector of Florence, whom do I start reading again but Dante Alighieri. This time I began again with the *Inferno*. I hadn't touched it since 1933 – seven years ago this fall, when I was a freshman at Cambridge. I am surprised how much I remembered of Bullough's explanations. For example in the first Canto:

> "*Ripresi via per la piaggia diserta,*
> Si che il pie fermo sempre era il piu basso"
> ["I started again on the path along that barren slope,
> *so that my lowest foot was at all times the firmer.*"]

I remembered very clearly how it meant he was going up a hill, and wasn't misled by Piaggia (*plage*) into thinking about beaches for a moment.

Limbo is the most common sort of medieval treatment – The Castle where the good pagans live belongs to any run of the mill Medieval Allegory. I like the four figures of Homer, Horace, Ovid and Lucan, led by Homer with a sword. I wouldn't say Canto V. and the Paolo and Franciscan episode was my favorite episode. Far from feeling Dante is too tough, I am impressed by the Inferno as more or less pagan poem. I don't know if I'll go right on through again. I'd like to some time. Nor do I think the end of the Paradiso satisfying when regarded as a *real* mystical vision, which it obviously wasn't. It is only good as the culmination of an *Itinerarium* proceeding the whole way through natural reason aided by theology: it is what reason says God would be like, but not *a* vision of God.

But it is still the best epic poem, the best poem, I ever read – I mean the whole *Divine Comedy*.

I don't know how many people I ever knew it was possible to really revere. Father Thomas [Plassman] is one. Mgrs. Ruegel another. Aunt Maud another. Maritain is impressive in a different way and anyhow he's younger.

Tonight Father Thomas sat in his office with the proofs of the new English translation of the Bible, and open books all around him on the desk – and with his hands he moved the pages of books, and the books themselves, and the galleys of neat proof with a great slowness and patience. He is a man of the most immense and unshakeable calm I ever saw, and underneath his calm is this tremendous simplicity and pleasant humor: a good humor that is so simple that the word kindly would be shocking, for it would imply . . .

[Two pages are missing here.]

How can any one tell how much he owes to the goodness of those who love him? If we knew what people in their love for us do to save us from damnation by the simple fact of their friendship for us, we would learn some humility. But we take for granted we should have friends, and are not at all surprised they should come seeking our company and liking us; we imagine we are naturally likable, and people flock to us to give us our real due, as if we were angels, and attracted them by our great goodness to love us. And it is only love that gives us life, and without God's love we would cease to be, and perhaps without their good, natural love and charity which argues for us always in God's sight without their always knowing it, He would long ago have given us up to our punishment, and turned His face away, and let us hurtle over the edge of the abyss, where the love of friends still holds us in their spoken or unspoken prayers.

I don't know what I have written that I could really call mine, or what I have prayed or done that was good that came from my own will. Whose prayer made me first pray again to God to give me grace to pray? I could have fought for years by myself to reduce my life to some order (for that was what I was always trying to do – even to ridiculous extremes and the most eccentric disciplines, all pseudo-scientific and pretty much hypochondriacal too; keeping records of what I drank, trying to cut out smoking by reducing the number of cigarettes each day, noting down the numbers in a book – weighing myself every few days, etc.!) and yet I would have slowly eaten myself out, I think. But someone must have mentioned me in some prayer; perhaps, again, the soul of some person I hardly remember – perhaps some stranger in a subway, or some child – or maybe the fact that someone as good as Lilly Reilly happened to think I was a good guy served as a prayer – or the fact that Nanny may have said my name in her prayers moved the Lord God to send me a little grace to pray again, or, first, to begin reading books that led me there, again – and how much of it was brought on by the war? Or maybe, Bramachari, in some word to the Lord in his strange language, moved the Lord to let me pray again! These things are inscrutable and I begin to know them better than I can write them. How many men have become Christians through the prayers of Jews and Hindus who themselves find Christianity terribly hard? . . . We cannot know all the movements of Christ's grace: we only know one thing, that in the Church it is sure – that everywhere else where there is grace, it is Christ's grace, but we can't be sure it is grace.

February 9, 1941

I've got a book of poems by Dylan Thomas and I can't put the book down. I read him in *Horizon* and it was a good poem. I read him now, and he is a good poet.

The poems stand on the page and look very valuable. His writing is very strong and sinewy and has much craft and wit but it is musically tremendously coherent. This musical coherence, and the terrific coherence of the imagery, combined with the mysteriousness of what is actually being said, the recondite idea of the poem – which I always suspect to be an idea having some bearing on religion, Heaven or Hell, give him great worth and you can't stop reading the stuff over and over.

There is not one tinny note in anything I have read except a line ending a poem – "Hands have no tears to flow" but that may not be as bad as I think (I don't like trimeters). He is so much better than T. S. Eliot that Eliot and Auden and even Spender, all those guys, become very insignificant, trivial, chatty, slightly mystical, drawing room boys, which we always knew they were anyway. Only next to Thomas they are that more inexcusably because there *is* somebody writing real poetry. Before, we thought poor Eliot, he can't write better than that tinny stuff because the whole age is impotent, rotten in the first place.

Thomas has got a couple of obvious tricks which could be overdone by someone less smart than he. Mixing up the functions of various senses and the senses to which they belong, and pairing them off with the wrong partners – Ears see, hands hear, lips hear, eyes feel around, etc.

He writes about hell: he is like everybody else, walking through hell, and the crime is not to see that hell, and see the damnation all around. Vergil points out the damned to Dante, but hides his eyes so he won't see the Furies hold up the head of Medusa: the problem for Dylan Thomas also is to see everything in hell but Medusa.

He is concerned some bit with the Sacrament of the Eucharist, and always with Christian problems concerning sin not with Christian answers concerning sin – I mean the answers of Faith. But of reason, generally, yes. Reason not specifically Christian; natural reason. Some of his writing is reverse-puritan stuff. His prose especially is like Robert Green, or Dekker's pamphlets – the Groatsworth of Wit, *Plague Pamphlet* style. But more sensational and, of course, modern. I don't like what I've read of the prose. Good writing, too much incest and witchcraft.

He is very much concerned with the itch of lust and the devil in the loins.

He gets some shattering effects by speaking of fleshly organisms being put together like things being carefully made of wood and string and sacking and so on. Analogies of crude crafts. A lot of very solid syntactical effects. I thought if you read all the titles of his poems in the table of contents one after the other it would make a parody of one of his poems but it didn't (The titles are all made up of first lines).

Seven or eight things I liked, reading in the book at random:[6]

> The fences of the light are down
> All but the briskest riders thrown,
> And worlds hang on the trees.
> The force that through the green fuse drives the flower
> Drives my green age; that blasts the roots of trees
> Is my destroyer.
> Once in this bread
> The oat was merry in the wind.
> Man broke the sun, pulled the wind down.

[6] This must have been *The Map of Love*, published in 1939. Although long out of print, his parenthetical remark ("This is more recent. He gets better and better.—1936") bears this out.

(This from a Eucharist poem. I think I understand)

> The hand that signed the treaty bred a fever. . .
> The ball I threw while playing in the park
> Has not yet reached the ground.
> Now Jack my fathers let the time-faced crook,
> Death flashing from his sleeve,
> With swag of bubbles in a seedy sack,
> Sneak down the stallion grave.

(This is more recent. He gets better and better. – 1936)

> In the groin of the national doorway I crouched like a tailor
> Sewing a shroud for a journey
> By the light of the meat-eating sun.

Everything he writes is very striking, and easy to remember. And when you go back over it, it is still more striking. This baby is some poet. Reading him, I feel awed to think he is only a year older than I, as I used to be awed when Joe Louis won the championship of the world, and only a couple of years older than I!

February 11, 1941

S. Bonaventurae – Itineris Mentis in Deum. Cap. II.7.

Nam cum species apprehensa sit similitudo in medio genita et deinde ipsi organo impressa et per illam impressionem in suum principium, scilicet in objectum cognoscendum, ducat; manifeste insinuat, quod ille qui est imago invisibilis Dei et splendor gloriae et figura substantiae ejus, *qui ubique est per primam sui generationem, sicut objectum in toto medio suam generat similitudinem, per gratiam unionis unitur, sicut species corporali organo, individuo rationalis naturae, ut per illam unionem nos reduceret ad Patrem sicut ad fontale principium et objectum.* [For since the species grasped is a likeness to the medium generated and thence impressed on the very organ, and through that impression it leads to its very essence, namely into the object to be known; he clearly implies this, because *he is the image of the invisible God and the splendor of his glory and the figure of his substance,* who is everywhere through his first generation, as an object generates its likeness through the whole medium, and is united by means of the grace of union, as the species is united to a corporal organ, in an individual of a rational nature, so that through that union he might bring us back to the Father as to the beginning source and object.]

———

Last year in the early winter I walked around and around the blocks enclosed by Perry, Eleventh and Bleecker Streets and Waverley Place. The other night in those blocks of houses, my exlandlady was writing me a letter and Mark Van Doren, in another house, another note. They arrived on different days, because one was mailed in the evening and the other late at night.

The other day I thought of the crazy small laundry on Waverley Place, where the laundryman, hearing I taught English at Columbia, would have long discussions with me on the difficulties his little boy was having with French in high school.

Now I think of the days I sat in the May sun, cramped and curled on the loose rotting boards of the little balcony outside the Perry Street front room, and held a bottle of coke in my hand and looked at the warm sun on the buildings – like Decoration Day 1939. That was before there was a war, and the World's Fair was just beginning, and I sometimes had hangovers. Sometimes – often. That was what the cocacola was for.

I am beginning to think the war has a lot to do with my not drinking anymore. Maybe if there were no war, I would still be having hangovers. But I doubt that, too.

That spring in that front room on Perry Street I read some good books. Hopkins' letters; Bridges' *Milton's Prosody*; R. Hughes' *In Hazard*, E. M. Forster's *Passage to India*; Herodotus; Thucydides; Curzon's *Monasteries of the Levant*; Saint John of the Cross; maybe some Leon Bloy, I forget. Then the big thing that happened that spring was *Finnegans Wake* came out, and I remember the fine day it was when that happened.

There were some good things about that front room in Perry Street. The shiny new telephone. The grave and delicate writing desk. The sun pouring in the windows. The too-many street cries. Calling Wilma Reardon on the shiny phone. Lax called up and told me he had heard the election of Pope Pius XII announced on the radio, and that day, too, I had been crouching on the balcony, in the sun. Another good thing was the record of "And the Angels Sing."

But just the same, I once in a while had hangovers. Also, I had no real work to do: but just thought some about writing a Ph. D. dissertation on Hopkins.

The room was a great expensive luxury. No more of that, in my whole life: I hope I can live always in monasteries or college cubicles, or corners of libraries. The thought of having "one's own establishment" – one's own telephone, one's own six-month lease, a name in the phone book "my apartment" – a civil status, disturbs me tremendously. It is no sacrifice to renounce it now.

The back room was dark, but I spent a lot of time in it, and it wasn't pleasant as a room; it was pretty dank. But starting at the end of August 1939 in a hell of heat and sweat and hangovers and wisdom teeth torn out of my hacked jaw with saws and hammers, I began to learn a lot of things in that room, and work there, too. The country's better.

That summer, when me and Lax and Rice were at the cottage up here, was a good summer.

This is the feast of the Apparition of the Blessed Mother at Lourdes. Both last night and tonight there was brilliant full moonlight, with a sort of soft-summer-haze hanging in the snowy valley. But it is cold, and the snow is so frozen that it cries under my rubber boots on the road, and grinds and complains like iron. I walked on the road around the field – very sad and ashamed that I can't sing at all, but have a silly braying voice, and no control over it. If I could sing very well, I would like to go around making up songs and singing them for Angels and for Our Lady, but I can't sing: and my voice is an offense and a joke. It would be a lot more pleasing to them if I tried more seriously to do penance for my sins, and said my prayers properly when I try to say them!! Not so much fiddling on two sticks, as if I thought I were Saint Francis!

February 19, 1941

Tonight I was received into the Third Order, under the patronage of Saint Gregory. I was thinking of entering the Order long ago – last fall. Things happened, or didn't happen and I am not in it until now. And even now my entry into it seemed unpremeditated, and I am ashamed. But at least I was able to bow my head before the Holy and Blessed Sacrament, conscious that the cord of penance was tied about my waist and know that I was in the presence of my Lord God and that now I have no other Master but Him.

To give away my goods to the poor – I had to give away a symbol.

The other night I awoke in the middle of the night in terror.

Several weeks ago I was praying in the chapel at night and I saw the edge of the abyss and sat on the edge of it all night, in a strange inexplicable way – no image can convey it; it was not exceptionally terrible. No image can convey it. It was terrible enough: it was a consciousness of something definite.

Every time it is the consciousness of a baffling person. I have no words, no images, no analogies, no quantitative or qualitative term to describe this person – *no feeling or emotion I can reproduce.*

Imagine a sensation being at the same time extreme and neutral, if that were possible, extreme terror or no terror at all, so much so you don't know whether it is something or nothing except that you are in the presence of that which is utterly unexpressed in words in every possible sense. I don't know if this is God or what it is. God knows what this is, He has given it to me for some reason. Then I go to Mass the next day walking along the hall, feeling in some way very terrible in a way I can't describe, understanding, not understanding the feeling. A good tertiary, ordinarily my enemy in spite of myself, says me a good word. It was as if I were relying on him to carry me into church, carry me to the altar rail. When I come from Communion every heaviness is lightened. The whole thing has vanished. God meant this for me: I have not understood it.

I understand most of these things half-way when I formulate the words "Thou art not as I have conceived Thee." I have made very many concepts of God.

I cannot formulate my own inability to formulate anything about God. Today, before the seventh and eighth stations of the Cross, I was terribly conscious that I was only saying words. The Lord permits our indifference before the Stations of the Cross so that we may realize that at best we are still indifferent to His sacrifice, and can't be anything but indifferent. We cannot suffer His pains, unless He lets us do so in a miracle – we can suffer our own indifference to His pains. To realize that God is dying and that we are indifferent is to stand on the edge of an inconceivable agony. But the agony is caused by our indifference in His Passion. Therefore for us to cry out in agony because He permits us to be indifferent to His Passion is to want to learn what His cry meant: "*Eloi, Eloi, Lama sabachtani*, My God, My God, why hast Thou forsaken me!"

I who write this, am the rich man who came to Christ and said: "Lord, what shall I do to be saved." Christ said: "Keep the commandments." But I have repeated the question. He has said "Go, give all thou hast to the poor and come, follow me."

Now the whole problem of my life is the question – am I that same one who turned back sorrowing because he had many riches? Will I irritate my Lord all my life, crying: "Lord, am I still following Thee?" as if I didn't know?

I learned one thing, at the Forty Hours at the Convent – two weeks ago tomorrow night. I can have one prayer – to belong to Him, to be able to renounce the whole world and follow Him. I say that prayer now: when it pleases Him, He will show me what to do. When – not next year, every next instant. If I love Him I will hear.

"*Anima mea in manibus meis semper*" ["Constantly I take my life in my hands"][7]

This is what I read in the Bible today:

Isaias. 47.1. "Come down, sit in the dust, O virgin daughter of Babylon, sit on the ground: there is no throne for the daughter of the Chaldaeans, for thou shalt no more be called delicate and tender."

(I did not open the Holy Bible for prophecies; I found this chapter about the vanity of Babylon's astrologers. I also read the Canto in the *Inferno* about the seers and sorcerers.)

55.1. "All you that thirst, come to the waters; and you that have no money, make haste, buy, eat; come ye, buy wine and milk without money, and without any price."

58.10. "When thou shalt pour out thy soul to the hungry and shalt satisfy the afflicted soul, then shall thy light rise up in darkness, and thy darkness shall be as noonday!"

February 22, 1941

Today there is a good set of complaints I would fill this page with except that it galls me to write about the stupid things that gall me. For example: the stupid new artist on *New Yorker* – bad drawings, bad signature "Chon Day."

The new song I heard last night, "They're making me over in the Army / They're making me over over there." Deliciously reminiscent of "we won't be back till it's over there."

I pray for the war to stop. The only moral justification for such a prayer is to pray in shame and terror, begging God that He miraculously implant the will to do penance in the souls of men, so that they may freely do the penance which He now imposes on the innocent and everybody in this

---

7 Part of a couplet in Psalm 119: "Though constantly I take my life in my hands, yet I forget not your law" (New American Bible).

war. But the world is going clean contrary to that way: they are crazy for the war itself, they would never do a penance. What scared me is how true this is likely to be, above all of Catholics.

I don't have to look farther than myself, I mean as far as the weakness and indifference of my prayers and the strength of my selfishness and spite.

Anyway, there has been nothing in the papers for weeks. It is like 1937, 1938. Politics. Everybody pretending to be ready to rabbit punch each other.

Some seminarians skated up the frozen river all the way to Olean. It is snowing again, more. This Wednesday is Ash Wednesday. This time last year, I suppose I was in St. Elizabeth's Hospital.

Illuminating thoughts I have had lately:

1. When I was in Cuba, once or twice I drank a lot of anisette. I think I must have been still crazy. Of all the foul drinks!

2. Place I'm glad I'm not at: The Eden Concert, Havana.

3. It must be a comfort to the nuns who go to Dr. McCarthy, the Dentist in the First National Bank Building, to look out the window and see with their wild helpless eyes the crosses on the towers of Saint Mary's while he violently drills their teeth. I fix my eyes on them – and I mean *fix!*

4. I am learning about the Appointment in Samara Catholic Culture of a town like Olean. Interesting. Player pianos. Big signed pictures of Father Thomas. Photographs of daughters more beautiful than the daughters themselves. A picture of Christ Our Lord – stamped on a small bronze plaque. Business faces shinier than Protestant business faces. More friendliness, less wit – (fortunate). Generally, no membership in the Country Club. Invite the Friars up to Cuba Lake all the time. Etc. Interesting. Neutral. Harmless.

Other things I have thought about:

1. Oyster stew looks better than it is.

2. Cold oyster stew is nauseating.

3. The little clammy club of gray oysters I leave in the bottom of the dish like a family of frogs, when I put down my spoon, scares me no little.

4. Oyster stew in the Cooks Diner is uninteresting. So is the Cooks Diner.

5. Nine girls from Mercyhurst ride on a bus and sing all the way from Erie to Olean. In the bus, I gathered, were a blind man, a Nazi, a business man who was coming to make reports on everything he saw in Olean, to take back to Erie.

6. A girl from Mercyhurst who does not drink is better than one who does, but I commend nor condemn neither.

7. Father Philotheus may or may not be homesick for his monastery at Dorsten, but I can't figure out which.

8. They got *quite a plant* at that Saint Bernard's Church at Bradford what with all them schools and convent, etc.

9. That I hope Rice sells the new children's book about night clubs he just wrote.

10. The name of Charles Henri Ford. How Henri is pronounced. Whether I am interested. Glad he wrote to me, asking to look at poems.

11. Washington's Birthday – no feast.

12. The dames from Allegheny jealous of the dames from Mercyhurst.

13. My own surliness.

14. Where is my brother John Paul?

15. The decline and fall of the *New Yorker.*

16. The lousy poem I wrote at 35 Perry Street around May 1939 called "The Informers." I only realized how lousy today.

17. Where is a copy of the poem "Verses for a Party Hat"? Weaver said that was like T. S. Eliot, which is certainly not true.

18. Lipperts. The big fight we heard about.

19. Walking along Healy's road – well macadamized, that road. The small steam roller stands a little off the road, in the woods, but is very often used.

20. Tippy, the dog in the chicken house.

21. Willy, the guy who washes dishes.

22. The medieval, friendly guy who drives the garbage wagon and the team of those two big dirty horses – and wears modern clothes looking exactly medieval.

23. Hitchhiking to Erie and Cleveland last summer. Knight and I were outside Geneva, Ohio, and it was six or six-thirty and the sun was slanting pretty on the country and the cars went by like lightning on this big wide highway. Across the road was a clean, painted up farm house, surrounded by green and neat grass, and given over to renting of rooms, to tourists. On the green lawn were white wooden chairs, and a woman on the porch rocked in a hammock and, possibly, sewed, and breathed the cool, happy, sweet air of that country. I was tired, and I think this was one of the nicest places I ever saw!

The place where Knight and I had dinner in Geneva – at a slicky slick counter. And people all dressed up in Miami clothes, Geneva being a resort.

24. Slate's job. His office. Me and Slate and Seymour and Helen eating bad delicacies at great expense in the New Yorker [Hotel].

25. The phony perfume a man said was stolen, and sold me, in the dark, behind the New Yorker, one night. Jinny and Lilly took it, although they knew at once how phony it was, the minute I gave it to them.

26. What about Gibney's cat?

27. How I condemn *Life Magazine*.

28. What are Charles Henri Ford's chain poems?

29. How come I had forgotten about finding the neat little calf-bound 1836 French edition of Saint Augustine's *De Musica* which I found myself, uncatalogued, this summer in the Library, and, told Father Irenaeus, was precious? (meaning interesting).

Saint Francis' prayer to the Blessed Virgin is one of the best prayers I know – the one that begins "O Holy Virgin Mary, there is none like unto thee among women . . ."

Shrove Tuesday. February 25

First it was bright, then an interesting storm with the snow flying parallel to the ground, then bright again with a Rome-Florida-Bermuda sky making holiday all over the sunny hills. And small orange clouds, dazzling with a kind of light and lovely fire, hung in the sky like clouds in a Giovanni Bellini picture, and the whole business was gayer than any world's fair I ever heard or dreamt of.

Walking from town – I saw a crazy collie running around a house as though he were herding it like a herd of sheep. His barks rang down the sunny road and disappeared. He was afraid of the cars. They set him to running like a fire.

God made this a very fine day. Past the place where the dog was, I came to the line of trees where the road comes over the rise and faces the monastery, off across the fields. And there on my right was a white house and a red chimney, bright as it could be and silent, the happiest house in the world. I have been knocked down by the vivid being of the air and the light on top of that rise before, and this was another time. I thought of houses on their knees in the snow praying like big fat women to be saved from the melodrama of an ordinary storm.

What do I care if I was shocked by a ranting article in *The Sign* about Philosophy in Literature. It is unimportant. Catholics think hanging tags on things is philosophy; instead of thinking, they shout, and it is a shame. They have some good will and no sense, and often not enough good will either, just a stubborn love of bad rhetoric and the Catholic culture they picked up from the nuns. But it is unimportant! Should I be mad and vituperate the same way? The article on Huxley I wrote was some little bit silly, in the same way.

I care less too, or pretend to, for the news I won't read in the papers for Lent. Invasion of England, Spain, Greece, Turkey, Germans capturing Suez Canal or getting bopped on the head in Smyrna. I don't know. By not reading the papers I will not know many of these things. I will not know my history and that is not important either.

My brother is in Mexico again. He would do well to put his money in a trap which would spring at his hand when he reached out to take some, not because Mexico is bad but because it won't make him any less unhappy.

All these things are unimportant.

Don't begin Lent as if you'd learnt everything. But brush your hair and start fasting, and fast because you know all these other unimportant things are important not in their above aspects, but inasmuch as they depend on your fasting – the state of the Church, peace and my brother.

March 2, 1941. Sunday

I can scare myself to death anytime by reading last year's journal. I was very happy last year up to the time I learned I had no vocation for the priesthood and was not acceptable. After that the year complicated itself terribly.

In the middle of wondering stupidly, in the middle of the vile heat of Virginia, if there was any such thing as determinism, a determinism of passions, I came upon a Christian theory of the will by experiment. The experiment was terrible, unpleasant, not deliberate, half-conscious, passionate. Above all, it wasn't necessary. I knew the truth of the doctrine before I proved it by using my will freely in a wrong course. There was no necessity. But if I never know anything again let me dread that!

Every minute a man reflects on himself he is compelled to cry out for the grace to renounce everything and carry his cross, for the sight of himself is astounding. Our will leaps out, overreaches itself, and we are caught by the neck, and strangle. God cuts us down. We begin again. Our will flies out and returns upon us like a net. To will pleasures is to spit in the wind, and have our own filth fly back in our face. Every time. Every time.

Walking up from the river, on the rutted asphalt, among the oil tanks, seeing, ahead of me, pine trees in the hearth of Gargoyle Park, I wonder if I am beginning to know more surely now that there is nothing for me but to pray and do penance and belong to Christ in poverty, in my whole life and without compromise. On the paper the marks are the same, the words are the same I would say coming down the steps of Our Lady of Guadalupe, on 14th Street, when I really was a complete prisoner. As if I were free now! I think then I was more confused. Now because I hope to be less confused, perhaps I also seem to myself to be. All I know is, it rests with God. It rests with me to ask Him. If I ask, He will answer. No matter what happens.

But what sun, today! It is the first Sunday of Lent. There is still snow in the fields. But there are small, unnoticeable buds on bushes, locked up, but swelling, ready to open. Breaking ice rustled in the river, and exploded.

Ever since the day of my reception in the Third Order I have written a lot of poems. I know what it is to wear a religious habit.

This has only a shadow of externality. It is an external habit which is worn, and which nobody sees. And, externally, it is as near meaningless as it can be, that is, in its pure externals. It is the bare anatomy of a religious habit, a string, a couple of squares of cloth.

But that is good, because that way it also has much meaning. Its meaning belongs only in the will of him who wears it. The cord, without penance, mocks the wearer, cuts him worse than a whip. And penance is always still only a beginning. You look back, and see no progress. Before, you were much worse off, yes, but then you hadn't really begun. Now you have begun. No, no, tomorrow. You know this was not yet the beginning. Perhaps it really starts, or you really know you start in Purgatory.

But you know where it will end: when it ends, when it is completed, that is: Heaven. Unknowable now. So it appears less than this bright day, which recommends itself forcibly to us by its actuality. And yet this is only a smudge in the shadow of heaven.

March 4, 1941

This has been a very remarkable day to have looked in the face. I don't think of the contents of a day as "a day," ordinarily; but this one has to be seen that way. To begin with, it is a day I have feared – it is the day I got all my notions together about war, and said them, briefly all at once, on a few sheets of paper, on a prepared blank and put them in the mail for the Draft Board.

I mean I made out my reasons for being a partial conscientious objector, for asking for noncombatant service, so as not to have to kill men made in the image of God when it is possible to obey the law (as I must) by serving the wounded and saving lives – or that may be a purely artificial situation: by the humiliation of digging latrines, which is a far greater honor to God than killing men.

The thing was that I wrote these things out without trepidation, and was amazed. Went quietly to Father Thomas and Father Gerald and got their approval. Went to Olean and had the thing notarized, mailed it. And all through it, I was tremendously happy in a strange quiet way. It was as if this were one of the good things for me to have done in my life – and all along I kept wondering at it. When the thing was in the box, I knew I was completely in God's hands. Everything goes according to His will. *I am free.* I have never felt such a cool sense of freedom as when I realized that I now belong to a decision by the board of strangers, which I will know is God's will, for He expresses His will through laws of states also. Whatever His will is, may it be done, through Christ Our Lord.

Riding in to Olean in a small old car with one of the workmen from the monastery farm was as pleasant as any time in my whole life; outside was good blue sky, and the hills in shadow from the sun going down gradually, aslant of them somewhere. In Olean the wide streets were almost empty and people were coming home from work. Riding back to Saint Bonas I came with Bob O'Brien, the plumber from the Olean House. Now the sun was below the hills, but the sky was the cleanest and clearest blue you ever saw and in it a couple of light, fiery, orange clouds, like in Bellini's pictures, again.

Bob O'Brien said "Isn't it good to be here in the country now? Where else would it be better than in this good country?" We had been talking about how people get mad in the city. A simple topic. Everything Bob said about the country he meant completely; it had the greatest depth of conviction. He is a big happy guy and means what he says; I never meant anything so much as when I agreed with him, either.

I walked up the road to the monastery, and saw the cross on top of the low cupola, over the rim of the roof, and saw that bright, clean, fiery sky, and heard the bell ringing, blowing down the hill from the open belfry up at Saint Elizabeth's for the Angelus, and once again I remembered clearly how I belong absolutely to God – for this thing in the mail only demonstrates that, does not make it so, for it always *was* so and will be, in a sense. But my consent is more open than ever, and I pray it be more and more and more so, until I am all His.

Then tonight I read *Robinson Crusoe* and when he comes on the island I was knocked flat at the wonder of what a marvelous book this is, maybe one of the best books ever written, and not a freak at all. No wonder kids like it! Like religion, it is perfect play.

Propter Sion non tacebo
et propter Jerosolymam non quiescam,
donec egrediatur ut splendor justus ejus,
et salvator ejus ut lampas accendatur.
Super muros tuos Jerusalem,
constitui custodes; tota die et tota nocte
in perpetuum non tacebunt.
Qui reminiscimini Domini,
ne taceatis,
et ne detis silentium ei
donec stabiliat et donec ponat Jerusalem
laudem in terra.

Isaias. 62.1 & 6.

[For Zion's sake I will not be silent,
for Jerusalem's sake I will not be quiet,
Until her vindication shines forth like the dawn
and her victory like a burning torch . . .
Upon your walls, O Jerusalem,
I have stationed watchmen;
Never, by day or by night,
shall they be silent.
O you who are to remind the Lord,
take no rest
And *give no rest to him,*
until he re-establishes Jerusalem
And makes of it
the pride of the earth.

(Isaiah 62:1, 6–7, New American Bible)]

Only a repeated miracle of God from minute to minute keeps me from falling into hell. I am made out of earth and ashes and spittle and a little mud. I don't know why I don't vanish like smoke. I am astounded and terrified at the tenacious pride of life that sticks in me. It says somewhere in the Breviary how God will confront you, *and show you that he is not like you.*

I walk around with temptation sticking in my stomach like a dagger, so bad I could vomit. Yet I hang by a thin thread of grace: when I go to take in my mouth the Blessed Sacrament, how can I do it without crawling on my face the length of the chapel? Every minute I am like a man condemned to death. If God wills, He can pardon me. If He does not will, I am executed. The knife falls. Every minute I am forced to plead for my life.

I read in the Gospel – "Blessed are ye when ye mourn." I cry desperately, hopeless of being able to understand what is so clear; that Christ, my judge, meant that line for me today, that everything I do, I read, I think, I touch, I do with meaning and a purpose. All these things are put in my way on purpose by everlasting, almighty God, who sees me write, who sees my fear.

I am terrified because I know I will sit up in the night crying "Jesu, Jesu, Jesu, Jesu" and will have to call Him until He, with His grace, rescues me from my cowardice that is terrified because I am finding out I am nothing, and yet still stubbornly refuse to believe it, and still puff myself up, still think I am something – because I seem to be, because I seem to be, only to find out that I am not, that I am in His hand, that life is a gift I have to beg Him for, because I am condemned to death by every movement of my self-will.

This is the day I should have feared, not that of the questionnaire!!

Today I walked up on the Two Mile in the new snow that is part of the blizzard that covered New York. It was a wonderful day, with level gray clouds, snow on the hills, woods. The Two Mile is a wonderful road, dipping and turning among small farms, lined with spectacular, small trees, and climbing gradually, into the woods, the mountain. It is like mountain country in Germany somewhere. The shapes of the hillsides are marvelous. Then, along the tops of the hills, the woods of young, straight trees. Icicles on the eaves of the small farm houses. Snow, drifted against the black or dark red barns – small barns. The two crazy dogs at one of the farms, one that looked like a fairy-story wolf-bear mixed, who stood up comically on his hind legs when he barked, and knew he was a character in a farce, but tried to be fierce, spoiled it by wagging his tail, got mad at himself, stood up, nearly rolled over backwards. Some vaudeville dog-wolf, shaggy in his black coat!

Where the farms and field ended and the woods began the snow-plough had stopped. Climbing the mountain in the deeper snow, with a sled-track to follow, was hard. Half way up I found a dead Studebaker.

At the top I came out on the Rock City road near the cabin where we were all summer, or rather near Healy's road and the cut – where I got a ride.

I thought of the last time I was up there in the snow – scared in much the same way as today, but I got through it then, too. That was in November. The day I remembered the phrase "O for the pencils of a Rembrandt" as used by Curzon in his *Monasteries of the Levant.*

Thought of a night in August when I hitchhiked up from Olean alone, and as we came through the cut, there in the headlights was Peggy Wells, standing at the foot of Healy's road by the mailboxes we never used. (Maybe they were *all* Healy's.)

> *Qui reminiscimini Domini,*
> *ne taceatis,*
> *ne detis silentium ei*
> *donec stabiliat et donec ponat Jerusalem*
> *laudem in terra.*
> [O you who are to remind the Lord,
> take no rest
> And give no rest to him,
> until he re-establishes Jerusalem
> And makes of it
> the pride of the earth. (Isaiah 62:6c–7, New American Bible)]

I am a small, weak place in the wall of Jerusalem, the most frightened sentry, blubbering in fear – *"bonus miles, Christe Jesu!"* ["good soldier Christe Jesu!"] Pray for me, you forty Holy Martyrs!

March 11, 1941

S. Bonaventure, *Itin. Ment. in Deum,* Cap III.

The Image of God – in us. *"Videre per speculum in aenigmate."* "To see through a mirror indistinctly" (1 Corinthians 13:12, New American Bible).]

"Intra igitur ad te et vide, quoniam mens tua amat ferventissime semitipsam; nec se posset amare nisi se nosset; *nec se nosset nisisui* meminisset, *quia mihi capimus per intelligentiam, quod non sit praesens apud nostram memoriam."* ["Go therefore into yourself and see, that your soul loves itself fervently; that it can't love itself unless it *knows* itself; neither does it know itself unless it *remembers* itself, for we understand nothing through intelligence, which is not also present in our memory."]

"Non invenit intellectus noster ut plene resolvens *intellectum alicuius entium creatorum nisi* invetur *ab intellectu entis purissimi, actualissimi,*

completissimi et absoluti, quod est ens simpliciter *et aeternum, in quo sunt rationes omnium in sua puritate. Quomodo autem sciret intellectus, hoc esse ens defectivum et incompletum, nisi haberet cognitionem entis absque omni defectu?"* ["Our intellect does not arrive at *full knowledge* of any created being, unless it *is helped* by an intellect of the purest, most actual, most complete and absolute being, which is *Being simple* and eternal, in which are the reasons of all beings, in its purity. How is the intellect to know this, it being a defective and incomplete creature, unless it has knowledge of a being without any defect whatsoever?"]

"Tanta est vis summi boni, ut mihi nisi per illius desiderium a creatura possit amari, quae tunc fallitur et errat, cum effigiem et simulacrum pro veritate acceptat." III.4. [Such is the power of the Supreme Good that everything a creature loves is loved out of desire for that Good; creatures are deceived and fall into error when they take the image and copy for the thing itself.]

In speculo. [Through a mirror indistinctly.]

"Mens humana, sollicitudinibus distracta, non redit ad se per memoriam; phantasmatibus obnubilata, not redit ad se per intelligentiam; *concupiscentiis illecta, ad se ipsam nequaquam revertitur per desiderium suavitatis internae et laetitiae spiritualis. Ideo totaliter in his sensibilibus iacens, non potest ad se tanquam ad Dei imaginem reintrare."* ["The human soul, distracted as it is by worries, does not return to itself *through memory;* clouded by images, it does not return to itself through *intelligence;* torn by disordered desires, it cannot return to itself through a desire for internal pleasantness and spiritual joy. Therefore, lying totally in these sensible things, it cannot thus return to itself and the image of God."]

"Et quoniam, ubi quis ceciderit, necesse habet, ibidem recumbere nisi apponat quis et adiiciat, ut resurgat (Isa. 24–20); *non potuit anima nostra perfecte ab his sensibilibus relevari ad contuitum sui et aeternae Veritatis in se ipsa,* nisi Veritas, assumta forma humana in Christo, fieret sibi scala reparans priorem scalam, quae fracta fuerat in Adam." ["And because, where someone falls, he will of necessity lie in the same place unless someone comes by and *helps him,* so *that he might get up* (Isaiah 24:20); nor can our soul be lifted up perfectly from these sensible things to the clear view of itself and eternal truth in itself, *unless the Truth, having taken a human form in Christ, becomes for it a ladder that repairs the first ladder, which had been broken in Adam."]

March 18, 1941

The first insult of the day, after getting off the five-thirty train into the freezing storm, was when I found the letter from *New Yorker* saying a poem containing a parody on "Beauty is truth etc. . ." was a parody of Emily Dickinson and their readers would mostly be unfamiliar with that poem "of hers" so they couldn't use it.

I never read a line of Emily Dickinson. I struggled back to my room, through the blizzard, shaking my head, like Brother Juniper in the book and saying: "How true! How true! How true!"

Now I really think I shouldn't send anything more to them.

However yesterday in the *New Yorker* office sitting quiet in the room full of desks, where Lax works with Mrs. Sayre and some fuzzy-headed dame who keeps calling up and asking what's on at the movies – in that room around noon time I started a good poem – good enough. Mark Van Doren read it in the subway, and liked it.

Things kept happening like on a timetable. Many small inexplicable things: enough for a completely tedious novel.

1. Wednesday night I was writing a poem when this very dull student brings me notice I'm to take my medical for the draft. I finished the poem, stupefied: then started to think about this. First I interpreted it as a summary rejection without trial, hearing, question or anything of my application for only partial military service – i.e., in the Medical Corps or somewhere like that. It took a trip to N.Y. to find out this wasn't exactly so.

2. Thursday afternoon I walked in the sun through the snow down to the river. The hills were pretty, and, as a matter of fact, I mostly walk down there in the morning, so everything looked rather different in the afternoon light. I suppose being called in the draft makes you yearn after everything familiar and pretty and good like a man with TB clutching at pleasant experience, knowing he is going to lose it all soon. So I felt very melancholy, and the hills were indescribably beautiful, and all in all everything was like the feeling I used to get at the end of the summer holidays when I was 15 or 16. "So fair a summer look for never more." It is very unpleasant. That was when I decided to go to New York.

3. Everything has been very much complicated by the publication, in *Time* of a stupidly written card I sent them complimenting them on an article about the dead Joyce. On the train, I met a friar from Calicoon who had read the thing and it had made him mad. The thing came out Thursday. Everybody in the world has seen it – except me. But, true enough, they had sent me a note. I do not regret them sentiments, as they say. But I

wrote the thing in a blunt and brutal sounding fashion of a kind to enrage all good fellows who are touchy about the dead Joyce, and it was not meant for publication. It was written in kindness and not to enrage. But it looked as though it had run from the pen of some admirer of James M. Cain. (I read it this morning. That, also, was in the mail.) Prof. Davis had read it, and some of my students, and the kid who waits on the Profs' table – Lax, Gibney and Seymour, none of whom ever read *Time*, had read this one: but they were only a little surprised. Probably thought it was a card from R. Ewing, or somebody, and saw my name. Also the Protestant minister in Douglaston, Lester Leake Riley: he had seen it.

People who didn't mention having seen it: Mark Van Doren, my family, Fred Ritter, whom I met on the L.I. train. That's about all.

4. In New York the women in the Subways reeked with perfume more than ever before, and there were many men in uniforms. I forget what was on the headlines – Oh yes, bombing of Glasgow and of Hamburg. The first I had seen, even of a headline, since Lent's beginning.

New York looked unpleasant even from Rutherford, N.J. Secretly I admired the new place for telephoning near the Eighth Ave. end of the L.I. concourse in Penn Station. It has armchair stools and clear, warm booths, and no dialing but an operator at a switchboard outside to put the numbers through while you are on your way to the booth. Luxury. But I still didn't like being drafted.

If I had seen myself writing that line, last year this time, I would have been sick for seven hours. This year – it is the first emotion I have felt about the whole thing, and I suppose I am more or less resigned to everything.

5. I went out to Long Beach, where Lax was at Seymour's. There the weather was warm, and there was a moon. Lax and I walked on the empty boardwalk, and our feet shattered the clam shells scattered all over the boards by the seagulls. At Seymour's house I got the greatest pleasure out of a 1925 *Pleasure Guide to Paris* written in Frenchy English for tourists, illustrated with portraits of French actresses: very funny, very pretty pictures. The pictures were ridiculous: the women were, you could tell, pretty, but only by guessing. Photographs never really do what they are thought to do – show you what people look like, or rather what they *are* like. A photograph of Saint Paul, if there were one, would be nothing at all – only a photograph of a First Century man, not of a Saint. (And yet the photographs of the Little Flower are more interesting than the terrible statues of her that we see. I admit that.)

6. On the way down I found out the name of the theater in Waverley that always makes me laugh:

Amusu Theater.

It's good when the "u"s are pronounced in the French manner.

On the way down, it was all like a well run schedule. I bit into a piece of bread and butter as we were entering Waverley. I got the rest of my dinner as we were entering Oswego. In Corning Station I had read Sext [Little Hours of the Divine Office] by mistake before Terce, and had to go over it again.

7. Long Beach was all right until we began to feel imprisoned, in the middle of Saturday afternoon. In the Lafayette Grill, where we went for sandwiches, cokes – a long picture showed a line of 1925 dames in 1925 bathing suits, lined up for an International Beauty Contest in Galveston, Texas. The waiter looked as if he had mercurochrome in the cracks of his teeth. Saturday night we rode from Long Beach to Port Washington, Lax and I hunched up on the floor of a grocer's truck, sitting crosslegged with not too much discomfort. The grocer's truck belonged to a friend of Seymour's brother, who questioned me, later, concerning Catholics in the field of liberalism, etc. as we were sitting in Gibney's cellar, among the drawings, chairs, and things for making statues.

8. I am very familiar with Gibney's house. It is associated, in my mind, with the World's Fair. In the alcove leading into the kitchen is the phone on which I tried to call Wilma Reardon, at the fair, the 4th of July 1939. I didn't get her. She was home. I didn't know that number. There was a slight misunderstanding. Gibney and I went to the fair, and she sat with no date, and was a little sore, I guess. The sheets in the guest room at Gibney's smelled strongly of camphor. Sunday morning, the nice weather was all gone, and it was raining. I left the house before anyone was up, and went to Church, and then to Douglaston.

That night Gibney and I went to North Beach, and watched the planes, as a sort of World's Fair surrogate and not such a good one. The terrible orchestra in the place where we drank ginger ale played a conga that made coming from Olean to New York sound like coming from Paris to remotest Iowa – as if I cared about congas.

I was glad to get back here. This monastery is more of a home than anywhere I have had since my father died – or since Pops died in Douglaston, which emptied the house, in a way: but that house was my home, too, last year, before I went to Cuba – at exactly this time of the year. It would be, except that – it isn't, and they are always thinking of moving out. The only thing that made it no home before was my own ingratitude. You have to be grateful for goodness before you know goodness, in a way.

March 19. Feast of Saint Joseph

I was the first one at the Draft Board to be examined, and got out about a quarter to nine, or nine o'clock into the icy wind and snow. The air was bright. I was cold standing around naked, passing from doctor to doctor. The room was full of respectful doctors and quiet, naked farm boys walking around being examined, one standing on the metal scale, another squinting at the chart, beginning with a big O.

They didn't do anything much to me except take blood out of my arm for a syphilis test. The blood, in the glass syringe, looked surprisingly dark. Then they took the blood in a test tube and corked it and put it to keep warm in a big pan of water heating over a gas ring. After that they took some of my urine in a bottle also. I bent over and a man looked cursorily into my anus.

I stood around frozen as much by the cold as by my own shame and was glad they didn't do too many things that would have kept me standing around. No blood-pressure was taken. They knocked me on my knee for the reflexes only as an afterthought.

Then the Doctor, with a sort of apologetic grin, gave me a folder which had a picture of some soldiers leaving in a train and it said: *"So Long Boys – Take care of yourselves"* and inside there was some crap about venereal diseases. ("If you are bored and lonely don't get picked up by loose women because they only want your money; and besides . . .") So I put this into my pocket and rode back in a bus to the monastery.

March 23. Sunday (4th in Lent)

The Four Mile Valley is less interesting than the Two Mile. To begin with the road is flatter, the fields are wider. Also my feet were full of cinders I had picked up along the railroad track, and got sore.

I got a ride up into Lippert's Hollow, which is a high bowl in the woods, full of neat and painted farmhouses inhabited by people called Lippert – and the woods resound with the clangorous thumping and pounding of oil pumps.

In every house I passed, walking, happy people looked out from the curtains with expectations of my being a visitor – but I passed all the houses and went up the steep, muddy road into the woods. All the snow has been melting.

I came out up by Ho-Sta-Geh, a house on top of the hills, with a stone verandah where you can eat steaks and look for miles out over the hills. All the hills are level at the top, and you can clearly see how all this is a peneplain. My other geological word for this region is Olean Conglomerate. I stood next to a big block of it to thumb a ride, and on this Olean Conglomerate were painted, in white, inexplicable numbers 00203.

A robin came in a tree, making a dull and enervated sort of chirping noise. I was not thrilled by the first robin. The other day, in the pasture behind the college, I saw a sea gull, probably blown in by Saint Patrick's Day's storm – and attracted to the place where they throw the garbage and old tin cans out back of the observatory.

I haven't any idea what the drafters are going to do with me. I find myself wondering about a lot of stupid things – the most consistent preoccupation being: how will I write things in camp? On what kind of a box will I set down my typewriter? Under what flickering yellow bulb will I scribble, with this here big volume on my knees.

What will I say to the sergeant when he comes up and says "What do you think you're doing?" I suppose that is the most artificial problem of all: thinking about the sergeant's attitude towards soldiers who read and write.

Or will I not be in camp at all? Put here teaching Dante, 18th Century Drama and Bibliography! I might have known they would soon enough get around to the teaching of completely stupid subjects. What is 18th Century Drama? What do I have to do? Talk four weeks about George Lillo? Bibliography: reading indexes aloud, I expect.

Or will I be somewhere in Texas hoping against hope for a weekend in the glittering city of San Antonio?

Some drab ideas. So drab I can't grasp them. I have fewer thoughts about all this than anything I can conceive. I can't comprehend the draft at all. I don't know what it's all about.

Now what do I expect to do? Stimulate my mind and happy myself up by reading Thomas Love Peacock? I was happy with the *Cuban Journal* I made last year. I looked in it again today. I think it is a good book. I have been too happy about all the poems I have been writing lately: now, for a change, I am a little sick of them.

What else do I keep thinking about?

This inferior pen, this third rate ink.

Whether I will get to Gethsemani Monastery, near Louisville, for Holy Week.

Wouldn't it be nice to go to Mexico, and write a Mexican journal?

That I haven't any idea what's going on in the world: and I also believe that nothing much is going on in the world: a sure enough sign that something will be soon.

It's a long time since I drew any pictures: and my Christmas cards weren't much good, either.

My father's death, in the Middlesex Hospital: for a long time he could not speak. On blue letter paper, with a fountain pen, he drew Byzantine saints. I told him one day I was going to learn Italian. That was a dreary hospital. This is another thing I cannot understand: his death. His illness was something that was being "kept from me", that is, how bad it was. I knew all along father would die, but didn't reflect upon it, because I couldn't: I mean I didn't know how. Anyway, I was too young and too selfish, and I had been away at school too much, and at Aunt Maud's and other places too much in holidays. I didn't reflect about it, but on the other hand I have never ceased to dream about it. I never doubted the fact that father's soul, or mother's, were immortal – never. It was never possible – even when I said I didn't believe anything.

Today, in the Four Mile Valley, hearing the rush of waters down the ditches of the mountainside, I was reminded of Murat and Le Puy du Cantal. On the rock at Murat is a huge image to the Blessed Virgin: she was in my father's pictures, and I hope she prayed for him when nobody else did. All the saints to whom were dedicated the churches and cathedrals that my father loved, pray for him. The Saint of St. Antonin, where he was building a house, where we lived looking at the river and Rocher d'Angears, pray for him. I have never stopped thinking about that town or all the places around it. It is thirteen years since I was there.

Again today I thought of the time we were in Clermont-Ferrand. Or the time we were in Marseilles – the restaurant where everybody was afraid of the towels. The first day we were in Montauban. My exhilaration at the sweet-smelling barbershops in Montauban. I often think of the Marist College in Montauban, a place I wondered at; very mysterious. The brick tower of St. Jacques. The Musée Ingres. The guidebooks I devoured. Father working on the land he had bought, on summer evenings, making flowers grow. The drawings of the house. The beginning of the house itself. His room, my room. Mine full of sun. His smelled of tobacco, a little. The kitchen, where we made cocoa out of goatsmilk. I thought of the source du Prince Novi, the Medieval tanneries, the legend of the Saint, the rocks, the stunted oaks, the causses, the tough little *chateaux*, the Calvaire where the rich people from Lille were trying to be country gentry. The Protestant cemetery, where there were nightingales in the cypresses. Eating at the Hôtel des Thermes: but above all: summer. And the rains of winter. And all father's pictures. The big screen he did for Bennett. The tunes he played on the piano in the movie house, for the Buster Keaton movies: I want to be happy. Chicago. Tea-for-Two. Toodle-oo.

Sometimes I think I don't know anything except the years 1926-27-28 in France, as if they were my whole life, as if father had made that whole world and given it to me instead of America, shared it with me.

I have not ceased to dream all this, or won't, ever. Also, I want to write another novel.

March 26. 1941

Saint Bonaventure on the problem of the relation of the intellect, memory and will, to the substance of the soul. Are they three separate substances, of which the soul is made up? Can that be? No. Are they three accidents of one substance as Saint Thomas thinks? No. When he says they are accidents, he has to immediately qualify them as accidents in no ordinary sense, because the substance of the soul cannot be considered apart from them. Ordinarily a substance must be able to be considered apart from its accidents, or it is no substance. . . . They are *"mediae inter substantiam et accidens"* ["means between substance and accident"] – they are, perhaps, properties of the substance? With the substance of the soul they form a *totum potentiale* ["full potential"].

Father Philotheus would say "No pure position!"

SAINT BONAVENTURE

Considering the soul abstractly, in itself, it is still inseparable from intellect, memory and will. These are not accidents of its substance. Nor are they its substance. But they are consubstantial with its substance:

> *"istae potentiae sunt animae consubstantiales,* et sicut in eodem genere per reductionionem." (I. Sent. 3.2. 1.3. Concl. T-I. p. 86.) ["These potencies are consubstantial souls, and they are the same kind, through reduction."]

They are to the soul what a man's image in a mirror is to the man . . .
Technical notion of *reductio:*

"Prima enim agendi potentiae quae egressum dicitur habere ab ipsa substantia, ad idem garus reducitur quae non adeo elongatur ab ipso substantia ut dicat aliam essentiam completam." (II. Sent. 24.1.2.1. ad 8th T.II. p. 562.) ["For first, the potential of acting, which is said to have an exit from that very substance, is reduced to the same kind which is not further drawn out from the same substance, so that it is called another complete essence."]

Difference between the two points of view. Thomist – denies the soul contains in its essence, as such, the sufficient conditions for any of its acts. According to St. Bonaventure – the soul draws from itself its own operations and their content – passing immediately from its substance to the acts that spring from it. . . .

April 5, 1941. Cincinnati, Ohio

Q: Well then, how are you going to begin?

A: Chronologically, perhaps: The *Felsenbrau* sign that impressed me as we came in to the city on the Big Four train. It was up on a big real Felscliff. Light went on and off. *Felsenbrau – aged in the hills: Felsenbrau: aged in the hills.* My only question was, did Felsenbrau themselves go and hack up that monadnock of a cliff where the sign was?

Q: You are full of ideas about Cincinnati, since you express yourself so volubly even on so small a matter as this. What other thoughts do you have concerning the city?

A: How many "n's" in its name?

Q: Have you expressed this thought elsewhere?

A: Yes, on a postcard to Lax.

Q: Did you put in that postcard everything you at first intended?

A: No. I omitted the statement that the Cincinnati R.R. Station was as big and as pretty as the whole N.Y. World's Fair of 1939.

Q: Why did you leave this out: taste?

A: No. Forgot.

Q: You had thought it up before? In the station itself?

A: Yace!

Q: What other thoughts did you have in the Cincinnati station?

A: Whether to go on at once to Louisville.

Q: Obviously enough, you did not, since here you sit on the 3rd floor of the quiet Hotel Parkview, overlooking the statue of Gen? Garfield (President of U.S.). I take it you were attracted by the city?

A: O, I intended to stop over anyway. But I was instantly seduced by its freshness, as they say.

Q: Who say?

A: They. Them. Rousseau. Voltaire.

Q: Over there? Was Europe a success?

A: I thought of that in the coffee shop of the Hotel Sinton, Stinton or Stimson. I thought of that title. Of J. W. Krutch speaking the title (his own words), and of Mark Van Doren laughing at J. W. Krutch saying, with a sniff, "Was Europe a success?" Then I thought of me laughing at something said by Seymour. Previously, in the train, near Springfield, Ohio, I had thought of Seymour's name for the hero of his novel – Simon Kelwey and wondered if he lived anywhere but Long Beach, would he have made it Calloway? Kelwey – a very Jewish non-Jewish name! The kind a guy called Calvaz would change his name to. (There goes a fire engine.)

Q: What else occurred to you in the Hotel Stinson, Slimpton or Shimpman?

A: That the dinner I had there was the worst food I had ever eaten. That I had been eating grapefruit and eggs all day (travelling), instead of potatoes and beans and bread, as at school (fasting, working). And was this fasting?

Q: Was it?

A: The food was no pleasure; especially the vegetables.

Q: What is the first thing you remember about Galion, Ohio?

A: That I cleverly called it *The Tobacco Road of the Universe*, to a woman, when we stood on the platform of the Erie Station desolate, while hopeless of ever seeing any taxis to take us over to the Big Four Station.

Q: Did anything subsequently bear out your idea that Galion was cheerless?

A: Yes: the Steel Burial Vault Works, next to the Big Four Station, Best steel burial vaults in the world. Worst station.

Q: What trains were late at Galion?

A: The Erie, 36 minutes. The Big 4 – 20 minutes. Normally there is a wait of one hour between trains. If the Big 4 had been on time the wait would have been reduced to 24 minutes. As it was, we waited 44 minutes.

Q: To whom did you converse?

A: Correction please: *with* whom. . . . Well, the principal of some elementary school in Youngstown.

Q: What acquaintance of yours from Youngstown, whom she had never heard of, did you mention to her?

A: Bob Burke, Columbia '38 – expelled for rioting.

Q: Were you surprised she had not heard of him?

A: Well, so what! Let's get back to Cincinnati!!

Q: As you wish. How did you happen to get to the Hotel Slimpton in the first place, to eat, since you are yourself staying at the Hotel Parkview, and writing with their pen?

A: I was walking, looking for a place to eat.

Q: What places had you passed up?

A: Old Vienna. Mill's Rest., The B and G, The Canary Cottage, The Netherland Plaza Julep Bar, Wiggins' Bar – where it was very crowded and beery.

Q: O, holier than thou! Why did you pick the Sinton?

A: Looked like a good hotel – if it is, it has the worst coffee shop in the universe, for its food, emptiness, old ladies.

Q: Neither *crowded* nor *beery.* . . .

A: Shut up!

Q: What public building, or buildings, impress you in Cincinnati?

A: The Station. The housing project on the way from the Station – not in itself, but as a symptom of Cincinnati's good will, in making a nice clean new avenue, through a slum, to the station.

Q: Others?

A: The Cincinnati Club. Saint Francis Xavier's Church. The other, newer church, on 8th St. just beyond Vine, where I hope to go to Mass tomorrow morning (Palm Sunday).

Q: What else pops into your head, concerning Cincinnati?

A: Count Cincinnati, in E. Waugh's *Vile Bodies.*

Q: Where are you glad you didn't take a room.

A: The Y.M.C.A. The Interlaken Plaza, or whatever it is. The Slipshod.

Q: Come, no puns. Where did you first tell the taxi-driver to go, before changing your mind?

A: The Y.M.C.A.

Q: I thought so! Well: what other project have you abandoned in Cincinnati?

A: Going on to Louisville by bus. Looking for an art museum, it is so late. Taking any interest in Covington.

Q: What is Cincinnati full of?

A: Starlings, going north. Soldiers, going north, south, east and west and, all too soon, to Europe. Warmer air than St. Bona's. Happiness.

Southerners. Old houses, distinguished, dilapidated. A pleasant air of charm; a character of its own.

Q: With whom did you converse concerning the draft?

A: The elevator boy in the Hotel. He said: "They're going to reach out and grab me."

Q: What surprised you about him?

A: His age. He seemed to be 18; is, or says he is, 34.

Q: What contribution did you make to the discussion?

A: The statement that I had been deferred: unexplained, as I had a frog in my throat.

Q: What movies tempted you to come in their portals?

A: None. Lay off the portals.

Q: To what other cities do you prefer Cincinnati?

A: Buffalo, Erie, Dayton, Columbus, Cleveland, New York, Boston, Washington, Richmond, etc. etc. Miami, etc. etc.

Q: You name almost all the cities in America you have seen!

A: Yes, as a matter of fact, I do. Cincinnati is the best city I have seen so far in America.

Q: What do you like about it?

A: Fountain Square. The Carew Tower. The streets. Garfield Place. The atmosphere. A grain elevator I saw on the way in. The Station. The Cincinnati Club. That little new church. The attitude of the people. Well dressed. Happy. Larfing. The air is invigorating.

Q: What important body of water have you so far not, to your knowledge, seen?

A: The Ohio River.

Q: Why not?

A: Darkness. Sore feet. Fear of empty streets and sudden floods. Fear of walking around too much lest someone think I was sauntering about with the purpose of molesting women. Hunger. Lack of interest.

Q: What do you like about this part of Ohio?

A: The country is more rolling. Fine long views, towards the sky, glaring brightness in the west, under the blowing rain clouds. Fine farms. All over Ohio you see miles all around: it is all but flat, but not quite. Trees on the horizon seem to be cities, smokestacks – you can't tell. The view of the city from the station, down the long sweep of that avenue. The lighting on the high buildings, at night. Palms on the altar of the church, for Palm Sunday. The voice of a Jesuit giving absolution to somebody else, in a confessional – and I myself on my way to the Trappists at Gethsemani.

April 7, 1941, Our Lady of Gethsemani

I should tear out all the other pages of this book and all the other pages of everything else I ever wrote, and begin here.

This is the center of America. I had wondered what was holding this country together, what has been keeping the universe from cracking in pieces and falling apart. It is this monastery if only this one. (There must be two or three others.)

Abraham prayed to the Lord to spare Sodom if there should be found in it one just man. The Blessed Mother of God, Mary Queen of Heaven and of Angels, shows Him daily His children here, and because of their prayers, the world is spared from minute to minute, from the terrible doom.

This is the only real city in America – in a desert.

It is the axle around which the whole country blindly turns.

Washington is paint and plaster and noise-making machines and lunacy: this country hasn't got a capital, or a heart, or any focal point to it, except Gethsemani, and Gethsemani holds this country together the way the underlying substrate of faith that goes with our own being and cannot be separated from it, keeps living a man who is faithless – who does not believe in Being and yet himself, *is*, in spite of his crazy denial that Being made him, mercifully, be.

This is a great and splendid palace. I have never in my life seen a court of a King or a Queen. Now I am transported into one and I can hardly breathe; from minute to minute. I have been in the greatest capital cities of the world, but never seen anything that was not either a railway station or a movie, instead of being the palace it tried to be. Here, suddenly, I am in the Court of the Queen of Heaven, where She sits throned, and receives at once the proper praise of men and angels. I tell you I cannot breathe. (I tell who? When I am in the palace of the Queen of Heaven, who do I talk to? I only ask to kiss the earth this Holy Place is built on.)

"What hath man deserved that Thou shouldst give him Thy grace?
    Lord, what cause have I to complain if Thou forsake me? Or what can
I justly allege if what I petition Thou shalt not grant?

This most assuredly I may truly think and say: Lord, I am nothing, I can do nothing, I have nothing of myself that is good; but I am in all things defective and ever tend to nothing."

Imitation of Christ, Bk. 3. Ch. 40.[8]

What *right* have I to be here?

I am like a man, a thief and a murderer, put in jail and condemned for stealing and murdering all my life, for murdering God's grace in myself and others, for murdering Him in His image; and I have broken roughly out of the jail where I lay condemned to death, justly, and rushed to the King whose Son I murdered – to the Queen, too, to His Mother whom the sword of sorrow pierced so that I all but murdered her! – and I break into her palace, and run bloody and foul, screaming like a gluttonous, bullying child, scattering her courtiers who pay her just honor for Her Son's love, and I implore her mercy; and Her Son grants, for a while – for a while – until I can implore more and more and more, life and life, for fear that I be destroyed from minute to minute.

What right have I here? What right have I to this mercy? I have no rights: I am absolutely without rights. Slaves have no rights. Rights are all lies. Because as soon as you claim by right the gift that is given you as pure gift, pure love, then the gift is lessened and lost!

When the slave is set free by pure love and claims it was his right to be free, he enslaves himself again: he puts himself back in chains, asserting the gift did not make him free, after all; he must be free not by gift, but *by right*. But if he only remembered to be free! And stop clamoring for a right that only enslaves him again, although the giver would make him free!

I have never had any right to anything in my life – and least of all, to this. What hath man deserved that thou shouldst give him Thy grace?

April 8. 1941. Our Lady of Gethsemani

PARADISUS CLAUSTRALIS

Abbeys are paradises, but in two different senses – and that the abbey is at the same time an earthly and a heavenly paradise is a paradox: especially because it is both only because it is also a purgatory.

What is a purgatory? The souls in purgatory are burned by the same substantial fire as the souls in hell: but they bear the burning with love and not hatred, for they love God and know through this fire they come to

---

[8] It is not certain what translation of *The Imitation of Christ* Merton was using at this time, since there were several that appeared in the early 1900s. In other places in this journal, Merton does not rely on translations but quotes directly from the Latin version.

Him, while the souls in hell hate God and hate their pains because the pains are just, and hate them because they are terrible and inescapable. The souls in purgatory bear their torments for the same reasons – they know they are inescapable and just: but justice is of God: to bear justice for the love of love is to be like God: it is in loving God that we are like Him: it is in realizing how little we love Him, how unlike Him we are, that we see it is just that we suffer to learn to love Him.

So one by one we gladly tear away our sins like plasters, and they hurt us. We love – not the pain: God. The pain is just – it is the only way we can get to him, the way that involves *this pain*.

An abbey, a cloister, is an earthly paradise because it is an earthly purgatory.

But if we fix our eyes on the mere *earthliness of its paradise* the abbey will eventually cease to be even an earthly paradise. The abbey has a beauty and an order and cleanness and stability in the physical and political order. It is beautiful, and it is ordered, and it is strong, simply as community: simple in its buildings, its gardens, its farms. I mean a true abbey which is, now, taken only as an expression of Medieval Christian culture. But this beauty, order and soundness and *social* symmetry are not there for the monks to enjoy, or for anybody else to enjoy, because they cannot be enjoyed, according to the proper sense of enjoy – to rest in a thing for itself alone. It has to be used.

But even the *uses* of this material paradise are limited. A monk does not use his abbey, its gardens, its beautiful chapel, its lovely, quiet cloister to save his soul – not in a real sense. He uses the chapel to pray in and he saves his soul by praying: he uses prayers to save his soul. Thus, the chapel itself only comes in at one remove. He uses a bed to sleep on. If the bed happens to have a mattress of straw and husks, he is not using a straw mattress to save his soul, but using it to sleep on. He is using self-denial to save his soul.

To sleep on a straw mattress or a board is not to save your soul, it is merely to sleep on a straw mattress or a board. To sleep on a straw mattress for the love of God is to use self-denial. The use of self-denial for God's love helps to save your soul. To enjoy self-denial for its own sake is a perversion: it always has to be *used*. But perhaps no one was ever perverted enough to enjoy self-denial in itself, for its own sake.

How does it happen that this abbey is an earthly paradise? It is as a result of a hierarchy of uses. For the good Trappists (and they are good, holy men), work is important – it is a mixture of penance and recreation.

However hard it is, it is still a form of play. Even the strictest penance is play, too. The liturgy, too. The Trappist uses work to save his soul. To be as little children, we must play like them, do things not because they are physically necessary, but *freely*, as if arbitrarily, almost: for love. Behind the strictness of the Trappist's discipline is this complete metaphysical freedom from physical necessity that makes it, ontologically speaking, a kind of play. This use of work as play to save the monk's soul results, indirectly, in the abbey being an earthly paradise – because work necessarily produces results, and the results, in this case, are a perfect community, a marvelous farm, beautiful gardens, a lovely chapel, woods, the cleanest guest house in the world, wonderful bread, cheese, butter – all things make this abbey the only really excellent community of any kind, political, religious, or anything, in the whole country.

This accident, by which the Trappist monastery is a material, as well as a spiritual paradise, is an illuminating example of medieval culture. The Cistercian monastery is the product of the accidents of the Benedictine Rule and medieval society and economy and techniques of living. But it isn't merely medieval – I think, as a matter of fact, the Cistercian monastery is the perfect product of harmony between a Christian religious rule and an agricultural life. Since agricultural communities must necessarily co-exist with man's world as long as it lasts, and, since it is promised our faith will also, this combination has nothing temporary about it either! This monastery is *modern* as well as *medieval*.

I merely brought up the point about medieval to suggest that – in those days – most of society depended on techniques of living so much more successful than our own. This would be an example. As a matter of fact, in the south of France, which is still largely medieval, the satisfactory balance of things, the order and the beauty of life in agricultural communities – (as compared to the rotten condition of farms in New York state – and the degenerate state of the farmers!) seems to bear out what I am saying.

But, however, the *Imitation of Christ* says (Bk. 2. Ch. 9):

"For whether I have with me good men, or devout brethren, or faithful friends, or holy books, or beautiful treatises, or sweet canticles and hymns, all these help but little, give me but little relish, when I am forsaken by grace and left in my own poverty."

All the monastery's beauty, the beauty of the chapel, of the liturgy – cannot only not be enjoyed in themselves, but even their uses are fickle, and desert us sometimes, too. So anyone who comes to a monastery for them alone is bound to be deceived and betrayed, even by them. And they are only the accidents of religious life: which is in the soul, and exists in the soul not as a "good feeling" but in the constant and unyielding practice of patience, humility, mortification – the steady unwavering love of God even though the most beautiful expressions of His glory to our senses should turn against us and betray us. And they must; that is part of His kindness: for if church windows and psalms and hymns always filled us, every time, with the same consolation, the deception, then, would be real and terrible: for then we should mistake them for God, and turn to them from Him, just as we are apt to turn to human love, from His love, and be deceived in that, also.

"I would not have any such consolation as robbeth me of compunction; nor do I wish to have such contemplation as leadeth to pride.

For all that is high is not holy; nor is every pleasant thing good; nor every desire pure; nor is everything that is dear to us pleasing to God."

Imitation of Christ, 2. 70.

S. Bernardi *De Diligendo Deo*.

Causa diligendi Deum, Deus est; modus, sine modo diligere. ["The cause of loving God, is God Himself; the way to love Him, is without any limit."]

Dignitatem in homine liberum arbitrium dico: in quo ei nimirum datum est ceteris non solum praeeminere, sed et praesidere animantibus. Scientiam, vero, qua eamdem in se dignitatem agnoscat, non a se tamen. *Porro virtutem, qua subinde ipsum a quo est, et iniquirat non segniter, et teneat fortiter cum invenerit.* ["I call free will the dignity of man: in this he is set above and also rules over all other living things. His knowledge consists in knowing that he has this dignity, but also that it doesn't come from him. His virtue, which he immediately recognizes as coming from free will, consists in seeking out his Creator and holding on to Him strongly when he has found Him."]

Nosce Teipsum

Scientia quoque duplex erit, *si hanc ipsam dignitatem vel aliud quodque bonum in nobis, et nobis inesse, et a nobis non esse noverimus.* [*Know Yourself*: "Knowledge is two-fold, for we know we have this dignity – or any other good in us – and we know that it doesn't come from us."]

Utrumque ergo scias necesse est et quid sis, et quod a teipso non sis, ne aut omnino videlicet non glorieris, aut inaniter glorieris . . . Homo factus in honore, cum honorem ipsum non intelligit talis suae ignorantiae merito comparatur pecoribus, velut quibusdam praesentis suae corruptionis et mortalitatis consortibus.

["You therefore should know two things: first, what you are, and next, that you are not what you are in and of yourself, so that you neither glory in yourself, nor glory in vain. . . . Man was made in honor, but since he does not understand this honor through his ignorance, he can justly be compared to sheep, or to other companions of his present state of corruption and mortality."]

(Ignorantia) [Ignorance]

. . . efficitur una de caeteris (creaturis) quod se prae caeteris nihil accepisse intelligat [". . . he is made one with the rest of the creatures, but doesn't understand that he is to be ahead of the rest."]

(Superbia) [Pride]

Si bonum quodcumque in nobis esse, et a nobis decepti putemus. ["if there is any good in us, and we wrongly believe that it is from us."]

Per illam (ignorantiam) quidam Deus nescitur; per istam (superbiam) et contemnitur . . . Est quippe superbia et delictum maximum, uti datis tamquam innatis, et in acceptis beneficiis gloriam usurpare benefici. ["Through the one (ignorance), God is not known; through the other (pride), God is despised . . . pride is indeed also the greatest sin, in which we deem gifts that were given us to be ours, so that we usurp the glory of the Giver of the gifts."]

Quamobrem cum duabus istis, dignitate atque scientia, opus est et virtute, quae utriusque frustus est, per quam ille inquiritur ac tenetur, qui omnium auctor et dator merito glorificetur de omnibus.

["Therefore, with these two, dignity and knowledge, there is also a need for virtue, which joins both together, through which we seek and hold onto Him, Who is the Author and Giver of everything, and is justly glorified by all."]

Meretur ergo amari propter seipsum Deus, et ab infideli, qui essi nesciat Christum, scit tamen seipsum. ["Therefore, God deserved to be loved because of Himself, and by the infidel, who *does not know Christ, but nevertheless knows God.*"]

April 9 – Wednesday in Holy Week. Our Lady of Gethsemani, Ky.

> "Write My words in thy heart, and think diligently on them; for they will be very necessary in the time of temptation."
>
> "What thou understandest not when thou readest thou shalt know in the day of visitation."

Imitation of Christ, 3. 3. 5.

(It is not a book that is being spoken of here. The reading that is meant is intuition, understanding, – the clarifications of our reason and will, from time to time by God's grace and His truth.)

Sometimes we see a kind of truth all at once, in a flash, in a whole. We grasp this truth at once, in its wholeness, as a block, but not in all its details. We see the whole perspective of its meaning at once, and easily. We get a vast, large, pleasing, happy general view of some truth that's near to us. We contemplate it a while, from this standpoint – as long as the truth stands vividly before us: we hold this new, luminous whole figure of truth in our minds – we do not understand it thoroughly by any means, but anyway we possess it to some extent, and with a kind of certain knowledge. But we do not yet know it through and through, but we know it by its general outline: we know the character of the whole figure, in the rough, in block. Any idea will do as an example: a mathematical notion or a philosophical one or a religious one – any idea with some scope to it.

But once this general figure has become our property and, we think, part of us in this first easy-seeming intuition – then by a series of minute, difficult, toilsome steps we begin to find out, separately, as if with great trouble, over and over again, things that are just _parts_ of this same idea we already possess as a whole. At first we don't recognize the connection – and we cannot: because, in fact, though we already know the whole of which these are parts, yet to discover these things as parts, and in themselves, and in their connection to the general figure we know, as it were, in a sketch, is a new discovery.

The process may take days – or years. We think we possess some idea; then, by a series of accidents, through a long desert of difficulties, we come upon little scraps of intuition and dialectic with great labor, and all these are only part of the same old idea. But we never begin to understand the idea really well until this arduous and discouraging process also is under way. And in this, we are really living that idea, working it out in our lives, in the manner appropriate to our own sad contingent and temporal state where nothing is possessed but in scraps and pieces, imperfectly, successively. Yet we always long to possess truth as it is eternally in God's Divine Mind – "_tota, perfecta, simul_" ["complete, perfect, together"] (Boethius), and sometimes He gives us intuitions that, in a flash, resemble heavenly intuitions with a kind of _image_ of completeness. But it is not real completeness. We have to make it up, afterwards, in our own rag-picking way, grubbing around in our own rubbish, like a man whose house has been burned down scraping around in the ashes for something that might have survived.

——

The same is true also in another way: first we see something as a whole, a general figure: but we do not know what it is. The figure stays with us, and confronts us, like the sphinx for years: and piece by piece, in our tribulations, we discover fragments of this truth, and piece them together until, in the end of this arduous and bitter business, we have some notion of what the truth is. And all these fragments we do not find by looking for them: they come in our way as if by accident. They get put there.

The same process, the same pattern of development holds good for a big image in the mind of a poet – a big figure, a big analogy – big enough to be the subject of a whole poem, of a *Hamlet*, confronts the poet. He may write it all out simply in one first, short poem – then write a hundred poems, developing and complicating metaphors and images that are all parts of this big central figure. Sometimes a poet's whole work is nothing but the development of one big central figure into a series of its constituent images. Marvell's imagery is all pretty much of a parcel – and Coleridge's: but there is more than just "The Garden" or *The Ancient Mariner,* to all their poems. But Wordsworth does it – all that series, from "Lines Left on a Seat Under a Yew Tree" through "Tables Turned," "Ode to Duty," "Resolution and Independence" are a series of ineffective attempts to work out the features of one big figure. Only "Resolution and Independence" finally succeeds.

The same pattern holds good for spiritual consolations, which is what Thomas à Kempis means, in this passage.

Thomas à Kempis and Saint Bernard are a lot alike. More alike than à Kempis and Saint Bonaventure, for example. For both, the fact of tribulation is very much present.

The life in this abbey is not understandable unless you begin the day with the monks, with Matins at 2 a.m. If you get up for the low masses, at 4:30 (when each priest says his mass), it still does not make the day completely comprehensible: because even then it is not clear that the high point of the day is High Mass at 8 o'clock. The hours from 2 to 8 (6 hours) are all devoted to prayer, and all pretty much filled up with prayer, by the time Matins, Lauds, Prime and all the little hours (at least in Lent) are said. The High Mass is the fullest, most sustained and most splendid ceremony of the whole day and unquestionably the most significant – not excluding

Compline and the Salve Regina, which is also very moving and significant. But in the High Mass everything is deeper and more tremendous, naturally, since, after all, it is a High Mass, the highest kind of Liturgy. This is the heart of the whole day, its center, its foundation, its meaning: it is the day. But if you are up at 4 or 5 you don't immediately realize this – High Mass, then, still seems to be only the day's beginning: then, the work in the fields seems to be the important part of the day (9-to-11:30 [Vespers] and 1-to-5 perhaps) when of course that is really not much more than recreation.

This is of course the way it should be – the whole business of the day is really prayer, culminating in High Mass. Work, study, etc. are all merely recreation. But it is shocking to see how little prepared we are to understand this completely – we are so corrupted with our own selfishness and our own concerns for money or fame or pleasure that we are brought up short at finding a place where prayer is really everything – and not merely a prelude to something else. For instance, we unconsciously assume the Mass is really only a prelude to – anything: even penance, self-mortification – anything so that the day is balanced as we would have it balanced, centered on the individual man, not centered on Christ and His Passion at all.

I had not realized this was why this abbey is one of the last good places in the universe – and truly a court of the Queen of Heaven. But it is so because it is not only dedicated to God – it also really belongs to God. How terrible it is to think, now, that for hundreds of thousands of priests all over the world, Mass and their Divine Office are nothing but preludes to something else – even admittedly good things, like the care of souls, or of the poor, if not bad things like the care of their own bellies or their own parish's bank account, or their new car or their poker games. But Mass must not be secondary to anything, even the care of souls: charity begins in the love of God, and that centers in Mass.

And for me, what has Mass been? Something that begins the day. But the important work of the day has been teaching and writing, and this is all wrong. I can say it, now, because I see it confusedly. How long is it going to take me to live this truth, and find this true balance in my life? Through how many tribulations? How will I find all the pieces of this truth, that tells me I must belong to God, not to myself: and so far all I have thought about has been myself, even kneeling before God in His tabernacles, even at Mass, asking Him to give and give me more, never thanking Him for anything, praising myself for everything He gave me. Now I can say this, because, in a vast, confused way, I know it: when will I truly know it?

I am still afraid of the hardness of learning so much, because to know this humility is to know, in a sense, everything about mankind, and I haven't even the beginning.

It disgusts me to write this down as if it were part of a treatise, or a book review – or of some cool and chatty little Catholic pamphlet, smearing a delicate little brushful of piety over some business man's soul – make it writer's soul, some crucifying poet!

To love the Liturgy merely because it is the greatest art the world has ever seen or dreamed of is to crucify Christ all over again. To make His passion nothing but a drama that stimulates our emotions like any other good drama is to be Pilate and Caiaphas and all His executioners in one – it is to be Judas. That is to take Christ's passion, in the Holy Mass, for ourselves, as a luxurious enjoyment to our senses and our minds.

Because the Drama of the Liturgy is not there to please us but to *kill* us: in that Drama we must die, or we are Judases, betrayers.

Christ was crucified once and for all on Calvary. He is not given to be crucified over and over again on our altars every day just to make a spectacle for a gang of self-indulgent aesthetes – the crucifixion of Our Lord, Our King, Our Judge, is given us again, every day, not only that He may die, but that we may die, and we must die in it, or else be Pilates or Judases – or else merely beasts without understanding.

There are people who go to Mass and hear it, and love it for themselves, because it delights them, pleases *them*. This is satanic, and yet God forgives it, because we are become so, by our sins, and this is the only beginning, perhaps: we can only begin to love Him for the wrong reason and never find out the right one until later.

There are people who go to Mass and participate in it – are not only there, and see and hear it, but themselves die in it, and are offered up entirely to God. This is man's part, and the least he could do for Christ, who died for him. And yet Christ makes them saints who really die to the world and give themselves to Him again freely, at every Mass!

S. BERNARD – DE DILIGENDO DEO

"Quid ergo retribuam Domino pro omnibus quae retribuit mihi? In primo opere me mihi dedit, in secundo se: et ubi se dedit, me mihi reddidit. Datus ergo, et redditus, me pro me debeo, et bis debeo." ["What therefore shall I give back to the Lord for all that He has given me? In the first place, He gave me myself; in the second place, He gave me Himself. When he did this, he gave me back myself. In order to give Him back what He gave me, I owe myself as payment for myself, and I owe this twice."]

"Verus amor seipso contentus est. Habet praemium, sed id quod amatur."
["True love is happy with itself. It has its reward in what it loves."]

"Causa diligendi Deum, Deus est. Verum dixi, nam et efficiens, et finalis. Ipse dat occasionem, ipse creat affectionem, desiderium ipse consummat . . ." ["The cause of loving God, is God. I speak the truth, for he is the efficient and the final cause. He Himself gives the occasion, He creates the feeling, and He Himself consummates the desire."]

"Bonus es, Domine, animae quaerenti Te: quid ergo invenienti? Sed enim in hoc est mirum, quod nemo te quaerere valet nisi qui prius invenerit. Vis igitur inveniri ut quaeraris, quaeri ut inveniaris." ["You are good, Lord, to the soul that seeks You. How much more to the soul who finds You? For in this is something to wonder about, for no one can seek You unless he has first found You. You wish therefore to be found, so that You may be sought, so be sought, so that You may be found."]

And in the way of thy judgments, O Lord, we have patiently waited for Thee – Thy name and Thy remembrance are the desire of the soul. My soul hath desired Thee in the night, yea, and with my spirit within me in the morning early I will watch to Thee. (Isaiah 26. 8–9)

Holy Thursday. *April 10, 1941. Abbey of Our Lady of Gethsemani*

"So you also when you shall have done all these things that are commanded you, say: *We are unprofitable servants; we have done that which we ought to do*" (St. Luke 17.10).

(This is at the end of the Parable of the man who does not thank his servant for doing his job.
The disciples had asked Christ to give them more faith –

"And the Apostles said to the Lord: increase our faith." (St. Luke 17.5)

This parable and its conclusion above is the answer – as also that of the grain of mustard seed.)

"He cometh therefore to Simon Peter; and Peter saith to Him: Lord dost thou wash my feet?
Jesus answered, and said to him: What I do thou knowest not now; but thou shalt know hereafter.
Peter said to him: Thou shalt never wash my feet.
Jesus answered him: if I wash thee not, thou shalt have no part with me." St. John 13.6.

"If you shall ask me anything in my name, that I will do. If you love me, keep my commandments." St. John. 14. 14. 15.

"He that hath my commandments, and keepeth them, he it is that loveth me. And he that loveth me shall be loved of my Father: and I will love him, and manifest myself to him." St. John. 14. 21.

"He that loveth me not, keepeth not my words. And the Word, which you have heard is not mine, but the Father's who sent me." ib. 14. 24.

"And now *I have told you before it comes to pass: that when it shall come to pass, you may believe.*" ib. 14. 29.

What does this sentence mean: I have told you before it comes to pass, that when it shall come to pass, you may believe? I think it does not have much sense if we only take it to mean that it is a sort of prophecy of the crucifixion, and when the crucifixion bears out the prophecy, it is proof of Christ's power as a prophet – or as God, then. For it would be unnecessary.

What He means is more [than] that: Now they have received His teaching, they possess His words and parables; they have taken them easily, but without much comprehension. They possess the truth, but they do not rightly know what it is, and they cannot rightly believe it until they know what to believe, and they cannot know until His words are fulfilled and their meaning worked out in the terrible agony on the Cross or the secret glory of the resurrection.

So it is with every one of us. He tells us His truth – then it has to become alive in us by working itself out within each one of us in our crucifixion and resurrection.

SAINT BERNARD *DE DILIGENDO DEO* [ON THE LOVE OF GOD].
AMOR CARNALIS [CARNAL LOVE]

Amor tuus et et temperans erit, et justus, si quod propriis subtrahitur voluptatibus, fratris necessitatibus non negetur. Sic amor carnalis efficitur et socialis, cum in commune protrahitur. Ch. VIII.23 [Your love will be both temperate and just if what is taken from your own pleasures is not denied to your brother's needs. Thus carnal love is made to belong to our neighbor when it is extended to the common good.]

Ut tamen perfecta justitia sit diligere proximum, Deum in causa haberi necesse est. Alioquin proximum pure diligere quomodo potest, qui in Deo non diligit? Porro in Deo diligere non potest, qui Deum non diligit. Ch. VIII.25. [Nevertheless, in order that it may be perfect justice to love one's neighbor, it is imperative that it be referred to God as its cause. *Otherwise how can he love his neighbor without alloy who does not love him in God? He surely cannot love in God who does not love God.*]

Qui naturam condidit ipse et protegit. Nam et ita condita fuit ut habeat jugiter necessarium protectorem, quem habuit et conditorem: ut quae nisi per ipsum non valuit esse, nec sine ipso valeat omnino subsistere. Quod ne sane de se creatura ignoret, ac perindi sibi (quod absit) superbe arroget beneficia creatoris, vult hominem idem conditor alto quidem salubrique consilio tribulationibus exerceri: ut cum defecerit homo, et subvenerit Deus, dum homo liberatur a Deo, Deus ab homine, ut dignum est, honoretur. Ch. VIII.25. [He who fashioned nature, it is He who shields it from harm as well. For it was so fashioned that it should have, as a necessary Protector, Him whom it had as Maker, in order that, what could not have come into being save through Him, should not be able to subsist at all without Him. And lest the creature might not know this about itself and consequently (which God forbid) in its pride arrogate to itself the benefits it had received from its Creator, the same Maker in His high and salutary counsel wills that man should be harassed with troubles, so that when man has failed and God has come to his assistance, while man is being delivered by God, God, as is fitting, may be honored by man.]

(This is a philosophical statement of the basic idea underlying the 3rd Book of the *Imitation of Christ*. It is the statement of the ontological foundation of humility.)

As soon as we know ourselves – even a little, we have to become at least a little humble. To know ourselves is to know our nature, the nature of man: (not merely to have experience of our individual tastes and eccentricities, as some might take self-knowledge to be) and to know, or begin to realize, the existence of the condition we live in: to be aware of our contingent nature, our helplessness, our dependence. The world has forgotten it, and it stands armed today to kill any man who remembers his dependence upon God, who holds in the palm of His hand all life from moment to moment. We are taught that change is its own foundation, or worse, needs no foundation: (for if we said change was its own foundation in some *unimaginable* way we would hit the boundaries of a theology of some sort, but one without any revelation, and we would get so far, leaving no argument of any value, one way or the other, and be powerless to say anything at all about the basis of all existence except that existence *is*, but we don't know what – which is the starting point of all argument, and not the end of any argument at all). Any man who does not want to accept himself as the cornerstone of the universe is liable to be crucified today. But if he is not willing to be crucified for believing something else, then his state is much more miserable, because he lives on the edge of lunacy all the time, and knows it every time he pauses and thinks and is forced to half-admit that the universe does not rest on him.

As soon as we know ourselves, we know our dependence. And to know this is to become humble. The more truly we know this, the more humble we are, because it is a hard truth to grasp. On account of our rebellion, our nature is perverted in such a way that, because it desires only its own satisfaction, and turns only towards itself, it tends to set itself up as the center of the whole universe, and to deny God. We are born in sin – that is, in an illusion, in blindness, and this blindness is the reason for our falling into all evil. As soon as we begin to see, we see God. Otherwise we remain blind, seeing only ourselves – our false greatness, that overlays our real, craven, helpless nothingness.

As soon as we know our dependence, if we really know it, we begin to turn to the One on Whom we depend, and seek to learn, no longer from ourselves, but from Him: not now His secrets, as if to possess them made us powerful over Him, but the secret of our own nothingness, which He alone can show us, which we long for so that we can receive His love into ourselves, and become like Him – that is, like ourselves, because we were once made in his *image and likeness.* (cf. Bernard – image – dignity – remains with us.)

As soon as we know our dependence, our own nothingness, we begin, by dying, to live. In this is our only hope: that knowing our nothingness, we come to learn from tribulation – and then tribulation, instead of paralyzing us and beating us to death and despair, is the necessary condition for us to learn how to live and tribulation teaches us the truth: it teaches us that our philosophy in which everything is centered on ourselves is false and deadly, because evil, in it, is inexplicable, and increases more and more as we try to avoid it more and more.

It is only tribulation [that] can teach us where our strength lies – not in our independence but in our dependence – God is our strength. Dying to ourselves, we live in Him.

In tribulation He teaches us. The most unfortunate people in the world are those who know no tribulations. The most unhappy are those who try to buy their way out of them, and to escape them by pleasures, by wars, by suicide in some political cause like Nazism, which is only an illusory self-sacrifice to an illusory religious ideal.

Christ washed Peter's feet – not only to purify him.

We are so low and so weak that unless Christ is our servant we cannot be in Him, or He in us! "If I wash thee not, thou shalt have no part in me." He washes us clean, we cannot wash ourselves. Unless He serve us, we cannot live. He gives us the sun and the light and the fine air, the land and the rich fields, the blossoming fruit trees, the song of birds for our joy. He gives us ourselves: He makes us, and we are free. He gives Himself for us, hiding in a small host, the Crucified Christ, Our Lord! Thus we live again.

Unless He serve us in His Love, we cannot live. The servant gives all Himself to whom He serves. Unless God give Himself to us, we cannot live: but, serving us, washing Peter's feet, He gives us His life and back our own, for then we know that we also are servants, and His Love is this – and it is to love Him and love one another even as He loved us, our servant, washing the feet of Peter, crucified on the cross – infinitely. How can our love be infinite, if we are contingent, finite, small and poor? It can be if it is His love, and no other. His love is infinite. He gives it to us. We only possess it by giving it back at once to him.

But as much of His love as we demand for ourselves, we lose.

As much of His love as we try to keep and turn to our own power, is lost to us, which is never diminished in itself.

I have not written what a paradise this place is, on purpose. I think it is more beautiful than any place I ever went to for its beauty – anyway, it is the most beautiful place in America. I never saw anything like the country. A very wide valley – full of rolling and dipping land, woods, cedars, dark green fields – maybe young wheat. The monastery barns – vineyards. The knoll with the statue of St. Joseph in the middle of a great field where the road goes through a shallow cut towards the village – and the station on the line from Louisville to Atlanta.

And in the window comes the good smell of full fields – *agri pleni.*

The sun today was as hot as Cuba. Tulips, in the front court, opened their chalices, but widened and became blowsy and bees were working, one in each flower's cup, although it is only April. Fruit trees are in blossom, and every day more and more buds come out on the trees of the great avenue leading to the gate house.

The Trappist brothers in their medieval peasant hoods and their swathed legs and big home-made boots tramp along in a line through the vineyards; bells ring in the steeple.

All the spring which I had looked forward to finding here, from St. Bonaventure's, is here, and I haven't been looking at it – for fear of trying to claim I owned it, for fear of taking out title deeds to it, and making it my real estate, as I have everything else. For fear of devouring it like a feast, making it my party, – and so losing it.

This morning after High Mass – a Pontifical High Mass celebrated by the Abbot at 8:30 – I walked along the wall of the guest house garden, under the branches of the fruit trees, and in the hot sun, in the midst of more beauty than I can remember since I was in Rome. I remember Rome a lot, here.

Then I went inside: the monks washed the feet of some poor men [Holy Thursday Liturgy], put money in their hands, kissed their hands, gave them a dinner. I had been afraid to see this, thinking it would be an artificial thing: instead I heard Christ speaking to St. Peter, because these monks had heard Him, and were doing – not a series of gestures, but what He said, in a living act of liturgy. I never knew that charity could be spelled out so simply, so innocently, without any complications or confusions. Of course, like all liturgical acts, it has plenty of inner complications: but its content, in this case, is still as simple as possible: and I am ashamed of what I feared, because Christ spoke in the cloister, in that act, and made me love Him a little more, and all I want is to love Him, all I beg for is that.

Good Friday. *1941. Our Lady of Gethsemani*

"Man when he was in honor did not understand: he hath been compared to senseless beasts, and made like to them." Ps. 48. 21.

The world is hanging itself like Judas, with a halter, and the body of the hanged bursts open in the air. Man when he was in honor did not understand. Therefore, like beasts we have to be reined in and beaten out of our stubbornness. And if we will not be humiliated by our bridles we will be destroyed – but if we will be humiliated willingly, tribulation can, with God's grace, become the "mild yoke of Christ." *Onus meum leve.* [My burden is light.] The rattle makes its terrible clack in the cloister like the winds of death in our desolate ribs, and our heart is abandoned to itself, not through God's will but through our own. He first loved us that we might love Him. We abandoned Him, not He us, and because we abandoned Him, His only revenge is to sometimes let us remember we are alone, not to be revenged on us, but to bring us gently back to Him.

———

"But what great matter is it if thou, who art but dust and a mere nothing, submit thyself to man for God's sake, when I, the Almighty and the Most High, Who created all things out of nothing, have, for thy sake humbly subjected Myself to man?

I became the most humble and most abject of all men, that thou mightest overcome thy pride by My humility."

Not only by the example of His humility, not only by the imitation of it, do we overcome our pride, for merely by imitating Christ, by ourselves, at a distance from Him, we can do little. But in His humility He not only showed us an example to follow, but nourishes us with Himself. He gave us not only a pattern of life but Himself, Life itself, He gave to us, bodily and spiritually and totally on the Cross. We must study His life – but that is little. Atheists study His life, and cheap biographers, and heretics, and quacks; everybody, some time or another, studies Christ's life, and how many absurd lives of Him are written, from Renan to Sholem Asch – not to mention the Catholic ones. What do we need with lives of Christ, when we have the New Testament. This is the wrong kind of meditation on Christ's life, to reshape its *story*, and tell it over in our own words. We cannot tell it in better words than those in which it has been told, or with a better or more interesting attitude, or interpretation. Everything else is dull, beside the New Testament. Lambs Tales from Shakespeare are weak enough, but they are enough to sweep you off your feet compared with lives of Christ in cheap fiction.

It is not enough to study Christ's life with the intention of imitating it – first we must receive Him; before we understand the pattern of life, we must receive Life and Being into ourselves, and He gives Himself to us in His passion and in the Blessed Sacrament, in Communion.

This is Good Friday. The tabernacle is empty.

Yesterday, at Lauds, they blew out the altar light, and the world froze.

"*At si frequens ingruerit tribulatio, ob quam et frequens ad Deum conversio fiat,* et a Deo aeque frequens liberatio consequatur, *nonne, et si fuerit ferreum pectus vel cor lapideum toties liberati, emolliri necesse est ad gratiam liberantis, quatenus Deus homo diligat, non propter se tantum, sed [et] propter ipsum.*"
["But if trouble often comes to someone, who also turns to God just as often because of it, *and if that person is delivered by God as a result,* isn't it so that, even though the chest were made of iron, and the heart made of stone in one so often liberated, it must be softened by the grace of the Deliverer,

so that man might love God, not just for his own sake, but because of what God is?"]

This is not to be taken as if Saint Bernard were deceiving himself and us by saying everyone who is in tribulation and then liberated from it knows in this God's grace. Nor does he mean he thinks that if a person is in tribulation, it follows necessarily he may be sometime liberated from it. It might happen to someone *never* to be liberated from terrible sorrow. But what he is speaking of is those who (1) love God for their own sakes, (2) and it is usual and frequent that when we pray, God answers our prayers and, unless we are stupefied with pride, we know He has delivered us and not we ourselves. (How do temptations come and go, for no apparent reason?) Except that we pray, and lament, and with God's love they are taken away again for awhile. But it is not our doing: we can seem to pray just as fervently, or more so, and the temptation will still remain. It is not merely a question of some "psycho-physical mechanism" working in us, guaranteed to produce always the same result: it isn't that we calm our own minds with prayer. Try and see how much success you have in stopping yourself from sinning if your will is to sin and all you have to offer against it is a series of psycho-physical mechanisms all dominated by yourself! (It is so hopeless that you give it up at once, and call the sin a good, and say there is no such thing as sin.) You have to will what is good, i.e., God's Will – and He will help you with His grace. And if you believe you are alone, He will leave you alone, to show you how you want to be: then try and will something good, without goodness in you! The answer you fall into, in despair at the evil that follows, is that the evil is a good – or else that there is no goodness at all. Both answers show clearly enough what remains – our *dignitas* – a capacity for goodness and a fundamental need to possess it, but the liberty to deny it, and the inability to fulfill that capacity by ourselves!)

"Quomodo Deus omnia esse voluit propter semetipsum, sic nos quoque nec nosipsos, nec aliud aliquid fuisse vel esse velimus, nisi aeque propter ipsum, ob solam ipsius videlicet voluntatem, non nostram voluptatem. Delectabit sane non tam nostra vel sopita necessitas, vel sortita felicitas, quam quod eius in nobis et de nobis voluntas adimpleta videbitur . . ." ["Just as God willed that everything is to be for Himself, so we also desire neither ourselves, nor any other thing in the past or the present, unless it is for Him equally, namely for His will alone, and not our own will. Clearly we will not take as much pleasure in the fulfillment of a need or a want as we do in the knowledge that we are fulfilling His will."]

"In corpore spirituali et immortali, in corpore integro, placido placitoque, et per omnia subiecto spiritui, speret se anima quartum apprehendere amoris gradum, vel potius in ipso apprehendere amoris gradum, vel potius in ipso apprehendi, quippe quod Dei potentiae est dare cui vult, non humanae industriae assequi." ["In a spiritual, immortal body, that is complete, calm and pleasing, and subject to the spirit in all things, let the soul hope to grasp the fourth level of love, or rather, to be grasped in it, because it is within God's power to give to whom He wishes, and not within human strength to attain this by itself."]

"Bonus plane fidusque omnes caro spiritui bono, quae ipsum aut, si onerat, iuerat, aut, si non iuvat, exonerat, aut certe iuvat, et minime onerat. Primus status laboriosus, sed fructuosus; secundum otiosus, sed minime fastidiosus; tertius et gloriosus." ["Obviously, the flesh is a good and faithful companion to a good spirit which, if a burden, is also a helper, or if it is not a burden, frees up the soul, to such a degree that it is not a burden at all. The first state is toilsome, but fruitful; the second is leisurely, but not boring, and the third is glorious."]

April 12. Holy Saturday. Our Lady of Gethsemani

"Qui magis aut certe solum diligit suum (bonum), convincitur non caste diligere bonum, quod utique propter se diligit, non propter ipsum." ["For he who only loves his own good, or loves it more than anything else, is guilty of loving this good unchastely, since he loves it for his own sake, and not for God."]

"Est qui confitetur Domino quoniam potens est, et est qui confitetur quoniam sibi bonus est, et item qui confitetur quoniam simpliciter bonus est. Primus servus est, et timet sibi; secundus mercenarius, et cupit sibi; tertius filius, et defert patri. Itaque et qui timet, et qui cupit, uterque pro se agunt. Sola quae in filio est caritas, non quaerit quae sua sunt." ["One man might praise God because He is powerful, and another might praise Him because He is good to him, and still another might praise Him because He is simply good. The first is a slave, who is afraid for himself. The second is a hired hand, who seeks his own gain. The third is a son, who honors his father. And so, the one who fears and the one who desires both seek their own good. Genuine love is found only in the son, and this love is that 'which does not seek its own good.'"]

"Nec timor quippe, nec amor privatus convertunt *animam. Mutant interdum vultum vel actum, affectum numquam."* ["For neither fear nor self-love *convert* the soul. They sometimes change their external appearance and action, but never their affection."]

"Facit et mercenarius (opus Dei), sed quia non gratis, propria trahi cupiditate convincitur. Porro ubi proprietas, ibi singularitas; ubi autem singularitas, ibi angulus, tibi sine dubio sordes sive rubigo. Sit itaque servo sua lex, timor ipse quo constringitur; *sit sua mercenario cupiditas,* qua et ipse arctatur, *quando tentatur abstractus et illectus. Sed harum nulla, aut sine macula est, aut animas convertere potest.* Caritas vero convertit animas, quas facit et voluntarias." ["A hired hand also does the work of God, but not because he is motivated by greed. Indeed, where there is personal ownership, there is distinction of persons. Where there is distinction of persons, there is a niche that inevitably collects dirt and rust. And so, the slave is held bondage by his own fear, as if by a law. The hired hand is limited by his own greed, since by it he is tempted, allured and drawn away. Neither of these two are without fault, nor can they convert souls. But genuine love converts souls, for it makes them free."]

Inseparable from the notion of charity is that of freedom. The *servus* and *mercenarius* are bound and restricted, one by fear, the other by self-love. Only *charity* is perfectly free. Love is loved for itself: that means, it is not drawn by any necessary attraction towards the satisfaction of anything less than itself, or conflicting with itself. Only in charity is love perfectly spontaneous, and free from determination or necessity. Hence the notions of charity and purity, for example, imply *liberty* and *freedom*, pure spontaneity.

All imperfect love, short of charity, ends in something not itself; perfect charity is its own end, therefore is free, because it is not determined by anything outside itself. Love that loves itself is God, and only God is absolutely free – and because He is absolutely free, He is omnipotent. The two are the same. But we are constituted in His image by our own *quasi ascitas* [quasi asceity] our seeming absolute freedom, because, in the last analysis, we are *free* in another sense – that finally no one determines our choices but ourselves: and we are free to resist God, and we know it to our sorrow! But we are free to love Love for itself, and to find ourselves again in that truly perfect freedom of Love's own self-sufficing and eternal action which is perfectly free because it is above all limitation, all imperfection of ends outside itself.

"Lex ergo Domini immaculata, caritas est, quae non quod sibi utile est, quaerit, sed [quod] multis." ["Therefore, the pure law of God is love, which does not seek its own usefulness, but rather what is good for the many."]

Love is God's "Law" (the "Law" by which He lives, and by which He makes all live – to call this a law is the greatest paradox –) because it is His

Being, His Essence, His Perfection, His Eternity, His Infinity. Therefore all being participates in it, because there can be nothing that does not come from God. (evil = non-being) To love that which no one else can participate in, but which *is absolutely restricted* (Anything whose good is only restricted to me, and cannot possibly be shared, is not a good at all. *Bonum est diffusivum sui* [The good is diffusive of itself]) is to love what is separated from God and deprived of His love – that is, to love death. Pride, self-love, are the love of death, because these turn away from God, in whom is *all* Being: therefore they necessarily turn to non-being, or death.

> *"Lex autem Domini (caritas) dicitur, sive quod ipse ex ea vivat,* sive quod eam nullus, nisi eius dono, possideat. . . . *Quid vero in summa et beata illa Trinitate summam et ineffabilem illam conservat unitatem, nisi caritas? Lex est ergo, et lex Domini, caritas, quae Trinitatem in unitate quodammodo cohibet et colligat in vinculo pacis."* ["For (love) is called the law of God, either because He himself lives by it, or because none has it, except through Him, as a gift. . . . Thus, what is in that highest and most blessed Trinity which maintains that supreme and ineffable unity, except love? . . . Therefore, love is the law, and the law of God, which holds the Trinity in unity, and keeps it always in the bonds of peace."]

Charity is not a quality, or accident of God, it is His substance. *Deus Caritas Est.*

> *"Dicitur ergo recte caritas, et Deus, et Dei donum. Itaque caritas dat caritatem, substantiva accidentalem. Ubi dantem significat, nomen substantiae est; ubi donum, qualitatis."* ["God is love. Therefore, love is rightly called God, and also God's gift. Thus, love gives love, and the substance gives the accident. When the term means the Giver, then the term means substance; when it means the gift, then it refers to quality."]

> *"[Ceterum] servus et mercenarius habent legem non a Domino, sed quam ipsi fecerunt. . . . (qui a Deo noluit suaviter regi, poenaliter a seipso regeretur: quique sponte iugum suave et onus leve caritatis abiecit, propriae voluntatis onus importabile sustineret invitus)."* ["The slave and hired hand have a law, but not from the Lord. Rather, it comes from themselves . . . he who refused to be gently ruled by God is ruled harshly by himself, and he who freely threw off the sweet and light yoke of love unwillingly bears the unbearable burden of his own self-will."]

> *"Bona itaque lex caritas, et suavis: quae non solum leviter suaviterque portatur, sed etiam servorum et mercenariorum leges portabiles ac leves reddit, quas utique non destruit, sed facit ut impleantur. . . . Porro timori permixta devotio*

ipsum non annullat, sed castificat. . . . *Deinde cupitas tunc recte a superveniente caritate ordinatur, cum mala quidem penitus respuuntur, bonis vero meliora praeferuntur, nec bona nisi propter meliora appetuntur. Quod cum plene per Dei gratiam assecutum fuerit, diligetur corpus, et universa corporis bona tantum propter animam, animae propter Deum, Deus autem propter seipsum.*" ["And so, the law of love is good and sweet, for it is not only lightly and sweetly carried, but also makes bearable and light the laws of the slaves and the hired hands, which it doesn't destroy, but fulfills. . . . Indeed, devotion mixed with fear does not cancel or nullify these; rather, it purifies them. . . . Also, greed is governed by the gift of love, so that evil is rejected completely, and what is good is desired, nor are good things sought except for those things which are better. When all this has been fulfilled through the grace of God, the body and all the goods of the body will be loved only because of the soul, and the soul will be loved only for God, and God will be loved only for Himself."]

"For you are dead: *and your life is hid with Christ in God.* When Christ shall appear, who is your life, then you also shall appear with Him in glory."

Coll. 3. 3–4.

This was in today's Mass. I had never read the prayers. Perhaps I had never even been to Mass on Holy Saturday: in fact I think not. It is, anyway, the first time in my life I ever knew what Easter was all about. I don't see how any Christian can go without being at Mass these three days – Holy Thursday, Holy [sic] Friday, and Saturday. Their significance is terrific, and above all so plain. And here, I have found my whole life dominated by them, so that I have not merely followed the feasts, as if with a kind of curiosity, but as it were lived the Liturgy, thanks be to God; and that is what the Liturgy is there for. If it is properly used by the priest, and attentively followed by the hearer, it cannot be anything else but *lived.* But to be followed, it is not to be followed as literature or music or merely as art: it must be accompanied by humble and unceasing prayer, and if I had prayed better I would have understood more. Yet always there is the temptation to forget the depths of prayer and be lost in a series of futilities by which we are drawn away from the depths of the Liturgy: temptations, vanity, scruples, all huddling one after the other. God permits them, to show us how little we can do to come to Him, even though the best of the Liturgy is there to draw us on and help us, without the infusion of His Grace. But He is always there, too, and gives us a little of His Grace at the best times for it, so that we know it is He by His presence and His voice instructing us, and not our memory or our own instruction or our own merit or any devotion belonging only to us alone.

To people who only pray a little, God is a servant – they treat Him as a servant, and order Him about: and still He will hear them, and out of His great and infinite mercy, He leads them to pray a little more, a little more, until little by little they come to pray as much as a Christian ought to pray – more than an hour a day, at any rate – and then God begins to show them He is not a servant only, but a master, our King, our Father. Then to those who pray the prayers of Saints, He must also come as a friend, as the soul's spouse.

It is a great and terrible insult to pray as little as most of us do, and yet order Him about as a slave. That is the same attitude those took who condemned Him to the slave's death – crucifixion.

And it is an insult to woo Him like a spouse when we don't yet even know Him as King; this is what the pious books of devotion do! And what did the Queen of Heaven say, in terror, to the angel? "Be it done unto me according to Thy Word!" Mary read none of these sacrilegious books of devotion!

In the few days I have been here trees that were barely budding have now begun to screen the air with greenness of small leaves. Petals are beginning to fall from the apple trees that are crowded with blossoms – and full of bees filling the sunlight with the sound of their swarming.

Bees are mentioned in today's Mass, too. The Paschal Candle is spoken of as "made from the work of bees"; it is a great honor for the bees to come in such an important place in such an important Mass. I wonder what it signifies.

The nights have been moonlit, and much warmer. Everyone has been going to bed at seven or seven-thirty, except, starting tonight, the monks all go to bed an hour later and are allowed a nap in the middle of the day to round out their seven hours which, most of the time, they don't get anyway.

It is disquieting to see anybody lead so hard a life. I thought at first I envied them, but I don't really. But I do wish I had a chance to be a Franciscan, as I had wanted to be last year! If the Franciscans in this country stuck to their rule and didn't have so many dispensations, so many radios, such taste for golf and creature comforts – if they were tonsured, and said Office in Choir more, and knew something about the Liturgy and about singing and about poverty, it would be a fine Order. But they are all fine fellows. It is just that this country has ruined their rule for them. Only the Trappists, here, have not let America soften them up. Consequently, it is said, they get the best vocations! This is one Order where you don't have to make faces like a business-man, to keep up your self-esteem. It is one order where self-esteem no longer matters. In America, that has become the thing every priest imagines has been demanded of him by the people: unless he has new suits, and a shiny car, and a line of lousy jokes, like a salesman, he thinks the people would desert him. All the people, however, are waiting for nothing so much as real Saints: then they could show their true colors: the real Christians would follow the saints: the others would have somebody they could stone.

Now the sun is setting. Birds sing. Lent is over. I am tired. Tomorrow is Easter and I go, for no good reason, to New York. Out there, a couple of jaybirds are fighting in a tree. I wonder if I have learned enough to pray for humility. I only desire one thing – to love God. Those who love Him, keep His commandments. I only desire to do one thing – follow His Will. I pray I am beginning at least, to know what that may mean. My Lord and My King and My God!

April 18 Friday. Douglaston

Leaving Gethsemani was very sad.

After Benediction, Easter Day, in the afternoon, the monks had almost all left the church, and it was quiet and sun streamed in on the floor. I made the Stations of the Cross, and also wished I were going to stay there – which is impossible. I wished it was not impossible.

I left early in the morning Monday, and got to Louisville at 8 – everybody was going to work – it would have been the middle of the day at the Abbey, not its beginning. I was very confused. There is a huge gap between the monastery and the world, and Louisville is a nice enough town but I wasn't happy to be thrown back into it. Then there were the papers with Germany about to enter Egypt in the war. There had been a big robbery on Fourth St., Louisville. I couldn't figure out, half the time, whether it was morning or afternoon. The sign "Clown Cigarettes" on, I think, Walnut Street, made me laugh wanly. There was a lot of sun. I didn't want to see any of the city, or any of the people. I went to the Cathedral, then to the Public Library: there I read a chapter – the one on Free Will – in Gilson's *Spirit of Medieval Philosophy*. In the Public Library I didn't even feel like reading any of Evelyn Waugh's fine travel book *They Were Still Dancing* which I read between trains there before. Very funny Coptic monastery. And something about Rimbaud having fled to Ethiopia and lived there and died there at peace with the church – anointed by some Capuchin Missionary. (If the Capuchins there are Saints, Waugh doesn't seem to know, or want to.)

It is terrible to want to belong entirely to God, and see nothing around you but the world, and not see Him. In the monastery you don't see Him, either, but you have nothing to do but lament your separation from Him, and pray to Him, and pray for the world. In the world itself, your prayers are drowned by the noise of traffic: you have to watch out for cars, falling buildings, brimstone, thunder.

The world is beautiful with the sunlight, but the objects in the sunlight are not beautiful – they are strange. Candy in a drugstore window. Newspapers. Mannequins in store windows. Women's clothes have military insignia all over them, now. Speech is violent and hard and blasphemous. And you weep because already you see how terribly difficult it is to hold on to the cleanness and peace you had at the Abbey!

I go everywhere talking about the Abbey.

Difference between the First and Second Times I spent a few hours in Louisville, between trains:

1. The first time it was gray and cool. The second, bright and warm.

2. The first time was on a Sunday, the second on a Monday.

3. The first time, I went to the Library and read Evelyn Waugh's *They Were Still Dancing* – dipped into Graham Greene's *Journey without Maps* – (which was about Africa, not Mexico as I had imagined) – and Blake's *Poems*. The second time I read a little of Gilson's *Spirit of Medieval Philosophy*. Both times I read most of G. M. Hopkins' poems. (Poem of his I still haven't read carefully enough to understand: *Spelt from Sybils Leaves*. Poems I have, for the first time, read and understood. "The Candle Indoors." "Brothers." "Felix Randall." The despair poems. Poems I read before and reread and understood more – most of them. I like better the priestly poems – "The Bugler's First Communion." I like best the despair poems.)

4. The first time I ate lunch at the Hotel Brown, the second at the Union (world's dirtiest) station.

5. The first time I arrived on the L. & N. from Cincinnati by day, and left, after dark, by the L. & N., from Gethsemane [station], on the line to Knoxville and Atlanta. The second time I arrived early in the morning from the south, Gethsemani, and left, early in the afternoon, Cincinnati.

6. The first time I neither bought, read nor glanced at any newspaper – being off them for Lent. The second time I got a lot of false information

from some Louisville paper that went like this: "British smash Nazi division and retreat 60 miles."

7. The first time I got very sore feet looking, in all the wrong places, for a Catholic Church. The second time I found the Cathedral easily, having asked a bell hop at the Hotel Brown and a doorman at the Kentucky Hotel – upon neither of which I had any claim as a guest.

8. The first time I was happy to be going to the Monastery. The second time I was sad to be leaving the Monastery.

9. The first time I walked down Fourth Street to the Ohio River – a huge wide river as wide as a sea, having, as I think, a levee where boats tie up – if that long sloping stone-paved bank is a levee. The second time I didn't bother. The Ohio River is the most beautiful thing in Louisville. Both Van Doren and Jim Knight remarked on it at once, when I spoke of Louisville.

[Pages 131–142 missing from holographic journal.]

May 3, 1941. Saint Bonaventure

"Nature laboureth for his own profit and taketh heed what lucre may come to himself alone, but grace considereth not what is profitable and advantageous to one but to many." [Imitation of Christ. III. Ch. LIX.]

The problem of salvation, of charity, takes on two pretty different aspects as it is looked at from two points of view – subjective or objective. Objectively the problem is social – but we forget it is the same problem in both cases. The subjective dichotomy is that of flesh and spirit – self-love and the love of God. That is, love of the flesh, love of matter: but here is an ambiguity, at once because introduced into this subjective context is a term that belongs to the objective – the *social* aspect of the problem.

When Saint Augustine speaks of self-love coming first (to love ourselves truly is to want salvation, and this is natural: without it we could not live), it seems like a paradox, but only to those who are confusing this aspect of the problem with its social aspect.

In the subjective sphere to love yourself is to really love your own soul so as to save it. In the objective sphere, however, "self-love" comes into a quite different context – it is there that it is opposed to something else. It is not really opposed to *anything* in the psychological sphere – even to the love of God – for to love ourselves perfectly we know we must lose ourselves in the bliss and peace and love of God – for His sake, not for ours. Yet it is self-love – for we love God to save ourselves: but to save ourselves we must love Him more than ourselves. However, in the other realm, there is a clear opposition – love of yourself – love of others.

Love of a private good; when *you* enjoy it, someone else cannot. All this in accordance with natural law. In a way you fight to get your own good by force from someone else – and when you have it, he hasn't. But, by the law of grace, you seek not what is private, but what is everybody's good, yours and your brother's – to seek peace is to seek that kind of a good, because it is only good by being shared. *Bonum est diffusivum sui.*

May 5, 1941

This is the forest primeval, the blundering blind and the padlocks. As to the forest primeval – I had the name Fenimore Cooper in my head because I mentioned it in this novel course: what I mean – mentioned! Then in the *National Geographic* is an article on the Finger Lakes, with those same excessively colored, excessively summery pictures, making everything unbelievably rich and bright and hot-looking, too. Making the whole world look like the first week of a long summer vacation.

All these things go together appropriately: the hexameter about the forest primeval; the *National Geographic*; James Fenimore Cooper; Lake Keuka; The Gliders at Elmira: Also Allegheny State Park and that Indian reservation, where I was last week in John Paul's Buick. All that flat, grubby-looking land – the only really poor and barren-looking land it is possible to find around here, they gave to the Indians. And the Indians probably burnt it over, or did the one thing that remained to make the whole thing look even worse.

Anyway the Indian reservation is a lot of flat and sandy land with dirty, scrubby little brown trees and bushes growing all over it; here and there is a black and shabby and charred looking sort of a house where some Indians live, making poisonous herb medicines. That is all. Indian children in neat clothes – or relatively neat, were playing softball near Quabar [?] bridge. A sixteen year old Indian, hanging his head, lolled along the road kicking a tin-can ahead of him. My brother kept saying they all looked like Mexicans. That is probably one of the things wrong with the Mexicans.

John Paul had just come back from Mexico. The Mexican newspaper he had was full of useless and funny violence.

"*Porque no pago la denda, fue herido.*" ["Because he didn't pay the debt, he was wounded."]

"*Estupido salvage hirio a un Joven.*" (*Solo por pasar el rato le infirio terribles Heridas en el estomazo.*) ["Stupid savage knocked down a young man (just to pass the time away, he inflicted terrible wounds in his stomach.)"]

"*Celosa nuyer que incendia a la casa de presenta rival.*" ["Jealous wife who burned the house of her rival."]

Also I had just finished reading Greene's book about Mexico. The one about Africa, that I glanced at in Louisville, hadn't seemed so good. But this one was a good book – maybe the best travel book I ever read: not so funny as Waugh's one about Abyssinia but more exciting.

The part about the ruins of Palenque was horrifying – and funny, too. All about Tabasco and Chiappas was very exciting. The first part, about being in Texas, wasn't much. It begins rather badly. But it is a good travel book. I wasn't terribly interested in his interview with General Cedillo. I wasn't interested in the poor stupid guy from Wisconsin. He made Orizata sound interesting. He made Puebla sound like a nice place. He made dysentery sound terrible. But the worst thing was the trip to the ruins of Palenque, where he didn't want to go anyway: but he had given it as his reason for going to Tabasco. Nice pictures in the book.

While we were riding along the Allegheny river, on the other side, on a road coming from Chipmunk, down around the Nine Mile, somewhere John Paul told me about the Mexican earthquake, which he missed. He was driving in to Mexico City when it happened, but passing through a place that wasn't affected. People in Mexico City fell down a lot. The bartender of his hotel came rolling out into the street and hung on to a palm tree. Maybe it was a waiter.

That day it was nice in the country. We were up to the cottage on the hill, and hacked down a bush with a machete. Everything was very neat, as opposed to last August when even the woods were very untidy, with discarded scraps of novel or of food hanging in all the bushes.

But I still keep thinking how nice it was writing the novel up there the year before last, and drinking coca-cola and eating sardine sandwiches, or looking out over the hills towards Eldred – everything green and blue and clear and clean and airy and full and pretty, not as exaggerated as a National Geographic picture, but full of real opulence and real peace.

They have now got new white paint on the window frames, and cleared the tangle of raspberry bushes that was beginning to choke up things along the front, in the little paved place outside the bedrooms: the place where Flagg sat in the sun combing her long red hair last June.

I had almost forgotten those meals of skinny pork and wet, gray potatoes; and all the canned peas, and canned beans.

Down towards Chipmunk there was a nice brook in the woods, running among scrub, along the road, and through many clear, sunny, grassy patches. I suppose there were some little blue flowers about. If there weren't, there should have been. Then we came home and there was a check for twenty-two dollars from the *New Yorker*, for they had taken a poem I like a lot; one about last summer, Lake Erie.

That is all part of that Finger Lakes context too (grapes) though not of any hexameter about the forest primeval. Also, has less than nothing to do about the Indian reservation.

Two days running we ate breakfast of scrambled eggs in the Olean House, and read the Buffalo papers. Wednesday we drove around in a bigger circle than Tuesday: bigger, and duller. And there really isn't much point in driving around in a car. I thought of the pleasure it was going to the Circus in Bradford, last summer. But even driving around in a car in order to look at the country is very disquieting because it is futile, and I don't want to be doing it, either.

What is one recreation I am happy about, and the only one? Writing – not this, but a letter in a crazy new language to Gibney yesterday, and a macaronic poem.

Friday. May 9, 1941

Things I don't understand – how that novel I wrote last fall could have been so bad. I looked at it again for the first time today – the first time this year. (I finished it after Christmas, before New Years – that is some revisions which made it no better.)

All the while I was writing it I would make jokes, in letters to people, about how bad it was. I really knew all along how bad it was. How dull. Every time I would read it, I knew that. That long tedious first part, about an apartment on Sutton Place: all the stuff I wrote on the hill. Then a terrible scene about two old men in a bar. Frightful stuff. After that an abominably dull episode at Heiniken's at the World's Fair. An awfully phony beggar comes into it for no reason at all: I was trying to be smart, and now I forget just how. I thought a scene in Miami I wrote in later (after the man in Boston kicked the novel out his door) was better. Why did I think it was better? Well, because I was indignant at having been made to realize, by the letter of rejection, that it was really a bad novel, and I thought the indignation would make me write better. But it didn't. The part I thought would be better was the same all over again, only worse.

Still there are two parts I remember liking – and I reread neither today – one about the French building at the World's Fair, the other about a boat coming into the harbor at Havana. Just because I liked the French Building and Havana, that doesn't make it any better of a novel.

I now realize that when John Paul was here last week it was very pretty. Especially coming over the hill and down that valley into Chipmunk. The road down that valley is more mountainous than any around here, a lot of crazy turns, and big drops over the rocky talus down among the oil wells and the trees. Wild cherry trees were out everywhere, covered with, like a powder, greeny white little blossoms. Like greenish white smoke.

But now the apple trees are out. The other day I was walking past the greenhouse. The sun drowned in the apple tree. The greenhouse looked like a big aquarium tank, all around in the breeze, petals of apple blossoms snowed down and fell noiseless on the fresh, damp, very green, new mowed grass. Now I write about it not terrifically fast, but fast enough so that my hand aches.

Things nature has been doing while I have been doing what I have been doing: making that big supple red dog behind the greenhouse grow up out of a small crazy thing that looked like it was going to be a chow. Now it's the prettiest mongrel you ever saw: a big quiet, lithe, gay, red dog with floppy ears, but like a collie, except also like a police dog as to the feet and head. This dog laughs and sings a lot, and talks and jumps up quietly and plays when a guy goes past the greenhouse. I like this dog. That is what nature has been doing, between fall and spring. Last fall when the dog was a pup he got under my feet and got stepped on, accidentally. He does not remember – or if he does, not with malice. I guess he isn't smart enough to know anything. Just playful.

Things history has been doing: I saw a picture from another planet: Germans with a machine gun on a mountain in Greece. And that happened since I got back from Kentucky, even. That's the kind of thing I don't easily believe.

But anyway if I ever refused to be a Trappist on the grounds that it might interfere with my writing another novel as bad as *The Man in the Sycamore Tree* I would be crazy. I would sure like to see the first one. I haven't seen that for over a year. I certainly wonder how that one looks. I say that because I have a feeling it might look better. Might.

If I was writing with a typewriter this minute I would try to write some more of the fake esperanto I wrote to Gibney in the letter Sunday.

I wonder if there is any point to putting in a journal items of news that come to one in a letter. For example, in a letter from Lax: that Gibney got a fever in Florida, or something. I think everybody has got the same fever every place.

Item, I wonder. (O Baby! what a bad word *item* is! Sterne!!!) how much of the stuff in this journal I also put into letters just because the stuff got into my mind by being put in the journal.

"I wonder" is the wrong way to begin a sentence, as soon appears when you begin more than one sentence with it.

List of Things I Saw With John Paul, in His Car:

In Eldred, the home of amateur boxing, a lot of amateur boxers, standing in the sun in front of the post office.

The Pennsylvania Train parked in the street in front of the Snow White Laundry, where I went with all my shirts.

A wide assortment of bridges over the Allegheny river.

Galani's in Bradford. That is a very dreary place, really. And so is the whole of Bradford.

The very dullest part of Allegheny State Park, which is, at one end, as close to Bradford as it is, at the other, to Salamanca.

Bovaird and Seyfang – is that the name? You see the sign, crossing the tracks into Bradford. How many million times have I made the Fu Manchu joke about *that* I wonder. Shall I explain? Well, you see, Dr. Fu Manchu has this secret organization called the Si-pang, or maybe Sey-pan, or Si-pen, or anyway, it *sounds* like Seyfang, if that's the correct name of Bovaird's partner. Or is it Bovard?

Other things we saw.

Too much of the Emery Coffee Shop. Too much of the *New York Herald Tribune.*

Too much of Bob Hope, Bing Crosby and Dorothy Lamour in a very vicious movie, all about hatred, trickery, treachery, cheating, embezzlement, stealing, lying, etc. All this being idealized. No good movie. The last I'm going to for plenty long time.

Too much "chicken in the rough" at a place outside Portville.

Somehow Portville surprised me by having a big avenue of trees and seeming a neat, prosperous and well ordered little town. That is, more of all these than Allegheny.

I still think Valéry is a fine poet. Better than ever. And Lorca, too. For the first time I read the *Ode to Walt Whitman* and it is a real fine poem; in fact for a single big poem, it is maybe the best that's been written in thirty – well, one hundred years. Or since "The Wreck of the *Deutschland*" maybe? Maybe. It has a whole lot to say, and it is a very clean poem, its indignation is very beautiful and very nice. Lorca is a fine guy, a real clean, nice guy, and the poem is the only poem written to defend anybody from filth that I ever read in this age. Everybody else is scared to write such a good poem for such a good reason: and, if they were not the poems they would write, would probably be shocking anyway. But Lorca's poem is all full of moral goodness, too. It is a nice poem, innocent and just and full of love.

Then I was less happy reading Mandonnet's *"Dante le Theologien."* It makes you slightly unhappy to read a guy want to write in such a way about Dante and Saint Thomas Aquinas, and making so many smug statements about Saint Thomas being the Truth Itself; and if every line of Dante is not based on Saint Thomas, the only reason is he was not able to get hold of enough of Saint Thomas' books, and had to be content with theories from someone else. Also, when he talks about the literature as such, he makes very gross mistakes, all from assuming things in a vacuum and twisting the lives to fit his own idea. Why should I criticize anybody? The last thing I want to be writing is criticism. More esperanto. Esperanto is in some way better than Joyce-talk. I'd also like to write, for once, a good novel, after so many bad ones. Now to try to read Scotus with [Fr.] Philotheus and them two seminarians.

May 12, 1941

Words culled like flowers from a page of George Eliot.

    bad odor

    disgusted

    licensed curate

    sore throats & catarrhs

    bilious

    'a soup tureen gives a hint of the fragrance that will presently rush [?]
      out to inundate your hungry senses'

    'the delicate visitation of atoms' (smell)

    'dinner-giving capacity'

    'keen gusto'

    'ill flavored gravies & the cheaper Marsala'

    heavy meat-breakfasts

    whiskers

    undertaker

    monitor

    useful practical matters

    an agreeable book

    mangold-wurzel

corrupt
focore
gull
'ugliness is past its bloom.'
inflamed nose
'Mr. Duke turned rather yellow, which was his way of blushing.'
dyspeptic
peptic   (Amos Barton)

May 13, 1941

"And the tongue is a fire, a world of iniquity. The tongue is placed among our members, which defileth the whole body and inflameth the wheel of our nativity, being set on fire by hell."

Saint James – 3.6.

"For the anger of man worketh not the justice of God."

Saint James – 1.20.

"And the fruit of justice is sown in peace, to them that make peace."

Saint James – 3.18.

This is the Epistle Luther called the "Epistle of Straw." And look what happened! Luther thought he had the truth in him; he was as convinced of that – more convinced – than I am in all my arguments for the faith, for God, for the Church. The world is full of argument, and I have just begun to ask myself questions about that. "The anger of man worketh not the justice of God." The hell of the schismatics, in Dante. All believed they were defending the truth. Sometimes I argue so much in a day I am already disemboweled like Mahomet [?], by argument! And it has just for the first time occurred to me that my opinions, judgments, arguments, defending the highest things I believe in, may all be foolish! That my justifications of myself in arguments are stupid. What does a man want with opinions, if he has beliefs? And if he has beliefs, what is there to argue about?

May 14, 1941. Saint Bonaventure

I wonder how many of the stupid and contentious and stubborn arguments I have had in my life I could remember? There are millions of them – and it is hard to say which ones are more embarrassing to remember and which ones were the most absurd. Theoretically argument is a wonderful thing. But when I think of all the arguments I have ever had I don't think I can find one that did me, or anybody, any service at all, or really meant anything at all: they were mostly stubborn and stupid and pointless and mixed up – and even if I did have something to say, these arguments were the worst ways of getting it said.

1. An argument I had, defending communism, with Russ and Ruth, the day after I landed in N.Y. from England in 1934 – In the living room at Douglaston. I forget what anybody said: only it was a hot argument.

2. An argument I had with Bill Fineran in the Gold Rail Bar, in 1936; I was attacking the Church, and said the existence of God couldn't be proved at all. An extreme position, I took. But I had been reading Gilson's *Spirit of Medieval Philosophy*, without understanding it very well. I had heard, from that, of Saint Bernard; and mentioned him, but Fineran hadn't heard of him.

3. Another argument I had in the Gold Rail Bar, with Robert Krapp, Columbia graduate student. This time defending the Church against a communist argument of some sort. I don't remember the arguments but I remember the strained sound of Krapp's voice and the increased activity of his Adam's apple when he made an objection of some sort.

4. An argument I had with my brother in 1934(?) as to whether Newark was or was not to be considered part of greater New York. A very violent argument in which we both lost our tempers, and my Grandmother, who had heard it from upstairs, lost her temper, too, without participating in the argument or being at all concerned with the point at issue. This was just before dinner, and dinner was spoiled.

5. An argument with Lax, about the value of writing articles for *Southern Review*, in a street, N.Y., at night, rainy, I think, his birthday (1937?), I had said I would like to write a critical article, just any critical article, and get it published in *Southern Review*. He said why would anybody want to do that? He was right. We argued for a very long time, however, as to the value of getting an article published in *Southern Review*.

6. An argument which I had with Tom and Iris Bennett in London, 1933, January (maybe.) They said Ravel's "Bolero" was phony. I had just heard it for the first time, and said it wasn't. The argument didn't last. They were right.

7. An argument I had in Spanish with half the population of Matanzas, Cuba, which was less an argument than a speech defending the Catholic Religion against a couple of agnostic students of Havana University. The majority was with me, and probably found it curious to hear the arguments in broken Spanish.

8. An argument I had with a French Canadian student from the Sorbonne, on the Cunard Liner *Ausonia*, in the bar, in which I said Victor Hugo was a lousy poet and he said the opposite, but in a tolerant way.

9. Under the trees at Oakham, on a little plot of grass between the school rooms and that ancient non-conformist chapel which was now a gymnasium – an argument with Doherty, concerning, I think, the possibility of proving the existence of God. I said it wasn't possible to prove God was first efficient cause of the world – or that once a first efficient cause was proved, that cause couldn't be shown, just from that fact, to be an infinitely perfect will: it was only some first efficient cause, more or less anonymous, not necessarily having a will.

10. In the living room at Douglaston, with my Uncle Harold – that the prose of *Of Time and the River* was really a kind of poetry; that poetry didn't have to be verse. He said poetry had to be verse. 1935.

11. Before one of Van Doren's classes, a short sharp argument with a crazy student who protested against being made to read *A Tale of a Tub* which he said was irreligious and immoral. The argument didn't get anywhere, because the class started. I suppose I was going to say how reading broadened the mind, and what did he want to do, interfere with academic freedom?

12. The big argument at Jacobson's party and afterward, when I first told everybody I was going to become a Catholic. It was a big absurd argument. I forget about what: probably again about how much could be proved by reason, in religion.

13. The argument at Mrs. Wilson's apartment in Great Neck (the mother of my cousin's girl) about how religion is true and the Catholic is the true faith. I still don't think there was much purpose to the argument as argument – which began when Mrs. Wilson asked me what the Trappists were all about.

14. Easter Sunday – the argument I am most ashamed of – I got into an argument with a Thomist from Notre Dame about Faith and Reason again, this time me *against* the Thomist proofs for the existence of God, but not able to say anything about the Scotist proof which I didn't know except [to] say they were good but I didn't know them. Some occupation for the afternoon of Easter Sunday after a retreat in a Trappist monastery! To argue! I was sick of every word I said right after I said it, and yet I went on arguing.

It is silly to *argue* that charity and peace are greater than contentions! Now that I am in the position of doing that in my arguments, I find it would undoubtedly be a good thing intellectually, as well as every other way, to shut up.

15. Not an argument, but a big monologue about life with Wilma Reardon, in Heiniken's Cafe, World's Fair, 1938. I forget what about; I guess writing came into it. It might have been very like a Thomas Wolfe speech, since I was full of beer.

16. I had dozens of arguments with Bobbie Chase. She liked to argue. I forget what they were all about.

17. An argument with Joe Roberts in my room in 548a West 114th St. He said if Catholicism was such a good religion, why had his governess, who had gone frequently to church, been such a heel in her treatment of him and his mother?

18. A big argument with Slate, about 11 p.m. in Tilson's drugstore, concerning the novel which, he said, had a moral purpose. I said the first function of the novel was not to teach but to delight.

19. An argument up at the cottage last summer when I got into hot water with the fellows for saying Hitler hated God, and not that he hated the church, which, to me, is more nearly the same thing than it is to them.

There was another argument up at the cottage last fall where everybody got very nervous: about what should people do in this war. I didn't believe it was absolutely wrong to kill anybody in war. Lax believed it was. Everything was very confused because nobody knew what was going to happen except that the Draft law was going through. Now the uncertainty is over – as soon as it was over, too, things became clear all by themselves. What to do, how to object, etc. We both put in exactly the same kind of objection.

20. An argument in Rome, with the people in the Pensione being very firm, in a strange way, about the fact that Fascist restrictions were good for a nation, and that the press *had to* be regulated, and people *had to* be restricted in what they could say or not say. (1933)

21. A big argument last summer with Father Joe Vann as to whether art appealed primarily to the intellect or to the emotions. He said the emotions. We both got very sick of the argument. Almost all the big arguments I have been in have been long, tenacious and exhausting and – pointless, in the end, getting nowhere, mostly depending on differences of personality or of temperament.

Now I suppose the next thing is to get into an argument to prove to someone that arguments represent differences in personalities as much as they do real, important issues. The issues are real. They can be treated adequately in books, and understood in meditation. In arguments, however, when people aren't at crosspurposes altogether, by equivocal use of terms, they are often just butting against one another's personality, each one seeing the same thing but not able to see it from the same aspect by reason of his own personality, his own individual peculiarity which determines that his point of view shall not, shall never be quite the same as mine, nor mine the same as yours.

That same old game of my happy childhood, entitled "Where was I this time last year, two years ago, etc. etc. . . . .

May 14, 1940:

Either in Havana, Cuba, or just leaving Havana. Maybe I sailed on the 15th. If I was in Havana, I was living in the Hotel Andino. There was an afternoon as hazy and indefinite as this one when I sat with this Manolo, the head waiter of one of those places at the Plaza – Oh! Club Pennsylvania was its name, and ate ice-cream. But the day before I left I went to Rio Cristal and had a fabulous lunch that was much more than I wanted to eat.

Last year: flowers, birds, waterfall, arroz con pollo, a special soup, frijoles, people playing guitars; a veranda. Back in Havana – the Church of Our Lady of Carmel. The Parque Central, leading to many places, via the streets that opened into it. Mostly to the Church of El Santo Cristo, and San Francisco. The only really good thing about Havana was the mornings – going to Church and Communion, then having breakfast, with a great huge glass of orange juice and reading, in the *Diario de la Marsua*, about the English being chased out of Norway. The big fight in Belgium was just beginning. When I landed in N.Y. after two days without news, things had suddenly become very terrible, Belgium folding up, British and French armies being cut to pieces, etc.

May 14, 1939:

35 Perry Street. I would sit on the unsafe balcony of that front room, while the loose boards rattled under me. I would wait for my telephone with the soft, subdued, and happy, expensive bell to ring. I would go to the World's Fair, with Lax and Gibney, to the Cuban village, to the French Building – or maybe that wasn't open yet. And I was reading *Finnegans Wake*, and writing what? Those rather lousy poems. Except around that time I wrote "Dido," which is all right. I thought I was going to write a Thesis on G. M. Hopkins for my Ph. D. at Columbia.

May, 1938:

We would sit in Dona Eaton's big room, with no sunlight, in the heat, typing very fast to finish Lax's novel for Nobbe's novel-writing course, about Mr. Hilquist and Mme. Choppy. Maybe drink Rhine wine. I had just been to Ithaca, and would soon come to Olean with Lax. Just then we thought we would come to Olean on an oil barge up the Erie Canal to Buffalo, but we didn't, we took the train. It is three years since I first came here.

May, 1937:

I guess I was sitting in Douglaston holding my head in confusion. I had just had most of my front teeth yanked out, and I guess I was waiting for nothing more important to happen than the appearance of the College Year book, as I was Editor, and wanted to see all the pictures of myself I was having printed.

Around this time was Russ Boyer's wedding, when we all – that is a lot of people from Douglaston – drove out to Rothman's and I was relatively content to be full of champagne, and it seemed like a good party.

May, 1936:

This game gets more distressing as the years go back. I suppose we had all just had a jolly jolly party in the old Alpha Delt house, and I was being interviewed about getting the job at Radio City. What an unhappy summer that was.

May, 1935:

I sat in the garden at Douglaston and typed a stupid term paper for Irwin Edman on the function of art. Further than this I refuse to remember, in 1935.

May, 1934:

Cambridge. Stab me with swords and shower my head with garbage, at the horror and embarrassment I feel upon remembering Cambridge in May 1934. I would rather be instantly dead than do one thing or say one sentence or think one thought that I was likely to have been happy about at that time.[9]

---

[9] The "horror and embarrassment" Merton felt thinking of this time at Cambridge was undoubtedly the report that he had fathered a child, and that his guardian, Dr. Tom Bennett, who had apparently made a settlement with the girl, had insisted that Merton go to the United States and live with his maternal grandparents, who had financed his education.

May, 1933:

I was in Douglaston. I had been in Rome, and I was just beginning to forget and stamp out of myself the grace that had been given me momentarily in Rome to try, in an obscure and proud and protestant way, to love God by trying to pray in shame and secret, and trying to read the Bible when nobody was looking, and trying to do good, or be good in some way. But I was also very busy reading D. H. Lawrence, and wondering more about how experienced I was and how shameful it was to know so little of "life" as I imagined I knew. I found out, I suppose.

May, 1932:

I had been in the Sanatarium with blood poisoning up to now, only more than my blood was poisoned. I thought John Dos Passos was the world's greatest novelist, and was busy writing an essay on modern novels.

May, 1931:

I can bear remembering this year, when I believed in God and was still a kind of a child, anyway. But I was beginning to wonder when I would be a great man of the world – not so much, though. I was just going to sail on the *Minnetonka* for America. I was writing very silly and no good poems indeed, and I thought Vergil's *Georgics* were swell (which they are) and I liked Tacitus, and I was just going to be Editor of the School Magazine, and I had been reading Shelley.

Ten years is enough. And this is not a satisfying game to play. It feels very much like hara-kiri.

May 15. 1941

I wouldn't rather write this journal than anything else. I looked at the one with the gray cover yesterday or the day before: no, yesterday. I got disgusted with that, too. Next time I go back to it I'll tear out a handful of pages, once again. That is the best way to read these journals. Read the leaves and tear them out and throw them away.

HISTORY

Rudolf Hess, whom I am not sure I had heard of before, but who was apparently one of the Nazis, flew from Augsburg to Glasgow in a stolen Messerschmitt and gave himself up to the British.

How did I know? Someone told me at breakfast, when I had my mouth full of cornflakes, if not Pep. There were a whole lot of bullets in the tail of his plane. The story's more romantic if the bullets were German.

Things I like about the story of Rudolf Hess' flight from Germany.

1. He had never flown a Messerschmitt before.

2. He headed for, reached, and landed on by parachute, the estate of a friend of his in Scotland. He either broke, sprained or twisted his ankle. A Scotch farmer with a pitchfork held him up. He got up smiling and polite. He had on a good uniform.

3. As soon as he disappeared the Germans gave out a story that he had gone crazy, taken a plane and committed suicide with it. That he had been crazy for a long time. Which was a most unhappy thought for the Propaganda bureau: because what would he be doing in the perfect government if he was a crazy? They were excited, I guess! Myself, I'm sure he was crazy, like all of them.

4. Hitler had said he wasn't to fly any aeroplanes. That is the first utterance or act of Hitler's that has ever seemed at all interesting to me. "Hess shall not fly any aeroplanes!"

5. Hess was the most obedient Nazi. Everybody is probably going to make out he was the symbol of *real* Nazis, and the one *good* Nazi, no doubt on account of all his bungling victories in France, Norway, Greece, etc.

6. But the thing that amuses me most about Hess is a little detail about his personal asceticism. He is another vegetarian, non smoker, non drinker. Since I have stopped drinking and smoking and don't eat much meat I can see very readily how a person might give up things – if only because it makes you feel good, which it certainly does. The one thing that is *not* perverse about the Nazis is their urge to discipline themselves and to be, in a way, ascetic, except they probably do it for not quite the best reason, i.e., charity.

Well, Hess landed, and even while the Scotchman was bringing him in, the Scotchman's wife was up making tea. But when Hess was offered tea, "he smiled," said the paper and he refused, saying he "never drank tea that late." However he took a glass of water. Baby, do I know that smile, of this man who has jumped out of a parachute and five minutes later is exercising a minute act of conscious self-denial, a little embarrassed. This situation is very haunting. Hess, beetle-browed conscientious, embarrassed, scared, refusing tea, politely. I feel very sorry for him that he had to be a Nazi party official, rather than a monk in some obscure, little monastery where he would have no importance at all and some real religion – and no feeling of embarrassment at having to practice asceticism in the absurd context of spies, machine guns, parachutes, etc. of a John Buchan novel. Here is a man in the middle of *The 39 Steps*, refusing tea politely because of his secret little resolutions. It is a great shame to set such a guy to parachute jumping and flying Messerschmitts – when all he really wants to be is preoccupied with small and intimate problems.

But it is a real problem: the strangeness of private asceticism – especially asceticism detached from any Church. The paper – (*The Times* printed his obituary) told how much he mentioned God and Providence in his speeches. He believes in God. He is a strange, scared, beetle browed guy, looks a little like [Max] Schmeling or like nine hundred German waiters I have seen in New York. I wonder if they are all unhappy the same sort of way?

May 18, 1941

Today is Sunday. Outside my window – (it is sunny and cool) a seminarian in his black cassock, is preparing to take a picture of a group of seminarians standing in front of a flowerbed of thin, low, scraggly tulips. I have just found very little to say in a letter home to my uncle and aunt.

Now the picture is taken. The seminarians fall out of their group, with a short burst of general laughter. But they fall back in again, for there will be another picture – this time everyone with his biretta off. All the birettas are thrown on the grass, off to one side. Maybe these are the ones who will be ordained priests next month, these seminarians.

I remember for some inexplicable reason the Sunday the war started, the Sunday of Labor Day weekend in 1939. I was on the dock at Southside, Urbanna, Virginia. Inside the musty store room, next to the red cooler full of bottled coca cola and Dr. Pepper, a radio spoke – with the voice of a man from London, saying how quiet it was there. And I had a terrible toothache, and was full of despair about the war, but the sun was blazing hot and it was the finest day on the river you'd ever hope to see!

I remember coming home from the services at the Episcopal Church in Douglaston, where I had started to go in 1937 again. It is funny how little I think of that – but in the spring of 1937 I had started to go to Church again. 1938, more so, I guess. I remember I even went, once, to something they had in the middle of the week. Thus I would come home pleased, and kid about having been to church, but I really felt quite happy. I hadn't remembered this.

The minister, at the request of one of his parishioners, had preached a couple of sermons about various controversies in the ancient church – Pelagians, Manichaeans, etc. He did not speak of the theological quarrels, but only took each struggle as a struggle for "liberty" against "dogmatism" and compared the whole thing, by inference, to the loyalists fighting the tyrannical fascists in Spain. Politically, at that time, I was with him: and still the sermon made me sore, because I wanted to hear about Doctrine, and nobody told me anything about Doctrine, about what to believe.

There was a sort of Calvinist cenacle in St. Antonin, on the road out of town Eastward, just at the edge of the town, under the plane trees. The interior was whitewashed. There was no altar, it looked like a courtroom. My father and I went there once. But it was too grim for him, and I myself didn't mind when we didn't go again.

I remember the protestant chapel at the Lycée – a cold, brick affair like a desecrated tomb, like an abandoned mausoleum. It was very cold in there in winter. We huddled around a stove and the pastor spoke of the parables – the vine and the branches. We nearly froze to death. We were fine branches, we were! That chapel was like an abandoned brick kiln. The Catholic chapel wasn't used at all, it was boarded up. The boys marched to Mass at the Cathedral, and I wasn't at all curious about it, either. Quite a few just stayed in *"étude"* with the little Corsican – I suppose you'd call him prefect. I forget what his title was. Petrolacci, was his name, and he was very unpopular.

Going to church at Ripley Court was a very good affair. We went to the village church, and I remember how happy I was to go to that church the first time. Also, Sunday, evenings, in the wooden "drill room" at the school, we sat on squeaking benches, and the birds sang in the elms, and Mr. Onslow read aloud from *Pilgrim's Progress*, and I liked that, too. I have since sneered at Bunyan, but it wasn't thoroughly sincere. I haven't anything against *Pilgrim's Progress* except the scene at the gate of heaven – where the devils took the boy who wasn't predestined – didn't have the secret password – and there wouldn't be anything against that either, except that it seemed completely arbitrary who had the password and who didn't: both he who got in (Pilgrim Christian) and the other had made the same difficult journey, and apparently for the same end. But the difference is a mystery that is not explained. That is not the place for a mystery, but for a straight and simple explanation. There is no such explanation for Bunyan – only confusion and fear.

As a child I was sent to the Christian Scientists once, but couldn't make any sense out of anything that was going on there. It was also in a shed, and I looked out of the window, and longed to be away.

I remember being happy at church in Rye, at a Lutheran Church in Strasbourg, in Saint Clement Dane's, in chapel at Oakham, especially at Communion Service in early summer, in the Quaker Meeting House in Flushing, in Church at Ealing (or coming out of it), in Church at West Horsley – at Seaview I.O.W. – at Brooke I.O.W. – even in Haughton's little church in Scotland, where he officiated and his tenants prayed – though I don't know what orders he had, I'm sure. But it was all in a completely different sense from anything I ever felt say at Corpus Christi, or Saint Josephs, 1st Ave., or La Merced in Camaguey, or Nuestra Senora du Carmen in Havana, or St. Mary of the Angels, Olean – or here – or at Gethsemani!!!

June 11, 1941. New York

Now I really have three journals going at once – _The Journal of My Escape from the Nazis_ which is already in the hands of Miss Burton, England's Jewel, at Curtis Brown Ltd., England's Helicon. The second is what I write on the typewriter but not for the _Escape from Nazis_, and the third is what goes in this longhand book.

What is the difference? I don't know yet. This one to be more private, more nondescript, and more religious – more personal, I guess. I have a lot of things to say personal like that don't belong in the fancy journal – the one I don't mind if people read over my shoulder in the subway.

What do I know that is rather for this diary than the others? That in New York I eat too much; that I don't like to eat meat. My belly should be lean. It is so full of food my tertiary cord bites into the flesh.

That twice today I went into Saint Agnes' Church on 43rd Street near Lexington, and it was a good place to go and get a little collected after walking around all over the place. I do not like the streets of this city.

That today I was walking all over New York for nothing – but for things I would have thought very important a year ago – talking to people who one way and another, do, or could, publish my stuff or were connected with something that had published my stuff. All unnecessary. It can be done by mail.

About all these people is, if anything, material for the other journal.

Both my brother and Gibney got notice to appear for a pre-induction Army Physical Exam, that is, a further stage than the civilian physical that I got, for my 1-B classification. My brother worries – and rightly – over the draft, but he worries in the wrong way, in a sort of a helpless way that makes me unhappy, because he rebels against it in a weakly crazy manner, thinking of joining air forces, foreign legions, etc. The idea that if you *choose* your own jail you are free, even if it is a longer term.

And Knight is already taken off to the army in Georgia. He had the very small consolation of being given the highest I.Q. of those so far drafted in Atlanta. And I think of how last summer, Knight and I hitchhiked to Cleveland together, and the evening we stood outside Geneva, Ohio, by a pretty, quiet, farm, dead tired, waiting for a ride at sunset on the big fourlane highway.

June 21, 1941. Saint Bonaventure

I just refrained from heaving out the window the only book I've tried to read in weeks except stuff about Dante, Coulton's *From Saint Francis to Dante.* It contained some fine material, all drowned in Coulton's opinions – argument after argument to vindicate his Victorian optimism, his love of moderate progress, etc. and his belief that asceticism is simply impossible and that saints are really only gentlemen, saints in a nice dull way, not in a mad crazy 13th century way.

The way to discuss whether or not asceticism is morally and physically impossible to live by is not to argue about it in terms of a lot of contradictory documents from the 13th century which say that sometimes the monks fell asleep in church – but to look around and see if there is anywhere in the world where there are ascetics. But there are true, good ascetics now, in America – for instance at Gethsemani. Therefore, as far as the possibility or impossibility of asceticism is concerned, arguments about the immorality of some medieval monks are quite unimportant. But that immorality is very interesting in other terms, and it is interesting to study – but from a completely different point of view from Coulton's. What did those men think? Did they justify themselves? Was the church very different then from what it is now? In what way? etc.

Also I don't like Coulton's coyness – always bringing up some subject and then saying "But modern decency forbids my further quotation of Salimbene's original which, by the way, was written for a *nun!*" Guys like Coulton love that – especially the part about the nun.

Coulton hates asceticism, and that means that he simply doesn't know what it is all about, and when he talks about it, he is talking about something fierce in his own mind, that scares him – and he is not really capable, hating asceticism as he does, believing in progress as he does, of understanding what Saint Francis and Dante were really after. However, he sure knows a lot of interesting facts about Saint Francis and Dante.

June 26, 1941

It is all the time hot and bright. In the mornings I sometimes write something in the _Journal of My Escape from the Nazis_. In the afternoons, read Dante and dull stuff about a course I have to give in Bibliography. Last summer we were all up at the cottage – or rather, I was here, thinking to be a novice and reading a lot of Saint Thomas Aquinas.

I looked at the ten first pages of _Brighton Rock_ and was not as happy about them as the very first time. The novel I wrote last fall, _The Man in the Sycamore Tree_, came back from Curtis Brown. I am not so sore at it as I was a few weeks ago. Last night I reread the Cuban part and liked it. Only, the beginning is terrible.

The place is full of secular priests from Erie on retreat. Down outside my window in a car, a radio gives out the serious and sincere sounding voice of Lowell Thomas broadcasting something I can't hear about the German invasion of Russia – which the guy in charge of ROTC here thinks is all a trumped up bluff to fool England into letting down her guard.

The other night I read some of Saint John of the Cross' _Cantico Espiritual_ which I understood much better than last spring (1940) in Havana. Also, I realized it is a much better book than I thought then. The opening is wonderful.

I was happy to find out in Lorca a version of the song which La Nina de los Penios[?] sang on one of my records – for her, it was a _sombrerito de rule_ [little hat of the rule]. Lorca called it _"Los Tres Pelegrinitos"_ and I finally found out what it was all about. Some poem! Also, Lorca's _"Oda a Salvador Dali"_ which I had heard about long before I met Latouche and Calas in the Golden Horn Restnt. It is one of Lorca's very best poems – very neat and elevated, like _"Garulaso de la Vega."_ Classical.

I am distressed at having to pay so much attention to things like Mudge's _Guide to Reference Books_ but other bibliographies are so dull that it was a kind of a pleasure to read entries in the _Cambridge Bibliography of English Literature_ – new this year, or anyway, last.

Right this minute I am inclined to think G. Greene's book about Mexico is better than *Brighton Rock*, and also to agree with Gibney that *Confidential Agent* is (better than *Brighton Rock*). I was surprised to find out Greene is 11 years older than I am – 37, now. I thought he was the same age, or 2 or 3 years older. I hope Auden is *at least* 11 years older than I am. I believe MacLeish is 4 times as old as I am, namely 104.

I got a lot of tame laughs out of an elaborate Irish *Capuchin Annual* for 1940 – partly in Gaelic, partly with pictures of Ireland like the pictures of England that used to come on the *Times* calendars – pretty landscapes, – partly with pictures of Irish patriots in their various types [of] regalia. It was a very Irish document, and they had pictures and notes on contributors in among advertisements in the back. One was a guy called O'Neil who had been born and always lived in Liverpool, but the note ended with the words – "He longs for the day when he'll set foot on Irish soil." Well, Liverpool isn't so far, no doubt the good young man shall have his wish.

Sunday. July 6

With the *Journal of My Escape from the Nazis* – it has a definite form: things seem to have to start in a certain way and what I write has to have some conscious reference to something I wrote the day before: there is enough of a thread of connection to be embarrassing. It will never sell, because of the Esperanto: and I am sorry, merely because now I have the feeling I had taken a little care with it, instead of just writing it carelessly from day to day, like any journal, which was what I wanted at first. Since it can't be sold, why not write completely at your ease? Simply because I can't write for fun. Everything I write begins to require effort as soon as it gets at all good – more effort and also gives more satisfaction; the two go together.

When I write merely automatically, one idea after another, the first thing I do is get in an argument with myself, which is hell.

Today I reread the scene where Jacques and Germaine quarrel over the stupid lines from Victor Hugo, *"Gall, amant de la reine, etc."* in Cocteau's *Grand Écart.*[10] It is one of the funniest scenes I have ever read anywhere. So is the character Stopwell funny – but especially this scene, with Germaine and her mother.

---

[10] *Le Grand Écart* was the title of a short novel published by Jean Cocteau in 1922. In French, the expression *grand écart* refers to a dance step, that is, "the split." Yet the original meaning of *écart* is that of separation or distance between. In this novel of his adolescence, Cocteau has in mind the gap between a woman of the world (with whom he was in love) and an inexperienced young man.

The dorms are full of clerics and nuns for summer school. Upstairs, some cleric is playing an ocharina. I guess if I had joined the order I could have played the bongos – they are more respectable than an ocharina. I would have wanted to keep the bongos, too.

The English are sore at P. G. Wodehouse for making broadcasts from Berlin saying he was well treated in the prison camp.

I also like Lorca's _"Asi que Pasen Cinco Años."_ The rugby player, the child and the cat (some scene) the mannequin and the young man: some scenes. That is the first of his plays I have read.

It seems like a long time since May 6 – like 2 months. It seems like years since Easter, at Gethsemani. In that time all the cigarette ads have become full of soldiers, and Knight has been drafted and is bursting out into boils in a camp in Louisiana [Fort Polk], and Gibney has been called to go in 5 days from now. Things moved fast since last summer, all right, when we all sat up on the hill in worse garbage than you'd get in a camp of any kind.

Now to read maybe _Bodas de Sangre,_ maybe _Cantico Espiritual,_ probably the _Cantico._ I haven't yet touched the cheap Chilean edition of _Bodas de Sangre,_ which has been waiting for more than a year – year and a half – to be cut.

Sunday. July 13, 1941

"True metaphysics _does not culminate in a concept,_ be it that of thought, of good, of one or of substance. It does not even culminate in an essence, be it that of Being itself. Its last word is not _ens_ but _esse;_ not _being,_ but _is._ The ultimate effect of metaphysics is to posit an Act by an act, that is, to posit by an act of judging, the supreme Act of existing, whose very essence, because it is to be, passes human understanding. Where a man's metaphysics comes to an end, his religion begins." Etienne Gilson _God and Philosophy,_ p. 143.[11]

Tuesday. July 16

Today I got a letter from Gibney who is at Camp Upton. I answer him in 5 pages of Joycetalk Esperanto, which, if the sergeants ever peruse, sure means a merry dance for me. Published in the courtrooms. That's one way to get published: my subtle poems all read into the records of the court!

---

[11] This quotation is taken from the last paragraph of Etienne Gilson's _God and Philosophy_ (New Haven: Yale University Press, 1941), which was originally the Powell lectures at Indiana University.

It is very shocking, horrible, to write on an envelope *Pvt.* Gibney and like the other day *Pvt.* Knight. On the other hand you got to identify who you're writing to or they might tear the letter up, or eat it, or wear it on their heads, or do some dull savage thing with it.

Tuesday. July 27. 1941

Well Homer what news! Ou ghst spug! Hoover! Swat thews! First the piece of *Journal of Escape from the Nazis* that Kerr had in Boston came back and he said it wasn't commercial. What's commercial? Even if the word means something to him, even then he isn't right. Publishers must be crazy. On the other hand what does publication matter anyway? Already Lax, his sister, Brother-in-law (oil man), Seymour, have read parts of it as well as the Math instructor (Ray Roth) here and then of course Naomi Burton, Sam Sloan, C. A. Pearce, Chester Kerr, so before it is even part finished the book has at least 9 readers I know of, all of whom like it.

So far it has a perfect record. Of course it might be published and then there would turn up one guy who didn't like it and the record wouldn't be perfect any more.

Anyway I pieced this piece back with the rest and it makes a nice looking book.

As for the rest of today: I made a speech to the Rotary Club in Eldred, Pa., about the fall of France, under the auspices of the local priest, a very businesslike sort of a business-priest. (He told me how his new curate was losing the illusions he had picked up in Seminary.) The Methodist minister seemed interested in the speech. He asked a lot of questions, smiling. He didn't seem such a fool. The priest was consistently rude to him, publicly and privately. I wish I was a priest. I hope the five bucks will buy some books. That is my dream concerning Rotary Club speeches – money for books, which I read and then turn over to Library ½ price so as not to be soiled with too many possessions and love of property.

Then I get a letter from my brother – he is at Laredo, Tex. – (was when he wrote) going to Mexico *to climb Popocatepetl.* No fooling.

Gibney is now in Fort Bragg where there were 3 suicides in 3 weeks. He was knocked into the hospital by his typhoid inoculation. He says out of 75,000 soldiers at Fort Bragg 15,000 are in the hospital.

Lax called him long distance from the cottage but it wasn't much use. He was out of the hospital again and it took 3 hours to get him.

I think of making an Anthology of Poems, Religious or nearly Religious. So far I have got Donne's "Hymn to Christ at the Author's Last Going into Germany," "At the Round Earth's Imagin'd Corners," "Nocturnal on Saint

Lucy's Day," "What If This Present were the World's Last Night?," and Herbert's "Aaron" and Vaughan's "The Seed Growing Secretly" and Hopkins' "Felix Randal." Also I think Hopkins' "Leaden and Golden Echo-Bugler's First Communion," "Candle Indoors," "Wreck of the *Deutschland*" and despair poems. Then Blake's "How Sweet I Roamed," "Little Girl Lost," "Auguries of Innocence," "Mental Traveler," "Holy Thursday" (Innocence), a lot more Vaughan (e.g., "Night"), plenty Traherne – Southwell's "Burning Babe." In all maybe 150 poems – or half that – 75 would be a better number.

Monday. August 4, 1941

Concerning the anthology my thought at present is: not so much Traherne. He can be a lot vaguer than the other metaphysicals.

Other drab thoughts for this evening: wait until they hear the Hut-Sut song in England and Germany. It is just the song to sweep Europe. It is horrible. They'll love it.

Last night walking home from Olean on the river road was nice. Fields full of white flowers. Farm houses with the big dark blue woods behind them, on the steep hills: and the avenue of fairly old trees along the road: this is one of the few roads lined with trees, big trees, around here. The river was very much like the Aveyron. At first the setting sun was in my eyes. Then it was dusk. The road was empty for a long while until two kids came by on bicycles. Then the moon was out, pale in the clear sky, and, over the hill, a star. It was cool. I began to think of nights in autumn, but only abstractly: this was still a summer night.

Passing the mouth of the Four Mile Valley – warm lights in the kitchens of the houses, everything quiet and good. Those are the houses I see from my room, lights, in the distance, when I pray before getting into bed: I remember them in the winter.

Yesterday Lax and I go to this country club in Bradford – the Penn Hills. Half a dozen little polite, dumb rich children swim in the pool. Nobody else much around at all – club building as fancy as something for a Hollywood movie. Great big tiers all around it, and very hot sun. It was as if a very rich club suddenly appeared in the Four Mile Valley among the farms and oil leases. It was terribly dull. A lot of rich drugstore owners who had made millions digging for oil sat around rather unhappy I suppose. We went away fast, depressed.

This is the last week of summerschool. I have chalk dust all over my hands by twelve o'clock every day. I have written many absurd names on blackboards – Hugh Kelly's False Delicacy; Samuel Foote; Belcom the

West Indian; gentle old stupid old Mr. Hardcastle; Colley Cibber, you big fribble. The nuns are probably as tired of my explanation of why 18th century moral drama was really immoral because it tried so hard to be moral, as if I had rubbed it all over the board with sandpaper. I myself am pretty chafed with my own arguments. I don't know what I was about as a sophomore when I liked *Tom Thumb the Great,* and it seems likely I am soon going to forget names like Foote, Whitehead, Colman, Sr. and Jr., Isaac Bickerstaffe, not to mention (whatever his first name was) Murphy. Some waste of time.

This pen is no good either.

Things I don't need to do any more –

> Look for a good restaurant in Olean. (Bill Welch's last night, turned out no good, and I might as well have come home – O, I was late getting back from Bradford, that was it.)

> Visit people in Olean – happier and busier in my hut down here – only not so busy now.

> Well, I hope I won't have to study no more plays of Sheridan, of whom I complain more than I really mean to this minute, just for something to say. Maybe the *Rivals* is the one good – or half way good – 18th century play – as if I cared.

> I can't think of any book I'm crazy to own right now – and if I could, I'd probably think about it altogether too much.

I am getting suspicious of this diary: can't I write in it anything but lists of possessions I have or want – or think I want, or don't think I want?

The Baroness de Hueck: said to the nuns, "Baloney" like a communist. She was very good. The little S.S.J., Sister Immaculata, who writes poems, was very impressed: looked earnestly startled, like a child about to be taken to Grandma's in New Jersey, when hearing all about these new things the Baroness de Hueck spoke of.

The Baroness stood in a free and easy way when she talked, and made good, simple, unhysterical gestures, very natural, and had a strong and sure voice and talked about martyrdom without embarrassment, as if it wasn't something abstract, in a book.

The way she said some things was as moving as a propaganda movie or a sentence in a good sermon – and left you ready to do some kind of action: in this case, something good – renounce the world, live in total poverty, but also doing very definite things, ministering to the poor, in a certain definite way.

Now count up all the people you have insulted since you heard that speech – all your acts of pride and envy and selfishness and laziness and impatience and vanity. I sure don't have time to own books or go to Olean or eat in restaurants or wonder why country clubs are dead: I ought to be too busy with prayers and penances and supplications. Every good idea or good desire is too easily turned into pride and overbearing, and envious selfishness.

What books did I buy lately?
> *Decline and Fall*, by E. Waugh.
> *The New Criterion* – by J. C. Ransom.
And ordered:
> E. Chapman – *Saint Augustine's Theory of Beauty.*
> H. Read – *Form in Modern Poetry.*
the last two only because they were cheap. I don't really want to buy books of criticism – or books at all.

A cleric lends me Leen's *Progress through Mental Prayer* which is pretty good.

Tonight is the Feast of Saint Dominic. I think of the Dominican place at Washington – Sunday, Vespers, fall of 1939. Tomorrow feast of Our Lady of the Snow – the Basilica of Santa Maria Maggiore. I think of the romanesque spire, the mosaics high up in the nave.

This is prophecy week in everybody's journal starting right now, one two three go: the one I think least likely is the one that will most probably happen. By September 2 – the 2nd anniversary of the war – I think the Germans, by that time, may have broken through and taken over the Ukraine.

The guy who teaches Paleography thinks we will be in a war with Japan. I just haven't any idea.

The Germans will have invaded England. Maybe this is the least likely according to logic. (To what, stupid?)

The Germans may be on their way to India. Even less likely.

The Russians may have driven the Germans back into Poland.

Totally unlikely – the war may be over. I would say this was almost impossible, by Sept. 1 – maybe by Christmas?

By Christmas –

Maybe the war will be over, with a compromise peace between Germany and England with France as go-between, and a stalemate in Russia. I don't understand chess metaphors or these prophecies either.

Or maybe Hitler will be dead – or Mussolini and Italy will be nothing but a colony – or Churchill dead which, I guess, wouldn't make any difference.

Maybe this bloody pen will be busted and I'll have something decent to write with.

If I was to list very unlikely things that might happen between now and Christmas –

1. Peace and complete agreement between England and Germany, Russia and Germany.

2. War between England and America, with Germany and England fighting us.

If I say these are unlikely – which they are – it follows that they will probably happen. But that means they are – in my mind – likely – because the most likely thing to happen is the one we least expect. But if I *expect* this – it isn't the thing I least expect. Must be something else!

Saturday, August 15, 1941. 548 West 114th Street, NYC

Same kind of August as 1939 but it feels different. Here it is the same brown bedspread, the fat, square (oblong) brown cushions that make the bed a studio couch. Outside my window, in the back, and high up among the fire-escapes, is the noise and clatter of a party – with one dame's voice louder than all the rest.

Down in Harlem is the Baroness' Place. Yesterday full of Hail Marys I went there. Today I sorted dresses in the clothing center – and women's shoes until my hands were thick with the gray dirt of their whiteing.

Walking across 135th Street between the clothing center and the Library where the Baroness has her desk, you see (looking West) City College on top of the hill, looking surprised. A big building saying Y.M.C.A. – white letters on black. A movie. Seven or eight pushcarts. The drabbest Billiard parlor in the world. The subway at corner of Lenox Avenue, and hundreds of little negro kids, walking solemnly, holding kites.

A pair of army trucks go by, full of colored soldiers leaning very far out and laughing excitedly at the strangers of their own race, all along the street. Very fast, the trucks are gone.

I try to call Lax at Godfrey's on E. 18th Street. The phone has been disconnected. Later I go down – but first to West 18th – and have to cross town on the 23rd Street bus passing Saint Francis de Sales Church, Madison Square, P.S. 47 – a big post office, etc. Then under the elevated. It all ends up near a bar where the author Ernest Boyd, beard, bow tie, neat half-baldness, pepper and salt suit, maybe, sits alone at a sidewalk table.

In Godfrey's I find all the little short poems of Emily Dickinson to make a mock of. Roger Beirne makes a great Mr. Chips speech in the street, and a greater business speech to the Burroughs Adding Machine Company so funny as I've never heard.

I remember the kids in the play in Harlem – Merlin turns to a black and white cat. Wonderful costumes. The sad and earnest parents watching ready to laugh and cry, so scared, so colored. The children on the tiny little stage, in a converted store. It was very good. If I have done any work there it has no proportion to the 2 meals and cups of black tea they have given me, Friday and today.

Ad Bened. Ant [Benedictus Antiphon at Office] Xth Sunday after Pentecost

"*Stans a longe publicanus, nolebat oculos ad coelum levare, sed percutiebat pectus suum dicens: Deus, propitius esto mihi peccatori.*" ["The other man (the tax collector), however, kept his distance, not even daring to raise his eyes to heaven. All he did was beat his breast and say, 'O God, be merciful to me, a sinner.'" (Luke 18:13, New American Bible)]

I read this in Saint Patrick's Cathedral and thought of Harlem standing afar off like the publican – *stans a longe publicamus, nolebat oculos ad coelum levare*. . . . The gentle, ragged kids running fast in the dark warrens of the tenements and out into the street. The mother cries out to one, "don't go on the roofs to fly your kite, it might pull you over the edge."

You don't get sentimental or exalted, sorting dresses in an old store in a tenement. You work. It is safe; there is nothing aesthetic about it. And what happens? I don't know. I'll know better when I see the dresses given out Tuesday – but I know something from the faces of the scared, earnest, devoted parents, last night, sitting, outlandishly polite, like bourgeois, listening to the Baroness before the play.

August 21

Two newly ordained Jesuits visited the Baroness and stayed for dinner, laughing uproariously at all the jokes and criticism she threw at them like daggers, brickbats, etc. Full of straight from the shoulder, hail fellow well met tactics. They were all right, though.

I am not as sore at religious as the Baroness [is] – or Leon Bloy. No reason why I should not be except for the Trappists. Charlie – who worked for the Baroness and wore Maritain's cast off overcoat all winter – is going into the Trappists – and is a good, humble guy – but she kidded him a lot, too, probably because he was entering an order.

Reading Bloy's *L'Invendable* it is quite clear to me that what he was doing was a kind of "lay apostolate" (a fancy term I don't like so much), he had a definite vocation to write what he wrote – nobody knows, or can measure, the tremendous value of his writing, as apostolate. If he only converted one man, it would justify his whole life. But he converted Maritain and a pile of others, and was crucified for how many?

I sure don't want Francis Thompson [author of *The Hound of Heaven*] in my anthology.

August 22. Octave of the Assumption

For *The Journal of my Escape from Nazis:* title page:

> *"Quand il se commet un crime quelque part, qui de nous en est innocent et comment chacun etablira-t-il son alibi?"* Leon Bloy – *L'Invendable*, p. 197. ["When a crime is committed anywhere, who of us is innocent of it, and how has any of us established his alibi?"]
>
> *"Quand je veux savoir les dernières nouvelles, je lis saint Paul."* Ibid. 207. ["When I want to know the latest news, I read Saint Paul."]
>
> *"La sentimentalité, c'est d'avoir compassion des bourreaux de Jesus-Christ."* Ibid. 243. ["Sentimentality is having compassion on the executioners of Jesus Christ."]
>
> *"Les propheties ne pouvant être comprises qu'apres leur accomplissement, a quoi serventelles?"* Ibid. 305. ["What good are prophecies that can't be understood until they are fulfilled?"]

August 28

> *"Les Juifs ne se convertiront que lorsque Jésus sera descendu de sa Croix, et precisement Jésus ne peut en descendre que lorsque les Juifs se seront convertis."* ["The Jews will not be converted until Jesus comes down from His cross, and because Jesus can't come down from the cross, the Jews won't be converted."]
>
> *Le Salut par les Juifs.* p. 72.

August 31. Watch Hill, Rhode Island

I wish somebody would tell me what I am doing in Watch Hill, R.I. –

I am supposed to be on my way to the Trappists at Valley Falls, but they couldn't take me in until after Labor Day – which is tomorrow – so I spent a long time trying to figure out if there wasn't some place where I would like to spend a weekend in New England.

I spit on New England. The whole shore of Connecticut is a series of gnomes' nests, most of them recommended by S. [Seymour Freedgood] as delightful. Yeah? Some experience driving along the Boston Post Road last night, blinded by the headlights of the rich, trailed by a truck towering and flashing like a lighthouse and as long as a dragon or a train.

All this was as a result of Seymour's betrayal concerning Greenport L.I. – which I had thought of – but I don't know why – and to which he had offered to drive me. Betrayal! I thought of this a lot yesterday afternoon when we were stuck in traffic in New York around three o'clock.

I have no enthusiasm for Watch Hill, but anyway there isn't anything wrong with it – except I can't see anywhere a church of any kind, let alone Catholic.

Summer resorts are more boring to me the more ambitious they are as resorts. I would be least of all bored in a place that wasn't a resort at all – only a fishing village. There I could walk around, interested. In a summer resort everything you see when you walk around is boring: small shops selling vulgar postcards, sand buckets, bathing caps, Kodak Verichrome film, Skol suntan oil, Modern Library books (*The Short Bible*, *Farewell to Arms*, *Introduction to Psychoanalysis*, maybe *The Late George Apley*, I don't remember.)

The least boring place here is a mile and a half away at the end of a long sandspit: an abandoned and wrecked fort overgrown with grass, a good place to sit, perfectly quiet, and look at the sea. Nobody goes there. It is swell. I was out there almost all afternoon. All you could hear was the sound of waves and a bell buoy.

I don't know whether the island you saw from there was Fisher's Island or Block Island – or both.

I get a terrific sense of futility out of making in my mind a list of places in New England where I might possibly spend a week of vacation doing nothing but write and pray. All the places I have thought of, except Martha's Vineyard, appear, for one reason or another, impossible. That is – they are all totally uninteresting to me.

Bread Loaf, Vermont.
Old Lyme, Conn. (gave me the horrors last night: my reaction was
    probably exaggerated.)
Clinton, Conn.
Narragansett Pier, R. I.
Newport (!) (That's a lie – I never even thought of it.)
Sandwich, Orleans, Provincetown, Gloucester, Cape Ann. The truth is, first that I don't want a vacation in the accepted sense of the word, but I do

want some sun and air and leisure to pray, but I don't know where to go and have no where to go – can only get to the Trappists for 5 days. Probably it would be best back at Saint Bonas – but I'll be back there soon enough, and it will be good.

Great feeling of futility and shame, riding around with Seymour trying to make a choice of some place to spend the weekend as if it mattered; as if one place were any better than another, once you got where it was cool and quiet. And yet one place is better than another – the smaller and less phony it is the better.

As far as I know there is no artists colony in Watch Hill: that, at least, is one good thing.

The whole of New England is full of artists colonies – and no art.

I spit on New England.

I spit on vacation resorts.

All I want is a place to sit in the grass and look at the sea. At least there is that here. But this won't last long, thank heaven. Tomorrow night I leave again.

All that has to be done to the anthology is add ten or fifteen more poems of Donne, Blake, Vaughan, Hopkins and one or two others: all easy. Then Introduction – and notes, how elaborate? Or maybe no notes.

What I think of now is the whole "Wreck of the *Deutschland*" which is Hopkins' best poem, and his own favorite, too, I think, and some good poem, anyway!

Later:

It is absurd for me to consider whether one place is better than another for a "vacation." I am not looking for particular kinds of restaurants, hotels, beaches, people. Rather – no hotels, no people. No movies. No boats. No dances. All I want is the quietest and coolest place – apart from that I am not looking for a vacation.

All I want is *"fugire palulum occupationes meas . . ."* ["to retreat a little from my daily concerns"]. This is the thing I want to do. *"Intrare in cubiculum mentis meae, excludere omnia praeter Deum. . . ."* ["to enter into the cell of the mind, and exclude all but God."] (Saint Anselm); but if, while I want to do this, I get too exercised about the character of all the different places I could possibly go to, [I] only defeat myself and I betray myself into a very unpleasant and unprofitable rat-race. So long as the place is quiet, what does it matter where I am? Best is a monastery. I can only get five days there. Maybe Martha's Vineyard. Some place where I can be by myself. That is the only essential thing.

> *"Entre l'homme, revetir involontairement de sa liberté, et Dieu depouille volontairement de sa puissance, l'antagonisme est normal, l'attaque et la resistance s'equilibrent raisonnablement et ce perpetuer combat de là nature humaine contre Dieu est la fontaine jaillissante de l'inepuisable Douleur."* L. Bloy. *Dans les Tenèbres.* 104. ["Between man, taking on his freedom against his will, and God, freely doffing his own power, the conflict is expected, the attack and the resistance are a match for each other, and this continual conflict of human nature against God is the abundant source of inexhaustible sorrow."]

September 1. Watch Hill, R.I.

You for your part can draw up a new code of just laws: I for my part will go and give my coat to a beggar. And until you have given your coat to the poor and shared your own bread with those who starve, you will not know much about just laws and your code will be a joke, say the prophets and the saints.

What good is it if you propose an elaborate old age pension plan, and while you are working out your plan, the old cripple at your doorstep is dying of hunger? First feed the poor, and then you may know something about laws to help the poor. First be poor, and you may know how to make laws to help the poor.

What good are your charitable laws if you yourself are selfish?

The people who make up our society are selfish, avaricious, greedy, lustful, envious (they are also, for these reasons, pitiable, confused, lost, helpless, inarticulate) and, realizing obscurely that "society" is diseased with their own selfishness, they blame it on the laws, if not on somebody else. Somebody else is unjust. The laws are uncharitable. So, we eliminate an unjust class, a selfish group: we make charitable laws: society becomes, we hope, charitable. So then we return to our own selfishness and envy and pride and greed – and wonder why society hasn't improved.

Our laws are very charitable but we ourselves are very selfish. Consequently, "society" is not charitable, or healthy: it is disordered, unjust, sick. It doesn't do any real good to make new laws. When new laws do help, it is because they reflect our own desire for justice, our own justice: but our own justice is confused by our own selfishness – we soon forget to love our neighbors, believing the law will take care of that for us.

The Social Security Law does not make it unnecessary for me to feed the poor: and if I myself and all like me are uncharitable, the Social Security Law will never help the unemployed much.

Nevertheless, it is better that there should be such a law than that there should be no such law. But then what? I like the law. I vote for men who make such laws: so what? I persuade others to see the value of such laws and vote for those who make them: what kind of a hero does that make me? I am willing to do that, but don't think it worth mentioning: it doesn't seem to be important. But when someone is starving and asks me for money, that is important: when I give him money I have done something good. It doesn't make me any kind of a hero, either: but it is a definite kind of good action. If somebody asks me what is a good thing to do, I don't tell him "vote for the people who want Social Security": first I tell him "Give all you have to the poor and follow Christ."

If I am giving all I have to the poor, and live to feed the poor, heal the sick, clothe the needy, how can I help being in favor of laws that will help feed the poor, clothe the needy, heal the sick? How can I help, also, voting for the people who are going to make those laws, and persuading others, if I am able, to do the same? That is so obvious that it doesn't require any comment, any particular emphasis.

What does require emphasis is this truth: it is not enough to be interested in charitable laws. To vote for legislators who favor unemployment insurance, old age pensions, etc. is not to feed the hungry, cherish the needy, heal the sick.

Also, knowing the injustices and stupidities and inefficiencies that seem to attend the administration of all laws, I am not likely to get hugely excited over some new law, even if I approve of it. Certainly I will be happy enough, I suppose: but so what? Has poverty been abolished?

No law will ever abolish poverty.

No revolution will ever abolish poverty.

Because laws and revolutions are without love, without charity: if poverty is ever abolished, it will not be only because of laws.

Poverty will never be abolished as long as anybody loves riches.

Poverty will never be abolished until the whole world becomes voluntarily poor.

One thing, however, is certain: if I pretend to love God, and if I don't feed the poor, heal the sick, clothe the needy – how do I know my love is any love at all? "When I was hungry ye fed me not – Lord, when dids't

Thou come to me hungry?" To feed the poor is not only a counsel – it is part of the first of all the commandments, "Love one another."

If I pretend to love God, and hate laws that will feed the poor, my love is not love, but pretense. But how can you tell? Nobody hates laws that will feed the poor – they hate laws which they think will fail to feed the poor!

But if I pretend to love God, and hate laws which will prevent me from getting fabulously rich, I had better re-examine my conscience for the love of money, and cast out my own greed before I yell too loud about this law!

Laws that take money from the rich and give it to the poor (if there are such laws) will never abolish poverty and will never abolish riches. Only charity can even begin to do this. But such laws as these help make the poor hate the rich and the rich the poor. . . .

But a law that feeds the poor is a good law. And I don't know how you can say a law takes money from the rich and gives it to the poor, where everybody is taxed. Besides, I don't like people who yell about taxes. If you don't like to pay income tax, go live in poverty, where there are no taxes.

Is there any law we have now in our system, so admirable that it is worth dying for . . . especially when we cannot save the laws with our blood anyway? What is so absurd as dying to save a system of laws.

If we go into this war we will not be dying so that the poor may be fed, the needy clothed, the sick healed: after we are dead the poor will be poorer than ever, the needy nakeder than ever, and there will be millions more sick people and cripples and blind.

It is possible not to believe this: however I believe it.

Nor am I particularly excited by a foreign policy like Roosevelt's which aims at getting us the things we would fight for without actually fighting for them: that means that somebody else is fighting for us: and besides it is only a temporary state: we know what happened to Russia who was winning the war without fighting!

Watch Hill

It is Labor Day. I am living in a sort of a shed – I am over a row of stores. This afternoon I leave for Providence.

What gems of recollection or of thought glisten in my holiday mind?

1. I think of Seymour and myself, crawling, dead beat, out of a car and into a fish restaurant on the road out of Saybrook, Conn. just next to the bridge over the Connecticut River into Old Lyme.

2. I think of the comical sea captain in a hut selling clams at Old Lyme. He tried to induce me to take rooms in some place, in Old Lyme shore. We fled like spies – back across the bridge – the border of Ruthenia. At Old Lyme there was no beach. The houses of the village have (some of them) a view of the river across marshes and mud-flats).

3. Outside my room (the wells shake when a door bangs) a woman cries quietly "Nelson?" "Nelson?" and an old man answers "Heh! Heh! Heh!" Immortalized forever by my pen! (I defy the proud full sail of Hemingway making for the all too precious galley of life with a capital L. So, Poetry makes immoral the fleeting aspics of existence.)

4. I think of the abandoned fort down at the end of the sandspit.

5. Four very light colored girls walked under the porches of the wooden shops, last night, laughing because one couple, a boy and one of them, friends had walked away on the beach: the girls had said "Don't get lost." The other had answered "We won't get lost." The girls were laughing.

6. I wonder where is my brother, and in what perplexity, and what confusion.

7. This time tomorrow I should be in the monastery: this will seem like a week ago, this moment in which I write.

8. I think of the big, wooden, out-of-date Olean House hotel, with huge verandas smelling of wood soaked in sea-mist.

9. I still can't remember the name of the place where I went to church. Maybe Misquamicut: not four miles down the beach as the girl said: but anyway $2\frac{1}{2}$. Saint Clare's Chapel.

I read Damon Runyon whom I never, until this, read. He is good because of his style. I laughed more at him today than I did last night. His stories are artificial and stupid and weak. He would be much better without plot: the plot only spoils what he is saying. But in a story like "Blood Pressure," an ending is necessary because a lot of suspense is built up. However the surprise ending is no surprise; it is unimaginative, trite and a let-down. The rest of the story is very funny.

There ought to be some way for Damon Runyon to write without those stupid plots to hang such good stuff on!

Our Lady of the Valley. R.I. September 2

I am ashamed to start out making a speech as if I had pulled myself hand over hand up a ladder into a new experience, and I am ashamed to write as if I were analyzing something new. I am not able to analyze anything of the kind I want to write about and what it is not new and yet it is new, too. I am ashamed to start out talking about writing instead of writing about God. I am also ashamed of the number of times the first person singular clangs like somebody hitting a stone with an iron bar through all these sentences.

To come back into a monastery is to find liberation. First, say that, and then say the other thing: this is a different monastery from Gethsemani. Not totally different, but very different. The difference is important. This place is such that its material beauty and order is less striking than that at Gethsemani. The guest house is less handsome, less spacious, poorer, slightly ramshackle. The guests are poorer people. To love this place, just as a pretty place, is harder than to love the pleasantness of Gethsemani, with the hills and fields all around it.

The first good thing, then, was to find out this didn't make any difference *at all!* The place is less beautiful: but the exterior aspect of the place has nothing much to do with my being here, and is almost totally unimportant.

All this had nothing whatever to do with the immediate liberation of my spirit as soon as I closed the door of my room and was alone in it. I said a prayer in the church. I came back to my room and read the little hours in the Breviary. In what does this sense of liberation consist?

"I am perfectly free – now I can say these psalms, the best things I know how to say, the best way I know how – clearly and quietly. I am free. I can read these words well! There is nothing to stop me! I can do this very important thing well."

The weight of three cities falls off my shoulders, and I am free to pray.

But this freedom, I do not deserve it, I have done nothing to deserve it, no act of mine has caused this freedom to be given me – not my coming here, even. It is a gift of God. I could have crawled here on my face from Los Angeles, and if God had not wished in His great love to give me this freedom to pray to Him with all the words of the prayer making sense, then nothing could gain that grace for me.

Then at High Mass – the same grace, heightened. Once again I see, and how clearly, that this Church is the Court of the Queen of Heaven, and that she is most certainly present in great glory in the midst of it!

Mystery within mystery: in her arms is her Son, the Child Jesus, opening His arms to the world, and in Him and with Him are also the Father and the Holy Ghost; and this Child holds, in the abyss of His Heart, all Being! Everything that ever is, was, or shall be for ever and ever there only truly lives, in the breathless and blinding light of that abyss which I dare not even hope to be able to imagine!!

What am I talking about? O God, I don't know! Have pity on me! I loved You in the Church as though I were going to break; and I could not breathe. It is absolutely impossible to take the sticks and pieces of iron and scraps and strings in my mind and build one intelligible idea about you and your immense Love from such sticks and scraps and strings!

Your great glory is not otherwise present, even in all the churches of the world – even where Your body is consecrated before murderers, let along such holy men as these! But You love us to love You in such a place as this, where men have elected to suffer in penance and sacrifice and holiness, in memory of the terrible agony of Your crucifixion! Your glory is most present where men suffer for Your Love, for we cannot love You and not suffer, Lord: to love You is to suffer.

To love You is to suffer at once as if our soul were trying to tear itself violently out of the prison of our body, and return to You, to the deep and blinding abyss of Your Love! How can this happen and we not suffer to know our imprisonment in our own infinitesimal smallness and unworthiness and selfishness and blindness and incapacity and helplessness?

Lord, you have given this liberty to us that we may suffer for our imprisonment. You will free our minds enough, momentarily, to know that we are prisoners and to lament! What a great freedom is this, nevertheless: it is the highest kind of freedom most of us will ever enjoy on earth – and almost everybody never asks for it, never wants to be liberated.

"Fili, cum tibi desiderium aeternae beatitudinis desuper infundi sentis, et de tabernaculo corporis exire concupiscis, ut claritatem meam sine vicissitudinis umbra contemplari possis: dilata cor tuum, et omni desiderio hanc sanctam inspirationem suscipe.

"Redde amplissimas supernae bonitati gratias quae tecum sic dignanter agit, clementer visitat, ardenter excitat, potenter sublevat ne proprio pondere ad terrena labaris." ["Son, when you feel in yourself a longing for eternal happiness, a longing given to you from above, and you desire to leave the tabernacle of your body, so that you can contemplate my clarity without the shadow of change: open your heart and accept this holy inspiration with deep desire. *Give total thanks for the goodness of God,* who acts so worthily for you, visits you so gently, stirs you so fervently, and bears you up so mightily, *lest you fall to earth with your own weight."*]

De Imitat. Christi. iii. 49.

Then when we are torn out of ourselves with the desire to be able to love God, we must know at once that this love is His gift. We must ardently long to love Him, and this love is sweet but, at exactly the same time we most acutely realize our own inability to love Him and that is bitter and makes us suffer. Almost as soon, too, as we feel this desire to love Him (for that is what this love is – a desire for Love, a love of Love) we instantly feel also our own weight dragging us down and keeping us prisoner. Then it is like being in the middle of a brawl, or a pack of hounds. All kinds of ideas leap on us and drag us back – especially as soon as we begin to *enjoy* the love we feel and not suffer it – (e.g. supposing one says to himself, with a burst of complacency – This is absolutely new. This is better than before. I am making progress – right away he falls back and comes to with a jolt big enough to break his back. It is like being hit with a whip, to hear such temptations to complacency. How many such temptations are there we don't recognize, but fall for them? Oh God, show them all to me, so that I may *suffer* them, not enjoy them in false complacency and die in them!)

The thing to do, the book tells us, is not to get mired right away in our own beastly complacency, which is like a grinning death, but to offer up thanks to God. Then, right away, we suffer more, because we realize how impossible it is to thank Him; the more we love Him, the more will we know our own pride and ingratitude and suffer from it. The more we suffer from the acute awareness of our own nothingness, our own imprisonment, the more we love Him. The greatest saints who loved Him most, suffered, in their love, to the point of being, like Him, crucified. Saint Francis loved Him so, he bore the marks of the crucifixion on his flesh.

How will I ever learn to suffer for God's love? I am aghast at how little meaning this has for me. What am I talking about – my mouth is open, and I go ah – ah – ! I am unintelligible, especially to myself.

I found myself doing, almost involuntarily, a totally inconceivable thing: praying to suffer pain, to be sick.

I am asking the Blessed Mother to pray that I might suffer for God's love. I had no conscious reason for doing this totally irrational thing, according to natural reason and the natural law. Also, I believe my prayers can be answered: why am I not terrified to ask for suffering physical suffering? How can I do such a thing?

O God, what is this gift You have given me now, that I should pray to be killed: for this is most certainly Your gift, nothing coming from me.

But I pray, in real earnest, and in no coy, quixotic, literary sense, to suffer for God's love, to be sick, to be despised, to be killed. I prayed for this in the midst of my weakness and my cowardice. Imagine a hypochondriac suddenly praying to be sick!

Yet one thing is comprehensible: it is better to be sick and in agony than go through the insane circus I went through this weekend, New Haven, Watch Hill, etc. looking for a good place to be happy over a holiday. I do not pray to be happy. I cannot any longer pray to be happy or successful. I pray to be unhappy.

When I found myself praying to suffer, in *spite* of every natural instinct, which at that very moment all rose up in horror and clamored against the prayer, then at once the ardent struggle of desire in me became almost unbearable, and I nearly broke in seven pieces. O my God, you desire us to suffer freely in love of you, because in voluntary suffering is most liberty and least deception: give me grace to enter into your Love through this narrow gate of suffering, I don't know how, I don't yet know what I ask, but let me ask it – although all I know is that I am terrified of the slightest toothache, terrified even of colds, of any pain in the stomach, of any weariness. Who am I to pray such a prayer?

I have also been ashamed to pray for my books and my poems to be published: better to pray that they should not be published, I don't know.

If I pray that my body may be saved from all pain, and that my life be all ease, prayer may or may not be answered, according to God's will. If I pray that my body may suffer sickness and torture and even be killed for God's love, my prayer may or may not be answered: but whether it is or not, it is by making such prayers that men besiege God into giving them strength to become Saints.

That I cannot conceive myself really praying such a prayer means I cannot conceive myself becoming a Saint. But I have to conceive that: or anyway I have to begin trying to be holy. O God, teach me how!

This time I have no perplexities about a vocation to be a Trappist – so far! I cannot be a priest.

Nor is this any time to begin worrying about going back to the Baroness' at once, instead of back to my job. This is not the time to worry about anything, but to pray.

September 3. Our Lady of the Valley

Rather than pray that my books and poems be published, perhaps I should pray that they should *not* be published. Why is that absurd? It is. Because it means I forget that whatever writing I do is done by God's grace and only through Him: but it is a talent; He has given it to me for Himself, for use, for Him. But writing is useless unless it is read: I could never pray that my writings should never be read, or should not be read. All right. After that, if they are read without being published? What do I know? But I ask that I write in humility, knowing that I am nothing, that all my desire to write comes from God's grace, and what is good in it is from Him and what is weak and poor comes from my own weakness and poverty.

Once I have written what I have written, what have I to ask, what is there left, except that the writings be disposed of according to God's will. I see no reason why my first two novels should ever be published – they are not good, they give God no glory. As for the *Journal of My Escape from the Nazis* – how do I know it is worth being distributed around for everybody to read?

(Whether it is better or worse than a lot of other books now being published is totally irrelevant, when the question is looked at from this aspect.)

But what should I pray for? – only to do God's will. To suffer. I can also suffer as a writer: *"Quod alii dicunt, audietur: quod tu dicis, pro nihilo computabitur . . .* ["What others say, will be heard; what you say, will be considered worthless."]

> *"Erunt alii magni in ore hominum: de te autem tacebitur. Aliis hoc vel illud committetur, tu autem ad nihil utilis judicaberis."* ["Others will be greatly praised in the world's view; but they will be silent about you. This or that task will be given to others, but you will be considered worthless."]
>
> *"Propter hoc natura quandoque contristabitur: et magnum, si silens portaveris."* ["Because of this, your nature will be saddened, and this will all be difficult for you if you bear it in silence."]
>
> De Imitat. Christi. iii. 49.

There is nothing wrong with praying to be, as a writer, as everything, obscure, unknown.

There is everything wrong with praying to be a bad writer.

I would pray to be the best writer of a certain time and never to know it, and to be also the most obscure. Saint Therese probably never even considered herself a writer. Bloy was one of the best writers in a time when there were some good writers: and also the most despised, one of the most obscure: *"L'Invendable."*

But I am not here to think about being a writer: except I am here to try to learn humility and how to do God's will and serve Him the best way I can, and writing has something to do with all these things, accidentally, because it happens that I like to write, and try to know how.

> *"Haec est enim gratia ad amicum tuum, pati et tribulari in mundo pro amore tuo, quotiescumque et a quocumque et quomodocumque id permiseris fieri."*

["This is your grace to your friend, to suffer and have trouble in the world for your love, whenever, and from whomever, and however you may permit it to happen."]

De Imitat. Christi. iii. 50.

"Bonum mihi quia humiliasti me . . . "

["It is good for me that you have humbled me . . ."]

Why should we pray for tribulation? In order to rejoice in God, because in God is our only true joy, and we see Him clearly and best when we suffer tribulation for His love. Therefore we pray to suffer not because we love suffering but because we love joy and peace: any joy that cannot survive suffering and tribulation of the flesh is inconstant and a deception. But the joy of God's love overcomes and withstands all things, and we come at it through suffering, not because we love tribulation but because we love peace.

"Laetatur in te servus tuus, non in se, nec aliquo alio, quia tu solus laetitia vera, tu spes mea et corona mea, tu gaudium meum et honor meus, Domine." ["Let your servant rejoice in you, not in myself or in anything else, for you alone are true happiness, you alone are my hope and my crown, you alone are my joy and my honor, Lord."]

De Imitat. Christi. iii. 50.

"Tu scis, quid expedit ad profectum meum, et quantum deservit tribulatio ad rubiginem vitiorum purgandam." ["You know what is beneficial to me, and how much the experience of suffering helps to remove the rest of vice from me."]

De Imitat. – ibid.

"Nam quantum unusquisque est in oculis tuis, tantum est et non amplius, ait humilis sanctus Franciscus." ["For whatever a person is in your sight, he is only that, and no more, says humble Saint Francis."]

What we are – our identity – is only truly known to God – not to ourselves, not to other men.

The greatest terror of the particular judgment is that, the moment after our death we instantly appear before the face of God and learn our own identity – truly; we finally see ourselves as we really are!

The measure of our identity, of our being (the two are the same) is the amount of our love for God. The more we love earthly things, reputation, importance, pleasures, ease, and success, the less we love God. Our identity is dissipated among things that have no value, and we are drowned and *die* in trying to live in the material things we would like to possess, or in the projects we would like to complete to objectify the work of our own wills. Then, when we come to die, we find we have squandered all our love (that is, our being) on things of nothingness, and that we are nothing, we are death. But then most of all in the terrifying light of pure Being and perfect love, we see the hatefulness of nothingness, of death. But if we have loved Him, and lost ourselves in Him, we find ourselves in Him, and live forever in joy.

But tribulation detaches us from the things of nothingness in which we spend ourselves and die. Therefore tribulation gives us life, and we love it, not out of love for death, but love for life.

Let me then withdraw all my love from scattered, vain things – the desire to be read and praised as a writer, or to be a successful teacher, praised by my students, or to live in ease in some beautiful place – and place it all in Thee, where it will take root and live, instead of being spent in barrenness.

My life is measured by my love of God, and that in turn is measured by my love for the least of His children: and that love is not an abstract benevolence: it must mean sharing their tribulation.

September 4. Our Lady of the Valley

One thing seems to be clear: that, when I was at Gethsemani, I nearly ruined my retreat with wondering whether or not it was possible I could ever have a vocation to be a Trappist – and, if so, if I would be able to stand the discipline all my life.

To begin with, when you have a vocation: that question doesn't make sense. You will be given strength to stand *anything* by the Holy Ghost and you have perfect hope in this. Doubts and misgivings are irrelevant and, in fact, vicious, because this is a situation out of reach of natural reason. Is it naturally reasonable to deny yourself, take up a Cross and follow Christ? No, it takes grace and faith, supernatural help.

Anyway, I took to arguing with myself about whether or not I had a Trappist vocation (at Gethsemani) – (irrespective of all impediments) and as a result I was much more occupied with this irrelevant question than with anything else. Besides, wearing myself on this futile argument, I soon got very tired of the getting up at 1:30, etc. By Good Friday I was getting rather disgusted, physically, and so, as an act of rebellion, went for a walk! All the time telling myself some absurd thing about the necessity to love God's creatures – nature etc. The only answer to that is: there is nothing in the Trappist discipline to prevent you loving nature the way I meant it then and do now: loving it in God's creation, and a sign of His goodness and Love.

But the whole thing was a silly, and scrupulous self-deception, only fortunately it only occupied me when there were no offices or prayers, or when I got tired of trying to read and meditate. So the retreat wasn't ruined altogether!

This morning, after Communion – the dawn was as clear as glass and the whole white earth praised the Immaculate Mother of God. I thought of her suddenly, in the silence and the light without stain. All created things are a sign of Love and goodness; the most perfect created love is the pure, stainless humility of Our Blessed Mother.

Her love of God, her humility, her stainless conception, her poverty, all these are the same thing. She was perfect in poverty because she was perfect in love: perfect in humility because perfect in love.

All things that are, are good, just because they have being. Their being is a gift, and it is therefore a sign of love: God so loves all things that He creates them, and so loves us He gives us being, and so loves us that though in our murderous ingratitude we murder our loving being with our pride, then He recreates us, making His own Son flesh to dwell among us.

I pray over and over – make me love You, Lord, and Mary, our Mother: make me love and love. I am no longer scared to say it over and over. And how can I love You? Not only by kneeling and saying over and over I love You, for the goodness of all things and thank You for the being of all things, and especially of myself: but by praying to be able to thank You more humbly and with more love. Why should I pray for love, but only in order to thank You more lovingly for all Your sweet creation. Because if I pray for love to *have it* and *enjoy it*, I lose it at once. Only if I ask for enough love to give back to You (because in my own complete poverty I have nothing I can give) is the prayer answered, full of grace, so that I want nothing more, but only to stay there praying for more love to give back.

There is nothing else but this to live for: to pray for love to give to Him, to receive it, and give it back to Him praying for more love to give Him again.

And as we receive more love, all we ask is that it finally consume us altogether so that we are totally offered up in sacrifice to God.

Therefore if I love Him, I will at once be poor.

If I love Him, I will become humble – the more I love Him, the more I will want to be both – and now that I realize how I am neither poor nor humble, how can I give him any thanks except in tears?

Then I will want to kiss His feet and wash them with my tears. How, Lord? By washing with my tears the feet of the least of His children after myself, who am the very least: for it is absolutely impossible to understand why He should give me any grace at all, in my pride, selfishness, weakness, envy, triviality, pettyness, stupidity, coarseness, impurity, and repulsive vanity: for all I do is devour Him like a hog, and wait for His graces as though they were some rather refined kind of worldly pleasure. But when it comes time to suffer the least thing for Him, or do the least thing for Him, even give Him thanks, I only do it half-willing, or as an afterthought, but mostly not at all.

When God gives us His graces so that we are aware of them, it is good to remember that they will presently be replaced by tribulations alone, and suffering without consolation.

To pray for suffering is not to pray for total suffering without consolation, and yet He sends us that, too, and we must accept it patiently, in love of Him. And then what do we do?

> *"Tunc expedit tibi ad humilia et exteriora opera confugere, et in bonis actibus te recreare: adventum meum et supernam visitationem firma confidentia expectare, exilium tuum et ariditatem mentis patienter sufferare, donec iterum a me visiteris, et ab omnibus anxietatibus libereris . . . Expandam coram te prata scripturarum: ut dilatato corde currere incipias viam mandatorum meorum."* ["Then it is good for you to resort to humbling, external labors, and to perform good works: expect my coming and my heavenly appearance with a firm confidence. Endure your exile and the dryness of your soul patiently, until you are visited by me once again, and you are delivered from all anxieties. . . . I will lay open before you the meadow of the Scriptures: that with a joyful heart you can begin to run in the way of my commandments."]
>
> *De Imit. Christi.* III. 51.

(Incidentally tribulations and physical suffering are by no means the same thing.)

I am disgusted to read myself writing like an ascetic when I have never suffered anything or denied myself anything. Lord, forgive me! It is because I want to belong to you entirely, and I *believe* that I can best belong to You in suffering – and also tribulation. Before I ask You to send them to me, it is true, (I am ashamed) I should go seek voluntarily what I can do by my own choice: how can I be poor? (One answer to that is easy: give up everything and go to Harlem. But before that I have another answer to try.)

First, be totally, voluntarily, poor!

(Also, may God give me a better way of writing about this sort of thing. What I have written is cheap and sloppy and, compared with what I want to say, phony.) Remember all these things.

"Domine, non sum dignus consolatione tua, nec aliqua spirituali visitatione: et ideo juste mecum agis, quando me inopem et desolatum relinguis." ["Lord, I am not worthy of your consolation, or any spiritual visitation, and therefore you act justly to me whenever you leave me needy and desolate."]

To love God so much that you are sad to be anywhere but in a church, or on your knees, or, at least, quiet.

All day the thought of Him, or of the Blessed Virgin, comes to you in the midst of the things you are doing, and flies like an arrow through you!

Where is it gone? Have I lost it already by talking about it?

If the thought of God's goodness ceases to flash through us unexpectedly from time to time, then, in the same way, can still come the thought of our own unworthiness of His gifts, as fast and as piercing, but, this time, bitter. It is another aspect of the same thing.

My God, Your goodness (that is, Your Love) is infinite. How can I understand it, or talk about it without filling myself with horror and shame, as if everything I said about You were as inadequate as to be almost a blasphemy? I want to tear this page out and throw it away.

Let me be obscure and despised, only because that is all I am worthy of: and not because I am really good and smart and so on, and merely want to be despised as a kind of exercise in humility made easy by other people! I think of myself as a good writer, and look at this stuff!

"Si enim ad instar maris lacrymas fundere possem, adhuc consolatione tua dignus non essem. Unde nihil dignus sum, quam flagellari et puniri, quia graviter et saepe te offendi et in multis valde deliqui. . . . Sed, tu clemens et misericors Deus, qui non vis perire opera tua, ad ostendendum divitias bonitatis tuae in vasa misericordiae, etiam praeter omne proprium merituum dignaris consolari servum tuum supra humanum modum." ["For although I might be able to pour out tears like the ocean, I would still not be worthy to have your consolation. I am only worthy to be beaten and punished, for I have often seriously offended you, and sinned greatly in many ways. . . . But you, clement and merciful God, who do not desire to destroy what you have made, to show the richness of your merciful goodness, you even deign to console your servant, beyond anything I deserve, and beyond the limits of my human condition."]

De Imit. Christi. III. 52.

September 5. Our Lady of the Valley

I just finished reading Bloy's *Dans le Tenebres.* One of the things I liked best about it was his wife's preface.

His ideas about the last war: that it wasn't really a war but something infinitely more revolting than a war. His ideas about [Henri] Barbusse's *Feu* are smart in a way we are just beginning to find out.

He says Barbusse's emphasis on the horribleness of war, just isolated from everything else, is crazy. "War is totally horrible, so let's not fight," and his solution that "The principle of equality will kill war forever" is terribly dangerous.

To begin with, the best reason for loving peace is not that war is horrible. A nation that loves peace because war is degrading, disgusting, unpleasant, brutalizing, filthy, etc. will get in plenty of trouble. No matter how horrible anything is there has to be a better reason, than its horribleness, for our hating it.

But since 1917 all nations have hated war (all men in these nations, that is) because of the filth of trenches, the horrors of mutilation, the pain and agony of wounds, the whole physically disgusting business of warfare. We have been hating war because it is horrible. That is not a good enough reason. To hate war because of its horrors is no guarantee that we are never going to fight, or that we understand what war is about, or that we have a moral attitude about war.

Another favorite reason for not going to war was – it is not profitable! What does it get you? That, too, is a wrong reason for hating war. When I say a "wrong reason" I mean it is neither a rational nor a moral reason for hating war. Fighting is a question involving morals, and questions of the material profitableness of war have no bearing on its morality.

Also, because war is horrible, and because it is "unprofitable" (is it? – probably is – certainly is for *a capitalist economy as a whole*) is not only no reason for not going to one war but is certainly no reason for saying all war is immoral. Bloy says this, too.

Barbusse was bad enough: [Archibald] MacLeish is worse. He reproaches himself and his generation for weakening the whole country with their attitude – describing the horrors of war, saying "Never again," etc. He is quite right: that attitude has made all the youth of the country detest war, and now we are going to war again, everybody is going in in a very equivocal and dangerous frame of mind, hating war and fearing its horrors and skeptical of its profitableness.

But you get the impression that now MacLeish is only trying to reverse his own position and say that war isn't really so horrible if you can stomach it, and that it *is*, in a way, profitable under certain circumstances.

A. MacLeish used to say:

"War is horrible, degrading, filthy; look at the mutilated men, the degeneration of men into beasts in the trenches, all this is totally disgusting, and it must, therefore, never happen again: for, since war is so horrible as to be almost unbearable, it is a crime. This crime must not be repeated. Moreover: there might be some sense in fighting if there were something to be gained by it: but we have gained nothing by it, it is totally unprofitable. We are only kidding ourselves if we think war will gain us anything but more misery."

Now he says, which is even more foolish (or I imagine he says, because I am not quite sure):

"We have committed a great sin in painting war in such horrible colors, because, as a result of this, the young men hate and fear war and have no stomach left for fighting. And now is the time to fight! And if it is the time to fight, that means we have something to gain by fighting, and will lose by not fighting, contrary to what I said before!"

What has happened to MacLeish is merely that he has finally realized war would not be abolished by common consent of men who had had enough of its horrors (which was the Barbusse, Remarque, idea) and yet enough men fear its horrors so that they won't fight when they are attacked by those more ruthless than themselves.

But war is still horrible, and if it is true to say so, then there is no sense in trying to pretend it *isn't* so. Also war is no more *profitable* now than it was then. It will certainly wreck our particular culture. It might be worth while, under such circumstances, to fight anyway. But AM does not make that clear. He only says that he was wrong: and whereas he said it was a lie war could save democracy, now it is true war can save democracy.

It seems to me, for those who *want to* go to war, that their position would sound a lot better if it went like this: War is terrible, but its horrors must be endured if the war is the only way to finally establish peace for a long while: a peace in which certain human values and spiritual values will be respected, and not a fake peace like the one between 1917–1939 (during which everybody was grabbing what he could get for himself until this real anarchy finally became apparent in a general collapse of the whole economic system). If Hitler wins, there will be peace, yes, but intolerable oppression of everybody except the Germans, and actually everybody except the Nazis, the Church will probably be wiped out in parts, if not all, of Europe, etc. Democracy will probably cease to exist even if we win, but it is worth losing all our comforts and even the shadow of our economic security and many of our liberties, if we can only destroy Nazism for good. And there is no chance of any real peace until Nazism is destroyed for good.

If this is true, then war is justifiable – and that war is bound to be one in which we will practically be destroyed ourselves but there may be something for the people who are left. . . .

However, this is merely a reverse of the Nazi argument, which says "unless England and the capitalistic democracies are wiped out *there can be no peace*. . . ."

How true is it that, if Germany were wiped out, there would be peace and justice on earth, with guys like Roosevelt running the world? It isn't that he's ill-willed, just incapable – and what capitalists would be cashing in on everything behind him: how real a peace would it be, and how just?

But anyway, let them not say Democracy would be saved, or would profit: let them say, it means the ruin of democracy on *the chance* that Hitler would be destroyed and on *the chance* that some new, just order would grow up, somehow, somewhere. Then most people would merely answer that they weren't interested in taking that chance. Whether they should be or not, I can't be certain.

I myself am not taking that chance until somebody comes out and says what kind of order he is prepared to enforce if he wins the war. Roosevelt has given no satisfactory answer, not satisfactory to me: because a repetition of 1921–29 would be impossible, as well as totally vile. Roosevelt merely points to some vague continuation of what we've got now, and what England has now. What we've got now could stand a lot of cleaning up: what England's got now would stand a total, fundamental change! As a matter of fact, neither will survive.

September 6, 1941. Our Lady of the Valley

Holy Father Saint Francis

I believe that, in your immense and inexpressible love of Jesus Christ our Lord, you can look into my dumb, crooked soul and see what is there before I can say it in the selection of cheap, vulgar, stupid words presently about to flow from my inexpensive fountain pen. And because of the immensity of your burning and immaculate and humble love of Jesus My God, I know you will pray to him for me that I may be granted whatever I pray that may bring me to Him in love and humility.

Therefore I pray you, Holy Father Saint Francis, first that I may be filled with tears and with the love of God, continually, not in order that I may delight in these things and be filled always with nothing but consolation, but in order that they may keep me silent from pride, and fill me with strength and desire to abandon the world altogether, even though I remain in the midst of it.

And when I am not filled with the strength of consolation then, even more, do I need your prayers Holy Father: because then the resolutions I made when I was full of love, look as if they were about to be wrecked on my rocks of pride and fleshly self-love.

When I pray for suffering – and then get a cold, the world's most ridiculous disease; sneezing in church; running nose; sweat; no sense of devotion; very unpicturesque: what is the result? I am mad and impatient – and mad at myself for being impatient. But if I am mad at myself for being impatient it is a great new flourishing exercise of my pride and nothing else.

So then I go back to bed for a long nap after dinner, missing None, and I am mad at myself for doing that. Going to bed or not going to bed makes little difference to the love of God. But pride makes a lot of difference: and I am mad at myself because of pride. – It would have been good if I hadn't gone to bed. I might still have the cold, which is gone. It doesn't matter. But I got mad and impatient, and that was a gross imperfection because it was nothing but pride.

Holy Father, take away, by your prayers, this pride; but for such pride, I would have something less absurd to write here. Because I am so aware of the absurdity is only a sign of more pride.

But for this pride, also, I wouldn't be so self-conscious about language to express what I feel: but that is only part of it. I wish I could write it better out of respect for God, Who gave me these small and very usual and familiar and unstartling and generous graces.

But I am also thinking it would be better to write about it in good words, not cheap words, so that the reader may (if it is ever read) respect me, *my* experience (as opposed to *the* experience but it isn't *my* experience really, and if *I* claim respect for it, I lose all the good it brought me, of love and devotion to My Lord.)

Yet, Holy Father, pray that I may write simply and straight anything I ever have to write, that no dishonor come to God through my writing rubbish about Him.

But if I am humble, I will write better, just by being humble. By being humble, I will write what is true, simply – and the simple truth is never rubbish and never scandalous – except to people in peculiar perplexities of pride themselves.

Holy Father Saint Francis pray for me: for you will never refuse to hear prayers that will help me to come to Our Lord. Then pray for me that I may give as much as I can to the poor. And that soon I may be able to go hungry so that someone else may eat. And that soon I may be able to suffer so that someone else may not suffer. And that I may laugh and sing when I am despised for God's love, and that I may dance and play when I am reviled for God's love, and called a mad man, and a fool and a crook.

Pray for me to be poor, meek; to hunger and thirst for justice, and be merciful; to be a peacemaker, clean of heart, to be reviled, to be persecuted for God's sake.

Pray for me, Holy Father Saint Francis, to do all these things although I have never gone hungry except for silly reasons (couldn't get my claws on the icebox) and never suffered except for silly reasons (hangovers; blisters from walking around all night in World's Fairs).

Pray for me, Holy Father Saint Francis, in all things to sing to God very humbly and childishly and sweetly, and not to be sore at myself when, instead of heroic temptations I get nothing but silly and absurd and insulting and stupid temptations: who do I think I am? The others will come soon enough!

Only pray for me, my Father Saint Francis, to give up everything for My Lord, to be the least of His children and the most insignificant of the poor for love only, and that in all things I may have grace to pray meekly and patiently and happily, and not in the confusion of pride, and the scruples pride puts in our heads and the fears pride freezes us with. Pray for me for enough humility to always pray for humility, poverty, and tears.

Through the merciful intercession of Christ Our Lord Who reigns eternally with the Father and the Holy Spirit, one God, the life and joy and bliss of all things and only object of all love! Amen.

September 14, 1941. Saint Bonaventure

I am inarticulate in the presence of the sorrows of the Mother of God – whose feast (The Seven Dolours) is tomorrow. Her sorrows surpassed all the pains of martyrs, and she is the Queen of Martyrs.

Am I to stand and look at the sorrows of Mary, Mother of God, as though at some spectacle? I sit as still and dumb as if my mind were a movie: and I am afraid, because those sorrows are not only for a spectacle. "Come and see if there is any sorrow like to mine!" That means: "taste, with me, of my sorrow, which is the bitterest of all sorrows. If you can look at my tears without weeping yourselves, or if you look at my grief and then tears come as a kind of a luxury into your own eyes, it is that, also, that adds to my sorrow, the very moment you look at me with no more than such selfishness!"

"Child! How can you taste my sorrow? How can you know what sharp swords of Dolour [Sorrow] have pierced my heart if you only weep because you see me weeping, and no more?

"Have you forgotten, O my lost children, why I wept and with what anguish, when my Son died on Calvary?

"Have you forgotten that, I, poor and immaculate, could taste no bitterness but the bitterness of your sins, for I myself was without sin!

"Have you forgotten the words of my Son to those women of Jerusalem who followed Him in wailing on the road to Calvary: not to weep for Him but for *themselves* – for their own sins!"

How can I speak, I am nothingness and dust. My brutality and the brutality of the whole world has turned to swords of Dolour, which *had to* pierce Her heart!

How can I express the huge, bestial ravening chaos of the world around me except by saying it is sick for judgment, sick for the devouring fire and whirlwind.

Have done with us, Lord, finish us, we are crying out to be destroyed, we are yearning for the Last Judgment! Yet who would ever dare to pray for such a thing? To do so would only mean whoever spoke the prayer didn't realize what he was talking about, was talking lightly and abstractly of an unimaginable terror: for who can stand up and *ask* Almighty God to judge him!

For if He judge us, who shall survive His judgment?

She prays, from moment to moment, to her Son to spare us. What does that prayer mean: what does it mean that He spares us? It means that He continues sweating blood in the agony in the Garden, and that the three hours on the Cross are stretched out into an eternity –

And her own sufferings on Calvary, with Dolours fast and dazzling as lightning passing from His Sacred Heart to Hers, these sufferings also stretch out and become eternal.

When she prays Him to spare us, She prays for the continuance of His agony and Her agony: and the longer He spares us, the more pain we heap upon Him and His Mother hurling into their faces our mountains of sins, getting worse and worse and worse!

Even what Jesus suffered on the Cross for me alone would be unbearable agony for me – even what His Mother suffered on Calvary because of me, I could not bear – maybe I would not even be asked to bear such pains in hell – how could I? Yet every man's sins caused Christ _infinite_ suffering – every single sin caused Him _infinite_ suffering, so great only God could bear it!

Yet what can I do but ask to have back a little of this suffering, so that I may weep with the Blessed Mother! Give me back, Lord, a little of what You have suffered for my sins: let me see a little of their horror, and of the horror of what I have desired on earth as it all appeared to Thee. Then I can truly share our Blessed Mother's sorrows, and not merely _look at_ them and snivel a little like a man in a movie.

O Mary, my Mother, Thy loving heart is a terrifying abyss of loves and sorrows, because, itself immaculate, it was capable of perfect suffering at the horribleness of my sins and the sins of the whole world! Mercifully let me share a little of thy sorrow, and, although it may be a bitterness more than bearable, pray I may have love enough to bear it, and I ask for no more than this grace to bear it – no more! But that is everything! If I have this, I have God's love, and that is the only joy, the only everlasting bliss that no tribulation can overcome!

September 18, 1941

Leon Bloy's Vocation (in a letter – _Mon Journal_, p. 71.)

> "_Pourquoi ne supposeriez-vous pas que ma vocation est peut-être unique? Longtemps avant d'avoir écrit une seule ligne, j'avais compris que le sacrifice de tout bonheur terrestre m'était demandé et j'avais accompli ce sacrifice. Je recommande a votre attention les pages du_ Désèspere, _de 179 à 184. Ce sont, je crois, les plus centrales de ce livre, celles qui expliquent tout...._" ["Why don't you think that my vocation is at all unique? Long before I wrote even one line, I knew that I was required to sacrifice all earthly happiness, and I fulfilled that sacrifice. I bring to your attention the pages of _Désèspere_, 179–184. These are, I believe, the most important pages of the book, the ones that explain everything...."]

> "_Vous me jugez humainement sans prendre garde que je suis précisément hors de tous les points de vue humains et que c'est là toute ma force, mon unique force. La vérité bien nette et qui éclate dans tous mes livres, c'est que je n'écris que pour Dieu._" ["You judge me from a human point of view, without taking into consideration that I am precisely outside the human point of view, and in that consists all my strength, my unique strength. The naked truth, which resounds in all my books, is that _I only write for God._"]

> " ... _Eh bien, si le don d'écrire m'a été accordé, n'est-il pas infiniment plausible de conjecturer que j'ai surtout la mission d'agir sur les âmes?_" ["And so, if I have a writer's talent, isn't it quite reasonable to suppose that I have a primary mission to work for souls?"]

September 26, 1941

In spite of a stupid, pompous, inanity stuck in the front of the Phoenix Library Edition of [Coventry] Patmore's *Poems*, I have again made some kind of effort to read him but I guess it's no use. The quotation which should have kept me out of the book in the first place is:

"I have respected posterity; and should there be a posterity which care for letters, I dare to hope that it will respect me!"

It is enough to make you want to throw the book on the floor and stamp on it. I give up wondering what he could possibly mean by "I have respected posterity." But if he does mean anything by it at all, as for instance "I have worried a lot about whether or not I would be remembered after I died," then he is confessing himself to be a man with very trivial concerns. Sure, everybody is likely to wonder about the same thing: but nobody but a fool would take the thought of fame seriously in such a naive and simple sense as this poor old Patmore does. Shakespeare thought about his poems being read after his death, too, but in a vastly different and more complex way: he was terribly perplexed by the problem of whether or not he was immortal (or seems to be, in the sonnets, Hamlet, etc.) and the sonnets say "at least my poems will last a long time, even if I myself die," which is a totally different statement from the one old Patmore makes, because in Shakespeare's statements is implied all the terrific seriousness of the whole problem of the immortality of the soul. Here this big simple self-satisfied Victorian with no anguish and no problems implied in almost anything he says, gets off this completely absurd, clumsy and meaningless remark that has nothing to recommend it but an inflated rhetorical tone which only makes it all the sillier.

Patmore was a Catholic. He believed in the immortality of the soul. Then *that* was all settled! All he had to worry about now was whether also his poems would be read on earth while he, Patmore, sat grinning in heaven with folded hands and his eyes, probably, shut, so as better to enjoy the delicious music and the gorgeous aroma of all the incense.

Unfortunately the true sign of a Christian is not complacency about the fact that he will someday go to heaven. On the contrary the saints are more often than not tormented with problems that only begin to exist when you have had your complacency knocked out from under your feet! Whether Patmore ever had any spiritual tribulations to deal with in his life. I do not even try to know. It is written "Judge not and ye be not judged," and I am not judging Patmore, only his poetry, which is sentimental, not religious.

And his poetry is complacent, mediocre, sensuous, vague; it is, especially, vague. No vaguer than some of his contemporaries' work, perhaps. But that is no merit – to be less vague than Swinburne.

I like the way he writes a poem on *Saint Valentine's Day* and treats it as the hearts-and-flowers feast and nothing else. Just the feast for him! The feast that has nothing to do with the saint! You can't even call it a pagan feast, because "pagan" suggests some life: it is just a cheap, sentimental, phony feast of middle class adolescents.

> "O, Baby Spring
> That flutter'st sudden neath the breath of Earth"

is at the same time ambiguous, confused, vague and in vile taste. One interesting line

> "The children, noisy in the setting ray"

crumbles like the apples of Sodom as soon as you look at it for its sense, which is about as meager and abstract as the average line of Thomson who learned to substitute circumlocution for metaphor, and that's all this heavy monster seems to do, too.

September 27, 1941

There was just now some sharp discussion in the hall about whether or not Daylight Saving Time ends tonight. It does. That's good. All of a sudden it is 9:30 not 10:30 and so I take out this fat book, no less tired than ten minutes ago – with absolutely nothing to write –

Except that I feel very sick from having read a short story I wrote last January. A short story like that is so dull it is almost a mortal sin. I believe that, in hell, such stories are read aloud to the damned, like the afternoon papers are read to the workers in the Havana cigar factories.

This was not only dull: it had complexities, and the complexities were working, but the wrong way: tightening up the story when there was nothing in it to tighten. Each new twist ground some more dust out of the empty frame until the whole thing disappeared like yellow dried-out paper of cheap Victorian books – crumbles and flies away in flakes. Some horror!

Temptation is leave it there as a humiliation and lesson.

Yeah? It was hard to rip out of the binders – 20 pages!

It was a pretty day; and a pretty evening, with a clear half moon – and the hills not misty yet. I keep seeing the pastures as they were last winter. But when I look towards Martiny's Rocks I am filled with awe, thinking of the earthly paradise I found under the tree last Sunday – a view over a road and farms and woods, the road leading back to a wild place, perhaps a wooded plateau, and I don't know what miles of woods, or what uninhabited valley full of oil wells.

The grass like green silk under the tree: and the sun and the silence and the wind moving in the branches and the heat pouring on the landscape: and I sit under the tree full of all this, not able to say anything to myself about it, because it was all incomprehensible as soon as I tried to describe it as a possessed experience. An individual material reality is unintelligible: what I was trying to describe was not an experience, it was nothing comprehensible, the matter of an experience, raw matter. That you can describe so as to seem to describe it, but you are really describing another thing, an experience – not this moment itself, but your experience in it.

The trick is to order your experience so that it doesn't get possessive, but is lost in the object, instead of trying to contain its object. That way it *does*, in fact, contain the object: but only by not trying.

It is the feast of Saints Cosmas and Damian, and I remember their church in Rome, with the mosaic of Christ standing among red clouds, small, firm clouds in a mackerel bank on a blue ground, receiving the two saints into heaven.

This was done when the Goths were at the gates of Rome and Saint Gregory the Great saw the avenging angel on the top of Hadrian's Tomb, putting the sword back into the scabbard . . .

I shall never cease to wonder at the love I suddenly got for these mosaics: it was certainly God's grace, and I cannot know in this life how much that love meant: but it may have meant my whole life, through the prayers of these Saints and others of the earliest times of the Church, who won by their prayers that I should love their churches, and by their more prayers that I myself should also pray and read the Bible – and after that, no matter where I went and what I came to for five years after, they still prayed until I came dragging back again, much more beaten and about ready to be dead!

They were physicians, and they were martyrs, and, I think, Arabs. The mosaic showed Christ in Glory, receiving them – and not smiling: My True God, teach us to see Thee, in Thy true glory and power and strength – teach us (for our own use of the words power and glory suggest bad opera, or a racket of machines, or something cheap and drunk:), cauterize our sore intellects and scabby imaginations, and let us see straight towards Thee – in Faith and Fear and Wisdom, not straining our eyes at the confusion of the hopeless imagery we make up to deaden our hunger for Thy Love and Justice. We cannot see Thee with eyes at all, yet in those days, the mosaics were there to teach us the Faith and Fear with which to begin to see Thee, with the inward eye of your intellect, and love.

September 28. Sunday. Saint Bonaventure

I had to go and borrow the news section of the New York and Buffalo papers from some of the other faculty members and read them. Better if I had not. Why are the Sunday papers always ten times more repulsive, even, than the ordinary week-day issues?

In this Sunday's I came across a story about the "world's most humane" poison gas. It had been invented in the last war, and even manufactured in a small quantity, but came too late to be used. It is still available for "defense only," naturally. Was ever any poison gas used except for defense? Cannibals eat human flesh in self-defense, don't they? They have to have meat in their diet, don't they? Self-preservation is the first law of nature, isn't it? Well?

Anyway, this is a very humane gas – it kills much more quickly and effectively than any other. It has a low freezing point and can be used (but for defense only, of course,) in the Arctic. Best of all, it is extraordinarily hard to disperse: it remains in corners and hollows _for days_, making sure of the last dog, cat, woman, child, grandfather, cripple, every neutral bird and beast, every living thing, or breathing thing: probably blasts the plants, too, in its terrifically efficient humaneness.

But the most shocking part of the whole story was that this gas was developed in the labs of _Catholic University._

I am ashamed to get sore at such a dumb thing as a newspaper story about poison gas. Why is poison gas the thing people get most exercised about? It is dramatically dirty, and an extremely indiscriminate weapon, as universal as pestilence, only far nastier.

Why is it that in war you can bear use of a violent weapon, a bomb, even a flame thrower, but the mind is revolted by this stealthy, filthy stuff? Is there a distinction?

Sometimes it gets easy to see the position of complete, uncompromising pacifists – as long as it is only an abstract question. (In the concrete, supposing there were pacifists in Czechoslovakia who preferred to let the Germans take over without a fight – these hypothetical pacifists are now in the German army, maybe, instead of the Czechoslovakian. A democracy might allow you to be an uncompromising pacifist, but not a dictatorship – of course if it is something you will die for, perhaps you get the opportunity – or else, perhaps, you are just shoved in the army and left to figure out how you got there!)

If you justify wars of defense; if you justify wars that are supposed to bring "peace as quickly and effectively as possible," then you have to accept the most drastic and beastly and horrible and disgusting and cruel weapons and tactics imaginable, because they are all "necessary for defense."

Obviously you have to *win* – there is no point in defending yourself if you just mean to put up a good losing fight for no purpose. You always hope to win, or at least damage the enemy so much he can't hurt you if he wins. But, you can't do this without bombs, total-war . . . everything goes: you defend yourself by hitting the enemy the most dangerous and terrifying kind of blows you can conceive.

But if that is what war is, and if wiping out civilian populations becomes "justifiable," it gives you pause, when you come to ask if, when the whole thing is carried this far, it isn't morally intolerable, and shouldn't any clean conscience rather die than participate in it . . . ?

I don't know how to argue any of this yet, without getting into crazy and artificial questions, and more pure fantasy than I would care to stomach, when there is so much of it everywhere else at the same time!

If you are defending yourself against an enemy who exterminates *in lethal chambers* its own citizens when someone decides they are "unfit," "weak" elements in society, is it charitable to refuse to fight them, or to have anything to do with an army fighting them?

Is it loving your neighbor to acquiesce in a bunch of completely unprincipled murderers getting control of the world? Supposing you don't know they are "completely unprincipled murderers" – which probably the army officers, etc. are not, even if they are impossible brutes – even then, you know it is part of their policy, even at home, to kill "in a sanitary and humane fashion" people who are sick or nervous; or, in just an ordinary brutal slugging, someone with the wrong kind of ideas.

Do I know anything this clear about the war?

When the issues become so clear, of course, you have to run to arms. They never really are that clear at all: but it is true the Germans are putting the whole world in danger of brutal and irresponsible and horrible and maniac policies of government, including slavery and the extermination of religions (ultimately) and a certain amount of "hygienic" killing of sick or nervous people.

The question is: after we have defeated them in a total war in which every kind of barbaric and immoral seeming weapon has been used, will any situation be possible in which the political life isn't barbaric and evil and tyrannic and cruel?

We go off to war on the assumption that if we win, we will have preserved a situation we now know, and live in, which has its faults, but its injustices are largely accidental; whereas we are defending ourselves, and staving off a situation in which the injustices are not only more acute and more horrible, but also *deliberate*, and a matter of policy.

We are inhuman in our stupidity, but the Germans are more often inhuman as the result of deliberate plans: they claim to know what they are doing. All that is intolerable. But is there any chance of the war ending in any way tolerably for anybody? Won't the state of affairs that follows, no matter who wins, be worse than anybody has seen for centuries? Or, perhaps, ever in history?

The only answer to that is we have no way of knowing, at all. It is a fair guess, but that is all. But the fact that this war, going on, is particularly bloody and indiscriminately cruel adds to the chances that, no matter who wins, the world will be in a much more barbaric and chaotic state than ever, when "peace" comes. There is nothing new about this: it is what almost all people are thinking now. I myself haven't any definite opinion.

I only understand the war as a religious, not as a political or sociological or economic problem: that is, it has created a frightful situation for the whole world in which hundreds of thousands of people are crippled, or starve, or are in prison and absolutely everybody else is in an agony of confusion and doubt or else a worse agony of lunatic certainties of a political order, that only tend to increase all the chaos and suffering in the world.

My function, morally speaking, in this situation, is to help stop the suffering, and try to feed those who are starving, or talk to those who are going crazy, *or do something* to bring relief from the pain in the world. Whether I am fulfilling that function the best way I can is not the question: of course I am not.

It seems to me this is the time to heal the sick, to bury the dead, and console the dying, or calm those who are going out of their heads, or talk to those who are driven silly by their sense of being lost in a storm. This last, and with clear evidence of the work of Divine Providence, I get a chance to do, and the rest will come soon enough, I think.

But if you ask me if I don't extend this conception of my function in the war to killing other people who are "causing all the suffering" I can only answer that I do not believe I can name any one group in the world which is "causing" all the rest of the world to suffer. I just don't know. I do not refuse to fight, and if we go to war I *want* to be in the army medical corps or something like that, rather than anything civilian.

Fighting is something I will suffer, but won't pretend to clearly understand, unless it gets [a] lot clearer to me than it is now. But what I know a Christian should be doing is praying, fasting, talking, feeding those who starve, healing the sick, consoling the dying, burying the dead, and suffering all things in atonement for his own and everybody else's sins.

I think the whole issue whether to fight or merely suffer is unimportant for Americans anyway, because all the suffering is not going to really begin for us until the war is, if not over, changed from what it is into a general upheaval with hundreds of scattered battles and revolutions all over the face of the earth.

Then we will begin to starve and riot, and it is going to be unimaginably bad.

Or even worse: maybe the whole world, the British and the Germans and the Russians, will rise up and fall on us in a mass, because we are going to be the most hated people on the face of the earth, more hated even than the Germans! For making the money we are now making out of their war: it is abominable, our prosperity now!

The breakdown won't come here for ten or fifteen years, is my guess. Next year or in 1943 the European war may break up into ten small wars, and we will be feeding them all with arms and men and ships, driving into the European continent, holding patches of Europe and Africa and Asia, campaigning around for ten years until the whole thing gets more and more chaotic and the chaos finally spreads to America.

And all the time the important thing will be to pray more and more, and suffer more and more, *voluntarily*, and do more and more for the others that suffer, and beg God to spare us, and send us the Spirit of true contrition and penance, on earth, and saints to lead us. . . .

Tomorrow is the Feast of the Dedication of Saint Michael: in the successive Gospels of these 2 saints' day (today is the Martyr Saint Wenceslas) the Lord says "*unless* you do a certain thing *you cannot be saved.*"

In one He says: "Who would come after Me, let him deny himself and take up his cross and follow Me." (Matt. 16–24)

And in the other, even more strongly "Unless you be converted, and made like to little children, you shall not enter into the Kingdom of Heaven." (Matt. 18.3)

And then, for tomorrow, the especially terrible message:

"Vae mundo a scandalis! Necesse est enim ut veniant scandala. Verumtamen vae homini illi per quem scandalum venit!" (Matt. 18) ["What terrible things will come to the world through scandal! It is inevitable that scandal should occur. Nevertheless, woe to that man through whom scandal comes!" (Matthew 18:7, New American Bible)]

September 30, 1941. Feast of Saint Jerome

Maybe it is going to become absolutely necessary to sleep less. I don't seem to have done anything at all today and yet I have been busy all the time – and now, soon I will have to sleep because I am getting tired.

Half the time, I believe, I only think I'm tired – it is some kind of dull protesting trick my laziness is playing on me to make me stop trying to work, and sleep. And yet I have done altogether too much sleeping with my face in a book – today I went to sleep in Chapter I of Gasquet's _Henry VIII and the English Monasteries._

Where did all the rest of the time go – ? I taught two classes, corrected some papers, read a few pages of [Christopher] Dawson's _Progress and Religion,_ wrote a letter trying to sell the anthology, wrote four very stinking pages in the typewritten journal, discussed part of Saint Augustine's _De Beata Vita_ which we are beginning to read with Fr. Philotheus – and said various prayers. This has filled up a lot of time and nothing valuable has been done.

But what am I looking for? What am I asking for? What do I mean, and what is it I think I need?

"If the salt have lost its savour wherewithal shall it be salted?"

This comes from the Gospel for the feast of a Doctor of the Church, and today is St. Jerome's feast. For three days in succession the Gospel has contained some _conditional_ statement of our getting into heaven. First – if you would come after Me – take up your cross, deny yourself! Second – woe to him through whom come scandals. Be like little children, for unless you are such, you shall not enter into the kingdom of heaven. Then, today, this: (Matthew V.)

"He therefore that shall break one of these least commandments, and shall so teach men, shall be called the least in the kingdom of heaven: but he that shall do and teach he shall be called great in the kingdom of heaven."

And:

"So let your light shine before men that they may see your good works and glorify your Father, who is in heaven."

I was at first confused, as usual, by this sentence, which I had never thought about much. But when I began thinking about it, the first reaction was a sense of false, pharisaic humility saying "What, am I the salt of the earth? Shall my light shine before men?"

But such humility as that (a humility which suggests itself so easily to the irresponsible individual consciences of Protestants), is really nothing but pride – if we were not proud, it would never even occur to us that "your light" meant anything but God's light shining through us, not for ourselves but for His glory!

Am I not the salt of the earth? Has not Christ, by His infinite grace and mercy, chosen me for the poorest child in His Church, but nevertheless, for His Church? Did He not give Himself in His entirety, into my vile mouth, in a thin and tiny host to be devoured by me, this morning? Did not He who is all glorious, become the most humble and abject of things, a little host as white as paper, with no taste or no beauty or no outward character at all, but to nourish me with life, because, any other way, His glory would not feed me but destroy me by its magnificence!

"But if the salt have lost its savour! . . ."

It would be the falsest, diabolical false-humility for Catholics to deny that we are the salt of the earth, because it means we are not refusing this glory, but refusing to be responsible for our own reflection of the glory by pride and lust and anger and envy: for we are *also salt without savour* – if we deny that we are the salt of the earth, we can remain complacently ignorant of the terrible fact that *we have lost our savour!*

"Wherewith shall it be salted?"
"Let your good works so shine! . . . do and preach! . . ."

If we renounce our wills (deny ourselves) and desire nothing but to do God's will (take up our crosses), we will love our neighbors as God loves us – and love Him in them, and forget our own desires in our desire to serve Him in them. We will give all we have to the poor, we will pray and deny ourselves, renounce all care what we will eat, where we will sleep, how we will be clothed, but feed, shelter and clothe others. We will pray for peace and preach it and be peacemakers, doing good to our enemies. We will be pure in heart and merciful, and there will be no pride or self-ishness left in us. And when this is done truly, in true charity, we ourselves will disappear in our good actions, and no one will see us, or praise us, because they see only God's love in us, and praise Him – or if they hate Him, they will hate what they see in us and we can suffer for Him! Naturally, if we do something so that we are praised, and not God, for it, the action has that much of imperfection, and we will lament and sorrow it was not perfect!

October 1, 1941

Supposing anybody were to be so rash as to ask why there aren't any good poets among American Catholics today: what would be the real answer, besides the loud mockery of everybody who ever read a true poet?

Why is it that modern Catholic poets in America are, of all groups, perhaps the most trivial and the most commonplace, not even saved by the fact that they are well-disposed towards God, and intend, sometimes, to praise Him? We are worse poets than the liberals and the communists even, and that is going far! They are worse than all the surrealists, who are mostly phony and frantic and diabolical and crazy, and yet sometimes knock you out of your chair with a good line. They are worse than all the accepted, and not too blameworthy, corn-belt people, American scene fellows, who are, at worst, pompous and boring!

What is one thing all poets need to know? They need to be reminded of their nearness to the Saints, just as everybody has to be reminded of this. To do anything any good in the world, you have to renounce the world in order to do that thing: you have to love it and give it your whole life.

Joyce was a good writer. You can't say whether it was because he suffered every kind of pain, tribulation and sacrifice for his writing, that he was a good writer, or whether it was the fact that he was a good writer made him do all these things.

A man who will make any sacrifice in order to sell his poems is not, by that, a good poet, and this is more likely to be the sign of a mediocre writer.

A man who will make any sacrifice to get his poems in print is also probably only a mediocre writer.

A man who will sacrifice anything merely in order to write almost certainly loves writing enough to become, sooner or later, some kind of a good writer. Joyce did that, and he was a good writer. The best in our time.

If a man can develop a technique in this way, in a purely natural order, what shouldn't we be able to do, who know prayer, and study sacrifice and tribulation, and believe in a God who died for us like a criminal and a beggar? What shouldn't we be able to do, who believe in becoming beggars for the love of what honors Him?

The answer brings us to the scandal that Joyce blamed for his leaving the Church – (the scandal itself is not significant reason for anybody especially as well-informed as Joyce to leave the Church. But that is another question) – and that is that we have become, in the cultural sense more than we ever were, _salt without savour._ This is true culturally and also, to some extent, religiously: although about that it is hard to tell. We are pompous, selfish, vulgarians, suspicious of art and of saintliness.

There may be just as many saints now, in the Church militant, as there have been before in any other century like ours: but if there are, they are in strange, hidden places, and nobody hears of them, outside of Harlem, or the slums, or contemplative monasteries where they happen to be in hiding.

The reason there are so few good Catholic poets is the same as the reason why there are so few Catholics, of the educated classes, anyway, that have really shown a great desire for saintliness – we are all mediocre, indifferent, concerned with trivialities, or small questions of pride, or are drawn into various political traps: many men of good intentions are trapped into Fascism, because they think they can serve God with political crusades before they have given everything to the poor and taken up their spiritual crosses of poverty and humiliation before men! And after they have done that, no military crusade makes too much sense, if it is predominantly a crusade, and an offensive!

Weren't we punished enough for the second, third and the horrible blasphemy of the Fourth Crusade (when the crusaders were diverted by Venice to the conquest of *Christian* Constantinople) by those Crusades themselves and the Black Death and the Reformation? (There was nothing essentially unholy about the First Crusade, as it started out, although that turned into an imperial conquest before it was over, too!)

All this is not to say that if we are not saints, we are all great sinners. We are not even that. The tragedy of modern Catholics is their indifference and their terrible mediocrity. When we are good, even our goodness seems hardly more than a negative thing: we resist temptations, but are not heroically saintly! If we are not cruel, grasping, lustful, pharisees, it is often only because we are sheltered from temptation in a safe social level where there are no grave dangers from either riches or misery. Half the time we are not even tempted by anything, or seem not to be – except there is always our own monstrous complacency.

And if this is true of our spiritual life, which nevertheless truly means more than anything else to us, for we do have our Faith, and by it we know this, how much more true is it likely to be of our poetry, which is something of only amateur interest to us, compared with first the salvation of our souls and (if we are any good) second (and not first) the feeding, clothing and sheltering of our bodies.

When even our highest aims, the salvation of our soul and the service of God, are seen by us with such indifference and set at so low a level as we have set them, how is something like the writing of poetry going to command any sacrifice, any zeal of us?

There is no reason for confusing the sacrifice an artist must make to learn a technique with the goodness of any artistic technique. But the sacrifice has to be made, because the technique has to be learned: and the technique is not a system of rules, either. If a man is going to be a good poet, he must generally choose between working in a bank and making money, and starving merely in order to write and write and write. He does not necessarily *have* to starve. But he must be prepared to. He does not have to starve to be a Saint, either: yet if he is a saint, he will seek poverty and seek starvation, too, of his own will.

The same with poets, who have to write in fear and trembling, prayer and fasting – and be like Saroyan with his typewriter, or Blake with his begging and his engravings, and Hopkins with his religious tribulations, and Langland begging, and Dante exiled, and all the others.

Was Donne a happy, prosperous citizen?

Show me the poets who were happy and prosperous, and who are they: a flock of Brownings and Tennysons. The only one I can think of who was both prosperous and a good writer is Shakespeare, but he is in the class with the others: because his prosperity is accidental and has nothing to do with the tribulation underlying *Hamlet* – whereas the *Idylls of the King* reeks of horsehair sofas, barouches, hair-lotion, and pommades, and port, and cigars.

The one Catholic writer in this century, who knew that being a writer was a vocation to be followed in poverty and fasting and love, was Leon Bloy. And [Eric] Gill, too, was an artist in the same right way. What was important: they were prepared to suffer and Bloy did. Once that is sure, then they don't have to starve, they will voluntarily fast: they don't have to be poor, they will give away everything in order to write and by their writing show God's light among men, that men may praise Him!

October 3, 1941. Feast of Saint Theresa of the Child Jesus

It would not be true to say I got mad reading the review of Huxley's new book *Gray Eminence* in *Time*.

Getting mad is not the thing to do at a thing like that: I don't know what is the thing to do – but getting mad is not it, because that is what they want: they want to sting people to anger, they want to hurt people, and our anger is a satisfactory result to them because it is a sign they have succeeded. However, *not to* get angry is not, in itself, the proper thing to do either. To keep your temper in order to show them that they have failed to hurt you is also absurd, more absurd and less honest than getting angry.

I don't know what to do except pray for Huxley and for the stupid, sly, crafty, pedantic little life-smurching mental dwarf that wrote this review for *Time*. I am not mad at him, but still can't see straight when I think of the vices of his beastly, smug little review.

That is the first thing these poor, pathetic hacks on *Time* are trying to keep from learning, lest it kill them: that smugness is the characteristic of crafty and petty and envious and unimaginative and jealous minds, no matter where they are. It is not just a trait of the old ladies in temperance societies that these smart "liberal" *Time* boys have been brought up by Ernest Hemingway to fear and detest and hate. *Time* is the smuggest magazine I have ever read.

What about *Gray Eminence?*

The book is probably smarter than the *Time* review made it seem. The reviewer on *Time* concentrated on the more sensuously exciting passages, the little shivers of horrified amusement at this poor old Capuchin's mortifications: but especially did they not only shiver and practically expire in the throes of convulsed, almost sensuous, delight at the fact that relics of St. Fiacre were applied to the piles of Cardinal Richelieu without any success. They described it – maybe the trick was Huxley's leaving the description cut off in mid-air and trailing away in dots – the way the daring parts of dirty books are always supposed to be. "The relics were applied. . . ." "O throes of blissful smug giggling! Save me before I stifle! Whoops! Did you *ever.*" Then they quote a big, equally "delicious" piece of satire from Huxley, describing the picture Rubens would probably have painted if the cure had worked: the idea was a good one, but it only seemed dull the way it was carried out. Maybe the fault was with *Time* – in its context, maybe Huxley's joke is all right, but I doubt if the best writing in the world would look good in *Time*: they would probably find some way of quoting it that would make it appear totally repulsive.

All this occurs to me on the feast of a saint so holy that this is incomprehensible when we try to see any relation between the world where it occurred and her: and there is none. She was in the world, and such things were all around her, and she saw them and yet never saw them because she was a child, fulfilling that condition which, if we don't fulfill, we are told with absolute finality by the clear words of God, we cannot enter the Kingdom of Heaven.

The joke of the problem of "being as little children" is that "being as children" was the solution [Sigmund] Freud was aiming at for all our psychic breakdowns, too, but he went about finding the solution of this perfect innocence where it is impossible to find it: he was looking for the effects of the innocence rather than innocence itself. He wanted to have the peace of innocence and yet enjoy all the pleasures that destroy innocence because, since we are human, we are self-conscious and self-critical, and there are things we can't do without creating problems which are solved by self-criticism. And Freud himself worked up some mechanism that explains, in one way, the psycho-physiological sources of this kind of giggling and petty malice about mild obscenity, here spiced with what the gigglers rather hope is blasphemy, too.

All this applies to *Time* more than to Huxley.

The answer to *Time* – is that you don't have to answer them, or tell them anything: but be, ourselves, as little children, innocent, and that beats anything they can ever say against us or against anything we believe. The reason they can say so much against us and anger us so much is in our own comparative lack of innocence, and proportionate stubbornness and pride.

As for Huxley: maybe I'd like to read the book.

The point of it I have to guess at, because you couldn't clearly tell from *Time's* review. But the point probably is: here was an ascetic, a man of great faith and principles, who confused the temporal and the spiritual orders, bringing about terrific disaster in the latter. He projected into the political problems of his time the problems of his own conscience and the struggle with his own flesh, and, failing to realize they were only analogous (or maybe they had no relation at all, even analogical) to one another, he believed his political intentions were God's will, just as his intentions concerning his own self-sanctification were inspired by God's grace. Then he proceeded to suggest courses of action as cruel and terrifying to his own flesh (in Huxley's eyes). The result was religious wars and massacres and tortures that made a chaos out of central Europe.

The conclusion Huxley probably means to draw from this is that saints and ascetics are as terrible a scourge, when they get into politics, as murderers and thieves – or perhaps even worse. Further, he probably means to say that the realm of politics is the realm of evil, and no good can be done politically at all, and the biggest temptation of saints is to get into this realm – and when they do, by virtue perhaps of the doctrine of *corruptio optimi pessima*, it means disaster. There can be no political action based on religious principles because the two spheres are absolutely distinct, and so on. As a corollary to that – Catholic asceticism is a kind of reverse sensuality, and is, as such, also evil: that goes for certain extreme disciplines, but just *what* it would cover for Huxley, I don't know.

The big problem of his book will be to show that the chaos and bloodshed in Europe were the result of this Capuchin's work and not the work of Richelieu who, as everybody knows, was neither an ascetic nor a saint!

Whatever may be the way Huxley deals with it, he has got a good problem.

There are kings who have been kings and also sanctified themselves and fulfilled the duties of their kingship with justice and charity. For them, there is no particular problem. They were saints because they were good and loved God and as a result they were also good kings – they rendered unto Caesar what was due to Caesar, and to God what was due to Him – that is the more important part. No problem.

But there are saints, like Joan of Arc, who have been sent by God to save a people, and that by political and even warlike action – there is less of a problem here, than in the case of Huxley's *Gray Eminence*. Either you believe Saint Joan was filled with true visions and was used as a miraculous instrument by God to accomplish His will in a striking way in history, or else you believe she was crazy. Between these points of view there is little argument possible.

But supposing you agree that God exists and is the kind of God the Christians believe Him to be – "pure actuality" – the perfect and eternal actualization of Being and Goodness, containing in Himself the sufficient reason for His Being, being Being itself, and for the being and goodness of all things, which He preserves from moment to moment by His own will and love of Being (love of Himself for Himself). He alone is worthy of the highest love, since He is the pure Actuality which alone can satisfy our love of actuality and of Being. Our life is to love Him; and unless we do, we are lost in unhappiness and confusion.

(Huxley would probably not admit this statement in terms of love – but would say the same thing over again making God the object of the intellect – God knows Himself, and His self-knowledge is the realization of Pure Being and the acts of knowing Himself and of loving Himself are simultaneous. Unless we know Him we are in confusion, etc.)

Supposing you see God in this way, and can conceive, then, that our life must be devoted to the striving to come to know Him as fully as possible. The Buddhists purify their intellects and wills so as to sink to a knowledge of Him where He awaits them in a kind of terrific passivity of nothingness, and Christians purify all their acts of will or of knowing, and are lifted, by His help, to the participation in His infinite actuality, where the most perfect and complete of all *acts* is to *receive* the vision of His actuality, "pure working."

This is the end of all our striving.

Supposing we had reached that end: no activity of ours, no matter how "perfect" according to all our notions of charity, the perfection of moral action, would be anything but imperfect, not to say sinful, if we abandoned the highest of all acts – that of being lost in the contemplation of God's Pure Actuality. *Mariam meliorem partem elegit.* ["Mary has chosen the better portion." (Luke 10:42, New American Bible)] However, we have not reached that end.

On the contrary, that we strive to reach it means that we work to possess this vision. Through our acts, we come closer and closer to this Purest Act. The purest activity is contemplation.

We reach contemplation, it seems, through acts of our own. But the strength to carry out those acts, and their success, depend on God's grace and His will. What are the acts His will drives us to do?

Acts of love of Him and of our neighbor. But acts of love. Love is the purest kind of activity we know. The highest love, that of God, is the most perfect activity possible to us – that is, again, the contemplation of His Divine Essence, Pure Being.

But the love of our neighbor is part of this perfection, charity: and until all distinctions are brought back to harmony in the terrific singleness of the act of the contemplation of God, there remains a distinction between different acts of charity. Some are directed towards God, in prayer, and mental prayer, etc., others are directed towards other people.

Even the present contemplative orders are orders, that is, societies, where men live together. It is precisely in such orders as these that acts of love of God and acts of love of one another are continually practiced very clearly and simply and properly. The men in these orders follow a straight way: where both aspects of charity are made very clear.

These acts of love for other men also can be distinguished into two kinds: the higher is expressed in charity towards individuals, the lower in loving care of the society as a whole.

Thus the following kinds of things done for the love of God are charitable acts – meditation; penance; healing a sick man; feeding a starving man; ruling a community of monks.

For the greatest saints, like Saint Theresa of Avila, all these acts were merged into a single habit of perfect charity. She was at the same time a great contemplative and a great reformer of her order. The same with Saint Francis – complicated, however, by the problems brought up by his immediate successors in the order. His success was not so clear as Saint Theresa's.

All this is simple and obvious. The political and economic aspect of charity is evident when you are dealing with a religious community.

This is where the problems begin.

It is easy to see how taking over the temporal and spiritual administration of a community dedicated to the salvation of the souls of all its members is a holy and charitable duty. But can a man, whose whole life is dedicated to holiness, call it a holy and charitable duty to make it his life work to rule or serve a society which has no clear purpose except to guarantee that the worldly interests of the individuals who belong to it shall be protected from one another and from enemies outside?

When it is quite clear that a society (like every state in the world except Vatican City, which doesn't count as a state, and is really a religious community) has no interest whatever in the spiritual salvation of its members, but only their temporal interests, how can a holy man rule or serve the government of that society without bringing into all his actions a clear division between what is done in his work, and what is done for himself? *Render unto Caesar.*

And then his whole life will be a struggle to reconcile the two – a struggle to do nothing as a ruler he would regret as a Christian! Even in ruling so small a community as a household that cleavage is present: but it is not dangerous, whereas in the rule of a whole big state the cleavage gets to be so big that to be a ruler of such a state is not a means to holiness, but perhaps a peril to it.

Then in Political Science, can there be such a thing as a Christian form of government – anything that would correspond to a monastic rule for a religious community? Or is the best thing we can get, merely a set of laws and practices that don't actually conflict with Christian principles?

Can there be a Christian form of government for any society whose only aim is to control the conflicting temporal interests of its members?

When a Christian ecclesiastic gets power over a nation in which there is complete religious and temporal disunity of interests, and attempts to reform it the way you would set about reforming a monastery which everyone has voluntarily entered for the same religious purpose, you get disaster and breed not peace but war and massacres and persecutions and chaos. (He may not try any reforms and merely compromise and try to keep some kind of order. Then there is nothing particularly Christian in his form of govt. It is just an ordinary, prudent government.) It would be better if he had never come near the government of that state, which he has ruined: and if he has done so, not out of mistaken love but also out of stubbornness and pride, he is also accountable to God for all the blood that has been shed.

This was the tragedy that took place when the Popes wanted to rule the world the way it was their holy duty to rule the Church! And I believe the Crusades were the punishment for such mistakes and such sins as this! The Crusades, the Black Death and the Reformation.

Yet in the Middle Ages the problem was not so acute: *if the whole of Europe were Catholic, there would perhaps be nothing wrong with the Pope ruling Europe as absolutely in the temporal as in the spiritual sphere.*

That is only true, however, if it is true to say the whole of Europe was *really* Catholic – that is, was inhabited by people who *lived* the faith, who actually lived in order to come at last to God, making God their supreme end over all things.

The trouble is, the world is the world – and Europe was Catholic, in the Middle Ages, certainly in a social sense: but the interests of too many of the temporal and even ecclesiastical rulers were too worldly for the immense cleavage between the two cities, of God and of the world, to be much less wide than it is today. And that cleavage is fundamental.

If ever this is so, there can never be a situation where temporal and spiritual rule will be capable of being successfully united in the hands of a single perfectly Christian government, except perhaps in very small states, over small areas, over not too many people. (Of course a Christian could start a good govt. that would not, however, be essentially Christian – but prudent according to the moderation of the world.)

But nevertheless, that is the only rule that will ever give anyone any *real liberty!*

October 7. Feast of the Holy Rosary
Today I walked about in the dry grass of the tank lots – where it was very warm, warm as summer, yet many of the trees and bushes were already bare, and leaves flew in the warm wind. The hills were full of color, the sky had in it piles of white cumulus cloud – I forget where I thought I had ever

seen a sky exactly like that before. Yet in any case I was sorry it was hot and glad it was going to be fall – glad to see through the trees – there is a severer and stricter beauty about the bare woods that appeals to me sometimes, more than anything summer brings to the country – I like every season, is the answer, and the season I like best is the one I am in at the time. I like all the seasons best in turn, one after the other – but one I do get tired of, and that is winter.

Enough about seasons, which mean more than I ever admitted before, to me, but I have followed them all my life with great love, and their rhythm should be the basis of all decent cultures – the Liturgy has something to do with them – no culture can ignore them and live. Maybe no culture can ignore agriculture and live. But anyway, enough about the seasons.

A silly, cheap, red, new plane came skidding clumsily over the trees and landed in a field near where I was sitting, and instantly a man and a dog came from nowhere and ran to it – I thought it was a rendezvous of spies and didn't go near. Five minutes later running men began to arrive through the fields from every part of the landscape expecting an accident.

I went back and sat down where I was before. Presently the sky got full of fancy gray clouds of the kind that were carefully and dramatically and shockingly realistically painted by Romantic artists of the 19th century.

The papers are full of a lot of fretting about religion in Russia – something political that has been cooked up by Roosevelt in connection with the war, of course. The whole thing is very blatant and stupid on both sides. Some days ago Roosevelt made a statement that "Religious Freedom was respected in Russia," which it is, in an article of the constitution. Then everybody opposed to that pointed out that the constitution didn't mean much, and in effect, Religious Freedom in Russia was a myth, since, although going to church is "allowed," it is discouraged in many ways, by the fact that no member of the party can go to church, and by the fact that the government allows no religious schools, but sees to it that "atheism," whatever that is, is taught in the schools everywhere.

So then somebody challenges Russia to come on out and guarantee "real" religious freedom. The Russians then reply that religious freedom is guaranteed by their constitution.

The whole thing is a very sad and stupid farce. What do they expect Russia to do? Promise not to use any more "atheistic" teaching in the schools? Promise anything? What does any political agreement mean in a case like this? The whole thing is a joke.

And even suppose Russia threw out all the "atheist museums" set up in the old churches and allowed religious schools to be opened, what difference can that possibly make in our attitude to the war? If American Catholics made a deal to agree to fight on Russia's side on condition Russia promised to be nice about religion it would be the most stinking immoral act I ever heard of! But we won't do that – not because we are above such immorality, but because most of us just don't want to fight anyway, on Russia's side or anybody else's.

The thing that is depressing is the *manoeuvre* being carried out by Roosevelt in such a blatant way: it assumes that Catholics are simply waiting to be bought by some deal like that – that maybe the Pope can be persuaded to call the cause of the democracies "Just" and proclaim a crusade against Germany, if the Russians will make some kind of a polite gesture about freedom of religion.

This assumption is insulting to Catholics in two ways: first by its implication that we are dumb enough to believe in a promise made by a government like Stalin's in a matter like this! Second by its implication that the Pope is nothing but another political boss who can be won over by a suitable "deal." All this hurts all the more because it is all partly true – it depends on a half-truth, and on some sins of political intrigue we wish we could forget!

Which doesn't mean that, if by some political means something can be done to bring back priests and preachers and teachers to Russia, it shouldn't be done: but not in this kind of a bargain, involving the spiritual authority of the Church being degraded to further some temporal purpose (declaring the war "just" to help 3 highly suspicious and materialistic nations win a war against one even more suspicious and even more dangerous to the Church). Admittedly, this has been done a lot before: but I don't think this Pope will do anything like that, but pray that he will be led by grace to save us and create for us a situation where we can do God's work and his and the Church's saving souls in Russia, or anywhere but not at the cost of any false crusades with a material value and none other – some crime!

October 8, 1941

This political trick of Roosevelt's about the Russians and their religion has got an equivocal twist to it which adds to its slightly crazy and suspect character. There has really been *no definite political move* at all – nothing you can call an action, and yet it very definitely is a political act. Roosevelt merely remarked, in public, somewhere – that the Russians possessed, and dearly loved, religious freedom. Then a lot of people disagreed, also in public. Nobody is saying anything to Russia, not directly (unless I missed it).

Russia, stirring as if in a distant dream, remarks absently to the autumn wind: O yes! we have religious freedom! And, nice kind of dream gesture, the reds abolish a couple of significant atheist magazines, mumbling all the while: "We are not abolishing anything, but merely ceasing publication on account of the shortage of newsprint."

Then the Archbishop of Canterbury, smiling in his sleep, announces like the incoherent mumbling of ice-floes breaking up in the wastes of the Antarctic, "you know, Russia is gravitating back towards religion. The people will insensibly return to God because they have to."

I am not the one to deny that "atheism" is so stupid, once it gets on paper as a doctrine, that it becomes comical. And even the biggest dopes in the world are capable of seeing this stupidity. That doesn't alter the fact that the habit of unbelief (which is an entirely different thing from the "doctrines" of atheism and independent of them) is very tenacious and dangerous and stubborn. What is important about unbelief, as well as about Faith, is the part played in it by the *will*. The doctrines of systematic unbelief are fantastically stupid, and the real unbeliever never insists on them – only the amateurs and the sophomores do. What is important in unbelief is, not the inability of the intellect to believe (because believers also know that Faith starts only where the intellect has to give up) – The intellect can't believe, and belief can't know with certitude – the two ideas are mutually exclusive.

Reasoning about unbelief, especially reasoning about the fact that Faith offers no *certain knowledge* of God (who therefore doesn't exist) is completely absurd, because it is arguing about something so misunderstood that the argument has no meaning and the problems argued do not even exist.

The important thing about unbelief is the *refusal* to believe; the one thing important about faith is the submission and acquiescence in "believing" what we can't certainly know one way or the other. In both cases it is more or less an emotional question. Even agnostics, who seem to have an intellectual position worthy of some respect – "I don't know because I can't know – " are still making the same mistake. We know they can't *know* the things that are the objects of Faith – neither can anybody else. Of course there is always the argument whether God's existence can be *proved* or not. The existence of a first principle can be proved, even to the satisfaction of some agnostics – but it is hard to get anyone to admit that this first principle is a personal God Who loves us infinitely because here some faith necessarily comes in – a matter of experience that no amount of Christian rationalism can do away with! And at this point they simply refuse to acquiesce, or else consent to. It is a matter for the will.

"He who is not with me is against me."

Agnostics hope to be neutral in this, but they can't be either, because it isn't a purely intellectual matter. Very soon we get to the point where we simply say: "I believe" or "I refuse to believe." Agnostics try to avoid that crucial choice by saying they are never even confronted with it. But that is another way of saying, "I refuse to believe," for it is merely to be translated into this: "I refuse to let myself be faced with a choice between belief and unbelief in which I will certainly choose unbelief."

Nobody can avoid this choice between believing in God and not believing in Him – and it is almost never an intellectual decision, but a question of an affective movement, an expression of a desire, "the assertion of a 'drive' in one of two clear directions," or whatever else you want to call it: an act of will.

The Russians' abolishing a couple of "Godless" magazines are merely cleaning their atheistic house of a lot of jabber that never causes unbelief, but is one of the accidental externals of an unbelief that isn't sure of itself. Now maybe they can develop a real, radical unbelief, like that of the rich descendants of some Protestant (or even Catholic) families, who not only never argued their unbelief but long ago ceased even to think about God, even in blaspheming Him.

Now that the Russians have abolished their "atheist" papers, it may only be a sign that they are becoming truly "godless" like some capitalists have been, already, for years!

"Atheism" was a silly term used by the nineteenth century (and 18th), applicable to a lot of jabbering idiots who didn't know quite what they wanted, or what they were talking about, and is to be carefully distinguished from the satanic and systematic godlessness of those who, without wasting time in talk, really love evil – greed, and lust, and avarice, and power and war.

I have just read straight through Gheon's book about Saint Theresa of Lisieux and am knocked out by it completely. What the book is about, if not the book itself, is the most exciting thing I have read for I don't know how long: this story of a middle-class French child who went into a convent, who never, according to the world or to nature, did *anything*; who died; and who was inexplicably hailed right after her death by Catholics in every part of the world for her great saintliness (because of countless miracles following the invocation of her name) – all this story is more terrific than any I have read since the story of the works of the First Apostles, in the Acts, or the story of Saint Francis.

Added to this is the terrific complication of the scandal of cheap, molasses-art and gorgonzola angels that surrounds the cultus of this great saint. About that, I'll make ideas maybe some other moment, not this one.

In reading the story of this saint it is not possible to doubt from the very first word about her parents that she was a totally extraordinary saint, more extraordinary than even Saint John of the Cross or Saint Theresa of Avila, who rejoice in heaven in her, their little sister's immense simplicity and love which includes also their love and their wisdom, because all their love and wisdom came from God and was all His.

Not only is she a saint but her father was one very obviously, too. What are they waiting for, to beatify him, too? His goodness is terrific, and the very thought of it makes you weep for joy at God's generosity, to give us such souls for our edification! This completely good man, a clockmaker, who loved to pray and meditate and read holy books, allowed himself one peaceful and harmless recreation – fishing – loved chastity – was miraculously matched with a saint for a wife, who gave him five daughters, all nuns and one of them a great saint! This good man, who after a great grace of God's – a mystical experience of high order, prayed to be allowed to suffer, being unworthy of such favours; and so was paralyzed, and lay paralyzed, dying slowly for months! This good man in his simplicity and goodness and complete carelessness of anything outside of ordering his quiet, obscure life and that of his daughters, to God – he makes me understand something of the justice of the just man, Joseph, whose justice we know too abstractly, since he has come to us only obscure and shadowy in his great humility.

As to the saint herself, I repeat, everything in her story knocks me flat – her childhood, no matter how bourgeois in its externals, was like the childhood of Blake in its spirituality: and, once again, no matter how vile the statues (there's a reason) of her, her life in her convent was not sentimental, not sweet, but a life of great heroism and austerity and simplicity and charity and wisdom as great as that of the greatest saints and martyrs: this little child was a Saint Peter and Paul, a Saint Francis, a Saint Lawrence, a Saint John of the Cross, mighty, in her childish weakness, as the great apostles, except she was no longer a child, but a nun.

It is remarkable how well Crashaw's "Poem to the Elder Saint Theresa" fits our younger Theresa, our own terrific child! (Never forgetting that in her childhood she was imperfect – as a nun, she was perfect. In her real, not metaphorical, childhood, she was even, in a sense, spoiled a little – but in her mighty and innocent service of Christ in the cold and obscure convent of Lisieux she was the least of all her sisters, suffering terrible spiritual and then physical tribulations in obscurity, for the love of God – and *without consolations.*

Not only was she not one whose religion was mawkish, or sentimental, or sloppy, or a luxury of polite and sensuous ecstasies, that her cultus suggests, but as a nun she enjoyed no ecstasies, not even consolations at all – only the terrors of the abyss and the *Dark Night*, and in the midst of this she continually renounced, over and over, the benefits of all her prayers, rejected consolation, offered herself up as a *total* sacrifice – allowed herself to be totally annihilated for Christ, in favor of sinners – with no reward, *no recompense*, not even heaven, which she would sacrifice to *"faire du bien sur la terre."* ["Do good while on earth."]

The implications of this are tremendous and unimaginable: nobody seems to have reflected for a moment on how much this means! But in any case, one thing is clear (while it is impossible to grasp the seriousness of her sacrifice of heavenly reward – which was undoubtedly accepted – and see what this means), and that is that in Saint Theresa as in Saint Francis is the complete perfection of Saint John of the Cross's way, the perfect pattern of the *Ascent of Mount Carmel* more perfect than Saint John of the Cross himself, perhaps, ever conceived possible!

In Theresa we are face to face with a terrifying miracle – of complete childishness and unbelievable maturity of tribulation: but the tribulation is hidden – and is only expressed – in terms that are totally innocent, totally naive, and even more or less gay.

It is no easy figure of speech to say she illustrates the counsel – the command – that we should be as little children merely because she talked always like an innocent child: she lived in her life this mystery: that being as a child was to be crucified, but crucified in a kind of innocence which makes the crucifixion not only a secret, but absolutely incomprehensible.

All we know is – the tribulation is there, and it is terrific – and only she and God knew how terrific – and she is still, only a child. But a child whose childishness involves maybe a maturer mysticism than all Saint John of the Cross, something that rejoins the awful mystery of the Stigmatization of Saint Francis.

Everything about her and her father illustrates Kierkegaard's remarkable intuition that the greatest and most perfect saints are those whose saintliness *cannot* be contained except beneath some exterior that appears totally mediocre and normal, because it is an incommunicable secret. The height of Saint Francis' saintliness came when he was a poor little sick man, kicked out of the command of his own order, and hiding his bleeding hands wherever he went, and not talking. He was greatest when he ceased to be a romantic hero of humility and became so humble he was incomprehensible; in the same way with Theresa: she is a little middle-class nun in a French town who sticks closely to her rule and is outwardly just like everybody else – zealous, but ordinary, simple, childish, even appearing to be contented and happy – in fact *being* happy – and yet accepting, the way a lesser saint would accept a consolation of grace – the utter desolation of Gethsemani and Calvary!

The Ascent of Mount Carmel and Kierkegaard's *Fear and Trembling* and the "Book of Job" and the *Dark Night of the Soul* do not suffice to explain the heroism of this mighty child who is still, with all that, under this appearance of mediocrity which has allowed her memory to be surrounded by statues that revolt anyone who ever knew what taste was, and be desecrated by a commercialism that calls to heaven for vengeance – and yet doesn't!

I cannot rest since I have read this book. I am terrified and excited at the thought that a soul so great should suffer so much on earth, and after her death remain on earth with us, foregoing until after the Last Day her heavenly reward – and this, while the memory on earth is desecrated by the ones who seem to love her most and who probably actually do!

This is the saint that is given us for our terrible, ugly, cruel, maniac, blasphemous, murdering age, the Saint that suffers for us and remains with us in the thick of everything that is most horrible about our dying, rotting civilization, and she herself most pure, most perfect because only such intense and incomprehensible perfection of innocence is capable of saving us, of suffering for our sins. Close as Saint Francis is to Christ, is Theresa, I believe, to His Blessed Mother: Saint Francis shared the wounds of the Passion, Saint Theresa [shared] not only Mary's joys but her Dolours. I cannot rest, thinking of this great and glorious saint that is given us: I beg and beg her to pray for me and help me to be filled with love and belief to give myself to Christ and lose myself in the terror of His perfection as it manifests itself in us when we suffer Him to come to us on earth. JMJT. [Jesus, Mary, Joseph, Theresa]

October 10, 1941

It is a good bright windy morning, with clouds, and it is half past ten. Half past ten is a good time of day – you stop and look up in the middle of work that is going along fresh, work that has not become intense and hot and sleepy and perplexed, like it will in the afternoon when it becomes more of a fight. But work, at this time of day, is nothing but a pleasure.

I read in F. L. Lucas' *Decline and Fall of the Romantic Ideal* a series of quotations illustrating the term "Romantic." Most of them mean nothing to me: they are slightly or often very ridiculous ("Forlorn – the very word is like a bell". . . . *"La Belle Dame sans Merci"* ["The Beautiful Woman with no Pity."] / Hath thee in thrall." *"Es war ein Konig in Thule."* ["It was a king in Thule."] *"Le vent qui vient a travers la montagne/me rendra fou."* ["The wind that blows across the mountain makes me crazy."] – This last couldn't be anybody but Old Victor Hugo roaring in his liberal whiskers. I shake with delightful laughter over this sublime line for nearly ten minutes). Then, all of a sudden I come across a couple that not only do not make me laugh, but knock me right off my chair, I find them so impressive and excellent.

"And Branwen looked towards Ireland, and towards the isle of the Mighty, to see if she could descry them. 'Alas,' said she, 'that ever I was born; two islands have been destroyed because of me.' Then she gave a great groan and there broke her heart. And they made her a four-sided grave and buried her on the banks of the Alaw." And the other, not so good, was from Pushkin. But this was out of the *Mabinogion*, which I had always avoided and laughed at.

What is being talked about in the *Mabinogion* is more like Homer than Keats or Hugo, and therefore it is Romantic in a very different sense from *Endymion*. It has a sense of desolation, but desolation like that of the Old Testament prophets. It is the Religious desolation of real myth, and experience, and not the sentimental desolation of a fake myth and a vicarious experience – which is all the regular romantics, mostly, achieved. Coleridge sometimes gets up to the heights of real myth, too. Keats, seldom. Coleridge, like a surrealist, describes the content of his own imagination and the result is good because the content of his imagination is interesting in itself (*Kubla Khan* and *Ancient Mariner*, anyway). Keats takes the content of his imagination and builds a fairy palace and invites himself to a poor substitute for a physical feast in this unreal palace. Keats describes what is unreal, Coleridge what is real. (Keats' experience is usually unreal, because at one remove from reality, but Coleridge's experience is real because of the complete integration between the poem itself and his imagination.) His poem *is* the world in his mind. Keats takes what is in his mind and uses it to build an unreal world for his poem. The *Ancient Mariner* is thoroughly well geared to Coleridge's imagination because it *is* his own experience retold as a myth. The *Eve of Saint Agnes* represents not a myth for a real psychological experience but a daydream of some physical experience that Keats never had, and is therefore unreal.

"*La Belle Dame sans Merci*" – insofar as it is more a mythical embodiment of a real psychological state, is a better poem: but insofar as this melancholy of Keats is itself vague, the poem is far inferior to those sentences from the *Mabinogion*, which have a terrific and definite kind of reality about them, and can serve as a myth for anybody's religious desolation over sins or mistakes.

—

Somebody has just wowed *Life* magazine with a ridiculous series of drawings illustrating the struggles of Democracy and Totalitarianism under the aspect of a world of dogs dressed up in suits and uniforms; dignified dogs in cutaways, Puritan dogs, Indian dogs, Boston Tea-Party dogs, Civil War dogs, World War dogs, and now Nazi dogs, Isolationist dogs, a Lindbergh dog, a young drunk intellectual swing-music dog, and some responsible dogs who want to fight Hitler.

It isn't the stupidity of the whole conception that is scaring: nobody is scared just by stupidity alone. It is the effect of the notion that we are dogs: the notion is terrifying, and for one very obvious reason.

One might expect that portraying Nazis as big dogs in uniforms would insult them, degrade them: not at all. It merely makes them look incomprehensible, harmless and foolish, even kindly. The insult is rather to the dogs. All the more foolish and inoffensive are the Nazi dogs when they appear in this context of a whole world of big, sincere, mute, dogface creatures which are presented to us as all on the same level, the good and the bad: for it is a dog world. We are all good or bad doggies. Some snap and growl, some are big noble watchdogs and some are good earnest gundogs and some are peppy, zippy, sporty, upright little terriers. Good dog! Up Roosevelt, up Churchill, up Mr. Nicholas Murray Butler, up Col. Lindbergh!

What a conception of the world! It fills me with terror, not because it is a weak and vulgar fancy, but because it happens to be *true*.

When men were conceived as having souls, the term "dog" was an insult, implying baseness, servility, fitness only to fight for scraps of flesh, under the tables of men. Now that men lavish on their dogs the respect we once had for men and for angels – it is not the fault of the poor good dogs – we have come to be a civilization of dogs, sitting up earnestly begging for nothing more than our daily Ken-L-ration. Up Einstein! up Stalin! (I wonder why *Life* thinks safe to call the war, as openly, a dogfight!)

JMJT.

October 11, 1941

"I like Blake often, but I like Hardy better." This, which is not the best written short sentence in the English language either (the lack of logical correspondence between "often" and "better" is an offensive sloppiness) is one of a million clues to what is wrong with F. L. Lucas' *Decline and Fall of the Romantic Idea:* that, and his naive idea, somewhere, that Blake was a diabolist. Lucas is smart enough to see what is obviously wrong with Shelley, Keats, Wordsworth, but not smart enough to see what is obviously right about Coleridge and Blake – to whom he is capable of preferring bleak, pompous, pedestrian dullards like Housman or Hardy who are about as interesting to me as a cold in the head.

Lucas doesn't know what the imagination is or what literature is, and his book is intolerably composed and sloppy. Perhaps you can't condemn him completely on account of his bad taste (he uses the phrase "enchanted cigarettes of Romanticism" several times as if it were serious!) but you can condemn him for his lack of ideas and for his inability to understand that when Blake saw the thistle before him as an old man gray, the only consequence that vision could lead to in terms of action would be *not* to "put a penny in its hat" but, possibly, to pray for innocence and love because such a vision does not really demand any particular action. It is a statement about the universe which makes morality itself intelligible, indirectly. So first, Lucas doesn't know that such visions have no direct, particular material or moral purpose, being visions [lead]ing us to contemplate the *moral character* of the universe as a whole.

Then again, if the metaphor of the thistle as an old man gray were what Lucas thinks could possibly deceive us into giving it a penny, it would be merely fanciful; whereas it is, in Coleridge's terms, *imaginative.*

Finally, Lucas didn't even read the metaphor right anyway. If he thinks Blake meant the thistle looked like an old beggar, he's crazy. The old man gray is a beadle, a gaoler, and a guardian of the poor. What is prickly or harsh about beggars? Or about mercy?

October 12, 1941

Whatever may be wrong with I. A. Richards' notions of Coleridge on Imagination, Lucas is far more wrong about Richards. He evidently doesn't understand the first thing about Richards' theory. When Richards takes a metaphor and breaks it down into all the "connections and cross-connections" of meanings it contains, finding scores of relevant things there that make the metaphor powerful and vital and terrifically significant – Lucas is merely scandalized at this excess of subtlety. He has a sort of Baconian distrust of any theory which says a metaphor can contain so much!

In the first place, Richards' method is best when it is applied to the most complex and most highly imaginative poetry – works wonderfully on

Shakespeare's sonnets and on metaphysical poetry. Lucas, by preferring Hardy to Blake, and by certain other statements of preference in his book (he definitely can't see as much in the metaphysicals either, as in men like Housman) shows at once that he does not really appreciate poetry of this intensity. Consequently, how can he understand a theory which attempts to show *how much* is packed into the metaphors of this intense and complex verse.

However, Lucas shows he has no conception of how to use Richards' critical apparatus as soon as he tries to apply it. First he takes the obviously imaginative metaphor of [Thomas L.] Beddoes, showing the air in time of pestilence to be

> "Transparent as the glass of poisoned water
> Through which the drinker sees his murderer smiling."

This is what poor Lucas has to say: "Poisoned transparent air – poisoned transparent water," there do not seem to be many 'links of relevance.' And so he thinks this terrifically complex metaphor is perfectly simple.

What about the initial ambiguity:

1. Air – which is *more transparent* then water, is compared to water. The notion of the water gains a suggestion of opacity from the poison dissolved in it. The air is then really being called transparent in a weird, unnatural way, a transparency that is really queerly and horribly opaque.

2. What about the murderer smiling through the poisoned water – more complexity. What is this smile, where is its correspondence in the air of the pestilence? That is vague, but the smile of the murderer is terrifyingly definite. There doesn't have to be a perfect balance in both members of the analogy. The smile of the murderer is a smile of certainty in his triumph – the water is half-drunk.

3. What complexity in the notion that whoever is drinking this water only begins to half realize the desperateness of his situation all at once. The water has been poisoned, he has drunk half of it, his murderer is smiling. . . . All this throws itself with terrific force into the idea of the pestilence and its terror and desperateness!

4. In other words, this metaphor is jammed full of ambiguities rich in meaning, produced by the fact that a lot of things turn out, in it, to be other than they are, and all these discoveries are terrifying and their terror is all gathered together and attributed to the air of the pestilence to make it a totally successful metaphor!

This is only the beginning of the complexities this smug Lucas failed even to imagine possible. What a man to be writing about the imagination!

However, he also takes one of Pope's (fanciful) metaphors and tries to show there are so many "cross-connections" of meaning with that, according to Richards, it should be called imaginative. (Whether that is so, or not, doesn't matter to me, now.) Lucas takes the lines:

> Words are like leaves, and where they most abound,
> Much fruit of sense beneath is rarely found.

Lucas finds five uninteresting ways in which words are like leaves and 4 equally uninteresting ways in which fruit is like sense and the total result of this list is to show very clearly that the two members of the analogy (words: sense = leaves: fruit) are not fused in a synthesis of something new and vital, but just a juxtaposition of "fixed and definites" – a "barren wedding" good as far as it goes, but *not* reaching the intensity of fusion demanded of an imaginative metaphor like the one by Beddoes. But Lucas thinks because there are more than one way in which the words are like leaves here, Richards must retire in confusion! Lucas seems to understand neither Richards nor Coleridge, and the reason is, he is himself a little suspicious of the imagination, which he cannot fathom: he applies the mind of a Bacon to what requires more the mind of a Blake. No wonder he can't understand mysticism, when he bumps up against it! His motto is *"Mens sana in corpore sano"* ["A sound mind is a sound body"] which would be a smart motto if only it didn't turn out that those who use it eventually betray their position by admitting their conception of *"mens sana"* is the mind of Thomas Hardy, or the miserable J. S. Mill, or poor old Ruskin, or maybe crazy D. H. Lawrence!

October 18. Feast of Saint Luke

When the Pharisees attacked God's disciples for forgetting some of the hand-washing ceremonies of the Jews, before eating, Christ answered them quoting Isaias:

> "This people honoreth me with their lips, but their heart is far from me
>   And in vain do they worship me, teaching doctrines and precepts of men"

and then the Lord added this comment:

> *"For leaving the commandment of God you hold the tradition of men, the washing of pots and cups . . ."*

and He goes on to throw in their faces an instance where one of their ritual traditionalistic laws had worked around to a position actually *excluding* a charitable act – establishing a negative value, instead of a merely trivial one.

This offers several interesting points for meditation.

1. We can know how this happens, first of all, even in our own religious life. As soon as we begin to desire to serve God, and pray to him, He leads us, and we come upon certain ways of prayer that suit us, and seem to open our minds and wills, and raise us up to Him, at the time. Then naturally we return to these same prayers again, until some forms of worship we have come upon, by God's goodness, become habitual with us. Then we add to them, we modify them to suit ourselves, and they become solidified in the habit, and we become very attached to the habit, especially if some habit of prayer carries with it a kind of reward, and satisfaction, and is pleasant. But when we have grown to love saying a certain prayer at a certain time (for no other reason than that it is a pleasant habit) and then something happens, to interfere with that habit – we have to do something for somebody else, that keeps us from following our habit to the letter (when we could carry out its religious intention any time, later), we rebel and get annoyed, as if we were being insultingly led from our charitable work to waste our time, when actually, this second duty may be much more pleasing to God.

2. If this happens to individuals, how much more does it happen to worldly societies – to cultures that are based on religions. A culture that takes its life from a religion is no doubt better than one that does not – because, taking its character from religion, a culture is liable to be intimately connected with the deepest springs of the spiritual life of the people; otherwise, as in artificial modern cultures, the basis is no more than a rationalization of the group's material needs, and this rationalization is generally abstract and the result is general barrenness and impotence and confusion in the culture as a whole. All religious cultures, primitive, pagan, Greek, Christian, Jewish, Mohammedan, Confucian have proved themselves more healthy and orderly and fruitful than essentially non-religious cultures – even that of the Renaissance which contained in itself the seeds of much disorder and ruin, while at the same time the culture of the Roman Empire, in which religious life had become dead formality, and not a vital force in the culture itself, produced a pretty poor culture, materially rich, with the same kind of super-heated, hot house development as our own decadent culture.

But the distinction between religion and culture must always be clearly made, because when we give to Caesar through a culture the energy and devotion and love that belong to God through His religion, the result is ruinous for ourselves, for our religion, and eventually, also, for our culture; but cultures rise and fall, flourish and decay, just of themselves – their nature is instability and imperfection and change.

In religious cultures, the distinction often becomes lost between the kind of acts that belong to the religious life and the kind of activities that are merely customary and traditional and totally human in their significance. This happened, for instance, in the case of the ritualistic traditions of the Jews that were concerned more with the health of the people than anything else. This happens in the case of certain social taboos, in animistic religious cultures, etc. Then the tradition gets so solid, and with it, the confusion between it and religion, that the two become inseparably confused – to attack the social tradition is to attack the whole structure – and to attack the gods themselves.

For the Pharisees, the religious and social traditions had become so inextricably confused that they were *incapable of understanding* Christ was the Messiah when He came. Understanding: I mean, they were incapable of reconciling the notion of Messiahship with that of a Christ who cared nothing for their *social* tradition. Fundamentally, of course, nobody was capable, or is yet, of understanding Christ to be the Messiah. It is a matter of submission and belief. But the Pharisees' very pride was objectified socially in their submersion of religion in a formalistic social tradition.

In this sense they had imposed man's will over God's – only continuing to attribute, to the whole structure, Divine sanction, not human. Their pride consisted in the subtlest kind of rebellion against God – that unconscious rebellion which we all should mortally fear, – in which we unthinkingly let our self-will deceive us that it is God's will – and everything our pride demands is right, is the voice of God!

This is the reason for the terrific importance of humility in the Christian life – a social, as well as a personal humility.

The Pharisees had a long tradition behind them. The tradition was religious and social, and its fountainhead was the Divine Will, as He had certainly expressed Himself to them in the past. They had kept all the rules and laws in their tradition – they were sure of this.

But the only thing that was failing them was humility enough to realize this system was not all divine but partly human, and the human part was of their own making: and who offended against it, only offended them, not God. Besides, Christ was not asking them to admit that their confidence and complacency in their own perfection was false, because they based it on keeping rules that did not make for any perfection. No rules make a man perfect: only love and humility.

The Pharisees had built up a strong social tradition saying it was "Divine" and as a result, they not only refused to believe in Christ when He ignored that tradition, but definitely expected a Messiah who would come to fulfill all their expectations in *a social sense:* deliver them from their enemies, and make their nation prosperous and secure for ever.

The Catholic cultures of the late Middle Ages tended to make the same mistake – and it ruined them. The interests of the Church, the City of God, became confused in men's minds with the interests of worldly nations.

There are certain instances where the two sets of values are practically inseparable, and when the armies of Charles Martel defended the Christian culture of Europe against the attacking Moors it certainly also involved the defense of Christianity in a more than cultural sense. This defense was vitally necessary for the salvation of many souls to whom the faith came through the medium of a flourishing Christian culture.

(But we must never mistake the flourishing of a Christian culture for the flourishing of the Militant Church, which is only measured by the numbers of Saints, and sainthood is independent of culture. Also, the decadence of a Christian culture does not signify the decadence of the Church, as Protestants, Communists, and so on, believe.)

The First Crusade for the recovery of the Holy Land seems to me, in my ignorance of it, to have been largely a social rather than a religious enterprise: at best, the reconquest of the Holy Sepulchre was an endeavour more proper to a Christian culture as such than anything proper to the prosperity of the Church as Mystical Body.

How much the conquest of the Holy Sepulchre had to do with the reality of Faith it would be hard to say – probably much. But after the first, all the rest of the crusades certainly degenerated – and degenerated so far that by the time of the Fourth Crusade they were not even any longer *crusades to save Christian culture but to enrich the growing materialistic cultures inimical, in the end, to Christianity,* of trading cities like Venice. The Crusades destroyed a very flourishing Christian culture and brought on the Renaissance and the Reformation –

And these were, I believe, a punishment for the confusion between the social and the spiritual orders in the time of the Crusades!

However, the military and Christian culture of the Middle Ages presents problems I cannot thoroughly understand, and I don't know enough about them. But it presents the following problems to my mind: when you have a Christian culture – when, and how far is it true to say that a military defense of that culture is a defense, also, of the Church? Is there ever such a thing possible as a military defense of the Church, or when we say that do we only mean the defense of a Christian culture? Can it ever be that a military *offensive* favoring a Christian culture will benefit the Church?

I think this last one is easy to answer. It is a false problem. As soon as there is any question of an offensive war even though it may widen the empire of a "Christian culture" – if that empire is such that it can lead an offensive war, it can be called Christian only in a cultural sense, because offensive wars are absolutely incompatible with Christianity in the real (spiritual) sense. Then such an offensive will never benefit the Church, but, on the contrary, be harmful to it.

All this is very pleasant to talk about – there are no Christian cultures left in the world – and all wars are described by both sides as clearly defensive, so that questions of the "justice" of any war are so tough as to drive you crazy – without your getting a solution!

Today, the problem of culture and religion is a different one.

The confusion modern Catholics can fall into is to treat whatever culture they are born into as if its traditions – although they have nothing to do with Christianity at all – were part of our religion. One clear instance of this is the acceptance by some Catholics of the American social tradition of race prejudice, in complete and *sinful* contradiction of the doctrine of the Mystical Body of Christ.

Words culled like big imitation gems from a page of Spengler.

Faustian distance – tactics.

in the birth pangs of Caesarian emerges a trait of the buried springtime.

the arc of happening is about to close on itself.

a naive heart-need.

man becomes plant – namely as peasant.

feelings and woodland rustlings beat together.

Poor old heavy Mister Spengler! But he does once in a while get a very sharp intuition!

October 29, 1941

THE MAN WITH A LOT OF MONEY

Once there was a man who became very rich in the defense boom and he said to himself: all this money embarrasses me, for several reasons. First I don't like the idea of having made so much money out of a war in which millions of people are being killed. But second, even if the way I had made the money did not make me feel dirty all over; – even if I had made this money out of producing something good to make people live happier – clean houses or good food (instead of gasses to kill them) – even then I have so much money that I have to get rid of it. It embarrasses me.

What will I do? I can spend it on pleasures, perhaps. But I find that all the pleasures of the world I live in seem to have to become coarse and disgusting and stupid and they give me a feeling of sickness in the pit of my stomach, and I want to spit out even the thought of them. But anyway, these pleasures would only embarrass me as much as the money itself; I do not want these pleasures any more than the money.

What will I do? Buy a house, and a car and a lot of radios and pianos and books and pictures and live like a cultured and comfortable gentleman? I am satisfied with what I have already, and besides I don't want these expensive things any more than the money, they embarrass me.

Well, then what will I do? Put the money away in case I should get sick? There is too much left over that I would be embarrassed with it, besides, if I get sick, the country is full of hospitals and clinics, and maybe in a few years the money won't be worth anything anyway.

So what will I do with the money? Give it to "charity"? But I don't want to hand over a check to a polite white-haired lady and have her pass the check along to somebody else, who will pass it still further along and divide up the money as it goes until finally, when a percentage has been taken out for the advertising agent and the renting agent and all the other agents, the money will get to the poor only after they have been put through the third degree to see whether they are *poor enough* to really get it, after all. Besides that, when I give to such charities as these, I am only buying myself a sort of a cheap luxury in my own mind: I feel good, and I have done a duty easily, without trouble or headaches, and besides my name gets in the paper and I have got out of paying the income tax and everything is swell: I sit down and think of the beautiful sweet-faced crippled children my money has helped, or the cute little babies glad to get milk my money can buy, and the world is full of everything cute and sweet, and I don't feel right, I feel that what I have done was just some kind of a lie or a trick – and I am as embarrassed as if I still had the money.

Then what will I do? I will take the money and find out not the big charities that advertise on the billboards, and have the big rallies in Madison Square Garden, but find out someone who knows the poor and lives among them: I will go to a priest in a poor parish, or someone who can tell me who are the very poorest people, the ones who live where everything is ugly, and as evil as death, and I will see that they get all the money I have, and all the money I make, for the rest of my life, except for my bare necessities. . . . And then the man took all the money he had and gave it directly to the people, in the poorest places in the city without asking any questions of them, but giving his money to every body that was sick, or down and out, starving, in rags, and in this way he gave away ten thousand dollars.

And if you believe that, you're crazy!

November 1. All Saints, 1941

I don't know how it started: maybe the Baroness' letter saying I should write for the poor, for those who would scarcely read, for those who held a magazine clumsily; Anyway – big problem: how can I write for the poor? How can I tell them poverty was the condition of Christ and the Blessed Mother on earth, and suffering was Christ's portion when, although I do not make any money ($45 a month and room and board) yet the life I lead here is as happy as the richest kind of life, and as comfortable. How can I write about poverty when, although I am in a kind of a way, poor, yet here I am in this happy country club? If I am to write for those who are poor and can hardly read, I cannot do it from this place. But that does not mean that if I live here and give away my salary – or live here and spend my salary, I am any less Christian than if I live among the poor.

But why do I ask myself questions, all the time, about what I ought to be doing? Why am I always unsatisfied, and wanting to know what is my vocation if it is my vocation to stay here reading and praying and writing and sometimes teaching a class? I came back under a condition that occurred to me at the Trappists – wait and see about any other vocation. Meanwhile go back to work and give away half your salary. All this merely postponed a lot of questions.

Did I know in advance that, when I had prayed to be poor, it would not satisfy me to give away $20 a month of my salary? Yes, I knew. Still, it didn't hurt to try it.

Wednesday I had decided to make Friday (Vigil of All Saints) the beginning of a Novena of Saint Francis, offering myself and all I have to the Holy Ghost, with Francis' aid, and begging that there would be sent to me, any time in the future, any one to whom I could give whatever was asked in the name of God.

Friday morning after beginning the Novena, and preparing to go to Buffalo to meet Baroness de Hueck and drive down with her, here, where she decided a couple of days ago (after my decision) to come and speak – I make the following things clear in my mind: that she will probably ask me to come to Friendship House. That if she did, it would not necessarily be a sign that I *had* to go, that it was definitely God's will – that I wouldn't decide anything before hand, make any decisions before hand: but the general idea was a sort of tentative defense *against* going to Friendship House.

Then I renewed my prayer to do God's will, in any terms He saw fit – give Him whatever He asked (this time again in terms of the money and goods I was thinking of when I began the Novena).

Then, riding to Buffalo was like any other auto ride. I wasn't thinking of anything or expecting anything, consciously. Fr. Hubert, Fr. Roman and I sit in Buffalo station talking about Rome, Paris, Cologne; about *Life* magazine being banned from Saint Bona's Library for a couple of issues; about the big stuffed Buffalo; about politics: I don't think of anything much. She arrives. We start off in the car.

Pretty soon the question comes: am I going to do Catholic Action?

Somehow I give it a clumsy parry (not excited or scared).

About half an hour later: "When are you coming to Friendship House?"

I make a bad parry, try to ask if I would be able to write at FH. She says why? and anyway, I must come without conditions or reservations, prepared to give up writing as well as everything else.

Fr. Hubert and Fr. Roman excited as I am, in a calm sort of a way.

Fr. Hubert says "Why don't you put the matter in the Baroness's hands?"

I say "Well, I'll have to stay until February at Saint Bona's!"

Everybody laughs.

From that moment it seemed settled. Just before saying the words, a very sweet and fast sensation: then the dive. Afterwards, all the rest of the ride, completely calm; everything seemed absolutely perfectly good, normal: talk about it or not talk about it: nothing more to be said.

Before asking the questions – she and Fr. Hubert say (concerning a problem of her own) about God's will: that it is known through persons and through events. At that moment, before the questions, which I knew would be asked, were asked, I knew what my answer must eventually be.

Now it is possible to doubt again. Then, not. But it is immaterial. I have until February to leave it indefinite, and give my mind, freely, a chance to change: in advance, I wonder whether I will have any desire to change it?

In all the places where I have walked, restless (like the grove), I walk with a different feeling: leaving places that have become agreeable to me through past prayers said there, and which I must not confuse with the love of God, thinking *them* to be part of that love. If I become separated and detached from those places that feed my devotion for the moment (and now give a kind of retrospective consolation which was never felt in them before), and go somewhere where I know the peace will be hard and sad with poverty and squalor, that detachment takes me closer to God, for He is not in this grove in any particular way: only my associations, my own imagination make it seem so.

I have been happy here in a way, never content, never completely at rest in a sense this was where I belonged.

Whatever this vocation is, it involves a whole different attitude to the future. A sense of calm. A sense that I am going to do something hard, murderous to my pride and my senses. That it doesn't make much sense to fear it or love it, but that I must refer everything to God. In the natural course of events I would never desire to do this unnatural thing (leave what is pleasant for what is unpleasant) and I have no natural powers that will ever enable me, by themselves, to stand Harlem. If God has called me to that life of poverty, He will make it quite clear what I am to do and also provide me with enough strength to do it. No sense in worrying or planning: only in continuing to pray that I may put my spirit entirely into His hands. Which means: doing at the same time what is better and harder, more holy and less rewarding, more merciful and less delightful. To do those things in which *I* am last and least. To submit my will to the Baroness', and to the priests.

All the arguments against going are jokes – transparently easy to see through, since they are all denied by the Gospels, the Beatitudes, the Baroness herself in asking me and by me myself, who really desire no other thing than this, which I have been praying for ceaselessly since August: that I may give myself entirely to God's service!

Before I had given the Baroness the first argument (about writing) I realized how foolish all the arguments would be.

That I am meant to stay here and write!

That I am meant to stay here and teach!

That I am meant to stay here and pray and meditate a lot!

If I am meant to write, I will write there also – and perhaps to more purpose. If I am meant to teach – the same thing. Pray and meditate – the same. And there I will be living in poverty and doing the holy work of God's apostolate, *all* the corporal and spiritual works of mercy, instead of, here, a couple of the spiritual!

Yet I do not say I will do this or I will do that. I pray God that in February I may do His will, and between now and then, hope to invent no arguments to sell myself one way or the other, but only continue working, praying and writing exactly as I am doing.

By His grace, that was the most I felt, upon answering the Baroness: that it seemed to be God's will that I would go in February. Between now and then I should go on as I have all term – no need for anything new or for any excitement whatever. If I pray, either I will change my mind or will not, but He will guide me. No need to be up in arms. No need to be anything other than what I am, but *pray and fast harder.* None of the excitements, arguments, tearing of hair, trips to Cuba, or big "farewell world!" gestures. No need for anything special, big joy, big sorrow, big excitement, big torments. All action until then indifferent except prayer and fasting and meditation – and work. But, I thank God and all saints, no running around in circles – not yet. Defend me later O God! against scruples. JMJT.

I have got *Gray Eminence* – which seems good so far. There, the big problem is that a man who convinced himself that his own natural will was God's will. This is always the great danger, but a danger that absolutely has to be faced.

In a question like that of a vocation the danger is met with faith and patience and humility and love and constant prayer, and in time the answer comes clear. Also, in cases of vocation, it can generally be assumed that when you are attracted to some course that involves doing much good and at the same time sacrificing all natural desires for ease, rest, consolation, comfort, leisure, security, personal independence, etc., the higher course is God's will unless something special happens to make that course impossible. It is God's will that we do good. He attracts us to do good. We try to follow. From then on it is necessary to pray and have great faith. All the arguments against the higher course only bring the answer: "O you of little faith!" except the one answer "I have no desire to follow that course – I am not attracted to it. I have forgotten the enthusiasm I had about it for 10 minutes, once, and now the idea leaves me cold, completely." If that answer is the true one, and in grace, then it is sufficient denial of the vocation. Every other answer against the vocation is a fake.

November 4, 1941

The reason for my going to the Trappists (in September) was to find out whether I should consider that I had a vocation to work in Harlem. The priest told me – without my having mentioned this idea at all – that the first thing was self sanctification, then to develop my talents. I resisted a strong impulsion to tell him about the vocation – for what reason I can't imagine. I didn't know how to bring it up? Any reason is absurd: I suppose I was trying to kid myself that the whole thing wasn't serious anyway.

The result was; I was waiting to find out in some other way – a rather superstitious process! What was I expecting – an angel to wake me up in the middle of the night and tell me? I realize more and more that I am certainly a very great fool. Why didn't I discuss what I wanted to discuss, in the confessional?

The best reason I can give is – maybe I was afraid of kidding myself and the priest with a story that had no real importance. Was it something I was going to forget in two days, or six? I wanted to wait and see: and there, too, I was fooling myself. But it turned out all right, too. The idea was to wait and see: the priest would have probably told me that himself.

We have to be very careful about asking God questions and then answering them ourselves and saying: "God answered."

Such questions are to be asked in the confessional – or of a spiritual director anyway – and perhaps argued a little with your friends, but not too much. And then you pray and wait, and look again at the question and answers after the passage of time.

After all, I believe it was quite reasonable to go on retreat to see whether or not I wanted to ask myself any questions concerning a vocation. And it was all right to wait and still not ask myself any. But it was not so smart to assume that perhaps the question that I had decided not to ask had definitely been answered by my not asking it.

In any case, it was all right. The question was bound to come up again and it did.

Walking down from Martiny's rocks on a day late in September, I think of the cowbells and the fields and the tree I have been sitting under – and I compare it all with Harlem – and I do not quite convince myself that it is my calling to be "a contemplative" in the country.

One thing I cannot see myself trying to be now, even if I could be, is a Franciscan in this province. But I still think of the Trappists. And I still wonder if what was an obstacle to the Franciscans might not be one to the Trappists: and I still keep thinking: maybe I could write to them and find out. And still I do not.

The choice between Saint Bonaventure and Harlem is definitely not a choice between two clear possible vocations. Harlem may be a vocation, but Saint Bonaventure isn't. Ever since I came here I have not regarded the place as anything permanent for myself: have always been wondering what else it was I was looking for. At first I thought, another job. Then I feared I would be drafted into the army. Then I wondered if maybe I couldn't be a Trappist. Now this Harlem business. One thing is sure: I had better get settled on something. To me, my life means two things: writing and voluntary poverty, both for the love of God. So far, here, there is no voluntary poverty – no sacrifice. Harlem will bring that, too. Beyond that, the Negro apostolate doesn't have to be the only thing I will ever turn to; but it begins to seem certain I should try the lay apostolate of poverty and writing and works of mercy and give my life to that.

One of the illusions I have had here was that this was a sufficient lay-apostolate: to teach, write a little, etc. But it is all indirect. It is Catholic Action but it is *not enough*. Teaching English is not enough – nor is writing novels in doubletalk. Both of these are sidetracks, and this place is too remote from the places where people suffer most, and cry out in agony for some kind of help.

Besides that, I imagine I can teach the people here something that will turn them towards helping those others. But how can I? How do I know what I am talking about? And why should they listen to me?

But when I have gone across the gulf and into Harlem then I will learn what to say and they will see where my news is coming from – from experience and not out of my big quixotic imagination.

Now at least I have been told by others what I am to do.

Be prepared to even give up writing for a while, if necessary.

Learn to write for the poor – who are those who are hungriest for words telling them what to do. The only way to learn that is to be one of them. To become poor, a liver in a slum, with no security and no worldly consolation, no possessions, no resources except faith!

I am scared of rushing at this with too much rowdy eagerness, the way I have rushed at other vocations and lost them, because I want this to be the one. I desire beyond everything that I may be really poor, give up all things, sell all I have and give it to the poor and follow Christ, and live for His love, and ask nothing but His love, give myself entirely to his love by being the lowest servant of His poorest and most abandoned children – and not only of them but of all His children. To be the poorest of them all, even as He makes Himself a tiny and obscure and weak white host of flour and wine to be eaten by the mouths of all of us even the most unclean, according to the laws of the Pharisees.

It is no use waiting now, I desire very much to begin to live in poverty, more than anything on earth. And this is a chance, and I pray that I may take it, and not lose it, and begin now to really follow Christ as He told us to. And this in great earnestness and love and devotion, not for the peace and relief it must give anybody, at first, to follow the Gospel _literally_ and without any further sophistry to make him sick with unquietness and secret shame and unfulfillment.

But I pray I may follow Him all the more devotedly when, through tribulation, even the _sense_ of peace is taken away for a while as it must be. And when I am left in physical poverty and total spiritual desolation! I dread it, but I must also _seek_ this, because most certainly in this tribulation He purifies us and brings us to Him!

O my God! Whether or not Harlem is the place of my vocation, help me soon to begin to live in perfect Holy Poverty according to Your Word, that my whole life may be given over entirely to Your love and to Your Almighty Will! Saint Therese of Lisieux, pray for me that I may refuse my God _nothing_ – not the greatest sacrifice, and not even the very smallest! Amen.

It is beginning to seem that when the Baroness came and told me again to get out of here and come to Harlem, it was right, it was time for me to go.

It does not seem to me either tremendously right or tremendously important to go to Olean, put my paycheck in the bank, get my statement and a couple of checks saying "Cistercian Monastery" punched and endorsed and cancelled among the others to show I am trying to be holy. It doesn't seem to me to mean anything of any kind to be called "Hi prof!" or to read in the _New York Times_ about the coal strike and the threatened war with Japan and the other horrors.

Everything that is important here is important anywhere else, and maybe more so: prayer, meditation, writing, work. This is not the best, or the worst, or the only place in the world for any of them.

If the Baroness came back and told me to stay, I'd stay, until somebody, who knew as much as she, came along with some other idea.

And all the time there is the rich youth in the Bible, who, when he was told he should give up all he had to the poor and follow Christ, turned away sad, "For he had great possessions," is in my mind. I can't be content here and think of that man, too. It seems to me this is a nice job which is valuable only because it can be given up, left, renounced, which is all I can think, right now, of doing with it.

November 24, 1941

I guess I am full of the kind of distress that means I ought to be writing a poem – or else what? Return to the chapel.

I got back from New York by the night train, having been wedged in various positions in the hard green seats of the day coach all night – but I am not physically tired, merely filled with a deep, undefined vague sense of spiritual distress as if I had a deep wound running, inside me, and it had to be stanched – and I should go back to the chapel, or try to say something in a poem. And that wound is another aspect of the fact that we are exiles on earth.

The sense of exile bleeds inside me like a hemorrhage – it is always the same wound, whether it is a sense of sin, or of loneliness, or of one's own insufficiency, or of spiritual dryness: they are all really the same, in the way we experience them. In fact, spiritual dryness is one of the most acute experiences of longing we can have – therefore, of love.

I got back to this wonderful, quiet place. There is a little snow on the hills, a light, hard frozen powder. The roads are like iron. The air is cold and gray. The rooms are silent. Water runs in the pipes.

It is still, and peaceful: but there is no peace for me here.

I am amazed at all this quietness which does not belong to me: for a moment, I get the illusion that the peace is real: but it isn't – not as soon as I hear the talk of the people. The peace here is not the peace of poverty and sacrifice, merely the "peace" of the absence of trouble, and that is not for me now, nor can be any more. And yet the peace is beautiful and quiet, and the people are good.

Yesterday, on retreat with the workers from Friendship House, Father [Paul] Furfey said: "You must be despised by the world: and if you are *not* despised and rejected, begin to think there is something wrong, somewhere." When he said this, I saw Betty Schneider smile to herself like a kid that had been told something, asked to a party, and that was some nice smile, a very glad smile, and there was more joy in it than I have ever seen here, because it was a joy that was pure of any mere contentment or earthly satisfaction, or false peace.

Before I was a Catholic I was half crazy with restlessness and boredom and sorrow. When I became a Catholic I ceased to be bored at all, or restless – in any natural sense. Most practising Catholics are sure to lead a life full of more or less natural satisfactions, natural patience, even-temper, contentment, the level-temperedness of stoics. But that is not enough, either – there is a lot of purely natural happiness around, among Catholics and people who are not. I have seen more of that, anywhere, in this last year, than for 10 years before, in spite of the war. It probably comes of the fact that people are making money and are comfortable but not in so safe a way that their comfort palls on them.

When I was in the quicksand of my own exaggerated restlessness, I thought this firm ground was all that anyone needed, for peace. And there is plenty of this natural happiness, this evenness of life, at Saint Bonaventure.

But that evenness is illusory and dangerous: it is *based*, economically speaking, on violence and injustice: the war and every injustice that led to the war. And also, it is a purely natural contentment and even if it were just, we cannot be content in merely natural satisfactions, our own selfish quiet and freedom from worry. We have to leave all and follow Christ, for only in Him is true peace: and Christ is where men starve, and are beaten.

We can either renounce all worldly quiet, and ease, and absence of trouble, and live our lives out in the Liturgy, before the tabernacle, as pure contemplatives loving one another in our community – or else we must renounce all our own ease and minister to Christ in the poor as much as we can. But if we renounce nothing except our cares, and if our only idea is to live together without friction so that each of us may remain at peace, materially, unruffled, we only get a false peace. It is a good enough peace in worldly terms, but it is not enough for Christians: for us, our peace is only in Christ, and is only come by through mortification, sacrifice and the Cross.

November 25, 1941

Aldous Huxley's letter with five dollars in it, for Friendship House: I am more impressed with this kindness the more I think of it. The more I think of the article in *Catholic World* I wrote about him, the more I regret it. In general, I think I was right: but I made many glib individual statements which I would gladly eat. One was "Huxley, as a philosopher, is not distinguished." Maybe he isn't. But I'd still gladly eat the words.

I read two words by Hitler in a stupid book by Rauschning: Hitler believes the cupidity and selfishness of priests and of all Catholics will make it quite easy for him to destroy the Church. Precisely: that is the one big danger: and they say that Hitler has a knack of seeing the weakest point of whatever it is he is about to attack. There doesn't seem to be much wrong with this intuition, about Catholics – in the purely natural order. However four saints can make up for all the materialists in the world, because theirs is God's power: and Hitler is crazy because he thinks he can prevent people from being saints merely by treating them as common criminals, not letting them appear to be martyrs. In the natural order, Hitler has made a very smart intuition: one which would be perfect except that he doesn't understand the supernatural strength which is the *only* strength of saints. And as long as Catholics rely on worldly defences against Hitler, they are lost. Therefore there is only simple defence: to take the Gospel literally, and *be saints*.

November 26, 1941

All day long through the walls of this building comes the sound of radios, from all sides, all playing the same terrible stuff, from the same place, the local station. I don't know whether it is anything very new, because I haven't even listened to radios much – at least not in the last four years: but it seems that nearly all the singing has turned into horrible, discordant, monotonous wailing and hooting, in the style of those Andrews Sisters. They take one fundamental discord and never change it, simply go on hooting it like a steam siren, in a sort of obvious rhythm, and the effect is horrible. Now all the singing is like that – never changes. No inventiveness, no taste, no rhythm, no harmony, just this offensive and monotonous hooting and wailing – not even melody: in fact, melody less than anything. It has become so that melody, the last stronghold of people who weren't sure enough of their taste to let it go, for rhythm etc., even that has been lost. Now there is just the pure vulgarity of this wailing – incessant, unrelieved.

And then there is Superman: he is supposed to fly in the air. His program is introduced by a sort of hysterical snatch of dialogue, or maybe there are three voices. (1) "It's a bird" (2) "It's a Plane!" (3) It's SUPERMAN!" Invariably I roll on the ground tearing at my collar, gasping for air! This building is full of students and even priests absorbing, with a very intent seriousness, all this stupidity.

One of the recent copies of the *New Yorker* made me very sore by being particularly bad. One of the worst features was a story about a Norwegian boy who had run away from Quisling to England: it was all in pidgin English.

Gibney has been taken prisoner in the manoeuvers in South Carolina.

November 27, 1941

I spent maybe the whole afternoon writing a letter to Aldous Huxley and when I was finished I thought "who am I to be telling this guy about mysticism" and now I remember that until I read his *Ends and Means* just about four years ago, I hadn't known a thing about mysticism, not even the word. The part he played in my conversion, by that book, was quite great. Just how great a part a book can play in a conversion is questionable: several books figured in mine. Gilson's *Spirit of Medieval Philosophy* was the first and from it more than any other book I learned a healthy respect for Catholicism. Then *Ends and Means* from which I learned to respect mysticism. Maritain's *Art and Scholasticism* was another – and Blake's poems; maybe Evelyn Underhill's *Mysticism* although I read precious little of it. Joyce's *Portrait of the Artist* got me fascinated in Catholic sermons (!) What horrified him began to appeal to me! It seemed quite sane. Finally, G. F. Lahey's life of G. M. Hopkins: I was reading about Hopkins' conversion when I dropped the book and rushed out of the house and went to see Fr. Ford. All this reading covered a period of a year and a half, or two years – during which I read almost all of Fr. Wieger's translations of Buddhist texts – without understanding them.

Anyway, what do I know to tell Huxley when I should have been asking him questions.

I am ashamed of everything I sent him, including a couple of poems.

Today I think – should I be going to Harlem or to the Trappists? Why doesn't this idea of the Trappists leave me? Should I do the thing I have wanted to do since spring: write and find out if the thing the Franciscans took to be an impediment might be passed over by the Trappists?[12]

If you asked me what I thought they would answer, right now I would be almost certain they'd let me in. . . . But I may be afraid to write and find they wouldn't, and have that last hope taken away, as if it were a hope. If I feel this way, does it mean anything?

Shouldn't I at least find out if there is some choice between Harlem and the Trappists? Does the choice exist for me?

Would I not say, just now, that if it did exist, I wouldn't hesitate to join the Trappists? Is that why I hesitate to ask – is this a curious, roundabout way of resisting a vocation?

If I really had a choice, what would send me to Harlem rather than the Trappists? Would it be the following combination of good and bad rea-

[12] Apparently, Merton's frankness about his past, especially fathering a child while at Cambridge, cautioned the Franciscans about receiving him into the novitiate. When entering Gethsemani, at the time of his first profession, he made provision for the (unnamed) person, if such could be found, by making available to his guardian, Dr. Tom Bennett, a part of his inheritance for this purpose. See *The School of Charity: Letters of Thomas Merton on Religious Renewal and Spiritual Direction*, edited by Patrick Hart (New York: Farrar, Straus and Giroux, 1990), 7–8, for a copy of this important document.

sons: that there would be real poverty (insecurity) but also I would be independent, continue to write, be able to circulate in the world and its life . . . but be able to help people and work in a place which cries out for help.

The good reasons do not apply only to Harlem. I would have to renounce perhaps *more* to enter the Trappists. That would be the one place where I would give up *everything*. Also, anyone who believes in the Mystical Body of Christ realizes I could do as much for the Church and my brothers in the world at Gethsemani, as in Harlem. As to the independence – and writing! Be prepared to give them all up. It seems monstrous this minute, that I should think of my writing as having any particular importance – that is, enough to get mixed up in this problem. If God wants me to write, I can write anywhere.

And Harlem will be full of confusions – and I don't particularly like the idea of working with a lot of girls.

Or do I want to go to Gethsemani because it is a perfect society, even in the natural order? Is it because last night, reading Mumford's *Culture of Cities* I got very depressed with the rottenness of New York? I think that made me want to be in Harlem, though – the most desperate of all places, to preach God!

Going to Harlem doesn't seem like anything special – it is good, and is a reasonable way to follow Christ: but going to the Trappists is exciting and fills me with awe, and desire: and I return to the idea "Give up *everything* – *everything!*" and that means something.

Now what will I do? Pray? Speak to one of the friars.

November 28, 1941

The one thing that most appals me is my own helplessness and stupidity: a helplessness and stupidity that come from a complete and total and uncompromising self reliance that, to the world, appears to be a virtue in me, and a great source of strength! What a lie and what a crazy deception that is: to be self reliant is to be strong and smart: to be self reliant will get you through all your problems, without too much difficulty or anguish.

Ever since I was sixteen, and travelled all over Europe, some of it on foot – by myself (always by preference alone) I have developed this terrific sense of geography, this habit of self-analysis, this knack of getting along with strangers and chance acquaintances – this complete independence and self-dependence which turns out to be, now, not a strength but, in my big problem, a terrific weakness.

My instinct, when I have been faced by any such problem, has always been to go off and walk restlessly somewhere by myself until the problem turns itself over and over so many times that I get sick of it. Maybe a solution comes out later. Maybe the problem is not terribly tough – but this time it is a tough one.

At least I went first to the chapel – as I did when the Baroness asked me to come to Harlem. Last spring, I walked with the vocation problem, in the woods. Two years ago – 1939 – I walked with the same problem, vocation to the priesthood, on the chicken dock, Greenwich Village.

First, in the chapel, my heart was pounding so fast I couldn't even see straight, and I could hardly make the words of the prayers. And all I could think was that it was very bad to be that disturbed. Eventually I calmed down, and prayed. Then the idea it would be a good notion to see Fr. Philotheus gradually crystallized out.

I left the chapel. I went first not to his room but mine. Then said a couple more prayers. Looked at a book about the Trappists: all the time knowing I was being a fool, I had no reason for standing around. (When my heart had pounded so fast in the chapel, I was saying to myself: "You are crazy: wait! wait! wait!")

When I got downstairs I went into the hall of the monastery and took two steps towards his door and rushed back out, and walked up and down with ten conflicting ideas in my head: first that I was being a fool – to be as disorganized as the French army was by the German fifth columns – second that waiting was not relevant because it just protracted this confusion – third that waiting was prudent – etc.

The next time I go in, I nearly get to his door, but then it is almost as if I were physically pushed away from it: the idea that pushed me away was: "This is absurd! This huge big problem in this small, familiar room, thrown like a bomb in the middle of some routine piece of philosophical manuscript he is reading... disturb him . . . etc." I rushed out again.

Finally I walked across the campus and back and when I got back he was out of his room – I could see the light was out.

So then the first impulse was to say "Now, see, let it all go for a few more days."

So I pray to Saint Theresa, in the grove.

While I am praying to her the question becomes clear: all I want to know is, do I have a chance to be a priest after all. I don't want him to argue for or against the Trappists. I *know* I want to be a Trappist. I remember the terrific sense of holiness and peace I got when I first stepped inside Gethsemani, something more certain and more terrific than ever hit me anywhere else – and which stayed with me until I got all mixed up about the vocation, the end of the week, in that terrible impasse: I want to be a priest – but I am told there is an impediment. Therefore the desire is just an emotional luxury: I am kidding myself.

While I am praying to her, Saint Therese of the Child Jesus, it is like hearing the bells in the tower, ringing for Matins in the middle of the night. I walk through the grove saying she will help me to be her Trappist – Theresa's Trappist, at Gethsemani.

I come back. No light in Fr. Philotheus' room. He is in the rec. room. I get him from there, without any great fuss. I tell him my questions.

Instantly he says that, in his opinion, there is no canonical impediment in my case. And he advises the thing that was so obvious I hadn't thought of it – go to Gethsemani as soon as the Christmas vacation begins, and tell the whole story to the Abbot. (I thought of writing – he said that would be bad.)

Also he advises me to be very careful about deciding to be a Trappist. What about my vocation to be a writer?

That one has absolutely no meaning any more, as soon as he has said what he has said.

So I run upstairs bursting with *"Te Deum laudamus – Te Dominum confitemur – Te aeternum Patrem omnis terra veneratur. . . ."* ["We praise you, God; we glorify you; all the earth adores you, Eternal Father. . . ."] And then to the chapel, and prayers and prayers and prayers.

I can't go to bed, and when I do, I can't go to sleep.

I go through the grove again – my head full of a big doubletalk mixture of *Te Deum* and goodbye to everything I don't want.

In bed suddenly I am amazed – in four weeks, with God's grace, I may be sleeping on a board –

And there will be no more future – not in the world, not in geography, not in travel, not in change, not in variety, conversations, new work, new problems in writing, new friends, none of that: but a far better progress, all interior and quiet!!! If God only would grant it! If it were only His will.

But I am most impressed with the fact that here I have been praying to find out His will and stopping myself from finding it out mostly by my own stupidity and stubbornness, which are both connected with this absurd idea of self-reliance and self-dependence which was going to be my greatest strength and turned out to be my biggest handicap.

As to all this self-analysis on paper – it isn't important either. If the twenty other things I have to say are important, I will find a chance to say them. That I waited this long to ask Fr. Philotheus this question about the vocation, and open the question again, it did no harm. All the waiting I have done, and possibly must still do, is all quite important and significant.

But I earnestly pray to give myself entirely to God, according to His will, and no longer get in the way with my own stupid will – only He can help me out of my own clumsiness.

November 29, 1941

The beginning of Advent. All the antiphons knock me down: Advent opens out like a night full of mystery and brightness and wonder, in which Christ is coming.

O God, whether it is true or not that there is no impediment to my being a priest, the mere chance that I *might* someday be one fills my life with the brightness and goodness of the year's spring: and the liturgical year begins!

O Holy Lord God! What a wonder and what a gift, that with the beginning of the liturgical year, I should be allowed to feel that there was even the mere possibility of my becoming a Trappist! With the birth of the new liturgical year, I am born new, too! Even if it is not possible, to be a priest – yet this Advent has begun like a real Advent!

The darkness before morning, when it is quietest and brightest, and Christ comes to be born!

"*In illa die stillabunt montes dulcedinem. . . .*" ["On that day, the mountains will drip sweetness."]

What a word "*dulcedo* – sweetness" has none of its dignity and holy goodness – How terrific it is in the *Salve Regina – Vita* – Dul-ce-do – *et spes nostra, Salve!* ["Our life, our sweetness and our hope, Hail!"] The word almost *is* a grace in itself, it has the fullness and cleanness and strength of grace in it!

In the long quiet night of Advent, *(dulcedo)* sweetness falls from the skies of Time's darkness like a radiance that is just beyond our vision! O Holy Grace!

The Lord is coming!

Yesterday morning I was serving Mass and I heard, behind me, a reader (it was Fr. Thomas) read in English words from the day's Gospel for the students' congregation:

"Blessed are those servants whom the Lord, when He cometh, shall find watching" and I was shot through with a strong and happy desire of belonging entirely to God's service, and was filled with a kind of exaltation all the rest of that Mass.

―――

O Lord, I want nothing more than never to have to argue with anyone again as long as I live! Argument with words only strengthens us in our stubborn resistance to everything that gives us peace – only increases our own prejudices and does little for the truth at all. First, we must argue by our example: and when we are totally devoted to God then we can speak truth, which is not our own opinion, but the truth we would rather die than violate or corrupt – and then we will either keep silent, or only talk to praise what is good and true.

Why should I ever criticize anyone else? The world is full of evil, and it is our duty to fight evil and teach truth: but if I want to do that, why can't I first start with all the evil that is in me – I can teach others what to avoid by making plain not their faults but my own. That carries much more conviction! But when I start out to do it, the first thing I find out is how stupid I am, how little discernment I have – when I was so subtle and discerning in seeing what was wrong with everybody else.

I am not trying to say what is God's will, concerning my life, because I cannot say before He shows me Himself – I won't know until after the word, in fact the event, that tells me: if it is His will that I become a Trappist, I will know when they admit me, and when they let me start out, and when I become a Novice, in strong love and desire to serve Him. I don't know God's will yet – I pray to know in time. Now I only write down what occurs to me today – I don't know any more than a couple of facts of present experience. They are simple.

The Breviary had become a little dry: now, suddenly, it is full of more meaning and life than it ever had for me, at any time!

One thing I never dared write in this book: last May, when I was worrying about the vocation – worrying and pounding my own silly brains rather than praying and meditating – I did nevertheless pray for guidance, in the wrong sort of spirit, perhaps: but anyway, I prayed and opened the Bible three times, and the second sentence was *"Ecce eris tacens"* – the first having been something I couldn't make out – but good, – from the Book of the Macabees. The third something of the same sort from a Gospel. But this *"Ecce eris tacens –* behold, thou shalt be silent" struck me dumb beyond any emotion or thought – I could only pray in a daze, and I was scared of what I had done – it seemed to me to be a kind of insolence on my part to have done this, and a worse insolence, now, not to do anything about it, because

I still couldn't see what to do – I had only asked for an answer to a question of fact concerning the future, really, and nothing about *how* to go about getting there. Besides, I certainly believed (and believe) God guided my hand, but am still left dumb because there is no certainty it necessarily means I will be a Trappist – it might mean something quite different. However, from the moment there is a possibility there is no canonical impediment to my vocation, the sentence has a clearer meaning. I pray it may mean that I can become a Trappist!

I haven't truly been all alive since the time I was told to withdraw my application for the Franciscans. Today, everything in the world was simple and harmonious and good like the spring I thought I could enter the Franciscans.

The feeling of fearful anticipation of trials, mixed with a belief they will never be too hard for the grace God gives one to bear them – is the same. I looked forward to the easy Franciscan novitiate as though it would be as hard for me, physically, then, as this whole hard life.

When I wanted to be a Franciscan, I was glad to hear from clerics that the novitiate had been made much easier. Now I am sure that I would not have been satisfied as a Franciscan in this province at all: and as to the Trappist life – haven't I been praying for a chance to give God *everything* and refuse Him *nothing?* If I am admitted, that prayer will have been answered: it is no more than the strict duty of a Christian to refuse God nothing He asks, and the rule of St. Benedict merely makes all that task at least clear on every point: we can never fail to see each opportunity for giving God what He asks us, by the light of a religious rule perfectly kept!

His will be done. If I am to be made to desire ardently a cloistered life and then be refused it, His will be done. The desire is surely from Him – it must be supernatural, there can be nothing *natural* in wanting to lead such a life!

But when I wanted to be a Franciscan, I now know there was much that was very imperfect about my motives.

No doubt there were supernatural motives, too. I had the same sort of desire to be a priest and belong to God then as now. I had the same exalted desire for that Holy sacramental power to bring into the world its Life and its Hope, the Light of the World! each day at Mass – to save the world by becoming the instrument of God's coming into it daily! To hear confessions and comfort and advise souls! (I long for that! To be given up entirely to that work.)

But also there were very strong and bad material motives, too.

The poverty meant less to me than absolute poverty – it meant security and no worry! It meant comfort and carelessness. In the Trappists, it *is* poverty, and labor, and hardship.

The chastity I welcomed.

The obedience – I was full of mental reservations about that (and would have got away with them, too). But in the Trappists – absolute, unquestioning obedience!

Also, there was the fact of the war and the draft. I would get out of the draft – useless to deny I thought of this: it was the war that drove me, in one way, to decide about becoming a Catholic, and it helped me to decide quick that I wanted to be a priest. It wasn't the real motive, I now know: and did know very soon. But it was there.

Now, thanks to God, I have not only had to face the problem of the draft as a moral issue, and decide, and submit – and make my objection the law allowed me and ask to be put in ambulance work, and take the chance of being put in a combatant unit anyway, as they did to Gibney who was granted the same (partial) objection I was. But I was in I-B – and I am out of the draft for a long while and then only in limited service and even if I am not, I am ready to do whatever I am told: so going to the Trappists has nothing to do with the war. (Somebody who reads the paper tells me we are about to fight Japan, this time for sure!)

All these things, these great evils and imperfections, some of them almost mortally sinful, perhaps, have much to do with the fact I wasn't accepted – I mean show that in God's sight I was not ready – Fr. Edmund only advised me concerning the "legal impediment" and would never have stopped at such imperfections as I now realize I had.

Even now, my unworthiness to be a priest is colossal – my pride is terrific, and my selfishness. But I dare ask again because I am sick to death and the Trappist rule will heal my pride and heal my selfish-greed and envy and graspingness for the world, if I fast and pray, fast and pray!

I give this whole Advent, every minute to the Blessed Virgin, begging her to help me to bring me to her house at Gethsemani to be her loving child and servant, a child of God in silence and labor and sacrifice and obscurity! JMJT.

November 30. First Sunday in Advent

"*Rorate caeli desuper et nubes pluant justum.*" ["Drop down dew, you heavens from above, and let the clouds rain the just."]

The music of the anthem from the Seminarians' High Mass, stayed with me until after dinner – now it has been confused with the tune of some psalm.

And tomorrow is the feast of another apostle – and I read again of an apostle's vocation – Saint Andrew's. He left his nets *instantly* and followed Christ – left all he had *instantly!* Lord, where dost Thou live? "*Veni et vide* . . . come and see!"

For two years I have been wondering and waiting and trying to see what was my vocation: it would be pride and madness to be angry at having perhaps "wasted" two years, because all the waiting has been forced on me by events, by what appeared to be confusions and are now becoming clear.

True, my vocation, when I was thinking of the Franciscans, was imperfect. But it was no less imperfect than the vocations of many others who have since, probably, become good holy priests. That in itself wasn't enough of a reason.

After living here a year and a half, I know one thing: I am terribly glad I am not one of the Friars here. You can become a Saint anywhere, and here as well as anywhere in the world – but there is not much distinction between here and the world – *cannot* be, because it is a college, and the monastery is in the college building and there is no cloister – etc. The friars are all good, peaceful fellows, the clerics that come in the summer are full of a healthy kind of zeal: but all their zeal is only the zeal you would expect in an honestly run business house, in a club of decent salesmen. Everything is below its proper standard: this monastery is good and honest the way the world *could* be – but is not *holy* the way a monastery *should* be.

All the priests here realize there is something wrong, but don't seem to know what it is. They all complain of it – they all want to remedy it – by human action, like running a business. They have the feeling they are part of a business that could be better run. The atmosphere is one of a complete stale-mate: everybody is sincerely devout in a way and wants to be more so – everybody knows there is something lacking here, and everybody who really wants to do something feels condemned to frustration.

The trouble is that when you run a supernatural society like a natural society, it goes dead. When *you run* a supernatural society it goes dead – period. Only God can make live a supernatural community, and here all the work is being done, perhaps, by men: of course, the individuals all pray – but they need a sort of reform.

God forgive me for talking so much about the Friars. I could say all these things over, better, about myself. All I have been doing here, with all my prayers, has been determining my life – grace has had to work in me in spite of, against my own human pride. If I pray – I am merely praying to have *my* way, – in a slightly less crude form than the kids and friars who offer up masses so that the team will win a football game!!!

About Harlem:

What made me want to go to Harlem: first, the one real thing: after I had worked at night there two weeks and then left to go to the Trappists, in Rhode Island, *one* thing made me think of staying in Harlem. A saintly woman, in the tenements, was dying of cancer – still is – day by day: but she was very holy and her holiness was in this suffering, and the Blessed Virgin had appeared to her a few times.

There is no doubt that the Blessed Virgin, where she appears to people in this country, appears in places like Harlem – or Gethsemani. Harlem – or Gethsemani – are the stables of Bethlehem where Christ is born among the outcast and the poor. And where He is, we must also be. I know He is in Harlem, no doubt, and would gladly live where He is and serve Him there.

There is no question I can't stay at Saint Bonaventure any more: I must go and find Christ where He really is – in real poverty and real sacrifice.

But then, what about Friendship House: it has this one great thing: it is real poverty, it is real sacrifice; it is real love of Christ in the poor. It is holy. The work is holy. The Baroness is a saint. Harlem is full of saints. And in Harlem there is no doubt a possibility even of martyrdom, in which my sins would all vanish at once and I would be certain of pleasing God, and coming to Him as His child, spotless, clean and holy and a saint!

What else about Friendship House?

It makes it possible to serve God perfectly – but is it the best possible way for *me* to serve God perfectly? Each individual has a different way, appropriate to him.

There are a lot of things that would make it hard for me to serve God – First of all, being with girls: I might be the only man on the staff – with five or six girls, and that situation is, to me personally, intolerable. To someone else it might not be. To me, it is. It inevitably means you are a sort of a center of a certain obscure kind of attention, and if you are not, you feel you are, or at any rate, I would either be so, or have to fight like a tiger with myself in order not to *try* to be. When I was there before, only for a few days, I got into a lot of situations where I was talking loud and asserting myself just because there were women around. I had eyes in the back of my head that followed the women around the room. But I don't want to get mixed up in such situations; I can't take them. If I am with women, I know they are women, every minute: and when I was in the world altogether, that was what I liked to be aware of. Now I cannot dare to. When I am away from women, I do not think about them, however, and can be at peace to pray. My prayers would be very confused in Harlem.

The other thing: standing around watching kids play ping-pong would seem to me no less fruitless and unsatisfactory than saying hello to all the sophomores on this campus, as I do every day. Both occupations could lead a man, be used by him, as a means to sainthood: but not by me. They are not the means I need. When I think of the Trappists – it is all different. I cannot think of one thing that would not help me towards God, with His grace!

December 2, 1941

Now I know!

The whole business has burst into fire and flame like a terrific battle! I can see some of the significance of the crisis the other night. This is a *battle* and a real one, and maybe the most real one I have ever had to face in my life – and the tremendousness of the forces engaged in it, for me and against me, begins to be apparent, and it appals me.

I remember how an almost physical force tried to keep me from going to Fr. Philotheus and finding out there was, at least in his opinion, every reason for me to take my vocation seriously! I was tempted to let the whole thing wait several days. . . .

Yesterday afternoon, in the mail, was a notice from the Draft Board – completely unexpected. I thought my classification (I-B) last March was final for a good long time: now I am to appear for re-examination. They have changed the rule about teeth. If I pass this time, it means I might be in the army by January – in I-A.

But at least I had made up my mind and written to the Trappists, saying I wanted to come there December 18. I spent yesterday writing out documents asking for time to find out whether or not the Trappists would have me.

And I have been praying without ceasing.

If, as soon as I decide on this vocation, obstacles appear, that has some importance! Today, all day, I am ground between two millstones. I keep praying to Saint Therese of the Child Jesus, whom I know to be my friend, and I remember her own vocation and her Holy impatience to be admitted to Carmel.

I am beginning to believe quite firmly that, whether I am drafted or not, I may sometime be a Trappist, and that this trial is a definite part of my vocation. There is no other conclusion. Overnight, over the weekend, all the force of my previous desire to be a priest (which had always still been in me) returned even stronger. Now my whole soul is gathered up in one desire: to pray and pray that I may do God's will.

What God's will is, depends on what happens – if the Draft Board refuses my plea for a delay – if the Abbot accepts me, etc. If the army takes me and the Abbot refuses me – the worst thing that could possibly happen – I have a feeling it is still only the beginning of a long struggle leading to the cloister.

I can't think of desiring anything else but the cloister, or of doing anything else but praying and striving to get there, and suffering in patience every trial, everything there is to be suffered, everything that makes the vocation seem hopeless!

For one thing, it seems to me God's will is, for me, the cloister: or that I should strive for it above all things. Notice that this letter from the Draft Board makes a sudden end of Friendship House, for me, unless I once again fail to pass with my teeth, which doesn't seem likely from what the secretary at the Local Board here told me.

Even this business of the army seems to make more sense than Saint Bonaventure, which is completely neutral ground, a realm of inertia. If I am not to be in the cloister, then it is well I should not be separate from the universal penance of military service and the war outside of the cloister. After all, there are certain points where the crisis is acute, and there the Christian is called to be – one is the cloister, the other, Harlem, any slum; another, the camp, especially concentration camps of prisoners; another – the front, too. The war is in all these places, under different aspects.

I have no interest in any human wars. Wherever I am, I am a citizen of the Kingdom of God and fight only as a soldier of Christ – killing nobody.

The big problem of the army: would they simply dump me in combatant service as they did Gibney, although my Draft Board gave me non-combatant status? What about Mass every day? Would it be possible? etc.

I have absolutely nothing that might make me *worthy* of becoming a Trappist. On the contrary I am totally unworthy of any grace or favor at all from Almighty God, Our Loving Father in Heaven. But I can pray and pray to Him because He is all loving: out of the infinite depth of His Love.

He wills our perfection, in love of Him: and I can beg Him to give me, out of His mercy and absolute generosity, what I could never hope to deserve. And if he sends me trials, should I not thank Him, instead of complaining? For by tribulations He perfects us; they are the surest sign of His love. And I take this trial as a sure sign of a vocation. Yet I cannot really say, although I try to, the terrific words of the *Magnificat* antiphon from Saint Andrew's Second Vespers last night:

> "*O bona crux, diu desiderata, et jam concupiscenti animo praeparata: securus et gaudiens venio ad te [ita] et tu exsultans suscipias me, discipulum ejus qui pependit in te!*" ["O good cross, long have I desired you, now prepared for this longing soul. I come to you, safe and happy, and you joyfully receive me, the disciple of Him who hung on you."]

When it comes to the words "*securus et gaudiens*" I only realize my own weakness and inadequacy and helplessness and *absolute isolation.*

I know in advance there is no hope of my saving myself, and only God can lead me; yet I am confused and hesitant about following where He wills, since it leads to a conflict: but I have to come through conflict to the cloister.

I cannot but pray for the trial to be short, and that I may come to the cloister. I can see where it might be altogether insane simply to assume that since the army was the *least pleasant*, the most arid and trying course, that therefore that should be the one to be prayed for. Absurd! That would be purely fanciful and absurd. If you have a vocation to the cloister you pray to get there with every breath in your body, I should think, and no fancy tricks with logic.

Every moment of the day – even before I got any notice involving a problem I was crying out as loudly as I could to God to bring me, now, to the cloister. Now it is the same – with an added urgency yet an added confidence.

Before the notice came there was the desire for the cloister. Since the notice of reexamination for the draft – a funny thing: a terrific combination of fear that I might *not* get to the cloister, and of confidence that the vocation is true and from God – and the trial is from God.

And if you had a true vocation for the cloister, and were yet taken off to the army? Simply have to suffer it. I don't know how. God would have to show me how. There is no force in me, but in Him is all strength.

But before I got this surprise notice from the Draft Board, I had a great desire, for the cloister. After the notice I also got *confidence* in the vocation!

As for things that have been totally forgotten, or become absurd: questions of the publication of anything I have ever written – books or poems or anything – and yesterday the anthology came back from Boston.

There is only one thing to do: pray incessantly. God's infinite goodness and mercy are such that He may take pity on me, and allow me to become a Trappist right away. Meanwhile, fast, and pray, and try harder than ever to avoid the least sin or imperfection from day to day. And you, holy Therese, Little Flower, do not fail me or desert me! Miracle worker, be by me! Holy Father Francis, and you, our glorious and immaculate and all-merciful Lady, Queen of Heaven and Mother of Sorrows, let me be ever with you, and fill my heart and soul and mind with your love, so that I may be always in the Kingdom of God even though on earth! And lead me safely and soon to the cloister! Amen.

JMJT.

December 3

I say over and over again: my prayers have no merit in themselves; nothing that is mine has any merit at all. If I had been praying all my life to become a Trappist, I would have no *right* to expect to become one – no right to demand, as a return, that I be accepted by the Abbot!

Yet I fall on my face, in tears, and beg God that I may become a Trappist at all hours of the day, not because I think to deserve anything by that, but because I believe that if He wills, I can be admitted to the cloister – even as soon as Christmas.

Do I expect anything? Am I schooling myself to expect anything? I am too full of tribulation, too ground up between the great turning millstones inside me to expect anything. How can I make any judgments about how God is going to answer my prayer? I am in absolute helplessness, ignorance, stupor. I can only pray and believe that if He wills, I shall be a Trappist.

I never saw the full significance of sentences beginning: "If God wills . . ." I had only thought of those words as a formula – something to place the future in God's hands and thereby avoid pride. But these words are no formula! When Saint Therese of Lisieux, devoured with desire to be in the convent, cast herself at the Pope's feet and asked him to intercede for her, he answered in what I thought at first was a formula: "If God wills, you will enter Carmel." But that means everything. Everything! Even the highest gift is possible to us, not that we can deserve it, but that we can *ask for it*. God, in His infinite bounty and love and mercy, can will it. "Lord if thou will," said the leper "I can be clean!" "Say but the word" said the centurion "and my servant shall be healed." If the Lord but turn His eyes towards, and look upon us, He fills us with all His love. But unless He turns His eyes, stretches out His hand; unless He wills – we are lost utterly. "Knock and it shall be opened unto you!" I fall on my face in tears.

Lord, I only desire to be in the cloister for one thing: to belong *entirely* to Thee! That is what the angels have made me pray (Your holy messengers) day and night since last Lent when I went to the Forty Hours up the hill at the convent. For nine months I have prayed for nothing so much as to know how I am to give myself all to Thee – and have not listened nearly attentively enough when Thou didst seem to answer!

Today I threw the worst novel[13] into the incinerator – both copies: only kept out a few pages, and I don't know why!

I turn over the page and am scared by this blank page. Tomorrow is the fourth day of a Novena to the Little Flower, begun as the result of a chain letter from some total, mysterious stranger who didn't even spell my name right and didn't even sign the letter. The letter had come to this person, previously from "Rose" – I know no Rose except the cleaning woman, here, and she denied all connection with the affair. The letter came from New York.

A special favor is promised for the fourth day: and I beg and pray that it may have to do with only one thing: how can I give myself most perfectly and entirely to God – how can I join the Trappists?

I am ground up by the millstones of this tribulation, and yet I thank God for sending them, because they mean I am on my way to him: but I am in terror at this crossroads!

How every value has changed overnight! How many preoccupations have I altogether lost, in this flailing! No more concern with opinions about worldly ideas, politics, or books: they are knocked out of me: and if I may come to be a Trappist, I hope they are knocked out of me for good!

---

[13] This conflicts with what Thomas Merton wrote in *The Seven Storey Mountain* (New York: Harcourt, Brace and Co., 1948), 338: "I took the manuscripts of three finished novels and one half-finished novel and ripped them up and threw them in the incinerator." Here he writes that he only threw the "worst novel" into the incinerator. This could have been *The Man in the Sycamore Tree*, since he said he only kept out a few pages, which were found in the "Fitzgerald File" at the Merton Archives of the St. Bonaventure's University library. *The Labyrinth* was found in typescript form, in what seems to be its entirety. *My Argument with the Gestapo (Journal of My Escape from the Nazis)* survived the flames, as we know, and was published by Doubleday in 1969 (and later as a New Directions paperback), under the title, *My Argument with the Gestapo: A Macaronic Journal.*

On the contrary: a great source of consolation – I served Father Conrad's Mass. Something in the clear and unaffected and childlike tone of this great big priest's voice saying the prayers after Mass filled me with consolation, as if the Blessed Virgin were suddenly there, radiant, with us, her children, because of these simple prayers! And she was!

Another thing: I know the Sisters of the IC [Immaculate Conception], in the convent over the kitchen, are praying for me, too – the Baroness told them I might come to Harlem. Strong prayers! O these good little sisters! My sisters, quiet and simple nuns working hard in that big kitchen, working fifteen times as hard as I ever saw anybody work, and always up to their arms in dirty work, and always insulted by the students and always perfectly – not resigned, but more active – busy and happy and holy, showing nothing but great self-effacement in their work, but full of real goodness and real peace! Their prayers are an army!

December 5, 1941

Lord, how little I am! How little I know! How I am appalled at the mere idea of some of the things I have thought, even as recently as – the day before all this began, a week ago. The idea that I was something. That my judgments and opinions were important. That it mattered what I wrote when I haven't had anything to write (except in poems) ever since September (not counting this journal, which never pretended to be important). The idea that I was a writer, a teacher, or something else, that I was a something, as if I could be anything without roots at all. All the time, I believed God gave me everything and yet did not seem to _experience_ it – now I experience my own nothingness, and long for God!

Lord! you have left the real beginning of my conversion until now! How long I have prayed to only serve Thee, only desire Thee, only belong to Thee, and not known what it meant! Now, Thou makest me pray all day, all day, in great thirst, repeating over and over: let me only belong to Thee, give _everything_ to Thee – when I am not praying I am dry and sick. When I am praying, O, sometimes, You give me the cleanest, quietest peace. I cannot stop! Never stop praying! It hurts to stop praying – it hurts to go to eat, but that, too, is sweet, if I only say "I will only eat very little, for Love of my God!" Then the meal is very sweet – a bit of bread, some vegetables, the way it is always at Gethsemani!

Still, the terrible fear of not getting there. But, nevertheless, yesterday, at the 12th Station of the Cross, an incomparable sense of desire and sweetness gave me, for a few moments, complete and unshakeable confidence that You intend me for a Trappist, that You may well answer all these unworthy prayers out of that great bounty and love! Later, I was just as scared all over again. But the confidence returned. When I pray, there is no fear, Thou art there.

No letter has come – not from Gethsemani, not from the Draft Board, not from the Franciscans in N.Y. concerning my documents I gave them, before. But when I pray, there is no fear, for the Lord shelters me, who am nothing, in the immensity of His being and His silence and His love!

O God, My God! Why am I so mute? I long to cry out and out to Thee, over and over, and Thou art nameless and infinite. All our names for Thee are not Thy name, infinite Trinity. But Thy Word is Jesus, and I cry the name of Thy Son and live in the love of His heart and believe, if He wills, He will bring me the answer to my only prayer: that I may renounce *everything* and belong entirely to the Lord!

Saint Theresa, Little Flower, never cease praying for me!

JMJT.

Index